90.00

DYSLEXIA, READING AND THE BRAIN

DYSLEXIA, READING AND THE BRAIN

A SOURCEBOOK OF PSYCHOLOGICAL AND BIOLOGICAL RESEARCH

Alan A. Beaton

Psychology Press
Taylor & Francis Group

HOVE AND NEW YORK

First published 2004
by Psychology Press
27 Church Road, Hove, East Sussex BN3 2FA

Simultaneously published in the USA and Canada
by Psychology Press
270 Madison Avenue, New York, NY 10016

Psychology Press is a part of the Taylor & Francis Group

Copyright © 2004 Psychology Press

Typeset in Times by RefineCatch Limited, Bungay, Suffolk
Printed and bound in Great Britain by Biddles Ltd, King's Lynn
Cover design by Sandra Heath

This publication has been produced with paper manufactured to strict
environmental standards and with pulp derived from sustainable forests.

British Library Cataloguing in Publication Data
A catalogue record for this book is available from the British Library

Library of Congress Cataloging-in-Publication Data
Beaton, Alan.
Dyslexia, reading, and the brain: a sourcebook of psychological and biological research / by Alan A.
Beaton.–1st ed.
p. cm.
Includes bibliographical references and index.
ISBN 1-84169-506-8 (hardcover)
1. Dyslexia.   I. Title.

RC394. W6B437 2004
616.85'53—dc22   2003026192

ISBN 1-84169-506-8

To Ute, Alison and Alexander

Contents

Preface

Anyone familiar with conferences on reading and developmental dyslexia will be aware that practitioners and researchers in different aspects of the field often have little contact with each other and with each other's literature. It was in an effort to redress this intellectual isolationism that I wrote this book. I do not pretend that it makes easy reading, but then it is not intended to be read from cover to cover in one sitting but dipped into as and when required. I hope that those starting out in reading research will find it a useful source of reference and that those who have been rather longer in the field occasionally will be surprised as well as informed.

It is a brave — or foolish — man who claims to be expert in all fields and I freely admit that I am more at home in certain domains of research than in others. This will no doubt be apparent to those with a keen eye for such things. I have, however, done my utmost to ensure that lack of expertise in some areas has not led me into making false claims. I have been conservative in what I have written and tried to remain faithful to the original sources.

There are fashions in the field of reading research, as there are in other academic arenas, fostered in part by funding pressures and the exigencies of publication, and, I suspect, by the sheer volume of literature and the lack of time in which to explore it with an open mind. In reading published articles, I received the distinct impression that many papers were simply not being properly interpreted. I was struck by how the findings of an investigation can be transformed by subtle shifts of meaning when reported as a summary by others. Ideas or findings were frequently attributed to authors without justification. What authors actually wrote or did was misquoted or inaccurately summarized — in some cases, by people who should have known better. Many valuable insights and opinions were overlooked that deserve to be more widely known. Conversely, some authors were accorded more credit than their work deserves. Quoting Kerr (1897) as providing one of the first recorded descriptions of congenital word-blindness is a case in point: his statement that "a boy with word-blindness, who can spell the separate letters, is a trouble" is the only mention of the topic in the entire 67 pages of his paper. Hallgren (1950) may well be the source of this error for modern writers.

In writing this monograph, I consulted many hundreds of references (as will be apparent from the length of the reference list). I have tried not only to do justice to the historical sequence of events in the field but also to portray the thrust and parry of debates in the literature. Although I do not make any claims for the worth of my own ideas, I have taken inordinate pains to ensure the accuracy of my summaries of those of other people. Some errors and misinterpretations are no doubt inevitable: I would welcome being informed where this is so.

Given the scope of the work, decisions as to how the material should be organized were not always straightforward. At the outset, I felt that cognitive and biological research should be reviewed in more or less separate sections. The book is therefore in two main parts, with some overlap between them. I acknowledge that separating the cognitive and biological fields is not a strategem that everyone would have adopted; nor is it always obvious why, within this main division, I have placed some material in one category rather than the other.

For example, the last chapter of Part I, Chapter 6, is devoted largely to auditory and temporal aspects of speech and to motor deficits in dyslexia. These converge on the functions of the cerebellum, so the cerebellar hypothesis of dyslexia is discussed not only in this chapter but also in Chapter 10, where neuro-anatomical and neuro-imaging findings relevant to this hypothesis are discussed.

I decided, rightly or wrongly, to keep material on visual aspects of reading and dyslexia in Part II. Although research on eye movements or coloured lenses, for example, would not not normally be treated as "biological", detailed aspects of retinal topography do not sit altogether comfortably within a section on cognitive psychology. The magnocellular deficit hypothesis of dyslexia is quite clearly biological in origin and I have provided a more detailed neurophysiological intro-duction to this idea than is usual in a book on reading. This fits more appropriately within a biological than a cognitive context. Because of the potential links with various aspects of visual function, it did not seem to me unreasonable to keep all the visual material together in one section, even if it does violate the conceptual (but arbitrary) distinction between cognitive and biological aspects of vision.

Much of the material on auditory or temporal functions in Chapter 6 might have been treated along with visual aspects of the magnocellular hypothesis. However, as far as dyslexia is concerned, there is comparatively little neuro-physiological research directly related to a "magnocellular" auditory system. Theories invoking this concept are something of an extrapolation from research on the visual system. I made the decision, therefore, to keep the material based on auditory psychophysical studies close to studies on speech perception rather than place it alongside visual functions. In this case, as elsewhere, I am aware that others might have organized the material in a different way and covered the various topics in a different order.

I confess to being exhausted by the effort of producing this monograph, as anyone else with an equal degree of temerity (or obsession) will readily appreciate. Notwithstanding the claims of the RAE, TQA (and whatever other systems of "accountability" the so-called assessment-jockeys come up with), I hope I can once again give to my wife and children the energy and time that they deserve and of which in recent years they have had too meagre a portion. It is to them that this work is dedicated.

Alan A. Beaton

Acknowledgements

I wish to express my appreciation to Professor David Oborne and Professor Rodger Llewellyn Wood, my former and current head of department, respectively. Both protected me from petty restrictions and excessively onerous administration, which enabled me to bring this work to completion. In doing so, they kept faith with a tradition of scholarship that is becoming increasingly rare in these days of relentless audits and unending bureaucracy. I wish also to thank my colleague, Dr Siné McDougall, whose characteristically quiet words of support gave me more encouragement than she probably realizes. In my years of working at Swansea I have never received anything other than friendly and courteous assistance from the library staff of the university. I am grateful to them for their help in different ways.

It gives me great pleasure to place on record my intellectual debt to my former tutor, Professor Tim Miles, OBE. His writing achieves a clarity of thought and exposition which I never attain myself but to which I always aspire. It is appropriate, too, to mention in this context Dr Neil Cheshire, though I doubt he will ever read these words.

I am delighted that a conversation long ago with Mike Forster has at last borne fruit. I have enjoyed collaborating with him and his editorial team from Psychology Press, especially Ruben Hale and Kathryn Russel. The manuscript could not have been completed without the technical assistance of Neil Carter, who always gave freely of his time. Juliette and David James did a thoroughly professional job in typing many of the references; Zoe Fisher was always willing to lend a hand wherever it was required. I thank them all.

Finally, I thank my wife, Ute, for putting up with many late nights and for shouldering an unfair share of domestic and family responsibilities during preparation of this monograph. Most of all, I thank her for putting up with me at a time when I cannot have been easy to live with.

A Note About Grade Levels

Many published papers in the reading literature give only the grade level of the participants used in the research, rather than their age. Although there is some variation between the school systems in different states of Australia, Grade 1 can be taken to refer to children of 5–6 years of age, Grade 5 to children roughly 10 or 11 years of age and so on. In the USA, first grade normally refers to children approximately 6–7 years of age and 12th grade to students aged 17–18 years.

Part I

The Cognitive Context

1

What is Dyslexia?

INTRODUCTION

If the emergence of speech marks the greatest intellectual advance of our species, perhaps even defining *Homo sapiens*, then the invention of writing must be counted a cultural landmark almost equally as significant, for it is the printed word that has been the repository of knowledge and allowed its dissemination across space and time. Even today, in the modern world of computers and information technology, an inability to read can have profound social and psychological consequences (Maughan, 1995). Yet reading has been called an "unnatural act" (Gough & Hillinger, 1980) and the majority of the world's population is functionally illiterate.

Reading is a complex behaviour that calls upon a range of cognitive skills The very word "reading" itself refers to a variety of different activities, a fact commented upon by Freud in his monograph on aphasia. He wrote:

the process of learning to read is very complicated indeed . . . Everybody knows from self observation that there are several kinds of reading some of which proceed without understanding. When I read proofs with the intention of paying special attention to the letters and other symbols, the meaning of what I am reading escapes me to such a degree that I require a second persual for the purpose of correcting the style. If, on the other hand, I read a novel, which holds my interest, I overlook all misprints and it may happen that I retain nothing of the names of the persons figuring in the book except for some meaningless feature, or perhaps the recollection that they were long or short, and that they contained an unusual letter such as x or z. Again, when I have to recite . . . I am in danger of caring too little about the meaning, and as soon as fatigue sets in I am reading in such a way that the listener can still understand, but I myself no longer know what I have been reading.

(Freud, 1953, pp. 75–76)

The effects of fatigue remarked upon by Freud are no doubt familiar to us all. They are reminiscent of the effects that damage to certain parts of the brain can produce on previously good readers.

Loss of the ability to read or to understand what one has read following stroke or other injury to the brain was commented upon by several authors in the nineteenth century (e.g. Dejerine,

1891, 1892). A British ophthalmologist working in Glasgow, James Hinshelwood, published a series of papers describing acquired cases of what were called word (1895, 1896, 1898) and letter (1899) "blindness" in the absence of conspicuous speech difficulties. These were followed in 1900 by a report of "congenital word-blindness" in two boys aged 10 and 11 years (Hinshelwood, 1900) and a further report of four cases from the same family (Hinshelwood, 1907).

In his papers, Hinshelwood referred to previous work by Kussmaul (1877), who apparently coined the term "word-blindness" (*wortblindheit*) to describe the reading difficulties of previously literate brain-damaged patients. No less a person than the president of the Neurological Society, Sir W.H. (Henry) Broadbent, pointed out (Broadbent, 1896), however, that the condition of word-blindness was not first described by Kussmaul, as might have been inferred from Hinshelwood's (1895) report. Broadbent (1872) himself had described patients who were unable to read following brain injury, albeit that they also showed some evidence of "verbal aphasia" (p. 150). On the other hand, Broadbent (1896) conceded that it might have been Kussmaul who first described difficulty with reading as "an isolated condition"—that is, as occurring in the context of intact speech (see also Dejerine, 1891, 1892). The word dyslexia was first used (see Hinshelwood, 1896) by a German ophthalmologist, R. Berlin, when referring to reading difficulties caused by cerebral disease or injury (Berlin, 1887).

Inspired by Hinshelwood's (1895) report, a general practitioner in Sussex, W. P. Morgan, wrote to *The Lancet* giving an account of the reading problems experienced by an apparently normal boy who had suffered no brain damage. Thus it is to Morgan (1896) that we owe the first description in the medical literature of what is now referred to as developmental dyslexia or specific reading disability. His account of what he called "congenital word-blindness" ran as follows:

Percy F.—a well-grown lad, aged 14—is the eldest son of intelligent parents ... He has always been a bright and intelligent boy, quick at games, and in no way inferior to others of his age. His greatest difficulty has been—and is now—his inability to learn to read. This inability is so remarkable, and so pronounced, that I have no doubt it is due to some congenital defect ... the greatest efforts have been made to teach him to read, but, in spite of this laborious and persistent training, he can only with difficulty spell out words of one syllable ... The schoolmaster who has taught him for some years says that he would be the smartest lad in the school if the instruction were entirely oral ... His father informs me that the greatest difficulty was found in teaching the boy his letters, and they thought he never would learn them.

(Morgan, 1896, p. 1378)

The relation between acquired and developmental forms of dyslexia has been the focus of discussion ever since these early reports (see Jorm, 1979a, 1979b and reply by Ellis, 1979, 1993; Baddeley, Ellis, Miles, & Lewis, 1982; Castles & Coltheart, 1993 and reply by Snowling, Bryant, & Hulme, 1996a). Both in the preface and elsewhere in his monograph on *Congenital Word-Blindness*, Hinshelwood (1917) compared the acquired varieties of reading disorder with congenital word-blindness, stating firmly his belief that "An adequate knowledge of the former condition is an essential preliminary to the proper understanding of the latter" (p. 40). In a report of "congenital word-blindness" in a father and two sons, Drew (1956) wrote: "It is impossible to avoid comparison of the findings in these patients with hereditary dyslexia and other patients who have dyslexia as a result of acquired cerebral lesions" (p. 455). More recently, Marshall (1985) and Coltheart (1982) also felt that insights gleaned from the study of the acquired dyslexias shed light on developmental forms of dyslexia. However, Ingram (1963) pointed out that "the clinical syndromes found in the developing child do not conform accurately to those of the adult with brain injury" (p. 200), while Critchley (1970) cautioned: "The acquired dyslexic shares with the developmental dyslexic a certain lack of facility in the full appreciation of verbal symbols; but there the likeness rests, and the analogy should not be pressed further" (p. 105).

Somewhat surprisingly, in view of the initial report by Pringle Morgan and subsequent papers by (among others) Thomas (1905), Fisher (1905), Stephenson (1907) and Hinshelwood (1895, 1896, 1898, 1917), all British medical men, the notion of congenital word-blindness or dyslexia did not quickly catch on among educationalists in the UK. More than half a century later, Gooddy and Reinhold (1961) remarked: "Cases of reading and writing difficulties are well known to neurologists and psychiatrists, but they are regarded as very uncommon in Great Britain. In Denmark, however, the condition is considered to be quite common" (p. 231).

One reason for the reluctance in the UK to accept the idea of a specific reading disability might have been that the terms used to refer to the condition (see, for example, Drew, 1956, p. 449) were inconsistent and even unhelpful. Fildes (1921), for example, regarded the term "congenital word-blindness" as misleading, an opinion with which it is hard to disagree. Long before the current emphasis on speech-related difficulties, Ingram (1963) made the point that "Naturally, psychologists are reluctant to diagnose children with difficulties in auditory discrimination or in synthesis of the spoken word (which are more important causes of reading retardation than visuo-spatial difficulties) as being 'word blind'" (p. 200). More importantly, perhaps, the concept of dyslexia was, and remains, unclear to many people.

For reviews of the early history of research on dyslexia, see Drew (1956), Vernon (1957), Critchley (1970), Naidoo (1972), Sampson (1975), Vellutino (1979) and Richardson (1992).

THE CONCEPT OF DYSLEXIA

The concept of specific reading impairment or specific developmental dyslexia has often been distinguished from that of general reading backwardness. Vernon (1962) suggested three categories of backward readers: (1) those whose difficulty

was due to environmental factors, "such as lack of culture in the home, inefficient teaching, etc" (p. 144); (2) those who suffered "some form of emotional maladjustment" (p. 145); and (3) "Those whose backwardness is often severe and may be attributable to some organic or constitutional factor ... These are the cases which should properly be classified as 'specific dyslexics'" (p. 145). Ingram and Mason (1965) were of the view that "children with specific reading and writing difficulties (specific dyslexia) constitute a small proportion of backward readers" (p. 465).

Thirty years ago, Naidoo (1972) bemoaned the "multiplicity of terms" used to refer to reading difficulties, while according to Rutter and Yule 1975:

> The terminology used in referring to reading difficulties is chaotic and confusing ... In part, this chaos stems from a vagueness of definitions and a general looseness in the use of words, but to a much greater extent it stems from fundamental disputes about the nature of the reading problems. This dispute is most evident in the continuing controversy about the existence of dyslexia. Conferences on reading are full of heated exchanges about whether the condition does or does not exist.
>
> (Rutter & Yule, 1975, p. 181)

Reviewing 50 years of research, Sampson (1975) wrote: "What is even more striking is the heat and sometimes acrimony which have fuelled discussion almost from the start" (p. 27). *Plus ça change, plus c'est la même chose*! As recently as 1994, an influential paper was published under the title "Does dyslexia exist?" (Stanovich, 1994a). The fact that this question could still be asked was regarded by the author as "an affront" to the field of reading disability research (Stanovich, 1994b).

Critchley laid out his argument in support of the concept of dyslexia as follows:

> The arguments in favour of the existence of a specific type of developmental dyslexia occurring in the midst of but nosologically

apart from the *olla podrida* of bad readers, has been said to rest upon four premises. These comprise: persistence into adulthood; the peculiar and specific nature of the errors in reading and spelling; the familial incidence of the defect; and the greater incidence in the male sex. To these criteria may be added: the absence of signs of serious brain damage or of perceptual defects; the absence of significant psychogenesis; the continued failure to read despite conventional techniques of instruction; and *the association of normal if not high intelligence.*

(Critchley, 1970, p. 11; emphasis added)

The final part of this defence of the concept of dyslexia may unwittingly have contributed to the belief of many people that dyslexics are, *ipso facto*, highly intelligent. This is a view that some parents of dyslexic children are happy to maintain, even if there is evidence to the contrary. Consequently, there is in some quarters (at least within the UK) a tendency to refer disparagingly to dyslexia as a middle-class condition. The underlying assumptions are probably manifold but no doubt include the idea that affluent parents want to avoid facing the "fact" that their child is not very bright and have the financial and other resources to manipulate the educational "system" to their own advantage. There may also be an unspoken assumption that poor reading ability in the lower socio-economic groups is less likely to be a handicap to progression within manual occupations than is the case within the more status-conscious middle class. Such attitudes are clearly unhelpful towards children from economically disadvantaged backgrounds. In fact, a distinct sub-group of reading-impaired or dyslexic children may be found even among a much larger group of children whose generally low level of literacy might be attributable to unfavourable social environments (Whitehurst & Fischel, 2000). But it is equally true that regarding a middle-class child's dyslexic difficulties as somehow manufactured to excuse or disguise a supposed low level of intelligence (see Nicolson, 1996) may be simi-

larly unjustified, hurtful and damaging. As Ingram and Mason (1965) point out, "A child may be having difficulty with reading simply because he is expected to keep up with children of his own chronological age but of higher mental age. This is particularly apt to occur in the higher socio-economic groups" (pp. 463–464).

The issue of classification is fundamental to scientific progress in any field, no less so in the field of reading disability than in any other. Where the taxonomic boundaries are placed has important implications. Lumping certain observations together draws attention to important links between them, whereas new advances in knowledge might give grounds for splitting concepts or phenomena that were previously lumped together. Miles (1994) asserts that "disagreements over the concept of dyslexia are in effect disagreements over the issue of lumping and splitting" (p. 208)—that is, over where one draws a dividing line between one group and another. In his view, some taxonomies are strong while others are weak. Miles refers to the field of medicine to illustrate his point:

> For example, the terms "fever" and "nervous breakdown" still survive in common use since neither is wholly uninformative; if, however, they are contrasted with terms such as "tuberculosis" and "phenylketonuria" the differences are plain. It is characteristic of strong medical taxonomies that they imply a theory of causation, accurate prognosis, and distinctive methods of treatment.
>
> (Miles, 1994, p. 197)

The term dyslexia, Miles argues, has "more power" than the term "poor reading", since the latter "draws the boundaries in the wrong place". This is because it diverts attention from things that in his opinion ought to be lumped together, such as slowness or weakness in non-reading tasks and the persistence of such difficulty into adulthood. Miles argues: "The advantage of the dyslexia concept is that it lumps these seemingly disparate manifestations together; and this is precisely what a good taxonomy does. To be a splitter in this area is to miss important links" (p. 205). Further arguments in favour of the concept of dyslexia as traditionally defined can be found in Miles, Haslum, and Wheeler (1998).

It is a truism that the population of poor or disabled readers is not homogeneous (Denckla & Rudel, 1976b, Mattis, French, & Rapin, 1975; Seymour, 1986). Perhaps it is not surprising there is no universally agreed definition of dyslexia. Much of the research carried out in the field of reading difficulty has defined poor, disabled or dyslexic readers simply in terms of a reading score or reading age that is considered low for the age of the children concerned provided that each child's IQ is 90 or above and that socio-educational, emotional, neurological or psychiatric reasons for the poor reading can be excluded. According to Siegel:

> The [sic] definition of learning disabilities assumes that (a) a learning disability is not the result of an inadequate education; (b) the individual does not have any sensory deficits, such as hearing or visual impairment; (c) the individual does not have any serious neurological disorders that may interfere with learning; and (d) the individual does not have any major social and/or emotional difficulties that might interfere with learning.
>
> (Siegel, 1999, p. 311)

The exclusionary criteria no doubt owe much to the 1968 definition of the Research Group on Developmental Dyslexia of the World Federation of Neurology, who described dyslexia as "a disorder in children who, despite conventional classroom experience, fail to attain the language skills of reading, writing and spelling commensurate with their intellectual abilities". This definition of dyslexia, it will be noted, entails the notion of some discrepancy in skills. According to Critchley (1970), "It is dependent upon fundamental cognitive disabilities which are frequently of constitutional origin" (p. 11). This claim is explored later in this monograph.

There are a number of problems with

exclusionary definitions of dyslexia, as has been pointed out by many authors (see, for example, Catts, 1989a; Kamhi, 1992). Rutter and Yule, for example, wrote:

> A negative definition of this kind not only fails to aid conceptual clarity but also it implies that dyslexia cannot be diagnosed in a child from a poor or unconventional background. In short, it suggests that if all the known causes of reading disability can be ruled out, the unknown (in the form of "dyslexia") should be invoked. A council [sic] of despair, indeed.
>
> (Rutter & Yule, 1975, p. 192)

Rutter and Yule (1975) further stated: "it is generally argued that specific reading retardation is usually multi-factorially determined, whereas it is claimed that dyslexia is a unitary condition" (p. 193). Mattis et al. (1975) also claim that a common assumption is that "a clinical entity exists called 'the dyslexic child' and that ... one can determine the single causal defect" (p. 150). To my mind, however, there is nothing in the concept of dyslexia that requires either that it is a "unitary" condition or that it has a "single" cause.

A working party of the Division of Educational and Child Psychology of the British Psychological Society recently proposed the following definition of dyslexia: "Dyslexia is evident when accurate and fluent word reading and/or spelling develops very incompletely or with great difficulty" (Reason, Frederickson, Heffernan, Martin, & Woods, 1999). This somewhat anodyne statement is probably helpful in the contexts for which it was intended (to secure attention and provision for all children with literacy problems) but for other purposes it can be claimed that it suffers from the opposite failings of the much-maligned exclusionary definitions in so far as it is over-inclusive.

Miles (1992) points out that "Basically, in exploring dyslexia we are exploring a proposed *taxonomy*, or method of classification, and as with any other proposed taxonomy its advocates are logically committed to showing what can be done *with* it that cannot also be done *without* it" (p.152, emphasis in original). What can be done with the dyslexia concept is to draw attention to the wide range of problems and to the putative constitutional nature of the difficulties encountered by dyslexic people, which may include undue difficulty with mathematics (Hermann, 1959; Miles, 1993a, 1993b; Knopik, Alarcón, & DeFries, 1997; Miles, Haslum, & Wheeler, 2001).

The Danish neurologist Hermann (1959) emphasized that "congenital word-blindness does not involve only difficulties in reading and writing, but is a more widespread disturbance of function relating also to other symbols, e.g. numbers and [musical] notes, and is thus a general asymbolia" (p. 17). Although he acknowledged that difficulties in reading, and especially writing and spelling, are paramount, he argued that a diagnosis of dyslexia cannot be made on the basis of a single symptom that is always present. Miles (1986) wrote: "developmental dyslexia should not be thought of simply as difficulty with reading or even as difficulty with spelling . . . the reading and spelling problems of a dyslexic person are part of a wider disability which shows itself whenever symbolic material has to be identified and named" (p. 161). This view is reflected in the composition of the Bangor Dyslexia Test (Miles, 1982), which assesses performance on a variety of tasks, which, on the face of it, are unrelated to reading, such as difficulty in telling left from right, difficulty in reciting the alphabet or months of the year, or in recalling a series of digits in reverse order.

In similar vein, Nicolson and Fawcett (1990) argued: "It seems reasonable . . . to take a wider perspective than is normal in studies of dyslexia, and to investigate the hypothesis that the nature of the 'dyslexic deficit' is not limited to reading and that the 'dyslexic reading deficit' is merely a symptom of a more general and more pervasive deficit in the acquisition of skill" (p. 160).

Rutter and Yule (1975) claimed that it had not been possible to demonstrate any clustering of the developmental anomalies said to characterize dyslexia. In their words: "there has been a complete failure to show that the signs of dyslexia constitute any meaningful pattern. It may be concluded that the question of whether specific reading retardation is or is not dyslexia can be abandoned as meaningless" (p. 194). This may have been true in 1975 when these words were written; arguably it is not the case now (Miles, 1993a; Miles & Haslum, 1986).

Miles and Haslum (1986) analysed data from the 1980–81 follow-up of the 1970 Birth Cohort Study, a survey of children born in Scotland, Wales, England and Northern Ireland during a particular week in April 1970. Based on the data collected from nearly 13,000 cases, regression equations were calculated from which it was possible to calculate whether each child's obtained reading score or spelling score was higher or lower than that predicted by the regression equation. The data were then treated in two ways. First, for each child a "dyslexia index" was compiled. Positive dyslexia points were awarded if the obtained reading and spelling scores were lower than predicted and negative dyslexia points were given if the scores were higher. On a recall of digits test, positive or negative points were given according to whether the child's (standardized) score was above or below the mean for the cohort as a whole. Miles and Haslum noted: "In addition, positive and negative points of equal weight were allotted according to whether the child did or did not satisfy the criteria for dyslexia on the left–right, months forwards, and months reversed tests. All items were standardized and summed together" (p. 111). The distribution of dyslexia index scores was then examined.

Miles and Haslum (1986) argued that a normal variation in scores would lead to the two tails of this distribution being symmetrical. On the other hand, if dyslexia represents an anomaly, something over and above normal variation that requires to be explained, then the two tails should not be symmetrical. Miles and Haslum found that there were many more individuals at the dyslexia positive end of this distribution than at the dyslexia negative end, which they took as evidence against the hypothesis of normal variation, implying that dyslexia represents some anomaly of development. However, perhaps all they have shown (depending upon the meaning of their statement "All items were standardized and summed together") is that their "criteria for dyslexia" on the tests of left–right confusion, recitation of months forward and months reversed are too lenient. It is possible that many more children show some "positive sign" of dyslexia on these tests than carry them all out without any slight hesitation or error. Examination of Appendix 3 in Miles (1993a) shows that only 10 of 132 "control" children achieved a dyslexia index of zero, though admittedly on a larger battery of tests than used by Miles and Haslum (1986).

There was a second way in which Miles and Haslum (1986) treated their data. Children were defined as discrepantly good or poor readers (or discrepantly good or poor spellers) if their obtained reading or spelling score was more than 1.5 standard deviations on either side of the score predicted by the regression equation. This procedure yielded populations of discrepantly good readers or spellers to be compared with discrepantly poor readers and spellers. The number of dyslexia positive "indicators" was then counted for each of the four groups. The argument was that if positive indicators occur by chance, then the number of children showing from zero to five indicators should conform to a Poisson distribution. This was indeed found for the discrepantly good readers and spellers. However, for the discrepantly poor readers and spellers, the obtained distribution of the number of indicators was not what was expected for a Poisson distribution. Miles and Haslum concluded that "there is something other than randomness which requires explanation" (p. 111).

For those who are sympathetic to the notion of dyslexia as a "pattern of difficulties" (Miles, 1993a) or as constituting a "syndrome" (Critchley, 1970; Hermann, 1959; Miles, 1994; Nicolson, 1996)—and not everyone is (see, for example, A. Ellis, 1985, 1987, 1993)—poor reading and spelling are but two aspects of the problem, and not necesarily crucial ones. Miles and Miles (1990) make the provocative claim that "there is no contradiction in saying that a person is dyslexic while nevertheless being a competent reader" (p. ix). In such circumstances, one might want to point to additional factors suggestive of

an anomaly, maldevelopment or disorder of the central nervous system which is manifest in an array of cognitive and, possibly, motor tasks.

Not everyone agrees. Ellis, McDougall, and Monk state:

Our problem with such additional criteria are two-fold. First, if deficits in, say, memory span and repetition of long words were used as diagnostic criteria, then finding that dyslexics have phonological problems would be an inevitable by-product of the selection criteria, not the empirical discovery that researchers want it to be. Second, the use of such additional criteria raises the spectre of individuals who are intelligent and have unexpected and incongruous reading difficulties but who are denied a diagnosis of "dyslexia" because they do *not* have problems with left–right discrimination, repeating polysyllabic words or whatever ... Should researchers be prepared to include a category of "bright non-dyslexic poor readers"? That does not seem, to us, to be a promising way forward and hence we would defend the use of minimal criteria which only require that a dyslexic be of average or above-average intelligence and have unexpected reading difficulties which cannot easily be attributed to problems of perception, emotion, education, etc.

(Ellis, McDougall, & Monk, 1996, p.4)

The point here, presumably, is that while Ellis et al. would not wish to deny a diagnosis of dyslexia to the intelligent poor reader, they would be reluctant to classify as dyslexic the adequate reader who might not be reading at his or her optimal or expected level, or the intellectually dull person whose reading skills are abysmal. In any event, it may be important not to withhold special assistance just because someone has average reading skills (Pennington, Gilger, Olson, & DeFries, 1992) or below-average intelligence.

Elaine Miles (1995) has questioned whether there can be a single definition of dyslexia. She suggests that the concept of dyslexia does not lend itself readily to a definition and that "description" might be a better term to use. Different definitions or descriptions will be relevant in different contexts. In a useful analysis of how different definitions of dyslexia have been used for different purposes, Tønnessen (1997a) suggests that any definition should be regarded as a hypothesis, to be rejected if future findings show that it does not hold up. Tim Miles (1993b) argues that a diagnosis of dyslexia is, in effect, a sort of bet. On the basis of a limited number of signs, the bet or hypothesis is that further signs will be found if they are looked for; if they are not, then the hypothesis is rejected.

As Tim Miles (1957) pointed out in relation to the concept of intelligence, there is no single way in which the term "definition" is used, it is an "ambiguous" term. Defining, he argues, is not the name of a single procedure but a group of procedures having some resemblance to each other. I would argue that as with intelligence, so with dyslexia. There is no unique pattern of behaviour that constitutes intelligent behaviour and nor should we expect to find a unique pattern of dyslexic behaviour. Similarly, just as the phrase "intelligent behaviour" makes perfectly good sense without implying that there is some independent entity called "intelligence", so also should we be wary of reifying a certain kind of reading performance into a "thing", namely "dyslexia". Dyslexia is not something that we either "have" or do not "have"; we cannot catch it or pass it on to someone else. Rather, I would view it as a constitutional weakness that influences the way in which certain tasks are carried out.

One reads sometimes in the press statements to the effect that up to one child in five may be dyslexic. Such figures should be regarded with scepticism. In the more technical literature, rather more moderate estimates of the prevalence of reading disability are to be found. According to both Critchley (1970) and Pennington (1990), estimates within the English-speaking world typically fall between 5 and 10 per cent of the population. The prevalence of reading disability may be somewhat lower in countries with a more consistent correspondence between the sound(s) represented by a given letter than is the case in English.

Makita (1968) reported a figure of less than 1 per cent for Japanese school children (lower for the Kana script than for Kanji). However, as with all such endeavours, different figures will result from different definitions and the severity of dyslexia.

Miles (1993b) adopted a definition of dyslexia involving a discrepancy between reading or spelling and a measure of IQ together with the presence of a certain number of "signs" he considered to be particularly frequent among dyslexics. He applied his criteria to data from a large-scale longitudinal survey of all children born in the UK during a particular week in 1970. The results led him tentatively to suggest a prevalence of between 2 and 4 per cent covering a range of under-achievement in reading.

Whatever the exact prevalence of reading difficulty—and however it is conceptualized—it is clear that a substantial number of children (and adults) are handicapped in their acquisition of literacy skills. This fact alone justifies the continuing search for the underlying causes.

DYSLEXIA AND IQ

The relation between reading performance and general intellectual ability has assumed central importance in definitions of dyslexia. Ingram and Mason (1965) stated that "Specific (or developmental . . .) dyslexia is the name given to the difficulty encountered by a proportion of healthy children of average or superior intelligence in learning to read" (p. 464). According to these authors, "It is evident that the child with subnormal intelligence will learn to read late and slowly, if at all" (p. 464). They argued that "a 'bright' child is likely to have a reading age higher than his chronological age, whereas a 'dull' one's chronological age will usually exceed his reading age". Because of this presumed association between reading age and intellectual ability, Ingram and Mason felt that only children of average or superior intelligence should be referred to as dyslexic if their reading lagged behind their general intelligence. However, not everyone adopted this line (see Drew, 1956).

Hallgren (1950) noted that " 'Word-blindness' is found in individuals of subnormal, normal and superior intelligence" (p. 3). Similarly, Naidoo (1972) was of the opinion that "specific dyslexia can occur at all levels of intelligence" (p. 16). Despite Critchley's (1970) assertion that dyslexia is associated with "normal if not high intelligence", he too did not believe that dyslexia was confined to those of higher intellectual ability. That he was quite clear about this is shown by the following statement:

> This syndrome of developmental dyslexia is of constitutional and not of environmental origin, and it may well be genetically determined . . . It is independent of the factor of intelligence, and consequently it may appear in children of normal I.Q., and it stands out conspicuously in those who are in the above-average brackets. Of course there is no reason why the syndrome should not at times happen to occur in children of mental sub-normality, when diagnosis might then be difficult.
>
> (Critchley, 1970, p. 24).

Conversely, Ingram and Mason noted that:

> Because children suffering from specific or developmental dyslexia and dysgraphia may be of average or superior intelligence . . . their reading and writing difficulties are often attributed to laziness, inattention, or emotional maladjustment. If they are of very high intelligence their difficulties may escape notice, as they may be able to scrape along at the level of their chronological age group.
>
> (Ingram & Mason, 1965, p. 464).

Notwithstanding the belief of influential writers such as Critchley (1970) and Naidoo (1972) that dyslexia and intelligence are independent, there has been a continuing reluctance to follow through the implications of such a view. As Stanovich (1994a) pointed out, "The concept of dyslexia is inextricably linked with the idea of an etiologically distinct type of reading disability associated with moderate to high IQ" (p. 588). Stanovich is undoubtedly correct in what he says in so far as researchers have tended to recruit poor readers who fit this description. Indeed, the idea of the necessarily bright dyslexic has become part of the mythology of dyslexia among the lay community. Yet there is no reason why the IQ of dyslexics should not be low, if only because poor reading might be expected to lead to lowered scores on many standard tests of intelligence, which, in part, assess the kind of knowledge that is provided by books. Vocabulary scores in particular are influenced by exposure to the written word (Sénéchal, LeFevre, Hudson, & Lawson, 1996; Torgesen, 1989) and vocabulary differences between skilled and less able readers are often reported. Poor readers presumably read less than their peers and growth of their vocabulary would be affected (Siegel, 1999; Stanovich, 1986). Indeed, there is almost certainly a reciprocal relationship between vocabulary and reading proficiency (Aguiar & Brady, 1991).

A key notion in relation to the concept of dyslexia has been that of an *unexpectedly* poor level of reading (Miles, 1993a; Nicolson, 1996; Shaywitz, Fletcher, Holahan, & Shaywitz, 1992) and this, in turn, has usually been interpreted in relation to a child's general intellectual ability or intelligence. For example, "A definite discrepancy between proficiency in reading and writing and other school subjects" as well as "A definite discrepancy between proficiency in reading and writing and the child's general intelligence" (p. 7) was required for inclusion in the study by Hallgren (1950). Ingram and Mason (1965) advised that "In ideal conditions teachers would recognize early those who were not making the expected progress in learning to read and write. The expectation would be assessed in terms of the intellectual capacity of the child as measured by a reliable individual test of intelligence" (p. 463).

A definition of reading impairment in terms of a discrepancy between obtained reading score and that predicted on the basis of age and/or IQ is known as a "discrepancy definition". Discrepancy scores are usually defined as the difference between the score obtained on a given reading test and the score predicted on the basis of the regression of reading performance on some measure of IQ (i.e. on the correlation between reading and IQ). A discrepancy of a given value (say two standard deviations below zero, the value attained when obtained and predicted reading scores are equal) is taken as a measure of under-achievement in reading. The degree of discrepancy obtained will, of course, depend upon the particular test instruments that are used (Catts, 1989a).

Although foreshadowed in much earlier work (see Hallgren, 1950), the widespread use of a discrepancy definition of dyslexia can be traced to the seminal study of Rutter and Yule, who wrote:

> *Backwardness* describes reading which is backward in relation to the average attainment for that age, regardless of intelligence. Retardation, on the other hand, is a term used to describe a specific disability in reading—specific that is to say in the sense that the reading difficulties are not explicable in term's of the child's general intelligence. In short, specific reading retardation refers to a variety of what is usually called "under-achievement", whereas reading backwardness concerns *low* achievement but not under-achievement.
>
> (Rutter & Yule, 1975, p. 181, emphasis in original).

These are sometimes referred to as IQ-discrepant and age-discrepant definitions, respectively.

DYSLEXICS VERSUS POOR READERS

Yule, Rutter, Berger, and Thompson (1974) observed that a distinction between specific reading retardation and general reading backwardness was first drawn by Schonell (1935). In fact, it was foreshadowed in the earliest writings on the subject. In the first recorded case of specific reading difficulty referred to above, Pringle Morgan noted of Percy F. that "The schoolmaster who

has taught him for some years says that he would be the smartest lad in the school if the instruction were entirely oral" (p. 1378).

In discussing the hereditary basis of "congenital word-blindness", Hinshelwood (1907) refers to four boys from a single family and to their teacher who "in his long experience . . . had never before met with anything like the difficulties encountered in attempting to teach these four boys to read, and that he was greatly puzzled how to account for it, as in every other respect the boys seemed so intelligent" (p. 1230). The implication is, of course, that these cases of intelligent poor readers should be regarded as nosologically distinct from unintelligent poor readers. Indeed, Hinshelwood went on to write that "Congenital word-blindness is a local affection of the brain, and such patients, as a rule, are as bright and intelligent as other childen . . . Such cases must be carefully distinguished from those where there is, in addition to learning to read, a general lack of intelligence and general failure of the mental powers" (p. 1231). On the other hand, Fildes (1921) found that "No relationship existed between the subjects' intelligence quotients and their power in reading", leading her to argue that "inability to learn to read depends rather on a specific than on a general defect" (p. 287).

It has frequently been pointed out that "there is no practical utility in the distinction unless the two groups [of poor readers] are also distinguishable on other criteria not directly part of reading" (Yule et al., 1974, p. 11). In comparing a generally backward reading group (*n* = 79) and a specifically retarded reading group (*n* = 86) of 9- to 11-year-olds, Rutter and Yule (1975) found that in a number of task domains there were considerable group differences. Boys made up 54.4 per cent of the generally backward readers but 76.7 per cent of the specifically retarded group. Neurological disorders of one kind or another were significantly more frequent in the backward reading group, as were motor and praxic difficulties, including clumsiness. Language complexity was also more often reduced in this group, but left–right confusion and articulation defects were not. However, although more *frequent* concomitant difficulties in the backward reading group than in the specifically reading-impaired group might justify separation of the two kinds of poor readers, it does not follow that anything can be said about the relative severity or *nature* of the reading difficulty in the two groups.

Although the terms reading "difficulty", "disability" or "impairment" have tended to replace the earlier and arguably value-laden term reading "retardation", it has been common since publication of the articles by Rutter and his colleagues to distinguish poor readers of generally low intellectual or academic ability, operationalized as IQ, from those whose reading ability is not commensurate with their overall ability (see McDougall & Ellis, 1994). The first group are sometimes referred to as "garden variety" poor readers (Gough & Tunmer, 1986; Stanovich, 1991), reserving the term dyslexic (or specifically reading disabled) for the latter group. Dyslexics thus defined are then compared on some test or other with normal readers or, more recently, with younger reading-age-matched controls (or with both comparison groups). The underlying assumption has been that in the case of "garden variety" poor readers, the low level of reading might be a consequence of a generally low IQ. Note, incidentally, that the definition of "garden variety" poor reader in relation to IQ is not identical to that of "backward reader" used by Rutter and his colleagues, who identified such readers purely on the basis of a low reading score in relation to a child's age not in relation to their IQ.

The outcome of excluding children with a relatively low IQ from the designation "dyslexic" is that one is left looking at a restricted sample of poor readers. Whether this matters is a different question. After all, it might be important for some purposes to know whether a reading age of 12 years is above or below expectation for, say, a girl of 16 with a Wechsler Intelligence Scale for Children (WISC) IQ of 60 (Fransella & Gerver, 1965). Other definitions of dyslexia make exclusions of a different kind. For example, the common research tactic of only counting children as dyslexic if their IQ is at or above average and their reading is at or below 18 months below that expected for their age excludes other children. They are those children of high IQ whose reading is commensurate with their age but not at the level expected on the basis of the regression of IQ on reading level.

Rutter and Yule noted that in applying their definitions of reading backwardness and reading retardation to the same population of children,

> 155 backward readers [reading age 2 years 4 months or more below chronological age] and 86 retarded readers [2 years 4 months below the level predicted on the basis of the child's age and short WISC IQ] were identified in the total school population of some 2,300 children. The two groups overlapped considerably, having no less than 76 children in common.
>
> (Rutter & Yule, 1975, p. 186)

The analysis carried out by Rutter and Yule (1975) led them to state that "the characteristics supposedly associated with dyslexia are also a feature of specific reading retardation (p. 192). They argued that "if there is no recognizable pattern, then in the present state of knowledge there is no means of determining whether anyone has the hypothesized condition. Some kind of biological 'marker' would be needed and so far none has been found" (p. 194). Whether this remains the case, readers will be able to judge for themselves after reading this book. In any event, Fredman and Stevenson concluded from a study of 13-year-old children from a sample of twin pairs that:

> When both reading level and IQ were taken into account there were no apparent differences between retarded and backward readers on any of the tests assessing the reading process . . . reading level accounted for most of the differences between the two groups . . . The findings of this study therefore strongly suggest that retarded and backward readers do not differ in terms of how they read, rather in terms of how well they read.
>
> (Fredman & Stevenson, 1988 p. 104).

Using data from the Colorado twin project, Pennington et al. (1992) compared children defined as reading disabled either on the basis of a discrepancy between age and reading achievement or on the basis of a discrepancy between achievement and that predicted on the basis of IQ. Seventy per cent of the reading disabled children met both discrepancy criteria but the same proportion of the remainder (i.e. 30 per cent) met the criteria for only one of the definitions. Although there were few significant differences between the groups of disabled readers defined according to the discrepancy between age or IQ, there were a number of trends in terms of sex ratios, neuropsychological profiles and relationship to phonological or orthographic coding ability.

The classification of poor readers as either specifically reading retarded or backward readers suggested by Rutter and Yule (1975) was taken up by Jorm, Share, MacLean, and Matthews (1986), who compared normal, "retarded" and "backward" readers. These designations were based on non-verbal intelligence test scores and a test of reading ability at the end of the second grade at school. By the end of Grade 2, the designations were 14 retarded and 25 backward readers (of whom 9 also satisfied the criteria for reading retardation). They were compared with 414 normal readers. It is worth noting, however, that at the end of Grade 1 only 12 children were defined as retarded readers and 11 as backward readers and thus stability of classification was not high. Measures were taken on a wide battery of tests on children's entry to school (in Australia)—that is, prior to their learning to read. The significance of this is that any difference between the groups at this stage cannot be a *consequence* of reading experience. Jorm et al. (1986) reported that backward readers were significantly poorer than normal readers on almost all tasks and significantly poorer than retarded readers on many tests: "On no task were the retarded readers significantly worse than the backward readers" (p. 51). Generally speaking, the cognitive deficits of the retarded group were in the areas of early literacy (such as letter naming, discrimination of numbers and letters) and phonological processing (such as phoneme segmentation, sentence memory and object naming), whereas those of the backward group were far

wider and included motor impairment. This suggested to Jorm et al. that phonological impairment is a causal factor in reading retardation but that general backwardness in reading is multiply determined.

Taylor, Satz, and Friel (1979) found little to differentiate discrepancy-defined dyslexics from other "disabled readers" (defined purely in terms of reading level) on a battery of neuropsychological and neurological tests, whereas Ellis and Large (1987) reported that "garden variety" poor readers were impaired relative to dyslexics (termed specifically reading retarded) in some aspects of phonological processing. The question arises here as to whether any differences are quite simply a consequence of a lower IQ or reading ability in the former group. It is well known that IQ correlates with reading ability at the early stages of reading (though there is some evidence that at later ages reading contributes to IQ scores rather than the other way around). Unfortunately, Ellis and Large (1987) did not examine whether the differences they found between the two groups disappeared or remained after controlling statistically for differences in IQ. However, after conducting a regression analysis, Ellis, McDougall, and Monk (1996a) found no difference between discrepancy-defined dyslexics and other poor readers on phonological tasks or in the use of phonology in reading. Similar findings with regard to the generation and use of phonology in reading were reported by Johnston, Rugg, and Scott (1987a), who compared poor readers of average and below-average intelligence with groups of reading-age and chronological-age controls. The results of the latter two studies support the findings of Treiman and Hirsh-Pasek (1985), who compared dyslexics (mean age 11.75 years, full-scale IQ greater than 80 and at least one of verbal or performance sub-scale score greater than 90) with younger normal readers (mean age 8.5 years) on tests of irregular word and nonsense word reading. The two groups were matched for their ability to read regular words. No conspicuous difference was observed between the two groups in performance, leading Treiman and Hirsh-Pasek to argue that "Our results call into question the view that dyslexia is a syndrome that is clearly distinguishable from poor reading more generally" (p. 363).

Vellutino et al. (1996) showed that normally reading children categorized into those with average IQ scores and those with above-average IQ scores did not differ in either reading ability or on tests of phonological skill. They suggested that "one needs little more than average intelligence to learn to decode print and that, given at least this level of intellectual ability, degree of facility in print decoding will ultimately be determined by degree of facility in phonological skills such as phonetic decoding, name encoding and name retrieval" (p. 632). Subsequently, Vellutino, Scanlon, and Lyon (2000) argued that "measures of general intelligence do not discriminate between disabled and non-disabled readers" (p. 236).

The reading measures used by Vellutino et al. (1996) included measures of reading comprehension as well as of decoding skill and word identification. In support of the results of Vellutino et al. (1996), a longitudinal intervention study of 7- to 8-year-old poor readers by Hatcher and Hulme (1999) obtained evidence that IQ is unrelated to acquisition of decoding skills but significantly predicts responses to remediation when reading comprehension is used as the outcome measure.

In a study by Shaywitz et al. (1992), children were defined as reading-disabled in terms of a discrepancy between their reading scores predicted from a regression equation and those actually obtained. This group (Group D) was compared with children who did not meet the discrepancy-based criteria for reading disability but were considered to show low reading achievement in so far as their age-adjusted standard score placed them in the lowest quartile of reading ability (Group L). Retrospective comparison of measures taken in kindergarten and prospective comparison of measures taken in fifth grade indicated few differences between the groups, although both differed from a control group of normal readers. Those differences between the groups that were found could be attributed (through regression and discriminant function analyses) entirely to differences in IQ. Since differences in ability were inherent in the definitions of the low-reading groups, Shaywitz et al. (1992) argued that their results suported the view that there are no qualitative differences between (discrepancy-defined) dyslexic and other (garden-variety) poor readers (see also Fletcher, Stuebing, Shaywitz, Shaywitz, Rourke, & Francis, 1994b). In general, they hypothesized that "phonological processing is central to reading and . . . deficits in phonological processing are not specific to one type of reading disability but, in fact, may display a prominent role in reading disability no matter how it is defined" (p. 647). The only difference between children in the two groups of poor readers was, they surmised, that children who did not meet the discrepancy-based criteria not only had phonological impairments but also deficits in other domains measured by tests of general intelligence. In a word, their deficits were "not as modular as in the D group" (p. 647). Of course, the findings of Shaywitz et al. (1992) comparing garden-variety with discrepancy-defined poor readers do not necessarily imply that there are no differences between either or both of these groups and dyslexics defined according to traditional or clinical criteria (see Miles et al., 1998).

Fletcher et al. (1994a) analysed the cognitive profiles of children defined as reading-disabled according to a number of different criteria. The results of their very detailed analyses revealed that 79–98 per cent of the children were consistently designated as being reading-disabled whatever criteria were adopted. Phonological awareness correlated with reading disability regardless of how it was defined and "there was little evidence . . . for specificity of cognitive deficits in relation to IQ based discrepancies" (p. 18). The general conclusion that Fletcher et al. (1994a) drew from their study was that while there are individual differences between reading-disabled children, the "results do not provide strong support for the validity of distinguishing children who meet discrepancy and low achievement definitions of reading disability" (p. 19). They went on to argue that "The present study suggests that the concept of discrepancy operationalized using IQ scores does not produce a unique sub-group of children with reading disabilities when a chronological age design is used; rather, it simply provides an arbitrary subdivision of the reading–IQ distribution that is fraught with statistical and other interpretative [*sic*] problems" (p. 20).

The apparent illogicality of distinguishing between dyslexics and others on the basis of IQ was highlighted by Stanovich, who maintained that:

> the concept of a specific reading disability requires that the deficit displayed by the disabled reader not extend too far into other domains of cognitive functioning . . . if the deficits displayed by such children extended too far into other domains of cognitive functioning, this would depress the constellation of abilities we call intelligence, reduce the reading/intelligence discrepancy, and the child would no longer be dyslexic!
>
> (Stanovich, 1988a, p. 155)

While this is true—the child would then be described as backward in reading or one of the "garden variety" of poor readers, to use the term introduced by Gough and Tunmer (1986)—it is not necessarily illogical to distinguish between such cases and those poor readers whose IQ is in advance of their reading ability.

A forceful case for abandoning IQ-related definitions of reading disability was made by Siegel (1988, 1989a, 1989b; for a reply, see Torgesen, 1989; Siegel, 1992), who maintained that the co-existence of low IQ and average reading scores in some children of her sample demonstrates that low IQ is not a cause of poor reading. It does not follow, however, that low IQ can *never* be a cause of poor reading (see Torgesen, 1989).

After reviewing 21 relevant studies, Toth and Siegel (1994) concluded that "finding few differences between dyslexic and poor readers except on IQ related tasks, it seems unnecessary to include IQ at all in the definition of dyslexia . . . [and] . . . the IQ discrepancy based definition for [*sic*] dyslexia should be abandoned in favour of a more parsimonious definition" (pp. 66–67). They favoured a definition in terms of a core phonological deficit and/or the use of a cut-off score on a standardized test of word reading. Stanovich (1994a) maintained that "it has yet to be demonstrated that whatever distinct causes actually exist are correlated with the degree of reading–IQ discrepancy. Because the term dyslexia mistakenly implies that there is such evidence, the reading disabilities field must seriously consider whether the term is not best dispensed with" (p. 590)

The abandonment of IQ in defining reading disability was advocated by Vellutino et al. (2000), partly on the grounds that in a group of poor readers studied as part of their large-scale longitudinal investigation (Vellutino et al., 1996), IQ did not predict response to remediation, although general language skills did (see also Torgesen & Davis, 1996). Furthermore, Vellutino et al. argued:

> If the IQ–achievement discrepancy were a precise metric that could reliably distinguish between children with and without reading disability . . . then one might expect that children who were found difficult to remediate would have significantly larger IQ–achievement discrepancies prior to remediation than would children who were found to be readily remediated.
>
> (Vellutino et al., 2000, p. 233)

In the event, this expectation was not met; indeed, the opposite was the case. Children who profited least from intervention had significantly smaller discrepancies than those who benefited most.

In contrast to the above arguments, Rack and Olson (1993) expressed the view that "it is premature to abandon the use of intelligence testing in the disabilities field since the etiologies of reading problems may vary as a function of intelligence" (pp. 276–277). These authors discussed data (see also Wadsworth, Olson, Pennington, & DeFries, 2000) showing that individuals with high (full-scale) IQ (relative to their word recognition ability) tended to have higher heritability coefficients for reading than individuals with lower IQ (relative to their word recognition ability). Mothers of disabled readers with low IQ had fewer years of education than mothers of disabled readers with high IQ, and there were fewer books in the homes of low IQ readers. It might be, therefore, that environmental factors were more responsible for reading deficits where IQ was comparatively low, whereas genetic influences were stronger in readers of high IQ (Olson, 2002).

Torgesen (1989) also argued that "IQ is relevant to the definition of reading abilities for scientific research" (p. 485) on the grounds that many studies have shown a correlation between IQ and word-reading scores, which suggested to him that, all else being equal, IQ is causally related to reading acquisition. Relatively few cases of children with low IQ but good reading skill, as reported for example by Siegel (1988), might reflect an unusually powerful contribution of other factors known to affect reading, such as high motivation, exceptional teaching and parental support. In Torgesen's view, low IQ may not be a sufficient or necessary cause of poor reading but it can contribute to reading failure. However, Torgesen (1989) seems to want to have his cake and eat it, since he accepts that "a reading disability can affect level of general intelligence, at least as measured by current IQ tests" (p. 484). Although he is of the opinion that measurement of IQ is necessary for research purposes (to ensure comparability between different groups of readers before contrasting their performance on some other variable, such as academic performance, phonological skill or whatever), Torgesen is less convinced that IQ is relevant to the selection of children for remedial help.

It will be apparent from the studies reviewed above that the results of comparing discrepancy-defined dyslexics with other poor readers have been mixed. Differences between studies in the cognitive profiles or functioning of poor readers are in part attributable to differences in the criteria used to define reading impairment (Siegel & Ryan, 1989) and in part, perhaps, to differences in severity of reading defect and route of referral to an educational support service or other agency.

In attempts to tease apart the separate contributions of different independent variables to a particular dependent variable, researchers have often used regression analyses. In criticizing the use of regression equations to diagnose dyslexia,

Dykman and Ackerman (1992) argue that "Regression formulas are well and good if the purpose is to identify all students who are underachievers. But it defies common sense to diagnose the child with an IQ of 130 and a reading standard score of 110 as having dyslexia. Certainly the public school system should not be expected to offer special services to such a child" (p. 574). These authors recommend the use of a cut-off technique, whereby there are two steps in the diagnosis of dyslexia. First, a standard score on a reading test is chosen (say 85 or below), meaning that the child is a poor reader for his or her age. Next, there has to be a discrepancy of at least 10 points between standard reading score and full-scale IQ. Such a method maintains the idea of a discrepancy between general ability and reading ability, but avoids the intuitively uncomfortable position of referring to children reading at a superior level as dyslexic.

Rudel writes:

> There are almost as many questions raised by the discrepancy approach as there are questions answered. Is one justified in classifying as dyslexic an upper-middle-class child with a reading age equal to his chronological age when most of the others in his school are reading considerably above [grade] level? Or, in contrast, do we judge as perfectly adequate the poor performance of an economically disadvantaged child with a low RGL [Reading Grade Level] that is nonetheless on a par with, or even above, the ERGL [Expected Reading Grade Level] of others in his school district? What if both these hypothetical children can sustain the tested level of reading only with constant, intensive reading remediation? This may be somewhat akin to questioning whether a diabetic is still a diabetic if he responds favorably to insulin but cannot live without it.
>
> (Rudel, 1985, p. 34)

A similar question arises with regard to adults (Beaton, McDougall, & Singleton, 1997a). Does a person diagnosed in childhood as being dyslexic cease to be dyslexic if, by dint of sustained and unusual effort, he or she has reached adequate or conventional levels of reading proficiency as an adult? (Such individuals are sometimes referred to as "compensated" dyslexics.) And what of adults who have not been labelled dyslexic as children? In fact, diagnosing dyslexia in adults is difficult for a number of reasons, not least being the paucity of standardized reading tests designed for use with adults (Beaton et al., 1997b; Scarborough, 1984).

Quite apart from the problems surrounding discrepancy definitions of dyslexia, there are pitfalls in the assumption that conventional IQ tests are appropriate for testing dyslexic individuals. This was appreciated by Orton (1925), who described a reading-disabled boy aged 16 with a Stanford-Binet IQ of 71. Orton reports: "I was strongly impressed with the feeling that this estimate did not do justice to the boy's mental equipment and that the low rating was to be explained by the fact that the test is inadequate to gage [sic] the equipment in a case of such a special disability" (p. 584). Elsewhere he wrote: "it seems probable that psychometric tests as ordinarily employed give an entirely erroneous and unfair estimate of the intellectual capacity of these children" (p. 582).

Symmes and Rapoport (1972) found the poorest scores within a sample of 54 dyslexic children to be on Arithmetic, Coding and Digit Span subtests, arguing that "the common denominator to these tasks seems to be the sequencing of symbols" (p. 86). Thomson (1982) administered the British Ability Scale (Elliott, Murray, & Pearson, 1979) to 83 children aged 8–16 years referred for reading and spelling difficulties who had a variety of other problems traditionally associated with dyslexia. All children showed a discrepancy between their scores in accuracy of reading and their psychometrically measured intelligence scores. The sample was found to have comparatively low scores on the arithmetic, word reading, short-term memory and speed of information processing sub-scales relative to their normal performance on other sub-scales. The implication is that in assessing the intellectual ability of dyslexic children, it might be appropriate to derive an

overall score calculated by excluding the so-called ACID sub-scales on which they tend to underperform.

Under-performance on certain sub-tests of an IQ scale potentially provides useful diagnostic information. This use of IQ tests may not be unrelated to questions concerning the differential incidence of dyslexia in boys and girls. According to Turner:

> What seems not to have attracted comment is the particular role of the WISC Digit Span and Coding tests in diagnosing dyslexia ... there is a female advantage on Coding of about half a standard deviation ... For Digit Span there is also a female advantage, though a lesser one.
>
> Given that WISC has been the foremost instrument used in dyslexia diagnosis, the implications for identification of girls are impossible to ignore. Individuals in assessment have their test scores compared with the combined scores of boys and girls in the standardisation sample. Thus boys are more likely, and girls less likely, to have their scores deemed as exceptionally low. To attract a dyslexia diagnosis, a girl must perform at a lower level than a boy on these two tests.
>
> (Turner, 1997, pp. 67–68)

In view of the problems inherent in definitions of dyslexia couched in terms of IQ, (Ellis, et al., 1996a, 1996b; Fletcher, Espy, Francis, Davidson, Rourke & Shaywitz, 1989; McDougall & Ellis, 1994; Share, McGee, McKenzie, Williams & Silva, 1987; Shaywitz et al., 1992; Siegel, 1988; 1989a, 1989b; Siegel & Himel, 1998; Stanovich, 1986, 1991, 1994a, 1994b; Toth & Siegel, 1994; Van der Wissel & Zegers, 1985), an alternative, and arguably better, discrepancy to use might be that between an individual's reading performance and some measure of spoken language ability such as listening comprehension (Stanovich, 1991). However, Siegel (1999) believes that "The time has come to abandon listening comprehension as an alternative to IQ tests" (p. 313). Tests of listening comprehension, she argues, place a heavy demand on memory and are affected by one's knowledge of the material. Despite certain reservations, she advocates the use of reading comprehension tests, which allow the individual to refer back to what has been written. A discrepancy between performance on such a test and single-word (and nonword) reading ability would be informative as to the cognitive basis of any reading deficit.

IS DYSLEXIA PART OF A CONTINUUM OF NORMAL READING ABILITY?

Among many unresolved issues in the field of reading research is the question of whether "RD [reading difficulty] is just the lower tail of a multi-factorially determined, normal distribution of reading skill, or whether some cases of RD represent an etiologically distinct disorder" (Pennington et al., 1992, p. 562). This is an old controversy, each side having its adherents. Snowling (1980) presented pronounceable four-letter non-words to 18 dyslexic children (diagnosed on the grounds that their reading and spelling ages were significantly lower than their age and IQ would predict) and 36 reading-matched controls in visual–visual, auditory–auditory and cross-modal immediate memory recognition tasks. She found that the two groups performed similarly with auditory presentation of stimuli, but with visual presentation the dyslexics performed less well than the (younger) controls. While normal readers improved on this task with increasing reading age, the dyslexics did not. On the visual–auditory condition (considered most like real reading), which required grapheme-to-phoneme conversion, the dyslexic children were particularly impaired. Snowling argued from her results that:

> dyslexic children ... are not just like readers at the lower end of the normal distribution of reading skill, for they do not perform similarly to a group of reading-age matched younger normal readers. Although they can develop strategies to read whole words and hence build a considerable sight

vocabulary, they find it difficult to decode unfamiliar words into sound.
>
> (Snowling, 1980, p. 303)

Other authors argue the contrary position with equal conviction. Bryant (1985) used data from Rodgers (1983) and elsewhere to argue that reading difficulties should be considered as falling on a continuum with variation in the normal range of reading ability. He believes that underlying this continuum is the capacity of phonological awareness. In his view, the processes underlying the abilities of poor readers are quantitatively but not qualitatively different from those in normal readers.

Stanovich claims that:

> with regard to reading and reading disability ... we are dealing not with a discrete entity but with a graded continuum ... I think it is also important to conceive of all of the relevant distributions of reading-related cognitive skills as being continuously arrayed in a multi-dimensional space and not distributed in clusters. In short, I accept the model of heterogeneity without clustering.
>
> (Stanovich, 1989, p. 368)

Elsewhere, Stanovich (1988b) argues that "the fact that the distribution is a graded continuum does not render the concept of dyslexia scientifically useless" (p. 599) and goes on to commend Ellis's (1985) example of dyslexia as being somewhat akin to obesity. Ellis argued:

> For people of any given age and height there will be an uninterrupted continuum from painfully thin to inordinately fat. It is entirely arbitrary where we draw the line between "normal" and "obese", but that does not prevent obesity being a real and worrying condition nor does it prevent research into the causes and cures of obesity being both valuable and necessary.
>
> (Ellis, 1985, p. 172)

As discussed elsewhere in this monograph, some people regard dyslexia not simply (or even) in terms of poor reading, but as a distinct clustering or pattern of cognitive skills. Nicolson (1996), for example, in criticizing the views expressed by Stanovich (1991, 1994a), was moved to write: "I consider that serious damage is done to the concept of dyslexia if dyslexia is viewed merely as one end of the poor reading continuum, or if all children who read poorly are considered dyslexic" (p. 196).

ONE HUMP OR TWO?

The question of the aetiological distinctiveness of dyslexia has often been addressed in terms of whether reading achievement scores are normally distributed (Fletcher et al., 1994b; Hermann, 1959; Rodgers, 1983; Share et al., 1987; Shaywitz, Escobar, Shaywitz, Fletcher, & Makuch, 1992a; Van der Wissel & Zegers, 1985) or whether the distribution contains a "hump" at the lower end (Dobbins, 1988; Rutter & Yule, 1975; Stevenson, 1988; Yule et al., 1974).

In a well-known paper, Yule et al. (1974) derived regression equations of the relation between non-verbal IQ and reading for five samples of children, four from the Isle of Wight and one from London. The children were aged 9–14 years and separate equations were determined for each age and sample. This enabled Yule et al. to calculate the numbers of children of each sample whose reading score (on a group test of reading) fell into various categories above and below the predicted mean for each sample. For reading scores at the extreme of the lower end (less than two standard errors below the predicted mean), there were significantly more under-achievers observed than predicted, a pattern seen in three of the samples individually. Significantly fewer over-achievers were observed at the extreme higher end of the distribution but this was due, it was argued, to a ceiling in performance on the test of reading ability. Since children with an IQ of 70 or less were excluded, the greater than expected number of under-achievers cannot be attributed to very low IQ scores.

In a further analysis, children who were selected on the basis of the group tests were administered individual tests. Specific reading retardation was defined in terms of a score on the Neale test of reading ability (which has separate accuracy and comprehension scores) at least two standard errors below that predicted by the regression of WISC-IQ on the Neale test for randomly selected control children from each of three of the five samples of children. In terms of accuracy, it was concluded that:

> In all three instances . . . the prevalence of specific reading retardation was well in excess of the expected 2.28 per cent. The individual tests confirm those based on group tests. Severe degrees of underachievement in reading occur much more commonly than would be expected on the basis of a normal distribution . . . *Extreme* under-achievement in reading occurs at appreciably above the rate expected on the basis of a normal distribution and so constitutes a hump at the lower end of the Gaussian curve . . . and the finding implies that there is a group of children with severe and specific reading retardation which is *not* just the lower end of a normal distribution.
>
> (Yule et al., 1974, pp. 9, 10, emphasis in
>
> original).

Given the departure from normality (that is, from a truly normal distribution) in the distribution of the discrepancy scores obtained by Yule et al. (1974), they maintained that "This suggests that there is a meaningful group of children with specific reading retardation which is not explicable simply in terms of the bottom of a continuum" (p. 1). Note that Yule et al. (1974) drew a distinction in their work between specific reading retardation and general reading backwardness (see above), a distinction drawn earlier by Rutter, Tizard, and Whitmore (1970).

Van der Wissel and Zegers (1985) criticized Yule et al. (1974) and Rutter and Yule (1975) on the grounds that a ceiling in the reading test scores led to the distribution of discrepancy scores being negatively skewed (see also Rodgers, 1983). In such a distribution, the proportion of children with scores less than two standard deviations below the mean is larger than in a truly normal distribution and thus:

> there is no need to introduce the notion of a meaningful group of children with specific reading retardation, as Yule et al. do, to explain the non-normality of the discrepancy scores. The relative ease of the reading test and the consequent negatively skewed disribution of discrepancy scores give us a much simpler, and in our opinion, more plausible explanation.
>
> (Van der Wissel & Zegers, 1985, p. 6)

Data associated with the 1970 British Birth Cohort Study, a survey of all births in Great Britain and Northern Ireland during a particular week in April, which were followed up in 1975 and 1980, were analysed by Rodgers (1983). The data from over 8000 children included scores on a short reading test and scores on four sub-tests from the battery comprising the British Ability Scales. Rodgers was unable to confirm the finding of a "hump" at the lower end of the distribution of under-/over-achievement in reading by 10-year-olds. In contrast, Stevenson (1988) claimed for 1547 children aged 11 years (but not for most of the same children as 7-year-olds) that "there is an unexpectedly large group of children with severe underachievement in relation to their general intelligence. This excess of children at the extreme of underachievement is not found when non-language-based school achievement, such as maths, is investigated" (p. 83). This finding was replicated for a group of 13-year-old children (*n* = 570) in a twin study (285 pairs); in addition, a "hump" was found for nonword reading.

Share et al. (1987) analysed data from a cohort of children from New Zealand who were assessed at different ages. These authors reported no evidence for a "hump" in the distribution of reading scores (corrected for age) regressed on performance IQ. By introducing successively lower ceilings on the scores (by allocating the same score to successively larger proportions of scores at the top end), they found that the proportion of under-achievers increased, while the proportion of over-achievers decreased. They also found that introducing negative skew into the distributions produced an excess of under-achievers even in the absence of floor and ceiling effects. They discussed the possibility of ceiling effects and evidence of skew (see Rodgers, 1983) in the data of Yule et al. (1974), which Rutter and Yule (1975) relied upon in formulating their distinction between specific reading retardation and general reading backwardness. Share and his collaborators suggested that the "hump" reported by the latter may have been artefactual.

Share et al. (1987) acknowledged that the absence of a "hump" in the distribution of under- and over-achievement in reading does not necessarily rule out the possibility of "two qualitatively distinct subpopulations of readers" (p. 38). The appearance of bimodality in a distribution depends upon the degree of separation of the sub-distributions and their relative sizes. However, as Share et al. also point out, "The validity of any distinction between types of disorder ulimately rests upon whether the disorders can be differentiated on dimensions other than those used to define the disorders" (p. 41). There was little in their own data to support such a distinction. Their conclusion was that "it seems best to treat under-achievement as a continuum" (p. 42).

Despite the confident assertion of Stanovich (1988b) that "There is in fact no hump in the distribution" (p. 599), a definitive answer to the question of whether there is a "hump" is remarkably elusive despite its apparent simplicity. This is perhaps because, according to Dobbins (1988), "the magnitude of the increased frequency of that expected is 23 children in a distribution of size greater than 5000" (p. 343), which, in the words of Miles and Haslum (1986), is "a slight pimple rather than a substantial hump" (p. 106). This might explain failures, such as that of Share et al. (1987), to find a "hump" in samples of less than 1000.

Although the supposed significance of the existence or otherwise of a "hump" is tied up with the question of whether dyslexia or specific reading disability can and should be distinguished from other forms (and causes) of poor reading, Stevenson maintains that:

> the presence or absence of a "hump" in reading underachievement is only marginally related to the issue of there being a qualitatively distinct group of poor readers. The *absence* of such a "hump" does not represent strong evidence against such an aetiologically distinct group ... Similarly the *presence* of the "hump" is only indirect evidence of the presence of an aetiologically distinct group.
>
> (Stevenson, 1988, p. 83, emphasis in original)

It follows from this view that justification for the term "dyslexia" does not stand or fall on the supposed presence or otherwise of bimodality in the distribution of reading achievement scores. The other arguments discussed in this chapter for and against the concept of dyslexia, as distinct from poor reading, have been based on the notion of a syndrome, or pattern of difficulties said to be associated with poor reading, and on the putative relevance of IQ or, more specifically, on a discrepancy between IQ and reading level. At the time of writing there is still no consensus in the literature as to how dyslexia should be defined. This constitutes a problem for the conscientious reviewer, since different authors use the term in different ways. The almost universal practice of including in the research sample only research participants who have an average IQ or above almost guarantees that a high proportion of participants satisfy a discrepancy definition. On the other hand, very often little else is known about the participants. What proportion, for example, show deficits beyond those of poor reading and spelling? Furthermore, the standard use of exclusionary criteria means that the research literature refers only to a restricted proportion of poor readers.

Seymour wrote of the World Federation of Neurology definition of dyslexia as difficulty in learning to read despite conventional instruction, adequate intelligence, socio-cultural opportunity and dependence upon cognitive disabilities of constitutional origin in the following terms:

> It can be seen that there are two parts to this statement. The first is a definition by exclusion which advises neurologists that a diagnosis of dyslexia might most confidently be made when a severe reading disability was [*sic*] found to occur in the absence of other negative influences ... The second part asserts that the disorder is dependent on fundamental cognitive disabilities which may well have their origin in the genetic programming of the development of the brain in early life. Since genetic influences of this kind can not be expected to respect the boundaries of poor intelligence, poor social circumstances or poor schooling, it is implicit that dyslexic problems may occur at any level of intelligence, social staus or adequacy of schooling. It follows that the definition by exclusion contained in the first part of the statement is no more than an admission that "dyslexia" is easier to diagnose in children who are intellectually, socially and educationally advantaged than in those who are not.
>
> On these grounds I would argue that the restrictive use of the term "dyslexia" constitutes a category mistake. It involves a pragmatically motivated stipulation that a general term should be applied restrictively to a subset of the larger class to which it refers. My own view is that no useful purpose is served by promulgating or seeking to defend this stipulation or indeed by arguing about its validity. In this monograph the term "dyslexia" will be used simply as a label for a disturbance affecting the establishment of basic reading and spelling skills. Dyslexia is defined as "difficulty in learning to read"
>
> (Seymour, 1986, p. 2).

Given the unresolved controversies discussed above, that is how the term "dyslexia" will be used in the present work, without implying thereby a commitment at this point to any particular view as to what dyslexia "is". In particular, I do not wish either to distance myself from, or necessarily align myself with, the view that dyslexia constitutes a syndrome that includes difficulties in domains other than reading and spelling. It is simply that it is virtually impossible to review the relevant literature without embracing the kind of broad definition adopted by Seymour. It has the merit of being about as theoretically neutral as it is possible to be. It will only occasionally be possible (see also Tønnessen, 1997a) in the present work to distinguish between different categories of poor reader as the relevant data are rarely presented in research reports. Thus whether the impairments identified should be seen as applying to "poor readers" generally or only to "genuine dyslexics" is an open point. This monograph should therefore be consulted with this in mind.

2

The Theoretical Context of Normal Reading Development

Dyslexia is but one side of a coin, the other being normal, skilled reading. It might be expected that discussions about the nature or causes of dyslexia would be carried out within the context of attempts to understand the processes involved in the acquisition of normal, unimpaired reading. Although this is to some extent the case, it is not always so. Many researchers of dyslexia seem quite oblivious to developments within the field of reading research more generally (and vice versa). Yet for many it is intuitively obvious that a theory of normal reading acquisition provides an essential framework for consideration of dyslexic difficulties. Such a theory may be important in determining how reading difficulties are assessed and remediated (Seymour & Duncan, 1997).

THEORETICAL APPROACHES TO READING

Dual-route theory

Early in the nineteenth century, neurologists in Germany such as Lichtheim, (1885), Wernicke (1974) and others produced simple diagrams to represent their theories of how the brain processed language. Although these "diagram makers" were ridiculed by the British neurologist Henry Head (Head, 1926), something of the flavour of their endeavour survives to the present day.

Over the past 20 years or so, cognitive neuropsychological analyses of the acquired dyslexias (see, for example, Coltheart, 1982, 1985; Ellis, 1993) have led to the development of so-called "box-and-arrows" models of a functional architecture that represents the state of affairs in adults who at one time were able to read (see Figure 1). This development is encapsulated in what is currently one of the main theoretical approaches to reading aloud, so-called "dual-route" theory. According to this approach (e.g. Baron & Strawson, 1976; Coltheart, 1978; 1985; Coltheart, Curtis, Atkins, & Haller, 1993, Coltheart & Rastle, 1994; Coltheart, Rastle, Perry, Langdon, & Ziegler, 2001; Funnell, 1983; Humphreys & Evett, 1985; Patterson & Morton, 1985), there are two routes, procedures or mechanisms whereby letter strings are pronounced. (Note that we are not here concerned principally with the issue of access to meaning.)

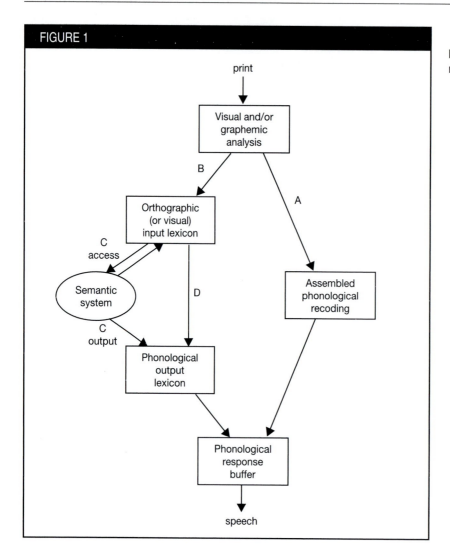

FIGURE 1

Figure 1 Model of oral reading routes

The first route or process posited by dual-route theorists entails words being read by a process that treats each word as an indivisible whole. A word is recognized by accessing an entry in a memory store of all known words, a visual input dictionary or lexicon. The pronunciation of the word is then given by accessing or addressing an appropriate entry in a dictionary or lexicon of the sound structure of familiar words. This is the lexical routine, and it is assumed to be required for the pronunciation of idiosyncratic exception words, such as *colonel*, *pint*, *quay* and *leopard*, which cannot be pronounced correctly by decomposing the word into separate constituent sounds according to grapheme–phoneme or other correspondence rules.

The second process or route of dual-route models is thought to be required for the pronunciation of nonwords or pseudowords, since they do not have a lexical entry. Letter strings are pronounced by decoding a given letter string into smaller units and the phonology of each unit is assigned according to a set of context-dependent rules to provide the appropriate pronunciation. This way of reading is known as the phonological recoding, assembled or sub-lexical routine and can be used for reading familiar regular words as well as nonwords.

Individual differences in the use of these two routes led Baron and Strawson (1976) and Baron (1979) to describe adult readers as being either Phonecians (predominantly rule-based) or Chinese (word-specific) readers. It should be noted that in referring to the two routes, Baron (1979) writes as follows: "Two general mechanisms are of interest. One, an orthographic mechanism, uses spelling–sound correspondence rules. This kind of mechanism can be used to read nonsense words, but it is less useful for words such as 'sword' and 'broad', which are exceptions to the rule" (p. 60). Thus Baron (1979)—and Baron and Strawson (1976)— used the word in the opposite sense to that in which the term "orthographic coding" tends to be used today.

Although the sub-lexical route is often referred to as the grapheme–phoneme correspondence route, it may not be the case that only single letters or graphemes (such as *ph* in *elephant*) are converted into sound units (see Baron, 1979; Norris, 1994; Shallice & McCarthy, 1985; Shallice, Warrington, & McCarthy, 1983; Treiman, 1992), therefore, a more theoretically neutral term would refer to an orthographic–phonological conversion route where the size of the relevant units varies between single letters, graphemes, sub-syllabic components and syllables. It will be noted that in the limiting condition an entire word might be the appropriate size of unit, in which case the distinction between a direct lexical route and an indirect sub-lexical conversion route disappears. Note, too, that use of this route presupposes an ability to segment letter strings into units of varying size before assigning the appropriate phonology. It is also worth noting that as well as converting a visually based unit (of whatever size) into a sound unit, an unknown word can be read by analogy with a word that is already known (Baron, 1979; Glushko, 1979; Kay & Marcel, 1981). This process also seems to require segmentation of a word into onset and rime (so as to read, for example, *cat* by analogy with *bat*). The underlying mechanism of analogizing has not been specified in any detail but, for the present, analogy theory can be seen as falling into a similar theoretical grouping as the multiple-levels view.

The key components of the lexical route, then, are: a visual input lexicon that feeds into the semantic system, which, in turn, activates candidate entries in a phonological output lexicon. The key components of the sub-lexical route are an orthographic–phonological conversion route and a phoneme assembly mechanism. (Both routes must lead at some point to generation and execution of an articulatory programme for a letter string to be pronounced overtly; for discussion of this issue see Rastle, Harrington, Coltheart, & Palethorpe, 2000.) To accommodate writing, the converse process to reading, the components need to include a phonological–orthographic conversion procedure and an orthographic output lexicon (for written spelling). Coltheart and his colleagues consider that the sub-lexical route operates in a left-to-right sequential manner, whereas the lexical route processes a letter string in parallel, each letter being processed at the same time (see Rastle & Coltheart, 1998, 2000b).

Since learning to read and discriminate letters undoubtedly involves some kind of visual discrimination learning, it may be as well to make clear that the component of the cognitive neuropsychological approach to skilled adult reading (see, for example, Ellis, 1984, 1985, 1993), which is called the visual input lexicon, refers not to a mechanism for visual pattern recognition but to a more abstract entity. This is a word recognition device that enables recognition of the spelling pattern of a visually presented word as a whole regardless of the precise format in which the word is presented. The alternative term, orthographic input lexicon, captures this meaning more precisely than the vaguer term visual input lexicon (see Figure 1 on page 26).

The two putative routes for reading may be regarded as being to some extent under the strategic control of the reader rather than immutably tied to particular types of stimulus (Baluch & Besner, 1991; Rastle & Coltheart, 1999a, 1999b; but see Waters & Seidenberg, 1986). In one study, dyslexic children performed at a significantly higher level than control children matched for reading on a test of orthographic awareness that required them to select which of a pair of letter strings most "looked like" a word (Siegel, Share,

& Geva, 1995). The basis for this choice was whether particular letter bigrams are found in the relevant postions as part of genuine English words. As the dyslexic children were less successful than controls in reading aloud pseudowords that could be read on the basis of grapheme–phoneme correspondences, this result suggests that under normal circumstances dyslexics may preferentially attend to the visual (orthographic) structure of words rather than sound them out. When children are highly skilled at recognizing words as (abstract) orthographic patterns in the context of pronounced cognitive and linguistic deficits, or when their word recognition ability is substantially in advance of their comprehension and other cognitive skills (for a review, see Nation, 1999), they are sometimes referred to as being hyperlexic.

It was argued by Pennington (1999) that the dual-route model should be questioned on the ground that "phonology is more central to reading than it assumes, and because the putative direct route is not independent of phonological coding" (p. 635). There are two main reasons why Pennington made this rather odd statement. The first is that there tends to be a high correlation between exception word and nonword reading performance (Gough & Walsh, 1991). The second is that much research with skilled readers (see Frost, 1998; Van Orden, Pennington, & Stone, 1990) has shown that "virtually every instance of printed word recognition involved phonological activation and that this activation happened very quickly, perhaps before the activation of spelling knowledge or meaning" (Pennington, 1999, p. 633). This is a debatable point (see Waters & Seidenberg, 1986). In any event, no dual-route theorist would wish to argue that under normal circumstances phonology *cannot* be activated. The theory is, after all, first and foremost a theory of how written words are pronounced. Dual-route theory explicitly distinguishes the activation of sub-lexical phonological units (assembled phonology) from the activation of whole-word (addressed) phonology. The question of whether phonology is activated before spelling or semantic information is a red herring. Nor is the frequent co-activation of semantic and phonological information evidence against the psychological or neural independence of these processes.

Some of the confusion in this area probably arises because some reading theorists conceptualize a single lexical entry as representing both semantic and phonological information. On the other hand, evidence from neuropsychology suggests that semantic information and phonological information *can* be separated—which is not to say that for all theoretical purposes they need to be. Cognitive neuropsychologists who argue in favour of dual-route theory separate these two aspects of lexical entries but not everyone does. The issue might seem to hinge on the time course of phonological activation: Does it occur before access to semantic representations or not? On this point, the evidence is equivocal, as shown by Pennington's use of the word "perhaps" in the above quote. More importantly, it is not at all clear that arguments based on temporal aspects of reading can ever falsify dual-route models.

Despite the label dual-route theory, it has been proposed that there are in fact three routes. In using the direct lexical route to pronounce irregular words such as *quay*, it is assumed that a semantic code representing the meaning of the word is activated and that this is used to address the word's entry in a phonological output lexicon. It was observed in a study of patient W.L.P., who suffered from dementia, that she could pronounce correctly irregular words such as *leopard* and *bear*, but apparently had no understanding of their meaning (Schwartz, Saffran, & Marin, 1980; see also Schwartz, Marin, & Saffran, 1979). This suggests the existence of a route (see Figure 1 on page 26) that directly links an entry in the orthographic input lexicon with the corresponding entry in the phonological output lexicon, bypassing the semantic system (see Baron, 1979). The condition is therefore sometimes referred to as lexical-nonsemantic reading (e.g. Lambon Ralph, Ellis, & Franklin, 1995; Weekes & Robinson, 1997). Further and more convincing evidence was provided by Coslett (1991), who reported that patient W.T. could read highly irregular words but was unable to read nonwords (implying a non-functioning conversion route). She showed an effect of imageability in repeating auditorily presented words and in writing to dictation, suggesting that performance on these tasks was semantically mediated, but she showed no imageability effect in oral reading. In addition, she was impaired in comprehension (as well as repetition and writing) of the low-imageability words that she read accurately. This pattern of results is consistent with the view that her oral reading was accomplished through a non-semantic whole-word route (see also Cipolotti & Warrington, 1995).

The existence of a non-semantic whole-word route for reading, and one perhaps for spelling to dictation (Patterson, 1986), is somewhat controversial and other interpretations have been offered. Cipolotti and Warrington (1995) favoured the view that direct links exist between phonology and orthographic units of different size (Shallice et al., 1983) and that the co-occurrence of good but not perfect exception word reading with poor or non-existent definitions of these same words by their patient D.R.N. reflects the greater vulnerability of larger (whole-word) units compared with smaller units to the effects of progressive neurological disease. For present purposes, the important thing to note is that the putative existence of a third route can be (and usually is) subsumed under the label of a direct lexical route.

The main evidence favouring the dual-route theory comes from cognitive neuropsychology (Coltheart, 1982, 1985, 1987) and, in particular, intensive individual case studies. There is considerable debate (see papers in Volume 5, Number 5 of *Cognitive Neuropsychology*) as to whether the best method in neuropsychology involves testing groups of patients (e.g. Grodzinsky, Pinango, Zurif, & Drai, 1999; Zurif, Gardner, & Brownell, 1989; Zurif, Swinney, & Fodor, 1991) or intensively studying the pattern of deficits and preserved abilities shown by single patients (e.g. Caramazza, 1986; Caramazza & McCloskey, 1988). In either case, the principle of double dissociation (Jones, 1983; Teuber, 1955; but see Plaut, 1995) has been invoked to support the view that there are two independent routes or procedures for reading.

The variety of acquired dyslexia known as surface dyslexia (Marshall & Newcombe, 1973; see Patterson, Marshall, & Coltheart, 1985) concerns the recognition of the orthographic (spelling) pattern of words and/or production of the correct pronunciation. Patients can read regular words and nonwords very well but have difficulty with irregular or inconsistent words, which they tend to pronounce as if they have applied a phonological recoding procedure. That is, they make what are called regularization errors, for example pronouncing the word *quay* as *kway*. This suggests (but does not demand) some impairment of the direct lexical route. In these circumstances, the patient may be more or less obliged to use the sub-lexical route to pronounce words (in a way that reflects the relative frequency of particular letter combinations in the language; see Patterson & Behrmann, 1997). Conversely, patients with phonological dyslexia can pronounce familiar regular and irregular words but have difficulty with nonwords. This suggests either that some aspect of their orthographic–phonological conversion route (including graphemic parsing, phoneme activation or phoneme blending) is impaired or that there is a weakness or impairment in the representation of phonological information (see Harm & Seidenberg, 1999, 2001).

The two sub-varieties of acquired reading disorder, surface dyslexia and phonological dyslexia, should be regarded as convenient descriptive (but not explanatory) labels, since the same pattern of deficit may be produced by difficulty in or surrounding more than one component of the cognitive architecture assumed to support oral reading. That is, a given impairment may be brought about by more than one functional lesion. For discussion of this point in regard to surface dyslexia the interested reader is referred to the collection of papers edited by Patterson, Marshall, and Coltheart (1985). With regard to phonological dyslexia, Volume 13 (1996) of the journal *Cognitive Neuropsychology* should be consulted.

Connectionist models of reading

In contrast to the dual-route theory of reading are the so-called connectionist or neural-network models exemplified by that of Seidenberg and McClelland (1989) and its more recent modifications (Plaut, McClelland, Seidenberg, & Patterson, 1996; Seidenberg, Plaut, Petersen, McClelland, & McRae, 1994). Connectionist networks consist of units (analogous to neurones) that are connected together in such a way that each unit has many links to other units. A layer of input units is connected to a layer of output units either directly or indirectly via an intermediate set of so-called hidden units. A stimulus is encoded by the input units and a response is produced by the output units. Initially, the network might be set up such that the strength of connections, or weightings, between the input and output units is random. The response to a given stimulus is provided by the output units taking the weighted sum of the activity of all input units. If the sum exceeds some predetermined threshold, then an output is produced. This output can be compared with the correct response (using a variety of algorithms) and, if incorrect, the weightings can be adjusted (in several models through a process known as back-propagation). The weightings between input and output units are altered according to the frequency with which particular graphemic and phonemic sequences co-occur. This process can be repeated until the network produces the correct response. Thus from the input provided to it during the training phase, the model or network abstracts or "learns" the statistical regularities between orthography and phonology. The critical question then becomes how the network "behaves" when confronted with stimuli (words or nonwords) on which it has not been trained. A second question is how it deals with (or how quickly it learns to respond to) stimuli that vary in lexicality, regularity (consistency), frequency or some other feature. The behaviour of the model can be compared with that of humans. To the extent that both behave in the same way, it is argued, the model provides a computationally explicit account of reading. The closer the correspondence between the behaviour of the model and the performance of humans, the greater the plausibility of the psychological theory upon which the model is based. This is not to say, of course, that the model necessarily pro-

vides a biologically plausible account, although it may do so. In addition to simulating normal reading processes, a "lesioned" model may provide insight into the behaviour of brain-damaged patients with acquired forms of dyslexia (Hinton & Shallice, 1991; Hinton, Plaut, & Shallice, 1993).

An early connectionist model was the interactive activation model of McClelland and Rummelhart (1981), according to which there were three orthographic levels: visual feature detectors, letter recognition units and word recognition units. Activation was held to spread in both directions between units at different levels, but there is inhibition between units within the same level. This approach is partially maintained in some more recent computational models, such as that developed by Seidenberg and McClelland (1989) and the model developed by Coltheart and colleagues.

Seidenberg and McClelland's (1989) model is based on 400 orthographic input units connected to 200 hidden units, which, in turn, are connected to 460 phonological output units. There are thus 80,000 connections between the input units and the hidden units and 92,000 connections between the hidden units and the output units. According to the model, there is no route specifically dedicated to irregular or exception words, all words being pronounced using the same procedures. The model was criticized (for reply, see Seidenberg & McClelland, 1990) on a number of counts by Besner, Twilley, McCann, and Seergobin (1990), most notably because it performed relatively poorly when presented with nonwords. In a sense, it behaved as a phonological dyslexic. Other criticisms were made by Coltheart et al. (1993), who argued that although the model gave a plausible account of exception word reading, it failed to provide satisfactory accounts of a number of other phenomena, including lexical decision performance.

The mere fact of implementing a computational model does not of itself distinguish between dual-route and single-route theories. The dual-route model, for example, has been implemented in Coltheart's dual-route cascade (DRC) model as applied to English (Coltheart et al., 1993, 2001) and German (Ziegler, Perry, &

Coltheart, 2000) and in the model outlined by Zorzi, Houghton, and Butterworth (1998).

The computational version of dual-route theory is termed cascaded because as soon as activation begins at any one level it is assumed to flow on to subsequent levels; it is not necessary that a particular threshold of activation must be reached in one component before being passed on to other components. The model of Seidenberg and McClelland (1989) is also interactive in this sense. Both models, however, constrain how activation flows between levels or layers. In Seidenberg and McClelland's (1989) model, for example, activation does not flow (at least directly) from the phonological to the orthographic level and in the DRC model letter units are activated by features but not vice versa.

In the DRC model, there are three routes: a lexical semantic route (not yet implemented), a lexical non-semantic route and a grapheme–phoneme correspondence (GPC) route. Each of the three routes is composed of three different layers corresponding to visual letter features, abstract letter units and phoneme units. The abstract letter units layer is common to the lexical non-semantic and GPC route; diversion of the two routes occurs after this level. Subsequently, there is a convergence of the two routes at the phoneme unit level as each unit in the phonological output lexicon is connected to the appropriate phoneme units in the phoneme layer.

Words are represented as abstract visual whole-word units in the orthographic lexicon, one unit per word. Thus in this model each word in a person's sight vocabulary has a local representation, whereas in other connectionist models (Seidenberg & McClelland, 1989) words are represented not as discrete entries in a lexicon but as patterns of activation distributed across a number of relevant units. The updated version of Seidenberg and McClelland's (1989) model (Plaut et al., 1996) uses local representations of graphemes and phonemes, but words are still represented as distributed patterns of activation across these units. At the present time, explicit computational models have been developed mainly for monosyllabic words (up to a given length), although Rastle and Coltheart (2000a) have

attempted to confront some of the complexities presented by bisyllabic words (see Humphreys & Evett, 1985; Patterson & Morton, 1985) within the context of dual-route theory. Ans, Carbonnel, and Valdois (1998) have also developed a model of polysyllabic word reading but without assuming any explicit (or implicit) conversion rules (that is, it is not a dual-route type model in the sense in which the term is usually used).

According to Seidenberg and McClelland's (1989) and related models, there are two mechanisms for oral reading: a semantically mediated mechanism and a mechanism that operates by converting print to sound according to context-sensitive mappings between graphemes and phonemes. These mappings are not generated according to specific rules as they are in the DRC model, but reflect the settings of the links between a set of input units (letter sequences), so-called hidden units and output units (phonology). These settings are weighted or biased according to the corpus of words on which the programme is trained. That is, the relative frequency and consistency of correspondences between orthographic and phonological units have to be learned. There is no specifically lexical procedure; the mappings "learned" by the system are entirely non-lexical, regardless of whether a letter string constitutes a regular word or an irregular word. According to this model, any discrepancy in performance between words and nonwords (as seen in phonological dyslexia) is due to the use of the semantically mediated procedure for reading; any difference between regular and irregular words (as in surface dyslexia) is attributable to different weightings operating on the mappings between input and output units. It is claimed that the model is not only capable of accommodating data on normal reading but can account for different kinds (and degree) of dyslexia (see Harm & Seidenberg, 1999; Seidenberg, 1993), as has been claimed for the DRC model (Coltheart et al., 1993, 2001).

Semantic representations are an integral part of the triangle model of word reading. This stands in contrast to most other theories of reading (but see Ehri, 1992a, 1992b 1995), although it should be clear that these other models do not deny the influence of semantic factors in word reading so much as ignore them. Because word processing is regarded as involving the interaction between orthographic, phonological and semantic representations in the model of Plaut et al. (1996), as well as in the earlier Seidenberg and McClelland (1989) version, this approach (shared by a number of other authors not necessarily associated with connectionist models) has been termed a triangle model.

Semantic factors affect the ease with which lists of words are learned (Ellis & Beaton, 1993), the probability with which individual words are read by deep dyslexic readers (Beaton, Ved, & Guest, 1994; Coltheart, 1980; Newton & Barry, 1997) and the speed with which they are recognized by normal adult readers (Strain, Patterson, & Seidenberg, 1995). It is not inconceivable, then, that they influence how readily children learn to recognize words during early reading development. Some support for such a view comes from a study by Laing and Hulme (1999). These authors found that children in the early stages of reading development more readily learned abbreviated spellings for highly imageable words than for words lower in imageability. Imageability is thought to reflect richness of semantic representation, ease of prediction or some such and is universally seen as a semantic variable. The results of the study by Laing and Hulme (1999), therefore, imply that semantic factors influence early word reading. It should be noted, however, that although Laing and Hulme controlled for familiarity and age of acquisition of the target words, they did so by asking a panel of 15 professionals who worked with children to rate both familiarity and the likely age of acquisition of the words on a 7-point scale in addition to rating degree of imageability. It may be that these ratings were not independent of each other, in which case the effect reported for imageability may in fact turn out to be an artefact of age-of-acquisition or of familiarity. Of course, the converse is also possible. Regression analyses were not carried out, so the relative contribution of each variable is unknown.

The claim of Seidenberg and McClelland (1989) and Plaut et al. (1996) that there is no need

to postulate separate routes or mechanisms to explain exception word and nonword reading entails the proposal that sub-varieties of developmental dyslexia can be explained without postulating damage to separate routes or processes. This issue was recently discussed by Harm and Seidenberg (1999), who manipulated aspects of the Plaut et al. (1996) model so as to simulate different patterns of dyslexia. In the simulations, differing levels of phonological impairment were found to differentially affect reading of exception words and nonwords (Harm & Seidenberg, 1999). In the simulation (of phonological dyslexia), the representation of phonological information was impaired prior to training of the model. With only mild impairment, nonword reading was slightly below that expected, leaving exception word reading relatively intact. With more severe impairment, both nonword and exception word reading were seriously affected (that of nonwords more than that of exception words). Harm and Seidenberg (1999) argued that this showed that damage to a single mechanism rather than to two routes is sufficient to produce both the characteristic mixed pattern of impairment shown by most dyslexic children and the more rare category of pure phonological dyslexia. However, the simulation did not lead to the pure case being very severely impaired in nonword reading. Although this is what was found by Manis, Seidenberg, Doi, McBride-Chang, and Petersen (1996) in their study of school children, pure and severe cases of nonword reading (phonological impairment) have been described in adult case studies (see, for example, Howard & Best, 1996, 1997). This was not regarded as embarassing by Harm and Seidenberg (1999), who stated that "Our view is that these patients' performances reflect other factors outside the scope of our models" (p. 514), which, despite their discussion of how such cases could come about, might be regarded as avoiding the issue!

In the simulation by Harm and Seidenberg (1999), developmental surface dyslexia was regarded not as a selective impairment in reading exception words, but as a general delay in reading, on the grounds that beginning readers are poorer at reading exception words than nonwords.

According to Harm and Seidenberg (1999), "surface dyslexic children can be said to be developmentally delayed" (p. 505). One way in which this pattern could be brought about was by providing less training for the model, which was seen as analogous to impoverished reading experience or a failure to adequately profit from such experience in school children. The fact that adult cases of severe developmental surface dyslexia have been described in the literature (Goulandris & Snowling, 1991; Hanley & Gard, 1995; Hanley, Hastie, & Kay, 1992) was not discussed by Harm and Seidenberg.

The role of learning in theories of the development of skilled reading has been somewhat ignored in the recent past, although there are signs (e.g. Ehri, 1992a, 1992b; Share, 1995, 1999; Windfuhr & Snowling, 2001) that it will have more attention paid to it in future. This will be a particular challenge for dual-route theorists, although one need not agree with Windfuhr and Snowling (2001) that "the finding that phonological awareness and paired associate learning *both* make unique contributions to word and nonword reading processes is not compatible with the idea that lexical and nonlexical reading systems are independent" (pp. 170–171, emphasis in original). According to dual-route theory, novel words and nonwords are read by means of phonological decoding. Grapheme–phoneme correspondences (or associations between units of a different size) have to be learned and there is every reason to expect that both phonological awareness and paired associate learning contribute to this process. The association between a given orthographic pattern or whole word and its pronunciation also has to be learned (lexical route). The implicit question posed by Windfuhr and Snowling (2001) is: "Why should phonological awareness be important for whole-word learning?" One answer might be that the first time a word is encountered in print it has to be treated as a nonword even if it is subsequently recognized as a whole-word single unit. Although this could be regarded as a form of rapid learning (see Share, 1995), which for some words might be accomplished in a single trial, initially some phonological segmentation is required.

The tasks used by Windfuhr and Snowling (2001) to assess phonological awareness were a rhyming (odd-man-out) task and phoneme deletion task. The odd-man-out task has been criticized as involving a number of components including a memory load (see Wagner & Torgesen, 1987), a view acknowledged by Bryant (1998). This being so, it may not be a good measure of children's awareness of the onset-rime structure of words. Furthermore, the stimuli used in the phoneme deletion task were such that the correct response always resulted in a real word (e.g. *bice* with /b/ deleted), which might have led to a high proportion of correct responses purely by chance. In any case, the task might well be tapping a knowledge of vocabulary, which, in turn, might be expected to influence the ease with which word-specific associations are acquired in the development of reading.

By their very nature, connectionist models provide an account of how associations are established between orthographic input and phonological output. In short, they learn over time. That is what children do; they do not become skilled readers immediately. However, the way in which the models "learn" (i.e. their learning algorithms) is not intended to model the learning process of children. Rather, they are descriptions of what is learned. Nor, indeed, does learning to read end suddenly. As Perfetti notes:

"What we know a lot about is *skilled* word recognition and *skilled* comprehension. What we still know much less about are the processes of word recognition (and comprehension) that serve a child as he or she learns how to read. Even less is known about the processes by which the learning reader acquires higher levels of word recognition skill, moving from 'novice' to 'expert' ".

(Perfetti, 1992, pp. 145–146, emphasis in original)

While attempts have been made to discuss developmental dyslexia and normal reading development within the theoretical context of dual-route theory, some authors feel that this approach does not do justice to the developmental aspect of acquiring what in the words of Coltheart and Leahy (1996) is "no more 'natural' an ability than skilled piano playing" (p. 137). They argue that a cognitive analysis explains the "how" but not the "why" of any reading deficit (Zoccolotti et al., 2000). Frith (1985), for example, sees the assumption that the same information processing model is sufficient to explain both acquired and developmental varieties of dyslexia as "a challenge to those of us who believe that it is necessary to have a developmental framework when considering developmental disorders" (p. 69). She maintains that a static model of adult performance, such as dual-route theory, is inadequate for understanding how children learn to read (see also Ehri, 1992a) and why some children learn to read easily while others have difficulties. However, Frith concedes that "the 'outcome' of the developmental sequence is the skilled reader. Structural models of skilled reading are therefore helpful when considering developmental models and vice versa" (p. 303). More recently, Snowling et al. (1996a) have gone so far as to assert that "The idea of trying to formulate a theory of developmental dyslexia in terms of a theory of adult reading is fundamentally midsguided" (p. 444). In their view, reiterated recently by Snowling and her collaborators (Snowling, 2000a; Snowling, Bishop, & Stothard, 2000), reading is a skill that is learned and we therefore need a theory of how this learning takes place.

It has been argued, then, that developmental dyslexia should be understood in relation to a theory of how learning to read normally takes place and how it fails to proceed in certain cases. However, there is, to my mind, no necessary incompatibility between cognitive neuropsychological models used to explain patterns of impaired and preserved reading in adults and developmental models of the acquisition process in children. As Coltheart (1987) pointed out, "learning to read must involve these two procedures" (p. 98). The challenge is to specify how the final components of the adult model are arrived at. Thus a cognitive developmental analysis of reading (or any other) disorder requires a description of the functional or cognitive architecture supporting reading (and writing) plus an account of the developmental processes that lead to skilled reading. Attempts to provide such an analysis can be seen in the experimental investigations of Seymour and his colleagues (e.g. Seymour & MacGregor, 1984; Seymour, 1986, 1990, Seymour & Elder, 1986; Seymour & Evans, 1993) and in the attempts of some theorists to to link the training of their connectionist models to the development of reading (e.g. Harm & Seidenberg, 1999).

STAGE THEORIES OF READING DEVELOPMENT

A number of theorists have proposed that reading development occurs in recognizable stages. There is, of course, no doubt that reading develops. What is entailed in the notion of stages is the idea that children necessarily pass through a developmental sequence in a fixed order. These stages are identified by the strategies children use as evidenced by the types of error which they make. The most well-known stage theories are those of Marsh, Friedman, Welch, and Desberg (1981), Frith (1985) and Ehri (1980, 1992a, 1992b, 1995). For a brief account of stage theories, see Rack, Hulme, and Snowling (1993).

Ehri (1980) presented a model, referred to as word identity amalgamation theory, which she has developed over a good number of years. She states that "The term 'amalgamation' is used to denote the special way in which orthographic identities get established in lexical memory" (p. 313). According to Ehri (1992a), there are three stages or phases of reading acquisition: visual cue or logographic reading, phonetic cue or rudimentary alphabetic reading, and cipher reading. In the first phase, children select salient visual features "in or around words" to access their meaning. In the second phase, once they have some letter–sound knowledge, children establish partial associations between some, but not all, of the letters in a word and the phonemes that they represent. This second stage requires at least some phonemic segmentation skill. In the third phase, "Not only are individual letters or digraphs linked to phonemes but also the sequence of letters is connected to the blend of phonemes such that part–whole relations are established leading from print into memory" (p. 132).

Ehri (1995) subsequently identified four phases termed the pre-alphabetic, partial alphabetic, full alphabetic and consolidated alphabetic phases. The first two of these phases correspond to the first and second phases of earlier versions of the model. "During the full alphabetic phase, beginners remember how to read sight words by forming complete connections between letters seen in the written forms of words and phonemes detected in their pronunciations … spellings become amalgamated or bonded to pronunciations of words in memory" (p. 120). By the final phase, "letter patterns that recur across different words become consolidated … Consolidation allows readers to operate with multiletter units that may be morphemes, syllables or subsyllabic units such as onsets and rimes" (p. 121).

A feature of Ehri's model, which is in keeping with the computational model developed by Seidenberg and McClelland (1989) and Plaut et al. (1996), is that "information about the spelling of specific words is retained in memory and amalgamated with information about pronunciations and meanings" (Ehri, 1992a, p. 108).

A common element in the stage theories proposed by Ehri, Marsh et al. and Frith (see also Gough, Juel, & Griffiths 1992) is that at the very beginning of reading there is a stage at which children respond to certain familiar features of a word but without taking account either of the whole word or of the letter–sound correspondence of individual letters within it (see also Seymour, 1986, 1990; Seymour & Elder, 1986). This stage is termed "logographic" by Frith (1985) and "visual cue" or "pre-alphabetic" by Ehri. Essentially, it incorporates two sub-stages (linguistic guessing and discrimination net guessing) postulated by Marsh et al. (1981). At this stage, children rely heavily on partial visual features of words to make context-based guesses. For example, a word like dog might be recognized by the hook of the g (the "waggy tail") or perhaps by

the whole of the letter g (Seymour & Elder, 1986). As a child's vocabulary grows, it will become increasingly difficult to distinguish between words that which share a common feature (compare *dog* and *pig*) and attention will need to be given to individual letters and their positions within a word. The key element at this stage is the realization that written words consist of letters that represent the sounds of the corresponding spoken words. This stage is referred to as the alphabetic (Frith) or sequential decoding (Marsh et al.) stage and refers to the process of sounding out the pronunciation of a word by applying letter–sound correspondence rules from left to right of a letter string. Children in the second year of instruction in reading show evidence of using such phonological recoding alongside a more holistic word-recognition strategy (Masterson, Laxon, & Stuart, 1992).

A refinement of Frith's theory is that reading and spelling may be out of "phase" with each other. She proposes that spelling may be "alphabetic" while reading is still "logographic". The development of grapheme–phoneme correspondences derives from their use initially in spelling and subsequent availability for use in reading (see also Cataldo & Ellis, 1988). This "pacemaker" hypothesis can explain why young children are occasionally able to spell regular words that they cannot read (Bryant & Bradley, 1980; Gough et al., 1992).

Ehri (1987, 1989, 1997), too, has explicitly addressed the relation between reading and spelling, which she sees as "one and the same, almost". She argues (Ehri, 1997) that they are almost the same because both depend upon the same knowledge base—that is, knowledge of the alphabetic system and knowledge about the spellings of specific words (see also Gough et al., 1992). They differ in that reading and spelling are different responses. "The act of reading involves one response, that of pronouncing a word. In contrast, the act of spelling involves multiple responses, that of writing several letters in the correct sequence. More information is needed to accurately spell words than to read words" (Ehri, 1997, p. 264). In Ehri's view, the same phases that characterize reading apply to spelling.

As mentioned above, the earliest stage in Frith's (1985) theory is termed a logographic stage, during which children's word recognition is dominated by familiar visual cues ("salient graphic features") that form part of a word. Seymour, too, specifies an early stage, which, somewhat confusingly, is also referred to as "logographic development" (Seymour, 1986, 1990; Seymour & Elder, 1986).

Seymour (1990) refers to Frith's model as postulating three strategies, the first of which is logographic, "the direct recognition of whole words" (p. 163). This is not quite the same as using partial cues to "guess" a word, although Frith referred to writing systems such as Japanese Kanji, in which a single character stands for a whole idea, as logographic. Seymour writes of a sample of children studied by Seymour and Elder (1986):

> The children in this sample were considered to display the characteristics of logographic reading. They possessed a system for recognition and pronunciation of words from a finite vocabulary but no general-purpose procedure for letter–sound analysis of new words. More detailed analysis of the errors suggested that the children recognised the words by a feature discrimination process, relying on overall word length, the presence of some salient letter shapes and, at a later point, letter position. Presentation of familiar words in a zig-zag or vertically oriented format was *not* seriously damaging to accuracy for many of the children. This suppported the conclusion that recognition was based on feature analysis rather than on identification of picture-like word shapes or *gestalts* . . . Seymour & Elder concluded that most of the children in the sample were "logographic readers". It was suggested that they were in the process of establishing a "logographic lexicon".
>
> (Seymour, 1990, p. 171)

More recently, Seymour wrote the following:

> The term *logographic* is used here to refer to a process that is concerned with the direct recognition and storage of *words*. The Shorter Oxford Dictionary defines *logography* as a "method of printing with entire words" and *logographic* as "consisting of characters or signs, each of which represents an entire word". The assumption is that English words, although composed of letters, may be treated as units in this sense. This does not imply adherence to the connotations that have (erroneously in my view) been attached to the word *logographic* in recent debates. Hence it is *not* equated with recognition of logos or reliance on visual cues even though these primitive processes may represent the early stages in the development of the process.
>
> (Seymour, 1997, pp. 324–325)

Clearly, there is great potential for confusion over the way in which the term "logographic" can or should be used. Gombert, Bryant, and Warrick (1997) refer to the term as "ambiguous", presumably because it has been used to refer (a) to recognizing words on the basis of partial cues, (b) to single characters representing whole ideas and (c) to recognizing words as gestalts or holistically.

The final, somewhat underspecified, stage proposed by stage theorists is termed orthographic by Frith, hierarchical decoding by Marsh et al. and consolidated alphabetic by Ehri. This refers to the use of rules—for example, that a final "e" changes the pronunciation of the middle vowel or that the combination "-ight" rhymes with "bite" or that "-tion" is pronounced in the same way as the word "shun".

As with the term "logographic", there is some ambiguity in the literature with regard to the term "orthographic", as was noted by Ehri (1995) and others. Seymour refers to an orthographic processor which has two levels:

> The first is concerned with functions which precede recognition, including identification of features of letters and words, selective allocation of attention to elements, and the analysis of the input into significant groupings (orthographic parsing). The second level is concerned with categorisation

and identification . . . [of] . . . graphemes . . . and . . . morphemes.

(Seymour, 1990, p. 147)

Thus this conception includes what other theorists refer to as early visual analysis plus the orthographic (or visual) input lexicon and to what Seymour and Evans (1993) refer to as the "visual (orthographic) processor".

Seymour (1990, 1997; Seymour & Evans, 1993) refers to his model as a dual-foundation model of reading development because "it is assumed (a) the foundations of literacy must have reached a certain level before orthographic development can be initiated and (b) orthographic development must have proceeded some distance before the construction of the morphographic framework becomes possible. However, no necessary sequence in the ordering of the foundation developments is proposed" (Seymour, 1997, p. 331).

The notion of stages might be taken to imply a stepwise rather than smooth progression through the early stages of reading. Contrary evidence comes from a longitudinal study by Stuart and Coltheart (1988), who suggested that there is a gradual rather than a stepwise change in error patterns. Furthermore, Stuart and Coltheart (1988) noted that some children (who were phonologically skilled) seemed to use alphabetic knowledge from the start without passing through a logographic stage. Stuart and Coltheart (1988) therefore disputed that it was always necessary to pass through a logographic stage before reaching an alphabetic stage at which children apply letter–sound correspondences. In a critique of their paper, Wimmer (1990) pointed out that as phonological scores in the first year of reading were not on their own predictive of reading scores but became predictive in the second year, the conclusion of Stuart and Coltheart was not justified. Indeed, the pattern of results obtained by them was precisely what would be predicted by the idea of an initial logographic stage. Citing evidence from Seymour and Elder (1986) that logographic reading was linked to whole-word attempts by teachers to establish a sight vocabulary, Wimmer raised the question of whether a logographic

stage is universal or is instead a by-product of a whole-word approach at the beginning of reading instruction.

In their influential monograph, Goswami and Bryant argued against the stage theories of Marsh et al. and of Frith in the following terms:

We can summarise our conclusions about Marsh's and Frith's theories quite briefly. The claim made by both of them that children read logographically first and alphabetically later seems to us to have been entirely justified by later research. So has Marsh's idea that children learn complex, conditional rules about orthography at an even later stage. But the claim that children spell logographically before they spell alphabetically—again made by Marsh and Frith—does not seem to fit any of the facts. Both theories too seem to us to be too narrow in their discussion about phonological awareness, as they mention only phoneme awareness and grapheme–phoneme correspondence. The fact that Marsh and Frith ignore rhyme and the awareness of onset and rime probably also accounts for the apparent reluctance of both of them to suggest that children recognise sequences of letters and relate them to sounds at a relatively early stage in reading.

. . . we do not think that children take a series of discrete and identifiable steps when they learn to read and to spell.

(Goswami & Bryant, 1990, p. 146)

How the views of Goswami and Bryant (1990) differ from those of stage theorists will become clear in the following chapter. For the present, it is worth briefly considering at this point the methodological and theoretical implications of the fact that reading is a developmental process, regardless of whether it occurs in stages as postulated by the authors discussed above.

Reading level matched designs

At one time, it was common to compare groups of disabled readers only with normal readers of the same age and IQ (Jorm, 1979a). A problem with such a design is that it is impossible to say whether any deficit in the reading-disabled group is simply due to a lower level of reading experience in the reading-disabled group or whether it represents a causal impairment. An alternative design is to compare groups of children matched not on chronological age but on reading or spelling age or level. Any difference between groups is then unlikely to be due to reading experience *per se*. However, the reading level design is not without its own problems (Jackson & Butterfield, 1989). In particular, it is not easy to decide what the criterion for matching should be. Even normal readers matched on one aspect of reading, say single word recognition, may not be matched on other aspects, such as comprehension (Backman, Mamen, & Ferguson, 1984). Indeed, Stanovich, Nathan, and Zolman (1988) suggest that investigators should refer to decoding level or comprehension level matched designs.

The strengths and limitations of the reading level matched design were discussed by Backman et al. (1984). A reply to this was published by Bryant and Goswami (1986), to which a rejoinder was made by Mamen, Ferguson, and Backman (1986). Further critical appraisal of this kind of design was undertaken by Jackson and Butterfield (1989), who identified what they saw as seven misunderstandings, or "myths" as they called them, relating to the characteristics of the design. As a consequence of all this discussion (see also McDougall & Ellis, 1994), it is now customary in dyslexia research to include both chronological and reading or spelling age control participants. More complex designs are possible (see Backman et al., 1984) but even this does not enable one to assign unequivocally a causal role to a particular variable. The conclusions that one can legitimately draw from a reading level comparison or from a chronological level comparison depend upon the pattern of positive or negative findings in each case (Bryant & Goswami, 1986). Such a comparison, of course, represents the state of affairs only at a single point in time and does not obviate the desirability of adopting a longitudinal approach to the study of reading development, as advocated by several authors (Ellis & Large, 1987;

Frith, 1985; Snowling, 1987; Snowling & Nation, 1997). A particular pattern of difference between two reading groups at one time, and hence level of reading, may not be apparent at another time or level of reading skill.

The developmental lag hypothesis

One of the conclusions sometimes drawn from a comparison between dyslexic children and reading age controls concerns the so-called developmental or maturational lag hypothesis. The idea here is that if dyslexics perform in a qualitatively similar manner to children of the same reading level, then it is reasonable to assume that they are lagging behind their chronological age-matched peers (see Stanovich et al., 1988). Unfortunately, it has not always been clear what is meant by a "qualitative" difference between disabled readers and younger normal readers (Bryant & Goswami, 1986). A further problem with the developmental lag hypothesis is that it implies that dyslexia is something that one simply grows out of—one is expected eventually to catch up with non-dyslexic readers. In many cases, this does not appear to happen. Longitudinal studies have shown that although the phonological skills of dyslexic children may improve over time, they increasingly fall behind their chronological-age and reading-age peers in this regard (Manis, Custodio, & Szeszulski, 1993; Snowling, Goulandris, & Defty, 1996b; Temple, 1990). While it is true that many adults diagnosed as dyslexic in their school years attain adequate proficiency in reading (e.g. Silver & Hagin, 1964)—such readers are often termed "compensated dyslexics"—there is evidence that their spelling in particular remains poor (Scarborough, 1984) and that their weakness in the phonological domain persists (Bruck, 1990, 1992; Elbro, Nielsen, & Petersen, 1994; Felton, Naylor, & Wood, 1990; Kinsbourne, Rufo, Gamzu, Palmer, & Berliner, 1991; Pennington, Van Orden, Smith, Green, & Haith, 1990; Pratt & Brady, 1988; Stanovich, Siegel, & Gottardo, 1997a; Temple, 1988, 1990; see also papers in Beaton, McDougall, & Singleton, 1997a). This implies that at least a simplistic version of the "maturational lag" hypothesis is untenable. The findings are, however, not inconsistent with a formulation of the developmental lag hypothesis, according to which levels of reading are commensurate with what might be expected at a particular developmental level of phonological ability, regardless of age.

An alternative to the developmental lag hypothesis is that dyslexics show a pattern of reading that deviates from that of younger normal readers. On this view, dyslexia represents a deviant pattern of reading development. There is no reason, of course, why a child's reading might not be both delayed and deviant (see Temple, 1987).

It is universally acknowledged that the dyslexic population is not homogeneous. Seymour (1986), for example, found that his poor readers (dyslexics and poor readers defined without regard to IQ) showed greater variation than normal readers, although the groups were not well matched with respect to reading age (McDougall & Ellis, 1994). It has not always been appreciated, however, that heterogeneity is characteristic of young unimpaired readers as well. This point was emphasized in a well-known article by Bryant and Impey (1986). These authors repeated with a group of reading-age control children the tests that had been given to two older dyslexics reported as individual case studies showing phonological (Temple & Marshall, 1983) and surface (Coltheart et al., 1983) dyslexia, respectively. Bryant and Impey (1986) argued that the dyslexics were not qualitatively different in their reading from normally reading children of the same reading age, since relative reliance on whole-word (lexical) and sub-word (sub-lexical) procedures characterized some normal children to the same extent as has been shown for the putative dyslexics (see also Baddeley, Logie, & Ellis, 1988; Ellis, McDougall, & Monk, 1996b). It was therefore inappropriate to use the features identified in the case studies as explanations of the reading difficulties. In reply, Coltheart (1987) pointed out that this was precisely as had been anticipated by Coltheart et al. (1983). He further argued against the suggestion of Bryant and Impey that there was nothing abnormal about the reading performance of the surface dyslexic case C.D. by

pointing out that it was abnormal for her age (16 years) even if it was similar to that of normal but younger readers.

Snowling et al. (1996b) studied dyslexic children at two points in time. At time 1, the dyslexics were as accurate as control readers in reading regular and irregular words and nonwords and showed a similar word-length effect. That is, the dyslexic children performed in a similar way to their reading age controls and thus might be said to have been delayed in their reading development but not deviant. At time 2, two years later, the dyslexic children were not only delayed but were showing a qualitatively different pattern of reading. They had made significantly less progress than the original control group and were impaired in reading nonwords relative both to this group and to an additional control group carefully matched for current reading age (see also Stanovich et al., 1988, who studied poor readers who were not considered dyslexic). The dyslexic children also made proportionately more dysphonetic spelling errors and, as at time 1, were impaired relative to both control groups in a range of phonological processing tasks, including tests of rhyme recognition and production, word and nonword repetition, and verbal short-term memory. Snowling et al. (1996b) concluded that their results showed that the nature of the phonological deficits in dyslexia changes over time and can be interpreted within a developmental perspective. Specifically, they hypothesized that "the absence of well-specified phonological representations when the dyslexic children started to learn to read caused a delay in the acquisition of reading" (p. 667).

This chapter has considered a number of theories of reading that have been used as frameworks in which to view dyslexia. The theories differ in several important respects, one being the extent to which they explicitly address the developmental nature of reading and dyslexia. To understand how difficulties in learning to read arise, it is helpful to consider those factors that underpin the successful transition from being a non-reader to a reader. This is the subject of the next chapter.

3

The Development of Reading: The Role of Phonological Awareness

Proficient reading is one of the most important intellectual tasks a child will accomplish in his or her lifetime. It is an ability that depends upon a number of component skills and takes several years to master fully. This chapter outlines research concerned with the cognitive skills that have been investigated in relation to normal reading development. Gough et al. (1992) point out that there are only 26 letters in the English alphabet but more than three dozen phonemes and that "the process of reading acquisition is aptly and accurately described as a process of cryptanalysis or codebreaking" (p. 39).

KNOWLEDGE OF LETTER NAMES AND SOUNDS

One of the first things taught to children who will eventually be exposed to an alphabetic language is the letters making up the alphabet. Although most children learn the alphabet relatively easily, for a minority it is a serious hurdle to be overcome. Being able to recognize and name individual letters rapidly presumably reflects a high

degree of familiarity with them, which would be expected to correlate with early reading proficiency. Knowledge of the sounds and names of letters allows children to become rudimentary or beginning readers (Barron, 1986). In fact, pre-readers' knowledge of the alphabet is a powerful predictor of their later reading success (Adams, 1990; Ehri, 1987, 1992b, 1995; Macmillan, 2002; Muter, Hulme, Snowling, & Taylor, 1997; Roberts & McDougall, 2003). Those whose alphabetic knowledge is weak are less likely to make good progress. Some of the earliest articles on the subject of reading impairment emphasize how poor some of the children described were at learning to write the letters of the alphabet (Morgan, 1896; Thomas, 1905). Yet in some cases, at least, the children could recognize with ease what a word was when it was spelled aloud (Thomas, 1905).

Knowing one's letters involves both knowing the sounds associated with each letter and knowing the name of the letter. Not all letters are equally as easy (or difficult) to learn. Pre-school children find it easier to give the first letter of a word like "beach" than a word like "bone" (or the last letter of "deaf" compared with "loaf") where the sound of the name of the letter corresponds to the sound that the letter makes in a word (Treiman, 1992; Treiman, Tincoff, & Richmond-Welty, 1996).

Children appear to use their knowledge of letter *names* in learning the *sounds* that letters make. Thus they learn the sounds of *b* and *f* (which are contained in the *names* of these letters) more readily than than the sounds of *w* and *h* (the names of which are not present in the sounds these letters stand for in a word). Even between *b* and *f*, there is a difference. The sound *b* is easier than *f* because the phoneme /b/ is at the beginning of the letter's name, whereas the phoneme /f/ is at the end of its name (Treiman, Tincoff, Rodriguez, Mouzaki, & Francis, 1998). At the earliest stage of reading and spelling, children seem to use letter names in spelling (e.g. Treiman & Tincoff, 1997) as a spontaneous strategy. Adams (1990) provides an example of children spelling "people" as *Ppl*.

In an experiment by Treiman and Rodriguez (1999), children aged 4–6.5 years were presented with pairs of letters. In one condition (the letter name condition), the name of the initial consonant corresponded to the sound in the "word" being learned. For example, the letters BN were used to represent the word "bean", JL to represent "jail", DR to represent "dear", and so on. In another condition (referred to as the sound condition), the same letter pairs were used to represent different words, the pronunciation of which did not include the (full) letter name. For example, BN represented "bone", JL represented "jewel" and DR represented "door". Both pre-readers and those who had begun to read learned the "words" more quickly in the letter name condition than in the sound condition. Letter names, then, represent a kind of reading-related knowledge (Share, 1995; Wagner, Torgesen, & Rashotte, 1994) that children may draw on to help them in their early reading and spelling.

In the first year of school, letter knowledge correlates significantly with children's awareness of the sound structure of words (Roberts & McDougall, 2003; Stuart & Coltheart, 1988). This is not surprising. The realization that there is a systematic if imperfect relation between the way in which words are pronounced and how they are represented in a letter string depends minimally on an awareness that individual letters correspond to individual sounds. The generic term "phonological awareness" is used to refer to knowledge of the sound structure of speech, which may be explicit or implicit (Cataldo & Ellis, 1988; Duncan, Seymour, & Hill, 1997; Seymour & Duncan, 1997). Phonological awareness or sensitivity has been a central issue in reading research over the past 20 years or so.

Ehri and Wilce (1985) asked kindergarten children to learn simplified spellings of words. In one condition the spellings contained letters corresponding to some of the sounds in the word presented (e.g. *msk* for *mask*, *jrf* for *giraffe*). In a second condition, arbitrary letter combinations were used and there was no correspondence between the letters and the sound of the word (e.g. *uhe* for *mask*, *wbc* for *giraffe*). The results showed that non-readers learned the arbitrary spellings more readily than the simplified phonetic spellings, but children with some letter–sound knowledge learned the phonetic spellings more quickly than the arbitrary spellings. The latter finding was confirmed and extended by Rack, Hulme, Snowling, and Wightman (1994), who interpreted it in terms of the direct-mapping hypothesis. According to this hypothesis, children from the earliest stages of reading automatically establish direct mappings between letters and sounds without the use of rules or explicit decoding. Laing and Hulme (1999) replicated the "phonetic spelling effect" and showed that among early readers there is a relationship between performance on this kind of learning task and conventional measures of phonological awareness (see below).

Implicit in the direct-mapping hypothesis (Rack et al., 1994) is the supposition that children's learning of letter names and sounds depends upon their underlying level of phonological skill. However, Byrne and his colleagues have consistently argued that phonemic awareness and letter knowledge make independent contributions to acquisition of the alphabetic principle (Byrne & Fielding-Barnsley, 1989, 1995).

Tunmer, Herriman, and Neasdale (1988) suggested that "some minimal level of phonological awareness must be achieved by children before they can derive much benefit from letter-name knowledge" (p. 154). An argument has also been put forward that phonological sensitivity, at least at the phoneme level, cannot be acquired without some minimum level of letter knowledge (Johnston, Anderson, & Holligan, 1996). These authors reported that explicit awareness of phonemes was apparent only among those pre-readers who had some letter knowledge. In the absence of the latter, there was little evidence of phoneme awareness. Johnston et al. (1996) concluded that "childen who demonstrate no knowledge of the alphabet, or who know very few letters, are very unlikely to be able to segment or delete phonemes" (p. 225). Conversely, Bowey (1994) reported that novice readers who are high in letter knowledge are phonologically sensitive at the level of the phoneme. Thus, conceivably, letter knowledge helps to establish knowledge of the phonemic structure of words, which, in turn, facilitates phonological sensitivity at the level of the individual phoneme.

If it is true that letter knowledge assists in discovering the phonemic structure of words (in the same way that learning to read an alphabetic language promotes phonemic awareness in illiterate adults; see below), then a child's segmentation abilities will be relevant to the use of letter names in spelling and reading. The word "tar", for example, can be segmented into the onset "t-" and the rime "-ar". The latter segment is the sound of the name given to the letter "r". In their spellings, children in the first year or so of primary school may represent the rime segment "-ar" with the single letter "r", omitting the vowel "a" (Treiman, 1994). However, letter-name errors are not equally likely for all letters. According to Treiman (1994), the consonant most likely to elicit errors is "r", followed by "l". The sounds of the names of these letters /ar/ and /ɛl/ are difficult for young children to further divide into individual sounds /a/ and /r/ or /e/ and /l/, but as their phonological awareness develops they are able to do so. They then are able to spell words like "tar" or "bell" correctly by including the previously omitted vowel. Yet even young children may not exclusively use a sound-based strategy in their spelling. Some evidence suggests that they are also sensitive to orthographic factors, such as morphological structure (Stage & Wagner, 1992; Treiman & Cassar, 1996).

Learning to correlate letters with the sounds that they represent is first and foremost a learning task. Specifically, it can be conceptualized as a paired-associate learning task. By and large, however, theorists have been more interested in how letter–sound knowledge predicts reading skill rather than in investigating how this knowledge develops. This is a somewhat curious omission in view of the fact that there is an abundant literature on the role of short-term phonological memory or phonological sensitivity in learning novel words (de Jong, Seveke, & Van Veen, 2000; Gathercole & Baddeley, 1989; 1990a; Gathercole, Hitch, Service, & Martin, 1997; Michas & Henry, 1994). In fact, letter knowledge has been shown to correlate with other measures of phonological sensitivity (Bowey, 1994) and verbal memory (Johnston et al., 1996), including nonword repetition, nonword name learning and receptive vocabulary (de Jong et al., 2000).

THE ASSESSMENT OF PHONOLOGICAL AWARENESS

The terms "meta-linguistic" or "phonological awareness" and "phonological sensitivity" are used to refer to a wide range of skills involved in discriminating, manipulating or otherwise responding to the sounds of speech (Adams, 1990; Bowey, 1994; Chaney, 1992; McBride-Chang, 1995; Stahl & Murray, 1994; Stanovich, 1986, 1992; Wagner & Torgesen, 1987; Yopp, 1988). Commonly used tests of phonological awareness or sensitivity include asking for the odd man out in a list of words (Bradley & Bryant, 1978, 1983), asking a child to tap out the number of sounds in a word (Liberman, Shankweiler, Fischer, & Carter, 1974) and deleting (or adding) a syllable or phoneme to a given word (first used by Bruce, 1964). In the last test, the initial, medial or terminal phoneme may be deleted, although these are not equal in level of difficulty.

Children between the ages of about 3 and 5 years find deletion of the initial phoneme of a word rather easier than the final phoneme, but by the age of 5 years most children can be readily taught to delete the final or initial consonant from CVC syllables (see Content, Kolinsky, Morais, & Bertelson, 1986). As well as administering tests of phonological analysis, tasks such as blending individual sounds to form a complete word may be used to assess phonological synthesis.

A variation on the phoneme deletion task was was introduced by Perin (1983), who showed that performance on a spoonerism test (for example, reversing the initial sounds of the two words *Billy Holliday* to yield *Hilly Bolliday*) correlated significantly with spelling ability. Although such phoneme exchange tests have been used quite frequently since the publication of Perin's paper, the criticism has been made that this task is not exclusively phonemic, but is confounded with orthographic factors (Ellis, McDougall, & Monk, 1997). Certainly, there is evidence that orthographic knowledge influences performance of adults (Seidenberg & Tanenhaus, 1979) and children (e.g. Bruck, 1992; Ehri & Wilce, 1985; Landerl, Frith, & Wimmer, 1996; Perfetti, Beck, Bell, & Hughes, 1987; Stuart, 1990), including dyslexics (Rack, 1985), on auditorily presented tasks. Perfetti et al. (1987) noted that "spelling strategies played some role in the tapping task"— that is, orthographic factors increasingly affected the number of taps given as children were tested at succesive points in a year. This task, incidentally, appears to require other abilities in addition to phonological awareness. Bryant, MacLean, Bradley, and Crossland (1990c) comment: "Tapping the right number of phonemes may depend upon some form of counting the phonemes; thus the test may measure abilities related to number as well as to reading" (p. 433).

Although developmental psychologists have shown that even very young infants show the ability to discriminate between sounds such as /ba/ and /pa/ (Eimas, Siqueland, Jusczyk, & Vigorito, 1971; Jusczyk, 1994), this does not mean that they have any explicit understanding of the fact that words (or nonwords) are made up of individual segments and that differences between two words may lie only in one particular segment. Phonological processing tasks are thought to be difficult for young children because there is nothing in the acoustic spectra of spoken words that identifies individual phonemes within words. A word like *cat* or *dog*, for example, is perceived as a whole not as individual sounds. (Similarly, a tune is perceived as such rather than as individual notes). Indeed, the so-called "segmentation problem" not only applies to individual words but to the speech stream as a whole, since within a word there may be longer "silent" intervals (though still extremely short) at various points than there are between words. Such "silent intervals" or gaps, therefore, neither mark off individual words in speech, nor identify individual segments within words.

There are at least two questions relating to tests of phonological awareness. One concerns the level of difficulty of tasks used. Adams (1990, p. 80), for example, argued (on purely intuitive grounds) that the difficulty of tasks commonly used in the literature can be identified as falling into one of five categories. The other question has to do with whether phonological awareness should be conceptualized as a single construct— that is, whether different levels of phonological awareness represent a single ability, or whether two or more independent component abilities contribute to overall phonological awareness.

Level of difficulty

It is generally believed that blending is a more primitive (i.e. earlier acquired) skill than segmentation (Perfetti et al., 1987; see Chaney, 1992) and that young children find it easier to segment spoken words at the level of the syllable rather than the phoneme (Bowey & Francis, 1991; Liberman et al., 1974; Treiman, 1985, 1986). One reason for the greater ease of syllable than phoneme segmentation for pre-readers may be that phonemes, unlike syllables, rarely have an independent existence. The way in which a given phoneme is articulated depends upon both the preceding and following phoneme, a situation referred to as co-articulation. A syllable, on the other hand, exists as a temporally discrete phonetic unit (Liberman et al., 1974).

The speech flow can be broken down into separate words and a word (or a nonword) can be segmented at different levels. As indicated above, one basis for segmentation is at the level of the syllable; another is at the level of the individual phoneme. Between these two levels is an intermediate level, since the syllable can itself be subdivided in different ways. One sub-division is in terms of three components—the peak (the central vowel) and a preceding consonant or consonant cluster (the onset) and a following consonant or consonant cluster (the coda). For example, the (monosyllabic) word *ground* can be divided into *gr + ou + nd*. Another sub-division is in terms only of the onset (*gr*) and the rime (vowel and final consonants: *ound*) or of the body and coda (*grou + nd*).

Treiman (1983) showed that adults find it easier to segment a spoken syllable into onset and rime than into divisions that cut across the rime, a finding later extended to children (Treiman, 1985). Similarly, many pre-school children are able to indicate that pairs of spoken words share a common sound when these are onsets or rimes, although they are unable to do so when the words share only a single intra-syllabic phoneme (Treiman & Zukowski, 1991).

Kirtley, Bryant, MacLean, and Bradley (1989) reported that children "who were on the borderline between reading and not reading" (mean age 5 years 7 months) found "oddity detection" tasks that differed in the initial consonant (e.g. *man, mint, peck, mug*) easier than those differing in the end consonant (e.g. *pin, gun, men, hat*). Difficulty with the end consonant is in striking contrast to the ability of children of the same age or younger to detect the odd word out in a rhyming list. "They can see that 'mat' and 'cat' end in the same way but not that 'mat' and 'pit' share a common ending" (Kirtley et al., 1989, p. 233). This suggests that the onset–rime distinction is important in children's phonological development at the beginning of reading. Bowey and Francis (1991) also found that rime oddity tasks were easier than phoneme oddity tasks in pre-readers and very early readers. In a second experiment by Kirtley et al. (1989), performance of children (mean age 5 years 6 months) in the end consonant condition

correlated much more strongly with reading ability than did performance in the initial consonant condition. Kirtley et al. (1989) suggested that "a major step in learning to read may take place when the child learns to break the rime into its constituent sounds by detaching, in the case of the tasks we used, the preceding vowel from the final consonant" (pp. 243–244).

Treiman and Zukowski (1996) noted that the linguistic status of a sub-syllabic unit (syllable versus rime versus phoneme) may be confounded with its size. Thus studies showing that children find it easier to segment speech into higher-level units may reflect either the linguistic status of the unit or its size—higher-level units tend to be larger than lower-level units. Treiman and Zukowski (1996), therefore, carried out a study to determine which was the relevant variable. They compared pre-school 5-year-old children's performance in detecting word similarity with two different kinds of word pairs. Shared onset word pairs (e.g. *pacts–peel*) were compared with pairs of words in which only a part of the onset was common to the two words (e.g. *plan–prow*). According to the linguistic status hypothesis, performance in detecting similarity should be superior with the first type, since the word onset is the same. According to the unit size hypothesis, performance should be equivalent with both types of word pairs, since the unit size is identical even though in the second type of word pair only a part of the onset cluster is similar. The results favoured the first hypothesis (see also Caravolas & Bruck, 1993). Using a similar design and logic, Treiman and Zukowski (1996) examined performance at the levels of the syllable and rime rather than the phoneme. Again, their results favoured the linguistic status rather than the unit size hypothesis. They suggested that "Awareness of syllables may develop earlier than awareness of intra-syllabic units, which in turn may develop earlier than awareness of single phonemes" (p. 209).

The nature of phonological awareness

Yopp (1988) carried out a principal components analysis of scores on 10 tests of phonological awareness which yielded two factors. Tests of phoneme blending and counting (among others) loaded heavily on one factor, while tests of phoneme deletion or manipulation, such as producing Spoonerisms or Pig Latin (moving the initial sound to the end of a word and adding another sound), loaded highly on the other, although the two factors were correlated. Rhyming ability did not load highly on either factor. Yopp concluded from her analysis that performance on rhyming tasks may represent an awareness that is independent of the ability represented by performance on the other tests. On the other hand, Bryant et al. (1990c) noted that "there is a strong connection between the rhyme oddity test given at the age of 4 years 7 months and the first-sound phoneme deletion test given more than a year later. These significant connections are evidence that rhyme and alliteration are not. . .separate from phoneme detection" (p. 433). This is consistent with phonological awareness being a single ability.

Stahl and Murray (1994) used the same measures as Yopp (1988) but assigned a weight according to the level of linguistic complexity (onsets and rimes, vowels and codas, cluster onsets and cluster codas) represented by each item. Factor analysis of the weighted scores revealed only a single factor whether the data were analysed by tasks or level of linguistic complexity. In another study, however, principal component analysis suggested that a phoneme factor, a syllable factor and a rhyme factor contribute independently to overall phonological awareness (Høien, Lundberg, Stanovich, & Bjaalid, 1995). As always with such correlational techniques, what comes out of an analysis reflects what is put into it rather than some universal truth. Using the mathematical technique of structural equation modelling, McBride-Chang (1995) concluded that three components—namely, general intellectual ability, verbal short-term memory and speech perception—each contribute uniquely (but not equally) to the construct of phonological awareness. McBride-Chang emphasized the role of speech perception (itself not a unitary variable) in particular. She argued that "If these abilities can be shown to be predictive of phonological awareness in the very early years of life (e.g. pre-school or even from infancy), this could potentially have far-reaching consequences for developmental theory and for the early identification of those at risk for reading disability" (p. 187).

Subsequently, McBride-Chang, Wagner, and Chang (1997) showed that speech perception (defined as discrimination between *bath* and *path*) and measures of phonological awareness were moderately (and significantly) correlated in pre-reading kindergarten children, although they were less so among older readers (McBride-Chang, 1996; Werker & Tees, 1987). McBride-Chang et al. (1997) argued that "speech perception may be among the most important precursors of phonological awareness" (p. 629).

It seems, then, that there is reasonable agreement between investigators as to the order of difficulty of tasks but somewhat less agreement about the nature of phonological awareness. If phonological awareness is *not* a single homogeneous ability, this might explain some of the variation in performance on phonological awareness tasks seen in the literature.

THE RELATION BETWEEN PHONOLOGICAL AWARENESS AND READING

In recent years, a great deal of work has demonstrated that young children's phonological awareness or sensitivity is related to their current (Bradley & Bryant, 1978; Bryant & Bradley, 1985; Hansen & Bowey, 1994; Huang & Hanley, 1995; Muter, Snowling, & Taylor, 1994; Roberts & McDougall, 2003) or future (Bradley & Bryant, 1983; Ellis & Large, 1987; Fox & Routh, 1983; Jorm et al., 1986; Juel, Griffith, & Gough, 1986; Lundberg & Høien, 1989; Lundberg, Oloffson, & Wall, 1980; MacDonald & Cornwall, 1995; Muter et al., 1997; Stuart & Coltheart, 1988; Stuart & Masterson, 1992) reading and/or spelling ability (for useful reviews see Bryant et al., 1990c; Elbro, 1996; Goswami & Bryant, 1990; Macmillan, 2002; Rack et al., 1994; Snowling, 1995; Snowling & Hulme, 1994; Snowling & Nation, 1997; Wagner & Torgesen, 1987) The collection of essays edited by Brady and Shankweiler (1991) is a valuable summary of the evidence to that date.

It is surprising that it should have taken until the late 1970s and early 1980s before the relationship between phonological ability and reading was firmly established. As long ago as 1944, Schilder argued that "the congenital reading disability is due to an incomplete function of centers. It is the inability of the patient [*sic*] to differentiate the spoken word into its sounds, and to put sounds together into a word" (p. 85). He concluded: "the basic difficulty in congenital reading disability is the difficulty to differentiate the spoken word into its sounds and to put together the sounds of a word. Words and single sounds are brought into connection with a written word and a written letter, but the written word and the written letter cannot be integrated and differentiated" (p. 87). Vernon (1962) wrote that "failure to read might be due to inability to perceive and remember the shapes of printed letters, or to analyse word shapes into letter shapes ... A more frequent cause of breakdown seems to be the lack of any *systematic* knowledge of phonic sounds and an inability to combine them together in the correct order" (p. 145, emphasis in original). Ingram (1963) refers to children studied in his clinic as being unable "to synthesize the individual syllables into words. When they tried to write they could not break words down into their component syllables" (p. 8). Rozin, Poritsky, and Sotsky (1971) write of second-grade children whose reading was "backward" as having a motivational problem but in addition "the children seemed to have particular difficulty in giving phonological interpretations in response to visually presented letters; that is, they could not, at least overtly, recognize such letters as representing components of their own or others' speech" (p. 1264). Partly as a result of their finding that a small subset of these children could readily learn to read Chinese characters, Rozin et al. (1971) anticipated the conclusions of Vellutino's (1979) review when they wrote: "We suspect that the phonemic representation contributes most heavily to reading difficulty" (p. 1267).

Given the complexity of reading, it is to be expected that the relevant component skills develop at different rates and emerge as more or less important at different times during a child's development. Whitehurst and Lonigan (1998) distinguish what they call inside-out skills, such as phonological awareness and letter knowledge, from outside-in skills, such as conceptual knowledge and general language ability. Both contribute to what has become known as emergent literacy, which Whitehurst and Lonigan define as follows: "Emergent literacy consists of the skills, knowledge, and attitudes that are presumed to be developmental precursors to conventional forms of reading and writing ... and the environments that support these developments" (p. 849).

It is not sufficient simply to say that an ability to be aware of or manipulate the sound structure of words predicts reading or spelling performance. One needs to know what aspects of phonological skill relate to what aspects of reading and spelling and at what stage. The questions that need to be asked are: "What is it that a child of a given age is aware of and how does this relate to the development of reading?"

Jorm, Share, MacLean, and Matthews (1984) compared children who at the end of kindergarten had differed in phonological decoding ability (as assessed by nonword reading). Those who were high in decoding ability had progressed in reading further than those whose decoding ability was initially lower. This supports the idea that phonological recoding skill is important during the early stages of learning to read (Jorm & Share, 1983). Of course, whether any particular aspect of phonological awareness at time 1 is predictive of reading at time 2 depends upon the absolute levels of phonological ability and reading competence and on the times when such abilities are measured. Kindergarten children with relatively high levels of phonological awareness (at least as determined by phoneme elision) may further develop that skill more quickly than those low in phonological awareness (McBride-Chang et al., 1997).

De Jong and Van der Leij (1999) found that individual differences in phonological awareness in grade 1 children had an effect on subsequent reading even when early reading was taken into

account, but individual differences in phonological awareness in kindergarten children did not
influence reading acquisition in grade 1 (perhaps
because phonemic awareness tests were too difficult and only rhyme awareness could be measured). Which aspects of phonological awareness
are predictive of reading will also depend upon
which other aspects of ability are taken into
account (and on the nature of the orthography;
see below). Aro, Aro, Ahonen, Räsänen, Hietala,
and Lyytinen (1999) noted in their study of six 7-
year-old Finnish children (held back from starting school because of minor socio-behavioural
difficulties) that "the six children achieved decoding ability with varying sets of phonological abilities. In this study, only Syllable Deletion and
Phoneme Identification skills consistently
emerged before decoding ability" (p. 461). These
authors found that there was considerable individual variation in the development of different
phonological awareness skills and their relation to
reading acquisition even in the regular Finnish
orthography.

Although there is a consensus that phonological skills (including verbal memory; see Chapter 4) are related to reading, there has been less
agreement regarding the causal relations between
the two (see Jorm, 1983). A common assumption
is that the development of reading is assisted by
phonemic segmentation ability, since proficiency
in the latter enables knowledge of grapheme–
phoneme correspondences to be readily
established. This, in turn, allows a candidate pronunciation to be assigned to any new word that is
encountered, a procedure held by dual-route theorists to be crucial for learning to read words that
are not already in one's sight vocabulary (but may
be in one's auditory vocabulary). However, rather
than develop initially through reading, knowledge
of grapheme–phoneme correspondences may
partially depend upon, or be supported by, an
earlier application in writing and spelling of the
reverse knowledge—that is, of phoneme–
grapheme correspondences—as implied by
Frith's developmental hypothesis (Frith, 1985,
1986) and emphasized by Seymour (1987a).

THE SELF-TEACHING HYPOTHESIS

An alternative to the conventional hypothesis is
that phonological recoding acts as a self-teaching
device that enables children to acquire word-
specific orthographic representations used in
sight-reading (see Ehri & Saltmarsh, 1995;
Reitsma, 1983). According to this "self-teaching"
hypothesis (Jorm & Share, 1983; Share, 1995),
some minimal levels of phonological sensitivity
and letter–sound knowledge, allied to information provided by context, are used to derive the
meaning of novel or unfamiliar words. The ability
to generate words beginning with a particular
sound plus the knowledge that a particular sound
is represented by a particular letter may elicit a
number of candidate pronunciations that are con-
strained by the context in which the word appears.
For example, knowing the names of the letters J
and L may enable a child to read the word JAIL
(Treiman & Rodriguez, 1999) even in the absence
of any blending skill. However, letter–sound
knowledge alone is insufficient to generate candidate pronunciations unless the child is capable of
appreciating that letters map onto individual
phonological segments within words (Share,
1999). Nor is it argued that phonological recoding
alone determines orthographic learning; there are
presumably individual differences in the ability to
remember word-specific information.

Direct support for the "self-teaching" hypothesis was claimed by Share (1999) on the basis of
an experiment in which second-grade children
were asked to read aloud short texts containing
novel "words". Three days later the children were
shown four alternative spellings of the target
"words" and asked to choose which they had seen
before. One of the alternatives was a homophone
of the target, while the other three contained a
letter substitution or transpositions. The children
chose the target word in preference to any of the
alternatives, including the homophone, and were
faster to name the target word in comparison
with the homophonic letter string. They were also
more accurate in writing the target word. These
findings could not be attributed to visual learning

or attentional factors and were taken to support the idea of an item-based rather than stage-based interpretation of the development of word recognition skills.

The "self-teaching" hypothesis acknowledges that some level of phonological awareness is necessary before learning of unfamiliar words can begin. This is in line with the view of authors such as the Haskins group (e.g. Liberman et al., 1974; Shankweiler, Crain, Brady, & Macaruso, 1992) and Bryant and colleagues (Bradley & Bryant, 1983; Bryant & Bradley, 1985), who have claimed that phonological skills are a prerequisite for reading. Others have argued that the reverse may also be true—namely, that reading facilitates phonological, particularly phonemic, awareness (Bertelson, de Gelder, Tfouni, & Morais, 1989; Bowey & Francis, 1991; Cataldo & Ellis, 1988; Mann, 1986; Morais, Bertelson, Cary, & Alegria, 1986; Morais, Carey, Alegria, & Bertelson, 1979; Read, Zhang, Nie, & Ding, 1986). In fact, there is no necessary incompatibility between these views, since a different causal connection may characterize different levels of phonological analysis. There is, in addition, a third alternative, namely that the relationship among these variables is reciprocal (Ellis, 1990; Ellis & Large, 1987; Perfetti et al., 1987; Peterson & Haines, 1992; Stanovich, 1986), different patterns emerging at different levels of reading development. This is the position that, in general, commands most support at the present time (see Share, 1995).

ON RHYMES AND RIMES

The above discussion has emphasized the relation between phonological awareness and knowledge of the correspondence between graphemes and phonemes. It may be, though, that segmentation ability at levels other than that of the phoneme assists children's early reading development. For example, the nonword *fliend* may be read according to rules relating to individual graphemes and phonemes (in which the two vowels are clearly and distinctly enunciated as two sounds) or so as to rhyme with either *friend* or *fiend*. Either of the

latter pronunciations suggests reading by a process of analogy (Glushko, 1979; Kay & Marcel, 1981). In short, novel letter strings may be read either by grapheme–phoneme correspondence rules or by analogy with known words.

It may often be difficult or impossible to decide whether a regularly spelled novel word is being read by analogy with a familiar word or whether it is being read according to grapheme-to-phoneme conversion rules. With irregular, inconsistently spelled words, a decision may appear to be more straightforward. However, Baron (1979) noted that "responses by analogy to exceptions might also occur if a person uses rules (correspondences) for large units". He pointed out that the word *have* might be parsed into *h + ave* and each of these units might be stored separately in memory. The nonword *yave* might be pronounced either to rhyme with *have* or *gave*. Thus "responses by analogy (in a descriptive sense) to exception words might arise either from a true analogy mechanism or from the use of large unit rules" (p. 61). The large unit in this case is the rime *–ave*.

Treiman and Zukowski (1988) showed that adults (university students) are more likely to pronounce the vowel pair in nonwords like *frieth*, *chieth* or *chiend* so as to rhyme with the real word *friend* when the vowels plus final consonant match a real word. A similar effect occurs in spelling nonwords. This strongly suggests that adults use the rime segment to make analogies with known words. Bowey (1990a) reported that the latency to name visually presented words can be reduced by prior presentation of parts of that word (priming) only if the prime letter string corresponded to the sub-syllabic units of onset and rime. Again, this suggests that the rime is a salient unit of processing. Does the same hold for children?

The rime segment of a word or syllable bears an obvious relationship to the concept of rhyme. Many, if not most, 3- to 4-year-olds are capable of making correct rhyme judgements (Lenel & Cantor, 1981; MacLean, Bryant, & Bradley, 1987) and awareness of rhyme (and alliteration) has been said to be related to later reading ability (Bradley & Bryant, 1983; Bryant et al., 1990c;

Ellis & Large, 1987; Lundberg et al., 1980; MacLean et al., 1987; but see Macmillan, 2002). For beginning readers, there appears to be a close relationship between rhyming performance and the ability to use analogies to read new words (Goswami, 1990a; Goswami & Bryant, 1992). That this is not simply due to general intellectual ability is suggested by the finding that with IQ partialled out there is still a statistical relationship between children's ability to detect the "odd man out" in a list of words (e.g. cat, hat, *fit*, pat) and later reading, but not between the ability to categorize sounds in terms of rhyme and their later ability to do arithmetic (Bryant et al., 1990c). This makes good sense, as recognizing that words rhyme might lead to the realization that those words that sound alike are often spelled as well as pronounced in the same way.

Bryant et al. (1990c) compared three models of the link between phonological awareness and reading. Model 1 was that there was no connection between rhyme (and alliteration) and reading or spelling but that the latter gave rise to phoneme awareness. Model 2 was that rhyme leads directly to phoneme detection, which, in turn, assists reading and spelling. Model 3 was that rhyme and phoneme awareness independently influence reading and spelling. These authors present results (incorporating data from an earlier report) showing that rhyme and alliteration at 5 years 7 months were strongly related to measures of phoneme awareness and that there was a strong relation between the rhyme oddity task results at the age of 4 years 7 months and an initial phoneme deletion test a year later. They took this as evidence against Model 1 (that reading and spelling give rise to phoneme awareness). However, Macmillan (2002) points out that in the study of Bryant et al. (1990c)—and those of MacLean et al. (1987) and Bryant, MacLean, Bradley, and Crossland (1989)—the mean scores obtained on the phoneme measures were not above chance and "Conclusions based on this evidence, therefore, must be regarded as tenuous" (p. 30). She argues from an impressive methodological review of the relevant literature that there is as yet no good evidence that either rhyme awareness leads to phoneme awareness or that rhyme is

related to reading proficiency once the factors of prior reading ability and letter knowledge have been removed.

In a study of pre-readers, Walton (1995) found that after the effects of other variables (including phoneme identification) had been statistically removed, rhyme ability was significantly related to performance in learning to read new words (number of trials to criterion being the outcome variable) but did not make an independent contribution to reading test words by analogy with continuously present practice words. This latter finding contrasts with that of Bryant et al. (1990c). The explanation offered by Walton was that the discrepancy can be attributed either to the different tests of phoneme awareness used by himself and by Bryant et al. or simply that more experience of reading is necessary for an independent relationship between rhyming ability and analogy reading to show up.

The ability to detect rhyme may depend upon realizing that words with different onsets have the same phonological rime component (Goswami, 1990a; Kirtley et al., 1989). After some exposure to text, a child may come to appreciate that a given sound is often represented by the same spelling pattern. He or she might thus be able to draw on knowledge of the orthographic rime segments of words in his or her existing sight vocabulary to infer the pronunciation of new words that look the same. This would provide a basis for reading by analogy (Gombert et al., 1997; Goswami, 1990a) or, *mutatis mutandis*, for spelling by analogy (see Nation & Hulme, 1996).

THE ROLE OF ANALOGY IN CHILDREN'S READING

Goswami and Bryant (1990) suggested that there is a causal connection between a child's preschool awareness of rhyme and alliteration and later progress in learning to read and spell (Bradley & Bryant, 1978, 1983; Bryant et al., 1990c; Ellis & Large, 1987; Walton, 1995). They argued that this connection could be explained by children's use of analogies (see also Gombert et al., 1997; Goswami, 1999b) based on the associations between letter strings and onsets and rimes. Since the ability to segment words at the level of onset and rime develops without explicit instruction, the ability to use analogies, it was argued, is present from a very early age and at the beginning of reading development. Children who are good at the "odd-one-out" test make more analogies between the ends of words used in training and those presented at test sessions than do children who are poor at rhyme detection (Goswami, 1990a).

Goswami and her collaborators were not the first to consider the role of analogy in early reading. Marsh, Desberg, and Cooper (1977) investigated children's reading of nonwords like *puscle* and *biety*. Application of grapheme–phoneme correspondence rules would lead to these stimuli being read as *muskle* and *peety*. If, on the other hand, these were being read by analogy with words like *muscle* and *piety*, then this should be apparent in the pronunciations given to the nonwords. Marsh et al. discovered (not surprisingly given the nature of some of the nonwords used) that the use of analogy was much less evident in younger (fifth-grade) than older or more sophisticated readers (i.e. eleventh-grade school students and college students). Nonetheless, even the youngest group tested showed some evidence of reading by analogy. Baron (1979) also discussed the use of analogy for reading nonwords, arguing that "the use of analogies is a natural strategy for pronouncing nonsense words—and may even be the major strategy used" (p. 62).

THE CLUE-WORD STUDIES

In a series of much-quoted studies, Goswami made use of a clue-word paradigm to determine whether presentation of a clue word sharing a sub-syllabic segment with a target word would facilitate reading of the target word by younger children. For example, the clue word *beak* is presented (and remains visible throughout) and children are told how this word is pronounced. This is followed by the presentation of words that share either a common rime with the clue word (e.g. *peak*) or a common onset and only part of the rime (e.g. *bean*). These were compared with control words that shared letters at the beginning and end of the words (e.g. *bask* or *bank*). Words that share a common rime can be read by analogy with the clue word. If you are told how to pronounce *beak*, then this offers a strong clue as to how *peak* is pronounced. Goswami (1988a) reported that 5-year-olds who were at the very beginning stages of learning to read were better at reading words that had a common rime with the clue word than other words. Children aged 6 and 7 years were also able to read some words that shared the same beginning (e.g. *beak–bean*) but were better at reading words that shared the rime (*beak–peak*). Using the same technique, these findings have been verified by others. For example, Peterson and Haines (1992), found that end analogies were easier than beginning analogies for 5- and 6-year-old beginning readers, particularly for those who were already proficient at auditory onset–rime segmentation (see also Savage & Stuart, 1998).

Goswami's results arguably might have arisen as a consequence of an effect known as phonological priming. That is, they may have been due to the phonological rather than the orthographic similarity of the shared rimes (see Brown & Besner, 1987). However, Goswami (1990b) showed that when a clue word is presented that acts as a clue to an analogy with one word at the same time as a phonological but not orthographic clue to another (compare *head* as a cue to the pronunciation of *bread* and *said*), then children read the analogous word (*bread*) correctly much more often than they read the phonologically primed word (*said*). Nonetheless, the fact that a phonological priming effect was found implies that it should be controlled for in experiments investigating analogy effects (see Bowey, Vaughan, & Hansen, 1998).

Using the clue-word technique, Savage and Stuart (1998) also found that more rime analogies were made than beginning (or head) analogies by young children (mean age 6 years 3 months). In a "phonological priming" condition, however, children read as many rime and head clued test words as in the standard clue-word condition. Savage and Stuart (1998) argued that one interpretation of the analogy effects is that they "represent purely phonological activation of related words, rather than the use of phonologically underpinned orthographic units as suggested by Goswami (1993)" (p. 95). However, as Goswami (1999b) points out, in the phonological priming condition children only heard the clue words (rather than saw them), which might be expected to act as a prompt to the correct pronunciation—a situation encouraged by the experimental instructions (a point that did not escape Savage and Stuart). If so, this might explain why rime analogies and "beginning" analogies were equally frequent in this condition but not the other conditions of Savage and Stuart's study. Furthermore, Savage and Stuart were reluctant to attribute all the transfer effects to phonological priming. They argued that, "While at least part of the transfer effect in the present analogy task may reflect the activation of target word pronunciations without consultation of orthographic knowledge, there are some limitations to an explanation of all the transfer ... purely in terms of phonological priming" (Savage & Stuart, 1998, p. 103).

Although Goswami (1986, 1988a, 1988b) argued that very young children use onset–rime analogies to read and spell novel words, this does not mean (and nor did Goswami claim) that they cannot also use other sub-syllabic components to make analogies (see also Nation & Hulme, 1996; Savage & Stuart, 1998). While controlling for phonological priming effects, Bowey et al. (1998) found that different groups of first-grade children were able to make analogies between clue words (e.g. *beak*) and targets overlapping in initial consonant–vowel sound (e.g. *bean*), medial vowel sound (e.g. *neat*) or end vowel–consonant sound (e.g. *leak*). Correct responses to these following presentation of the clue word were referred to as beginning, middle and end analogy effects, respectively. There was no evidence that first-grade children produced larger end than middle or beginning analogy effects after taking account of between-session improvement. As a greater end analogy than beginning analogy effect provided the basis for Goswami's claim that novice readers use rime analogies, the results of Bowey et

al. (1998) led them to argue that (with effects of phonological priming controlled) their findings "imply that novice first-grade readers are not yet able to use orthographic rime units independently. Orthographic rimes may only be used when the reading task explicitly provides a substantial memory prompt that may enhance recall of the orthographic rime of the target word. The clue word methodology does just that" (p. 120).

Bowey et al. (1998) performed a second experiment to establish whether there may be a differential contribution of phonolological priming to end analogy and beginning analogy effects. The results of this experiment led them to conclude that there may indeed be a differential contribution. With priming and re-testing effects controlled, "improvement in target word reading following clue word presentation was actually stronger in the beginning analogy group than the end analogy group" (p. 129). The middle and end analogy groups of children showed no greater improvement in reading target words following presentation of a clue word than was observed for phonologically primed words. Bowey et al. concluded:

> The view that beginning readers use orthographic rimes as units of word recognition requires findings that there is significantly stronger use of end than beginning (or middle) analogies, *after phonological priming effects have been controlled*. It therefore follows from the current findings that beginning readers do not reliably use orthographic rimes as units of word recognition even within the clue word task.
>
> (Bowey et al., 1998, p. 129, emphasis in original)

In a reply to Bowey et al. (1998), Goswami (1999a) pointed out that "Our argument has consistently been that an analogy strategy is available to beginning readers, not that orthographic rimes are 'functional units of word identification' prior to the child having learned to read any words that could serve as a basis for an analogy" (p. 213). Whether analogies are actually used is, according to Goswami, a function of a child's phonological awareness, vocabulary size and the method used to teach reading.

Goswami criticized certain of the experimental methods adopted by Bowey et al. (1998), which, she argued, "prevent unambiguous comparisons" between her own results and those of Bowey et al. In turn, Bowey (1999) published a refutation of these criticisms. Both authors note the contribution of teaching practices to the results, which were obtained in experiments of analogy effects. Explicit emphasis on teaching the letters of the alphabet is strongly associated (Duncan et al., 1997) with experimental findings that favour small-unit theories. Hence explicit instruction regarding the relations between graphemes and phonemes may reduce an initial reliance on rime analogy.

Nation, Allen, and Hulme (2001) took up the question of whether, at the very beginning of reading development, analogical transfer effects are based on children making orthographic analogies (underpinned by phonological awareness), as claimed by Goswami, or whether phonological priming constitutes a sufficient explanation of analogical transfer. Using children aged 5½ to 6½ years, Nation et al. presented clue words either purely auditorily or in combination with visual clue words that varied as to whether they were spelled in the same way as the test words. For example, "bone" and "moan" rhyme but do not have the same rime, whereas "bone" and "cone" share the same rhyme and overlap orthographically. A visual clue word presented in the training phase was either present during testing or absent during this latter phase; in either case, the clue word was spoken aloud by the experimenter during the test phase. The results showed that there was as much transfer from clue to test words in the purely phonological condition as in the visual conditions. In the latter conditions, there was no significant difference in the amount of transfer as a function of orthographic overlap (none versus complete overlap in the rime) across all three clue-word conditions.

To eliminate the possibility that implicit orthographic knowledge was influencing the children's performance, Nation et al. (2001) repeated the experiment incorporating a number of methodological changes with rather younger children who were tested for their ability to read the clue words prior to the test phase of the experiment. Despite the methodological changes, the results obtained in the first experiment were replicated in the second. This suggests that the effects reported by Bowey et al. (1998) were not simply due to a different method of presenting clue words to that used by Goswami. More importantly, the findings of Nation et al. (2001), which controlled for children's ability to read the clue words imply that orthographic analogies play little role in the transfer effects shown by beginning readers. This, in turn, undermines the claim (Goswami, 1993) that reading development is based upon orthographic analogies (underpinned by phonological awareness). Nonetheless, Nation and her collaborators were of the view that phonological priming alone is insufficient to enable children to read "by analogy"; in addition, some limited orthographic knowledge (such as letter names) is used to enable them to read test words (see also Roberts & McDougall, 2003; Savage & Stuart, 1998).

Goswami claimed that for beginning readers the link between rhyming skills and the use of rime-based analogies is stronger than that between phoneme deletion and use of analogies (Goswami, 1990a; Goswami & Bryant, 1992; Goswami & Mead, 1992). Similarly, Bowey and Francis (1991) reported that performance on a rhyme oddity task was more strongly related to very early reading skill than was performance on a phoneme oddity task. This does not, however, mean that children cannot *use* alphabetic decoding to read *pari passu* with (or even before) reading based on rime analogies. There are two processes here: phonological skill required for onset–rime segmentation and alphabetic decoding and a sight vocabulary necessary for making analogies. Goswami's view is that the process of analogy is available to children from the outset of reading; how it is used depends upon sight vocabulary and level of phonological skill. Note, incidentally, that evidence that children can use analogies does not necessarily imply that this is a conscious or deliberate strategy (see also Nation & Hulme, 1996). Twenty years earlier, Baron (1979) asked the question: "If the analogy mechanism is so useful, why don't children use it all the time?" (p. 67). After all, Baron believed that "the use of analogies is a natural mechanism" in children (at least those who were poor readers and in the fourth grade of school). The response he gave to his own rhetorical question was "One possibility is that they do not think to try to use it" (p. 67). In short, "availability" and "utilization" of an analogy mechanism may not be the same thing.

Goswami tested her idea that beginnning readers use rime analogies rather than paying attention to individual phonemes (i.e. using phonemes as the basis for analogy) by examining children's pronunciation of vowels. The way in which vowels are pronounced is highly variable in English and depends upon the context. Goswami reasoned that if at the very early stages of reading children analyse single-syllable words into onset and rime, then they should learn about the pronunciation of vowel sounds in the context of the rime only (i.e. not independently) as vowels are always a part of the rime. She therefore designed experiments along the lines of her earlier ones to examine transfer from a clue word to a target word, this time looking at transfer to target words that shared an entire rime with a clue word (e.g. *beak–peak*, *bug–rug*) as compared with target words that shared a vowel but did not share the entire rime (e.g. *beak–heap*, *bug–cup*). Control words shared onset–vowel units only (*beak–bean*, *bug–bud*). Goswami's results showed that 5- to 6-year-olds only showed transfer to words that shared an entire rime, while older children made analogies between words sharing smaller units. She suggested that reading development can be seen as an increasingly refined process of lexical analogy (Goswami, 1993). Initially, the establishment of orthographic recognition units is phonologically underpinned at the level of onset–rime, but as reading develops this phonological underpinning becomes increasingly refined, "resulting eventually in complete phonemic underpinning to supplement the original onset–rime coding" (Goswami, 1993, p. 468). A child's knowledge of orthography is thus both affected by, and in turn influences, his or her phonological knowledge. This "interactive analogy model" stands in contrast (see also Stuart & Coltheart,

1988; Wimmer & Hummer, 1990) to other models (Frith, 1985; Marsh et al., 1981) that propose that children first pass through a logographic stage and then an alphabetic stage before reaching an orthographic stage.

In Goswami's paradigm, the clue word is present during both the initial stage when pronunciation of the clue word is given and throughout the test stage of the experiments. The presence of a clue word in the majority of Goswami's experiments should make one cautious in accepting her proposal that children use analogies spontaneously in the very early stages of learning to read, although there is no doubt from her own studies and those of others that they can be trained to do so. However, analogy effects have been observed in experiments with beginning readers in which the clue word is not visible during testing (e.g. Ehri & Robbins, 1992; Goswami, 1986). Although Muter et al. (1994) found a smaller effect of transfer from the clue word when this was absent throughout the test phase than when it was present, they were still able to confirm that their 6-year-old participants showed analogical transfer even when the clue word was not present during testing. Nonetheless, Muter et al. felt that their findings "lead us to doubt whether young children spontaneously use analogies with any degree of frequency" (p. 300). Savage and Stuart (1998), however, also observed spontaneous use of analogy without previously taught clue words being present during reading of target words by children aged 5 years 7 months to 7 years 4 months, as did Brown and Deavers (1999) with children of almost 6 years of age.

The tendency to use rime analogies apppears to increase with age and reading proficiency (Bowey & Hansen, 1994; Bowey & Underwood, 1996; Coltheart & Leahy, 1996; Duncan et al., 1997; Leslie & Calhoon, 1995; Marsh et al., 1977; Treiman, Goswami, & Bruck, 1990), a finding sometimes said to conflict with the view that children use analogies from the outset of reading. This is, of course, not necessarily true. There is no inconsistency between being able to use analogy (some of the time?) at the outset of reading and developing that ability (particularly with stimuli that have few lexical neighbours; see Coltheart &

Leahy, 1996) as reading proficiency increases. Nor does the use of analogy based on rime mean that skilled readers do not use grapheme–phoneme correspondences more than analogy even as adults (Coltheart & Leahy, 1996).

While rhyme and word onset may be important at the early stages of learning to read English, there is evidence that this might not be so true of a more regular orthography such as German. Working with Austrian children, Wimmer, Landerl, and Schneider (1994) found that rhyme awareness assessed by a German version of the odd-man-out test at the start of reading instruction was not statistically related to reading and spelling measures taken at the end of the first grade at school. It was, however, closely related to such measures at the end of grade 3. Wimmer et al. argued that the German orthography allows children to make an easy start with reading using grapheme–phoneme translation and blending rules. Only later does awareness of larger phonological segments such as rhyme affect reading fluency and spelling skill. This view of the importance of the phoneme early in reading of German is supported by other work from Wimmer's laboratory, which has demonstrated a strong correlation between performance on a vowel substitution task and reading and spelling at the end of the first grade (see Wimmer & Hummer, 1990; Wimmer, Landerl, Linortner, & Hummer, 1991).

The rime frequency effect

Goswami's view (see also Coltheart & Leahy, 1996) is that it is the number of words in a child's mental lexicon that mainly determines the developing use of analogy (Goswami, 1999a, 1999b) and this increases with age. A similar view was expressed by Bowey and her colleagues (Bowey & Hansen, 1994; see also Bowey & Underwood, 1996) in explaining the finding that both adults (see Coltheart & Leahy, 1992) and children (Bowey & Hansen, 1994; Treiman et al., 1990) read nonwords with relatively common or frequent rimes more accurately or more quickly (see Brown, 1987; Brown & Watson, 1994) than nonwords with less frequent rime segments. This is known as the rime-frequency effect (see also

Bowey & Underwood, 1996; Laxon, Masterson, & Moran, 1994; Leslie & Calhoon, 1995), which, incidentally, is regarded by Bowey and Hansen (1994) as inconsistent with a simple dual-route grapheme–phoneme correspondence mechanism. Bowey and Hansen (1994) found that among first grade Australian children, only those with "more developed word reading ability showed the orthographic rime frequency effect" (p. 475). The rime-frequency effect is attributed by Bowey and Hansen to two factors, each of which improves with reading proficiency: (1) the size of sight vocabulary on which analogies can be based and (2) grapheme–phoneme recoding skill, which enables nonwords with uncommon rimes to be read.

Frequency of a particular pronunciation of the rime segment can be separated from a word's overall frequency. Leslie and Calhoon (1995) reported that skilled readers were more likely than less skilled readers to correctly read the rime in a low-frequency word if they had previously read that rime correctly as part of a high-frequency word. As skilled readers were more likely to read rimes with a high number of orthographic neighbours (similarly spelled and pronounced words) than rimes with a low number of neighbours, the implication is that rime neighbourhood size is a more potent variable than word frequency in determining its pronunciation. This suggestion is consistent with findings with adult readers showing that large neighbourhood size facilitates lexical access, at least for low-frequency words (Andrews, 1989; Grainger, 1992; Peereman & Content, 1995; Sears, Hino, & Lupker, 1995).

Leslie and Calhoon (1995) found that children who read at third-grade level or above were more influenced in their word and nonword reading by the target word's (or nonword's) neighbourhood size than were children reading below this level. Laxon et al. (1994) reported a similar finding with regard to word type. The word reading of both 7- and 9-year-olds was affected by neighbourhood size but only the older group showed a sensitivity to word type, consistent regular words being more accurately pronounced than inconsistent regular words. As a child's sight vocabulary increases, he or she is clearly going to be exposed to more words with rimes from large neighbourhoods than from small neighbourhoods (see Laxon, Masterson, & Coltheart, 1991).

The role of segmentation ability in making analogies

Using fixed-step multiple regression techniques, Goswami (1990a) showed that performance on the "odd-man-out" test is statistically related to the tendency to make use of analogies in reading even after the effect of phoneme awareness (as measured by a phoneme deletion task) has been partialled out. In a later study, Goswami and Mead (1992) obtained evidence that the ability to make beginning and end analogies relates to different phonological skills, rhyming ability having a special relationship with analogy based on rime. In a cross-sectional experiment carried out with children aged 6–7 years, Goswami and Mead found that the ability to make end analogies (based on rime, such as *beak–peak*) was closely related to rhyme awareness as measured by the oddity (odd-one-out) task even after the effects of reading ability and nonsense word reading were statistically controlled. Measures of phoneme deletion did not remain significant after taking these variables into account. On the other hand, after controlling for both reading ability and nonsense word reading, the ability to make analogies between the beginning of words (beginning analogies, e.g. *beak–bean*) was related to the ability to perform successfully on tasks involving phoneme deletion, including final consonant deletion, but not rhyming ability.

Deletion of a final consonant entails breaking up the rime of a word and success reflects segmentation at other than the onset–rime boundary. Goswami and Mead (1992) suggested that the best explanation of their data would be that "children only begin to make beginning analogies once they have begun to read and can segment words at boundaries other than onset and rime" (p. 161).

Ehri and Robbins (1992) pointed to an apparent paradox. Goswami's findings suggest that reading by analogy is an easier process for very young children than phonologically recoding

words, yet Ehri and Robbins themselves found that only those children with some phonic decoding skill used analogy. They suggested that this paradox can be resolved if it is assumed that the individual phonemes making up the rime have already been blended (requiring some degree of phonological skill) and can be retrieved from memory as an existing unit, thereby "eliminating the need to blend phonemes in the rimes of new words because the blended rimes are supplied by readers' memory for known words" (p. 22). Thus, to read by analogy children must have adequate decoding skill to segment words into onsets and rimes and to blend a new onset with an existing rime.

In similar vein, the results of an experiment by Bruck and Treiman (1992), in which children were trained to make various kinds of analogy, led these authors to suggest that, "In order to take full advantage of their inclination to segment spoken and printed words into onsets and rimes and to use this information productively for pronouncing unfamiliar words, children must learn something about the relations between individual graphemes and individual phonemes" (p. 387). On the other hand, according to Leslie and Calhoon, only:

> A minimal amount of grapheme–phoneme correspondence knowledge, as measured by the ability to produce phonemes when presented with graphemes, may be needed for reading by analogy. Our students knew a high percentage of phonemes for single consonants, but . . . few could produce any phoneme for vowels . . . A highly developed knowledge of grapheme–phoneme correspondences may not be necessary for reading by analogy.
> (Leslie & Calhoon, 1995, p. 584).

Walton (1995) reported that (Canadian) kindergarten children (mean age 5 years 8 months) who were high in pre-reading skill (as measured by rhyme ability, phoneme identification and letter–sound knowledge) were able to use analogies to read test words. The mean number of letter-sounds known by this group of children was only

10.6, which supports the view expressed by Leslie and Calhoon (1995).

Ehri and Robbins (1992) based their argument that some degree of phonemic awareness is necessary for making analogies on their finding with kindergarten and first-grade children that (after training to criterion on a set of clue words) only those with some phonic decoding skill (two or more of five nonwords read correctly at pre-test) read test words (with unconventional but systematic spellings) by analogy. However, the measure of decoding skill used by Ehri and Robbins (1992) was level of performance in reading five simple nonwords (such as *bev* and *mal*), three of which could be read by analogy. Thus their decoding measure might actually have been a measure of the ability to use analogy (Muter et al., 1994).

Bruck and Treiman (1992) suggested that children need some level of knowledge or ability concerning the relations between single graphemes and phonemes (as well as between groups of graphemes and groups of phonemes) to make analogies based on rime. These authors assessed children's phonological awareness using tests of initial and final phoneme deletion and phoneme counting. A composite phonological awareness score was significantly related to the number of analogy trials required to reach criterion. Children with good phonological awareness required fewer trials to learn the clue words than children with poorer awareness. Bruck and Treiman suggested that:

> The type of phonological awareness that is important in learning to read words depends on the way in which children are taught . . . Our results suggest that instruction that is confined to larger units is not sufficient for beginning readers, who have a tendency to pronounce unfamiliar items on a phoneme-by-phoneme basis. Children need instruction not just on the relations between groups of graphemes and groups of phonemes but also on the correspondences between single graphemes and single phonemes, especially vowels. In this view, children may succeed in using analogical strategies to process larger orthographic units only when they know something about the correspondences between single phonemes and single graphemes. This interpretation is consisent with that of Ehri and Robbins (1992).
>
> (Bruck & Treiman, 1992, pp. 386–387)

In support of those authors who have argued that training or some minimal existing level of reading proficiency is a prerequisite for making analogies, Muter et al. (1994) noted that "all the children demonstrating the analogy effect had at least some reading and spelling skills" (p. 300). This was seen as conflicting with the claim attributed to Goswami that even non-readers use analogy. Whether in fact this claim *was* made by Goswami is not easy to decide.

Goswami and Bryant (1990) maintained that the ability to make analogies is already in place before the child receives instruction in reading. That is, the abilty to make analogies is available to young children from the outset of reading instruction and, without being explicitly taught, they can read novel words by using analogies based on rime. If this constitutes "reading", then the claim that "non-readers" use analogies is falsely attributed to Goswami and her co-workers. On the other hand, Goswami has also argued that whereas children may begin by recognizing a correspondence between the orthographic pattern of a word and onset–rime units, they go on to realize that the onset and rime itself are represented by a series of phonemes. This realization is thought to be based on, or at least assisted by, the process of learning to read and to spell (see Cataldo & Ellis, 1988). The obvious, if not strictly logical, interpretation of Goswami's view is that very young children may make analogies between words before any formal reading instruction. Such children might well be referred to as non-readers, in which case it is legitimate to attribute to Goswami the claim that non-readers use analogy.

RHYME VERSUS PHONEMIC SEGMENTATION IN EARLY READING: THE SMALL- VERSUS LARGE-UNIT DEBATE

There is evidence, some of which is outlined above, that children's awareness of spoken language develops from an awareness of more global features (such as the syllable) to awareness of smaller constituent features (such as onset–rime or phonemes). Goswami and Bryant (1990) argued that rhyme awareness and phoneme awareness are separate components of phonological ability that develop independently of each other, although it is probable that those who are most sensitive to rhyme are those who are, or become, most sensitive to phonemes (Goswami, 1999b). Goswami and Bryant (1990) maintained that rhyme ability is the crucial skill affecting the development of reading in the early stages. The ability to detect rhyme was said to lead to an awareness of the onset–rime distinction within words and this, in turn, influences the use of analogy in reading and spelling (see Goswami & Bryant, 1990; Goswami & Mead, 1992).

Contrary to the findings on children's early analogies that have been regarded as implying that early reading is based upon segmentation ability at the large-unit or onset–rime level, other research has suggested that small-unit or phonemic segmentation ability is the critically important factor from the outset of learning to read (Muter et al., 1997; Nation & Hulme, 1997; Seymour & Duncan, 1997; Seymour & Evans, 1994a, 1994b). Seymour and Duncan (1997) regard theories such as that of Frith (1985) as implying that children progress from using small units (phonemes) to larger units (such as syllables or sub-syllabic segments larger than the phoneme) in learning to read. This can be termed a small-units hypothesis and contrasts with the hypothesis that reading progresses from large units (such as the rime) to smaller units (such as the phoneme). Duncan et al. (1997) provide a lucid summary of the evidence available at that time in favour of the two competing positions.

Muter et al. (1994) refer to Muter's doctoral thesis in which she carried out a principal components analysis of scores of children of different ages on a range of phonological awareness tasks. This consistently yielded two factors that Muter et al. (1994) termed *rhyming* and *segmentation* factors. This, plus the findings of their own experiment, led them to conclude as follows:

> Segmentation ability, in interaction with letter knowledge, fuelled progress in reading, and in particular spelling, during the first year at school. Rhyming did not contribute to reading or spelling performance in the first year, but did have a significant influence, alongside segmentation, on spelling progress in the following year. In contrast, neither segmentation nor rhyming skills contributed to reading ability in the second year; the major contributors were in fact reading vocabulary from the previous year, together with concurrent letter knowledge. Taken together with the present results, these findings favour an interpretation of children, first using knowledge of sound-to-letter relationships to read and later, with increasing awareness of orthographic regularities and rhyme, using analogies. Spelling, on the other hand, remains phonological, with both segmentation and rhyming exerting a significant influence over its development.
>
> (Muter et al., 1994, pp. 307–308)

In a later investigation Muter et al. (1997) showed that in the first year of school (at 4 years of age), phonemic segmentation ability was highly predictive of both reading and spelling, while rhyming (tested by a set of questions each asking which of three alternative choices rhymed with a given word) was not. These results support the idea (Yopp, 1988) that rhyme and segmentation skill represent different components of phonological ability. They contradict those findings suggesting that rhyme ability plays a crucial role in the early stages of learning to read, whereas segmentation is crucial for spelling (Bryant et al., 1990c; Cataldo & Ellis, 1988; Goswami & Bryant, 1990). It may be that the different tests of rhyming used by Muter et al. (1997) on the one hand and those of Cataldo and Ellis (1988) and Bryant and his colleagues on the other (who used the odd-man-out or oddity test of sound categorization) are responsible for the different results. On the basis of an experiment showing that performance on a test of sound categorization is determined by the difficulty of the phonetic discrimination (Snowling et al., 1994), Muter et al. (1997) suggest that "the sound categorization task is best thought of as a phonetic discrimination task tapping the efficiency of speech perception mechanisms, rather than as a measure of rhyme awareness" (p. 388).

In the second year of school, neither concurrent nor earlier rhyming ability was found by Muter et al. (1997) to be associated with reading. Nor was segmentation ability a significant predictor of reading, although it did predict spelling. Rhyming was significantly associated with concurrent reading and spelling scores at this stage, far later than might be expected based on Goswami and Bryant's position. Muter et al. (1994) had earlier found a relationship between rhyming ability and concurrent use of analogy, but rhyme ability at age 4 and 5 years did not significantly predict the use of analogy at age 6 years. One possible implication of these findings is that phonemic and rime segmentation skills reflect independent abilities that relate differentially to different aspects of reading and spelling at different points in children's development.

The study by Muter et al. (1997) was criticized on a number of grounds by Bryant (1998). In particular, he pointed out that the instructions to children asking them to choose a word that "rhymes with or sounds like" a target word meant that choosing a word with the same onset as the target word was a legitimate response. Muter et al. (1997), however, scored only rhyming words as correct responses. As a good proportion of distractor words did in fact begin with the same letter as the target, Bryant re-analysed Muter and colleagues' data (corrected to take account of a few previous errors) to include same-onset choices as correct. He also used separate scores on two reading tests, whereas Muter et al. combined scores from the two reading tests into a composite measure. Not surprisingly, Bryant's re-analysis resulted in higher scores than those reported by Muter et al. This led to ceiling effects in the second year and, therefore, Bryant restricted further re-analyses to data from the first year. These showed that the onset-plus-rhyme score was a better predictor of reading and spelling than the rhyme score used by Muter et al. Bryant concluded that the onset-plus-rhyme scores "compared favourably" with the two phoneme scores (deletion and identification) in predicting reading. This does not establish, of course, that rhyming per se is a better early predictor, but it does imply that the possibility should not be rejected. However, in her methodological review of research on rhyme and reading ability, Macmillan (2002) concludes that "evidence to date does not support the idea that early rhyme awareness is importantly related to reading ability" (p. 23). She suggests that a link between rhyme and reading may only be found "when prior reading ability or knowledge of the alphabet is ignored as a factor that may contribute to the variance in reading" (p. 22).

Bryant's critique received a reply from Hulme, Muter, and Snowling (1998). They provide evidence that refutes Bryant's suggestion that children interpret instructions to choose a word that "rhymes with or sounds like" a target word any differently than they interpret instructions to choose a word that merely "rhymes with" a target word. Hulme et al. argue that Bryant's measure of onset-plus-rhyme is a global measure of sensitivity to sound and "not a specific measure of either rime or phoneme sensitivity" (p. 43). They maintain that "This global 'sound sensitivity' does not require awareness of onset–rime segments as Bryant has argued" (p. 42). This is tilting at a straw man. Nowhere in his critique does Bryant argue that his measure requires onset–rime awareness (although one can see why he might be expected to have said this). Indeed, his caution in interpreting the results of a factor analysis that produced two factors, onto each of which his onset-plus-rhyme measure loaded ("appreciably" in one case and "heavily" in the other), suggests rather that Bryant would not disagree with the position taken by Hulme et al.

The view that it is phonemic segmentation rather than rhyming skills that is the most important predictor of early literacy skills was reiterated by Nation and Hulme (1997). These authors used a number of phonological awareness tasks with nonwords as stimuli (to avoid any confounding effects of orthographic knowledge on this task). The participants were three groups each of 25 children aged 5.5–9.5 years. The results of hierarchical regression analyses showed that phonemic segmentation, as measured by the ability to segment an entire letter string into separate sounds, was significantly associated with reading and spelling performance even after all other variables (including age and digit span as a measure of memory) had been taken into account. Sound categorization (rhyming) was also a significant predictor but not always so after the effect of phonemic segmentation had been statistically controlled. The ability to segment nonwords into onset–rime units (unlike the other phonological awareness tasks) did not correlate with age, reading or spelling ability. Nonetheless, it is worth noting that the correlation between age and onset–rime segmentation just missed the conventional 5 per cent level, being significant at the 6 per cent level, and that with age controlled, the partial correlation between rhyme and reading was significant.

Nation and Hulme (1997) argued that "The failure to find a clear relationship betwen onset–rime segmentation and the early stages of reading and spelling development is a clear contradiction of the predictions made by Goswami & Bryant (1990)" (p. 165). With age partialled out, however, "the correlation between onset–rime segmentation and reading age—although small—was statistically significant" (pp. 160–161). Thus although Nation and Hulme identify phonemic segmentation skill as the more powerful concurrent predictor of reading and spelling, and although onset–rime segmentation and rhyme each failed to predict unique variance in the regression analyses, it is evident that the relationship between reading on the one hand and rhyming and onset–rime segmentation abilities on the other is not negligible. Furthermore, from this study of concurrent relationships, it does not follow that literacy skills might not be predicted by rhyme and segmentation scores taken at an earlier age than that of the youngest children studied in this investigation.

The claim that it is phonemic segmentation rather than rhyming skills that best predicts early reading and spelling skills receives support from Seymour and Evans (1994a, 1994b). These workers reported that in the pre-school period, children were able to produce rhymes to words spoken by the experimenter but were unable to perform segmentation tasks at any level. With the beginning of reading instruction, phoneme segmentation ability emerged before the ability to segment at the onset–rime level, a result that Seymour and Evans considered to contradict what they saw as Goswami and Bryant's position.

The relevance of attempts to refine which component(s) of phonological awareness best predict early reading and spelling ability is that they may help to specify which skills should be considered "primary" in the teaching of reading and in identifying children at risk for reading failure. Seymour and Duncan (1997) argued that "If the critical problem in learning to read is the establishment of correspondences between segments of sound and arrays of letters, then it seems to follow that reading and spelling development might beneficially follow the same larger-to-smaller pathway as phonological development" (pp. 126–127). Macmillan (2002), however, cautions that "it may be dangerous to design instruction according to a development view, according to what [sic] skills appear to be easier, when instruction targeted at developing the skills that are supposedly more difficult may be more effective" (p. 34).

Seymour and his colleagues report on experiments designed to distinguish between the small-unit versus large-unit hypotheses (Duncan et al., 1997; Seymour & Duncan, 1997). First, children's ability to read nonwords constructed from different sub-syllabic segments was compared with their ability to read known real words. It was argued that large-unit theory would predict that nonwords made from the onset of one word and the rime of another would be easier for children in the first year of primary school to read than nonwords made from body and coda or from onset, peak and coda taken from familiar words. Small-unit theory, it was argued, would predict that the latter nonwords would be easier to read than the former type. In the event, the results favoured small-unit theory. However, among second-year primary school children who had reading ages of 8 years and above, there was a rise in the frequency of rime analogies as compared with body analogies in reading nonwords. This was not seen for children whose reading ages were 7 years or below.

First-year primary school children were next presented with familiar written words one at a time. With a word visible to the children, the experimenter sounded out a sub-syllabic segment of varying size and the children were asked to mark on the word those letters corresponding to the appropriate sound segment. For example, given the word "ground" the child might be asked to mark the letters (orthographic unit) corresponding to the sound "ound". This test was given for different sub-syllabic units, including large (body and rime) and small (onset, peak and coda) units. Children were correct in identifying the rime segment 60 per cent of the time and in identifying the small onset and peak units over 90 per cent of the time. In another experiment, first- and second-year primary school children were presented with two spoken words and they were asked to say which bits of the two words sounded the same. Again, the word segments were varied in this "phonological common unit" task and again the children performed better with smaller units than larger units.

Seymour and Duncan (1997) conclude that the results of their study "strongly suggest that the progression in normal reading acquisition is from a small unit (phonemic) approach in the initial stage towards a large unit (rime-based) at a later stage" (p. 130). These results have been replicated in a study by the same group incorporating some methodological variations on the original study (Seymour, Duncan, & Bolik, 1999). As a result of considering teaching methods used with the children they tested, Seymour and colleagues suggested that the small to large unit progression in children's awareness of speech segments as

assessed by the phonological common unit task "appears to be linked to letter sound knowledge and reading progress and can be accelerated by focused instruction" (p. 125). This position is in accordance with those studies with illiterate adults that have shown that good performance on tasks requiring awareness of the phonetic structure of speech—for example, deleting or adding phonemes (phones) to nonwords—depends upon some experience of reading an alphabetic script (Bertelson et al., 1989; Mann, 1988; Morais et al., 1979, 1986; Read et al., 1986).

In some ways, the argument concerning small versus large units and the role of teaching instruction may be largely irrelevant, since there is evidence that children can, in effect, teach themselves by inferring knowledge of rules from their experience of written text—the so-called "knowledge sources account" (Thompson, Cottrell, & Fletcher-Flinn, 1996). Evidence from a study of children's reading of various types of nonword shows that even in the absence of explicit instruction, by the age of 7 years they have acquired a knowledge of grapheme–phoneme correspondence rules and are sensitive to the consistency of rime pronunciations (Stuart, Masterson, Dixon, & Quinlan (1999). Overall, however, the children were more likely to use grapheme–phoneme correspondence rules than rime units to pronounce nonwords (see also Coltheart & Leahy, 1992).

The results of studies such as those of Seymour and his colleagues have been seen as supporting a position contrary to that advocated by Goswami and Bryant (1990). The latter were said to have claimed that children make use of analogies based on onset–rime segmentation before using smaller sub-syllabic segments such as phonemes. How may the two positions be reconciled?

Goswami and Bryant (1990) certainly argued that the ability to segment words at the level of onset and rime develops very early without explicit instruction and relates to subsequent reading achievement. It is also clear that at a later stage of development, phonemic discrimination ability is a powerful predictor of reading and spelling ability (Nation & Hulme, 1997; Perin, 1983), but is in turn itself influenced by reading instruction. Thus one interpretation of the research findings is that the fundamental ability at the earliest stage of learning to read is onset–rime segmentation and that the ability to segment words at the level of individual phonemes, determined by reading instruction, influences reading ability at a later stage, perhaps by assisting in acquisition of the principle that in alphabetic languages, at least, individual phonemes are mapped onto their orthographic representations. However, the results of Seymour and his colleagues (and those of Muter and co-workers) suggest that even very young beginning readers are sensitive to units smaller than the rime.

Seymour's group refer to a distinction drawn by other theorists between epilinguistic or implicit phonological awareness and meta-linguistic or explicit awareness. They suggest that tasks such as the common unit task require only implicit awareness, whereas tasks such as phoneme deletion require explicit awareness. These two aspects of phonological awareness may be dissociated, in that a child who has an implicit awareness may not also show explicit awareness of the same size of phonological unit. This helps to make sense of the findings that pre-school children appear to have an awareness of large units (onset–rime) but that reading instruction (including letter–sound knowledge) leads to an awareness of phonemes. Seymour's proposal is that phoneme awareness is initially implicit but made explicit through instruction. The same applies to rime awareness. It is initially implicit (i.e. in the pre-school years) but becomes explicit as experience with orthographic structure increases. This proposal therefore throws into sharp relief the role of instruction and offers a potential resolution of differences in findings between the Dundee group headed by Seymour and Goswami's group.

The Dundee group was known to have had intensive so-called phonic instruction, whereas the earlier findings of Goswami (1986, 1990a, 1990b, 1993) were obtained with children for whom more global (look-and-say) methods of teaching were in vogue at the time. Goswami and East (2000) gave first-year primary school children a small amount of tuition in using onset–rime correspondences and found that their per-

formance with rime units exceeded that reported by the Dundee group. The role of reading instruction is thus crucial in determining the pattern of results obtained on the common unit task as on others. Methodological factors are also crucial. Goswami and East (2000) argue that in interpreting the results of studies comparing small units (phonemes) with large units (onset and rimes) in early reading, it is important to distinguish between *recognition* of shared segments and the *identification* and *production* of such segments.

Brown and Deavers (1999) believe that it is "clearly misleading to cast the debate in terms of a simple comparison between the small-units-first and the the large-units-first model" (p. 232). These authors presented children with two kinds of nonword. Regular nonwords (such as *deld*) were derived from regular, consistent words; irregular nonwords (such as *dalk*) were derived from irregular or inconsistent words. It was anticipated that regular, consistent words would be read by a grapheme-to-phoneme based strategy, whereby each letter was pronounced according to a simple vowel-based rule. Irregular, inconsistent words would be read either according to a vowel-based rule or would be pronounced by analogy to irregular words (so as to rhyme with *walk* or *talk* or *balk*). Thus the strategy used could be inferred from the pronunciation that was given. An analogy-based strategy would imply the use of a large unit (the rime), whereas reading by rule would imply the use of smaller units (but see Baron, 1979). (Note that regular nonwords might also be read by analogy, but there would be no difference in pronunciation from that produced by vowel-based rules.)

Brown and Deavers (1999) divided children on the basis of their reading scores and reported that, like adults, children with a mean reading score of 11 years 6 months on the British Ability Scale (BAS) made significantly more analogical responses than those with a mean reading age of 8 years 8 months. That is, younger, less skilled readers are more likely to adopt a grapheme–phoneme correspondence based strategy than are older, more skilled readers (see also Bowey & Underwood, 1996; Coltheart & Leahy, 1992; Leslie & Calhoon, 1995). Provision of a clue word as in Goswami's experiments led to a higher proportion of analogy responses without there being any difference between groups of skilled and less-skilled readers (see also Goswami, 1986). The extent to which analogies were made in reponse to provision of a clue word varied, however, with the number of target nonwords the children were asked to read. There were significantly more analogy responses made when reading single-target nonwords than in response to four-target non-words. Brown and Deavers intepreted their findings in terms of a flexible-unit model, whereby children adopt either a small unit or a large unit strategy according to the demands of the task facing them (see also Roberts & McDougall, 2003). This position is consistent with the multiple-units hypothesis of skilled adult reading developed by Shallice et al. (1983) and referred to in Chapter 2.

There may in fact be no contradiction between small- and large-unit theories that requires a "reconciliation". Goswami and Bryant (1990) did not assert that in learning to read children progress from larger units to smaller ones, only that at the beginning of reading children have analogies available to them and that to some extent they may make use of them (see Goswami, 1999b). Despite this, "As phonological awareness of rhyme develops prior to phonological aware-ness of phonemes, it was claimed that analogies based on rimes preceded analogies based on phonemes. However, the implicit process of analogy was thought to operate at multiple levels, e.g. onset, rime *and* phoneme, depending on phonological skills" (Goswami, 1999b, p. 223, emphasis in original). Nor did Goswami and Bryant argue that there is no relation between phoneme awareness and reading at the very early stages of learning to read. Thus to argue that there is a stronger relationship between rhyme and reading than between phoneme awareness and reading (or vice versa) is to create a false anithesis. Indeed, Goswami (1999b) is adamant that "the question of whether reading development follows a 'path' from small to large units . . . or vice versa . . . is misguided. Both causal connections are important for reading" (p. 226). Working with 4- and 5-year-olds, Roberts and McDougall (2003) have recently shown that while performance on rhyme-based tasks best predicts performance on the clue-word (analogy) task, scores on phoneme-based tasks are stronger predictors of single-word reading. These authors argued that "children are able to respond strategically to what they perceive to be the demands of the task and this changes the balance of skills that they draw upon" (p. 329). This compromise position seems a reasonable conclusion to what many now view as a somewhat long-drawn-out and arid debate.

4

Phonological Awareness, Phonological Recoding, and Dyslexia

The research discussed in the previous chapter indicates that phonological segmentation and blending skills play a key role in the development of reading. In particular, poor phonological awareness at the level of the phoneme may hinder acquisition of the alphabetic principle (Frith, 1985; Share, 1995; Snowling, 1995) although, as pointed out by Tunmer et al. (1988), "Phonological awareness is necessary but not sufficient for acquiring phonological recoding skill" (p. 150). Furthermore, the relationship between rhyme detection and the abilty to make analogies suggests that children who have difficulty in segmenting words at the onset–rime level will find it difficult to read some words by analogy with others. Indeed, dyslexic children have been found to make fewer analogies than reading age matched controls (Hanley, Reynolds, & Thornton, 1997; Manis, Szeszulski, Howell, & Horn, 1986). This may mean that they tend not to use analogies spontaneously. However, poor readers (Baron, 1979) and dyslexics can be taught to

make analogies and may do so spontaneously if provided with a clue word (Deavers & Brown, 1997a, 1997b).

THE PHONOLOGICAL DEFICIT HYPOTHESIS OF DYSLEXIA

An obvious corollary of the fact that reduced phonological awareness is associated with impaired reading skills is that poor phonological skills lead directly to poor reading. This is referred to as the phonological deficit hypothesis. Consistent with this hypothesis, children poor in phonological awareness generally show poor reading ability; conversely, children who are poor readers are usually poor in phonological awareness (Snowling, 1981, 1995; Stanovich, 1988a, 1988b; Stanovich & Siegel, 1994). Even many adult dyslexics, though perhaps only those of the so-called phonological sub-type of dyslexia

(Kinsbourne et al., 1991), continue to experience difficulties in performing successfully on tasks assessing phonological abilities (Bruck, 1990, 1992; Elbro et al., 1994; Felton et al., 1990; Kinsbourne et al., 1991; Leong, 1999; Miles, 1986; Pennington et al., 1990; Pratt & Brady, 1988; Scarborough, 1984; Stanovich et al., 1997a, 1997b; Temple, 1988, 1990; see also articles edited by Beaton, McDougall, & Singleton, 1997a), including discriminating speech-related stimuli (Cornelissen, Hansen, Bradley & Stein, 1996). Indeed, reduced phonological sensitivity remains one of the most persistent deficits in adult dyslexics, even if their reading of English has reached reasonable levels of accuracy (Bruck, 1990; Elbro et al., 1994; Gottardo, Siegel, & Stanovich, 1997; Hanley, 1997; Liberman et al., 1974; Pennington et al., 1990; Snowling, Nation, Moxham, Gallagher, & Frith, 1997; Watson & Miller, 1993). Nonetheless, the fact that not all dyslexic adults (see, for example, Hanley, 1997; Rack, 1997) and children (e.g. Nicolson & Fawcett, 1995a) have deficient phonological skills indicates that there may be a wide range of phonological ability among dyslexics (Stanovich, 1988a, 1988b).

In fact, a clear relationship between phonological ability and reading is not restricted to low levels of reading or even to an alphabetic script (Ho & Bryant, 1997). Ehri points out that:

> the individual differences in reading that are predicted by phonological awareness span the entire range of reading skill, not just the lower end consisting of disabled readers. That is, high correlations reflect the fact that differences in phonological awareness are associated with accelerated reading as well as retarded reading, not just retarded reading.
>
> (Ehri, 1989, pp. 361–362)

Stainthorp and Hughes (1998) have shown that a group of 5-year-old precocious readers, defined as those who read fluently prior to school instruction, had significantly higher scores at shallow intermediate and deep levels of phonological sensitivity (Stanovich, 1986) than non-reading children matched for verbal IQ.

PHONOLOGICAL RECODING IN DYSLEXIA

Despite all the research, there is no universal consensus as to how phonological awareness mediates success in learning to read. One commonly held view is that some phonological awareness is essential for an understanding of the idea that the sounds making up a word are represented by combinations of individual letters. As Seymour (1987b) noted, "A standard proposal . . . is that the contribution of phonemic segmentation might be mediated via the establishment of a system of grapheme–phoneme correspondences" (pp. 504–505). The existence of such a system is assumed by many, but not all, theorists to be most clearly demonstrated in the context of novel or nonwords.

Dyslexics find it difficult to apply grapheme–phoneme (or, more generally, orthographic–phonological) conversion rules. It is these that enable a child to recognize words that they have not encountered previously in print but are in their spoken or hearing vocabulary (Stanovich, 1986). If a child finds it difficult to segment a word into its constituent parts, it will be difficult to learn that particular sounds are represented by particular letters or letter combinations and hence to acquire a phonological (or "phonic") reading strategy. According to Rack, Snowling, and Olson (1992), among disabled readers "Phonological recoding is the most common source of word reading difficulties in dyslexic children" (p. 114). This accounts for the occurrence of a persistent (but not universal) nonword reading deficit in dyslexia (Ben-Dror, Pollatsek, & Scarpati, 1991; Brown, 1997; Rack et al., 1992; Van Ijzendoorn & Bus, 1994), first demonstrated by Snowling (1980) in an immediate memory recognition task.

The ability of children to read nonsense words (thought to depend upon phonological recoding at some level) is more predictive of the ability to read regular than irregular words (Baron, 1979). This suggests that, at certain stages in reading development, a phonological recoding strategy is used to read regular words as well as nonwords.

Impaired phonological recoding would be expected to follow from impaired phonological awareness. The finding from one study that phonological awareness scores predicted performance in reading regularly spelled words better than irregularly spelled words (Stuart & Masterson, 1992; see also Griffiths & Snowling, 2002; Hansen & Bowey, 1994) is consistent with this idea.

Brown (1997) points out that "The phonological deficit hypothesis, with its assumption that spelling-to-sound translation ability will be selectively impaired in dyslexia, leads to two critical predictions. The first prediction is that nonword reading will be selectively impaired in dyslexia; the second is that there will be reduced effects of spelling-to-sound regularity in dyslexia" (p. 209). After reviewing the literature, Brown comes to the conclusion that while there is consistent evidence for a nonword reading deficit in dyslexia (for reviews, see Rack et al., 1992; Van Ijzendoorn & Bus, 1994), there is far less consistency over the question of a reduced regularity effect—that is, a reduced advantage for regular compared with irregular (or exception) word reading. Individual cases may show a reduced regularity effect but, in Brown's submission, "most group studies do not find reduced regularity effects" (p. 212). An experimental investigation of his own with "highly dyslexic subjects" also failed to reveal any evidence of a reduced regularity effect, but did show an impairment in nonword reading. Brown believed these paradoxical results to be inconsistent with the standard interpretation of a phonological deficit affecting spelling-to-sound translation but to be consistent with the idea of dyslexia as a reflection of impaired phonological representations (see also Metsala, Stanovich, & Brown, 1998).

The quality of phonological representations

Most versions of the phonological deficit hypothesis account for poor reading in terms of poor phonological segmentation skills. However, the other side of the coin—the ability to synthesize or blend words from constituent phonemes should not be forgotten, since this also relates to individual differences in reading ability (Poskiparta, Niemi, & Vauras, 1999; Torgesen et al., 1989).

An alternative explanation of the relationship between phonological awareness and reading is that performance on phonological awareness tasks reflects the quality of the phonological representations that are used in learning to read and in other speech-based functions, such as object naming (Hulme & Snowling, 1992; Laing & Hulme, 1999; Swan & Goswami, 1997a, 1997b). Thus, whether the fundamental problem for dyslexics, at least for the majority of those considered to be phonologically impaired, is one of weak, insecure or indistinct phonological representation of words (Elbro, 1996; Katz, 1986; Snowling & Hulme, 1994), or relates to a difficulty in segmenting speech sounds at one or other level (syllable/phoneme/onset–rime) (see Muter et al., 1997) and then mapping these segments on to the relevant visual symbols (see, for example, Manis et al., 1997), is a matter yet to be resolved, although the two views are clearly not mutually exclusive. Swan and Goswami (1997a, 1997b) have presented evidence from picture-naming studies consistent with the view that dyslexic children are characterized by both weak phonological representations *and* poor segmentation ability. Either way, varying degrees of severity of a phonological deficit may have different consequences. A relatively mild deficit may have an effect only on reading acquisition, whereas a more severe impairment may influence both speech perception and production as well as reading (Harm & Seidenberg, 1999). It is important to appreciate, however, that poor phonological skills do not inevitably lead to deficient sight reading skills any more than good phonological awareness necessarily leads to good phonological decoding skills.

The notion of a phonological awareness deficit, as the term is used in the literature, is somewhat broad. A deficit may affect different aspects of phonological processing. Snowling (1987) suggests that difficulties with input phonology (auditory perception) would be expected to delay the acquisition of letter–sound corrrespondence rules. Difficulties with output phonology, the processing stage at which the codes for pronunciation of letter strings are retrieved or assembled, would impair phoneme blending. Problems with phoneme segmentation would be expected to interfere with spelling. Snowling described dyslexic children having different patterns of phonological skills and suggested that difficulties with different aspects of phonological processing might explain individual differences in reading and spelling performance found even in an apparently homogeneous group of "phonological" dyslexics (Snowling, Stackhouse, & Rack, 1986b).

For children with expressive phonological impairments, the problem may not simply be a motor deficit but reflect a more fundamental difficulty in analysing or classifying speech sounds at a sub-syllabic level (Bird, Bishop, & Freeman, 1995). Nonetheless, deficits in expressive or output phonology do not necessarily impair the development of normal reading skills (but see Hulme & Snowling, 1992) unless they are associated with other language impairments (Bishop & Adams, 1990) or are particularly severe (Bird et al., 1995).

Although it is now widely accepted that a deficit of phonological processing lies at the heart of developmental dyslexia (Lundberg, 1989; Snowling & Hulme, 1994; Stanovich, 1988a, 1988b; Vellutino et al., 1996; Wagner & Torgesen, 1987), there are some (e.g. Nicolson, 1996; Scarborough, 1990) who are critical of the phonological deficit hypothesis as a complete account of the difficulties faced by all poor readers (and spellers), never mind those designated as dyslexic and for whom reading and spelling are not the only areas of dysfunction. According to Scarborough:

> Plausible though this hypothesis might be, it may not provide a complete explanation of reading failure. There is abundant evidence that the reading difficulties of dyslexic children begin to emerge from the time that they start learning to recognize letters and to appreciate letter–sound correspondences. Moreover, the relation between metaphonological and literacy skills is apparently one of reciprocal causation, such that phonological proficiency facilitates the learning of letter–sound correspondences, which in turn enhances phonological skill and awareness. To

explain reading failure in terms of these phonological skills, therefore, may say little more than that a child's success in early literacy achievement is predictive of subsequent progress in reading, and raises the question of what underlies the early deficits in literacy and phonological processing to begin with.

(Scarborough, 1990, p. 1739)

Despite the huge amount of research showing the importance for reading of being able to analyse the sound structure of words, the mechanisms underlying the relationship between phonological segmentation ability and reading are not entirely clear. One might expect developmental changes in children's phonological representations, gradually moving from a more holistic to a more segmental level of representation with increasing age (see also Metsala, 1997), to lead to awareness at a phonemic level and hence to the acquisition of reading (see Fowler, 1991). Yet exactly how this ocurs, and how individual differences in phonological segmentation ability arise, has yet to be worked out in detail.

Phonemic awareness, literacy and non-alphabetic languages

Regardless of the exact mechanisms involved, a relationship between phonological awareness (at whatever level) and reading might arise either because poor phonological skills lead to poor reading (Bryant et al., 1990c) or because poor reading leads to poor phonological skills. Among adult non-literate speakers of Portuguese, phonological awareness is less developed than among current (Bertelson et al., 1989) or former (Morais et al., 1986) adult non-readers. Furthermore, readers of non-alphabetic languages such as Chinese or Japanese Kanji may be unable to add phonemes to, or delete them from, spoken words of their own language (Mann, 1986; Read et al., 1986). Chinese-speaking children who have learned an alphabetic system (pin-yin) for pronouncing Chinese characters have higher levels of phonological awareness than those who have not learned an alphabetic system (Huang & Hanley, 1995). The implication is that instruction in (and/

or experience of) the alphabetic principle develops awareness of the phoneme level of spoken language; normally, it does not develop spontaneously simply through speaking, although in some individuals it may do so (see Mann, 1991). Even in regular orthographies, such as Finnish, phoneme deletion and synthesis or blending may be a product, rather than a determinant, of reading acquisition (Aro et al., 1999). Given the above findings, it is likely that the more advanced phonological skills, such as phonemic segmentation and manipulation, are not attained by the majority of children until they have received at least some formal instruction in reading (Muter et al., 1997).

The research relating phonological awareness to reading implies two things. The first is that poor phonological awareness leads to poor reading; the second is that remediating the phonological deficit should lead to improved reading performance. These implications are, however, based on findings that are essentially correlational in nature. To find deficits in a variable such as phonological skill among disabled readers compared with children matched for reading level suggests, but does not prove, that phonological skill has a causal role in reading disability. A better strategy is to combine longitudinal research with strategies aimed at remediating the deficit (Bryant & Goswami, 1986). Intervention studies have therefore had two principal aims. One has been to confirm that good phonological awareness is causally related to good reading; the other has been to evaluate particular methods of promoting reading skills or preventing reading failure (see Blachman, 1991).

INTERVENTION STUDIES

The results of many intervention studies have been said to show that various training regimes can promote better phonological awareness in pre-readers and in somewhat older children low in such skills, including dyslexics (e.g. Lovett, Borden, DeLuca, Lacerenza, Benson, & Brackstone, 1994; Lovett, Lacerenza, Borden, Frijters, Steinbach, & De Palma, 2000). Positive results would be expected from interventions which directly target those skills on which reading is said to be based and several studies apparently demonstrate that training in phonological skills can have direct effects on subsequent reading (Byrne & Fielding-Barnsley, 1995; Hatcher, Hulme, & Ellis, 1994; Lovett et al., 1994; Lundberg, Frost, & Petersen, 1988; Torgesen, Morgan, & Davis, 1992). Significant effects on reading as a result of training phonological skills can be viewed as substantiating the claim for a causal connection between the two.

Bradley and Bryant (1983) reported that there was a non-significant trend for pre-readers who practised segmental language tasks to become better readers in the early grades of school than those who did not practise. In an attempt to identify which variables best predict children's response to phonological intervention programmes, Torgesen and Davis (1996) found that different pre-programme skills best predicted the level of segmenting and blending skills measured after exposure to the programme. While explicit segmentation skills were best predicted by a combination of general verbal ability and ability to spell nonwords, blending skill was best predicted by nonword spelling and digit naming. General verbal ability was less important. It was argued that nonword spelling "may be particularly sensitive to emergent levels of the kind of explicit phonological awareness required by both the segmenting and blending tasks. On the other hand, being able to rapidly access phonological representations from long-term memory was particularly important for growth in blending skills, but not segmenting" (Torgesen & Davis, 1996, p. 17). The authors are careful to point out that the pattern of results obtained may not hold for different training regimes or response measures or for samples having different demographic characteristics.

Intervention programmes may involve syllabic or phonemic analysis (segmentation) and/or synthesis (blending) or practice in the use of analogies. In a relatively early study, Fox and Routh (1976) examined the effects of training 4-year-old children (whose mean IQ was 112) in sound-blending. They reported that training was only effective in improving performance on a reading-like task for those children who were already proficient segmenters. Those who were less proficient at segmenting syllables into individual phonemes did not benefit from training in blending. It is possible that selection of groups on the basis of segmentation ability may also have selected for some other skill, including blending. A subsequent study by Fox and Routh (1984), in which 31 initial "non-segmenters" were divided into groups who were trained either in phoneme segmentation alone or in segmentation plus blending, showed that in comparison with an "untreated" control group and segmentation alone, the segmentation plus blending procedure was effective in allowing more children (8 out of 10) to learn to decode a "reading-analogue" stimulus. In both studies, some pre-training instruction in associating letter-like symbols with sounds was provided.

Peterson and Haines (1992) also found a differential effect of analogy training on high and low segmenters as determined by an auditory task requiring onset–rime segmentation. Before analogy training, the low segmenter group showed virtually no ability to use analogies to read unknown words. Though analogy training did result in some improvement in segmentation ability, this group showed no improvement in the ability to read by analogy. High (and middle) segmenters, on the other hand, showed a marked improvement in the ability to read new words by analogy.

Although training has been shown to be effective in some children at risk for reading disorders, as well as for children without any special risk factor (Schneider, Roth & Ennemoser, 2000), not all training programmes are effective with all children. In the view of Bus and Van Ijzendoorn (1999), "Children at risk for developing reading problems may be more difficult to teach phonological awareness skills just because they are at risk . . . [but] . . . special children may even need this type of training more than normal children, although they profit less from it than in the short term" (p. 412).

Lovett, Ransby, Hardwick, Johns, and Donaldson (1989) reported that training 10-year-old disabled readers in decoding skills, including phonemic analysis and blending, did not lead to improved nonword reading. In some other studies, too, a good proportion of those who were low in phonological awareness at the start of the programme failed to show much improvement (e.g. Lundberg et al., 1988; Torgesen et al., 1992). Yet despite the refractoriness of severely disabled readers in responding to interventions based on phonemic awareness training, there have been some encouraging reports.

Borstrøm and Elbro (1997) carried out a phonemic awareness study with pre-school Danish children who had at least one dyslexic parent; the children were referred to as being at risk of dyslexia. The training was administered to all children in a kindergarten class as a group each weekday for 17 weeks and did not include alphabetic instruction. Nonetheless, on measures of word and nonword reading at the start of grade 2, children at risk who had received the training outperformed at-risk children who had not received specific training in kindergarten. The prevalence of "possible dyslexia" in grade 2 was much higher (27 out of 88) in the two at-risk groups than in a normal control group (4 out of 88). However, among the at-risk children, there were 20 out of 52 possible dyslexics in the untrained group and only 6 out of 88 in the trained group.

It has been shown in several studies that training in phonemic awareness may have benefits for subsequent reading up to 3 (Byrne & Fielding-Barnsley, 1995) or even 6 years later (Byrne, Fielding-Barnsley, & Ashley, 2000) in children trained as pre-readers. On the other hand, others have failed to find lasting effects (e.g. Layton, Deeny, Upton, & Tall, 1998). Moreover, some children who show good phoneme awareness after pre-school training go on to become poor readers, perhaps as a consequence of weakness in other cognitive skills relevant to reading (Byrne et al., 2000).

In addition to research into the effects of training in phonemic awareness, several investigators have looked at training in rhyming skills and onset–rime segmentation skills and their possible benefits on reading or spelling. The results of at least some of these studies suggest that the benefits of short–term training in onset-rime segmentation and in making rime-based analogies might be relatively short-lived in comparison with training based on other units such as vowels (see Bruck & Treiman, 1992; Wise, Olson, & Treiman, 1990). Goswami (1999b) is dismissive of most intervention studies of this kind, claiming that "no methodologically adequate large-scale studies of the possible benefits of including tuition in rhyme and analogy in the early reading curriculum have been carried out" (p. 228). This, it should be noted, does not mean that intervention studies claiming to show an effect of training on some experimental measure or other are invalid. For example, Peterson and Haines (1992), working with 5- and 6-year-olds, present results showing that intensive and extended rime-based training can lead to an increase in the use of analogy to correctly read test words as compared with untreated control groups. However, as Goswami points out, the fact that the control group received no specific training raises doubts over the long-term benefits of analogy training because of the possibility that the effects reported were due to motivational factors associated with the treatment in the experimental group.

The same criticism cannot be levelled against Greaney, Tunmer, and Chapman (1997), who studied two groups of impaired readers. One half of each group assigned to two different trainers was trained with rime analogies, while the other half of each group was given item-specific training—that is, on particular words presented within the context of a sentence. The analogy-trained groups were better than the other groups in reading the target words on which they were trained and also showed greater transfer to a standardized reading test and in reading nonwords. At follow-up a year later the analogy group maintained its advantage and came close to the progress made by a control group of normal readers matched for reading age.

Macmillan (2002) reviewed the research literature on the putative relation between rhyme and reading from a methodological perspective. She concluded from a number ($n = 16$) of training studies that research involving rime instruction only produced positive effects among older children who were already reading. Among "beginning non-readers", other forms of instruction produced significantly superior progress in reading.

Troia (1999) reviewed a corpus of intervention studies, also from a methodological point of view, and concluded that many are characterized by a number of deficiencies, the most serious of which appears to be non-random assignment of participants to different treatment groups. Goswami's (1999b) criticisms of training studies include "unseen" control groups, failure to equate length of training between different groups and failure to ensure comparability of pre-treatment literacy experience. Bus and Van Ijzendoorn (1999) point out that a study comparing two groups—one trained, one untrained— "is not a fair comparison", as more attention is paid to the trained children, which can produce a halo effect. It is also difficult to be sure that normal classroom procedures are not contributing to any advantage. Moreover, it is important to test for the specificity of any claimed effect; that is, that the effect of intervention is specific to phonologically related skills and not, say, to arithmetic skills, yet this has not often been done.

Despite these criticisms, there is is sufficient evidence from training studies to substantiate the claim that phonological awareness at different levels is causally related to reading proficiency. In addition, it can be concluded that some forms of intervention are effective in promoting advances in phonological awareness and/or reading. Clearly, it is important to discover exactly what strategies are effective and how these link with pre-existing skills to promote efficient reading. The exact nature of the training may be crucial in determining whether positive effects are found.

Some evidence suggests that although training in spoken phoneme identity ("all of these words start with /s/") may be more useful than segmentation training ("su . . . n or bu . . . s") in allowing transfer of the relevant skill to new words (Byrne & Fielding-Barnsley, 1990; see also Murray, 1998), it may be that both phonemic awareness and letter–sound knowledge are needed (the phonological-linkage hypothesis) for the alphabetic principle to be grasped fully (Bradley & Bryant, 1983; Byrne & Fielding-Barnsley, 1990; Hatcher et al., 1994; Lovett et al., 1994), even in a regular orthography (Schneider et al., 2000). Macmillan (2002) concluded from her review of the literature that "the bulk of curent evidence suggests that while phonological training may improve phonological skills, it rarely has any effect on reading ability; in contrast, phonological training *combined with letter sound teaching* can produce some positive effects" (p. 34, emphasis in original).

Similarly, Bus and Van Ijzendoorn (1999) concluded from a meta-analytic review that, "In general, our data suggest that gains are more consistent and robust when phonological awareness has been trained together with letter sound correspondence" (p. 412). In the absence of explicit linkage between phonemic awareness training and letter–sound knowledge, there may be no lasting gains in reading or spelling from training in either segmentation or blending alone, although both together may have beneficial effects in pre-readers (see Torgesen et al., 1992). According to Hohn and Ehri (1983), teaching the letters of the alphabet is superior to purely oral segmentation training because it "teaches the correct size of the sound units to be segmented", enabling children "to acquire a visual sound-symbolizing system . . . to distinguish and represent the separate phonemes" (p. 760).

The ability to segment a stimulus into its phonemic constituents presupposes the ability to hold these in memory (Jorm, 1983). Commonly used blending and segmentation tasks thus tap both phonological processing skills and, to some extent, phonological memory ability.

PHONOLOGICAL AWARENESS AND VERBAL MEMORY

Problems in verbal learning and memory have been found in many studies of dyslexia (McDougall, Hulme, Ellis, & Monk, 1994; Snowling, Goulandris, & Defty, 1996b; Vellutino, Steger, Harding, & Phillips, 1975; for reviews, see Baddeley, 1986; Brady, 1991; Jorm, 1983). Such a deficit is not usually found with non-verbal tasks or material if steps are taken to ensure that verbal encoding is controlled (Jorm, 1983). The memory deficit appears to be specific to tasks that require phonological processes (Share, 1995). Even among non-dyslexic readers, measures of short-term phonological memory are significantly related to reading ability (Gathercole, 1995; Gathercole & Baddeley, 1989; Share, 1995; Wagner & Torgesen, 1987; Wagner et al., 1994).

In an early investigation, Fildes (1921) tested 26 children aged 9–16 years "selected on the report of their teachers as finding reading a very great difficulty" (p. 286). Twenty-two of the participants were attending "special schools for mentally defective children". The range of IQ was from 111 to between 50 and 69. It was said that no child was less than 4 years retarded in reading; some were designated as readers and others as non-readers. On a test of repeating a series of digits presented orally at the rate of one per second, those children designated readers performed better on average than the non-readers at each of 3- to 5-digit sequences. That is, in modern parlance, the non-readers had a lower digit span. Since the above study, many other investigators have found dyslexics to have lower digit spans than control readers (e.g. McDougall et al., 1994; Miles, 1993a) or lower than expected for their age (Thomson, 1982). However, they do not necessarily have lower spans than children matched for reading age (Pennington, Van Orden, Kirson, & Haith, 1991b).

Given the well-established difficulties of dyslexics in phonological awareness, it is reasonable to ask whether there is a connection between poor phonological processing and impaired verbal memory. If so, how might low verbal memory spans found in some dyslexic children relate to their phonological ability more generally? One possible answer is that memory problems contribute to difficulties in holding individual phonemes in mind as part of a phonic reading strategy. Indeed, memory span correlates with nonword reading scores and better than with measures of comprehension (Siegel & Ryan, 1988). Another possibility is that phonological representations at the segmental level of the syllable may be less easily applied to the recovery of novel stimuli during memory tasks than those which are specified at a phonemic level (Fowler, 1991).

The idea that a difference in memory span between good and poor readers is linked to poor phonological processing is supported by two main findings. The first is that the difference is found only for verbal stimuli or those that can be easily verbally encoded and not for visuo-spatial material (e.g. McDougall et al., 1994; Swanson, Ashbaker, & Lee, 1996). The second is that good readers appear to be more susceptible to acoustic (phonological) confusion effects than poor readers (Brady, Shankweiler, & Mann, 1983; Mann, Liberman, & Shankweiler, 1980; Mark, Shankweiler, Liberman, & Fowler, 1977 but see Holligan & Johnston, 1988). Both findings imply that good readers are better able, or more likely, to use verbal retrieval or rehearsal strategies than are poor readers (but see Mark et al., 1977), who may use visually based strategies to a greater extent than good readers (see Johnston & Anderson, 1998; Palmer, 2000; Rack, 1985).

Phonological awareness and phonological or verbal short-term memory have been shown in some studies to make independent contributions to reading ability (e.g. Gathercole, Willis, Emslie, & Baddeley, 1991b; Hansen & Bowey, 1994; Mann & Liberman, 1984; Windfuhr & Snowling, 2001) although the amount of variance predicted by verbal memory after phonological sensitivity or awareness has been taken into account is small and, in some studies, not significant (Bowey, Cain, & Ryan, 1992; Gottardo, Stanovich, & Siegel, 1996; Leather & Henry, 1994; McDougall et al., 1994; Rohl & Pratt, 1995). In short, the research findings concerned with this issue are somewhat inconsistent (Brady, 1991). Nonetheless, Bowey (1996a) argued that phonological sensitivity and phonological memory are independently related to phonological recoding ability and word recognition skill, with phonological sensitivity being particularly strongly associated with phonological recoding.

The task of learning to associate random shapes and nonwords was given to primary

school children aged 7–11 years by Windfuhr and Snowling (2001). Even after controlling for decoding ability, the children's performance on this paired-associate learning task independently and significantly predicted concurrent word and nonword reading skill (see also Vellutino et al., 1975). The same was true of phonological awareness. These findings imply that differences in learning ability underpin some of the individual differences found in word reading ability, a conclusion consistent with the "self-teaching" hypothesis of Jorm, Share and colleagues (Jorm & Share, 1983; Share, 1995, 1999). Conversely, Aguiar and Brady (1991) found that, with fourth-grade students, reading ability significantly predicted the number of trials required (and errors made) in learning a list of novel words.

Bowey et al. (1992) looked at verbal memory as indexed by receptive vocabulary or digit span (forwards and backwards) in relation to phonological decoding skills (assessed by nonword reading) and phonological sensitivity, as measured by a variety of oddity (odd-one-out) tasks, in three groups of children. These were less-skilled fourth-grade readers, skilled fourth-grade and skilled second-grade readers. Children at the same reading level (second-grade and less-skilled fourth-grade readers) differed on the measures of phonological sensitivity but not on digits forwards. It is possible that age differences in rehearsal strategies counteracted any difference in memory capacity (Bowey, 1996a). However, although rehearsal is crucially involved in short-term memory tasks, such as those used to measure digit span, Johnston et al. (1987b) have argued that differences in rehearsal processes do not distinguish between groups based on reading level. Rather "when task demands are high, both good and poor readers abandon verbal rehearsal as mnemonic strategy" (p. 209).

Using hierarchical mutiple regression, Hansen and Bowey (1994) separated the effects of phonological segmentation (analysis) skills from verbal working memory (phonological short-term memory). Consistent with the view that phonological analysis and verbal memory are independently related to concurrent reading scores (Bradley & Bryant, 1978; Goswami & Bryant, 1990), these authors found that each made a unique and significant contribution to variation in reading scores among second-grade children (mean age 7 years 4 months). Nonword repetition was strongly associated in second-grade children with measures of reading achievement, including phonological recoding as measured by nonword reading, but neither word span nor digit span was significantly associated with word recognition or phonological recoding.

It is conceivable, as Hulme and Roodenrys (1995) point out, that difficulty in phonological memory tasks is a result rather than a cause of reading problems. However, since verbal memory performance in pre-school children or those just beginnning school predicts later reading ability (e.g. Ellis & Large, 1987), it is unlikely that verbal memory deficits are a consequence of poor reading. This said, Ellis (1990) argues that the acquisition of reading underpins developmental changes in the strategies and skills used in short-term memory tasks.

Nor is it likely that poor verbal or phonological short-term memory in dyslexia is a direct cause of whole-word recognition difficulties (Pennington et al., 1991b). As Hulme and Roodenrys (1995) argued: "If . . . there was a clear and direct causal link between short-term memory problems and reading problems all children with short-term memory difficulties should have poor reading skills, and, conversely, all children with reading problems should have short-term memory problems. This is manifestly not true" (p. 392).

Nonetheless, problems with so-called working memory may contribute to some disabled readers' difficulties in reading comprehension (Swanson, 1999; but see Stothard & Hulme, 1992) and hence contribute to normal variation in reading skill (Pennington et al., 1991b). Alternatively, difficulties in verbal working memory may be an index of other phonological deficits. For example, Torgesen, Rashotte, Greenstein, Houck, and Portes (1987) presented separate phonemes to children who had to blend them into complete words. Dyslexic children with low memory spans were worse at performing this task than dyslexic children with spans of normal length. Problems

in working memory and deficits in phonological sensitivity or awareness might both reflect the quality of underlying phonological representations (Fowler, 1991; Wagner, Torgesen, Laughon, Simmons, & Rashotte, 1993).

Johnston et al. noted that:

A number of studies have found that poor readers are slower to name letters, objects and pictures. Furthermore, Jorm, Share, MacLean & Matthews (1986) found that children who subsequently had difficulty with reading not only had poorer immediate memories than normal readers before entering school, but were also slower and less accurate in naming pictures and colours. All these difficulties may have a common origin, which might take the form of dysfunction in one or more of the processes which "interface" between visual and verbal processing. These processes might directly affect word recognition, and indirectly affect memory span. As far as the latter is concerned, slowness and inaccuracy in the recognition and encoding of stimuli could lead to impaired memory span.

(Johnston et al., 1987b, p. 210).

If poor readers are relatively slow or inefficient in phonological encoding of visually presented material (see Ellis & Miles, 1978; Johnston et al., 1987b; Shankweiler, Liberman, Mark, Fowler, & Fischer, 1979) or in retrieving phonological information (such as word or letter names) from long-term memory (Gathercole & Baddeley, 1989), or do not use phonological codes as readily as good readers (see Rack, 1985; but see Johnston et al., 1987b, for a cautionary note and Johnston, 1982, for a dissenting view), then the amount of material that can be verbally encoded at a given presentation will be less than for good readers. If, in addition, the quality of such representations is poor, then it would be no surprise to find poor readers doing less well in tests of verbal memory, such as digit span.

Furthermore, if knowledge of the phonological structure of words is used in speech production and if the phonological representations of (at least some) dyslexics are weak or inefficient, this might help to explain other speech-related problems such as impairments in naming or in category- or letter-fluency tasks, all of which have been reported in some studies of dyslexia (see below).

Evidence that the phonological representations used in speech production also support auditory–verbal short-term memory performance comes from a study of a brain-damaged patient F.M., who is said to have progressive fluent anomic aphasia (Knott, Patterson, & Hodges, 2000). F.M. is profoundly anomic both in conversation and to confrontation (that is, when confronted with an object to name) and tests suggest that much of her difficulty lies in activating the phonological form of words from their semantic representations. F.M. was much more likely to reproduce a name correctly in a memory task when she had given it previously as a response in a picture-naming task than if she had been unable to name the picture. As her semantic system itself appears to be very largely (although not entirely) intact, her impairment can be regarded as a semantic–phonological output disconnection. She had no difficulty in activating lexical–phonological representations from auditory input as shown by good immediate word repetition (which deteriorated dramatically with a short delay interval) and by the fact that she exhibited normal priming effects in an auditory lexical decision task (deciding whether a spoken letter string does or does not constitute a real word). Knott et al. (2000) argued that "The frequency of F.M.'s phonological errors both in immediate serial recall performance and delayed single-word repetition therefore suggests that it is activation of the lexical–phonological representations that support *speech production* that is crucial to maintaining phonological integrity in STM" (p. 139, emphasis in original). Unlike many dyslexics, however, F.M.'s digit span was of more or less normal length.

Reading and nonword repetition

A well-established speech-related difficulty for children with reading problems relates to the repetition of nonwords (e.g. Stone & Brady,

1995). Snowling was the first to show that the ability to correctly repeat nonwords differentiates good and poor readers matched for reading age (Snowling, 1981; Snowling, Goulandris, Bowlby, & Howell, 1986a). This has been regarded as a phonological short-term memory task by Gathercole and her colleagues (Gathercole, Willis, Baddeley, & Emslie, 1994b), who found that six "language-disordered children" aged 8 years but with a reading age of 6 years were impaired on this test relative to controls (Gathercole & Baddeley, 1990a). Gathercole has also reported significant relationships between nonword-repetition performance and reading by unimpaired readers as well as others (see Baddeley & Gathercole, 1992; Gathercole, 1995). There is some debate, however, as to whether the test is primarily a measure of phonemic segmentation and blending ability or of memory (see Snowling, Chiat, & Hulme, 1991, and reply by Gathercole, Willis, & Baddeley, 1991a; see also Bowey, 1996a, 1997 and reply by Gathercole & Baddeley 1997) or, indeed, of something else.

Muter and Snowling (1998) reported that nonword repetition at ages 5 and 6 years predicted reading accuracy at age 9 years. They also found that phoneme awareness (measured between 4 and 6 years of age) was a good predictor of reading both in the short term (first year of school) and in the longer term (age 9 years). (By contrast, rhyme discrimination was neither a good concurrent predictor when given at age 9 nor a good predictor of reading at age 9 when given at the younger ages.)

Muter and Snowling (1998) wrote: "Nonword repetition has been most usually conceptualised as a measure of phonological working memory (Gathercole & Baddeley, 1989). However, our observation that nonword repetition correlated with phoneme deletion at age 9 suggests that it should not be construed purely as a memory test but rather as a measure sensitive to the integrity of phonological representations" (pp. 332–333). On the other hand, Michas and Henry (1994) found in a study with children aged 5–6 years that nonword repetition and nonword memory span were equally as strong in predicting new word learning, which arguably favours the view that nonword repetition is primarily a test of memory.

Certainly, the similarity to real words (held in long-term memory) of the items to be repeated significantly affects performance on the nonword repetition and other tasks involving memory (Gathercole, 1995; Gathercole et al., 1991b; see also Dollaghan, Biber, & Campbell, 1993; Hulme, Maughan, & Brown, 1991). Furthermore, nonword repetition ability is related to the learning of novel but not familiar words (Gathercole & Baddeley, 1990b; Gathercole et al., 1997; Michas & Henry, 1994). Both of these findings might be regarded as favouring a view of nonword repetition effects based purely on memory factors. Unfortunately, this so-called lexicality effect does not resolve the issue, since it is possible that ease of articulation and segmentation are both a function of item familiarity. Words will be more familiar than nonwords and they would therefore be better articulated.

In any event, the relation between performance on the nonword repetition test and reading is complex even in normal readers. There is little evidence of a relation during the first year of reading. The relationship is strong and significant during the following year but subsequently dissipates (see Gathercole et al., 1991a). It is conceivable that the relationship is mediated by an effect of vocabulary, as Gathercole and colleagues have shown that phonological memory as measured by nonword repetition is a powerful predictor of both native (Gathercole & Baddeley, 1989) and foreign (Baddeley, Gathercole, & Papagno, 1998; see also Service, 1992; Service & Kohonen, 1995) vocabulary learning. However, De Jong et al. (2000) have recently reported a study with Dutch children aged 4.5–6.5 years showing that, with age and non-verbal intelligence statistically controlled, the significant effect of nonword repetition on receptive vocabulary and nonword learning disappeared. With vocabulary, age, non-verbal IQ, letter knowledge and nonword repetition statistically controlled, phonological sensitivity (measured by sound categorization tasks) still accounted for a significant amount of variance in nonword learning. Based on the results of their hierarchical regression analyses,

De Jong et al. (2000) argued that phonological sensitivity might be more important than phonological memory in learning novel phonological forms. Increasing levels of phonological sensitivity might allow increasingly well-specified phonological representations of novel items from the time when they are initially encountered.

Verbal memory, articulation rate and reading

There is an undoubted relation between verbal short-term memory span and articulation rate (see Baddeley, 1986; 1990; Hitch & Halliday, 1983; Kail, 1992) as measured by such tasks as speed of word or nonword repetition. Among adults and children older than about 4 years of age, there is a significant correlation between articulation rate and span (Gathercole, Adams, & Hitch, 1994a; Hulme, Thomson, Muir, & Lawrence, 1984). Simply referring to a faster articulation rate, however, obscures the precise mechanisms whereby span improves with age. Hulme et al. (1984) suggested that "the development of memory span may be the product of continual improvements in the motor skills involved in speaking" (p. 253). A more fine-grained analysis in a later study, on the other hand, revealed that the situation is not quite so simple. Maximal speech rate was not the only determinant of memory span. In fact, older and younger children did not differ in the speed of pronunciation of individual words, or in the duration of pauses between responses, but they did differ in the time taken to prepare their initial response (Cowan, Keller, Hulme, Roodenrys, McDougall, & Rack, 1994). It is thus possible that individual differences in item memory search times and/or covert rehearsal processes influence memory span.

The speed with which words can be articulated is not related only to memory span. A relation between speech rate and reading was noted as long ago as the inter-war period. Monroe (1928) asked children both to read aloud and to repeat the letters of the alphabet. She reported that there is:

> a differentiation between normal and retarded readers of the same school grade in ability to read and repeat the alphabet.

For example, if a child is found in the third grade who makes more than seven errors in repeating the alphabet, takes longer than thirty seconds to do it, or makes three mistakes in reading the letters of the alphabet, it is almost certain that he is a retarded reader.

(Monroe, 1928, pp. 399–400)

(Reading retardation was defined as reading below school-grade level and below "mental-age level".) Since then, a good many workers have noted a link between articulation rate and reading ability (e.g. Ackerman, Dykman, & Gardner, 1990; Brady, 1991; McDougall et al., 1994; Torgesen et al., 1987).

The working memory model

The notion of a phonological loop component of so-called working memory has been widely adopted to explain a variety of effects in memory research (Baddeley, 1986, 1990; Gathercole & Martin, 1996). Briefly, the loop is said to consist of two components: a time-limited (rapidly decaying) acoustic store and a rehearsal mechanism that is used to refresh items in the store. Rehearsal is thought to be conducted using sub-vocal speech. The faster the covert or sub-vocal (and, by implication, the overt) speech rate, the greater the number of items that can be maintained in an articulatory rehearsal loop or acoustic store within working memory. All else being equal, those with a faster rate of articulation will have longer spans. It has therefore been argued that differences in rehearsal *rate* between dyslexic and control readers, as between younger and older children (see Hitch & Halliday, 1983; Hulme et al., 1984), give rise to group differences in verbal short-term memory performance (McDougall et al., 1994; Raine, Hulme, Chadderton, & Bailey, 1991). Another possibility is that speed of access to phonological representations decreases with age (McDougall et al., 1994) or with reading experience. Once again it may also be the case that the relevant factor is not so much the *rate* of processing as the *quality* of the underlying phonological representations (e.g. Brady, 1986; Elbro, 1996; Fowler, 1991). These two aspects of

performance could offset each other such that, for example, a faster rate of processing by dyslexics than by younger reading-age controls may be undermined by weaker phonological representations in the former (Hansen & Bowey, 1994).

The idea that verbal memory span depends upon an articulatory (Baddeley & Hitch, 1974) or phonological (Baddeley, 1990) loop component of working memory is underpinned by two major findings: the word-length effect and the acoustic or phonological confusability effect. Memory span is longer for short words than for long words (Baddeley, Thomson, & Buchanan, 1975) and memory for item order is worse for items that are phonemically similar than for items that are phonemically dissimilar. Both effects suggest that items are retained in memory through a process of overt or covert verbal rehearsal. Indeed, the presence of a word-length effect is often taken as an indication that sub-vocal articulation is being used. However, the source of the word-length effect from which sub-vocal articulation is inferred may be more variable than was once thought. Indeed, a length effect can be produced in the absence of rehearsal (Brown & Hulme, 1995). Consistent with this idea, Muter and Snowling (1998) found that the contribution of speech rate to reading accuracy was independent of the contribution made by both phonological awareness and phonological memory as measured by nonword repetition. Furthermore, the idea that the word-length effect is based on the spoken duration of the words has been questioned. Word duration is less predictive of span than is the phonological complexity, "the number of phonemes differing from their immediately preceding neighbours", of the items to be remembered (Service, 1998).

Assuming that the phonological loop component of working memory is used in vocabulary learning (Avons, Wragg, Cupples, & Lovegrove, 1998; Baddeley et al., 1998; Gathercole et al., 1997), it might be expected that this would be a pervasive feature of both general language ability and reading skill. Ellis and Sinclair (1996), for example, argued that phonological or short-term memory is intimately involved in the acquisition of syntax as well as vocabulary.

The term "working memory", incidentally, is not synonymous with the term "short-term memory". It was pointed out by Hulme and Roodenrys (1995) that "The latter has been used to refer to a hypothetical memory store and hence is a structural term. Working memory, by contrast, is a functional term in that it refers to the functions of memory processes within particular tasks. Thus working memory is both a broader and less precise term than short-term memory" (p. 374).

The contribution of long-term memory to short-term memory span

It is known that memory span for verbal items is not independent of the nature of the items—it is longer for words than for pseudo-words of the same length. This lexicality effect suggests that in remembering lists of items, words benefit from their established representations in long-term memory (Gathercole & Adams, 1994; Gathercole et al., 1991b; Hulme et al., 1991). This is consistent with the contribution of long-term memory to performance increasing with age—in other words, the length of time for which words have been known—and is separable from any effect of speech rate (Roodenrys, Hulme, Alban, Ellis, & Brown, 1994; Roodenrys, Hulme, & Brown, 1993).

An attempt to explain lexicality effects in recall was made by Hulme, Roodenrys, Schweikert, Brown, Martin, and Stuart (1997), who refer to a process of "redintegration" or reconstruction of originally presented material. A partially decayed memory trace may be re-constructed using stored knowledge about the structure of words. If such knowledge is inefficiently represented in dyslexics, then it would be less helpful in assisting the process of reconstruction than in control participants. This would result in a lower recall performance for dyslexics.

McDougall and Donohoe (2002) argued that a differential contribution of long-term memory to performance on span tasks might also play some part in accounting for differences between good and poor readers. These investigators compared memory for nonwords and for words of different frequency of occurrence. Their reasoning was

that (after differences in speech rate are taken into account) the two groups might not be expected to differ in recall of high-frequency words, since both groups are likely to have representations for such words in long-term memory. For low-frequency words, however, only the better readers might have such representations, as poor readers are known to have more limited vocabularies than good readers. Neither good nor poor readers would be expected to have long-term representations for nonwords. In the event, McDougall and Donohoe (2002) confirmed their predictions. Once differences in articulation rate were statistically controlled, memory span for high-frequency words did not differ between groups but span for low-frequency words was greater for the good readers than for the poor readers regardless of whether their relatively poor reading was accompanied by IQ scores that were average (dyslexic readers) or below average (garden-variety poor readers). The performance of the latter group was equivalent to that of younger children of the same reading level. McDougall and Donohoe (2002) also found that the good and poor reading groups differed in memory for nonwords. This they attributed to a difference in the ease with which the groups learned the nonwords during the experimental task, it being easier for the good readers.

Although much theorizing has been concerned with factors associated with speech production, it may be not so much speech ouput as speech input or perception that is important. Gathercole and Martin (1996) contend that "the capacity to retain verbal material over short periods of time is indeed an integral part of the speech processing system, but . . . it depends much more closely on the processes and products of speech perception than speech production" (p. 77). Research concerned with the relation between speech perception and reading is discussed in Chapter 6.

SIGHT READING OF WHOLE WORDS

Whatever the nature of the underlying deficit, deficiencies in phonological processing and memory can be compensated for by the development of orthographic skills (Funnell & Davison, 1989), which, in some individuals at least, may exceed average levels (Campbell & Butterworth, 1985; Holmes & Standish, 1996). Poor phonological skills and poor nonword reading can co-exist with levels of word reading that are consistent with what might be expected from general intellectual level or educational opportunity (Stothard, Snowling, & Hulme, 1996). That good or at least adequate reading skills can develop even if phonological awareness is severely deficient has been demonstrated by both single-case (Cossu, Rossini, & Marshall, 1993; Howard & Best, 1996, 1997) and group studies. The latter show that there is considerable overlap in phonological decoding abilities of proficient and poor readers (e.g. Olson, Wise, Conners, Rack, & Fulker, 1989; Stanovich et al., 1988; Treiman & Hirsh-Pasek, 1985).

The fact that good word recognition can occur in the context of poor phonological awareness implies than an adequate sight vocabulary can be built up simply through regular exposure to a sufficient number of words. This is not to say, however, that information about letter–sound or other orthographic–phonological relationships is not simultaneously being learned, however slowly or imperfectly. The inconsistency of English orthography (compare h-ea-d with b-ea-d) suggests that multiple orthographic–phonological correspondence rules must be built up. In the normal course of events, these presumably are applied according to the relative frequency with which the different pronunciations occur in the language (see Patterson & Behrmann, 1997).

Children may learn about the relationships between letters and sounds and other orthographic–phonological relations not only through explicit instruction but by abstracting information from what has already been learned about whole words and their pronunciation (Stuart, et al., 1999; Thompson, et al., 1996; Zinna, Liberman, & Shankweiler, 1986; Share, 1995). Such a process is apparent from a recent investigation of a highly precocious (hyperlexic) reader who, at the age of 37 months, read at the level of an average 8-year-old (Fletcher-Flinn & Thompson,

2000). Her performance on nonword reading tasks showed that she employed a phonological recoding strategy and was sensitive to the graphemic context in which sub-lexical units occurred, although at this age she had not developed an explicit awareness of phonemes as tested by phoneme deletion and other tasks.

There is evidence (Jorm & Share, 1983; Share, 1985) that phonological recoding ability contributes not only to efficiency of the sub-lexical route posited by dual-route theory (see Baron, 1979; Stuart & Masterson, 1992), but also to whole-word (orthographic) word-recognition ability. Gough and Walsh (1991) computed correlations between performance on nonword reading and irregular or exception word reading tasks. On examining the data closely, it turned out (contrary to the expectations of dual-route theory) that no children performed well on exception words and poorly on nonwords, although many children performed relatively well on nonwords but poorly on exception words. It was also noted that children with relatively high levels of phonological recoding ability (as judged by performance on nonword reading) learned to recognize unfamiliar exception words in fewer trials than did children who were relatively poor decoders.

The above findings suggest that under normal circumstances, phonological recoding does not operate in total isolation from learning to recognize words by sight. This is not, in fact, surprising. Despite all the fuss that is made about the vagaries of written English, it surely is true that sounding out an irregular or exception word provides some clue as to the correct pronunciation of the word and hence to its meaning. Furthermore, the context will often constrain a possible response to the correct one only. Some theorists have argued explicitly that single-word recognition requires an amalgamation of knowledge of a word's meaning, its phonology and its orthography (Bowers & Wolf, 1993; Ehri, 1992a, 1992b). By sounding out visually unfamiliar words that the child knows already through speech, a sight vocabulary can be built up more quickly than if no clues at all to pronunciation were derivable from phonological decoding.

The point being emphasized here is that lexical and non-lexical (or phonological and orthographic) strategies are likely to have a reciprocal relationship (see Manis et al., 1993). If so, then children with an inadequate whole-word system (lexical reading strategy) may have difficulty in acquiring a non-lexical reading procedure (Coltheart & Leahy, 1996). Consistent with this view, Stuart and Masterson (1992) reported that children with good early phonological awareness scores had well-developed lexical and sub-lexical reading skills, while for children with relatively poor early phonological awareness scores both skills were compromised. For the latter children, it was suggested that "their primary difficulty lies in the sub-lexical system, and . . . their inability to develop efficient sub-lexical procedures has jeopardized the development of their orthographic input lexicon and thus their ability to use the lexical system" (Stuart & Masterson, 1992, p. 186).

Evidence for the view that good phonological skills and letter–sound knowledge assist the process of learning a sight vocabulary is presented by Stuart, Masterson, and Dixon (2000). They reported that beginning 5-year-old readers who could segment initial phonemes and who had good knowledge of letter–sound mappings learned to read whole familiar words from repeated exposure to specific connected texts much more quickly than those children whose phonological and letter name knowledge was less developed. These findings are consistent with the idea that a sight vocabulary is acquired most readily if at least some of the segments of the spoken word can be matched to particular letters—that is, if there is at least some measure of phonological underpinning. However, the acquisition of a sight vocabulary is probably somewhat less "spongelike" (Adams, 1990) than might be thought, since the children in the study of Stuart et al. (2000) learned more words by sight using a flashcard technique than they did through repeated repetition of texts.

In a discussion of the development of word recognition within the context of dual-route theory, Barron (1986) argued that "experiments show that the non-lexical route can be influenced by lexical knowledge. This evidence is inconsistent with the independent lexical and non-lexical routes postulated in the standard dual-route model" (p. 112). Part of this evidence is that the output of the non-lexical system can be biased, as in word priming of nonword pronunciation. Following exposure to the word "pint", for example, individuals are more likely to pronounce, say, "wint" or "fint" so as to rhyme with "pint" rather than with "mint" or "dint". In the absence of priming, a nonword such as "wint" is unlikely to be given the highly infrequent pronunciation that rhymes with "pint". (For analogous effects in written spelling see Barry & Seymour, 1988; Burden, 1989; Campbell, 1983, 1985.)

Contrary to Barron's (1986) criticism, dual-route theory makes no claim that sub-lexical phonological decoding or assembly cannot be influenced by lexical knowledge, although it is not explicit about how this is achieved. This may be a limitation of the theory but the theory is, after all, a theory of how words (and nonwords) are pronounced, not of how pronunciations are learned. This said, it must be acknowledged that the standard version of dual-route theory requires to be "fleshed out" so that how the orthographic input and output lexicons are established within a developmental framework is specified more precisely.

ARE THERE SUB-TYPES OF DYSLEXIA?

The fact that not all poor readers demonstrate phonological deficits raises the question of whether there are different varieties or sub-types of developmental dyslexia. The issue is one that has exercised many investigators from at least the early 1960s. Ingram (1963) suggested three categories of impaired reading, namely visuo-spatial difficulties, correlating difficulties and speech–sound difficulties. By "correlating difficulties" Ingram meant difficulties in relating visual symbols and spoken speech sounds, for example "being unable to find equivalent speech sound for individual letters or group of letters" (p. 201). By speech–sound difficulty he meant "synthesizing words from spoken sounds". Today, these two categories would be subsumed under one heading of phonological difficulty.

Johnson and Myklebust (1967) distinguished between visual and auditory dyslexia. The former was said to be characterized by confusion between letters or words that are visually similar, reversal errors, visual memory deficits and a slow rate of perception. A person with auditory dyslexia was said to be unable to "synthesize sounds into words or analyze words into parts; consequently he does not learn with an alphabetic or phonic approach" (p. 173). No data were used to support this distinction between dyslexic sub-types.

Boder (1971, 1973) proposed a tripartite classification distinguishing between dysphonetic, dyseidetic and dysphonetic–dyseidetic (i.e. mixed) sub-types of dyslexics on the basis of their reading and spelling errors. According to Boder (1973), "The dysphonetic child typically has a sight vocabulary of whole words that he recognizes on flash presentation and reads fluently. He reads words globally as instantaneous visual gestalts—rather than analytically . . . Though he may have an idea of phonetics, he lacks word-analysis skills; he is unable to sound out and blend the component letters and syllables of a word" (p. 668). The dyseidetic child, on the other hand, "has a poor memory for visual gestalts . . . He is an analytic reader and reads 'by ear', through a process of phonetic analysis and synthesis, sounding out familiar as well as unfamiliar combinations of letters, rather than by whole-word visual gestalts" (p. 670). Children who show the mixed type of dyslexia "are usually the most severely educationally handicapped. They are both dysphonetic and dyseidetic, though not necessarily equally so. They cannot read either on sight or 'by ear' " (p. 670). In her sample of 107 children, Boder classified 67 as dysphonetic, 10 as dyseidetic, 23 as showing the mixed type of dyslexia and 7 were "undetermined".

For almost 30 years, Bakker has proposed a model of dyslexic sub-types based on the idea that, under normal circumstances, learning to read initially involves predominantly the right cerebral hemisphere as, at this stage, reading involves an emphasis on visuo-spatial aspects of text. At a more advanced stage, there is an emphasis on linguistic features that are processed by the left hemisphere (see Bakker, 1992; Bakker, Smink, & Reitsma, 1973). Thus at some stage there is a switch from predominantly right hemisphere to mainly left hemisphere processing. According to this "balance" model (for a critique, see Hynd, 1992), two kinds of reading problems may arise. One is when children continue to use right-hemisphere-based visuo-spatial strategies long after they should have been subordinated to linguistic strategies. This was said to give rise to so-called P-type dyslexia in which reading is slow and effortful. On the other hand, some children are said to make the switch to left-hemisphere-based strategies too soon, giving rise to L-type dyslexia, which is characterized by fast but inaccurate reading. Electrophysiological support for this typology was claimed by Licht (1994).

Not everyone has subscribed to the view that there are different varieties or sub-types of dyslexia. Naidoo (1972) applied the technique of cluster analysis to the data from a selected sample of 94 dyslexic boys. Although there were some indications of different groups based on aetiological considerations, Naidoo was more impressed by the fact that "Although some patterns of disability, [neurological] immaturity or atypical response occur with greater frequency in some groups than in others, none is confined to any one group . . . Not only are no disabilities confined to any one group but some occur frequently in all, particularly low scores on sound blending, Digit Span and Coding [on the WISC]" (p. 108). She concluded from her analysis that "The absence of clearly defined sub-groups and the indications of a multiple rather than a unitary causation do not support the view that aetiologically or clinically separate forms of dyslexia can be distinguished" (p.109).

The earlier classifications (e.g. Boder, 1971, 1973; Ingram, 1963; Mattis et al., 1975) were often based on the performance of clinic-based samples on neuropsychological tests—that is, on the basis of associated symptoms rather than on features of reading *per se*. For example, Mattis et al. (1975) identified from a clinic population three independent syndromes of dyslexia, which they termed language disorder, articulatory and grapheme dys-co-ordination, and visuo-perceptual disorder. This approach can still be seen in the work of some present-day authors. Morris et al. (1998) applied a series of cluster analyses to data from eight cognitive tests covering a range of verbal and non-verbal skills. The clusters that emerged were said to be consistent both with the notion that sub-types of reading disability exist and with the view (Stanovich, 1988a, 1988b) that the core problem in reading ability is a phonological deficit, which, across different individuals, is associated with other deficits that vary in their nature and severity.

The associations and dissociations that emerge from techniques such as cluster analysis are a function of the measures that are entered into the analyses. As Morris et al. (1998) point out, a cluster based apparently on visuo-spatial skills may be isolated if some measure of phonological awareness is not included in the test battery. This may be why some of the earlier studies emphasized non-verbal perceptual factors that today are not regarded as being especially salient in the aetiology of reading disability (see Chapter 11).

A different approach to sub-type classification takes as its starting point not the performance levels of different individuals (or groups) on a range of cognitive tests but rather classifies poor readers according to the pattern of performance that they show on reading itself. In addition to assessing verbal and performance IQ, Mitterer (1982) examined the reading of regular and irregular words as well as nonwords by school-based children selected as being poor readers. On the basis of his results, Mitterer argued that there were at least two sub-types of poor reader. One type was said to rely heavily on phonological recoding, while the other relied heavily on a whole-word approach. This kind of typology has been discussed widely in recent years.

The earlier typologies of Johnson and Myklebust and of Boder were largely descriptions based on clinical description rather than on an explicit theory of the processes underlying reading. The scheme applied by Mitterer to different types of poor reader may be applied equally to different processes used by one and the same reader (see Baron, 1979; Baron & Strawson, 1976). This, of course, is the basis of so-called dual-route theory (see Chapter 2), which underpins recent attempts to identify different sub-types of poor reader.

It has been claimed on the basis of individual case studies that there are sub-types of developmental phonological dyslexia (Campbell & Butterworth, 1985; Snowling & Hulme, 1989; Snowling et al., 1986b, Temple, 1985a; Temple & Marshall, 1983) and developmental surface dyslexia (Castles & Coltheart, 1993, 1996; Castles & Holmes, 1996, Coltheart, 1987; Coltheart, Masterson, Byng, Prior, & Riddoch, 1983; Hanley & Gard, 1995; Hanley et al., 1992; Manis et al., 1996; Samuelsson, 2000; Seymour & Evans, 1993; Seymour & MacGregor, 1984; Snowling & Nation, 1997; Stanovich et al., 1997b; Temple, 1985b) corresponding to the sub-types of acquired dyslexia in adults. This is not to say that there is agreement between all researchers as to the best explanation of the cause(s) of different sub-types, each of which is likely to be relatively rare (Snowling, 2001). There is, however, a consensus that many developmental dyslexics, probably the majority, show characteristics of *both* phonological and surface dyslexia (termed "morphemic dyslexia" by Seymour & MacGregor, 1984; Seymour, 1986). Snowling (2001) argues that "it does not seem particularly useful to classify dyslexic children into subtypes because all taxonomies leave a substantial number of children unclassified" (p. 42).

Wilding (1989) argued that even the individual case studies purporting to demonstrate sub-types of developmental dyslexia are not "pure" examples of the putative sub-types (see also Share, 1995; Wilding, 1990). In particular, he argued that all the single cases included in his review showed evidence of a phonological processing impairment. Yet even within a particular sub-population of, say, "phonological dyslexics", different individuals may show different profiles of performance on phonological tasks associated with differences in reading and spelling profiles (Snowling, 1992). Perhaps seeking absolute "purity" is to ask too much and what is important is the relative reliance of each supposed sub-type on lexical and sub-lexical processing routes (Castles & Coltheart, 1993; see also Seymour & Evans, 1993; but see Stanovich et al., 1997a, for an alternative conceptualization) or compensatory strategies for a common phonological deficit (Snowling, 1992; Wilding, 1989, 1990). Relative here may be in terms of either a chronological age or reading age comparison.

In a well-known study, Castles and Coltheart (1993) attempted to show that individual differences in patterns of reading ability in dyslexic children can be interpreted in terms of a dual-route theory of adult reading. In Coltheart's view, learning to use the sub-lexical route is abnormally slow, leading to the characteristics of phonological dyslexia, while for other children it is learning to use the lexical route that is abnormally slow, leading to surface dyslexia (Coltheart, 1987). Of course, differences in the relative rates of acquisition of these two routes also allow for a "mixed" variety with scope for considerable individual differences within both normally developing and impaired readers. On the other hand, Snowling (2001) argues that individual differences in dyslexia can be accounted for by differences in severity of an underlying phonological deficit (weak representations) combined with differences in compensatory strategies or abilities such as visual memory and perceptual speed.

Castles and Coltheart (1993) compared dyslexic children's reading of regular and irregular words and nonwords with that of normal readers of the same age. The results led Castles and Coltheart to argue in favour of two sub-types of reading difficulty based on a dissociation between irregular word and nonword reading tasks (see also Castles, Datta, Gayán, & Olson, 1999). Some dyslexic children showed evidence of nomal nonword reading but poor irregular word reading, whereas other dyslexic children showed the reverse pattern. Most, however, had deficits in both nonword and irregular word reading.

The paper by Castles and Coltheart (1993) was severely criticized by Snowling et al. (1996a) for not using a reading-age comparison group. Snowling et al. (1996a) pointed out that Castles

and Coltheart (1993) had based their assessments of normal word and nonword reading on the children's chronological age, not reading age or level of reading skill, and there was no evidence that these patterns of reading were in any way unusual for normal children of a similar level of reading skill.

Castles and Coltheart's (1993) study was criticized by Snowling et al. (1996a) not only for the failure to employ a reading-level contrast but, more fundamentally, for applying theory drawn from studies of acquired dyslexia in adults to the case of developmental dyslexia in children. The argument here was that though the findings from adult cases of acquired dyslexia might point to impairment of specific processing mechanisms (which in the adult have been established), data from children with dyslexia need to be interpreted within a "normal developmental framework". In short, Snowling and her colleagues considered that what they saw as methodological weaknesses in the study of Castles and Coltheart prevent any "meaningful conclusions" being drawn about the nature and origins of individual differences in reading by dyslexic children.

Stanovich et al. (1997b) re-analysed the data of Castles and Coltheart (1993) and claimed that "When an RL [reading level] control group is used, surface dyslexics defined by a CA [chronological age] match are almost completely eliminated, but phonological dyslexia (deficient nonword reading in relation to reading age) remains a common pattern" (p. 114). Nonetheless, the surface pattern was still seen in two members of Castles and Coltheart's sample (compared with 10 defined by Castles and Coltheart on the basis of a chronological age comparison). It may be that a relative impairment in reading irregular or exception words was not easy to pick up in dyslexic children, since the reading level control group with whom they were compared (younger readers of average ability for their age) would not be expected necessarily to have a very large "sight" vocabulary. (For further discussion, see Jackson & Coltheart, 2001.)

Manis et al. (1996), using different stimuli to Castles and Coltheart (1993), incorporated a reading age comparison in their study of dyslexic sub-types. These authors found that only those children who could be described as "phonological" dyslexics were impaired on a phonological awareness task, whereas those who were "surface" dyslexics were not impaired on the task (see also Hanley & Gard, 1995). The latter (i.e. surface dyslexics) could be regarded as developmentally delayed in that they performed like younger reading age controls. Thus there is some reason from recent research to accept that a surface sub-type of developmental dyslexia does exist, although as in the Castles and Coltheart study, Manis et al. found that most dyslexic children fell into a mixed category rather than a pure sub-type.

The procedure of Castles and Coltheart (1993) was adopted by Zabell and Everatt (2002) to classify adult student or graduate dyslexics into phonological or surface sub-types, although, because of ceiling efffects, reading latencies rather than accuracy scores were used. Thirty-one per cent of the sample of 45 dyslexics were classified as surface dyslexics and the same proportion as phonological dyslexics. (This is a more even spread of surface and phonological dyslexics than has been reported for children.) A control group of 28 non-dyslexics performed better than the phonological and surface groups on all tasks, but outperformed the unclassified dyslexics only on nonword reading accuracy. On tests of lexical access and word knowledge, there were some group differences in the direction one would expect. For example, surface dyslexics were poorer than phonological dyslexics at selecting the correct spelling from word–pseudohomophone (e.g. *goat–gote*) pairs. Of greater interest is the fact that phonological and surface dyslexics did not differ significantly between themselves on any of the measures of phonological skill (spoonerisms, alliteration and rhyme fluency), including nonword reading (used in the initial separation of dyslexics into sub-types). This finding is difficult to accommodate on the view that surface dyslexia arises purely as a function of an inefficient lexical processing route.

In some studies in which a distinction has been drawn between putative surface and phonological

sub-types of dyslexia, a difference in behavioural (Borsting, Ridder, Dudeck, Kelley, Matsui, & Motoyama, 1996; Cestnick & Coltheart, 1999; Ridder, Borsting, Cooper, McNeel, & Huang, 1997), neuroanatomical or neurophysiological characteristics might be regarded as providing construct validity for the initial distinction (see Cestnick & Coltheart, 1999) based on dual-route theory. Thus some authors have claimed that event-related potentials (Licht, 1994; MacPherson, Ackerman, Oglesby, & Dykman, 1996) or other electrophysiological indices such as power spectra analysis (Ackerman, Dykman, Oglesby, & Newton, 1995) distinguish different sub-types of dyslexics. The results of these studies are difficult to interpret, as the classification of putative sub-types has differed across studies. Licht (1994), for example, classified dyslexics according to Bakker's P and L scheme, whereas Flynn, Deering, Goldstein, and Rahbar (1992) and MacPherson et al. (1996) employed Boder's (1973) classification. The nature of the comparison group against which results from poor readers have been compared has also varied, from normal readers of the same age (Flynn et al., 1992; Licht, 1994) to adequate readers with a diagnosis of attention deficit disorder (Ackerman et al., 1995). Even the designation of a sub-type has not always been based on sufficient evidence. Ackerman et al. (1995) and MacPherson et al. (1996) classified poor readers purely in terms of their performance on a single test of nonword decoding skill. It would have been more appropriate to refer to different levels of skill rather than to two sub-types of disabled reader. In any case, as pointed out by Flynn et al. (1992), "To find that a child with dyslexia who is reading a passage with difficulty has different neurophysiologic activity from a non-disabled child who is reading the same passage with ease does not imply differences in cortical mechanisms" (p. 134).

Genetic analyses might provide a means of defining or validating phenotypic sub-types (Smith, Pennington, Kimberling, & Ing, 1990). Using behavioural-genetic analyses, Castles et al. (1999) have shown that phonological and surface sub-types of dyslexia are inherited to different extents (see Chapter 7).

It is widely recognized that proficient reading involves a variety of component skills, any one of which, if deficient, may impair the acquisition of normal fluent reading (see Snowling et al., 2000; Tunmer & Hoover, 1992). The importance, generally, of distinguishing between different dyslexic sub-types is that they may imply different causal mechanisms (Seymour & Evans, 1993, 1994a, 1994b), whether conceived of in biological terms or as specific loci of impairment within the cognitive architecture. Finding different cognitive correlates associated with different dyslexia sub-types might represent a useful first stage in helping to identify different causal mechanisms. Perhaps, too, different causal mechanisms would call for different strategies of remediation (see, for example, Seymour & Bunce, 1994). In the words of Morris et al.:

> The chief reason for seeking subtypes of reading disability is the hope that distillaton of more homogeneous sub-groups will provide a basis for future research designed to relate to biological and social factors that cause the underlying linguistic and cognitive deficits that lead to a reading disability. A better classification of children with reading disability would inform approaches to effective intervention.
>
> (Morris et al., 1998, p. 368)

The existence of distinct dyslexic sub-types is entirely compatible with there being a continuum of differences in the pattern of performance seen in poor readers. That is, the sub-types identified might be regarded as comprising those individuals who fall at the extreme ends of the distribution of performance on orthographic and phonological processing tasks (Castles et al., 1999). Nor does the occurrence of distinctive sub-types imply that intensive remediation (in, for example, phonological awareness) cannot produce a change in an individual's profile of performance. This does not mean that other environmental influences, such as exposure to individual printed words, may not have contributed to the pattern shown by any particular individual. The question of how particular profiles

actually arise is important but has not yet been fully answered.

Stanovich et al. suggest that:

> Surface dyslexia might arise from a milder form of phonological deficit than that of the phonological dyslexic, but one conjoined with exceptionally inadequate reading experience. The phonological dyslexic might become more apparent when a more severe pathology underlying the functional architecture of phonological coding is conjoined with relatively high levels of exposure to print ... The latter would hasten the development of the orthographic lexicon ... but the former would be relatively refractory to direct remediation efforts.
>
> (Stanovich et al., 1997a, p. 124)

Like Manis et al. (1996), Stanovich and his colleagues suggested that surface dyslexia might be seen as representing a developmental lag or delay, whereas phonological dyslexia might reflect "true developmental deviance". However, according to Jackson and Coltheart:

> The reason that surface dyslexia appears rarely in RL [reading level] matches between older poor readers and younger average readers probably is that younger average readers have had very little time to build up their orthographic lexicons. Therefore, a comparison of their exception word reading with that of older poor readers is not particularly meaningful.
>
> (Jackson & Coltheart, 2001, p. 135)

The interested reader is referred to their monograph for further discussion as to the theoretical significance of the surface sub-type of dyslexia.

The question of sub-varieties of dyslexia in English invites consideration of another question. Are manifestations of dyslexia the same in all languages? Indeed, are all languages read in the same way by unimpaired readers? This question obviously cannot be answered for all the world's 6000 languages (especially as many are not written and even those that are written cannot be read by a majority of its speakers). Relevant data are limited to a very few European languages.

READING IN ORTHOGRAPHICALLY TRANSPARENT AND OPAQUE LANGUAGES: THE ORTHOGRAPHIC DEPTH HYPOTHESIS

Until recently, by far the largest proportion of reading research has been conducted with English-speaking participants. However, there appears to be increasing interest among researchers in investigating reading in languages other than English (see Goswami, 1997; Seymour, Aro, & Erskine, 2003). Idiosyncratic aspects of a language—for example, the relative frequency of complex syllable onsets (e.g. /fl/ or /st/) in Czech as compared with English (Caravolas & Bruck, 1993)—may determine the age at which children explicitly acquire an awareness of such features. In short, it is quite possible that the different phonological input provided by different languages influences aspects of phonological sensitivity and hence reading. Certainly, there is some evidence that pre-school bilingual children have some advantage over monolinguals when it comes to explicit phonological awareness (Bruck & Genesee, 1995; Campbell & Sais, 1995). More interesting, perhaps, is the hypothesis that reading can be affected by the orthographic nature of the script in which a language is written.

In some languages, such as English, the relationship between orthography and phonology is not one-to-one. The same sound can be represented in different ways (such as the "ee" sound in *read* and *freed*). Conversely, a given letter string can be pronounced in different ways (compare, for example, the rime *-alk* in *balk* and *talk* or different pronunciations of the words *wind* and *tear*). The orthography of English and other languages with similar inconsistency in letter–sound relationships is said to be deep or opaque. In shallow or transparent orthographies such as German, Spanish, Italian or Welsh, the letter–sound relationships are more consistent or regular.

The orthographic depth hypothesis refers to the idea that languages differing in their orthographic depth are processed in somewhat different ways (Feldman & Turvey, 1983, Katz & Feldman, 1983, Katz & Frost, 1992). In terms of dual-route accounts, languages that differ in their orthographic depth are, according to the orthographic depth hypothesis, read using different relative contributions of lexical and sub-lexical strategies. On a connectionist account such as that favoured by Seidenberg and his colleagues, differences in orthographic regularity have consequences for the ease or speed with which connections are established between orthography and phonology (see Seidenberg, 1992).

Evidence that the depth of orthography has an influence on reading comes, *inter alia*, from the finding of Ognjenovic, Lukatela, Feldman, and Turvey (1983) that beginning readers of English (a deep orthography) and Serbo-Croatian (a shallow orthography) exhibit different error patterns. Furthermore, Katz and Feldman (1983) have shown that word reading in Serbo-Croatian is unaffected by semantic priming (prior presentation of a related word) and the advantage of reading latency over lexical decision time (time to decide whether a letter string constitutes a real word or not) is greater for Serbo-Croatian than for English readers (Frost, Katz, & Bentin, 1987). From the point of view of dual-route theory, both these findings suggest that Serbo-Croatian readers rely more on the assembled (sub-lexical) routine than do English readers, who rely more on the addressed (whole-word) routine.

A strong version of the orthographic depth hypothesis would propose that an orthographically shallow or transparent language such as Italian or Spanish is necessarily read using only the sub-lexical routine (Turvey, Feldman, & Lukatela, 1984). On this view, the sub-lexical routine always provides a correct pronunciation for any word or nonword (pseudoword); since there is no need for a lexical routine, none develops (Bridgeman, 1987). If this hypothesis were true, then it should not be possible to find an individual who can read words in a shallow orthography but not matched pseudowords, since they would be read using the same process. In other words, it should not be possible to find an acquired phonological or deep dyslexic reader of these languages. However, acquired phonological dyslexia has been reported for Italian speakers (De Bastiani, Barry, & Carreras, 1988; see also Basso & Corno, 1994) and deep dyslexia has been reported for Spanish speakers (Cuetos, Valle-Arroyo, & Suarez, 1996; Ruiz, Ansaldo, & Lecours, 1994). These findings provide evidence against any strong version of the orthographic depth hypothesis, unless it is argued that a lexical route develops after the onset of illness. Given the apparent difficulty of remediating acquired phonological dyslexia (Castles & Coltheart, 1994; De Partz, 1986; but see also Broom & Doctor, 1995; Klein, Behrmann, & Doctor, 1994), the time scales involved in the investigations of De Bastiani et al. (1988) and Cuetos et al. (1996) render this possibility unlikely. Ruiz et al. report two patients who were deep dyslexic at 6 and 8 years post-stroke, so in these cases it is more difficult to rule out the possibility of development of a lexical route.

If it is true that in shallow orthographies words are read purely by means of a sub-lexical (phonological decoding) mechanism, semantic errors in reading and writing should be less frequent than in deeper orthographies. The findings of Basso and Corno (1994) for Italian support this prediction. Further evidence against the view that a lexical processing route fails to develop in readers of orthographically shallow languages comes from demonstrations of lexical priming effects on pseudoword (nonword) spelling in Italian (Barry, 1992) and on lexical decision (Sebastián-Gallés, 1991) tasks in Spanish. In addition, Job, Peressotti, and Cusinato (1998) have observed lexical effects in naming pseudowords in Italian. A consistency effect was observed whereby pseudowords with inconsistent endings (more than one possible pronunciation) took longer to be named than inconsistent ones (only one possible pronunciation) in Italian.

While a strong version of the orthographic depth hypothesis does not appear tenable (Besner & Smith, 1992), it is possible that children learn-

ing to read languages that differ in orthographic depth tend to adopt whole-word and sub-lexical strategies to differing extents. This weaker version of the orthographic depth hypothesis has been investigated in a series of studies by Wimmer and his colleagues. For example, in an unpublished study, Wimmer and Frith found that in a lexical decision task, young readers of German (orthographically shallow) were more likely than younger English readers to accept pseudohomophones (e.g. *brane*, *blud*) as genuine words (see Wimmer, Landerl, & Schneider, 1994). This accords with the view that German readers tend to adopt a phonologically mediated strategy in performing this task (see also Goswami, Ziegler, Dalton, & Schneider, 2001). It is also consistent with other suggestions that beginning readers of other transparent orthographies such as Spanish (Goswami, Gombert, & de Barrera, 1998), Greek (Goswami, Porpodas, & Wheelwright, 1997) and Welsh (Beaton, Buck, & Williams, 2001; Spencer & Hanley, 2003) are more proficient at nonword reading than those of deeper or more opaque orthographies such as English or French (see Seymour et al., 2003). Note, incidentally, that any differences in reading or spelling (Wimmer & Landerl, 1997) transparent and opaque orthographies at the outset of reading cannot necessarily be taken as evidence that differences exist between skilled adult readers purely as a function of orthography. The orthographic depth hypothesis may apply to beginning readers but not to adult readers.

Wimmer and Goswami (1994) compared English children learning to read English with Austrian children learning to read German. The children were presented with real words that were numbers (e.g. *five*, *seven*, *funf*, *sieben*) and pseudowords derived from real words in such a way that the onset–rime segments were preserved. For example, the pseudoword *sen* was created from the onset *s* from *seven* and the rime -*en* from *ten*. Similarly, the pseudoword *zwhen* was created from the onset *z* as in *zwei* and the rime -*ehn* as in *zehn*. The children were also presented with the numerals corresponding to the written words (5, 7, and so on). The results showed that whereas the reading time and accuracy were very similar for the English and German words and numerals, many more errors were made by the English children attempting to read pseudowords derived from English than by the German children reading pseudowords derived from German. There were also differences between the two languages in the nature of the errors that were made. Austrian children's errors in reading pseudowords tended to be other pseudowords, but the English children often refused to give an answer if they could not read a pseudoword.

The results reported by Wimmer and Goswami (1994) are consistent with the view that children learn to read English and German using different strategies, the strategy for German being more analytic or phonically based than that for English. However, the Austrian children had been taught using a "rather systematic phonics approach", whereas the English children were taught using "a combination of phonics and a whole word reading scheme". This somewhat undermines support for any simple version of the orthographic depth hypothesis, since the different patterns of performance between the two groups of children may have been due to the different teaching methods to which they were exposed rather than to the orthographic depth of their language *per se* (see Frith, Wimmer, & Landerl, 1998). Furthermore, the English children had been reading for longer than the Austrians and the method of instruction may interact with age and orthography (Wimmer and Hummer, 1990). Similar reservations apply to a study of English and Italian readers by Thorstad (1991).

Wimmer and Goswami (1994) suggested that the orthographic depth of a language has both direct and indirect effects on the strategies adopted in reading by children. They argued that direct effects follow from the fact that in a transparent and consistent language, grapheme–phoneme correspondences are easier to detect and use than in an opaque language. In less consistent and more context-sensitive languages, it may be adaptive initially to use familiar spelling patterns and analogy in reading. On the other hand, teaching methods appropriate to different orthographies have an indirect effect on the

adoption of reading strategies. An orthographically transparent language, for example, is easier and more convenient to teach via a "phonics" than a whole-word approach.

With regard to "direct" effects, there is some evidence to suggest that readers of orthographies that are more transparent than English (that is, in which there is a more consistent correspondence between graphemes and phonemes) acquire an explicit knowledge of phonemes, as indicated by performance on phonological awareness tasks, earlier than their English-speaking counterparts. This was shown for Italian (Cossu, Shankweiler, Liberman, Katz, & Tola, 1988) in a cross-language study and was argued to occur for Turkish on the basis of a single-language study (Öney & Durgunoğlu, 1997).

Although beginning readers of a transparent orthography may acquire explicit knowledge of phonemes earlier than readers of a more opaque orthography, there is some agreement that, as has been claimed for English (e.g. Liberman, et al., 1974), children exposed to transparent orthographies acquire an awareness of spoken syllable and onset–rime segments before the individual phoneme (Caravolas & Bruck, 1993; Cossu et al., 1988; Öney & Durgunoğlu, 1997; Wimmer et al., 1994.)

In English, orthographic units consisting of vowel and final consonant (VC) are more predictable in their pronunciation than either individual vowel graphemes or CV units at the beginning of a word (Treiman, Mullennix, Bijeljac-Babic, & Richmond-Welty, 1995). This predictability may make the VC unit (the rime) a more salient unit for readers of English than it is for readers of languages in which the orthography is more highly predictable at the level of the phoneme. As Goswami et al. (1998) point out: "Nontransparent languages may be more predictable in terms of spelling-to-sound correspondence at levels other than the phoneme" (p. 21). The letter "a", for example, is pronounced in three different ways by English readers of *ball*, *park* and *hand*. However, apparent inconsistency at one level (such as grapheme to phoneme) may mask consistency at another level (such as the rime). The pronunciation of words such as *hall*, *dark* and *band* or *fall*, *lark* and *land* corresponds to that of *ball*, *park* and *hand*. This might be expected to lead readers of English to look for consistency at a larger unit size than the grapheme.

Goswami et al. argue that:

> For children who are learning to read a very transparent orthography, such as Spanish, a reliance on letter-by-letter decoding is the most efficient reading strategy . . . Children learning to read orthographies with less transparency, such as English or French, are faced with a much more difficult task. They have to learn a larger set of ambiguous orthographic–phonological relations . . . English and French children . . . seem to cope with spelling–sound ambiguity by coding orthographic–phonological relations in terms of larger spelling units, such as rimes.
>
> (Goswami et al., 1998, p. 46)

Degree of familiarity with larger orthographic and phonological units, such as rime or rhyme, might be expected to influence the relative ease with which young children (and adults) code these segments in reading nonsense stimuli. Goswami et al. (1998) varied phonological and orthographic familiarity and found that both affected speed and accuracy of nonsense word reading in English, French and Spanish. They concluded that the effects of familiarity interact with orthography.

Ziegler, Perry, Jacobs, and Braun (2001) concluded from their reading of the relevant literature that readers of highly regular orthographies rely heavily on grapheme–phoneme decoding strategies because the mapping of graphemes onto phonemes is relatively unambiguous. In contrast, children learning to read a less consistent orthography such as English use a variety of strategies to cope with the inconsistency. Ziegler et al. hypothesized that "consistency of an orthography should have a measurable effect on the grain size of units that are likely to play a role during reading and reading development" (p. 380). Specifically, adult readers of English might be expected to show evidence of processing larger units than readers of German, who would have

learned to read by processing letter strings in terms of smaller units.

Ziegler et al. (2001) tested their hypothesis by comparing speed of reading words and nonwords by English and German readers. They manipulated the size of letter strings to be read in two different ways. First, the neighbourhood size of words was varied—that is, the extent to which a given target word shares its rime with other words. For example, *hate*, *date* and *late* share the same rime as do *make*, *fake* and *lake*. Readers sensitive to the rime should show an effect of neighbourhood size (see Johnson, 1992). Second, the size of the letter string was varied. This should affect readers who are using a small unit size, such as the grapheme, to a greater extent than readers of larger unit size. Participants (30 English-speaking and 23 German-speaking psychology students) were presented with words that are spelled identically or very similarly and mean the same in the two languages. They were also presented with more or less identical nonwords (more or less because German nouns are spelled with the initial letter in upper case). The results showed that response latencies (i.e. the time taken to pronounce the stimulus items) were indeed influenced in the way predicted. Readers of English showed a larger effect of neighbourhood size than the readers of German, whereas string length showed the opposite effect, being stronger for German than for English readers. These statistically significant effects are impressive given that they were obtained with extremely similar stimulus items in the two languages and survived after statistically partialling out the effects of covariation between length and size of rime (body size). Ziegler and colleagues (2001) concluded that "orthographic consistency appears to determine the very nature of the orthographic and phonological processes and not only the relative contribution of orthographic and phonological codes" (p. 383).

It is quite possible that the relationships found for English between different components of phonological awareness and reading development, and hence between phonological deficits and dyslexia, may not be identical for transparent and opaque orthographies. If these are read in characteristically different ways, then one might expect to find that failure to acquire efficient reading of languages that vary in orthographic consistency is associated with differences in the nature of the reading deficit.

Orthographic depth and dyslexia

One of the earliest studies of reading problems in different languages appears to have been that of Stevenson, Stigler, Lucker, Lee, Hsu, and Kitamura (1982), who devised reading tests in Chinese, Japanese and English. Contrary to the prevailing view that reading difficulties were not found in readers of non-alphabetic languages, Stevenson et al. reported that a proportion of Chinese and Japanese children also experienced severe problems (see also Ho, Chan, Tsang, & Lee, 2002).

Lindgren, De Renzi, and Richman (1985) compared Italian and American fifth-grade boys on a wide variety of tests. Word-reading ability was assessed by a test of reading comprehension and three different discrepancy-based definitions of dyslexia were used. Dyslexia was significantly more frequent among the American sample than the Italian sample for two of the three definitions. The third, based on regression equations, did not show a difference. However, the regression equations were based on different correlations between IQ and reading ability in the two countries and this "tended to 'adjust away' cross-national differences in the proportion of children falling at the extremes of the score distributions" (p. 1410). In both countries, the dyslexics were significantly inferior to normally reading control children in nonsense word reading but "decoding appeared to present more problems for the U.S. dyslexics than for the Italians" (p. 1412).

The difference between American and Italian students in decoding ability was attributed to the greater sound–letter regularity of the Italian orthography compared with English orthography. The authors acknowledged that there are "cultural and experiential differences" between the two countries, particularly with regard to method of instruction. Such differences, rather than the nature of the two orthographies, might bring about the performance differences observed. It is

difficult to disentangle the effects of instruction from those of the nature of the orthography since, as pointed out by Lindgren et al. (1985), "it is very difficult to avoid using a primarily phonetic approach in Italian reading instruction. Thus whether differences are due more to basic characteristics of the language than to instructional methods becomes difficult to determine since the methods often follow directly from the structure of the language" (p. 1414). For example, it has been suggested that daily reading and spelling practice in a regular orthography in effect provides regular phonemic awareness training (Aro et al., 1999; Cossu et al., 1988).

Given the ubiquity of a nonword reading deficit in English-speaking dyslexics (Rack et al., 1992), including those of college age (Ben-Dror et al., 1991), the question is whether the same applies to readers of orthographies that are more regular or consistent than English. To examine this question, Wimmer (1993) compared German-speaking (Austrian) dyslexic children aged 8–10 years with younger reading-level matched controls on nonword reading. At the end of the second grade, the error rate of the dyslexics was 17 per cent; this fell to 8 per cent by the end of the fourth grade. Reading speed, however, was slow throughout both grades. Comparable results for Greek were reported by Porpodas (1999). Four Italian (surface) dyslexics tested by Zoccolotti, De Luca, Di Pace, Judica, Orlandi, and Spinelli (1999) were also said to to be markedly slow for their age in reading Italian words and nonwords (and showed some stress assignment errors and a significant word-length effect) but not in naming pictures. Despite being slow, participants in all these studies made few errors. The 10-year-old Dutch dyslexic children studied by Van der Leij and Van Daal (1999) showed "near perfect" accuracy in reading familiar words but were slower than both reading-age and chronological-age control participants in reading both words and nonwords (but not digits). It seems, then, from these studies that the reading speed of dyslexic children exposed to regular orthographies is slow for both words and nonwords, but particularly so for nonwords. In short, a nonword deficit appears to show up in terms of reading speed rather than accuracy, although González and Valle (2000) found that young Spanish children who were poor readers (mean age 107.5 months) made significantly more errors in nonword reading than control children matched for reading level.

Matching for nonword reading level as in Wimmer's (1993) experiment does not show whether German-speaking dyslexics are relatively more impaired at reading nonwords than words. To establish whether this is the case requires dyslexic and control groups to be matched for word reading speed. This was accomplished by Wimmer (1996a), who matched German-speaking dyslexic children and younger normally reading controls for word-reading speed before comparing their performance on reading nonwords. Despite the equivalent word-reading speeds for the two groups, Wimmer found that the dyslexics were much slower than the controls, but only a little less accurate, in reading (and spelling) nonwords. This confirms the existence of a nonword reading deficit in German-speaking dyslexics.

Given the regular nature of the German orthography and the method of schooling in Austria, Wimmer argued that:

> For our dyslexic children, after 4 years of schooling, it can be ruled out that the nonword reading deficit is due to insufficient knowledge of grapheme–phoneme correspondences. However, there are other plausible accounts for how a phonological impairment may affect nonword reading. One is that dyslexic children may suffer from slow access to phonological memory representations ... Another possibility is that dyslexic children's particular difficulty with nonword reading results from inefficient access to syllables or syllable constituents (onsets and rimes).
>
> (Wimmer, 1996a, pp. 88–89)

However, results from another regular orthography do not support this latter position. De Gelder and Vroomen (1991) compared 11-year-old dyslexic Dutch children with reading-age-matched controls on phonological awareness tasks at different linguistic levels: syllable, onset–rime and phoneme. The dyslexic group was impaired relative to both reading-age- and chronological-age-matched controls only at the phonemic level.

Despite there being a consistent letter–sound correspondence, slow nonword reading times and impaired phonemic awareness suggest that difficulty at the phoneme level is characteristic of dyslexia in transparent orthographies as it is in English. However, English-speaking poor readers have been shown to do less well on rhyme-oddity tasks than younger readers matched for reading level, implying that their difficulty extends to the onset–rime level (see, for example, Bowey et al., 1992; Bradley & Bryant, 1978). This has not been demonstrated for transparent orthographies. If a child's phonological representations are structured first at a holistic level and gradually become more segmentally refined (under the influence of reading experience), it may be that in contributing to very early awareness of individual phonemes a transparent orthography enables difficulty at the higher level of linguistic unit to be bypassed or overcome.

The competent, if slow, reading and spelling of nonwords in fourth-grade dyslexics studied by Wimmer (1996a) apparently masks the fact that at an early age Austrian dyslexic children may show considerable difficulty with phonological recoding and segmentation tasks. While this persists for some children, others have compensated for the difficulty by the end of the fourth grade. Thus the data of Wimmer (1993, 1996a) suggest that at the early stages of beginning to read, speakers of English and German who are diagnosed as dyslexic do not differ markedly, whereas by the fourth grade or thereabouts the difficulties for readers of English remain but are less apparent for readers of German. In a follow-up study of 12 children initially investigated by Wimmer and Hummer (1990), it was argued that "The reason why German dyslexic children—in contrast to their English counterparts—outgrow the initial difficulties ... quite plausibly has to do with differences in orthographic consistency and associated differences in teaching approaches" (Wimmer, 1996b, pp. 184–185). Nonetheless, the deficit in reading speed found for older German-speaking dyslexic children may still be tied to a phonological impairment. Blending individual phonemes to pronounce a word or nonword requires speedy grapheme–phoneme conversion so that the relevant phonemes can be co-articulated in the participant's response. A tardy conversion from print to sound will result in reduced efficiency of phoneme blending (Wimmer, 1996a, 1996b).

Wimmer, Mayringer, and Landerl (2000) have recently argued (see also Landerl, 2001) that a phonological awareness deficit does not on its own lead to inaccurate word and nonword reading in German, at least when a systematic teaching approach that emphasizes the correspondence between graphemes and phonemes is adopted prior to instruction in reading. Landerl, Wimmer, and Frith (1997) compared English and Austrian (German-speaking) dyslexic children aged 11–13 years on reading words and nonwords that were highly similar in the two languages and on a spoonerism task. In terms of reading speed, children of both nationalities were generally slower than their reading-level matched controls. The English dyslexic and control children made many more errors than their Austrian counterparts, especially of low-frequency words and of nonwords. The Austrian children made few errors (see also Beaton et al., 2001; Wimmer & Goswami, 1994). Normally-reading English control children of 8 years of age also made many more errors with nonwords than did the young Austrian control readers, although by the age of 12 years the difference between English and Austrian control readers was no longer present. It was suggested that "besides the consistency of orthography the reliance on synthetic phonics as the teaching and remediation approach may also be of importance for the observed differences in the manifestation of dyslexia in German and English children" (Landerl et al., 1997, p. 329).

Landerl et al. (1997) also compared their participants' performance on a spoonerism task. Somewhat surprisingly, in view of the relatively good nonword reading (and spelling; see footnote to p. 329 of Landerl et al., 1997), the scores of the Austrian dyslexic children on the spoonerism task

were as poor as those of the English dyslexic children. This poor performance of the Austrians stands in apparent contrast to the high level of phonemic awareness demonstrated on a vowel-substitution task (converting *Mama* to *Mimi*) demonstrated by dyslexic fourth-graders in Wimmer's (1993) study. Clearly, the task of phoneme-exchange differs from that of vowel substitution and appears to be more complex. The latter task requires stripping the initial phoneme from each word—deletion at the level of onset and rime—plus holding in memory a number of word segments that then have to be blended together to form two words as responses. For even one of the response words to be correct, the initial phonemes must have been correctly stripped from each of the two stimulus items. Given this reasoning, Landerl and Wimmer (2000) re-analysed the data of Landerl et al. (1997), scoring as correct any response for which the first word was correct (that is, disregarding the second word). Under this system of scoring, the performance of both the Austrian and English dyslexic children was, of course, enhanced. For both groups, performance was now comparable to that of reading-level control children, although it was impaired in relation to chronological age controls. Thus for children of this age, phoneme deletion at the level of onset–rime does not on its own appear to be a serious problem for either English- or German-speaking dyslexic children.

In addition to re-analysing their earlier data, Landerl and Wimmer (2000) carried out a small study with 13 poor and 23 control Austrian readers who were on average 2 years younger than the participants in the study of Landerl et al. (1997). The children were given a nonword spelling task (nonwords that differed considerably from real words to avoid the use of analogy) and a phoneme segmentation task requiring them to isolate the individual sounds of nonwords. This therefore required access at the level of individual phonemes rather than at the level of onset–rime. The results showed that even these younger Austrian dyslexic children performed well on the tasks. Landerl and Wimmer (2000) argued that, "Obviously, three years of experience with a consistent orthography is sufficient to induce access to the phoneme level even in dyslexic children" (p. 255) and that, more generally, "The present findings and the longitudinal findings on German-speaking dyslexic children seem to favor a version of the phonological deficit explanation that would posit a dysfunction of the phonological module that has little to do with segmental awareness difficulties" (p. 258). Rather, difficulties with phonological memory and building up word-level orthographic representations were seen as responsible, at least in orthographies with consistent letter–sound mappings acquired in the context of a phonics-based teaching approach. Data from Greek reported by Porpodas (1999) are consistent with these conclusions of Landerl and Wimmer (2000) for German dyslexic children.

Despite being a highly regular language with regard to reading, German is somewhat less so with regard to spelling. There is relatively little inconsistency in the way in which German graphemes are pronounced but rather more inconsistency in the opposite direction, since a given phoneme can be represented by different graphemes. Austrian dyslexic children (mean age 9.3 years) diagnosed in the third grade at school were found by Landerl (2001) to make more spelling errors than age-matched controls. Very few of these errors were phonologically implausible, suggesting that the dyslexics' sound segmentation skills were not grossly impaired. Landerl argued that "Obviously, dyslexic children's knowledge of orthgraphically correct spellings is very limited". She continued: "This deficit in orthographic spelling skills is one of the most typical characteristics of dyslexia in German, which quite often continues into adulthood" (p. 194).

At the time of writing, there is little in the literature on adult dyslexia with regard to orthographic depth. However, in a recent neuroimaging study, English, French and Italian dyslexic adults were compared, using stimuli appropriate to their own language, on a battery of psychological tests and on reading of words and nonwords as well as on phonological tests. Italian is a highly regular orthography compared with English and French. Participants from the three countries were equally impaired relative to controls on tests of reading and phonological skill and showed a similar pattern of performance on the remaining tests, although the Italians were more accurate in reading both words and nonwords than the English or French dyslexics (Paulesu et al., 2001).

If dyslexia is at least in part a constitutionally determined condition, then one would expect to see a common biological signature (or signatures) despite differences in the way in which the phonology of different languages is represented in their orthography. Brain scans (positron emission tomography) in the study by Paulesu et al. (2001) revealed that dyslexic participants from all countries had lower levels of activation than normally reading controls in the inferior, middle and superior temporal gyri and in the middle occipital gyrus on the left side. The authors argued from this that differences in reading performance across dyslexics from different countries are due to differences in orthography rather than differences in the organization of neural mechanisms involved in reading.

The research discussed in this chapter points overwhelmingly to a phonological deficit of some kind or another being the principal factor underlying difficulty in learning to read an alphabetic script. This applies both to orthographically opaque and transparent languages, although the precise nature of the deficit has yet to be elucidated. Learning to read, however, does not take place in a linguistic vacuum. The impact of a phonological deficit will be within the context of a child's overall language ability and experience and may well not be restricted solely to the business of reading. This is the topic to which I turn in the next chapter.

5

THE GENERAL LANGUAGE CONTEXT

It is arguable that too much attention has been paid in recent years to the role of phonological processing in reading development, as this has directed attention away from other aspects of the relations between general language skills and reading (Bishop, 1991; Snowling, 2000b), yet there can be little doubt that a child's general language ability and background feeds in to the acquisition of his or her reading skills.

POOR COMPREHENDERS

To become a skilled and proficient reader requires not only good word recognition skill, but an ability to understand what one has read. Neither of these is sufficient on its own; both are required if one is to successfully derive value (and pleasure) from the written word (Gough et al., 1992; Tunmer & Hoover, 1992). Although word decoding ability and comprehension normally develop hand in hand, and some dyslexics at least show comprehension deficits in comparison with younger children matched for reading level (see Guthrie, 1973a), these skills may become dissoci-

ated, even if the difference is not apparent at a younger age (see Guthrie, 1973b). Indeed, when we speak of dyslexia we normally mean that word recognition skills are deficient in the context of relatively intact comprehension ability. The opposite dissociation may also occur—good word recognition but relatively impaired comprehension. An extreme form of such a dissociation can be seen in so-called hyperlexic children, whose reading level is considerably in advance of what would be expected on the basis of their age or educational level (Richman & Kitchell, 1981; for a review of hyperlexia, see Nation, 1999).

Quite apart from hyperlexic children, who are often autistic or carry some other diagnosis of developmental disorder, there are normally developing children (and presumably adults) whose reading comprehension skills are lower than expected but whose decoding skills are adequate or normal (see Nation & Snowling, 1997, 2000; Oakhill, 1982; Siegel & Ryan, 1989; Yuill & Oakhill, 1991). Such children, sometimes referred to as word-callers, may experience comprehension difficulties even with auditorily presented tasks (Oakhill, 1982; Stothard & Hulme, 1992). Thus their poor comprehension is not restricted to reading but is part of a general language comprehension deficit. These children have been shown to have deficits in syntactic awareness by Nation and Snowling (2000), who propose that "poor comprehenders' impaired syntactic awareness is a manifestation of more general language processing difficulties, encompassing both semantic and grammatical weaknesses" (p. 237).

Poor comprehenders appear to have good phonological skills relative to those who have both comprehension and word decoding deficits (Stothard & Hulme, 1995), although they may score below average on some tests of verbal short-term or working memory (Siegel & Ryan, 1989; but see Stothard & Hulme, 1992). This is seen by Nation and Snowling (2000) as "a consequence of the same language processing limitations that contribute to their difficulties with syntactic awareness" (p. 237).

Because poor comprehenders show less facilitation from context than do normal readers or dyslexic children, it is to be expected that they will be less competent at figuring out the identity of irregular words (Nation & Snowling, 1998). This leads to the prediction that with increasing age there will be an increasing discrepancy in irregular or exception word identification skills between poor comprehenders and control readers.

READING AND GENERAL LANGUAGE ABILITY

The development of normal reading ability does not occur *in vacuo* but in the context of other aspects of language development. Semantic and syntactic problems often co-occur with reading problems (see, for example, Catts, 1989a; Ellis & Large, 1987) and reduced syntactic proficiency has been reported in children aged 30 months who subsequently turn out to be dyslexic (Scarborough, 1990). Furthermore, good readers perform better than poor readers on tests assessing the ability to recognize syntactically well-formed sentences even with general cognitive ability and vocabulary level controlled (Willows & Ryan, 1986).

The question arises as to whether dyslexia should be conceived of as a part of a general developmental language disorder or as a disorder specifically related to literacy skills. There are reports that in the early (Bowey & Patel, 1988) and middle years (Bowey, 1986) of childhood, syntactic or grammatical ability predicts, or correlates with, reading performance (Muter & Snowling, 1998), even when general ability and vocabulary level are statistically controlled (see Tunmer & Hoover, 1992; Tunmer, Neadsale, & Wright, 1987). In one study with children (Gottardo et al., 1996) and another with adults (Gottardo et al., 1997), the effect of syntactic ability was removed when phonological sensitivity (and working memory) were also entered into the regression equation. This may in fact be accounted for in terms of a relationship between syntactic ability and phonological processing skills, since there are a number of ways in which the former might influence development of the latter (Tunmer & Hoover, 1992).

In an experimental study of oral language production that controlled for IQ and social class, Fry, Johnson, and Muehl (1970) found that a group of 36 below-average readers (age: $M = 89.88$ months, $SD = 3.47$) used significantly less complex constructions in their speech than a control group of average and above-average readers of the same mean age ($M = 92.71$ months, $SD = 3.13$). This does not, of course, tell us about the causal direction of any difference between the two reading groups, or whether there would be a difference between dyslexics and younger readers of equivalent reading age. However, language variables measured at age 3 years have been shown to significantly predict word and sentence reading performance several years later (Olofsson & Niedersøe, 1999).

The fact that syntax-recognition ability and oral production is better in good than poor readers is perhaps not surprising. One would expect that good readers read more books and are therefore exposed to more instances of well-formed sentences than poor readers. In addition, it is not unreasonable to suppose that good readers can integrate what they read into an overall structure better than weak readers. However,

Bowey (1986) reported that, after controlling for general verbal ability as assessed by the revised Peabody Picture Vocabulary Test (PPVT–R), syntactic awareness (measured by tests of oral sentence imitation and oral sentence correction) correlated significantly more highly with measures of word decoding skill than with measures of comprehension in a group of Australian fourth- and fifth-grade children. One possible explanation of this finding is that both syntactic awareness and decoding skill correlate with some third variable, such as phonological awareness or general language ability and, furthermore, that this third variable influences decoding ability more than it does comprehension.

A particular question concerns the extent to which phonological awareness (sometimes referred to as a meta-linguistic ability) and general language ability are independent. If meta-linguistic ability is independent of general language ability, then it should account for a significant amount of variance in reading performance once the effect of general language ability has been statistically removed. To test this hypothesis, Bowey and Patel (1988) administered tests of syntactic awareness and the "odd-man-out" sound categorization test (using three rather than the usual four items per trial) as measures of meta-linguistic ability and tests of general language ability (including the PPVT) to 60 first-grade children (mean age 73 months). The dependent variables were reading comprehension and word identification. Bowey and Patel found that, with general language ability controlled, meta-linguistic skills did not predict significant additional variance for either dependent variable. However, neither did the measures of general language ability predict significant additional variance in word identification scores once the measures of meta-linguistic ability were statistically controlled, although they did account for a significant amount of additional variation in reading comprehension. Bowey and Patel argued that "we cannot conclude that meta-linguistic skill constitutes an ability that emerges independently of general language" (p. 379). They were careful to point out, though, that "The conclusion that meta-linguistic skill does not appear to

emerge or operate independently of more general language ability should not be construed as an argument that particular meta-linguistic abilities do not contribute in quite specific ways to the development of various aspects of reading skill" (p. 379).

The issue, then, concerns whether phonological ability makes an independent contribution to reading over and above general language ability. In their study, Bowey and Patel (1988) found no independent influence of phonological awareness on reading after the effect of vocabulary score and general language ability were statistically controlled. Bryant, MacLean, and Bradley (1990a), however, found that sound categorization, but not syntactic awareness, accounted for unique variance in early reading achievement after the effects of general language ability and IQ were statistically controlled. Bowey (1990b) discusses possible reasons for the discrepancy between the results of the two studies (and corrects four errors in the F-values reported by Bowey and Patel, 1988), including differences in the age of the children tested and differences in test materials. Despite such differences, Bowey felt that the discrepancy between the studies was relatively minor and "reduces to the issue of whether meta-linguistic ability accounts for unique variation in early reading achievement" (p. 443).

In a reply, Bryant, MacLean, and Bradley (1990b) pursued their view that "the connection between children's sensitivity to rhyme/alliteration and reading is an independent one" (p. 449). In an earlier paper (Bryant et al., 1989) they had reported that, with the effects of IQ, vocabulary, social class and phonological sensitivity at age 3 years 4 months statistically controlled, knowledge of nursery rhymes at age 3 years 4 months predicted phonological sensitivity at age 5 years 7 months and reading and spelling scores at ages 5 years 11 months and 6 years 3 months. When sound categorization scores at age 4 years 7 months or 5 years 7 months were included in the analysis, however, knowledge of nursery rhymes was no longer a significant predictor of early reading performance. Bryant et al. argued that early exposure to, and knowledge of, nursery rhymes sensitized pre-readers to the sound structure of language and that this, in turn, enhances early reading performance.

Bishop (1991) pointed out that "Nearly every study that had included relevant measures found strong links between syntactic and semantic competence and reading and spelling ability" (p. 98). She suggested that language, literacy and phonological awareness are all interrelated, but that within a particular subset of children there may be a specific link between phonological awareness and literacy. This subset of children she regards as theoretically, though not numerically, important "precisely because the dissociation between phonological and other language skills makes it possible to study the specific effect of phonological impairments on reading acquisition, without having to allow for confounding effects of other verbal deficits" (p. 100). In her view, the situation was now such that "Clearly, with sufficient imagination, any task that involves a verbal stimulus or response can be interpreted as reflecting phonological processing" (p. 99). Bishop's interpretation of the data from her own and other investigations was that there is a direct causal link between semantic and syntactic deficits and reading difficulties. This could come about in several ways. For example, if a word has been decoded but cannot be understood because it is not in a child's vocabulary, then it cannot provide useful context for decoding the surrounding text. If a child has difficulty with syntactictically demanding structures, then written sentences may overload the child's ability to remember or understand them.

The issue concerning the nature of the interaction between phonological awareness, general language ability and reading arises at a biological as well as at a cognitive level. Specifically, one can ask whether there are independent genetic influences on normal variation in general language skill, phonological ability and reading. Certainly, there is good evidence that genes play a role both in developmental language disorders (see Chapter 7) and in normal language variation (see review by Stromswold, 2001). There is also evidence (see Chapter 7) of a genetic influence on phonological coding in disabled readers (Olson et al., 1989; Stromswold, 2001) and on individual differences

in reading ability in a general population (see Stevenson, Graham, Fredman, & McLoughlin, 1987). The question is, are these genetic influences one and the same or independent of each other?

Hohnen and Stevenson (1999) attempted to unravel the relationship between general language skill, phonological ability and literacy ability in a sample of the general population by testing 126 pairs of twins. The extent to which individual differences in these abilities are produced by genetic, shared environmental and specific environmental factors was evaluated in monozygotic and dizygotic twins aged 5 years 10 months to 7 years 4 months using a model-fitting approach. The results suggested that there is a shared genetic influence on all three abilities (that is independent of any genetic influence on performance IQ) and that phonological awareness and literacy are jointly influenced by environmental factors that are independent of general language skill. That is, there was no evidence to suggest that there is a shared genetic influence between phonological ability and reading that is independent of the genetic influence they share with general language skill.

Hohnen and Stevenson (1999) point out that a shared genetic influence on general language and literacy would explain why some studies have reported a relation between the two. A shared genetic influence also explains the strong relationship between phonological awareness and language. Furthermore, a shared environmental influence (perhaps instructional) explains the findings in some studies of a unique relationship between phonological ability and reading after the effects of general language ability have been removed. Although all abilities develop together under genetic influence, more extreme environments could produce independent covariation between phonological awareness and reading in a subset of children (Bishop, 1991).

NAMING DEFICITS IN DYSLEXIA

Word-finding problems are frequently referred to in the clinical literature on dyslexia (e.g. Johnson

& Myklebust, 1967; Miles, 1993a) and often dyslexic people can be heard to complain aloud of "words! words!" Several studies have found dyslexics as a group to be less fluent in everyday speech (Stirling & Miles, 1988) or to be slower to generate words starting with a particular sound, though not from a particular semantic category (Frith, Landerl, & Frith, 1995; Griffiths, 1991), although this might not always be the case. In one Finnish study, the combined group score on two fluency tasks (generating words beginning with the letter *k* and giving examples of foods) of a small group of nine 18-year-old dyslexics was found to be inferior to that of a control group of normal readers (Korhonen, 1995). Unfortunately, it is not possible to disentangle the relative contribution of a phonemic from a semantic deficit to the combined score.

Dyslexics tend to be slower and/or more error-prone in naming letters, colours or objects (Catts, 1986; Denckla, 1972; Denckla & Rudel, 1976a, 1976b; Gladstone, Best, & Davidson, 1989; Johnston & Anderson, 1998; Katz, 1986; Landerl, 2001; Mattis et al., 1975; Miles & Gibbons, 2003; Rudel, 1985; Snowling, Van Wagtendonk, & Stafford, 1988; Wolf, 1986; Wolf, Bally, & Morris, 1986; Wolf & Goodglass, 1986; Wolf & Obregón, 1992) than age-matched controls or so-called "garden variety" poor readers (Wolf, 1991; Wolf & Obregón, 1992). A naming speed deficit was found to persist over 9 years in at least some of the dyslexic individuals studied by Korhonen (1995) and it is likely that difficulty in rapid naming is an unremitting problem for many dyslexics (see Felton et al., 1990).

Naming deficits are found not only for objects, colours and letters but sometimes also for digits (e.g. Denckla & Rudel, 1976a, 1976b; Wolf et al., 1986). This may simply reflect a difficulty with printed material or generally weak phonological representations and thus be considered part of the reading deficit (Share, 1995). On the other hand, digits can be regarded as ideograms, the processing of which need not be compromised in dyslexia. Rozin et al. (1971) reported that eight second-grade "backward" readers who were unable to read simple nonwords or three-letter rhyming words (e.g. CAT, FAT, SAT, MAT) after

being given the pronunciation for "AT" were able to learn to read a series of Chinese characters despite making little progress "in reading the English alphabet" (p. 1266).

For rapid serial naming of objects, Denckla and Rudel (1976a, 1976b) reported that dyslexics were slower not only than controls who read at an age-appropriate level but also other learning-disabled children matched for reading age. In comparison with such children, a matched group of dyslexic boys aged 8–11 years (*n* = 10) were said on the basis of a discriminant function analysis to be characterized by "slowness, circumlocution, and paraphasic substitutions on confrontation naming tasks" (Denckla, Rudel, & Broman, 1981, p. 126). Even adult "compensated dyslexics" (who have overcome their initial problems and read at adequate or normal levels) may be slower (but not less accurate) in reading a passage of prose than non-dyslexic contols (Lefly & Pennington, 1991). This perhaps reflects less automatic (Wolf et al., 1986) or efficient lexical access or retrieval and/or assembly of the appropriate sequence of phonemes for pronunciation.

It might be argued that vocabulary knowledge mediates the relationship between naming speed and reading. However, Wolf and Goodglass (1986) reported that confrontation naming performance differentiated groups of average, bilingual and disabled readers even though there was no "blatant" group difference in vocabulary. Semrud-Clikeman, Guy, Griffin, and Hynd (2000) reported that young reading-disabled children (less than 12.3 years old) were slower and more error prone in naming series of digits, letters and objects than both control readers of the same age and children with a diagnosis of attention deficit hyperactivity disorder. Older reading-disabled children were slower only on digits and letters. Despite being relatively slow, the disabled readers had vocabulary scores well within the norms for their age. Thus difficulty in rapid naming appears not to be due to an impoverished vocabulary, but rather to some difficulty in rapidly or automatically retrieving words from an internal lexicon or in storing or assembling their constituent phonemes.

Although some research has suggested that rapid automatized naming scores predict reading level only among poor rather than average readers (Meyer, Wood, Hart, & Felton, 1998), or that naming impairments may only be found in cases of more severe rather than mild reading impairment (see Bowers & Wolf, 1993), an association between reading and rapid naming of letters and digits or other symbols has been reported among normal beginning readers (see Wagner et al., 1994). Indeed, correlations have been reported between reading generally and naming speed (Manis et al., 1997; McBride-Chang, 1995, 1996). Picture-naming speed in Dutch kindergarten children predicts later reading achievement in grade 1 (de Jong & Van der Leij, 1999) and grade 1 Austrian boys who are slow at serial picture naming are slower at reading German words and nonwords than are children with a phonological deficit (Wimmer et al., 2000).

In one of their seminal papers, Denckla and Rudel (1976a) refer to the possibility of a deficit in "automatization, a kind of rapid retrieval function . . .", but point out that "Still to be explained is the source of the failure to 'automatize' in dyslexic children" (p. 477). On the basis of a causal path analysis of the performance of children aged 8–13 years, Kail and Hall (1994) suggested that the association between rapid naming and reading is mediated by age-related changes in speed of general cognitive processing conceived of as "a global mechanism that limits the speed with which most cognitive processes are executed" (p. 953). This view contrasts with the idea that good and poor readers differ in terms of the "automaticity" with which name codes are accessed in memory.

The double-deficit hypothesis

Wolf and her colleagues have put forward what they call a double-deficit hypothesis of dyslexia. In addition to the well-established phonological deficit in many, perhaps most, dyslexics, Wolf and Bowers (1999) argue that impaired naming speed is an important independent "second core deficit" of dyslexia. As evidence for this proposal they cite "generally modest rather than strong interrelationships between naming speed and the broad group of phonological-based tasks" (p. 420), together with differential contributions of

phoneme awareness and naming speed to the variance in word identification skill. This leads to the proposal that there are at least three different dyslexic sub-groups based on the presence either of one deficit alone or on the joint presence of a phonological processing impairment and a deficit in naming speed (see also Swan & Goswami, 1997a, 1997b).

The double-deficit hypothesis was examined in German-speaking children by Wimmer et al. (2000). They reported that children with only a phonological deficit prior to reading instruction (and subsequently taught using a systematic phonetic approach) were able to learn to read words and nonwords in the regular German orthography (and to spell phonetically regular words) despite their deficit. Children with an impairment only in naming speed, or who had a phonological deficit combined with a naming-speed deficit, were slower than those with a phonological deficit, alone. When the children had to read foreign words (predominantly English), both a phonological deficit and a naming-speed deficit were associated with less accurate performance. These results support the double-deficit view.

Other authors, too, regard a naming deficit as distinct from an overall phonological deficit. Referring to results unpublished at the time, Bowey (1996b) reported that with all other variables statistically controlled, letter-naming time accounted for 9 per cent of unique variation in word-reading skill in fourth- to sixth-grade children. She argued that: "In children of this age, the association between word reading and rapid letter-naming probably reflects letter-processing speed *per se* and probably reflects reciprocal causation" (p. 116). Bowey concluded that "Rapid naming may measure an ability that is largely independent of general phonological processing skills in children of this age" (p. 116). On the other hand, Landerl (2001) found a correlation between rapid automatized naming (RAN) scores and performance on a phoneme deletion task in German-speaking dyslexic children (mean age 9.3 years).

The double-deficit hypothesis predicts an additive effect on reading such that the joint presence of phonological and naming deficits leads to worse performance than is predicted by a single deficit (see Ho et al., 2002). From a statistical point of view, however, the inter-correlation between rapid naming, phonological awareness (PA) and reading skills means that a number of difficulties arise in attempting to evaluate the prediction of an additive effect (Compton, DeFries, & Olson, 2001). Nonetheless, Compton et al. (2001) tentatively suggest that "PA and RAN have an additive effect on the written language skills of children with R[eading] D[isability]" and "RAN-deficits primarily affect performance on reading tasks that require speeded/fluent response, and PA-deficits primarily affect performance on reading tasks that emphasize phonological processing skill" (p. 147).

From a genetic point of view, there is no evidence that the quantitative trait locus on chromosome 6 associated with deficits in phonological awareness and reading difficulties (see Chapter 7) also affects rapid naming (Davis, Gayán, Knopik, Smith, Cardon, Pennington, Olson, & DeFries, 2001).

Whatever the precise genetic and statistical relations, it is possible that impaired naming and a phonological deficit are both reflections of a common processing impairment, such as weak phonological representations, which has a differential impact on different aspects of reading. In any event, the precise nature of the naming difficulty in dyslexia is not yet clear and merits further attention (see Meyer et al., 1998).

ARTICULATION PROBLEMS IN DYSLEXIA

Mention was made in the previous chapter of experimental work concerned with reading and nonword repetition. As well as problems with nonword repetition, many poor readers—adults as well as children—experience problems in articulating phonemically complex or multisyllabic real words (Brady et al., 1983; Catts, 1986; Elbro et al., 1994; Miles, 1993a) even during everyday speech (Critchley, 1970; Johnson & Myklebust, 1967; Lovell, Shapton, & Warren, 1964; Miles & Miles, 1990; Rutter & Yule, 1975).

Difficulties in certain aspects of speech production have been reported in pre-readers who subsequently develop reading problems (Scarborough, 1990), school-age poor readers (Wolff, Cohen, & Drake, 1984) and college-aged dyslexics (Catts, 1989b). Korhonen (1995) found that in a small group ($n = 9$) of children with reading difficulties and deficits in rapid serial naming at the age of 9–10 years, both the naming impairment and impaired articulation persisted over a 9-year follow-up period (see also Bruck, 1992; Felton et al., 1990). It is unlikely that articulation deficits *per se* are causally related to reading (Catts, 1986; Vellutino et al., 1996) but rather serve as a marker for other phonological problems (Stanovich et al., 1988).

Speech output difficulties may reflect an impairment at the earlier input or encoding stage of establishing phonological representations. In a study by Kamhi, Catts, and Mauer (1990), reading-disabled children took longer than age-matched controls to learn to pronounce novel nonwords. Using a forced-choice recognition procedure, the poor readers were also less accurate in recognizing the novel words than were controls. Kamhi et al. suggested that encoding limitations might explain many of the problems experienced by poor readers. They argued that "innaccurate or poor quality (e.g. 'fuzzy') representations might lead to inferior performance on tasks tapping verbal short term memory, rapid naming, and phonological awareness" (p. 635). Elbro (1996) argued similarly in holding that "distinct representations will provide a less ambiguous (and thus better) input to the articulatory system" (p. 474).

Heilman, Voeller, and Alexander (1996) have extended the motor theory of speech perception expounded by Liberman and Mattingly (1985) to the development of reading, and specifically to phonological dyslexia, in what they term a motor–articulatory feedback hypothesis. In brief, the motor theory of speech perception (Liberman, Cooper, Shankweiler, & Studdert-Kennedy, 1967) holds that we perceive speech by reference to the articulatory movements that we make to produce it. Since it is possible to perceive speech while being unable to produce it, the relevant aspects of articulation are not the movements themselves but rather the neural commands that are set up in the brain to produce the "intended articulatory gestures". Given that infants perceive speech before they can produce it, the link between acoustic stimuli and these intended articulatory gestures is held to be innate.

Heilman et al. proposed that:

> The motor–articulatory feedback theory of speech perception may explain how one develops phonological awareness. According to this motor theory, the perception of spoken words is associated with the production of intended articulatory gestures . . . learning to read would involve coupling the specific articulatory gestures that are associated with specific graphemes . . . According to the articulatory feedback hypothesis, developmentally dyslexic children may be reading disabled because they are unable to spontaneously use articulatory gestures when attempting to convert graphemes to phonemes . . . and unawareness of one's articulatory gestures may also account for impaired phonological awareness.
>
> Heilman et al., 1996, pp. 409–410)

To avoid the logical difficulty that unawareness of one's intended articulatory gestures ought, in theory, to lead to a failure to perceive speech, Heilman et al. specify that in their theory "unawareness" means a "feedback failure rather than a failure to reach consciousness" and propose that "the articulatory awareness required for reading is greater than that needed for speech" (p. 411).

A neurological locus for articulation?

Apraxia of speech is a neurological disorder in programming the speech musculature to produce the correct sounds in the appropriate sequence and with appropriate timing. Patients with apraxia of speech consistently mispronounce words but know the word they want to say. Apraxia of speech is distinguished from the dysarthrias resulting from weak or paralysed muscles

performing the articulation as a result of cerebellar damage (Dronkers, 1996). On the basis of the common locus of damage in all 25 patients in a group with apraxia of speech (and spared in all of 19 patients without apraxia), Dronkers (1996) proposed that the pre-central gyrus of the insula on the left is specialized for coordination of speech articulation. Her view is supported by the findings of a positron emission tomography (PET) study, which found that repetition of single words strongly activated this region (plus left premotor cortex and the basal ganglia on the left) in comparison with control conditions (Wise, Greene, Büchel, & Scott, 1999).

It is tempting to speculate that the anterior insular region might be found defective in at least some dyslexics. Paulesu et al. (1996) found in their PET study that, in comparison with controls, the left insula of five well-compensated adult dyslexics was under-activated during tasks involving rhyme recognition and verbal short-term memory. During the latter task, individuals were specifically instructed to rehearse the stimuli silently. Presumaby, this involves some measure of subvocal articulation. However, it is not reported whether the dyslexic participants experienced articulatory difficulties in their everyday speech.

A deficit in rapid naming or articulation may be part of a more widespread difficulty in language processing. Before being taught to read and write, young children are already fluent speakers with a large vocabulary and a great deal of implicit knowledge about spoken language. Literacy skills are, as it were, grafted on to, or parasitic upon, this knowledge base. It follows that an impairment in the speech-processing system has the potential to interfere with or impede the acquisition of reading and spelling skills (see Stackhouse & Wells, 1997).

DEVELOPMENTAL LANGUAGE DELAY (SPECIFIC LANGUAGE IMPAIRMENT) AND DYSLEXIA

Some delay or difficulty in language development appears to be quite frequent among dyslexic children (Critchley, 1970; Ingram & Mason, 1965; Kinsbourne & Warrington, 1963; Miles, 1993b; Naidoo, 1972; Rutter & Yule, 1975; Thomas, 1905). According to Ingram and Mason (1965), about one-half of "patients" with specific developmental dyslexia and dysgraphia have a history of slow speech development. Critchley (1970) reported: "In my series of 125 children presented [*sic*] with reading or spelling problems, 41 had been late in the acquisition of speech. Besides late development of speech, and imperfections in articulation, there may also be demonstrable at times an immaturity of the faculty of *language* as opposed to speech. Thus inadequacies in syntax and in vocabulary may at times be discerned" (p. 81, emphasis in original). More recently, Gallagher, Frith, and Snowling (2000) retrospectively analysed the pre-school language development of a group of 6-year-olds whose literacy development was delayed. The results suggested that these children (all from families with at least one dyslexic member) had experienced at least some "mild delay in all aspects of spoken language" (p. 210). Among those subsequently classified as dyslexic, language impairments were found at age 8 years (Snowling, Gallagher, & Frith, 2003).

As well as dyslexic children frequently having a history of language delay, those diagnosed as having developmental language disorder often show difficulties in the realm of literacy. Tallal, Miller, and Fitch (1995) maintain that "the vast majority" of pre-school children diagnosed as having developmental language delay or disorder "exhibit inordinate difficulty learning to read" (p. 202). Certainly, such children frequently (e.g. Catts, 1993; Ingram, 1963) have difficulties learning to read and spell but it is by no means invariably the case (Bishop & Adams, 1990). Recent research suggests that there may be a heritable type of specific language impairment linked to reading disability (Bishop, 2001).

Exactly what aspects of impaired speech or language processing may have an impact on literacy attainment is a matter for empirical enquiry, since not every child with a speech-processing impairment becomes a poor reader and speller and the interaction between different component skills changes over time (Snowling, 2000b).

Research by Stackhouse and her colleagues (see also Bishop & Robson, 1989; Bishop & Adams, 1990) has suggested that 4- to 5-year-old children who have difficulties with speech output alone are less likely to have problems with later reading and spelling than are children who also have deficits in other aspects of language, such as speech comprehension, sentence recall or grammar (Stackhouse, 2000). This does not isolate the cause(s) of poor reading among speech- and language-impaired children but it does suggest that attention needs to be paid to a range of speech- and language-processing skills within a developmental perspective. The effect of individual weaknesses may show up at different stages in children's developmental trajectories.

Congenital or developmental aphasia (see Broadbent, 1872; Zangwill, 1978), now known as specific language impairment, refers to unusual difficulty or slowness in acquiring language. The term embraces a wide variety of developmental language problems that are addressed in a series of papers brought together by Bishop and Leonard (2000). Definitional issues (and a great deal more) are discussed in the excellent text by Bishop (1997).

In a series of articles collected under the title *Developmental Dysphasia* and edited by Wyke (1978) there is, with the exception of one article, hardly any mention of developmental dyslexia, although Menyuk suggests that it might be "a concomitant problem of children with developmental dysphasia since the reading acquisition process presumably entails unconscious awareness of linguistic categories and relations" (p. 155). The exception is the contribution by Zangwill. In his introductory chapter, it is difficult to discern whether Zangwill is thinking of dyslexia and dysphasia as being one and the same disorder or whether he is thinking of them as distinct nosological entities. In discussing a case described by the celebrated neurologist Henry Head, Zangwill writes: "This is a relatively mild case of developmental dysphasia in an intelligent adult in whom the principal difficulties were mainly, though not exclusively, confined to writing and spelling. Today it might be classified as developmental dyslexia rather than dysphasia" (p. 4).

Zangwill (1978) presents two other cases chosen, he tells us, to illustrate the familial incidence of developmental language disorders and "the links between slow speech development in childhood and difficulties in reading and writing later on" (p. 4). In the absence of conspicuous speech difficulty, both cases would undoubtedly be classified today as severely dyslexic. More recent research confirms an association within families between speech disorders and dyslexia. Lewis (1992) compared the familiy pedigrees of children with pre-school moderate to severe phonological/articulation disorder. She found significantly more dyslexic members were reported in the families of these children than in the families of children without phonological disorder.

The heritability of language and language disorder

Adoption (Felsenfeld & Plomin, 1997) and twin studies strongly suggest that there is a heritable component to specific developmental speech and language disorders (for reviews, see Stromswold, 1998, 2001). The probandwise concordance rate for monozygotic twins is higher than that for dizygotic twins (Bishop, Bishop, Bright, James, Delaney & Tallal, 1999a; Bishop, North & Donlan, 1995; Lewis & Thompson, 1992; Tomblin & Buckwalter, 1998), the exact values differing, of course, with the measure of speech or language function that is used.

Gopnik (1990) and Gopnik and Crago (1991) studied a British family with specific language impairment and tentatively suggested that there might be a single gene responsible for acquisition of certain morphological rules (but see Watkins, Dronkers, & Vargha-Khadem, 2002a). On the basis of the family pedigree, a single autosomal dominant gene with full penetrance has been implicated in the language disorder seen in affected members of the KE family. This has been localized to a specific region (7q31) on chromosome 7 (Fisher, Vargha-Khadem, Watkins, Monaco, & Pembret, 1998; Lai, Fisher, Hurst, Vargha-Khadem, & Monaco, 2001). However, Cholfin, Curtiss, Shields, Kornblum, and Geschwind (2000) reported that in a family whose

language disorder is similar to that of the KE family, there was no evidence of linkage to 7q31 (see also Bartlett et al., 2000). Other authors (e.g. Tallal et al., 1996) have suggested that rather than implicating genes specifically for grammar, the defects seen in developmental language impairment reflect a problem located further "upstream", such as poor discrimination of speech sounds, which impairs the acquisition of normal grammatical competence.

In general, evidence of a genetic contribution to an impaired function (or set of functions) such as specific language impairment is not evidence of an equivalent (or indeed any) genetic contribution to the normal range of variation in that function or set of functions (such as language development). Tomblin and Buckwalter (1998) compared monozygotic and dizygotic twins in which at least one member of each pair was specifically language impaired. Their results suggested that heritability of language scores from the general population was similar to heritability of poor language scores and that the heritability of language disorder is not simply a consequence of heritability of low levels of cognitive ability. However, heritability of developmental language disorder does not necessarily imply an equal heritability of normal language. It has been shown (using a different measure of language ability and with many more participants) that language delay at 2 years of age (indexed by vocabulary score) is highly heritable—meaning that there is a strong genetic influence—and much more so than individual differences in language ability in the range of scores considered normal. Furthermore, shared environmental influences are much more important for normal language ability than for language delay (Dale et al., 1998). However, this should not be construed to mean that there is no genetic influence on normal language development.

Evidence in relation to this issue was reviewed recently by Stromswold (2001). She concluded that "most genes responsible for language delay will not be associated with individual differences in normal language ability" (p. 327). On the other hand, she also argued that "specific-to-language genetic factors play a substantial role in the variation in linguistic abilities among both people who suffer from language disorders and those who do not" (p. 705). The relationship, however, is not simple. As Stromswold (2001) pointed out, children who are genetically at risk for developing language disorders may be "particularly sensitive to subtly impoverished linguistic environments" (p. 690). Stromswold (2001) calculated that "Genetic factors seem to account for more of the linguistic variance among language-disabled people than among normal people" (p. 688). As Tomblin and Buckwalter (1998) put it: "The path of genetic influence on language is no doubt long and complex and the mechanisms interposed between gene expression and language achievement may bear on many behavior domains, some of which may be principally involved in language and others more generally related to learning and behavior" (p.197). Even within the realm of language itself, different aspects may be under greater genetic control than others (see Bishop et al., 1995).

Is there a continuum of disorder between specific language impairment and dyslexia?

Although developmental dysphasia is apparent at a much earlier stage of development than is developmental dyslexia (Tallal & Piercy, 1978), specific language impairment and specific reading disability may lie on a continuum of linguistic deficit (Bishop & Adams, 1990; Gathercole & Baddeley, 1987; Kamhi, 1992; Stanovich, 1989, 1994b; Tallal, Allard, Miller, & Curtiss, 1997). Indeed, according to Gallagher et al. (2000), "It is now widely held that dyslexia is on a continuum with language disorders" (p. 203) and Stromswold (2001) argued that "Genetic studies also suggest that dyslexia and SLI [specific language impairment] are related" (p. 682). The idea is not new, having been proposed in Denmark 60 years ago (see Hermann, 1959, p. 133). However, specific language impairment and developmental dyslexia may be characterized by different cognitive profiles. Children with delayed language development may show poor reading comprehension in comparison with reading accuracy, whereas children classified as dyslexic tend to have poor word

decoding skills but relatively good comprehension (Bishop & Adams, 1990).

The severity hypothesis

One view of the relationship between specific language impairment (SLI) and dyslexia is that the two conditions reflect qualitatively similar impairments but differ in severity—the severity hypothesis. Children with either disorder have the same impairment in reading but those with a diagnosis of SLI have more severe spoken language difficulties than those diagnosed as dyslexic. That is to say, dyslexia is a less severe form of SLI.

Although developmental dyslexia was first studied within an aphasiological context, Critchley maintained that:

> There are weighty objections to the concept of developmental dyslexia as a fragment of congenital "aphasia". The idea is a specious one which must be scrutinized with caution. In the first place we know very little about the nature of the so-called congenital "aphasia". It would be better to speak in terms of a mere comparison with cases of loss of language in the adult or older child, and not to try and exalt an analogy to the status of a hypothesis. The comparison has a certain utilitarian merit, but no more.
>
> (Critchley, 1970, p. 104)

The severity hypothesis was distinguished recently from the idea that both conditions are associated with reading impairment but the impairment is due to different underlying mechanisms. On this view, there is a qualitative difference between dyslexia and SLI. To examine this issue, Snowling et al. (2000) tested a group of 15- to 16-year-olds who as children at the age of 4 years had been diagnosed as having SLI (Bishop & Edmundson, 1987) and at 15 years of age "had impairments in all aspects of spoken language functioning" (p. 590). On average, these adolescents were found to be significantly poorer than age-matched controls in reading accuracy, especially those SLI adolescents whose performance IQ was less than 100. Although there was a significant mean difference in non-verbal (as well as verbal) ability between the groups, the reading deficit of the SLI group could not be attributed to this factor, since differences in mean scores and incidence of literacy problems between the SLI and control children remained after taking this factor into account in a series of regression analyses.

In terms of the severity hypothesis, Snowling et al. argued:

> Our findings lead us to reject this hypothesis. While dyslexic children typically have problems with the development of decoding skills from the outset of learning to read, the tendency observed in the present sample of SLI children was for basic decoding skills to develop normally in the early years, with a relative decline in word recognition skills subsequently. For dyslexic children with good language skills, compensation for the reading impairment is usually possible ... but spelling difficulties are a residual sign of impairment. The developmental trajectory observed among the SLI children was quite different; reading difficulties became more marked with increasing age, and spelling levels, though also declining, did so [sic] less than reading levels. Furthermore, SLI children with PIQs [performance IQs] above 100 had spelling levels that were average for their age. Taken together, these findings provide unequivocal evidence that the developmental course of the two disorders is different. This argues against the hypothesis that dyslexia is a mild form of SLI, emerging when the language difficulties that cause concern in the pre-school years have resolved.
>
> (Snowling et al., 2000, p. 596)

A subset of the SLI group, who as 4-year-olds had isolated phonological impairments, were found to be normal readers as adolescents, contrary to the prediction that those with phonological impairments would turn out to be dyslexic. These young people did, however, exhibit significantly poorer phonological skills, as measured by tests of nonword repetition and spoonerisms, than controls and their nonword reading was relatively weak (though not significantly worse than that of controls). Snowling et al. (2000) point out that "The cognitive similarity between these children and those classically defined as dyslexic is striking" (p. 597). That being so, one may ask how these individuals have managed to avoid becoming frankly dyslexic. The suggestion that Snowling et al. make (see also Snowling et al., 2003) is that phonological deficits can be compensated for provided that vocabulary and other oral language skills, including syntactic and semantic abilities, develop sufficiently to provide textual aid, which, in turn, will help recognition of long or irregularly spelled words. If they do not, then young children with poor phonological abilities will fall further and further behind their peers.

Snowling et al. point out that:

> The relationship between dyslexia and SLI turns on the diagnostic criteria used ... To avoid the definitional issues surrounding the relationship between SLI and dyslexia, we suggest that a more productive way forward is to consider the child with a history of language impairment to be at risk of literacy difficulties in terms of the cognitive processes required for learning to read ... Children whose phonological impairments persist to the age of 5½ are at greater risk ... However, normal reading progress cannot be assured for children who make a good start with decoding skills. As the range of written vocabulary they encounter increases, and the texts which they read become more demanding linguistically, children with a history of SLI remain at risk of reading problems because of the contribution of syntactic, semantic, and pragmatic language skills to the development of literacy.
>
> (Snowling et al., 2000, pp. 597, 598)

The approach advocated by Snowling and her colleagues seems to me to be a useful way of looking at the relationship between dyslexia and other developmental problems of speech and language. It bypasses the theoretical issue but addresses the practical problem of children who fail to learn to read whatever label might be attached to them. Certainly, it seems from the research reviewed in this chapter that the speech-related difficulties of dyslexics are widespread rather than evident only in the task of oral (or silent) reading. Whether one chooses to lump or split dyslexia and SLI may turn out to be a less interesting question than addressing what factors cause one child to become specifically language impaired and another to be "only" dyslexic. The causal factors may overlap or they may be independent.

In an extension of the study of children at risk of dyslexia reported by Snowling et al. (2000), participants were classified into those who were considered dyslexic (n = 37) at age 8 years and those (n = 19) who were not (Snowling et al., 2003). The two sub-groups differed not only on measures of literacy but also on a number of oral language measures. At age 6 years, the non-dyslexic children had been impaired relative to controls in grapheme-phoneme decoding skills and had shown significant deficits in digit span and in rhyme-oddity detection but had had good oral language skills. This might be what enabled them to avoid becoming poor readers, assuming that at least some of the non-impaired group inherited a biological risk factor. Snowling and her colleagues suggested that "the better vocabulary of high-risk unimpaired children may facilitate the development of segmental [phonological] representations and therefore phoneme awareness. In turn, good phonemic skills may have gone some way toward protecting them from the reading failure that might have been expected given their poor grapheme-phoneme skills" (p. 370). Conversely, the poor oral language skills of dyslexic children might not have enabled them to compensate for poor grapheme-phoneme decoding abilty.

The difficulties experienced by dyslexic children are not related only to problems of speech output but, as the following chapter will show, to difficulties with speech input and non-motor output.

6

Auditory Perception, the Temporal Processing Deficit Hypothesis and Motor Skills

It is possible that poor phonological awareness and/or weak or insecure phonological representations in memory are a reflection of faulty speech perception processes (Godfrey, Syrdal-Lasky, Millay, & Knox, 1981; Watson & Miller, 1993). Correlations between speech perception scores and phonological awareness or phonological memory as measured by, for example, phoneme segmentation and digit span (Watson & Miller, 1993) or naming ability (McBride-Chang, 1996) have been reported by several workers (Hurford, 1991; Manis et al., 1997; McBride-Chang, 1995). However, to demonstrate a relationship between speech perception and phonological awareness does not establish that problems in speech perception are causally related to reading difficulties. However, since certain perceptual aspects of speech are important in developing phonemic awareness (Yavas & Gogate, 1999), it would not be surprising to find that reading ability is related to speech perception.

SPEECH PERCEPTION AND READING DIFICULTIES

The idea that reading difficulties may stem from speech perception problems is not new. Ingram (1963) believed that "difficulties in auditory discrimination or in the synthesis of spoken words are more important causes of reading retardation than visuo-spatial difficulties" (p. 200), and Shankweiler et al. (1979) proposed that "the possibility needs examination that subtle deficits might be demonstrated by children with reading disabilities in their perception of the acoustic cues for speech" (p. 543). Deficits among young dyslexics in discriminating between pairs of CV (consonant–vowel) syllables were reported by Hurford and Sanders (1990). These workers reported that training in making phonemic discriminations led to an improvement in performance on the task. No improvement in phonemic discrimination was observed after training with non-speech stimuli, but Hurford and Sanders (1990) did not assess whether an improvement in phonemic discrimination led to better reading. Without special training there may be little or no spontaneous improvement in discrimination ability. Cornelissen et al. (1996) found that 10 adult dyslexics were slower to respond, and made significantly more confusion errors between /pa/ and /fa/ and between /tʃa/ and / ʃa/, than matched controls, suggesting that the deficit is persistent.

It may be only very subtle deficits in speech perception which underpin some disabled readers' phonological problems (Mody, Studdert-Kennedy, & Brady, 1997) and hence (arguably) their word decoding difficulties. Such deficits are likely to require careful techniques for their detection. Tests of basic auditory discrimination ability, as assessed by tasks such as minimal-pairs word or nonword discrimination (in which participants have to indicate whether two sounds are the same or different), are not always sufficiently sensitive to differentiate between disabled readers and controls. Even using a rather more complex testing procedure than simple discrimination, Shapiro, Nix, and Foster (1990) failed to find any difference between aged-matched groups of different reading ability (as defined by a test of reading comprehension).

A deficit in speech perception may be more readily detected under conditions of irrelevant noise than under normal circumstances (but see Pennington et al., 1990). A difference between disabled and average readers on a speech (CVC) discrimination task (but not on a comparable auditory non-verbal task) was found by Brady et al. (1983) only under noisy listening conditions, although Snowling et al. (1986a) found that in repeating words and nonwords dyslexic children were no more influenced by the presence of noise than were age-matched and reading-level-matched controls.

Categorical speech perception in dyslexia

During the production of voiced sounds, such as /ba/, the vocal cords vibrate immediately the sound is released at the lips. In the case of unvoiced sounds such as /pa/, the vocal cords vibrate after a short delay. The duration between the release of air at the lips and vibration of the vocal cords is known as the voice-onset time; it is an important cue in speech perception. Using a synthetic speech synthesizer, it is possible to study how sounds with different voice-onset times are perceived. Presentation of a sound with a zero-millisecond voice-onset time leads to the perception of /ba/, but with a 40 msec voice-onset time people report hearing /pa/. At intermediate voice-onset times, individuals report hearing one or other sound, not something in between. This is referred to as categorical perception.

Brandt and Rosen (1980) compared 12 dyslexic and four normal readers aged 8–12 years on identification and discrimination of synthetic (computer-produced) consonant–vowel speech stimuli. They reported that the dyslexic children were "not markedly impaired in their ability to extract and encode phonetic information from speech syllables. On both the VOT [voice-onset time] continuum and the more highly abstracted place of articulation series, these children labeled and discriminated the speech sounds very much like normal-reading children and adults" (p. 335). However, "the dyslexic group produced somewhat flatter discrimination functions than expected [which] may, in fact, reflect a *less* categorical (i.e. less phonemically based) perceptual system than in the normal-reading group" (p. 336, emphasis in original).

A very similar investigation was carried out with 17 dyslexic and 17 control children by Godfrey et al. (1981), but they carried out more sophisticated analyses of their data than did Brandt and Rosen. While the results of the two studies were in many respects comparable, Godfrey et al. (1981) were able to demonstrate statistically significant differences between dyslexic and control readers. Both groups showed categorical perception of speech stimuli but "dyslexic children were less consistent in their classification of stimuli and changed more gradually from one phonetic category to another than normal children. The dyslexic group did not discriminate between syllables from different phonetic categories as well as the control group did" (pp. 418–419). Children classified in terms of Boder's distinction (see Chapter 4) between "dysphon-etic" and "dyseidetic" dyslexics did not differ in terms of their speech perception performance; the two groups performed similarly and both differed significantly from the control group.

While emphasizing that the dyslexics' performance on the tests of identification and discrimination of speech stimuli was not abnormal, Godfrey et al. explained what they felt to be the implication of the children's less categorical speech perception (see also Reed, 1989) in the following terms:

> Inconsistency in phonetic categorization might affect the dyslexics' ability to learn through the formation of inadequate long-term representations of phonetic units. Any such abnormality in the long-term stored "image" could be expected to adversely affect reading processes that involve the transformation of script to phonetic units of speech, as well as the ordering and combining of those units that make up words.
>
> (Godfrey et al., 1981, p. 420)

Thus inconsistent categorical boundaries might interfere with the establishment of stable representations of phonemes in long-term memory and contribute to the reading problems experienced by dyslexics.

Werker and Tees (1987) compared 14 disabled readers aged 8–14 years with 14 age-matched controls on four tasks designed to assess categorical speech perception. Their results showed that speech perception in the disabled readers was significantly less categorical than in the control readers. That is, the boundaries between different phonetic boundaries were less sharp in the disabled readers. On the basis of this and other findings, Werker and Tees proposed that disabled readers "could not access underlying abstract phonological categories and, instead, had to rely on sensorimotor (articulatory) representation of the sound/symbol correspondence". They stated that "more research is required to determine whether this less stable phonological representation is caused by a primary perceptual deficit. . .or is the result of other subtle language

difficulties resulting in lack of boundary sharpening" (p. 60).

Categorical perception, phoneme awareness and phonological decoding

The findings discussed above converge on the conclusion that categorical boundaries between different speech sounds are less distinct in people with dyslexia who may thus confuse phonetically similar sounds more readily than non-dyslexic persons. However, the findings that dyslexics as a group show flatter phoneme identification functions (less categorical perception) obscures the possibility that only certain dyslexic individuals show this effect. Manis et al. (1997) found that while most dyslexics in their study had normal phoneme identification functions, a sub-group of seven from the total of 25 dyslexics had significantly flatter functions than either age-matched or reading level-matched controls. Five of these seven school students belonged to a group of dyslexics labelled low in phonological awareness, whereas the remaining two were from a high-awareness group. Most of the low-awareness group had normal phoneme identification functions. Thus less categorical speech perception is not an inevitable correlate of low phonological awareness; nor does a high level of awareness necessarily protect against it.

Quite what determines whether speech perception will be normal or less categorical in individual cases remains to be established. The importance attaching to this derives from the possibility that there is a causal connection between less categorical perception of speech sounds and phonemic awareness. This, in turn, might be expected to influence the ease of learning the correspondences between graphemes and phonemes. As Manis et al. (1997) put it: "The basic argument is that children who do not perceive clear distinctions between phonemes may not form readily accessible long-term memory representations of these phonemes. This would lead in turn to difficulties in segmenting and manipulating phonemes, and in learning grapheme–phoneme mappings" (p. 231). Alternatively, less clear distinctions between phonemes may mean less well-specified phonological representations.

In a study of two adult phonological dyslexics and a group of 20 developmental dyslexic individuals aged 10–14 years, Masterson, Hazan, and Wijayatilake (1995) showed that phonemic discrimination problems were associated with difficulties in reading nonwords. Both adults and five of the six young dyslexics had problems in discriminating between pairs of auditorily presented monosyllabic words as "same" or "different". These same individuals made errors in reading nonwords, although the adults, at least, were said to be good at reading real words. (Only mean real word reading scores are given for the younger dyslexics.) Masterson et al. (1995) suggested that auditory perceptual (phonemic) problems lead to failure to acquire alphabetic strategies of reading in general and that this leaves individuals who have such problems with only a "primitive capacity" for non-lexical processing. However, as with phonological awareness, only longitudinal studies, allied to training studies, can show convincingly that deficits in the perception of speech underlie the difficulty in learning to read.

What might determine whether or not an individual shows an unusual phoneme identification (or discrimination) function? One factor might be reading itself. As discussed above, there is evidence in children of a reciprocal relationship between reading and phonemic awareness (Cataldo & Ellis, 1988; Ellis & Large, 1987) and it is well known that adults who have never learned to read (Bertelson et al., 1989; Morais et al., 1979; Morais, Alegria, & Content, 1987), as well as those whose script is not alphabetic (Mann, 1986; Read et al., 1986), are less proficient in manipulating phonemes than are those who have experience with an alphabetic script. In short, "Writing systems create the categories in terms of which we become conscious of speech" (Olson, 1996, p. 100).

Of the studies referred to above, the possibility that reading experience might affect categorical perception was considered only by Godfrey et al. (1981), who noted that their findings showing a relation between reading ability and performance on certain speech perception tasks were correlational rather than causal in nature. They entertained the possibility that "learning to read causes

the child to create or refine his or her mental abstraction of a phoneme, and failure to read may therefore result in poorer performance on auditory speech perception tasks" (p. 421). Godfrey et al. pointed out that comparing dyslexic children with a reading-age level control group as well as a group matched for chronological age would help to tease out the causal relationships involved.

Even if reading is mastered to some degree, it may be the case that phonemic perception remains faulty or imprecise. Steffens, Eilers, Gross-Glenn, and Jallad (1992) found evidence of less sharp phonetic boundaries in a group of adult "compensated" dyslexics, dyslexic men tending to deviate more than dyslexic women from the performance of the normal-reading groups. These authors concluded that "dyslexic subjects lack the degree of precision demonstrated by normal readers in laboratory tests of speech identification and discrimination" (p. 199). At the same time, they emphasized the heterogeneous nature of performance within their group of dyslexics.

In a group of 13 reading-disabled children, Adlard and Hazan (1998) found that a sub-group of four children with poor phoneme discrimination performance had particularly poor nonword reading scores. There was only one child with poor phoneme discrimination in the group of 24 controls. The group of reading-disabled children as a whole scored significantly more poorly on nonword reading (and repetition of nonwords longer than two syllables) than either reading-age or chronological-age controls. The sub-group showing what Adlard and Hazan termed "perceptual weakness" did not differ from the remaining reading-disabled children on any of four nonspeech psycho-acoustic tasks, but did have a higher mean nonword error score than the others. These remaining children had no difficulties in speech perception, suggesting that only a relatively small proportion of disabled readers have perceptual problems of this kind.

Among the "perceptual weakness" group, one child had a history of intermittent hearing loss, compared with two children from the remaining nine of the reading disabled group who did not show particularly poor phoneme discrimination performance. Comparable data are not given for the control groups. Masterson et al. (1995) noted that the two adult dyslexics whom they tested had a childhood history of hearing loss and "a large number of the dyslexics in the group study had a history of middle ear infection" (p. 252). The literature on the relationship between intermittent hearing loss and language ability (Bishop & Edmundson, 1986; Klein & Rapin, 1993), including reading and spelling (Klein & Rapin, 1993), is inconclusive and it would be interesting to examine more closely whether, and if so in what circumstances, hearing loss leads to perceptual discrimination problems.

ELECTROPHYSIOLOGICAL INDICES OF AUDITORY PROCESSING IMPAIRMENT IN DYSLEXIA

As well as impaired phoneme discrimination ability, other kinds of auditory processing impairment in some dyslexic people have been demonstrated using electrophysiological techniques. Twenty adult dyslexic participants were found by Menell, McAnally, and Stein (1999) to be less sensitive as a group to amplitude changes in acoustic stimuli than 20 control participants. The dyslexics also showed reduced auditory-evoked potentials measured at the scalp. The electrophysiological and psychophysical measures correlated positively and significantly. Performance on the psychophysical task also correlated positively and significantly with reading ability. All participants had their hearing checked and were said to have thresholds of 15 dB or better. Menell et al. concluded that "Because AM [amplitude modulation] in speech is important for its intelligibility, the insensitivity of dyslexic listeners to AM is likely to impair their identification of speech" (p. 802).

An electrophysiological paradigm was also used by Schulte-Körne, Deimel, Bartling, and Remschmidt (1998) to determine whether poor readers and spellers (screened to exclude those with any middle ear infection within the week

prior to testing) differed from age-matched controls in what is known as mismatch-negativity (MMN). This is a component of the event-related potential (ERP) recorded from the scalp that occurs in response to a change occurring in a sequence of repetitive auditory stimuli. Schulte-Körne et al. (1998) presented speech stimuli consisting of a series of sounds (/da/) among which a different sound (/ba/) was occasionally presented (an "odd-ball" passive discrimination task). The results showed that over the fronto-central regions of the brain, the group of 19 poor spellers/readers (mean age 12.5 years) had an attenuated MMN (measured as area under the averaged curves) for speech stimuli but not for non-speech stimuli (pure tones) in comparison with 15 control readers. This result converges with that of a PET study showing that, in comparison with controls, a group of 15 dyslexics had reduced activation in right fronto-temporal (but not left temporal) areas in response to a task requiring them to listen to a pair of tone sequences and decide whether they were identical (Rumsey, Andreason, Zametkin, King, Hamburger, Aquino, Hanahan, Pikus, & Cohen 1994a).

The MMN is thought to index pre-attentive processing and thus group differences in MMN are considered unlikely to result from attention or motivation. Schulte-Körne et al. (1998) believed their results to be consistent with other research showing deficits in phoneme perception and that their results "suggest that the deficits in pre-attentive speech processing can be considered a cause of dyslexia" (p. 340). Their study, however, was correlational in nature; a longitudinal study with pre-readers would, if their results were replicated, be more convincing evidence. There is also the possibility that their results with speech stimuli are a reflection of experience or skill in reading rather than a cause of reading difficulties. Moreover, the findings reported refer to group averages—Schulte-Körne et al. did not relate their electrophysiological results to reading or spelling scores to assess the relationship between these two variables within individuals or sub-groups of poor spellers/readers.

The MMN paradigm was used in a study of eight adult dyslexic participants by Kujala,

Myllyviita, Tervaniemi, Alho, Kallio, and Näätänen (2000). There were two conditions. In one condition a pattern of four tones was presented (pattern condition) and in the other condition pairs of tones (tone-pair condition) were presented. In the standard trials of the pattern condition, the four tones were presented with silent intervals of 200, 150 and 50 msec between them. In the deviant trials, the tones were presented at intervals of 200, 50 and 150 msec. In the tone-pair condition, the interval between the members of each pair was 150 msec in standard trials and 50 msec in deviant trials. It was found that at latencies of 400–450 msec, the MMN response distinguished the dyslexic participants from controls only in the pattern condition. Whereas the controls showed two consecutive MMN responses in the deviant trials, the dyslexics did not. Kujala et al. argued that "In dyslexic subjects, only the second MMN was elicited, suggesting that their auditory cortex discriminated the second but not the first change . . . These results suggest that dyslexic adults have problems in discriminating temporal sound features that are surrounded by other sounds (cf. phonemes) in words" (p. 265). Because the stimuli used were pure tones, the findings were interpreted by Kujala and colleagues as demonstrating a basic auditory processing defect, as opposed to a linguistic defect, in dyslexic adults.

Given that the MMN paradigm is regarded as an index of pre-attentive processing, it offers the promise of the early detection of possible speech-related problems that may impinge upon literacy acquisition. It has been used with infants from Finnish families in which at least one parent is dyslexic. Preliminary results from 18 6-month-old children compared with 17 controls show differences between the groups in the difference waveforms (the response to the standard stimulus subtracted from that to the deviant stimulus) recorded from the scalp (Leppänen & Lyytinen, 1997). Although it remains to be shown that the difference is predictive of literacy or language-related problems, this finding indicates the potential utility of the technique for the early identification of children at risk of dyslexia (see also Molfese, 2000). It needs to be appreciated, however, that anomalies of MMN responses are not restricted to dyslexic participants but have been reported to occur in children from a range of diagnostic categories including learning disability and attention deficit disorder (Bradlow et al., 1999; Kraus, McGee, Carrell, Zecker, Nicol, & Koch, 1996).

Many auditory discrimination and identification tasks require participants to compare a current stimulus with one held in memory or to compare two stimuli presented one at a time. In the case of the latter, the response requirement is often to indicate which stimulus came first. To operate effectively in the course of daily life, it is clearly of fundamental importance to perceive and remember the temporal order of occurrence of all kinds of events—auditory, visual or otherwise. This ability is held by some to depend especially upon the "speech-dominant" (Efron, 1963a, 1963b) or left cerebral hemisphere (Carmon & Nachshon, 1971; Goldman, Lodge, Hammer, Semmes, & Mishkin, 1968; Leek & Brandt, 1983; Mills & Rollman, 1979, 1980; Natale, 1977; Nicholls, 1996; Robinson & Solomon, 1974; Swisher & Hirsh, 1972), especially the left temporal lobe (Sherwin & Efron, 1980).

The question of how events are remembered and behaviour is organized in the correct temporal sequence has exercised many minds since Lashley wrote his celebrated monograph on serial order in behaviour (Lashley, 1951). Current contributions to thinking in the area include those of Brown, Preece, and Hulme (2000), Burgess and Hitch (1999) and Carpenter, Georgopoulos, and Pellizzer (1999). It is part of the "folklore" surrounding dyslexia that dyslexics have a particular difficulty in dealing with the correct sequential or temporal order of events. Hermann (1959) argued that what he termed "directional function" applied as much to chronological sequences as to spatial arrangements and that "Spatial arrangement and sequence are probably identical phenomena" (p. 146).

Although words are arranged spatially on a page, the position of the words, and at least sometimes that of their constituent letters, has to be computed from sequential visual fixations (Eden, Stein, Wood, & Wood, 1995a). Therefore, a reader must, at some level and in some cognitive code or another, maintain a representation of the serial order of the visual stimuli on which she or he has fixated. However, reading involves not only the eyes but an inner voice or ear. It is probable that an initial visual representation is recoded into an acoustic or articulatory code. As Bakker (1970) stated succinctly, "During reading a spatially ordered, visual configuration is transformed into a temporally ordered, auditory pattern" (p. 81).

TEMPORAL ORDER AND READING

During the 1960s, several researchers studied the ability of children to match a series of temporally ordered visual (Bakker, 1967) or auditory stimuli with a spatially ordered visual series. The seminal study was that of Birch and Belmont (1964), who presented a sequence of taps separated by intervals of 0.5 or 1 sec that had to be matched to a visual pattern of dots separated by small and large spaces. Children who were poor readers performed less well than control readers. Subsequently, Birch and Belmont (1965) reported that performance on an auditory–visual (crossmodal) matching task varied with level of reading "readiness" and with intelligence but this was not partialled out statistically.

Bryden (1972) pointed out that "The studies of Birch and Belmont do not permit one to determine whether poor readers have difficulty with crossmodal transfer, the temporal arrangement, or both" (p. 825). In his own study, Bryden showed that poor readers were impaired relative to age- and IQ-matched controls on same–different tasks that did not involve matching across sensory modalities (as well as those that did). He therefore concluded that, "The failing of poor readers, extending as it does to tasks involving both auditory and visual presentation, and both sequential and spatial patterns, must be an even more general one" (p. 831), which he thought might involve verbal coding. More recently, using a design involving sequential presentation of auditory and visual patterns, Rose, Feldman, Jankowski, and Futterweit (1999) confirmed that poor readers are impaired on intramodal as well as cross-modal temporal matching tasks. This is not to say, however, that performance on the two types of task is equivalent. In a recent study of Finnish dyslexic children, Laasonen, Tomma-Halme, Lahti-Nuuttila, Service, and Virsu (2000) presented auditory, visual and tactile stimuli in tasks requiring the participants to state whether or not two series of stimuli occurred simultaneously. It was found that the dyslexics' performance on cross-modal temporal judgement tasks was comparatively worse than on intramodal tasks.

In a comparatively early study, Bakker (1970) presented above-average and below-average readers with a series of stimuli in different sensory modalities. The stimulus items were each presented for 2 sec with an inter-stimulus interval of 4 sec. The items could be readily named (verbalized) in one condition but not in the other. The participants' task was to indicate which item they had seen—first, second, third and so on. The results revealed differences between the two reading level groups only for the readily labelled stimuli, leading Bakker to the idea that "the perception and retention of temporal order is related to the reading and speech process" (p. 94). However, Liberman (1993) expressed the view that "There must, of course, be temporal processes that serve the visual aspects of reading ... but it seems unlikely that these bear any relation to the temporal processes of speech" (p. 270).

On the basis of an experiment requiring reproduction of a sequence of taps on wooden blocks or repeating a sequence of digits, Corkin (1974) suggested that "reading disorders in children may grow out of a more general deficit in serial organization that cuts across sensory modalities and stimulus materials" (p. 353). Surprisingly, Corkin did not cite Bakker's work despite the obvious similarities between the two investigations. In any event, what seems indicated by both studies is that, however it is described, there is a close relationship between accuracy of recall of a sequence of events and level of reading proficiency.

A number of authors, then, have found poor readers to be less able than average or good readers to remember the serial order of events whatever the modality of stimulus presentation (Bakker, 1970; Corkin, 1974). This ability is sometimes referred to as perception or judgement of temporal order. However, as inferior performance by poor readers was often (e.g. Corkin, 1974) dependent upon a time interval being interposed between presentation and a recall attempt, *memory* for temporal order might be a more appropriate term in some circumstances. Certainly, it is not clear from some of the earlier studies (e.g. Bakker, 1967; Zurif & Carson, 1970) whether deficits distinguishing different groups of readers were due to memory requirements (that is, to a problem of memory for temporal order) or to a more perceptual level of impairment (Carmon & Nachshon, 1971; Eden et al., 1995b).

In a more recent study, May, Williams, and Dunlap (1988) presented participants tachistoscopically (100 msec) with two words, *box* and *fox*, separated by a very short interval of time. The words were presented in two of four positions (up, down, left, right). The task in one condition was to say which word had appeared first and in the other condition to indicate the position of the first word. The briefest time interval between the two words required to achieve 75 per cent correct performance was measured. In both conditions, poor readers aged 8–10 years required significantly longer between words than did good readers of the same age. The mean temporal order judgement (TOJ) thresholds varied between approximately 40 and 50 msec for good readers and approximately 60 and 80 msec for poor readers. A group of adult normal readers had thresholds around 30 msec. It was concluded that the "poor readers clearly exhibit a visual TOJ deficit" (p. 922). Whether poor performance on this task is best conceived of as a deficit in judging temporal order is a moot point. It may be more appropriate to think of it in terms of a purely visual phenomenon or as reflecting a verbal labelling difficulty. Somewhat similar finding to those of May et al. (1988) have been reported for adult dyslexics by Hari, Renvall, and Tanskanen (2001).

Another task that has been used with reading-disabled individuals also involves presentation of two visual stimuli separated in time by a short interval. The object is to discover how short the interval can be for the two stimuli to still be perceived as separate rather than one. Using such a task, it has been reported (with stimulus presentations of low but not high spatial frequency) that disabled readers require longer between the two members of a stimulus pair than do normally reading controls for the two stimuli not to be perceived as one (Lovegrove, Heddle, & Slaghuis, 1980b; see also Stanley & Hall, 1973). The separation threshold is held to be a measure of visible persistence—the length of time during which the neurophysiological activity associated with presentation of a stimulus outlasts the duration of stimulus presentation. Disabled readers report flickering stimuli as fusing into a single uninterrupted light at lower rates than do controls (Lovegrove, Martin, & Slaghuis, 1986). Thus disabled readers appear to experience both longer visible persistence (see also Slaghuis, Twell, & Kingston, 1996), at least at low spatial frequencies if not at high spatial frequencies (Badcock & Lovegrove, 1981), and to have lower flicker fusion rates than control readers. However, a demonstration of longer visible persistence in dyslexic than control participants seems to depend critically on the nature of the task from which increased visible persistence is inferred. It does not occur with the so-called "temporal integration of form" technique (Hogben, Rodino, Clark, & Pratt, 1995), in which a pattern is divided into two components presented in sequence to the participant who has to identify the complete pattern; longer visible persistence is inferred from correct performance over longer inter-stimulus intervals.

Working with a group of eight children with specific language impairment, Wright, Lombardino, King, Puranik, Leonard, and Merzenich (1997) measured detection thresholds for brief target tones presented before (backward masking), during or after (forward masking) different masking noises. In comparison with control children, those with specific language impairment were found to be impaired in detecting target tones presented before a masking tone of similar frequency. Bishop, Carlyon, Deeks, and Bishop (1999b) failed to replicate these findings. In contrast to results for specifically language-impaired children reported by Tallal (see below), the children studied by Wright et al. (1997) were said not to demonstrate an impairment in the perception of rapidly presented sounds. However, Wright et al. state in their paper (without giving details) that preliminary data from 12 children with reading difficulties show that "Five had excessive amounts of backward masking". They go on to state that their data are consistent with the view that "some, but not all, children with reading problems have difficulties accurately perceiving rapidly presented stimuli" (p. 178).

Eden, Stein, Wood, and Wood (1995a) presented reading-disabled children, backward readers (of lower IQ than disabled readers) and normal readers of approximately average IQ with two tasks. One was to identify the number of dots present at one time on a screen; the other was to count the dots as they were presented on a screen one at a time in rapid succession. Performance on the temporal dot task correlated with reading score and both disabled and backward readers performed significantly more poorly than controls on this task but not on the purely spatial version of the task in which all the dots appeared simultaneously.

Counting successively presented dots is obviously a verbal (if sub-vocal) task and one in which dyslexics might be expected to perform poorly, given the evidence of their poor speech-related processes. Is it possible that some of the difficulties faced by dyslexics in this domain are tied in some way to temporal factors? According to Share:

A general temporal processing deficit would offer a unitary explanation for all the phonological deficits observed in disabled reader groups. Poor quality phonological representations would be attributable to the high degree of processing overlap associated with the parallel transmission of speech. Difficulties in the rapid sequencing of speech motor acts necessary for serial naming and verbal rehearsal would constitute an independent expression of the temporal deficit.

(Share, 1995, p. 188)

TEMPORAL ASPECTS OF SPEECH PERCEPTION

The perception of speech depends upon the processing of rapid changes in acoustic energy (formant transitions) at different frequencies. As Liberman, (1993) expressed it: "speech perception requires the listener to respond to resonances that move rapidly up or down in center frequency. In the case of stop consonants, for example, the critically important resonances complete excursions as large as 500 Hz in about 50 ms" (p. 269). Discrimination between certain (stop) consonants (e.g. b versus d or p) in CV syllables such as /ba/ and /da/ or /pa/ depends upon the ability to detect formant transitions that occur in very short intervals of time, of the order of 10 or 20 msec. These acoustic events provide critical cues to the place in the vocal tract at which the consonant is articulated and hence to speech perception.

It is not only formant transitions that occur within very short temporal intervals. The duration between the release of air at the lips and vibration of the vocal cords, referred to as as voice-onset time, is also an important cue in speech perception generally, as well as being related to the phenomenon of categorical perception. It will be remembered that some dyslexic children and adults show less steep or more "fuzzy" boundaries between adjacent categories of phoneme.

The question arises as to whether some individuals' deficiencies in perceiving brief temporal events might relate to the existence of less categorical boundaries. This question was addressed by Reed (1989), who presented children with a number of tasks. One was to identify two sounds presented in close temporal succession. Twenty children who met a discrepancy definition of dyslexia showed a mean increase in errors as the interval between two tones or synthesized consonant–vowel (CV) syllables was decreased from 400 to 10 msec. A similar increase in errors was not seen for 20 chronological age control children, or, in either group, for vowel stimuli. The reading-disabled children were also less consistent than controls in identifying stimuli in a categorical perception task. Unfortunately, Reed did not carry out an analysis by individual participants to determine whether both effects were shown only by a specific sub-group of children. She did, however, ask a sub-set of the 10 most impaired readers to participate in a second experiment in which they were presented with a visual version of the temporal judgement task. No deficit was found in this task. Given the intact performance on the visual temporal judgement task, Reed considered that the auditory results she obtained "may reflect a basic perceptual deficit rather than a deficit in the retention of temporal order" (p. 287).

THE TEMPORAL PROCESSING DEFICIT HYPOTHESIS OF DYSLEXIA

In view of findings such as those discussed above, there has been considerable discussion about the role of auditory temporal discrimination and perception in dyslexia and other developmental language disorders. The basis of the argument and the nature of the empirical findings on which it is grounded have changed somewhat from the early days (e.g. Zurif & Carson, 1970) to more recent times (see Farmer & Klein, 1995 and associated commentaries and reply).

Currently, the idea is that a fundamental temporal processing problem leads to speech processing impairments, which, in turn, have a deleterious impact on reading development (for a review, see Farmer & Klein, 1995). Tallal, in particular, has argued that:

A sub-group of dyslexic children have phonetic processing difficulties . . . As data accumulate . . . they continue to support the hypothesis that phonetic processing deficits themselves may result from inefficiencies or deficiencies of the processing mechanisms essential for processing the rapidly changing acoustic spectra which characterize the ongoing speech stream.

(Tallal, 1984, p. 168)

Much of Tallal's research has been conducted with children diagnosed as showing specific language impairment (SLI; developmental dysphasia). In a series of studies (reviewed in Tallal, Miller, & Fitch, 1993, 1995), Tallal and Piercy (1973, 1974, 1975) compared SLI children on tests of discrimination and temporal order judgement using pairs of stimuli that were either short or long in duration. They were presented with either short or long inter-stimulus intervals. The language-impaired children differed from control children only on short stimuli and short inter-stimulus intervals. The conclusions that Tallal and Piercy drew from comparisons of SLI and control children's performance with different types and duration of stimuli and inter-stimulus interval (Tallal's auditory repetition test) were that language-impaired children have a perceptual deficit that affects the rate at which they can process incoming auditory information.

In relation specifically to formant transitions, Tallal and Piercy (1975) concluded that it was their "brevity not the transitional character" (p. 73) that causes problems for SLI children. Studdert-Kennedy and Mody (1995) pointed out that in a subsequent paper reporting the results of experiments with brain-damaged war veterans (Tallal & Newcombe, 1978), the findings with SLI children are described with some subtle shifts of meaning. Instead of referring to a deficit affecting the rate of auditory information processing, the children were said to show a deficit in "auditory temporal analysis" (Tallal & Newcombe, 1978, p. 13). The difficulty experienced by SLI children with formant transitions was attributed to "speech sounds that incorporate rapidly changing acoustic spectra" (p. 13). These subtle shifts of meaning have been the source of a good deal of argument and counter-argument as the "temporal processing deficit hypothesis" has been debated in the literature.

Using discriminant function analysis, Tallal, Stark, and Mellits (1985a) showed that six variables in combination correctly discriminated all but one of 59 individuals as language-impaired or control participants. These variables were said by Tallal et al. "to have in common the assessment of specific temporal capabilities, either in perception or production" (p. 317). This, in fact, is an arguable point. One of the variables, "a finger-identification subtest, assessed the subject's ability to identify two touches presented simultaneously on two different fingers" and another "assessed the ability of subjects to locate two touches presented simultaneously to the cheeks and/or hands on either side of the body" (p. 317). The fact that stimulus presentation was simultaneous does not necessarily imply that the ability being assessed is temporal in nature. Despite criticisms of the study of Tallal et al. (1985a) by Zhang and Tomblin (1998), Tallal (1999) maintains that "it was rapid temporal processing variables alone that entered the discriminant function equation" (p. 227). She and her colleagues calculated in a companion paper to Tallal et al. (1985a) that 72 per cent of the variance in receptive language ability of the dysphasic children could be accounted for by their ability to efficiently process non-verbal acoustic tones and stop consonant–vowel syllables. They argued that "a deficient timing mechanism ... may underlie the receptive language deficits of developmentally dysphasic children" (Tallal, Stark, & Mellits, 1985b, p. 533).

Although most of Tallal's work has been with SLI children, in one study she compared 20 children formally diagnosed as showing specific reading delay with a group of younger normal readers (Tallal, 1980). One test required the participants to press two buttons in succession to indicate the order in which a pair of tones had been presented at various inter-stimulus intervals (between 8 and 428 msec). In another version of the test, using the same stimuli and inter-stimulus intervals, the participants had to make a single keypress to indicate whether the two tones were identical or different. In both versions of the task, the disabled readers were impaired relative to the controls but only when the interval between tones was relatively short (305 msec or less). There was no difference between groups at the 428 msec interval. Performance on these tasks correlated significantly with scores on a nonword reading test; the more errors made on the auditory task, the more were made in reading nonwords. Tallal (1980) concluded that "reading-delayed children's

difficulty with temporal pattern perception may stem from a more primary perceptual deficit that affects the rate at which they can process perceptual information" (p. 193). However, not all reading-delayed children had problems on the auditory tests, as Tallal herself pointed out. She suggested that the test profiles of disabled readers may be related to the presence or absence of concomitant oral language difficulties.

Snowling (2001) also found that not all dyslexics have problems with auditory tests. Bishop et al. (1999b) reported the same in relation to children with SLI. Indeed, Bishop and her colleagues noted that even control children without SLI often show poor auditory procesing (including poor performance on Tallal's test of auditory repetition). This, they argue, "poses difficulties for any theory that regards auditory deficits as a necessary and sufficient cause of LI [language impairment]" (p. 1308), a view shared by Nittrouer (1999). The latter (see also Waber et al., 2001) found no difference between 110 children with poor phonological processing skills (who included 17 poor readers) and their controls in recall of sequences of non-speech tones presented at various rates or in the ability to use brief and transitional properties of speech (including formant transitions).

Tallal et al. (1993, 1995) discussed data drawn apparently from her 1980 study. Dyslexic individuals were classified into two groups on the basis of their oral language skills. One group had oral skills that fell into the normal range for age, whereas a second group was impaired. It turned out that only the latter showed a correlation between nonword reading scores and the number of errors made in the so-called tests of temporal perception. Tallal and Stark (1982) failed to find any difference between impaired and good readers in what was termed temporal integration. Reading-impaired children aged 7–9 years and age-matched controls were compared on a battery of perceptual and motor tests. Children with concomitant oral receptive and/or expressive language delay were specifically excluded from the reading-impaired group. Contrary to expectation, few differences were found between the reading-impaired and control groups in perceptual or motor performance. Tallal and Stark, therefore, suggested that "the pattern of temporal perception and motor deficits that have [*sic*] been reported ... may be specifically related to the presence or absence of concomitant receptive and expressive language deficits in this population" (p. 174). However, it might be argued that the groups compared by Tallal and Stark did not differ sufficiently in reading ability. Despite differences on tests of vocabulary and comprehension, there was no group difference on a test of nonword reading (although there was a difference in syllable segmentation ability).

The general conclusion that Tallal draws from her research is that "language- and reading-impaired children, due to their basic auditory temporal processing deficit, are unable to establish stable and invariant phonemic representations" (Tallal et al., 1995, p. 207). It should not be thought, however, that any such deficit is irremediable. Merzenich, Jenkins, Johnston, Schreiner, Miller, and Tallal (1996) have reported that within as little as 3–4 weeks of training, language-learning-impaired children aged 5–10 years benefited from a brief daily regime designed to improve their performance on a task of temporal order judgement. Furthermore, gains were made by almost all children on a phoneme-identification task. In conjunction with the regular presentation of audio-cassette recordings of acoustically modified speech, the on-line speech discrimination and comprehension of a subgroup of these children was also said to have improved (Tallal et al., 1996). It is possible that such training regimes may usefully be applied to dyslexia (see Habib, Espesser, Rey, Giraud, Bruas, & Gres, 1999).

Is a temporal processing deficit specific to speech?

Tallal (see also Farmer & Klein, 1995) uses the term temporal perception to refer to perception or processing of stimuli that are of short duration and/or are presented within close temporal succession. Studdert-Kennedy and Mody (1995) argued that processing should be considered temporal only if the defining features of the stimulus are changing in time. Stimuli should not be con-

sidered temporal simply because they are of short duration or have short inter-stimulus intervals. Studdert-Kennedy and Mody (1995) consider that Tallal and co-workers have entangled themselves in a "conceptual muddle" between temporal perception (i.e. perception of the temporal properties of stimuli) and rapid perception (i.e. perceiving rapidly). That is, they argue that Tallal and her followers (Farmer & Klein, 1995) have confused two different things. As they put it in a later paper (Mody et al., 1997), "Difficulties in perceiving very brief temporal events and/or events with very brief intervals between them indicate a deficit not in temporal perception, but in the perception of rapidly presented information. We should not confuse rate of perception with perception of rate" (p. 203).

Mody et al. (1997) also argue that "to discriminate between stimuli is merely to indicate that they are different in some respect. Identification therefore entails discrimination, but not vice versa. For temporal order judgement (TOJ), discrimination is not enough: identification is required" (p. 203). Mody and colleagues are here drawing attention to the fact that errors on a discrimination task do not indicate the reason for the error. A mistake in identifying a stimulus might lead to an error on a discrimination task that is unrelated to the temporal aspects of the task:

> Errors are therefore ambiguous, unless we have independent evidence of correct identification ... Arguably, all the supposed difficulties in "auditory temporal perception" or actual difficulties in perceiving rapidly presented information, so far reported for both reading-impaired and specifically language-impaired children, can be traced to difficulties in stimulus identification.
>
> (Mody et al., 1997, p. 203)

Mody et al. (1997) point out that no-one "has established, by means of an appropriate non-speech control, that rapid acoustic changes are indeed difficult to perceive for either specifically language-impaired or specifically reading-impaired children" (p. 206). They accept that a number of studies, such as those of Godfrey et al. (1981), Werker and Tees (1987), Reed (1989), Hurford and Sanders (1990), and Steffens et al. (1992) discussed above, have shown that poor readers have difficulty in discriminating or identifying phonemes such as /b/ and /d/, but "An auditory account of that effect, attributing it to a deficit in some aspect of so-called temporal processing, has not yet been subject to direct test" (p. 207).

The point here is that a deficit in speech-related tasks has been attributed by Tallal and some authors to a general auditory deficit in temporal processing rather than to a speech-specific impairment. There is independent support from electrophysiological research for the idea of a general-purpose (i.e. non-linguistic) temporal processing mechanism. Liégeois-Chauvel, de Graaf, Laguitton, and Chauvel (1999) studied 17 epileptic patients undergoing pre-surgical exploration who had micro-electrodes implanted into the auditory cortex before potential excision of (non-auditory) cortex for the relief of their intractable epilepsy. The patients were presented with a series of natural French syllables varying in voice-onset time and with non-speech analogues that preserved the same temporal structure as the syllables. Evoked potentials from Heschl's gyrus, and to some extent the planum temporale, on the left side of the brain, were similar for the two classes of material and reflected sequential processing of the different components of the stimulus. That is, a distinction between voiced and voiceless syllables (and between their non-speech analogues) was seen in the waveforms. On the right side, the waveforms were similar regardless of the duration and spectral complexity of the sounds. Liégeois-Chauvel et al. (1999) concluded that "Our results suggest that a single mechanism in the auditory cortex, involved in general (not only speech-specific) temporal processing, may underlie the further processing of verbal (and non-verbal) stimuli" (p. 484).

In a review of the neurobiology of speech perception, Fitch, Miller, and Tallal (1997) suggest that "anomalies evident in the brains of dyslexics may act, in part, to impair the encoding and consequent perception of rapidly changing auditory cues, such as those that occur in speech phonemes" (p. 339). This issue was addressed specifically in experiments reported by Mody et al. (1997). Matched groups of reading-impaired and normally-reading children were selected such that they differed on the task of discriminating /ba/ from /da/ as reported by Tallal and others. Next, the same children were tested on easier discriminations (/ba/ versus /sa/ and /da/ versus /ʃa/). The stimulus pairs of the harder discriminations differ only in one phonetic feature (place of articulation), whereas the pairs of the easier discrimination differ in three phonetic features (place, manner of articulation and voicing). If impaired performance on the difficult discrimination is due to difficulty in identifying the items because of their close auditory–phonetic similarity, then the children would be expected to have much less difficulty with the easier pairs. If, on the other hand, the difficulty is related to rapid rates of stimulus presentation (short inter-stimulus intervals), this would be expected to persist when the more difficult discrimination is presented. The results favoured the first explanation.

In a second experiment, the children were presented with comparable frequency-modulated non-speech stimuli that varied in formant "analogues" in the same way as the speech stimuli. As the control stimuli were not perceived as speech, they constituted acoustically matched control stimuli to the speech stimuli. Good and poor readers performed at an equivalent level on tasks using these stimuli, thus demonstrating that the deficit observed in Experiment 1 is not a general auditory problem but is specific to speech stimuli (see also Breier, Gray, Fletcher, Foorman, & Klaas, 2002). Furthermore, the fact that poor readers had no more difficulty than good readers on this task implies that their problem does not reside in perceiving rapid acoustic changes. Manipulation of the inter-stimulus interval in Experiment 2 had little or no effect on discrimination of the non-speech stimuli by either group, whereas the same manipulation significantly influenced performance with the speech stimuli in Experiment 1 only for the poor readers. Thus "whatever difficulties were induced in the poor readers by increasingly rapid presentation of synthetic stop-vowel syllables were not similarly induced by the non-speech control patterns" (p. 218)—nor were they induced in the good readers for either type of stimulus. Mody et al. (1997) concluded that "These results demonstrate that the poor readers' difficulties with /ba/–/da/ discrimination were specific to speech, and cannot be attributed to a general auditory deficit in the perception of brief patterns of rapidly changing acoustic information" (pp. 218–219).

In a final experiment, Mody et al. (1997) varied the extent of the first formant onset transition from one frequency to another. This manipulation is associated with a shift in perception from /seɪ/ to /steɪ/. The view that poor readers are impaired in phonetic processing of brief formant transitions would predict that they would require a more extensive formant transition than good readers to change their labelling of a stimulus from one category to another. In the event, poor readers showed the same labelling functions as good readers.

Mody et al. (1997) acknowledge that their results do not disprove the hypothesis of a deficit in auditory temporal processing but they argue that there is no evidence at all in its favour. Instead, they believe that the impairment shown by poor readers (in discriminating /ba/ from /da/) reflects a phonetic difficulty. They argue that "/ba/ and /da/ are difficult to discriminate and identify at rapid rates of presentation because, although phonologically contrasting, they are phonetically similar . . . [they] differ on a single phonetic feature" (p. 225). Deficits in non-speech auditory perceptual tasks (e.g. Nicolson & Fawcett, 1994a, 1994b; Tallal, 1980) may co-occur with speech perception deficits but, according to Mody et al. (1997), "Deficits in speech perception among reading-impared children are domain specific and phonological rather than general and auditory in origin . . . [but] . . . how poor readers' deficits in speech perception relate to their characteristically impaired phonological awareness, and so to reading, is a question we must leave to future research" (p. 227).

The article by Mody et al. (1997) has been criticized by Denenberg (1999) on a number of statistical and methodological grounds. He argued that "the report is so seriously flawed that it fails to address the controversies surrounding the Tallal hypothesis" (p. 379). One of the points made by Denenberg is that the groups examined by Mody et al. might more properly be referred to as normal and superior readers rather than poor and good readers. Thus they did not meet the criteria of reading-impaired as specified by Tallal and the relevance of their findings is questionable. The second main point made by Denenberg is that Mody and co-workers' experiments did not have sufficient statistical power to justify acceptance of the null hypothesis that the two groups of readers did not differ in discriminating highly contrasting (easy) pairs of stimuli (/ba/–/sa/ or /da/–/fa/) even though they differed on the less highly contrasting (difficult) pair (/ba/–/da/).

There are, then, two issues that have led to much controversy in the literature. One concerns whether or not Tallal and colleagues have actually demonstrated a temporal deficit (Mody et al., 1997). The second issue concerns the specificity of any supposed temporal perception deficit: is it confined to stimuli within the linguistic (speech-related) domain or is it a more general auditory temporal deficit? In fact, the temporal deficit has been seen as being multi-modal rather than confined to the auditory modality. Bishop et al. state:

> According to the current version of the theory, the impairment is not seen as specific to the auditory modality. Similar difficulties in coping with brief or rapid events can be seen in other sensory modalities. However, this multimodal rapid processing deficit is thought to have an especially severe impact on language development, which is crucially dependent on the ability to distinguish and identify brief and rapid auditory events.
>
> (Bishop et al., 1999a, p.156)

Bishop et al. (1999a) tested pairs of twins aged 7 years and above in which one or both twins satisfied criteria for a diagnosis of developmental language impairment. (These twins were a sub-set of the twins studied by Bishop et al., 1995.) A representative sample of twins from the general population was also tested. Participants were administered Tallal's auditory repetition test, which was regarded as providing an overall measure of how well children could discriminate and remember non-verbal auditory sequences (tones), and Gathercole's test of nonword repetition. If the latter is a fair test of phonological short-term memory, and if phonological deficits in learning-disabled children are a consequence of poor auditory non-verbal memory, then there should be a close relation between performance on the two tests. In the event, both tests discriminated between language-impaired and non-impaired children and on both tests the scores of twins and co-twins were significantly correlated for both monozygotic and dizygotic twins. However, performance on the nonword repetition test was found to be highly heritable but not that of the Tallal test, which appeared to be influenced largely by shared environmental factors. While acknowledging that the version of Tallal's test they used "was poorly suited for identifying rate-processing limitations" and that the nonword repetition test is not a pure test of "phonological perception", Bishop et al. (1999a) considered these findings to "pose a challenge for those who maintain that nonverbal and speech processing deficits have a common origin" (p. 164).

MORE ON TEMPORAL PROCESSING: PSYCHOPHYSICAL AND ELECTROPHYSIOLOGICAL STUDIES OF AUDITORY PERCEPTION IN RELATION TO READING

McAnally and Stein (1996) studied "auditory temporal coding" in 23 dyslexic adults. In comparison with 26 controls, this group was not impaired in the ability to detect a small interruption within a white noise stimulus. Specifically, the task was to indicate which of three short bursts of noise contained the interruption. However, using a similar paradigm, the dyslexics were significantly impaired at detecting small changes of frequency of pure tones around a base of 1 kHz (see also Hari, Sääskilahti, Helenius, & Uutela, 1999).

They were also impaired at exploiting differences between the two ears in the phase of a tone that was presented against a background noise. Since they were not impaired when the tone at the two ears was in phase, the results suggest "a reduced ability of the dyslexics to exploit differences in inter-aural phase" (McAnally & Stein, 1996, p. 963). With dyslexics and controls combined, performance in the "reverse phase" condition of the binaural task correlated significantly and separately with measures of word and nonword reading. When considering only dyslexics, the correlation was significant for words alone.

Snowling (2001) discusses an attempted replication of McAnally and Stein's (1996) study. Whereas McAnally and Stein reported adult dyslexics to be impaired only at low frequencies, Hill, Bailey, Griffiths, and Snowling (1999) found only a few of their participants (11 dyslexic university students plus one other adult) to have elevated frequency discrimination thresholds, or frequency modulation detection thresholds, at both low (1 kHz) and high (6 kHz) base (centre) frequencies. Snowling (2001) reports the absence of a significant correlation within individual dyslexics between the presence of a "temporal processing deficit" and the severity of a phonological processing deficit. She notes that this is unsurprising, since not all children show an auditory temporal processing deficit. She goes on to suggest that "there are many reasons why dyslexic listeners may show poor performance in auditory psychophysical paradigms. A major contender is the poor levels of attention control characterizing some dyslexic readers" (p. 40). It is well-known that dyslexic children often carry a co-diagnosis of attention deficit disorder; perhaps only these children show auditory processing deficits (but see Breier et al., 2002) . Certainly, there have been failures to replicate findings of auditory impairments in poor readers (Heath, Hogben, & Clark, 1999; Hill et al., 1999), although it seems that a growing number of studies report differences in auditory–temporal processing as a function of reading proficiency.

The magnetic field responses evoked in seven adult poor readers and seven control participants by "a variety of psychophysical tasks measuring perceptual interference between rapidly successive stimuli" were recorded in a magnetoencephalographic (MEG) investigation by Nagarajan, Mahncke, Salz, Tallal, Roberts, and Merzenich (1999). The MEG recordings revealed differences between the two groups of participants in responses in and around the primary auditory cortex, while behavioural data showed that the poor readers were impaired on a temporal ordering task. During this task, "Subjects signaled which of four possible tone pair sequences (high–high, high–low, low–high, low–low) was presented by pressing buttons strapped to their thighs" (p. 6484). Nagarajan et al. concluded that, in comparison with controls, the poor readers showed "fundamentally different cortical response dynamics generated by brief stimuli, along with substantially weaker cortical responses to rapidly successive stimuli across the same time-scale" (p. 6486). Inferior performance by the poor readers on the temporal order task may have resulted from a difficulty in labelling the response alternatives, yet Nagarajan et al. (1999) argued that "This study provides further evidence that most reading impaired individuals have an enduring 'deficit' in their cortical processing of brief and rapidly successive inputs, paraleled [*sic*] by a fundamental difference in the fidelity of the processing of detailed features of rapidly successive and rapidly changing acoustic inputs" (p. 6487).

A larger-scale attempt to correlate auditory deficits with reading impairments in adults was made by Ahissar, Protopapas, Reid, and Merzenich (2000). These authors administered an "extremely broad" battery of psycho-acoustic tests to 102 adults from a wide range of educational backgrounds among whom some (it is not clear how many, but it appears to be approximately half the group) reported themselves to have had a childhood history of reading difficulties (CHRD). Within each group, scores on specific sub-tests were said to be correlated with measures of word and nonword reading and with spelling, but no correction for multiple correlations was made. This makes it difficult to interpret the finding that, for both groups of participants, performance on a formant discrimin-

ation task was said to be "highly correlated with pure tone frequency discrimination ($r = 0.69$ and 0.64 for controls and CHRD, respectively) and with reading measures" (p. 6835). In fact, none of the correlations with the reading measures shown in the table of correlations was significant for either group, yet the authors stated that "This finding is consistent with the hypothesis that impaired phonemic awareness stems from impaired discrimination between basic speech elements" (p. 6835).

To separate the effects of overall intelligence from performance on the auditory tasks, 36 participants with a score above 90 on a test of non-verbal intelligence were divided into two groups. The groups were based on nonword reading scores that were respectively above and below participants' non-verbal intelligence scores, thus forming a group of relatively good and relatively poor (nonword) readers. The relatively poor readers were found to be significantly worse on certain of the psychoacoustic tasks. Once the effects of non-verbal intelligence were statistically removed, linear regression analysis of the data for the two groups combined showed that psychoacoustic performance accounted for significant unique variance in word and nonword reading. Ahissar et al. (2000) concluded that "impaired acoustic processing is directly related to reading impairment" (p. 6836). The authors proposed that, generally speaking, "For the poorer reader . . . the salience of representation of phonological parts of speech is degraded by an abnormal representation of inputs in the acoustic stream" (p. 6837).

Auditory effects have not been confined to sensory discrimination tasks. Hari and Kiesilä (1996) presented trains of binaural clicks to 10 dyslexic adults and 20 controls. With short inter-aural time differences between the clicks at the left and right ears, participants reported hearing the clicks "jumping" from side to side. This illusion was no longer present for the controls when the inter-aural time difference exceeded approximately 90–120 msec. For dyslexics, the illusory effect continued to be reported until the time difference between clicks at the two ears exceeded 250–500 msec. This auditory effect, which was not replicated in a study of Austrian dyslexic boys by Kronbichler, Hutzler, and Wimmer (2002), is reminiscent of a greater duration of visible persistence that has been said to occur in dyslexics (see Chapter 12).

It has been reported from the same laboratory that auditory stream segregation (hearing an alternating series of sounds presented to both ears simultaneously as two streams rather than one) occurs at significantly slower rates of presentation for adult dyslexics than for controls (Helenius, Uutela, & Hari, 1999). With stimulus onset asynchronies (SOAs) between alternating high- and low-pitch tones of 130 msec and above, control participants ($n = 18$) reported hearing a single connected stream of sound. At shorter SOAs they heard two segregated streams of sound. Adult dyslexics ($n = 13$) reported hearing two streams at a SOA of 210 msec and shorter. Thus the control participants perceived the sound sequences as segregating into two streams at faster presentation rates than the dyslexic participants. Helenius et al. suggested that this result "may reflect prolongation of the time window during which sounds can affect the perception of previous or subsequent sounds . . . It is possible that, because of an extended time window of perceptual integration in dyslexic individuals, previous speech sounds could interfere with the identification of later-occurring sounds . . . and thereby lead to phonological problems" (p. 911).

CORRELATIONS BETWEEN TEMPORAL ASPECTS OF AUDITORY AND VISUAL SYSTEM FUNCTIONS AND READING

An interesting feature of the data collected by Helenius et al. (1999) is that among the dyslexic participants, but not the controls, the correlation between performance on the experimental task correlated significantly with a measure of naming speed for words and nonwords. Those with slower naming speeds reported segregation of two sound streams at longer SOAs.

In their study referred to above, McAnally and Stein (1996) measured participants' auditory brainstem response, which was said to reflect "the synchrony of neural discharge in response to stimulus onset" (p. 964). Neither the amplitude nor the latency of this response differed between dyslexics and controls, which implies that their responses to onset and offset of stimuli were normal. McAnally and Stein drew the conclusion that "dyslexics are impaired in their ability to generate or exploit neural discharges which are phase-locked to the fine structure of temporal stimuli . . . [but] their neural coding of onsets and offsets is normal" (p. 964). This clearly has implications for the perception of speech sounds, which relies upon detection of very fine temporal perception for the discrimination of different phonemes.

The main finding of McAnally & Stein (1996), that dyslexics are impaired relative to controls in the processing of low rates of auditory frequency modulation, was replicated in a further study of 21 dyslexic adults by Witton et al. (1998). These authors also showed that their dyslexic participants had lower visual detection thresholds for coherent motion than controls. That is, the dyslexics required a greater proportion of random dots in a random dot kinematogram to move in the same direction for them to be just detected as moving left or right against a background of randomly moving dots. A further finding was that scores on the auditory and visual tasks were significantly correlated for the two lower rates of frequency modulation (FM) (said to depend upon frequency-sensitive mechanisms; a higher rate of frequency modulation, 240 Hz FM, is thought to be detected by mechanisms sensitive to tonal cues). In addition, performance on the auditory (low FM conditions) and visual tasks was correlated with a measure of performance that combined error rates and speed of response on a nonword reading task. This appears to be the first demonstration of a correlation between dynamic auditory and visual tasks and phonological skill in the same individuals. However, Bishop, Carlyon, Deeks, and Bishop (1999b) did not find a signficant correlation between FM thresholds and nonword reading (or nonword repetition) in their sample either of 11 children with specific language impairment or in age- and IQ-matched control children aged 8–14 years.

These auditory frequency modulation effects were extended to a group of 32 normal unselected school children (mean age 9.9 years) in a study that included a test of the ability to produce spoonerisms, as well as a test of irregular or exception word reading (Talcott et al., 1999). Again, there was a significant correlation between performance at the low rate of frequency modulation (2 Hz FM) but not at the high rate (240 Hz FM) and some measure (not specified in the paper) of nonword reading performance (and spelling). The authors predicted and obtained a lower correlation between performance on the auditory task and irregular word (compared with nonword) reading scores, but the correlation was still significant. Talcott et al. argued that their findings indicate that "basic auditory skills can constrain phonological development and therefore also reading ability" (p. 2047) and, "[al]though it is unlikely that FM sensitivity is directly responsible for reading and spelling ability, the effects of FM could mediate individual differences in speech perception. This could determine phonological ability, which in turn impacts upon reading skill" (p. 2049).

A futher report appears to relate to the same sample of 32 children, since the mean values (but not all the standard deviations) provided are identical to those given in the above study. In this later report, Talcott et al. (2000b) report that (after statistically controlling for individual differences in overall ability and intelligence) visual motion detection thresholds accounted for significant variance in orthographic coding ability as measured by performance on a test requiring a choice between a written (homophonic) word, such as *rain*, and a pseudohomophonic alternative (e.g. *rane*). In contrast, when phonological coding ability (apparently measured by a combination of nonword naming and phonemic substitution and exchange tasks; see their Table 3) was the dependent variable, performance on the 2-Hz FM task accounted for a significant proportion of the variance. Talcott et al. concluded that "Together these analyses suggest that normal children's orthographic and phonological decoding skills

vary with their temporal sensitivity to visual and auditory stimuli respectively" (p. 2956).

Baldeweg, Richardson, Watkins, Foale, and Gruzelier (1999) recorded the mismatch negativity potential (MMN) over the fronto-central scalp of adult dyslexic and control participants. The MMN is "elicited in response to infrequent deviant auditory stimuli embedded in an unattended sequence of frequent standard stimuli" (p. 496). Abnormal responses were found in the dyslexic group to (deviant) changes in stimulus frequency but not to changes in duration. Discrimination of tone frequency (pitch) was also impaired in the dyslexic group but not discrimination of tone duration. Correlations computed between MMN latency and frequency discrimination performance were said to be significant both for dyslexics alone and dyslexics and controls combined. The same applied to the correlations between MMN latency and reading errors on regular word and nonword (but not irregular word) reading tasks. Among the dyslexics, but not the controls, performance on a visual motion discrimination task was strongly correlated with performance on the tone frequency discrimination task. As the MMN is thought to originate "in the vicinity of the auditory cortex", it was concluded by Baldeweg et al. that "abnormalities in cortical development, particularly of the left hemisphere, may render the brain vulnerable to deficits in discrimination of those elements of speech that require the auditory cortex to process rapid frequency changes" (p. 501). This might have consequences, they argued, for the development of phonological skills.

It has been suggested that a deficit in extracting the suprasegmental attributes of the speech stream may contribute to the difficulties in phonological awareness shown by dyslexic children at the level of the syllable or onset–rime. The syllabic rhythm of speech is associated with the slow amplitude modulation of the acoustic waveform. Goswami and her colleagues designed an experimental task in which amplitude modulation was varied so as to affect the perception of discrete "beats" in the auditory stream (Goswami et al., 2002). The task was based on a sinusoid modulated in amplitude to a depth of 50 per cent. Within this, the rate of amplitude change was manipulated by varying the rise time of the modulation while the overall rate was kept constant. Very slow rise times (greater than one-quarter of a second) induce the percept of a continuous sound varying in loudness. With rise times of less than approximately 120 msec, however, individuals' perception changes to that of a continuous sound with a loud beat occurring rhythmically at the modulation rate. Goswami and colleagues hypothesized that dyslexic children would differ from controls in their psychometric beat-detection functions. In the event, the slope of the function for dyslexic children was significantly greater than that for age-matched control children. The slope of the function for younger children matched for reading age was intermediate between these two slopes. After controlling for age and IQ, the correlations between beat detection and phonological awareness measures, rapid automatized naming, phonological memory, spelling and word and nonword reading were all significant. Furthermore, a group of young precocious readers showed a steeper beat-detection function than similarly aged control children from the same cohort. On the basis of further analyses, Goswami et al. (2002) argued that "the ability to process amplitude envelope onsets accurately may constitute the primary deficit in developmental dyslexia" (p. 10915).

The findings discussed so far in this chapter strongly suggest some anomaly in the temporal aspects of auditory system function of dyslexics which is likely to have an impact on phonological skills and hence reading. Merzenich et al. (1996) made the interesting observation in connection with their training study, designed to improve performance of children with specific language impairment on temporal order tasks, that since the temporal processing deficit could easily be overcome, it was not due to some "irreversible defects in the molecular and cellular elements of the learning machinery of their brains" (p. 80). Rather, the language-learning problems of language-learning-impaired children may be due to abnormal perceptual learning that contributes to abnormal language learning. It is well known that in the first months of life, the ability of infants to

make particular phonetic distinctions is finely tuned to the sounds provided by their native language (Jusczyk, 1994; Werker & Tees, 1984). The auditory system feeds in to a young child's developing phonological system. Perhaps at least some of the problems in auditory, and hence phonological, processing reported to occur in dyslexia can be attributed to events occurring (or not occurring!) during this period. If so, it might be possible eventually to identify those children at risk and devise appropriate interventions. Either way, as Bishop et al. (1999b) suggested in relation to specific language impairment, it may be that auditory deficits will be important only in those at genetic risk of dyslexia. Bishop and her colleagues have found in a twin study that whereas phonological impairments are highly heritable, auditory deficits are linked more tightly to experiential factors (Bishop et al., 1999b).

MOTOR DEFICITS IN DYSLEXIA

The difficulties reported by dyslexic children are not restricted to the verbal domain but often extend to non-speech motor deficits. It has often been argued (e.g. Kimura, 1993; Tzeng & Wang, 1984) that speech and skilled motor actions have neural mechanisms in common. The assumption has been that these have to do with the timing and sequencing of movements. According to Farmer and Klein (1995), "The generation of motor movements depends upon precise and rapid temporal sequencing, and a disruption in this sequencing process could lead to motor difficulties. Some rapid sequential motor movements may originate in the same area of the language cortex that plays a part in discriminating rapid acoustic stimuli such as stop consonants" (p. 473).

Although it is usual to think of problems on phoneme discrimination tasks or in articulating phonemically complex words or nonsense syllables as linguistic problems, they might be regarded as impairments of motor control. As Munhall (1994), for example, noted, "One of the fascinating things about speech production is that it lies at the juncture between a linguistic symbol system and the physics and physiology of motor control" (p. 176). Certainly there appears to be a "tight association" between the production of individual speech sounds and single (but not multiple) non-verbal oral movements in left-brain-damaged aphasic patients with anterior (pre-Rolandic) lesions (Kimura & Watson, 1989; Ojemann & Mateer, 1979).

Speech is a serial activity extended in time, and so is reading, but they are not the only temporally organized or serial behaviours. Other human behaviours are exquisitely coordinated according to temporal (and spatial) constraints. Judging the duration of an event or the speed of a moving object, and adjusting one's behaviour accordingly, are capabilities that we take for granted, although not all children find them easy.

Clumsiness has traditionally been regarded as common in dyslexic children. According to Miles (1993a), dyslexics often have a history of difficulties of coordination in such tasks as learning to ride a bicycle or in tying shoelaces. The latter implies an impairment in bimanual coordination (see Chapter 9), although, as Denckla (1985) remarked, "one has to be careful about the word coordination and its implications" (pp. 189–190). She summarized many years of clinical experience by noting that:

> Both practical and theoretical implications follow from a careful description of the coordination deficits of dyslexic children. There is, for example, a common tendency among some clinicians to use the word *dyspraxia* rather liberally, even in reference to disorders that these clinicians regard as coordination deficits, related to brainstem or vestibular connections. This leads to considerable confusion.
>
> (Denckla, 1985, p. 187, emphasis in original)

Although frank dyspraxia may be rare in dyslexia, there have been many suggestions of subtle motor difficulties in children with developmental language disorders (e.g. Bishop, 1990a, 1990b; Hill, 1998; Preis, Schittler, & Lenard, 1997).

Using stepwise logistical regression procedures, Haslum (1989) found that failure on two tests of motor coordination carried out as part of the very large-scale British Birth Cohorts Study were associated with membership of a group defined (partly on the basis of under-achievement in reading or spelling) as dyslexic at age 10 years. The first test involved catching a ball, clapping a specified number of times between throwing it in the air and catching it again. The second test was walking backwards along a straight line. It appeared that a link between motor difficulty and dyslexia (as defined in this study) might be stronger for boys than for girls.

It is not just gross motor skills that are affected in dyslexia; fine motor skills have also been said to be abnormal in some dyslexic children. The handwriting of dyslexic children is notoriously poor and they often appear to find difficulty in copying figures, although they can accurately judge which of two reproductions is more faithful to the original (see, for example, Rudel, 1985). As there is no reason *a priori* why poor readers and spellers should also show difficulties in copying or handwriting, their poor graphic performance suggests a difficulty with fine motor coordination and skill. Denckla (1985) observed that "the elementary-school-age child referred for a reading problem often also performs below age level on copy-form tests. Further, the child appears to have some knowledge of his own poor performance, but he is unable to make the pencil do his bidding!" (p. 188).

Leslie, Davidson, and Batey (1985) compared the performance of 23 disabled and 23 control readers aged 9–12 years on the Purdue pegboard. Using the left or right hand alone, disabled readers moved significantly fewer pegs than controls, although in the bimanual condition the two groups did not differ. That disabled readers do more poorly than controls in unimanual peg-moving with either the left or right hand has been reported by others (Gardner & Broman, 1979; Nicolson & Fawcett, 1994a, 1994b). It has also been reported that children with specific language impairment do poorly on this task in comparison with controls (Bishop, 2001; Preis et al., 1997). Since there is significant shared genetic variance for impaired peg-moving and nonword repetition, as also for reduced tapping speed and speech production, Bishop (2001) suggests that "genes that put the child at risk for communicative problems also affect motor development, with the association being most evident when speech production is affected" (p. 56). In one recent study, children diagnosed as showng specific language impairment performed similarly to children diagnosed with developmental coordination disorder (and to younger normal control children) on a task involving the production or imitation of familiar (but surprisingly not unfamiliar) single and multiple hand postures (Hill, 1998).

It was predicted by Felmingham and Jakobson (1995) that dyslexics would show impairments on tasks carried out under visuo-motor control. These investigators compared the performance of nine dyslexic boys aged 9–12 years with that of a control group on a task requiring the individual to pick up a vertically oriented dowel rod from a moving conveyor belt when it reached a specified position. Although instructed to intercept and pick up the dowel rod using a pincer grip (thumb and forefinger), the participants did not always do so. Dyslexics significantly more often than controls used a non-pincer grip. Although kinematic measures of arm and hand movements showed no other significant differences between the two groups, there was a trend towards a longer time between maximum grip aperture and the object being lifted in the dyslexics compared with the controls. Taken together with the significant difference in frequency of "error" grips, this was regarded by Felmingham and Jakobson as suggesting "a subtle disturbance in the regulation of hand closure in dyslexic subjects" (p. 472). Such an impairment might well affect reading-disabled children in their everyday motor activities, such as catching a ball or picking things up.

Denckla (1985) refers to a study she and Rudel carried out with "purely dyslexic children" (i.e. without evidence of concomitant attentional deficits) referred to a neurological practice. The children were tested on:

Toe taps, heel–toe alternations, hand pats, hand pronation–supination alternations, and finger repetitive and successive opposition to thumb alternating sequences . . . Only at ages 7 and 8 years were the dyslexic children slower than controls on the toe taps, and only at age 8 were they slower on the sequence of successive opposition of fingers and thumbs. On formal examination the sequencing often appeared awkward and effortful; it had to be rehearsed to be gotten [sic] in the correct sequence. This kind of "dyspraxic" learning of finger sequencing was not, however, reflected in the speed of execution once the sequence had been mastered.

(Denckla, 1985, p. 191)

Denckla (1985) mentions that there "was a tendency toward large right–left differences, that is, a tendency for the left side, normally somewhat slower in a right-preferring population such as this one, to be even more so, excessively slow" (p. 192)

In relation (presumably) to these same children, Rudel (1985) concluded that "motor slowness, at least on these tests, appears to be outgrown by age 9–10 years" (pp. 49–50). However, Velay, Daffaure, Giraud, and Habib (2002) found slower manual responses in dyslexic adults than in controls. Fawcett and Nicolson (1995) reported finding certain motor deficits in dyslexics up to 17 years of age, which also suggests a persisting difficulty. Dyslexic individuals (predominantly male) performed significantly more poorly than chronological age controls on tests of bead threading (number threaded in 60 sec), peg moving (mean time to move a row of 10 pegs with the preferred hand) and articulation rate (of high-frequency words). Dyslexic participants performed at the same level as reading-age controls on the peg-moving and articulation tasks. They were significantly worse than their reading-age controls at threading beads. Kinsbourne et al. (1991) used the tasks of sequential finger tapping and alternating heel–toe taps with a group of adult dyslexics. The most severe dyslexics, but not those less severely affected, were impaired on these tasks when they were carried out with the right hand or foot. The authors raised the possibility that "neuromotor impairment characterizes those with the most severe dyslexia, and they are the most likely to be found in an adult dyslexic sample" (p. 771).

The above observations concur with those of earlier writers. Orton wrote of the (14 or 15) reading-disabled children referred to a specialist clinic as follows:

> Many of these children are clumsy with both hands, or had been so in early childhood. They are often of the "motor incoordinate" type with evidence of mild apraxia. Some of them give a history of delay in learning to talk and walk and of a lack of nicety of balance and consequent frequent falls and of indecision in the choice of the right or left hand in using the knife, fork and spoon, all of which speak for a definite delay in decisive dominant control of the motor mechanisms.
>
> (Orton, 1925, p. 595)

The reference to a "lack of nicety of balance" is interesting in the light of more recent research by Nicolson and Fawcett (1990). These authors showed that in comparison with control participants, 23 dyslexic children aged 11.5–14.5 years were impaired in balancing on a beam when they were asked to walk along it, arms outstretched while counting backwards in threes or while performing a choice-reaction task using a hand-held response button. The dyslexics were not impaired when performing the balancing task (see also Tallal & Stark, 1982) or either of the secondary tasks alone. However, this result has proved difficult to replicate (Yap & Van der Leij, 1994) except in dyslexic children who had high ratings on a questionnaire designed to assess attentional difficulties (Wimmer, Mayringer, & Raberger, 1999). Dyslexic children with low scores on this questionnaire, indicating no or few attentional problems, performed as well as age-matched control readers. It was argued, therefore, that attentional problems, rather than dyslexia *per se*, cause dual-task balancing problems. Interestingly, Wimmer

et al. (1999) found a significant interaction between group membership and balancing foot. Dyslexic children (with or without attention scores used as a covariate) did not show the right foot advantage shown by control children. Wimmer et al. (1999) noted that this was consistent with a left hemisphere deficit in dyslexics, but it is equally as consistent with an asymmetrical cerebellar deficit (see below).

THE AUTOMATIZATION DEFICIT HYPOTHESIS

As Nicolson and Fawcett point out, it is difficult to account for motor deficits on any hypothesis that is restricted specifically to reading (Fawcett & Nicolson, 1992; Nicolson & Fawcett, 1990, 1994a). They therefore suggested that under conditions where demands are made on (attentional) resource allocation, dyslexics may be at a disadvantage because of a failure to carry out various tasks, such as balancing, "automatically". Thus dyslexia was seen in terms of an "automatization" deficit, but one for which some degree of compensation was possible through conscious effort.

Fawcett and Nicolson (1992) repeated their earlier experiments, this time using a go/no-go reaction time task in place of their previous choice-reaction task (which was potentially a source of left–right confusion). The participants were of two broad age groups, namely older (mean age approximately 15 years) and younger (mean age approximately 11 years). The dyslexics were not impaired in simple balancing relative to their controls, or in accuracy of response in the reaction-time task alone, although they were slower than the controls in this task. However, within-participant analyses confirmed that the two groups of dyslexic children (some of whom had participated in their earlier studies) were impaired in the dual task of balancing on a beam combined with a reaction-time task, whereas age- and IQ-matched controls showed no such effect. Furthermore, in training the participants to perform a selective (go/no-go) reaction time task,

"The normal children needed little training to meet the criterion whereas the dyslexic children took up to four sessions of practice" (p. 513).

Fawcett and Nicolson (1992) saw their results as "a direct challenge to the phonological deficit hypothesis . . . [which] does not account for the full range of findings related to dyslexia" (p. 508). They proposed that "the disability suffered by dyslexic children is indeed one of learning, but . . . by no means specific to reading, rather . . . it is a *general* learning deficit (for *any* skill) which is confined to the final stage of skill mastery—the stage where the skill normally becomes so fluent that it occurs 'automatically', without the need for conscious control" (p. 508, emphasis in original). Effectively, therefore, theirs is a theory that relates to the distinction that has been made between controlled and automatic attention (Schneider & Shiffrin, 1977).

With practice, many tasks come to be controlled "automatically" as defined in terms of dual-task performance. Balancing on a beam would be expected to become "automatic" with practice, a view for which there is independent evidence from a study of people who had had one leg amputated. Initially, a concurrent arithmetic task interfered with standing still but as rehabilitation increased so the effect of concurrent arithmetic decreased (Geurts & Mulder, 1994).

Not that Fawcett and Nicolson (1992) deny the importance of phonological deficits in the aetiology of dyslexia. Far from it. They argued that:

Phonological skills are learned from experience. They are one of the earlier skills to be automatised and so a dyslexic automatisation deficit would predict exactly the decrement that has been found. . . . In short, the phonological deficits found among dyslexic children are interpreted naturally as a special case, albeit crucial to the development of reading skill, of an automatisation deficit.

(Fawcett & Nicolson, 1992, p. 525)

The reason non-phonological skills have not figured as prominently as phonological deficits in recent investigations is, according to Fawcett and Nicolson (1992), that problems only reveal themselves at higher levels of skill. Moreover, they can often be masked by an effort of conscious compensation. As acknowledged by Fawcett and Nicolson (1992), there is an extensive literature on visual deficits associated with dyslexia. They hold that "the visual deficits are found primarily in tests requiring rapid visual processing, exactly consient with the hypothesis of a dyslexic automatisation deficit" (p. 526). This argument, however, is less than convincing. It is difficult to see how some of the research on phenomena such as motion coherence or contrast sensitivity thresholds (see Chapter 12) can be regarded as learned skills (although there may be an element of learning involved in carrying out the experimental task). Thus if the data on visual impairments in dyslexia are accepted, the automatization deficit hypothesis does not provide an entirely comprehensive account of dyslexic difficulties despite the claim that it "appears capable of providing a plausible and coherent account of diverse characteristics of dyslexia" (Fawcett and Nicolson, 1992, p. 525).

One might wonder whether there is anything particularly unusual about the dyslexic individuals tested by Nicolson and Fawcett (1990) Fawcett and Nicolson (1990, 1992). Those tested by Fawcett and Nicolson (1992) had been diagnosed between the ages of 7 and 10 years on the basis of "standard exclusionary criteria and discrepancies of at least 18 months between chronological and reading age" (p. 511). There is nothing unusual in this selection procedure. However, the fact that they were recruited via local branches of two national dyslexia associations rather than drawn from school populations may have some bearing on their symptomatology. Arguably, parents and others sympathetic to the concept of specific developmental dyslexia are more likely than "non-believers" to consider their child's motor skills relevant to a diagnosis. They would be more likely to contact dyslexic associations, leading to a biased population of disabled readers. Unless one wishes to argue that these children represent unusually severe or unusual forms of dyslexia (a position that is not entirely indefensible), the implication would seem to be that motor deficits will be observed among many other dyslexics if the trouble is taken to look for them.

As an alternative to their "automatization deficit" hypothesis, Fawcett and Nicolson (1992) considered, and rejected, the hypothesis that their results could be explained purely on the basis that dyslexics are impaired specifically in motor skills. However, in a subsequent paper, Nicolson and Fawcett (1994a) reported that, on a battery of tests, dyslexic children showed "severe initial deficits in bead threading, pegboard manipulation, and normal balance but the latter two did at least improve with age. By contrast, the deficit in blindfold balance persisted into the oldest group [aged 16 years]" (p. 159). The motor deficits shown by dyslexics were in addition to "weak or transient deficits for nonword repetition and speech rate; small but persistent impairments for phonological discrimination and memory span; and a marked and persistent impairment in rhyme and segmentation" (p. 159).

THE CEREBELLAR DEFICIT HYPOTHESIS

In a later paper, Nicolson and colleagues (Nicolson, Fawcett, & Dean, 1995) proposed a cerebellar hypothesis of dyslexia (hinted at in Fawcett & Nicolson, 1992), although they were not the first to suggest involvement of the cerebellum in dyslexia (for further discussion of this hypothesis, see Chapter 10). Denckla (1985) had previously noted that "there is considerable misunderstanding of the non-specific developmental awkwardness often seen as a correlate of dyslexia which some may attribute to 'cerebellar' dysfunction" (p. 187). Somewhat earlier, Frank and Levinson (1973) had studied 115 selected dyslexic children referred for psychiatric evaluation on the grounds that they were making slow progress learning to read despite remedial help. Of these children, 17 were randomly selected for neurological examination and "all 17 cases . . . were found to have a cerebellar deficit" (p. 692). Indeed, 97 per cent (112) of the total sample were said to have shown "evidence of a cerebellar–vestibular dysfunction"

(p. 690). Unfortunately, the scientific quality of this work leaves something to be desired. Marshall's unforgiving opinion (Marshall, 1983) of a summary of Levinson's research (Levinson, 1980) was that: "This book is the most brilliant parody of clinical research this reviewer has ever read" (p. 72). More recently, Levinson (1988) claimed that 99.5 per cent of 4000 learning-disabled individuals, of whom "3,821 or 95.5% gave a past or present history of reading symptoms", showed one or more signs of cerebellar–vestibular dysfunction but no control data are presented.

Nicolson et al. (1995) argued that "A search for the underlying cause of deficits in balance, in motor skill and in automatization would generally point strongly to the cerebellum" (p. 43). In their article, they report research based on previous findings with patients who had damage to the cerebellum. Ivry and Keele (1989) had found that in comparison with Parkinson's disease patients, cerebellar patients were impaired on a task requiring them to judge which of two auditorily presented intervals of time was the longer. Nicolson et al. gave the same task to dyslexic children and found them to be impaired relative to age- and IQ-matched control children. Like cerebellar patients, the dyslexics were not impaired on a comparable loudness-estimation task. Ivry and Keele concluded that "The dissociation between time and loudness estimation strongly supports the cerebellar deficit hypothesis" and that "no other theory of dyslexia predicts this pattern of results" (p. 45). However, as discussed elsewhere, the idea that dyslexics have some temporal processing impairment has a fairly long history. What is novel is relating any such impairment specifically to the cerebellum. It is also arguable that the cerebellar hypothesis is not the only one to be able to accommodate many different aspects of dyslexic difficulties. If, for example, the putative magnocellular deficits of dyslexics (see Chapter 12) extend to the auditory modality, then arguably a magnocelluar deficit hypothesis can account for equally as broad a range of findings as the cerebellar hypothesis, though the two hypotheses are not mutually exclusive (see Rae et al., 1998).

Be that as it may, in a replication of earlier work, Fawcett and Nicolson (1999) tested a new sample of dyslexic children on a battery of tests that have been associated with cerebellar damage. The dyslexics were drawn from a school for dyslexics and two schools with large dyslexic units. All participants satisfied the usual exclusionary criteria and were of at least average IQ (taken as being greater than 90 on the Weschler Intelligence Scale-Children). The reading age of the older children (10–16 years) was at least 2 years behind chronological age but for the younger children (8 and 9 years) this was relaxed to a discrepancy of around 1 year. The "cerebellar" tests involved assessment of postural ability (degree of sway or movement in response to a gentle push in the back), arm shake (degree of arm movement when the wrist was passively shaken by the experimenter, a measure of muscle tone) and speed of toe tapping. Other tests administered were of accuracy in phonemic segmentation, repetition of nonsense words and speed of picture naming. The dyslexics were significantly poorer than their chronological age controls on all tests except speed of picture naming, especially on the "cerebellar" tests (as estimated from the effect sizes). Fawcett and Nicolson (1999) concluded that "Although it would be premature to assign the difficulties of dyslexic children to the cerebellum alone ... the severity of the classic cerebellar signs suggests that the cerebellum is one of the key structures involved" (p. 77). Neuroanatomical evidence relevant to this point is discussed in Chapter 10.

Before accepting Fawcett and Nicolson's conclusions, two points should be made. First, none of the 59 dyslexic children had participated in previous research, but 19 of the 67 controls had done so. No analysis was presented to show that these children had not benefited from their previous experience, thereby contributing to the group differences found. Second, the mean IQ of the dyslexics was significantly lower than that of the controls. To deal with this, Fawcett and Nicolson calculated the correlation between IQ and scores on the experimental tasks "for the control children only" (p. 72) and found no significant correlations. It would have been more impressive had

the same thing been reported for the dyslexics. As it is, the *lack* of significant correlations found in the control children does not indicate what is the case for the dyslexic children. Conceivably, some factor might account for a lowered IQ and the reading problems as well as for a reduced level of performance on the experimental tasks.

A second attempt by Fawcett and Nicolson (1999) to deal with the different IQ levels in the dyslexic and control groups was made by excluding children with an IQ greater than 120. After these exclusions (two dyslexics and 34 controls judging from the details provided), the mean IQ difference between groups (less than 2 IQ points) was no longer significant. Analysis of variance of scores on the experimental tasks obtained by the remaining participants again showed that the dyslexics performed significantly more poorly on all but the picture-naming test. While this suggests that the effects of a relatively high IQ were not critical to the original results, it is possible that the distribution of IQ scores in the two groups after exclusion of children with an IQ over 120 were not equivalent. Mean scores are provided but no indication of the variances or skew. It remains possible that some unacknowledged or unnoticed difference between groups can explain the findings. Further analysis involving, for example, analysis of covariance with IQ as the covariate would have been useful, even if it was felt necessary to prorate the dyslexics' IQ scores to take account of the common finding of relatively low scores on certain of the sub-tests (Thomson, 1982).

This chapter has ranged over a large number of seemingly disparate findings. The cerebellum might be what links them together. However, there are at least two difficulties that the crebellar deficit hypothesis has to meet. The first is that cases of frank dyslexia do not seem to be encountered in cases of cerebellar disease (Zeffiro & Eden, 2001). It is true that Moretti, Bava, Torre, Antonello, and Cazzato (2002) reported more reading errors in a group of adult Italian patients with cerebellar lesions than in a control group of neurologically intact volunteers. However, the errors made are not clearly related to those that are typically found in cases of acquired dyslexia (see Chapter 2). Patients were given 50 words and 50 nonwords to read, a passage of text and 10 sentences. Errors were combined over these different stimulus items and classified into a number of categories. One category was word substitution (e.g. "gatto" [cat] for "tavola" [table]); a second category included neologisms (e.g. "catrumpo" or "drimondo"). Neither of these errors is typical of acquired (or developmental) dyslexia. There were also a number of what were referred to by the authors as letter-level mistakes (anticipations, such as "totrino" for "tortino", reversals, such as "catavappi" for "cavatappi", and regularizations, such as "cat-rame" for "catrumo"). These might be regarded as errors in articulation of output, rather than as true reading errors. The data are reported as group mean scores for each type of error (combined over the different types of stimulus material) and analyzed without any correction for multiple testing or adjustment for unequal variances. In short, the data presented are less informative than they might be and should be regarded as suggestive rather than convincing evidence of dyslexia-related reading errors.

A second difficulty for the cerebellar deficit hypothesis of dyslexia is that, if dyslexia is caused by a disordered cerebellum, "it seems strange that individuals with developmental dyslexia ... do not exhibit more florid manifestations of the classic cerebellar clinical syndrome" (Zeffiro & Eden, 2001, p. 512). But maybe this is splitting hairs. Perhaps any similarity at all between the motor symptoms of cerebellar disease and the kind or motor deficits seen in dyslexia is all one should expect. Arguably, that similarity is to be found in the timing of subtle aspects of movement control. Indeed, it may not be just the timing of non-motor behaviour that is undertaken by the cerebellum. In reviewing the functions of the cerebellum, Ivry (1997) argued that "The timing hypothesis provides a general description of cerebellar function. This specifies a unique role of the cerebellum that is not limited to motor control" (p. 565).

The generic hypothesis that impaired temporal processes affect both perception and various forms of action is one that has enjoyed considerable currency. With regard specifically to dyslexia, Habib wrote:

> In clinical practice, there are numerous circumstances where dyslexic children seem to have trouble with various aspects of temporal processing, well beyond the sole sensory level. For instance, it is very usual to find severe delays in time duration awareness, sequential naming problems for concepts pertaining to time (such as days of the week), errors in time relocation of memories, and vagueness of temporal distance or remoteness appreciation ... the term dyschronia [see Llinás, 1993] could apply to dyslexia from more than one point of view. Whether or not these different levels of "temporal features" impairment are dependent upon the same mechanism is not yet known, but represents a reasonable and testable hypothesis.
>
> (Habib, 2000, p. 2384)

However, the resolution of time differences of the order of milliseconds on the one hand and the organization of everyday behaviour across much longer time intervals on the other do not strike me as likely to depend upon a single mechanism, impairment of which provides a cogent account of every aspect of dyslexia.

Finally, although not related to temporal aspects of behaviour or specifically addressing the cerebellar deficit hypothesis of dyslexia, a recent intervention study is of some interest. It appears to have been inspired by a belief that in dyslexia there is something abnormal about certain aspects of nervous system functioning associated with the control of motor output. Given that the cerebellum is intimately involved in the control of movement, there are clear affinities between this study and the cerebellar deficit hypothesis.

McPhillips, Hepper, and Mulhern (2000) reported the results of an investigation in which the effect of movement training was evaluated with 60 dyslexic children aged 8–11 years divided into three groups of 20 children each. One group was trained by being asked to repeat movements associated with an asymmetrical tonic neck reflex

(ATNR). This reflex is elicited in neonates by a sideways turning of the head when the infant is lying on its back. It consists of extension of the arm and leg on the side to which the head turns and flexion of the upper and lower limb on the opposite side of the body. The reflex becomes inhibited during development such that normally the ATNR is not seen after the age of about 6 months. Its persistence beyond this time is associated with central nervous system abnormality. In the children of this study, a persistent TNR was assessed by asking them to stand upright with their feet together while an experimenter slowly turned the head one way or the other. "Positive indicators of this reflex include movement of the extended arms in the same direction as the head turn, dropping the arms, or swaying and loss of balance" (McPhillips et al., 2000, p. 538).

The aim of the study by McPhillips et al. (2000) was to determine whether the ATNR could be inhibited by a training regime involving rehearsal and voluntary repetition of the movements involved in the ATNR and other primary reflexes. The rationale was that during infancy the occurrence of the reflex might contribute in some way to its eventual inhibition. The experimental group was provided with a regime of specific movements to carry out each day for about 10 min for 12 months. A placebo control group was also given a sequence of movements to carry out but these were not based on the primary reflexes. A control group of children was given no specific instructions. Tests of reading proficiency, verbal IQ, phonological ability and writing speed were administered to the three groups before and after the 12-month period. The three groups were well-matched in terms of group mean scores. The results were interpreted as showing that the experimental group made significantly greater gains in reading than either of the other two groups, which did not differ between themselves. Certainly, the data at first glance look impressive. However, full details of decomposition of the group-by-time interaction term are not provided in the report. It will be of great interest to see whether the results prove replicable by other groups of workers, especially since ideas as to why movement "therapy" should enhance reading ability seem somewhat vague. The conclusion of McPhillips et al. was simply that "persistent primary reflexes may have a critical role in early neurological maturation which, in turn, has repercussions for later reading development" (p. 540).

Part II

The Biological Context

7

Biological Aspects of Dyslexia

It is widely but not universally believed that dyslexia (however it is defined) has a neurobiological basis. Denckla and Rudel (1976b), for example, wrote: "in the past decade there has been growing recognition that children described as having 'developmental dyslexia' are heterogeneous both etiologically and clinically, although the consensus is that all suffer from some kind of neurologically based dysfunction affecting their ability to learn, spell, and write" (p. 1). More recently, Stanovich (1991) noted that "The typical 'media dyslexic' is almost always a very bright child who is deeply troubled in school because of a 'glitch' (assumed to be biologically based . . .) that prevents him or her from reading" (p. 10).

The International Dyslexia Association's definition of dyslexia states categorically that "Dyslexia is a neurologically-based, often familial disorder which interferes with the acquisition of language. Varying in the degrees of severity, it is manifested by difficulties in receptive and expressive language, including phonological processing, in reading, writing, spelling, handwriting and sometimes arithmetic". A similar definition is provided by the British Dyslexia Association, who maintain that "Dyslexia is a complex neurological condition which is constitutional in origin" (BDA, 1995, p. 9).

It is implicit in the view that dyslexia is of constitutional origin that there is a biological cause, which, in principle, is identifiable even if the exact cause is not yet known. Until recently, the nature of the supposed cause was left unspecified. In the last 20 years or so, however, considerable investment of research effort has gone into searching for the elusive biological "cause" of dyslexia.

The view that dyslexia is caused by some constitutional factor or factors is supported not only by evidence of a genetic component but by certain other findings. For example, significantly greater asymmetry in ridge counts between the palm-prints of the left and right hands among dyslexics compared with controls were reported by Jamison (1988). Since dermatoglyphic patterns are established before the 19th week of gestation, these findings imply that a predisposition towards dyslexia may be established by some factor(s) very early in development.

Liederman and Flannery (1994) reported that dyslexia is associated with a preponderance of summer births; specifically more dyslexics were born during May, June and July than during any other period of the year. A seasonal effect has also been reported for other neurodevelopmental disorders (Livingston, Adam, & Bracha, 1993) and for left-handedness (Leviton & Kilty, 1979; Rogerson, 1994). Such seasonal effects may arise from a variety of factors, including variation in prevalence of viral infections. These might affect the developing brain at a critical time during gestation.

Not all researchers have embraced a biological viewpoint. While reading failure may be caused by, for example, a phonological processing deficit, it does not necessarily follow that this deficit itself can be attributed to a specific biological impairment. Ehri (1989) writes, "Before we jump to conclusions about neurological abnormalities underlying phonological deficits and causing reading/spelling problems, we need to explore more fully experiential, instructional causes of the deficits" (p. 356). She goes on to argue that "the phonological deficits observed in dyslexics are largely experiential in origin and reflect the fact that they have not learned to read and spell. This is due primarily to inadequate instruction which has failed to develop dyslexics' knowledge of the spelling system so that it penetrates and comes to symbolize their phonological knowledge" (p. 356).

Thus it is possible to view the causes of reading difficulty as occurring at two broad levels, cognitive on the one hand and biological on the other (Frith, 1997). Within the biological domain, there are different levels or types of factor that might operate, possibly in combination, to produce unexpected difficulty in reading.

Behan and Geschwind (1985a) stated that they had noted "an unusually large number of spontaneous abortions or ... an unexpectedly increased number of children with cardiac malformations" (p. 77) in 45 mothers of dyslexic children. Hugdahl, Synnevåg, and Satz (1990a) also reported a "tendency for more frequent [spontaneous] abortions" among the mothers ($n = 29$) of 105 Norwegian dyslexic children than among the mothers ($n = 17$) of control children. In a more recent study, miscarriage in families selected on the basis of a reading-disabled proband was significantly higher than in control families selected through a matched control (Gilger, Pennington, Green, Smith, & Smith, 1992). The mechanism underlying this effect is obscure but may indicate that reading difficulty tends to occur among families in which there is an inherited

tendency for early fetal development to be compromised, perhaps by some kind of immunological attack on the fetus (Gilger et al., 1998).

Kawi and Pasamanick (1958) searched the birth records of 372 boys referred to a clinic for disabled readers. In comparison with control children chosen by being next on the register of births and matched for sex, IQ and socioeconomic status, hospital records revealed that the mothers of disabled readers had experienced complications surrounding pregnancy and parturition significantly more frequently than mothers of the control children. In fact, twice as many mothers of disabled readers experienced birth complications than mothers of controls and among the former multiple complications were also more frequent. The authors noted that "those that appear to be more highly associated with reading disorders are preeclampsia, hypertensive disease, and bleeding during pregnancy. These complications are more prone to produce fetal anoxia" (p. 1422).

It appears, then, that pre- or peri-natal brain damage can have lasting effects on the acquisition of reading skills. So-called soft neurological signs have often been reported (e.g. Critchley, 1970; Drew, 1956) to accompany dyslexia in many cases. Nonetheless, most authorities sympathetic to the notion of a biological cause regard developmental dyslexia as arising not from unidentified early brain damage, but from some anomaly or maldevelopment of areas of the brain critical for reading or from some other factor, or combination of factors, which include genetic and hormonal as well as structural mechanisms. Reading disorders are more frequent among epileptic patients than controls (Schachter, Galaburda, & Ransil, 1993), which is consistent with the possibility that early central nervous system damage, possibly in combination with environmental factors such as interrupted schooling, can interfere with the development of reading.

The following review deals principally with those areas of research that have been most actively pursued in relation to dyslexia. Although most authors regard dyslexia as having a biological basis, the evidence is correlational rather than causal and the problem of specifying precisely how biological mechanisms map on to cognitive functions remains a challenge for future research.

GENETIC FACTORS IN READING DISABILITY

Although reading difficulty may stem from social, educational or other causes, the fact that instances of very good and very poor readers co-occur within the same family (Finucci, Guthrie, Childs, Abbey, & Childs, 1976) makes it unlikely that reading disability is due purely to environmental circumstances. The familial pattern of dyslexia, together with the sex ratio, whereby males are said to be more frequently affected than females (e.g. Hallgren, 1950; Lewis, 1992; Rudel, 1985), have been viewed traditionally (Critchley, 1970; Miles & Haslum, 1986; Miles et al., 2001) as pointing to a constitutional basis, probably genetic, for the condition (see Grigorenko, 2001, for a review).

A familial component to dyslexia was recognized a long time ago (Fisher, 1905; Hinshelwood, 1907, 1917; Stephenson, 1907; Thomas, 1905). According to Dearborn (1929), "Family 'trees' or genealogies of word-blindness, extending back into the fourth and fifth generations have been described" (p. 129) and it is now widely acknowledged that dyslexia runs in families (Critchley, 1970; DeFries, 1992; DeFries, Fulker, & LaBuda, 1987; DeFries, Singer, Foch, & Lewitter, 1978; Finucci et al., 1976; Hallgren, 1950; Lubs et al., 1993; Lyytinen, 1997; MacKain, Studdert-Kennedy, Spieker, & Stern, 1983; Pennington, 1990; Rutter & Yule, 1975; Scarborough, 1989; Wolff & Melngailis, 1994). There are higher rates of reading impairment among the parents and siblings of reading-impaired probands than among first-degree relatives of controls. Not all probands have an affected parent but, if they do, then sibs are more likely to be affected than if neither parent is affected (Finucci et al., 1976; Hallgren, 1950) and to be more severely impared if both rather than one parent is affected. This suggests an additive genetic effect. Sibs are also more likely to have relatively low reading scores

(i.e. to be at risk) if the father rather than the mother is the affected parent (Wolff & Melngailis, 1994). Evidence for familial aggregation based on spelling rather than reading impairment has also been reported (Schulte-Körne, Deimel, Müller, Gutenbrunner, & Remschmidt, 1996). The exact percentage of affected relatives may vary according to the criteria employed for determining the presence of dyslexia in the proband and its severity.

A landmark study of 112 families was carried out in Sweden by Hallgren (1950) on the basis of which he concluded that dyslexia followed an autosomal dominant pattern of inheritance. This means that inheritance of a single copy of a specific allele (not on the X or Y chromosome) should be sufficient to cause reading disability. This, in turn, implies that at least one parent of every dyslexic person should be affected, although dyslexia in parents and/or siblings was reported by Hallgren to be present in only 88 per cent of the probands' families. While compensating mechanisms may obscure dyslexic tendencies in adults, some of Hallgren's conclusions are undermined by methodological weaknesses. His method of identifying dyslexia in the parents of the probands was not wholly satisfactory, being based solely on questionnaire, and his sample included a high incidence of speech disorders (approximately one-third of dyslexics compared with 7 per cent of controls). For some of his index cases, Hallgren relied upon a reported history of dyslexia rather on standardized tests of reading and writing. Noting that it was not possible to diagnose dyslexia on the basis of reading and writing test results alone, Hallgren (1950) stated: "In my opinion, it is often more important for a differential diagnosis to evaluate the child's proficiency in reading and writing as compared to proficiency in other school subjects and to the average level in the class rather than in relation to the norm for a certain age" (p. 36). Although not a view that obtains at the present time, there can be few who would not agree that it embodies a good deal of common sense.

Using psychometric tests with both probands and relatives, Finnucci et al. (1976) found no typical pedigree for dyslexia and proposed that this was "probably a reflection of genetic heterogeneity" (p. 19), compelling evidence of which was produced by Lewitter, DeFries, and Elston (1980). This undermines the case for an autosomal dominant mode of transmission (Pennington, 1999) and the idea that separate genetic mechanisms might operate simultaneously in the determination of reading difficulties now seems to be widely accepted in the literature. In the light of recent findings (discussed below), it is likely that one or a few major genes operate in the context of a polygenic background (Pennington, Gilger, Pauls, Smith, Smith, & DeFries, 1991a). However, different genetic factors may underlie similar reading problems in any two individuals and the same genotype in different individuals may be associated with different phenotypic expression (Decker & Bender, 1988).

The sex ratio in dyslexia

A difference between the sexes in the incidence of dyslexia has been regarded as one indication of a constitutional basis for the condition. In clinically identified samples, a ratio of approximately three or four males to one female is generally but not always seen (e.g. Hallgren, 1950; Levinson, 1988; Miles et al., 2001; Thomas, 1905; Wolff & Melngailis, 1994) and it may be even more extreme (e.g. Symmes & Rapoport, 1972). The sex ratio appears to vary with the discrepancy between reading level and IQ (see Lovell et al., 1964) and with severity of dyslexia.

A difference in the prevalence of dyslexia between the sexes might be explained on a number of different genetic models. Hallgren (1950) suggested that the expression of a relevant gene was modified according to gender, while Symmes and Rapoport (1972) proposed that reading disability was caused by a recessive allele carried on the X chromosome. However, little or no support for this hypothesis was obtained by DeFries and his colleagues (DeFries, 1992; Lewitter et al., 1980).

Sladen (1970) re-analysed Hallgren's (1950) data and noted that there were more males than females born to dyslexic mothers. The 70 sons and 34 daughters included 35 male and 7 female probands, so the gender ratio among the siblings

of probands with "dyslexic" mothers was 1.3 : 1. Sladen suggested that "this should be watched in further studies" (p. 32). Among the offspring of "dyslexic" fathers, the male to female ratio was 2 : 1. She suggested that dyslexia might be "largely recessive in females but dominant in some males" (p. 33).

While dyslexia is generally acknowledged to be more common among boys than girls, it has been argued that the imbalance between the sexes may have been over-emphasized due to a greater tendency to recognize or classify the disorder in boys than girls and/or to statistical factors (see Share et al., 1987). On the basis of a computer simulation, Van der Wissel and Zegers (1985) noted that the sex ratio in reading under-achievers (defined in terms of a discrepancy criterion) found by Rutter and Yule (1975) is entirely predictable, in that the distribution of reading scores for boys and girls differed both in terms of the mean (girls higher) and standard deviation (boys more variable)— "no additional hypotheses are needed" (p. 7). More recently, Reynolds et al. (1996) noted in a study of twin pairs that there was greater phenotypic variance in oral reading performance of boys than girls, although the relative influence of heritable factors was the same in the two sexes.

Gilger et al. (1992) argued that the traditional imbalance in the sex ratio can be accounted for by an "ascertainment bias". Their reason for saying this was that once probands were excluded, the sex ratio in four family samples ranged from 1.1 to 1.5 : 1, much closer to unity than the traditional figures (see also Wolff & Melngailis, 1994). A similar view was expressed by Levinson (1988), who discussed data from 4000 learning-disabled individuals aged 7–50 years, 95 per cent of whom were said to have a past or present history of "reading symptoms". Reading scores were available for 1399. Of the latter, 416 or 29.7 per cent read at or above grade level and 671 or 48 per cent read 2 years or more below grade level. Levinson's data on so-called "soft" neurological parameters apparently showed no differences between the sexes, leading him to propose that in general "although a sex-linked component may exist in some dyslexics, the male : female ratios are referral rather than incidence ratios" (p.

1003). However, the appropriate data to substantiate this claim were not presented by Levinson.

The absence of a difference between the sexes in frequency of neurological signs within a clinically referred sample, while suggestive, does not provide an adequate basis for inferring that there is no difference between the sexes in the incidence of reading disorder in the general population. However, in support of Levinson's claim that a high male : female ratio in dyslexia is due to a difference in referral rates between the sexes, one study in America (Shaywitz, Shaywitz, Fletcher, & Escobar, 1990) reported that there was no difference between the sexes in the prevalence of reading disability when this was defined in terms of a discrepancy between actual reading age and that statistically predicted on the basis of IQ. When reading-disabled children were identified by their schools, however, more than twice as many boys as girls were designated as being reading-disabled.

In some familial and twin samples used in genetic studies of dyslexia, the sex ratio has been reported to be much lower than 4 : 1 (DeFries & Alarcón, 1996; Lubs et al., 1993; Pennington, 1990; Pennington et al., 1991a) and it may not differ substantially from 1 : 1 (DeFries & Alarcón, 1996; Lubs et al., 1993; Wadsworth, DeFries, Stevenson, Gilger, & Pennington, 1992). Among research-identified probands of two (relatively small) twin samples, no significant departure from a 1 : 1 ratio was found by Wadsworth et al. (1992). Among the unaffected siblings of reading-disabled probands also, the ratio was close to unity. Nor did Wadsworth et al. (1992) find any difference in the sex ratio either of probands or their siblings depending on whether the mother or father was impaired. This is not say, of course, that as a rule dyslexia might not be more severe in males than females (Lubs et al., 1993). There is, however, no evidence of differential heritability in boys and girls (Wadsworth, Knopic, & DeFries, 2000a).

In line with the results of Shaywitz et al. (1990), Wadsworth et al. (1992) found a small, and arguably significant, excess of males among their referred or clinical populations. Shaywitz et al. (1990) suggested that the reason why they found more boys than girls in a school-based sample was that teachers are more likely to perceive boys than girls as being disruptive in the classroom. This interpretation was questioned by Miles et al. (1998), who suggested that the teachers in the study conducted by Shaywitz et al. (1990) recognized children who were in need of special help. Such children, argue Miles et al., may be those traditionally defined as dyslexic. In their own study, in which they analysed data from over 11,000 children from across Scotland, Wales and England, Miles et al. (1998) applied clinical as well as statistical criteria to the definition of poor achievers (and included poor spelling plus or minus poor reading rather than poor reading alone in their criteria). The sex ratio they found using these criteria of dyslexia (adjusted slightly for the sex ratio in the cohort as a whole) was 4.5 boys to 1 girl. However, when the criteria of poor achiever was poor reading (as assessed by a test largely of reading comprehension) in relation to intelligence, the sex ratio was much closer to 1 : 1. Thus the ratio obtained differed according to the criteria adopted to define poor achievement, a possibility foreseen by Wadsworth et al. (1992). Miles et al. (1998) regarded their results as confirming the over-representation of boys among dyslexics as traditionally or clinically defined. Furthermore, they argued that their data provide support for the view that dyslexia should be distinguished from specific reading retardation (defined in terms of discrepancy definitions) or poor reading generally.

Another possible explanation of the difference between studies reporting gender ratios showing a much larger proportion of males and those with ratios closer to unity may have to do with IQ rather than referral bias or teacher perceptions. Data from the Colorado Reading Project, where there is no initial gender bias, show that as selection for severity of word reading deficits becomes more severe (i.e. samples are selected by scores that deviate further and further from normal), the mean IQ of the sample tends to decrease and the samples include proportionally more and more males (Olson, 2002). If only individuals with a full-scale IQ greater than 100 are considered, then the trend is even more apparent. Thus there is a much greater bias towards males in samples where the deficit is severe and IQ is above normal. Compared with school-based populations, samples of clinic- or teacher-referred children may consist predominantly of children with this profile (Olson, 2002).

Twin studies of dyslexia

Although the familial pattern of dyslexia is highly suggestive, it does not constitute definitive evidence of a genetic contribution to reading difficulties. Families share environments as well as a proportion of their genes and there is some evidence of assortative mating for reading ability (McManus, 1991) and dyslexia (Wolff & Melngailis, 1994). One of the traditional approaches to this issue is that of twin studies. The assumption is that since monozygotic (MZ) twins share the same genetic make-up they should, if a condition is in part genetically determined, show a higher rate of concordance for the condition in question than dizygotic (DZ) twins, whose shared genetic make-up is no more than that of singleton siblings who on average share 50 per cent of their genes. According to Grigorenko (2001), "the first twin study of dyslexia" (p. 106) was that of Hermann (1959). In fact, Hermann refers to a study by Norrie (1954) published in a Danish journal. Hermann (1959) maintains that Norrie found that 7 pairs of "uniovular" twins "showed concordance in all instances, whereas the remaining 21 biovular pairs showed concordance in only 6 pairs . . . Norrie later supplemented her material with a further 11 pairs, of which the uniovular pairs showed concordance in both instances, the 9 biovular pairs showing concordance in four" (p. 87). Adding these data to 6 pairs of twins discussed by Hallgren (1950) led Hermann to calculate that all of 12 MZ twin pairs (not 10 as stated by Grigorenko) were concordant for reading disability in contrast to only 11 of 33 DZ twin pairs. Early twin studies were briefly reviewed by Zerbin-Rüdin (1967). From the studies she mentions, it has been inferred (Decker & Bender, 1988; Grigorenko, 2001; McManus, 1991) that the concordance rate among 17 MZ and 34 DZ twins was 100 per cent and 35 per cent, respectively. One of the DZ pairs and five of the MZ

pairs were reported as "single" case studies, the remaining pairs coming from Norrie (1954) and Hallgren (1950).

According to Bakwin (1973), who interviewed mothers of 338 like-sex twins, 97 of whom were said to be "reading-disabled" (no test scores provided), the concordance rate in MZ twins was approximately 84 per cent and about 29 per cent in DZ twins. Other studies have also shown identical (MZ) twins to have a higher concordance rate for reading problems than fraternal (DZ) twins and to have higher heritability of reading disability than fraternal twins (DeFries et al., 1987). A recent analysis of a large number of twins from the Colorado Reading Project suggests probandwise concordance rates of 68 per cent in MZ twins versus 38 per cent in DZ twins (DeFries & Alarcón, 1996). Thus despite some variation in terms of the exact degrees of concordance that have been reported, it has generally been concluded that MZ twins show a higher rate of concordance than DZ twins (Grigorenko, 2001; Stromswold, 2001).

Stevenson et al. (1987) pointed out that previous twin studies, with the exception of that of DeFries and Fulker (1985), suffered from one or more of the following flaws: (i) lack of independent assessment of reading problems in the twin pairs; (ii) lack of an adequate definition of reading problems; (iii) failure to take into account the possible genetic influence of general intellectual level or IQ on reading; (iv) possibility of bias in participant population leading to high concordance rates; and (v) lack of adequate determination of zygosity.

In their own study, Stevenson et al. (1987) used standardized measures of IQ, reading and spelling with 13-year-old twin pairs. After controlling for IQ, heritability estimates for reading age were 18 and 29 per cent on the Neale and Schonell tests of accuracy, respectively, while that for the Schonell spelling test was 73 per cent. (Heritability refers to the proportion of the phenotypic variance that is due to genetic variance; this is expected to be higher for MZ than for DZ twins if a trait is partly under genetic control.) Stevenson et al. concluded: "These results then indicate that genetic influences are identifiable which have an impact on individual differences in reading ability, independent of genetic contributions to individual differences in intelligence" (p. 237).

Taking account of the different incidence of reading and spelling difficulties in MZ and DZ twins—that is, in the base rate as a function of zygosity—Stevenson et al. (1987) reported probandwise concordance rates for reading and spelling difficulties ranging from 33 to 59 per cent for MZ twin pairs and from 29 to 54 per cent for DZ twins. There were no significant differences in corresponding concordance rates for MZ and DZ twin pairs. For spelling difficulties, however, the concordance rates for MZ twins was consistently higher than that for DZ twins. Heritability estimates for spelling scores adjusted for IQ were higher than for unadjusted scores, suggesting that heritable factors rather than general intelligence influence spelling performance. Stevenson et al. argued that "with the exception of spelling difficulties, no clear pattern of genetic influence is detectable" (p. 237). After considering possible reasons for the difference between previous findings and those of their own study (including the restricted age range of their own sample), Stevenson et al. wrote: "In conclusion, the results of this twin study indicate that by 13 years of age, genetic factors are not a major influence on most cases of specific reading retardation. However, for spelling difficulties they make a significant contribution to aetiology" (p. 245). This points up the fact that the contribution of genetic factors to different aspects of reading disability may differ with age. Stevenson et al. suggested that a genetic influence may be less important in older than younger children, a view for which there is some, admittedly weak, evidence (DeFries, Alarcón, & Olson, 1997; Wadsworth, Gillis, DeFries, & Fulker, 1989). There is also evidence for an interaction between age and the heritability of reading and spelling. Heritability estimates for reading tend to decrease with age, while those for spelling tend to increase (DeFries et al., 1997).

In the context of the above results, it is interesting that Osborne, Gregor, and Miele (1968) found a higher correlation for spelling achievement among 33 MZ pairs of adolescent twins (0.816) than among 12 pairs of DZ twins (0.256).

Although this was reported as a non-significant difference, Stromswold (2001) calculates that it *was* significant. Moreover, the heritability ratios used (plus Falconer's coefficient calculated by Stromswold) indicate relative high heritability. Schulte-Körne et al. (1996) found evidence for familial aggregation of spelling difficulty among 83 first-degree relatives of 32 German probands. Subsequently, Schulte-Körne et al. (1998b) reported the results of a linkage analysis of seven multiplex German families (multi-generational families in which several family members suffer from a disorder), which yielded evidence of a gene locus (15q21) for spelling disability (see also Nöthen et al., 1999). These studies were not concerned with reading disability and, therefore, it does not follow from these results alone that reading and spelling difficulties should be considered independent deficits. However, as Schulte-Körne et al. (1996) noted, "it is possible that there are pure spelling disabled families and another subgroup of families characterized by reading and spelling or pure reading disability" (p. 821). In this context, the report of Bryant and Bradley (1980) showing that children are sometimes able to spell words that they cannot read is of interest (see also Frith, 1980)

The possibility raised by Stevenson et al. (1987) that there are developmental differences in genetic aetiology of reading and spelling deficits has recently been supported in an analysis of a large sample of twins from the Colorado Twin Study of Reading Disability. When samples were selected for reading or spelling deficits, heritability estimates for reading (word recognition) were larger for younger (less than 11 years 5 months) than for older twin pairs; moreover, estimates decreased with age for reading but increased with age for spelling (DeFries et al., 1997). This might be explained by a relatively greater influence of environmental or remedial factors on reading than spelling with increasing age. It is interesting in this context to note that in a longitudinal phonemic awareness training study, Byrne and Fielding-Barnsley (1995) found an improvement in reading skills but no concomitant improvement in spelling ability (but see Bradley & Bryant, 1983; Lundberg et al., 1988).

The negative conclusions of Stevenson et al. (1987) with regard to genetic factors in reading disability are at variance with most of the literature. Olson et al. (1989) have suggested that the relatively small number of individuals with reading disability in the study of Stevenson et al., the failure to exclude cases in which reading difficulty might have been due to "inadequate education", and the fact that the rate of reading difficulty was, unusually, nearly twice as high in DZ than in MZ twins, might all have contributed to the negative findings for reading disability reported by Stevenson et al. It might also be relevant to point out that the latter defined reading difficulty in relation to either the children's accuracy or comprehension scores. Most studies in this field do not use measures of comprehension.

Despite the null results reported by Stevenson et al. (1987), there is evidence that at least some components of reading are heritable. Olson et al. (1989) studied reading-disabled and younger nondisabled twin pairs from the Colorado Reading Project in a reading-level-matched design. Word recognition scores were derived from a standardized test. Phonological coding ability was assessed by nonword reading and orthographic decoding was assessed by a timed pseudo-homophone test (e.g. *room* versus *rume* or *rain* versus *rane*) on which correct responses required the use of word-specific orthographic knowledge. Using a regression model developed by DeFries and his colleagues to estimate heritability (see DeFries, 1992; DeFries & Fulker, 1985; DeFries et al., 1987), there was strong evidence in both male and female twin pairs for a genetic contribution to the probands' deficits in word recognition. This was true whether probands were defined in terms of the lower scoring member of each twin pair or in terms of the lowest scores on the word recognition test. Among the reading-disabled children, both phonological and orthographic coding were found to make strong and independent contributions to the children's level of word recognition. However, virtually all of the heritable component of the variance in word recognition was accounted for by phonological decoding, which was itself heritable. Orthographic coding skills were not found to be heritable. In contrast to these findings, however, Gayán and Olson (2001) have maintained more recently that shared environmental factors do not play a greater role in orthographic than phonological decoding, since subsequent work with an enlarged sample has suggested that there is, after all, a heritable component to orthographic coding, consistent with indications of a common genetic influence on both word and nonword reading (Fisher et al., 1999; Gayán & Olson, 2001; Gayán et al., 1999). In relation to this more recent work, Gayán and Olson (2001) noted that: "The genetic effects that influenced group deficits in accuracy and speed in the reading tasks were partly common and partly independent ... This independence may ultimately be supported at a molecular genetic level if specific genes are found to have stronger effects on deficits in specific component reading and language skills" (p. 503).

Olson et al. (1989) argued that: "The phonological deficits of children with R[eading D[isability] were significantly heritable, but there may be prior deficits in segmental language skill that lead to phonological coding deficits in reading" (p. 345). They therefore calculated heritability estimates for the genetic correlations between word recognition and two tests of phonological skill, rhyme fluency (the number of words given as rhyming with the word *eel* in 1 min) and a Pig Latin task. The latter required a participant to strip the initial phoneme from a word, place it at the end of the same word and add the sound "ay". When probands were selected to be low scorers on the phonological decoding task (but not when probands were selected on the basis of low word recognition scores), the heritability estimates were significant for both phoneme segmentation ability and rhyming fluency.

In the study by Olson et al. (1989), poor readers were not classified by sub-type. In a later regression-based analysis of a large sub-set of the twin data from the Colorado Reading Project, a proportion of poor readers were classified as phonological or surface dyslexics (Castles et al., 1999). Heritability estimates for the two sub-types differed markedly. Although there was evidence for a significant genetic component to the deficit in surface dyslexics (just under one-third), the influence of shared environment was much larger, accounting for over 60 per cent of the deficit. In the phonological group, by contrast, the genetic influence was substantial (approximately two-thirds), whereas the influence of shared environment was relatively weak (approximately one-quarter). These findings support the distinction between two extreme types of disabled reader and are compatible with suggestions that exposure to printed material may be especially important in determining the surface dyslexia sub-type (Olson et al., 1989; Stanovich, Siegel, & Gottardo, 1997a, 1997b).

Identifying a genetic susceptibility locus

A search for the genetic locus of a condition can be carried out using the method termed "linkage analysis". If a trait can be linked to a known genetic marker locus, it is inferred that a major gene for that trait is located on the same chromosome as the marker locus. As explained by DeFries and Alarcón, this is because:

> Genes that are closely linked together on a chromosome tend to be transmitted together from parent to child, whereas those that are far apart on the same chromosome or are located on different chromosomes are inherited independently . . . Evidence of co-transmission between a putative gene for a disorder and a marker suggests that they are located in the same chromosomal region.
> (DeFries & Alarcón, 1996, p. 44)

In addition to the X and Y sex chromosomes, each individual has 22 pairs of autosomal chromosomes, each of which has a constriction referred to as the centromere. This separates the chromosome into a short arm (labelled p by convention) and a long arm (labelled q by convention). However, finding a chromosomal region linked to a condition such as dyslexia is not the same as finding the gene or genes, since "a marker that is linked could be millions of base pairs removed from the responsible gene or genes" (Olson, 2002, p. 155).

There are two main methods of linkage analysis for behavioural disorders. One method is the sib-pair method, in which it is assumed that:

> if a major gene for a trait is tightly linked to an easily typed marker gene, a pair of sibs who are both affected with the trait will also tend to be concordant for the same linked allele. If the trait and the marker are not linked, the sibs will inherit the same allele from the same parent only 50% of the time. Thus, a significant discrepancy from random assortment of the trait and the marker allele can be taken as evidence for linkage.
> (Smith et al., 1990, p. 208)

The second method is the family study. In this case, the pedigree of each family available for study is examined for evidence of linkage (as compared with random assortment). This is expressed in terms of the probability of linkage for each of several theoretically possible levels of recombination frequency. This refers to the frequency with which a set of alleles crosses over from the chromosomes from one parent to combine with alleles on the (homologous) chromosome provided by the other parent. (The probability of recombination between two alleles is smaller the closer the distance between the two alleles. Put another way, the recombination frequency (θ) is low. This value, therefore, is a measure of the genetic distance between two alleles.) For each family, the probability of linkage at each combination frequency is compared with the probability of non-linkage. The log of this ratio is termed a LOD score (log of the odds of the likelihood of linkage). A LOD score of 3 (odds of 1000 to 1 in favour of linkage) is conventionally taken as establishing linkage, whereas a LOD score of −2 or less (odds of 100 to 1 against linkage) is taken as showing absence of linkage. For an excellent straightforward explanation of genetic methods of analysis, see DeFries and Alarcón (1996).

Indications that reading disability may be related to a major gene linked to a specific chromosome first came from a small-scale study of nine North American families "in which specific reading disability appeared to be inherited through several generations" (Smith, Kimberling, Pennington, & Lubs, 1983, p. 1346). Smith et al. reported a possible linkage between dyslexia and a marker on chromosome 15, although not all families showed evidence of linkage (suggesting genetic heterogeneity or more than one cause). However, using a large Danish sample, Bisgaard, Eiberg, Møller, Niebuhr, and Mohr (1987) failed to find evidence of linkage to this chromosome. Subsequent work by Smith and her colleagues on an enlarged North American data set (Cardon, Smith, Fulker, Kimberling, Pennington, & DeFries, 1994; and correction by Cardon, Smith, Fulker, Kimberling, Pennington, & DeFries, 1995) provided evidence of linkage between reading disability and the short arm of chromosome 6 (but not 15) in the vicinity of the human leukocyte antigen (HLA) region. The HLA region was targeted because of suggestions of an association between dyslexia and certain auto-immune disorders (Bryden, McManus, & Bulman-Fleming, 1994a; Geschwind & Behan, 1982; Geschwind & Galaburda, 1987; see also Chapter 8). Evidence of a common genetic origin for dyslexia and one auto-immune disorder, insulin-dependent diabetes mellitus, has been provided by Hansen, Nerup, and Holbek (1986, 1987).

The definition of reading disability used by Cardon et al. (1994) was based on a weighted composite measure of scores on tests of word recognition, reading comprehension and spelling. Evidence of linkage of reading disability to chromosome 6, therefore, does not demonstrate which aspect of reading performance is linked to this chromosome. Nonetheless, the importance of a locus at chromosome 6 was independently confirmed in research by Grigorenko et al. (1997) with six extended families in North America. Probands were selected on the basis of childhood diagnoses of reading disability and each family had at least four affected individuals. The total data set consisted of 94 individuals. The linkage analyses carried out indicated which reading-related processes were linked to a particular chromosome. Phoneme awareness was linked to a region on the short arm of chromosome 6.

According to Field and Kaplan (1998), this "did not coincide well" with the region identified by Cardon et al. (1994), but Pennington (1999) noted that Grigorenko et al. (1997) "found a highly significant linkage between deficits in a phoneme awareness phenotype in dyslexic families and markers on essentially the same region of chromosome 6" (p. 647).

A locus at chromosome 6 was not the only locus identified by Grigorenko et al. (1997). Single-word reading was linked to a marker on the long arm of chromosome 15 (15q21–q23). The finding of breakpoints in translocation (between segments of chromosomes 2 and 15) in association with dyslexia is consistent with this locus (Napoli-Hemmi, Taipale, Haltia, Lehesjoki, Voutilainen, & Kere, 2000; Taipale et al., 2003. Evidence suggestive of a link between spelling, rather than reading, ability and chromosome 15 (but not chromosome 6) in seven extended families with a history of spelling disability in Germany was found by Schulte-Körne et al. (1998b). The locus identified (15q21) was the same as that identified by Grigorenko et al. (1997) despite the different phenotype definitions in the two studies (reading disability in the case of Grigorenko et al., 1997; spelling disability in the case of Schulte-Körne et al., 1998b). Given that the locus on chromosome 6 identified by Grigorenko et al. was linked to phoneme awareness, one might have expected that spelling disability would have been linked to the same locus (6p21–p22) rather than to chromosome 15. Schulte-Körne et al. (1998b) suggested that "if the gene residing on chromosome 6 has only a minor effect on spelling disability, then our sample size might have been too small for detection [of linkage]" (p. 281).

According to Grigorenko et al. (1997), their own results "suggest that there are at least two loci contributing to somewhat distinct phenotypes of reading disability" (p. 31) but caution about this was expressed by Pennington (1997). The latter commented as follows:

Grigorenko et al. found that their single-word reading phenotype was significantly linked to a marker near the centromere on chromosome 15 and that their phoneme-awareness phenotype was very significantly linked to markers on the short arm of chromosome 6, but they did not find a significant difference between the results for each measure at each genetic location ... Grigorenko et al.'s interpretation of their findings implies a genetic "double dissociation" between the genes influencing the two phenotypes ... But this implied double dissociation does not fit with the cognitive science understanding of reading ... Single-word reading is not cognitively separate from phoneme awareness, since phoneme awareness is essential for the development of single-word reading; thus their genetic influences should overlap, at least to some extent. In sum, any conclusion about their genetic independence is premature until there is a significant difference in linkage at each location, and even then it would be important to rule out problems related to the variation in phenotypes and markers.

(Pennington, 1997, p. 15)

In contrast to the findings of linkage between reading disability and a region of chromosome 6 (6p23–p21.3) reported by Cardon et al. (1994) and Grigorenko et al. (1997), replicated with an increased sample size by Grigorenko, Wood, Meyer, and Pauls (2000) and recently confirmed by Grigorenko, Wood, Golovyan, Meyer, Romano, and Pauls (2003), no linkage was found by Field and Kaplan (1998) despite using the same markers in a study of 79 families with at least two dyslexic siblings. Field and Kaplan (1998) suggest that "if a dyslexia predisposing locus does exist on chromosome 6p, it may be relevant to a subtype of dyslexia that was not well represented in our sample" (p. 1453). Field and Kaplan go on to point out that whereas Cardon et al. (1994) and Grigorenko et al. (1997) selected their families on the basis of reading disability generally, they themselves selected families on the basis of impairment in phonological decoding skills (as assessed by so-called word attack tests). Field and Kaplan (1998) also used a different method of data analysis, quantitative trait locus mapping, to the method of non-parametric

affected pedigree member analysis used by Cardon et al. (1994) and Grigorenko et al. (1997). That is, Field and Kaplan (1998) categorized individuals according to whether they did or did not show "phonological decoding dyslexia" (with a third uncertain category), as compared with the quantitative measures of reading disability or phonological awareness used by Cardon et al. (1994) and Grigorenko et al. (1997). However, re-analysis of the data of Field and Kaplan (1998) using quantitative measures of phonological awareness, phonological decoding, spelling and rapid naming again failed to reveal evidence of linkage to the p region of chromosome 6 (Petryshen, Kaplan, Fu Liu, & Field, 2000). On the other hand, using both qualitative and quantitative linkage analyses, Petryshen et al. (2001) found suggestive (but not statistically significant) evidence for a susceptibility locus on the long arm of chromosome 6 (6q11.2–q12).

Lack of agreement in the findings of Field and Kaplan (1998) and Petryshen et al. (2001) on the one hand and Cardon et al. (1994) and Grigorenko et al. (1997) on the other underscores the fact that different methods of selecting participants and classifying reading disability (i.e. the phenotype), not to mention the use of different markers and techniques of analysis, should not necessarily be expected to provide identical results (see, for example, Grigorenko et al., 2003). Petryshen et al. (2000, 2001) studied Canadian families in which there were at least two dyslexic siblings, whereas most other studies have used families with a single proband. Petryshen et al. (2001) argue: "Thus, the most probable cause of our inability to detect 6p linkage was that our sample contains different proportions of various dyslexia genes than other samples due to our stricter ascertainment criteria" (p. 515).

Gayán et al. (1999) analysed 180 individuals from 79 families who were entirely independent of the sample analysed by Cardon et al. (1994). Twin pairs, at least one of whom showed evidence of reading difficulty, were selected and administered a battery of tests, including tests of orthographic coding and of phonological decoding. Siblings of these twins and of a control sample of twins in whom there was no indication of reading problems were also tested. Analyses of the data revealed that both orthographic and phonological aspects of reading are influenced by a quantitative trait locus (QTL) on the short arm of chromosome 6. Gayán et al. (1999) point out that "The closeness of this putative QTL to the human leukocyte antigen region suggests the possible implication of a coding or regulatory gene related to the immune system on reading deficits" (p. 163). Recently, the samples analysed by Cardon et al. (1994) and Gayán et al. (1999) were combined in a sample of 127 families. Re-analysis of data from 104 families (not all were informative because of missing phenotypes and/or genotypes) using different methods confirmed linkage of a number of reading-related processes (including orthographic coding) to a particular chromosomal region, namely 6p21.3–22 (Kaplan et al., 2002). It should be noted, however, that the P-values were not corrected for multiple tests, Bonferroni tests being considered too conservative. Since all phenotypic measures were intercorrelated, the assumption of independence was not met.

Fisher et al. (1999) used a data set based on 82 families in the UK chosen for inclusion in the study if there were indications of reading disability in one or more of the siblings of the proband. The latter were drawn from children referred to the "dyslexia clinic" at a hospital at which orthoptic studies were carried out and reported by Stein and his colleagues (see Chapter 11), so arguably there may have been a bias in the nature of the difficulties experienced by the children who were referred. Probands were defined in terms of a discrepancy between their standardized reading score and that predicted on the basis of a test of their verbal or non-verbal reasoning ability. Four quantitative phenotypes were measured: word recognition, discrepancy between IQ and reading age, orthographic coding (as determined by a test of irregular word reading) and phonological decoding (as determined by a test of nonword reading). Analysis of the data suggested that a quantitative trait locus on chromosome 6, consistent with the region identified by the above studies using different analytic techniques (Cardon et al., 1994; Gayán et al., 1999), influences both irregular and nonword reading. Confirmation of a QTL related to reading disability located on chromosome 6 (and another on chromosome 15) has been presented (with more refined mapping of the relevant gene loci) for another British sample of over 100 unrelated probands and their parents by Morris et al. (2000).

Fisher and colleagues have provided evidence of a quantitative trait locus based not on targeting specific chromosomal regions but on a genome-wide scan, the first such study to be published in relation to dyslexia. As well as confirming a region on chromosome 6 (6p21.3) for the same UK sample as reported by Fisher et al. (1999), but using a different method, and a region on chromosome 2 (2p15–p16), as reported for a Norwegian sample by Fagerheim, Raeymaekers, Tønnessen, Pedersen, Tranebjaerg, and Lubs (1999), this latest analysis yielded evidence of a QTL for reading-related processes on chromosome 18 (18p11.2) in each of two samples from the UK and one from the USA (Fisher et al., 2002).

Summary and further considerations

Despite some negative findings, there appears from this brief review to be growing evidence of a contribution to components of reading from a gene or genes located on chromosome 6 and possibly chromosomes 15 and 18. This is not to deny that other gene loci may be involved. Rabin, Wen, Hepburn, Lubs, Feldman, and Duara (1993) in a brief report suggested a link between reading disability and chromosome 1 (see also Froster, Schulte-Körne, Hedebrand, & Remschmidt, 1993). Using non-parametric linkage analysis on data from a large Norwegian family ($n = 80$) with 36 affected members, evidence linking dyslexia to a gene on chromosome 2 (localized to 2p15–16) was found by Fagerheim et al. (1999). Thus at least five regions relevant to dyslexia have been identified and there may be more (Stromswold, 2001). For example, using 320 markers Nopola-Hemmi et al. (2001) studied segregation of dyslexia in a pedigree derived from 140 families. Linkage analysis revealed a new susceptibility locus on chromosome 3. Given heterogeneity in the phenotype and the different susceptibility loci identified, it is probable that individuals with reading difficulties differ in their genetic aetiology. However, identification of susceptibility loci does not mean that the mode of inheritance of susceptibility to dyslexia has been worked out, although future progress in this regard is likely to be rapid. A candidate gene on chromosome 15 (DYX1C1) has been recently proposed by Taipale et al. (2003).

It should be be appreciated that the gene loci implicated are unlikely to be concerned with reading *per se* (Ellis, 1985); there has been insufficient time for reading-specific genes to have evolved since the appearance of written language approximately 6000 years ago (but see McManus, 1991). Rather, the relevant genes must be involved in the fundamental phonological (speech-related) processes on which reading depends. As Pennington (1997) put it: "contrary to intuition, individual differences in reading skill have more to do with speech than with vision and at least as much to do with single-word processing as with the processing of connected text" (p. 14). Exactly how the genes have their effect has yet to be worked out. Given that they are not concerned with reading *per se*, it is to be expected that they will be associated with other aspects of developmental language disorder.

Gallagher et al. (2000) have reported data showing that early speech and language skills predict later literacy outcome. At the age of 6 years, 36 of 63 children at genetic risk of dyslexia (i.e. with at least one affected first-degree relative) scored at least one standard deviation below the mean of a control group of children on tests of literacy development compared with 4 of 34 control children. Those "at risk" children who showed delayed literacy at age 6 years were significantly impaired in comparison with the controls on a number of tests of speech and language at age 45 months. Gallagher et al. suggested that their findings show that "children from at-risk families who are slow to develop literacy skills at 6 years experienced a rather general language delay at 45 months" (p. 207). The findings could not be attributed to differences in parental support for reading-related activities and therefore suggest that some genetic factor affecting speech and language development is involved (see also Snowling et al., 2003).

The study by Gallagher et al. (2000) does not establish conclusively that their findings constitute a genetic effect as opposed to being environmentally determined. The causes of difficulty in learning to read are manifold and not all of them are heritable. One cannot, for example, inherit poor teaching or lack of opportunity (at least not directly). Reports that dyslexia is found more frequently among children of high compared with low birth rank and in families with large sibships (Melekian, 1990) are also difficult to square with a wholly genetic determination of reading disability. Furthermore, "A susceptibility locus, unlike a disease locus, is neither necessary nor sufficient to produce the disorder in question" (Pennington, 1999, p. 646). Nonetheless, it is now widely accepted that there is at least a genetic component to many, if not most, cases of reading disability.

Given the evidence of a genetic contribution to dyslexia, there is growing interest in the possibility of identifying children at risk even at a very young age (see Borstrøm & Elbro, 1997; Lyytinen, 1997; Molfese, 2000). The hope is that if children likely to become dyslexic can be identified early enough, then the possibility of effective intervention may be increased. Indications that children under the age of 5 who have one or two dyslexic parents are likely to score lower than control children on certain phonological (speech-related) tasks, such as rhyme awareness and production (Locke, Hodgson, Macaruso, Roberts, Lambrecht-Smith, & Guttentag, 1997), encourage this belief.

GENETICS AND DEFINITIONS OF DYSLEXIA

A question arises as to how the results of genetic studies relate to definitional issues surrounding reading disability or impairment. I know of no genetic study that has defined dyslexia in the way championed by Miles (1993a, b) and others of the same persuasion. Taking seriously the concept of "dyslexia" as nosologically distinct from other types of poor reading and spelling (as advocated by Miles) might lead to some unexpected results. In short, different definitions of dyslexia might lead to different conclusions being drawn.

Using data from the Colorado Twin Project, Pennington et al. (1992) compared children defined as reading-disabled either on the basis of a discrepancy between age and reading achievement or on the basis of a discrepancy between achievement and that predicted from IQ. Seventy per cent of the children who were reading-disabled met both discrepancy criteria but the same proportion of the remainder (i.e. 30 per cent) met the criteria for only one of the definitions. Although there were few significant differences between the groups of disabled readers defined according to the discrepancy between age or IQ, there were a number of trends in terms of sex ratios, neuropsychological profiles and relationship to phonological or orthographic coding ability. It could be, as pointed out by Pennington et al., that these:

> . . . reflect the different contexts in which the same genes for RD [reading disability] express themselves, instead of pointing to distinct etiologies. "Backward" readers have the genes for RD *as well as* genetic and environmental risk factors for other cognitive disabilities, whereas children with IQ-discrepant RD have, on average, fewer of these other risk factors and hence have more specific deficits and a better ability to compensate for their deficits.
> (Pennington et al., 1992, p. 571, emphasis in original)

Wadsworth et al. (2000b) analysed data from monozygotic and dizygotic twin pairs from the Colorado Reading Project and the Colorado Learning Disabilities Research Center. From an initial sample of unselected twins, pairs of twins were selected on the basis that at least one member of the pair could be described as being reading-disabled. Participants were then divided into two groups according to the full-scale IQ averaged for each twin pair. Heritability estimates

were then made separately for those twin pairs with average IQ less than 100 and those with an average IQ more than 100. The heritability estimates (using the method devised by De Fries and Fulker, 1985) were 0.43 and 0.72 for the low and high IQ groups, respectively. These values differ significantly and suggest that genetic influences are a more important cause of reading disability among children with high as opposed to low IQ scores. However, they do not speak to the issue of whether there is a different genetic influence as a function of IQ. Although different proportions of variance are accounted for by genetic factors, this might well be because the impact of environmental factors varies with IQ. In fact, Wadsworth et al. (2000b) suggest that "the environment for reading development could be both more favorable and more homogeneous, on average, for children with higher IQ scores, with the result that the environment would have less of an impact in producing individual differences in these children" (p.198).

GENETICS AND NORMAL VARIATION IN READING AND LANGUAGE ABILITY

Pennington et al. (1992) pointed out "the logical possibility that age-discrepant and IQ-discrepant definitions of RD [reading disability] may not be etiologically distinct from each other, but their common etiology may be distinct from that underlying the normal distribution of reading ability" (p. 570). Some years earlier, Stevenson et al. (1987) had argued that "the genetic mechanisms contributing to individual differences within the normal range might well be different from those producing very poor performance" (p. 231). DeFries and Alarcón (1996) made the same point when they wrote that "multiple regression analysis of twin data suggests that the etiology of reading disability may differ from that of individual differences in reading performance" (p. 44).

It does not necessarily follow from the fact that reading disability has a strong heritable component that the same applies to normal reading scores, although, as Pennington (1999) points out, a small number of (quantitative trait) loci may underlie the transmission of both dyslexia and normal variation in reading skill. In fact, a strong heritable contribution to phenotypic variance in oral reading performance (and a weaker but still significant shared environmental contribution) has been reported from a large-scale population study of twins unselected for reading disability (Reynolds et al., 1996).

Given the association between phonological awareness and early reading, it would not be surprising to find that phonological ability is to some extent inherited. A question would remain, though, as to the relation between phonological ability and other language-related skills. Hohnen and Stevenson (1999) point out that "even in studies that have found phonological processing to make a significant independent contribution to reading, the amount of variance explained is relatively small compared with the amount that it jointly contributes with general language. These findings suggest that the relationship requires further investigation" (p. 591).

The heritability of phonological ability with regard to normal variation (i.e., not simply in disabled readers) was examined by Hohnen and Stevenson (1999) in a study of 66 monozygotic and 60 dizygotic twins. A model-fitting approach was used to estimate the extent to which individual differences in literacy (single-word reading and spelling), general language skills and phonological awareness are caused by genetic, shared environmental and specific environmental factors. The authors reported that:

> After genetic effects on IQ were controlled, a separate genetic influence was identified that acted on literacy, phonological awareness, and language. No genetic link between phonological awarenesss and literacy independent of general language ability was found; such covariance was mediated through environmental influences. Individual differences in literacy ability are substantially influenced by genetic factors, some of which also act on phonological awareness and general language ability.
> (Hohnen & Stevenson, 1999, p. 590)

Hohnen and Stevenson concluded that their analyses "support the view that that there is a single underlying dimension of individual difference that is genetically mediated and is specific to verbal skills. This ability is independent of general intelligence and influences general language ability, phonological awareness, and literacy" (p. 598).

The fact that both language and literacy are influenced by a shared genetic factor explains both why a strong relationship between language and literacy has been recorded in the literature and why a substantial amount of variance in literacy is accounted for jointly by phonological awareness and language. Once the effects of general language ability have been statistically removed, phonological awareness accounts for independent variation in reading ability because both phonological awareness and literacy skills share an independent, environmentally mediated influence. This environmental factor may include such things as classroom instruction, which affects phonemic skills and reading.

Any genetic contribution to dyslexia is presumably expressed in the anatomy and/or physiology of the brain. The cortex or outer mantle of the brain consists of two heavily convoluted halves, which, to the naked eye, look mirror images of each other. These two halves or hemispheres are separated by the longitudinal fissure. The lateral fissure, the fissure of Sylvius, separates the temporal lobe from the frontal lobe (and part of the parietal lobe) on each side. The central sulcus or fissure (or fissure of Rolando) of each hemisphere is often regarded as marking the boundary between anterior and posterior regions of the the brain (see Figure 2, p. 154).

GYRAL PATTERNS

The pattern of convolutions or gyri is approximately the same within the left and right hemispheres. The basic pattern of gyral morphology appears to be fixed at birth, but there is evidence from animal research that gyral development may be disrupted by certain peri-natal and presumably

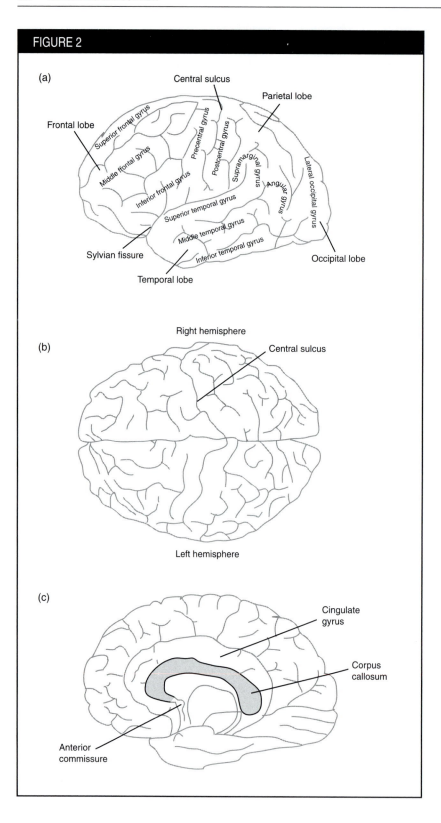

Figure 2 Lateral view of the left hemisphere (a), dorsal view of the cerebral cortex (b) and medial view of right hemisphere (c) in humans.

pre-natal events (Herman et al., 1997). In humans, any anomaly in the pattern of gyral development may be relevant to the biological underpinnings of dyslexia.

Although there is sufficient gross similarity across different brains for individual major gyri and sulci to be readily identified and thereby serve as cortical landmarks, there is also some degree of individual variability (Rademacher, Caviness, Steinmetz, & Galaburda, 1993; Steinmetz & Seitz, 1991; Whitaker & Selnes, 1976), which can make it difficult to specify comparable locations across different brains (Leonard, Puranik, Kuldau, & Lombardino, 1998). Indeed, Leonard et al. (1998) argue that "The identification of landmarks is not straightforward … It is time to recognise the arbitrary nature of landmark identification and the relatively abstract, derived and evanescent nature of concepts such as Heschl's gyrus and Heschl's duplications" (pp. 403, 404).

The first published report of a post-mortem examination of the brain of a purportedly dyslexic individual was of a boy named Billy, who died suddenly (presumably around the age of 12 years, but this is not explicitly stated) of a cerebellar haemorrhage. Drake (1968) wrote: "in the cerebral hemispheres, anomalies were noted in the convolution pattern of the parietal lobes bilaterally. The cortical pattern was disrupted by penetrating deep gyri that appeared disconnected. Related areas of the corpus callosum appeared thin" (p. 496). Billy was apparently subject to sudden outbursts of temper and showed frequent mood swings. He was said to have marked difficulty with reading and writing and some difficulty with arithmetic, although by age 12 years 2 months his performance on standard tests indicated that he performed at a more or less satisfactory level in reading and spelling. Other aspects of the report suggest that he would today be classified as showing attention-deficit hyperactivity disorder (ADHD). Billy's medical history included recurring left frontal headaches during the 2 years prior to his death and "dizzy spells" and "blackouts" occurring from 6 years of age. In short, the extent to which Billy could be regarded as a "representative" dyslexic person is unclear.

Steinmetz, Ebeling, Huang, and Kahn (1990a) classified human brains examined either post-mortem or by MRI scanning into one of four types according to their gyral morphology. Cases showing juxtaposition of the upward inclined branch of the Sylvian fissure (posterior ascending ramus, PAR) and the post-central sulcus were referred to as Type I. Cases where there was no PAR were classified as Type II. In cases of Type III there was an intermediate sulcus between the post-central sulcus and the PAR, and in Type IV cases the PAR was continuous with the post-central sulcus so that the supramarginal gyrus was absent. Type I (said to be the "classical" morphology shown in textbooks) was the most common variety encountered in both hemispheres, but significantly more common in the right than the left hemisphere. Type II was only found in the left hemisphere; Type III was significantly more common in the left hemisphere and Type IV more common in the right hemisphere. Using this scheme of classification, Leonard et al. (1993) compared the gyral patterns, as revealed by MRI, of nine adults aged 15–65 years with a history of reading problems, 10 unaffected first-degree relatives and 12 unrelated normal readers. Type III cases were relatively (and significantly) more common and Type I cases relatively infrequent in the left hemisphere among the poor readers compared with the unrelated control readers.

An association between gyral morphology and membership of a dyslexic group (n = 22), a control group of normal readers (n = 13) or a group of children diagnosed as having ADHD (n = 20) was not found by Hiemenz and Hynd (2000). These findings conflict somewhat with those of an earlier report (Hynd & Hiemenz, 1997) based on a larger number of participants in each group (27, 14 and 38 dyslexics, normal readers and children with ADHD, respectively). In the latter article, it is reported that, in the left hemisphere, dyslexics differed significantly from the ADHD group in showing a reduced incidence of Type 3. In the right hemisphere, dyslexics had a "significantly reduced incidence of Type 1 morphology (57%) and a higher incidence of Type 3 (37%)" (p. 51). Hynd and Hiemenz

(1997) suggested that there may be a familial component to gyral morphology (see also Bartley, Jones, & Weinberger, 1997). On the other hand, Steinmetz, Herzog, Schlaug, Huang, and Jäncke (1995) found no evidence for a genetic influence on the size of a particular region of the temporal lobe in monozygotic twins (who were discordant for handedness). In contrast, Oppenheim, Skerry, Tramo, and Gazzaniga (1989) reported that there was greater similarity in size and shape of the corpus callosum among pairs of monozygotic twins than among control twins.

Clark and Plante (1998) compared the brain scans of 20 parents of "developmental language-disordered" children with those of 21 unrelated "controls". The morphology of the inferior frontal gyrus (Broca's area) was classified in terms of the presence or absence of "extra sulci". The distributions by morphological type for these two groups did not differ significantly. However, when the participants were divided into those who were said (on the basis of the combined results from a short test battery) to show evidence of language disorder (15 and 4 individuals, respectively, from the original two groups), the distributions differed. There were relatively more individuals with extra sulci in the "language-disordered" group than among those without any evidence of language disorder. The tests used to classify participants into these two groups included tests of written spelling and articulation rate but not of reading. Other tests involved following oral instructions (the Token Test) and a test of vocabulary. The implications of these findings with regard to dyslexia are unclear. The same applies to the presence of more than one trans-verse gyrus of Heschl, which has been said to be more frequent among dyslexics than controls (Leonard et al., 1993) and appears to be a herit-able feature of brain morphology (Eckert & Leonard, 1999). Although a second gyrus of Heschl is more common on the right (see Chapter 8), a second gyrus has been reported on the left in seven of nine participants with a specific phono-logical deficit (see Eckert & Leonard, 2003), although this has not been a consistent finding (e.g. Green et al., 1999).

It has not yet been demonstrated that different gyral patterns in either developmental language disorder or developmental dyslexia are of any significance. However, it is of interest that Hiemenz and Hynd (2000) report differences on certain linguistic measures as a function of gyral type (irrespective of group membership). In par-ticular, children of Type 1 morphology scored more highly than those of Type III on a test of vocabulary (Peabody Picture Vocabulary Test – Revised), the data being analysed separately for each hemisphere.

In a series of post-mortem studies of the brains of people who were said to be dyslexic dur-ing their lifetime, Galaburda and colleagues noted a number of cortical abnormalities, including ectopias and microgyria, in peri-Sylvian areas of the left hemisphere in particular. Ectopias are abnormalities of cell migration between different cortical layers and were also reported to be pres-ent in the brain of the first case of learning dis-order to come to autopsy (Drake, 1968). Accord-ing to Rosen, Galaburda, and Sherman (1989), "Polymicrogyria is defined by the presence in the cerebral cortex of an area containing mutiple, narrow, short, curved gyri occupying a variable extent of the cortical surface. When the affected area is small and limited in the number of abnormal gyri, the condition may be referred to plainly as microgyria" (p. 237, footnote 1). It is possible that cortical microgyria and abnormal-ities of the medial geniculate nucleus in dyslexia (Livingstone, Rosen, Drislane, & Galaburda, 1991) are related in some way (Herman, Gal-aburda, Fitch, Carter, & Rosen, 1997).

It is not clear what should be concluded from the histological findings of Galaburda and col-leagues, since these abnormalities are also found post-mortem (Kaufmann & Galaburda, 1989), although to a lesser extent and more frequently in the right than the left hemisphere, in some pro-portion of brains from neurologically normal individuals. Galaburda, Sherman, Rosen, Aboitiz, and Geschwind (1985) suggested that focal dysgenesis in dyslexic brains might lead either directly to cognitive deficit or indirectly to restructuring of connections between associated cortical areas. The latter idea was thought to be supported by the case of a single rat fortuitously observed to have a type of microgyria in association with an abnormal pattern of callosal terminations (Rosen et al., 1989).

The search for the biological underpinnings of dyslexia has not concentrated on microscopic anomalies but rather on macroscopic differences between dyslexics and control brains. In particular, much attention has been given to how asymmetry in function and structure of the left and right cerebral hemispheres might relate to dyslexic difficulties. For a long time, interest centred on the functional role of the cerebral hemispheres; only more recently has there been research on possible structural factors. Historically, questions relating to the relative roles of the left and right hemispheres were pursued in relation to issues surrounding left- and right-handedness or other manifestations of sideness. These are discussed in the following chapter.

8

Laterality, Dyslexia and Hormones

Observations linking laterality of hand or eye with difficulty in learning to read have a long history. Samuel Orton is usually credited (if that is the right word) with the idea that reading disability is associated with anomalies of so-called cerebral dominance (Orton, 1925). This term refers to the idea that one half of the brain takes a leading role in specific functions. The notion of cerebral dominance current at the time, propagated with respect to stuttering in particular (Travis & Johnson, 1934), was that one cerebral hemisphere, almost always the left, was in some way dominant over its partner. There appeared also to be a tacit assumption that this state of affairs took some time to develop and that the lack of a strong preference for one hand or the other reflected an intervening or immature state of "sideness". From here it was but a short step to arguing that incomplete lateralization at the level of the hand and/or eye reflected a failure of one hemisphere to develop dominance over the other. This idea became especially popular within the context of mirror-writing and mirror-reading.

MIRROR-WRITING AND MIRROR-READING

It is well known that Leonardo da Vinci habitually wrote in mirror-fashion and with his left hand after his right became paralysed (Critchley, 1928; Ireland, 1881; see also Capener, 1952). The phenomenon of mirror-writing, however, had attracted attention much earlier. In his 1928 monograph on the subject, Critchley wrote:

> Probably the earliest reference in literature was made in 1698 by Rosinus Lentilius. In his Miscellanea medico-practica Tripartita he mentions briefly a left-handed epileptic girl who used to write with her left hand "inveris litteris", which were unreadable unless viewed in a mirror. A few years later he saw a second case in a soldier of Nordlinga whose right arm had been hacked off in battle; this soldier then started to write mirror-wise with his left hand ... For nearly two centuries no further reference was made upon the subject until ... 1878.
>
> (Critchley, 1928, p. 9)

Mirror-writing was traditionally said to be associated with epilepsy, stammering, "feeble-mindedness" and left-handedness (Gordon, 1921; Inman, 1924; Ireland, 1881; Orton, 1925; see Burt, 1958). Parson (1924) stated flatly that "spontaneous mirror-writing occurs only among *left-handed children, and among right-handed adults who have suffered right hemiplegia and a consequent change of eyedness from right to left*"

(p. 86, emphasis in original). Inman (1924) went so far as to assert that "the tendency to mirror-writing in left-handers is so well known that it needs only a [passing] reference" (p. 215). He described the case of a boy who was developing a squint and was writing double (e.g. 229977 for 297). The boy was "the youngest of six, of whom all but the first two were left-handed until the age of seven or eight, when they became right-handed. All these left-handers have tended to write backwards, mirror fashion" (p. 215).

In a review of mirror-writing, Blom (1928) referred to no fewer than 81 sources, a good many of which associated mirror-reading and/or -writing with left-handedness. More recent authors have also suggested that mirror-reading and/or writing is both more frequent and more efficient (Peters, 1983; Tankle & Heilman, 1982, 1983; Tucha, Aschenbrenner, & Lange, 2000) among normal left-handed than right-handed adults (but see Bradshaw, Nettleton, Wilson, & Burden, 1985; Vaid & Stiles-Davis, 1989).

Orton (1925, 1928) believed that letter reversals and mirror-writing were especially common in poor readers. His theoretical contribution to the field of dyslexia was to provide an explanation for poor reading based on ideas that already existed in the literature concerned with mirror-writing. He argued that the memories or engrams of letters and words were laid down in the correct orientation in one hemisphere but in the reverse orientation in the opposite hemisphere. Normally the dominant hemisphere "suppresses" the minor hemisphere but in cases of "weak" or "incomplete" dominance of one hemisphere, there is "incomplete elision of one set of antitropic engrams and there results confusion as to direction of reading which serves as an impediment to facile associative linkage with the auditory engrams" (Orton, 1928, p. 1051). Orton (1925) coined the term "strephosymbolia" to refer to "confusion, because of reversals, in the memory images of symbols" and (rather oddly) "as a descriptive name for the whole group of children who show unusual difficulty in learning to read" (p. 610).

Orton cannot have been the first to think of images being laid down in mirror-image fashion in the two hemispheres. Discussing mirror-writing by left-handers in schools and institutions, Ireland had this to say:

It may be asked, is the image or impression, or change in the brain tissue from which the image is formed, reversed like the negative of a photograph; or if a double image be formed in the visual centre, one in the right hemisphere of the brain and the other in the left, do the images lie to each other in opposite directions, e.g. C on the right and [reversed] C on the left?

(Ireland, 1881, p. 367)

Critchley (1928) stated (without providing any data) that "mirror-writing executed with either hand may be seen in the belated efforts at writing made by children with congenital word-blindness" (p. 17). This belief, allied to the idea that children with delayed reading showed an unusual proportion of reversal errors, led to a number of studies being carried out into mirror-reading and -writing during the inter-war years. Working as a research associate for Samuel Orton, Monroe (1928) reported that delayed readers were quicker at mirror-reading than normally developing children of the same reading grade and that the poor readers "were more successful at every reading grade in reversing the direction of writing than were the normal readers" (p. 412). She subsequently reported that "Left-eye preference . . . is associated with fluent mirror-reading, and fluent mirror-reading is associated with reading disabilities" (Monroe, 1932, p. 90). However, an association between either crossed eye–hand dominance or left-eyedness and accurate mirror-reading was not confirmed by Kirk (1934) in a sample of 61 children whose median IQ was 67. Given Monroe's results with "normal children", Kirk concluded from her own results that "mentally retarded children may be superior mirror readers when compared with normals of the same reading grade. This superiority may tend to eliminate the possible influence of ocular and manual preference in our group" (p. 200). More recently, Miles et al. (2001) did not find dyslexic children of average intelligence or above to be any faster than controls at reading reversed symbols.

Today, we know that mirror reversals are not especially common in cases of reading difficulty, as they are found in a great many children who are learning to read (see Fischer, Liberman, & Shankweiler, 1978; Hildreth, 1934; Liberman, Shankweiler, Orlando, Harris, & Bell-Berti, 1971), though it has been thought that they might persist for longer among younger dyslexic children (Critchley, 1970; Money, 1962). Reversal problems are restricted to the processing of symbols of one's own language and appear to reflect verbal rather than visual problems (Vellutino, 1979). It might be that people expect poor readers to confuse mirror-image letters frequently. In what is conceivably a telling response to a question about the difficulties experienced during reading, one child replied "I see letters backwards, Mum says so" (Eden, Stein, Wood, & Wood, 1994). We also now accept that Orton's theorizing was at fault—engrams are not laid down in mirror image at the two sides of the brain. Indeed, the theory was internally inconsistent since, as Critchley (1970) pointed out, it does not explain "why verbal–symbol arrangement alone is at fault, while surrounding objects, scenes and pictures appear in normal orientation" (p. 65).

HANDEDNESS AND CROSSED HAND–EYE DOMINANCE

Orton based his notion of strephosymbolia on the belief that dyslexic children were more often left-handed or showed crossed hand–eye dominance (right-handed but left-eyed or left-handed but right-eyed) than would be expected by chance. Hallgren (1950) was equivocal with regard to a high frequency of left-handedness but found no support in his data for the view that crossed hand–eye dominance was associated with dyslexia. In point of fact, crossed hand–eye dominance is common, occurring with a high frequency even in right-handers—though it is true that most right-handers are also right-eyed (Annett, 1999a;

Bourassa, McManus, & Bryden, 1996; Dellatolas, Curt, Dargent-Paré, & De Agostini, 1998; McManus, Porac, Bryden, & Boucher, 1999; Porac, 1997). It is possible that eye dominance is influenced by the same genetic factor(s) as handedness (Annett, 2000).

Although Orton's ideas about how memories are laid down were plainly wrong (Corballis & Beale, 1993), his theories were enormously influential despite the fact that he eventually came to realize (Orton, 1937) that even strongly right-handed individuals may become dyslexic (see also Annett & Kilshaw, 1984). Although not everyone accepted Orton's explanation of reading difficulties in terms of cerebral dominance, the idea of reversed images, along with ideas concerning the related problem of left–right confusion (Harris, 1957), certainly caught on despite the obvious difficulty that it was not clear why the images of letters should be reversed but not those of other stimuli, such as pictures or objects.

In short, Orton's ideas were taken up enthusiastically, with the unfortunate consequence that individuals were sometimes said to be dyslexic *because* they were left-handed or crossed-dominant. This has caused no end of confusion and misinterpretation in the literature, not least because the prophecy is likely to be self-fulfilling. Children who were left-handed and poor readers are more likely to have been referred to clinics for the reading-disabled in greater numbers than those who were right-handed (and right-eyed). When people investigated reading disability in such samples, therefore, there was indeed often, but not always, a greater frequency of left-handers!

IS LEFT-HANDEDNESS SINISTER?

In his book on *The Backward Child* (first published in 1937), Sir Cyril Burt devoted a chapter to left-handedness, which he clearly regarded as a defect. He opens the chapter as follows: "Of all the special motor disabilities found among school children, that which interferes most widely with the ordinary tasks of the classroom is left-handedness" (Burt, 1958, p. 270). In his preface he writes: "Since stammering and left-handedness are the defects that seem to cause most trouble both to the teacher and to the child, particular attention has been devoted to these two conditions" (p. ix). Indeed, around this time writers such as Parson (1924) talked of "curing" left-handedness as if it were a disease! We now know better than to regard left-handedness as a "defect", but it is still not unusual for sinistrality to be invested with unusual, but misguided, significance (see Bishop, 1983).

At the end of the nineteenth century, it was common for parents and teachers to make children write with the right hand. Ireland (1881) noted that "Teachers think it their duty to compel left-handed children to use their right [*sic*]" (p. 363). Subsequently, attempts to teach left-handers to write with the right hand (see Inman, 1924; Parson, 1924) and, much more rarely, attempts by native right-handers to write with the left hand (Inman, 1924; Munro, 1932), were thought to result in stammering. In her review of studies on laterality from 1924 onwards, Downey (1933) noted that "The belief that reversal of native handedness in writing may cause a speech defect is fairly wide [*sic*] extended" (p. 124). Fildes and Myers describe the case of a left-handed boy "between six and seven years of age" (p. 273) as follows:

> He had just begun to be taught to write with his right hand; but he found the greatest difficulty in doing so, owing to the coarseness and the want of coordination of the movements of that hand. For these reasons, and especially because he began to stutter, he was soon allowed to write with his left hand only; whereupon the confusion of the positions of letters and the disturbance of speech rapidly disappeared.
>
> (Fildes & Myers, 1921, p. 273)

There were, however, as noted by Downey (1933), many dissenters ("dissentients" was Downey's term) from the common (but not universal) view that teaching left-handers to write with their right hand leads to stammering. Parson

(1924) studied the effects of enforced writing with the right hand and concluded that "not a single case of defective speech could be traced to a reversal of manual habit . . . As the total public school enrollment at the time . . . was about 15,000, and as practically all lefthanded pupils were made to write with the right hand, this result in a period of four years was impressive" (pp. 102–103). Nonetheless, Parson conceded that "the present writer is led to believe that whenever stuttering occurs as a result of changing the native handedness of young children it lasts while the change is being made, and no longer . . . When the stuttering persists, all efforts to effect a change of handedness should of course be abandoned" (pp. 103–104). As a number of writers of the the time appreciated, if the means of enforcing a change of handedness are brutal, then stuttering may arise as a consequence of emotional upset.

Ojemann (1931) summarized data on 23 children who had been trained to write with their right hand though they were otherwise thought to be left-handed on the basis of the hand used for activities such as using scissors, dealing cards and throwing a ball. Two of the children showed some "speech defect" at the time they were tested and four had had a speech defect at some previous time. "In these cases no connection between the training in using the right hand for writing and the speech disturbance could be established" (p. 124). Ojemann's findings led him to conclude that "It appears to be the exception rather than the rule for a speech disturbance to be produced by training left-handed individuals to write with the right hand" (p. 125).

Travis and Johnson reviewed the literature, noting that:

> Ojemann's findings are very valuable in indicating generally the degree to which handedness may be changed in some cases without producing stuttering. It must be remembered, however, that other studies . . . have shown that in some cases even the shifting of a single skill, writing, to the non-dominant hand is followed by the onset of stuttering, so that it would be misleading to

regard Ojemann's findings in twenty-three cases as being universally conclusive.

(Travis & Johnson, 1934, p. 544)

Travis and Johnson (1934) argued that "changes of handedness occur with significant frequency in the history of cases of stuttering" (p. 559). They also concluded that stutterers show "a greater degree of left-laterality and ambilaterality" than normal speakers. Although they believed that familial left-handedness was more frequent among those who stuttered than among normally fluent speakers, they were at pains to point out that "The present writers have never contended . . . that innate left-handedness stands in a causal relationship to stuttering" (p. 560). Rather, in line with Orton's views, they supposed the relevant factor to be "a high degree of ambilaterality" in cerebral organization (p. 559).

In addition to stuttering (and squinting in the view of Inman, 1924; see also Previc, 1993), a raised incidence of mixed- and left-handedness has been noted in very many studies of diverse clinical populations, including dyslexics (Beaton, 1985; Hardyck, 1977). A higher-than-expected frequency of left-handedness in any particular clinical group does not, of course, establish that all left-handedness is pathological. Nonetheless, the idea that left-handers are in some way cognitively inferior to their right-handed peers even among individuals of normal or even superior intelligence was much debated in the late 1960s and 1970s (see Hardyck & Petrinovich, 1977).

Among a small group of graduate students, Levy (1969) found that left-handers had a lower mean non-verbal IQ than right-handers. Briggs, Nebes, and Kinsbourne (1976) reported that among undergraduates, full-scale IQ was lower in left- and mixed-handers than in fully dextral individuals. Following these reports, a flurry of papers were published, some supporting one or other of these positions, others offering contradictory evidence (for a review, see Beaton, 1985). Since then, more methodologically sound studies with large samples (e.g. McManus & Mascie-Taylor, 1983; Newcombe, Ratcliff, Carrivick, Hiorns, Harrison, & Gibson, 1975) have provided no convincing evidence for the notion that nor-

mal left-handers are intellectually inferior to right-handers. This is not to say that there is no relationship at all between cognitive processing and handedness (Annett, 2002; Lewis & Harris, 1990; Martino & Winner, 1995; O'Boyle & Benbow, 1990; Van Strien & Bouma, 1995), although the nature of the relationship has been much disputed.

Whittington and Richards (1987) analysed data from over 11,000 children in the National Child Development Study begun in the UK in 1958. They argued as follows:

The variations revealed in the pattern and rates of development of handedness, coupled to certain ability and attainment deficits, suggest that for a substantial number of children left-handedness and lack of consistent handedness may be associated with processing difficulties. On the other hand it could also be accounted for by a minority of children having more serious learning difficulties, which would be consistent with findings that indicate that left-handedness is a characteristic of learning disabled groups.

(Whittington & Richards, 1987, p. 54)

As Hardyck (1977) observed, "reports on clinic samples, particularly on learning disability cases, remain as the last bastion of evidence for the association of left-handedness and deficit" (p. 305).

LEFT-HANDEDNESS AND DYSLEXIA

Following Orton's lead, many investigators tried to ascertain whether a particular link exists between left-handedness or crossed-laterality and dyslexia. However, while some investigators claimed that there is an association between some aspect of laterality and poor reading (see Dearborn, 1931; Hallgren, 1950), others obtained contradictory results (Gates & Bond, 1936; Hildreth, 1934; Witty & Kopel, 1936). Many studies were methodologically inadequate. Statistical techniques were not often applied, numbers were frequently small in some categories and measures of both handedness and eyedness were usually unsatisfactory by today's standards.

Much of the earlier research on handedness and eyedness in relation to reading impairment (and stuttering) was reviewed by Vernon (1957). She is rightly dismissive of much of this research on the ground that one could not rely upon the accuracy of the assessment of handedness. She posed the question: "What is the upshot of all the experimental work on laterality and cerebral dominance, and of the theories to which it has given rise?" (p. 106). Vernon answered her own question as follows:

> It is of course possible that incomplete lateralization is a sign of a general lack of maturation in the development of cortical functions, which also affects reading . . . But all theories which attribute reading disability to some general lack of maturation are unsatisfactory in that they give no explanation as to why reading alone should be affected, and not other cognitive activities.
>
> (Vernon, 1957, p. 109)

On the other hand, Vernon accepted that lack of maturation might be a predisposing factor and that individuals lacking in maturation might have "no well-established laterality" and exhibit, among other difficulties, reading disability. However, she noted that many reading-disabled individuals are completely lateralized and that the cause of their disability must therefore be sought elsewhere. Annett (1970) emphasized that incomplete lateralization is part of a normal distribution of individual differences, mixed handedness being part of a natural variety of preference found among university students as often as in school children. She concluded that "it seems unlikely that laterality as such can be a causal factor in reading failure" (p. 79).

Critchley (1970) also reviewed some of the earlier literature, admitting that "Why only a proportion of ill-lateralized children should be dyslexic is not easy to understand" (p. 70). Like Vernon, Critchley noted that "undoubtedly . . . some dyslexics are unequivocal dextrals with no history of left-handedness or ambidexterity". He refers to the suggestion of Zangwill (1962) that there might be two sorts of dyslexia, one occurring in fully lateralized individuals and the other in poorly lateralized individuals. Critchley suggested that weak lateralization and reading problems might be associated with an unsuspected cerebral lesion or slow maturation involving a genetic factor controlling both handedness and cerebral dominance. Alternatively, the absence of strong lateral preference might be associated with a particular vulnerability to some sort of perinatal stress factor that also influences acquisition of reading. Critchley (1970) acknowledged that the relationship between cerebral dominance and dyslexia was complicated by the fact that "a child may be only 'relatively' right-handed or left-handed" (p. 72) and that poor readers are a heterogeneous group of people.

According to Gooddy and Reinhold:

> It is well known that many children suffering from congenital dyslexia belong to a family where one parent or relative may be right-handed and another left-handed. Many children with the condition are themselves not strongly right- or left-handed. Some patients are right-handed but left-footed or vice versa, or they may be right-handed and left-eyed. The lack of firmly established right- or left-handedness may indicate the lack of one markedly dominant function of the brain. The lack of differentiation of function of one hemisphere and the other may be a causal factor of the condition. We wish to put forward the theory that asymmetry of right and left cerebral hemisphere functions is normally established as the child grows up; and that this asymmetry of function is closely related to the performance of reading and writing. We believe that children with congenital dyslexia fail to establish asymmetry of function in the cerebral hemispheres.
>
> (Gooddy & Reinhold, 1961, p. 240)

The theory put forward by Gooddy and Reinhold (1961) was hardly original and clearly owes much to Orton's formulation. McFie (1952), too, argued that in cases of specific dyslexia, "the neurophysiological organization corresponding to dominance has not been normally established in either hemisphere" (p. 199). In short, the idea of incomplete lateralization at the cerebral level was implicit in many accounts that emphasized lack of strong dominance at a manual level.

The controversy over a relationship between handedness and reading disability has persisted until the present day, with some researchers finding that there is little or no raised incidence of sinistrality (left-handedness) among dyslexics or reading-impaired children (e.g. Hugdahl, Synnevåg, & Satz, 1990a; Lubs et al., 1993; Rutter et al., 1970) and others finding that there is a higher than expected proportion of left-handers (e.g. Steenhuis, Bryden, & Schroeder, 1993). Naidoo (1972), for example, found a slight but non-significant excess of non-right-handedness among a clinic sample of dyslexic boys compared with controls. There were said to be proportionally more dyslexic than control boys "whose families included one or more members who were wholly or partially left-handed" (p. 966), but relevant figures are not provided. It should be noted, incidentally, that finding an increased proportion of left- or mixed-handers in a group of poor readers does *not* imply that differences in reading ability will be found between left- or mixed-handers and right-handers in the general population.

A comparatively high incidence of left- or mixed-handedness (and/or mixed hand–eye dominance) has been reported among many clinically diagnosed dyslexics (Dearborn, 1931; Hallgren, 1950; Harris, 1957; Naidoo, 1972; Orton, 1937; Zangwill, 1962) but the sample sizes often have been quite small. However, in a larger-scale investigation, Harris (1957) studied a clinic sample of 316 children and reported an excess of mixed- and left-handedness (but not of crossed eye–hand dominance) in comparison with 245 unselected control children.

One reason why there appear to be relatively more left-handers among clinic than school-based populations of dyslexic readers may be a bias in self-referral. If people believe that there is an association between left-handedness and dyslexia, then left-handers with poor reading skills may be more likely to refer themselves to appropriate agencies (Beaton, 1985, 1997). According to Naidoo (1972), reports of an association between atypical laterality and poor reading have been particularly frequent among children referred for neurological investigation, but a response bias may be present even in non-clinic populations (Chavance et al., 1990). This might explain the finding of Steenhuis et al. (1993) that self-reported "dyslexia" was more common among left-handed (as well as among left-eyed) adult respondents to a questionnaire asking about laterality, health and developmental disorders.

In contrast to clinic-based samples, a study of a school-based population of 200 Scottish schoolboys aged 9–10 years found no evidence of an increased incidence of left- or mixed-handedness (based on a 10-item performance battery), eyedness or crossed eye–hand laterality in retarded readers (defined by a reading score at or below the 10th percentile) than in age-matched controls (Belmont & Birch, 1965). Delayed readers were, however, found to perform less well than controls on tests of left–right discrimination. Clark (1970) investigated reading in both sexes in a sample of 1544 normal school children, also in Scotland, and obtained no evidence that mean reading quotients differed for left- and right-handers (defined according to writing hand, or a combination of writing and throwing hand), or as a function of either footedness (kicking a ball) or preferred eye.

Sparrow and Satz (1970) found no difference in handedness between 40 normally reading and 40 poor readers from an American school population (although they did find that 28 per cent of the poor readers had a dichotic left ear advantage as compared with only 8 per cent among the controls, a significant difference in frequency). In the UK, Thomson (1975) compared 60 children whose reading age was 18 months less than their chronological age with controls whose reading level was commensurate with their age. He found that the probability of being a good rather than a "retarded" reader was highest for children whose preferred or dominant hand, foot, eye and ear were all on the same side. So-called "cross-laterality" was more frequent among the poor readers. Thomson pointed out, however, that "the whole question of laterality and attainment is much more complex than has previously been supposed, both by Orton and his followers, as well as his critics. For example, not all reading retardates show inconsistent laterality, and 58 per cent of this sample from the control group did at least one task with their non-preferred side" (p. 320). As will be discussed presently, whether an effect of handedness (or eyedness) is found depends not only upon the measures that are taken, and on the size and composition of the samples of participants, but also on how the data are analysed (see Annett & Turner, 1974).

In an unselected sample of Grade 2 children, no significant difference in reading or other cognitive ability between extremely left- and right-handed children defined by the Harris (1974) test of lateral dominance was found by Satz and Fletcher (1987). These authors argued that, despite the negative findings:

> The tendency to believe that sinistrality is a sign of possible deficit will continue to pervade much of clinical practice with learning-disabled children. The reason is probably threefold: first, myth; second, a small subset of the left-handed populaton [sic] exists who are pathological left-handers (PLH) because of early left-brain injury. However, their cognitive or reading impairment, if present, has nothing to do with left-handedness ... Third, approximately 10–13% of the normal male population are MLH [manifest left-handers], some of whom could become learning disabled for reasons unrelated to handedness.
>
> (Satz & Fletcher, 1987, p. 297)

Levinson (1988) found no relationship between handedness and reading ability in a sample of 4000 learning-disabled individuals of whom 95.5 per cent were said to have past or present reading "symptoms". However, Levinson's assessment of handedness was unspecified except with regard to mixed-handedness, which was said to be "present when a given individual was able to perform one or more functions better or as well with the nondominant hand" (p. 991). This is an unusual definition, especially since one of the tasks considered was that of batting (presumably with a baseball) yet many strong right-handers, at least among professional cricketers in Britain, bat in a left-handed fashion (see Edwards & Beaton, 1996). The participants in Levinson's study who were not considered mixed-handed on this definition were considered strong right- or left-handers. The breakdown of handedness types into right-, left- and mixed-handers was said to be 77.2%, 13.4% and 9.4%, respectively. Although Levinson argued that "The incidence of left-handedness and mixed-handedness in this sample was no higher than that characterizing a random sample" (p. 1001), the proportion of right-handers identified by Levinson is lower than that normally found in unselected populations. In any case, it is not appropriate to compare proportions based on one method of handedness assessment with those based on another. A further problem in Levinson's argument arises from the assessment of the "reading symptoms". These included "continually losing one's place, needing a finger or marker, or having to slow down the tracking activity significantly (slow reading) to fixate and refixate better" (p. 991), all of which are likely to be found to some extent among a wide sample of non-learning-disabled individuals, yet no comparison group of such individuals was included by Levinson.

Bishop (1990b) reviewed 21 studies in which handedness was measured objectively rather than by self-report and there was "some indication that reading level was well below mental age as well as chronological age" (p. 123). From her analysis, Bishop calculated that the rate of left-handedness was 11.2 per cent in dyslexics compared with 5.8 per cent in controls. She concluded that "on the most optimistic interpretation, the rate of left-handedness in dyslexics is twice that of controls" (p. 125). However, this applied only if the disproportionate influence of the negative findings

(Bishop, 1984) from the very large-scale UK National Child Development Study were excluded. She notes that these findings have important methodological implications in that a sample size of nearly 400 (half dyslexic, half controls) would be required to detect an effect of this size.

The literature on the relationship between handedness, cerebral asymmetry and reading disability has been reviewed by a number of authors (Annett, 1985, 2002; Beaton, 1985; Bryden, 1988; Hardyck & Petrinovich, 1977; Obrzut, Boliek, & Bryden, 1997; Satz & Fletcher, 1987). All note the inconsistency in definitions of both handedness and reading disability. Despite both this and the largely negative conclusions of Bishop's review, which has been quoted by some as the last word on this issue, a recent meta-analysis of the same studies (which include clinic samples) as those considered by Bishop (1990b) suggests that, though not great, there is a significantly increased incidence of non-right-handedness among poor or dyslexic readers in comparison with control groups (Eglinton & Annett, 1994).

The observation that there is a raised incidence of left-handedness among dyslexics does not, of course, entail either that most dyslexics are left-handed or that most, or even very many, left-handers are dyslexic. The theoretical challenge is to explain how it is that although there are more left-handed dyslexics than expected, only a minority of left-handers actually become dyslexic. One response to this challenge will be dealt with later; at this point, it is only necessary to emphasize that most dyslexics are not left-handed and that left-handedness or crossed hand–eye dominance in themselves are not indications of a propensity to dyslexia.

Pathological left-handedness

One explanation of the raised incidence of left-handedness among dyslexic individuals is to have recourse to the concept of "pathological left-handedness". The idea appears to have been first proposed by Gordon (1921) but was more formally developed by Satz (1972) as an explanation of the disproportionate number of left-handers seen in various clinical groups. Satz argued that

some proportion of left-handers might be right-handers who had suffered from some degree of very early brain damage. The idea is that in a proportion of cases of pre- or peri-natal unilateral lesion, the damage is such as to cause a shift in control of the preferred hand from one hemisphere to the other. If lesions of the left and right cerebral hemispheres are equiprobable, then the fact that most people are destined to become right-handers means that more individuals will have their handedness shifted from right to left than from left to right. This will have the effect of increasing the proportion of individuals manifesting left-handedness in the population of brain-damaged individuals.

While the pathological left-handedness model accounts for a raised incidence of sinistrality among people with brain damage, it does not explain an increased frequency of left-handedness among clinical but neurologically undamaged samples without further assumptions being made. One is that very early subtle cerebral insult or anomaly sufficient to cause a "shift" in handedness may occur at a particular stage of brain development yet not be serious enough to produce any conspicuous neurological impairment. Bishop (1980) argued that in such cases, one would expect to see particularly poor performance of the non-preferred hand compared with the preferred hand. She confirmed her prediction of a raised incidence of left-handers in a group of normal school children showing this pattern of hand skill. In a later publication, she calculated that in the normal population approximately one case in 20 of left-handedness is due to pathological causes (Bishop, 1990b). Such causes might be related to prematurity and very low birth weight (Coren, Searleman, & Porac, 1982; O'Callaghan, Burn, Mohay, Rogers, & Tudehope, 1993; Ross, Lipper, & Auld, 1987; Saigal, Rosenbaum, Szatmari, & Hoult, 1992) or to so-called birth stress, which has, controversially (see Beaton, 1985, 2003), been linked to left-handedness (Bakan, 1971, 1977; Bakan, Dibb, & Reed, 1973; Coren & Searleman, 1990; see Searleman, Coren, & Porac, 1989).

Not everyone is comfortable with the notion of pathological left-handedness. It was rejected by

McManus (1983), except for the theoretically trivial case in which a severely hemiplegic person cannot use one limb, and Peters (1990) has expressed doubts concerning its application to the "normal" population. With regard to dyslexia, it might be argued that any insult likely to lead to pathological left-handedness might also lead to some subtle disruption of language processing in the left hemisphere and hence to difficulties in the acquisition of reading. A counter-argument might be that an insult sufficient to cause a switch in handedness and to impair language processing would also be expected to produce a shift in lateralization of language from the left to the right hemisphere. There are at least two answers to this. One is that it may well be the case that a switch in language lateralization has occurred. In the vast majority of cases of dyslexia, one simply would not know one way or the other without special investigations. A second answer might be that a switch of handedness does not inevitably follow early unilateral damage (see, for example, Glass, Bulas, Wagner, Rajasingham, Civitello, & Coffman, 1998), although it may do so in some cases (see, for example, Isaacs, Christie, Vargha-Khadem, & Mishkin, 1996).

Despite the fact that some forms of peri-natal brain damage have been associated with difficulties in learning to read (Kawi & Pasamanick, 1958) there are strong arguments for believing that pathology is not the major cause of an increase in left-handedness among dyslexics. There are at least two theories that attempt to explain why this is the case. One of these is the right-shift theory proposed by Annett (1978, 1985, 1995a, 1995b, 2002).

Annett's right-shift theory

The starting point of Annett's theory is not which hand is preferentially used for which activity, but rather the distribution of differences in skill between the left and right hands (hereafter referred to as the laterality distribution). Skill and preference are systematically related (Annett, 1976; Bishop, 1989a) but the skill distribution, being approximately normal, is convenient to deal with. Annett has consistently argued that what has to be explained about human handedness is

not the variation, but the fact that this distribution is continuous and shifted to the right (relative to a hypothetical distribution which has a mean of zero, i.e. no mean difference between left and right sides). This is why her model is termed the right-shift (RS) theory.

It is important to understand that Annett's model is first and foremost a model of cerebral speech lateralization, rather than of handedness. It posits two alleles, rs+ and rs−, at a single gene locus. The rs+ allele (gene) provides some (at present unspecified) advantage to its possessor in speech acquisiton and ensures that speech processes are lateralized to the left hemisphere. In addition, the rs++ coincidentally leads its possessor to be more likely (but not invariably) to become right-handed. This influence is over and above those random factors which otherwise determine handedness. In some cases, the influence of the rs+ gene may not overcome the influence of those chance factors that otherwise lead to the individual being left-handed (the individual is still left-handed); in other cases, the influence of the rs+ gene is in addition to the other factors leading to dextrality. In the absence of the rs+ gene, both speech processes and handedness lateralize to left and right by chance and independently.

The laterality distribution (of differences between the hands in skill) is conceived as being made up of a sub-distribution of individuals who lack the right-shift gene (i.e. are of genotype rs−−) and one or more sub-distributions of individuals who possess the rs+ gene in single or double dose. In her earlier publications, Annett considered only two sub-distributions (rs−− on the one hand and rs+− and rs++ combined on the other) but more recently she has favoured an additive model (see Annett & Kilshaw, 1983) in which the sub-distributions of rs+− and rs++ are separated.

It is not yet possible to identify the different genotypes directly. It is impossible to say to which genotype any given individual belongs. However, the different relative positions occupied by the genotype sub-groups on the laterality distribution imply that the rs−− genotype is relatively more frequent at the left-hand end of the distribution, while the rs++ genotype is relatively more frequent at the right-hand end.

Individuals who make up the rs−− sub-distribution have no systematic bias towards either left hemisphere speech lateralization or handedness—the bias when it occurs is due to the presence of the putative rs+ gene. The various processes involved in speech perception and production may each lateralize to the left or right hemisphere. In some cases, they may be distributed between the left and right halves of the brain. According to the theory, left hemisphere lateralization occurs either due to chance (in half those who are rs−−) or because of the presence of the rs+ gene. The rs+ gene, it is hypothesized, ensures that all these processes come together in a single hemisphere, the left. This is thought to provide some advantage to native language learning. Annett writes:

A child listening to the sound of its own voice has the benefit of a shorter and more reliable feedback path from speech output to auditory input if both are served by the same hemisphere. A longer path across the immature callosum would be involved if input and output were served by different hemispheres. Voice play would be less rewarding for the child and as a consequence could be that the representation of relationships between sounds and phonemes is insecure.

(Annett, 1995b, pp. 437–438)

It follows that dyslexia (of the phonological variety) is more likely to occur among those of rs−− genotype than in those who are rs+− heterozygotes or rs++ homozygotes.

Annett and Manning (1990) argued that individuals weak at phonology are likely to be drawn largely from the rs− genotype and to be at risk of dyslexia. If so, one would expect to find that, as a group, the mean group difference in skill between the two hands is close to zero. The group will include a range of handedness as postulated for a sub-group of the total population that is not "shifted" to the right. If one accepts, however, that there exists another dyslexic sub-type, not

characterized by phonological impairment but by some other deficit, then another group of dyslexics might be found at the right-hand end of the laterality distribution. On average, these people would be strongly dextral.

In support of their predictions, Annett and Manning (1990) reported (see also corrigendum: Annnett & Manning, 1994) that, in a normal school population, mean reading quotients were lower at both ends of the laterality distribution than in the centre (although the data were not analysed statistically in terms of mean quotients). Annett and Kilshaw (1984) had found earlier that not only were there more left- and mixed-handers (and left-footers) among a clinic sample of 129 dyslexics (mainly boys), but also there were relatively more strong dextrals among the dyslexics than among the controls. Bishop (1990b) suggested that the excess of left-handers in the dyslexic group could reflect secular changes in handedness over the past two decades, since the control population used by Annett and Kilshaw was based on samples studied at different times over the past 20 years. However, Bishop's scepticism is probably unfounded. While it is true that there is a greater proportion of left-handers today than was the case 100 years ago (Coren & Halpern, 1991; Gilbert & Wysocki, 1992), there is little or no evidence that there has been any substantial increase in left-handedness over the past two decades (but see McManus, 2003).

Data from unselected school children (Annett, 1992a) provide support for the idea that those with poor phonological processing are more likely to be drawn from the left end of the laterality distribution or continuum. Annett has also claimed that 9- to 11-year-olds with a relative deficit in memory for word forms (orthographic coding) are more dextral on average than controls (Annett, 1992a). These results are unlikely to be due to some form of early pathological development or insult to the brain, since the effects found for school children have been replicated in undergraduates (Annett, 1999b), who might be supposed to constitute a select group that is unlikely to be intellectually handicapped.

Annett (1991) argued that undergraduates who performed relatively poorly in a spoonerism test were more likely to show atypical speech lateralization, as assessed by a dichotic monitoring task, than those who performed relatively well in the spoonerism test. That is, a left ear advantage, often regarded as indicative of right hemisphere speech, was more frequent in the former than in the latter group.

Further support for the idea that poor phonological processing is associated with Annett's rs−− genotype comes from Smythe (2000). She reported in her doctoral thesis that after exclusion of individuals with low levels of performance on tests of hand function (to eliminate those with impaired hand function due to undetected cerebral insult) and further exclusion of individuals with low levels of overall cognitive ability (which might in some way be linked to weak phonological processing and/or possible pathological handedness), children with low scores on a number of tests of phonology were significantly less dextral than children with relatively high scores.

Data suitable for testing the hypothesis have also been collected by Heinz Mayringer and Heinz Wimmer in Austria. Their approach to the data was determined by a hypothesis advanced by Crow, Crow, Done, and Leask (1998) rather than by Annett's right-shift theory. Mayringer and Wimmer (2002) found no support for the idea that children with almost equal levels of left and right hand skill are impaired in reading and spelling. Professor Wimmer has kindly made his raw data available to me, which we are currently analysing from the point of view of Annett's theory. As the number of children tested is the largest so far sampled in this context, the data should prove capable of providing an independent replication or refutation of the theory as it applies to reading (of a transparent orhography).

Bishop (1990b) argued that "What would give greater credence to Annett's genetic theory of dyslexia would be a demonstration that strongly right-handed and non-right-handed dyslexics had different types of reading problem" (p. 128). Annett, Eglinton, and Smythe (1996) classified children aged 10–12 years in terms of their scores on a number of different cognitive tests, including reading, spelling and phonological processing. Those who were considered to be poor readers

were sub-divided into those with relatively poor phonological processing ability and those who were not phonologically impaired. Approximately 24 per cent of the phonologically impaired poor readers wrote with their left hand, while there were no left-handed writers among the poor readers whose phonological skills were sound. The mean difference in skill between the hands of the phonologically impaired poor readers was much less (i.e. further to the left on the laterality distribution) than was the mean hand asymmetry of the remaining poor readers. These findings were seen to be consistent with the idea that different types of reading impairment are associated with different patterns of laterality (Annett, 1996).

The study by Annett and Manning (1990) prompted Palmer and Corballis (1996) to administer Annett's peg-moving task and a standardized test of reading to 203 children from New Zealand aged between 11 years 2 months and 13 years 11 months. As found by a number of investigators (Annett, 1985, 2000; Beaton, 1995, 2003; Resch, Haffner, Parzer, Pfueller, Strehlow, & Zerahn-Hartung, 1997), hand skill differences depended upon the performance of the left hand rather than the right. Following the procedure adopted by Annett and Manning (1990), the children in the study conducted by Palmer and Corballis (1996) were divided into four groups (quartiles) on the basis of the standardized difference between left and right hands in peg-moving. Unlike Annett and Manning (1990), these authors found no curvilinear relationship between reading ability and relative hand skill. However, using regression analyses it was found that after excluding left-handers, there was a significant correlation between reading and the square of the difference between the standardized scores of left and right hands. The square of the left hand score alone also correlated significantly with reading score.

As acknowledged by the authors, there are a number of reasons (other than the possibility that the null hypothesis is correct) why the study of Palmer and Corballis (1996) may not have yielded results similar to those of Annett and Manning (1990). First, the number of participants tested by

Palmer and Corballis (1996) was relatively low. Work from my own laboratory as well as Annett's suggests that numbers need to be relatively high for any effect of the hypothesized rs+ gene to show up against the chance distribution of hand differences. In this context, incidentally, dividing participants into quartile groups may not be optimal for maximal discrimination between the hypothesized genotypes (McManus, Shergill, & Bryden, 1993) because of the expected overlap between the three different genotypes (rs−−, rs+− and rs++) in the distribution of hand-difference scores. A more sensitive method is to classify for levels of cognitive ability first and then to compare hand scores within groups of different level of ability. A second reason for the failure of Palmer and Corballis to replicate the findings of Annett and Manning (1990) may relate to the composition of the participants tested by Palmer and Corballis. They were drawn from three schools with a socially restricted (middle-class) sample of children. Annett (1993) has reported that the chances of gaining entry to a grammar school in the UK (such schools are scholastically and hence socially selective) were related to handedness in a way consistent with the idea that individuals of rs−− genotype are under-represented in such schools. This means that it will be harder to detect any effect of the gene in anything other than a random sample of the population. Third, it may be that any relationship between handedness and reading ability shows up more readily during the early stages of learning to read rather than when reading is well established.

A small number of participants is not a criticism that can be levelled against Resch et al. (1997), who tested 545 German participants aged 17–30 years. Rather than reading, a test of spelling was administered. The authors reported that there was a linear relationship between quartile groups defined on the basis of hand differences on a test of tracing lines and spelling scores regressed on age. Although Resch et al. argued that this result was not as predicted by the right-shift theory, which would lead to the expectation of an inverted U-shaped relationship between the variables, it is possible to argue the contrary position, namely that the results are in fact consistent with Annett's theory. This is because German orthography is highly consistent in letter–sound correspondence and therefore might be regarded as a good test of phonological recoding. If so, one might well expect that with increasing dextrality, the effect of the rs gene would be to lead to better phonological ability and hence to better spelling in a consistent orthography. Reading an irregular or inconsistent orthography such as English, on the other hand, places demands on orthographic recoding. An over-commitment to phonological processing at the expense of orthographic coding might result in a pattern of reading analogous to surface dyslexia. In English, then, the right-shift theory applied to reading would predict an inverted U-shaped function relating handedness to reading ability, but the same might not be expected of spelling in a regular orthography.

CEREBRAL LATERALITY AND READING

The question of a relationship between laterality and reading or cognitive ability generally has been dogged by claim and counter-claim ever since the issue was first discussed by Orton. The interest of the early investigators in putative handedness differences between dyslexics and normal readers eventually gave way to a more direct search for hemispheric differences. A good deal of effort was expended on electroencephalographic and similar indices of asymmetrical hemispheric processing in dyslexia (see Rippon & Brunswick, 2000). Studies using either tachistoscopic hemifield presentation or dichotic listening techniques (e.g. Hugdahl & Andersson, 1987), in particular, were popular at one time and remain so, though other techniques (e.g. McFie, 1952) or modalities of presentation (e.g. Witelson, 1977) were also used. Many of these studies have been reviewed elsewhere (Beaton, 1985; Bryden, 1988; Hiscock & Kinsbourne, 1982; Young & Ellis, 1981). Hiscock and Kinsbourne (1982) cogently explored the theoretical and empirical bases of hemisphere-based accounts of dyslexia. Their analysis covered a range of interrelating issues leading them to end their selective review of laterality and dyslexia as follows: "The data base is inadequate, not only with respect to laterality and its significance in dyslexic children, but also with respect to the more fundamental issues of laterality and its relation to hemispheric specialization and cognitive function in children and adults who read normally" (p. 217). One might add that the level of theoretical and methodological sophistication applied to the design and interpretation of studies was often low. Differences in the scores obtained from the two visual hemifields or at the left and right ears were uncritically accepted as indicative of the degree of hemispheric dominance or asymmetry shown by different groups of readers. Relatively few researchers attempted to understand how laterality data are affected by strategic and other cognitive factors, including attention (see Hugdahl & Andersson, 1987; Obrzut et al., 1997).

In more recent years, interest has tended to centre on supposed neuro-anatomical differences between the hemispheres and on functional hemispheric asymmetry as revealed by neuro-imaging studies. These are discussed in Chapters 9 and 10.

THE HORMONAL THEORY OF DYSLEXIA

Pathological left-handedness and Annett's theory are not the only explanations to have been proposed to account for an increased frequency of left-handedness in dyslexics compared with controls. In a well-known, if methodologically somewhat dubious paper, Geschwind and Behan (1982) proposed that excessively high levels of pre-natal foetal testosterone circulating during early maturation of the brain are associated with increased rates of left-handedness and dyslexia. This was said to be due to a reduction in development of the left hemisphere relative to the right hemisphere in a region known as the planum temporale, part of the superior surface of the temporal lobe. Although the left planum was believed to be larger in adults (Geschwind & Levitsky, 1968), and in fetal brains by 31 weeks gestation (Chi, Dooling, & Gilles, 1977), the

homologous region on the right was thought to mature more quickly at earlier stages of embryogenesis. In addition, it was argued that by suppressing maturation of the thymus gland, testosterone influenced the immune system. These two postulates were considered to explain associations reported by Geschwind and Behan (1982)—on the basis of not very strong evidence—between left-handedness and elevated frequencies both of certain disorders of the immune system and of developmental learning disorders such as dyslexia. However, no definition of dyslexia was provided and selection of their participants was less than satisfactory. For a critique of this paper, see Satz and Soper (1986).

The theory was extended in a series of papers by Geschwind and Galaburda (1985a, 1985b, 1985c), subsequently combined as a single monograph (Geschwind & Galaburda, 1987). High levels of foetal testosterone were said to be associated not with left-handedness *per se*, but with "anomalous dominance" or shifts in lateralization (cerebral or manual) away from the standard or typical pattern of left lateralization for language and a preference for the right hand. (Right hemisphere functions were also included in their argument but will be ignored in the present context.) Geschwind and Galaburda argued:

> Our thesis is that although genes contribute importantly, many influences that lie outside the gene pool of the fetus can alter lateralization patterns. The most powerful factors are variations in the chemical environment in fetal life and, to a lesser extent, in infancy and early childhood. The factors that modify cerebral dominance also influence the development of many other systems, for example, the organs involved in immune response.
>
> (Geschwind & Galaburda, 1987, p. 10)

There is nothing scientifically untoward in the general idea that "the link between anomalous cerebral dominance and dysimmune states (especially in males) is due to genetic effects modified by hormonal factors" (Behan & Geschwind, 1985a, p. 77). In terms of specific detail, however, the theory has come in for considerable criticism (Tønnessen, 1997b). An attempt to formalize the major postulates of the Geschwind–Behan–Galaburda (GBG) theory was made by McManus and Bryden (1991) and an evaluation of the evidence for and against it was published by Bryden et al. (1994a) as a major target article (for replies to peer commentaries, see Bryden, McManus, & Bulman-Fleming, 1994b). An earlier qualitative review of the theory was provided by Habib, Touze, and Galaburda (1990).

With regard to dyslexia, research by Galaburda and his colleagues (Galaburda et al., 1985; Humphreys, Kaufmann, & Galaburda, 1990) suggested that the region of the planum temporale was symmetrical in four autopsied cases of putative dyslexia (see Beaton, 1997, for a critique and review). Subsequent work suggested that symmetrical brains were larger in total area of the planum (left plus right) than asymmetrical brains The implication was, then, that a symmetrical brain is due not (as originally proposed) to a smaller left hemisphere, but to a larger right hemisphere. The theory was therefore modified to suggest that excess testosterone in some way interferes with or arrests the process of cell death (epigenetic involution), whereby the right hemisphere is normally reduced in size (Galaburda, Corsiglia, Rosen, & Sherman, 1987).

It was not until 10 years after its initial proposal that the major postulate was tested directly. Concentrations of amniotic testosterone measured at 16 weeks gestational age were found by Grimshaw, Bryden, and Finegan (1995) to predict handedness in girls and language lateralization (assessed by dichotic listening) in boys at age 10 years. However, the results went in the opposite direction to that predicted by the GBG hypothesis (and thus in the direction proposed by Witelson, 1991; see below). That is, higher concentrations of pre-natal testosterone were associated with stronger right-handedness and stronger left language lateralization.

There are other indications of a relationship between handedness and testosterone. Tan and Tan (1999) found that 8.3 per cent of a sample of 327 neonates exhibit a stronger left- than right-hand palmar grasp reflex (25.7 per cent stronger

on the right, 66.1 per cent equal). Subsequently, these authors reported that for male infants, the strength of the grasp reflex of the left hand (but not the right) was significantly and negatively correlated with testosterone concentration measured from the mother's umbilical artery (Tan & Tan, 2001). For females, there was a negative relationship for both hands. For both sexes, strength of right-handedness (as measured by the difference in palmar reflex strength) increased with concentrations of testosterone (contra GBG). Tan and Tan (2001) proposed that "T[estosterone] acting on the rght and left sides differentially and slowing the development of both sides in different degrees, may create an asymmetric spinal motor system, which, in turn, may stimulate the development of a cortical motor laterality" (p. 190).

It has also been found (Moffat & Hampson, 1996) that adult right-handers show higher concentrations of salivary testosterone than left-handers (or that strongly lateralized individuals of either handedness group have higher testosterone concentrations than weakly lateralized individuals). This, too, contradicts the GBG hypothesis unless low concentrations of foetal testosterone are associated with high concentrations of adult salivary testosterone, which intuitively is unlikely.

Interestingly, it was subsequently reported (Moffat, Hampson, Wickett, Vernon, & Lee, 1997) that the salivary testosterone concentrations taken from a group of 34 pairs of brothers correlated significantly with the mid-sagittal area of the posterior (but not the anterior) half of the corpus callosum as measured by MRI. Testosterone did not correlate with overall brain volume and the correlation remained significant if the latter was controlled for in a partial correlation. If adult testosterone concentrations reflect pre-natal concentrations, this would support indications from animal work that the early administration of testosterone to female rats increases the size of the callosum (Fitch, Berrebi, Cowell, Schrott, & Denenberg, 1990).

According to the GBG theory, cerebral laterality, handedness, learning disorders and immune disease are all related through the action of fetal testosterone. Within this conceptual framework, therefore, researchers have tended to looked for the two- and three-way (occasionally even four-way, Flannery & Liederman, 1995) associations between these variables. Literally hundreds of studies have been carried out to test some aspect or other of the hypothesized associations (Bryden et al., 1994a, 1994b). Unfortunately, many of these studies are methodologically inadequate and/or flawed by small sample sizes and biased ascertainment of participants (Bryden et al., 1994a; Gilger et al., 1998).

With regard to immune disorders, investigations have been carried out to compare the relative incidence of immune disease in left- and right-handers in the population at large (or relatively large samples), or else individuals have been selected on the basis of their handedness and the incidence of immune disorders compared between groups of different handedness. Using the former approach with approximately 17,000 respondents, Bishop (1986) found no association between handedness, measured by skill differences between the hands, and frequency of asthma, allergies and eczema. Dellatolas, Annesi, Jallon, Chavance, and Lellouch (1990) analysed data from two samples. The first was of 698 volunteers using a 10-item handedness questionnaire; the second was of 8659 conscripts to the French army using two items relating to handedness, namely writing and drawing. In neither sample was there an association between allergies and left-handedness. Although different methods of analysis yielded different results, a failure to confirm the predictions of the GBG theory cannot be attributed to insensitive measures of handedness, as there was an association between left-handedness and stuttering and extreme right-handedness was associated with a lower frequency of allergic disorders, including asthma and hay fever. Negative findings with regard to allergies were also reported by Betancur, Vélez, Cabanieu, Le Moal, and Neveu (1990).

Steenhuis et al. (1993) analysed data from nearly 7500 individuals who were given questionnaires and obtained no evidence to suggest that the frequency of (a selected few) auto-immune disorders (and health generally) differs according to handedness (measured by preference questionnaire). The exception was that, contrary to the GBG hypothesis, arthritis was significantly more common in right-handers than in left-handers and ambidexters combined. No association between handedness and (a limited number of) auto-immune diseases was reported. Further negative findings from 11,578 mother–child pairs were reported by Flannery and Liederman (1995). However, their test of handedness in the children was the hand used to draw a cross on a piece of paper, which may not have been discriminating enough to pick up any potential effects.

Hugdahl, Synnevåg, and Satz (1990a, 1991) distributed a questionnaire to 105 Norwegian dyslexic children aged 7–12 years and to 105 age- and sex-matched control children. Their data are not presented in such a way as to be able to determine whether there was an association between handedness and immune diseases, but presumably there was not or the authors would have said so. However, they did report that "The single most important result was the significantly higher occurrence of immune diseases in the dyslexic group compared to the control group" (p. 675), but there was no significant association between non-right-handedness (assessed by a 15-item questionnaire) and dyslexia. Hugdahl et al. (1990a) point out that "if a triadic association involving immune disorder, dyslexia and left-handedness exists, it refers to a small subset of the population with either disorder" (pp. 678–679).

Very similar findings to those of Hugdahl et al. (1990a) were reported for a smaller North American sample of poor readers and their families by Crawford, Kaplan, and Kinsbourne (1994), who used a 5-item handedness questionnaire. An interesting aspect of this study was that steps were taken at the design stage to assess the possibility of biased responding by children who had an identified disorder. The responses of a sub-set of the control children were compared to those of 35 children with chronic eye problems. As there were no group differences in responses, it was assumed that there was no intrinsic methodological bias that would lead children with an identified disorder to respond differently to the controls. The fact that the results from the reading-disabled children differed from those of the controls therefore suggests that the findings are not artefactual.

An alternative approach to looking at immune disease as a function of handedness or reading group involves comparing the incidence of left-handedness in individuals who have a disorder of the immune system with the incidence in a control group of individuals free of immune disease. For example, Searleman and Fugagli (1987) reported an elevated incidence of left-handedness (defined in terms of a 7-item questionnaire rating strength of preference for each item) in 207 people with inflammatory bowel disorder (ulcerative colitis and Crohn's disease) in comparison with a control group. Salcedo, Spiegler, Gibson, and Magilavy (1985) reported that 14.8 per cent of 54 patients (age not given) with the auto-immune condition systemic lupus erythematosus (SLE) were left-handed as determined by the hand used for "writing and eating" elicited during telephone interview. It was reported that this incidence was no greater than that found in an unpublished study of 11- to 17-year-olds or in college students (Spiegeler & Yeni-Komshian, 1983).

No overall association between left-handedness and SLE (or any other illness) was found in 134 patients and 732 controls by Chavance et al. (1990). On the basis of certain features of their data, these authors proposed that much of the research within the context of the GBG hypothesis might suffer from a bias in the way in which individuals complete handedness inventories and health questionnaires (see also Dellatolas et al., 1990). Specifically, they suggested that there might be:

... a relation between the attitude towards questionnaires and the handedness index of right-handers: some subjects might be more ready to say they use the right hand for each of the 10 activities considered and to deny having suffered from a given disease ... Similarly, the right-handers who say they use the left or both hands for one or two activities might be the most apt to answer positively to questions about their health.

(Chavance et al., 1990, p. 437)

Reviewing the literature, Chavance et al. (1990) noted that a relation between handedness index and attitude towards questionnaires on health "can explain most findings confirming Geschwind's theory while no relation has been reported in surveys for which the sampling plan guards against such an information bias" (p. 438).

In their review of research related to the GBG hypothesis, Bryden et al. (1994a) carried out a meta-analysis of published studies. Excluding the data of Geschwind and Behan (1982, 1984), the results of the meta-analysis suggested that there is only a slight elevation of left-handedness in people with immune disorders but with significant heterogeneity. Considering allergies, ulcerative colitis and Crohn's disease as a single entity, there was a slightly higher incidence of left-handedness than among controls, but for the conditions of arthritis and myasthenia gravis there was a slightly lower incidence of left-handedness. If Geschwind and Behan's own data were included, there was a significantly increased frequency of left-handers but the analysis showed that their data were significantly discrepant from other reports in the literature.

Lahita (1988) reported (in a somewhat confusing paper) that patients with SLE were, as a group, less strongly right-handed than a control group of volunteers recruited from an advertising company and an (unspecified) clinic. This finding was, it seems, largely accounted for by the patient sample of 97 women (compared with 16 men) who had SLE (although statistically speaking sex differences were not significant). Lahita (1988) also reported that dyslexia (defined in a way that is difficult to establish from the report) was unusually frequent in the male offspring of women with SLE. Conversely, "none of the SLE fathers had dyslexic children" (p. 393).

There are two common types of diabetes, only one of which might be relevant to the GBG hypothesis (Searleman & Fugagli, 1987). Insulin-dependent diabetes mellitus (IDDM) or type 1 diabetes is an auto-immune disease linked to the major histocompatibility complex (HLA-D/DR region) on chromosome 6. According to Hansen et al. (1986, p. 165) and Hansen et al. (1987, p. 257): "There is a genetic connexion between chromosomes 15 and 16 through a gene on chromosome 15 involved both in protein synthesis for testosterone and in the structuring of the human immune system". These authors reported (Hansen et al., 1986, 1987) that among the relatives of patients with IDDM, close to 50 per cent were affected either by diabetes or dyslexia. This led them to suggest (Hansen et al., 1987) that "It would seem permissible to consider the possibility that IDDM and specific dyslexia are due to one common dominantly inherited autosomal genetic error that may, probably triggered by a viral factor (which could sometimes be operative *in utero*), come to expression as either IDDM or specific dyslexia" (p. 258). Although dyslexia among the relatives of diabetic patients was apparently high (there was no control group), the incidence of dyslexia was noticeably low among diabetics themselves. Hansen et al. (1986) argued that "it may not be unreasonable to speculate if [*sic*] IDDM and neurological dyslexia could be due to the same dominantly inherited genetic susceptibility with the environmental factor by early elicitation of dyslexia (possibly even *in utero*) largely establishing protection against a later elicitation of diabetes" (p. 166).

Gilger et al. (1992) reported on four large independent studies of reading disability in families, one of which appears to incorporate data from an earlier report by Pennington, Smith, Kimberling, Green, & Haith (1987). There was little convincing evidence of an association between non-right-handedness and either reading disability (variously defined) or immune disorders. However, the incidence of non-right-handedness as measured by the Edinburgh Handedness Inventory was said to vary between 23 and 35 per cent, which suggests that left- and mixed-handers were combined in the category of non-right-handers. It is perhaps not surprising that, overall, no association was found, although in one sample non-right-handedness as assessed by a single question was elevated in the families of disabled readers compared with controls. An increased incidence of auto-immune disorders was reported for the families of disabled readers in one sample (their Washington sample) in comparison with the families of non-disabled readers. Strangely,

the Washington-based sample reported a frequency of auto-immune disorders five times that of another group of the same mean age. (The third group was a twin study and the mean age was considerably lower; onset of auto-immune disease typically occurs at a relatively late age.) In this second (Iowa) group, the frequency of reported allergies was slightly but significantly elevated in the families of disabled readers.

Gilger and Pennington (1995) pointed out that there are a number of possible reasons for any observed statistical association such as between reading disability and immune disorders. They state that "the Gilger et al. article [1992] has been cited many times as support for a sub-type of RD [reading disability] that is etiologically related to ID [immune disorder] and non-right-handedness, even though our specific genetic tests for a common etiology were not significant" (p. 91). More recent work in their laboratory led Gilger and Pennington (1995) to affirm their view that reading disability and immune disorder are not linked as a result of a common genetic aetiology, although they left open the possibility that "some sort of genetic link may be found for immune system functions and RD" (p. 93) due to a mechanism such as proximity of genes for reading disability to the HLA (human leukocyte antigen) region of chromosome 6 (see Chapter 7).

If a link between dyslexia and immune function does exist, it is possible that dyslexic symptoms arise not from the action of testosterone, as suggested by Geschwind and his collaborators, but from maternal auto-antibodies (coded for in genes of the HLA complex) influencing the brain during the first 6 months of gestation. Alternatively, unusual immune system functioning might mean that the brain is particularly susceptible to the effects of viruses or other neurotoxins at a vulnerable period of its development (Stromswold, 2001).

A simple correlation between any two conditions may be determined by any one or more of a number of factors. Gilger et al. (1998) looked for an association between developmental reading disorder (DRD) and certain immune disorders using twin and family data to test specifically for genetic aetiology of the hypothesized link. Data were analysed from "approximately 846 individuals from DRD proband pairs (i.e. 423 twin pairs) and 496 individuals from control probands (i.e. 248 twin pairs)" (p. 313) and from "approximately 272 blood relatives from 19 three-generation kindreds" (p. 315). Even though in the twin sample both reading disorder and the presence of at least one reported allergy were heritable, there was no evidence, either in twins or in the sample overall, of a common genetic aetiology using either survey methodology or, in a sub-sample, immuno-assay data. Since both twin and pedigree data showed higher than expected correlations among relatives for allergies, it was suggested that "there may be a within-family environmental trigger that is in part responsible for the allergies common to relatives" (p. 329). Intriguingly, evidence was found of assortative mating for allergies. The same has been reported for reading ability (McManus, 1991; Wolff & Melngailis, 1994).

Tønnessen, Løkken, Høien, and Lundberg (1993) examined the triadic relation between dyslexia, handedness and immune disorders in a Norwegian sample of 734 12-year-old children from the school population. The percentage of dyslexic children (defined by a score below the 20th percentile on both a word–picture matching test and a nonword homophone recognition test) was twice as high among left-handers (13/64 = 20.3 per cent) as among right-handers (58/634 = 9.1 per cent). There was no association between dyslexia and immune disorders. Tønnessen et al. (1993) reported that 25/60 (41.7 per cent) of dyslexics had immune disorders, whereas 228/555 (41 per cent) of non-dyslexics had immune disorders. However, there were 4.2 per cent left-handed dyslexics among children with immune disorder as compared with 1.4 per cent left-handed dyslexics among those without immune disorder. Among 54 left-handers, 19 were positive for immune disorder compared with 225 of 547 right-handers.

Tønnessen et al. (1993) concluded from their data that there is a "slight but significant association between handedness and dyslexia and between handedness and immune disorders" (p. 414). The first association was significant for boys but not girls considered separately and the second

association was significant for girls but not boys. They further concluded that "immune disorders are less fundamental or important than left-handedness and dyslexia in the triadic association of these conditions" (p. 415). The discrepancy between their own data and those of Pennington et al. (1987) was attributed to the different ages of the populations sampled and/or to methodological factors surrounding the assessment of immune disorder.

Another potentially relevant methodological factor concerns the definition of handedness adopted by Tønnessen et al. (1993). The measure of handedness used in their study was derived from a translated 12-item version of the Oldfield Handedness Inventory. Handedness was defined as consistently right or left if all 12 items were answered with the same hand: "Any inconsistency in hand preference qualified for a classification as mixed-handedness". Only 3 per cent of the sample was classified as mixed-handed, with 8.7 per cent being classified as left-handed. The proportion of consistent left-handers is rather higher than is typically seen in other reports in the literature, but the proportion of mixed-handers is improbably low. For example, data collected by Annett show that approximately 25–35 per cent of individuals are mixed-handed (Annett, 2002). Even combining the percentages of left- and mixed-handers produces a figure that is relatively low. In comparison with a value of 11.7 per cent non-right-handedness in the study of Tønnessen et al. (1993), Gilger et al. (1992), who incorporated data from Pennington et al. (1987), identified 23–35 per cent of respondents as non-right-handed using the same (untranslated) inventory as Tønnessen et al. A strict criterion of left-handedness may explain why Tønnessen's group, in contrast to Gilger et al., obtained significant relationships between handedness and both immune disorder and reading disability, but it does not explain why Tønnessen et al. failed to find a relationship between immune disorder and dyslexia whereas Gilger et al. did so, at least for one of their samples, as did Hugdahl et al. (1990a).

The idea that genetic factors can be modified by intra-uterine hormonal factors to produce a wide range of developmental anomalies affecting not only the brain but the cardiac and skeletal systems (Behan & Geschwind, 1985b) helps to bring together a diverse range of findings and generates a very large number of hypotheses. It must be admitted, however, that despite a huge amount of research, not a great deal of value has been learned as far as dyslexia is concerned. To my knoweledge, no-one has shown, for example, either that "effective levels of testosterone" (McManus & Bryden, 1991; Tønnessen, 1997b) produce dyslexia or that there are higher concentrations of circulating testosterone in dyslexics than in controls. Almost all the research concerns associations between dyslexia and other characteristics, such as left-handedness or immune disease. The association between dyslexia and immune function, in particular, is not well established. Bryden et al. (1994a) noted that only about half of the relevant studies show a link and many of the studies have shortcomings. Yet despite all the flaws and weaknesses identified by its critics, the GBG theory helps to tie together a range of disparate findings and associations for which no other theory provides a convincing explanation. To this extent, it can be claimed that it has directed attention towards patterns of co-occurrence that might otherwise have been missed. Furthermore, its heuristic value is by no means exhausted.

9

Neuro-anatomic Aspects
of Dyslexia

The relationship between the two cerebral hemispheres with regard to dyslexia has been thought to be in some way anomalous ever since Orton first popularized the idea. Quite how dyslexics differ from normal readers was not always specified, although one proposal was that if dyslexia represented a developmental lag, then it must be the left hemisphere that is the laggard (see Chapter 2). Such ideas were difficult to test with the empirical methods then available, even allowing for conceptual woolliness. After reviewing the main theories and evidence, Hiscock and Kinsbourne (1982) wrote: "It must be concluded that, despite the current popularity of hemisphere-related explanations for dyslexia, there are strong logical and empirical arguments contrary to those explanations. Several decades have passed since it was first proposed that some forms of dyslexia stem from irregularities of cerebral lateralization, but the thesis remains unproven" (p. 218).

Cerebral lateralization, or hemispheric asymmetry, of function is assumed to be related to neuro-anatomic asymmetry. Despite appearing to the naked eye as two symmetrical hemispheres there are a number of subtle anatomic asymmetries as well as microscopic differences

(Galuske, Schlote, Bratzke, & Singer, 2000; Hayes & Lewis, 1995; Jacobs, Schall, & Scheibel, 1993; Seldon, 1981a, 1981b) between language-related regions of the left and right halves of the brain.

BROCA'S AREA

The inferior frontal gyrus, as its name suggests, is situated in the frontal lobe and on the left side is known as Broca's area, after the French surgeon and neuro-anatomist of that name who first identified this region as a speech "centre" (Broca, 1861, 1863, 1865; for translation and commentary on the 1865 paper see Berker, Berker, & Smith, 1986; for discussion of the views of Broca, his contemporaries and his successors, see Harris, 1991). It is bounded posteriorly by the pre-central sulcus, superiorly by the inferior frontal sulcus and inferiorly by the Sylvian fissure. Broca's area is said to correspond to Brodmann's cytoarchitectonic areas 44 and 45, although these vary quite considerably in size and location between individuals (Uylings, Malofeeva, Bogolepova, Amunts, & Zilles, 1998).

One might imagine that if anatomic asymmetry relates to functional asymmetry (that is, to the side of speech lateralization), then it is in regard to Broca's area that this is most likely to occur. However, from a lateralization point of view, research interest has tended to centre on a certain region of the temporal lobe, the planum temporale (Steinmetz, 1996) and it is only recently that much attention has been paid to the frontal area. Foundas, Leonard, Gilmore, Fennell, and Heilman (1994; 1996) noted a close correspondence between anatomic asymmetry in the region of the inferior frontal gyrus and asymmetry in the region of the planum temporale. Of 11 patients examined, nine showed a leftward asymmetry of both anatomic areas, one (for whom the Wada sodium Amytal test revealed speech lateralized to the right) showed a rightward asymmetry and one showed a larger left planum and right inferior frontal gyrus. However, this pattern has not always been found.

Albanese, Merlo, Albanese, and Gomez (1989) examined 24 adult brains post-mortem and found the posterior portion (pars caudalis) of the inferior frontal gyrus to be larger on the left in 62.5 per cent of cases and larger on the right in 12.5 per cent of cases. They also found on "visual analysis" (i.e. an eyeball approach) a similar asymmetry of the planum temporale. However, the authors state (without providing data) that "the predominant side was not the same for both regions in all the brains" (p. 310), which supports earlier observations of Falzi, Perrone, and Vignolo (1982). These authors reported that the posterior frontal gyrus on the left side has a greater cortical surface area than the corresponding region on the right. One MRI study (Foundas, Eure, Luevano, and Weinberger, 1998a) revealed that whereas a second portion of Broca's area, the pars triangularis (Brodmann's area 45), was larger on the left side in most of the 32 brains studied, the adjacent portion, the pars opercularis (roughly corresponding to area 44), was more frequently larger on the left in right-handers but on the right in left-handers (see also Albanese et al., 1989; Uylings et al., 1998). In fact, there was a significant correlation between scores on the Edinburgh Handedness Inventory and an

asymmetry quotient that reflected the relative degree of this left–right anatomic asymmetry.

In a study using MRI with teenagers and young adults, Pennington et al. (1999) examined brain morphometry in a sub-set of twins from the Colorado Twin Study. A randomly chosen number of 75 unrelated reading-disabled participants were compared with 22 unrelated controls who were normal readers. Handedness did not differ between the groups. After taking account of differences between the sexes, a significant interaction was found between group and brain region. The volumes of the insula and anterior superior cortex (which included Broca's area) were smaller, and a region termed the retrocallosal cortex was larger, in dyslexic than control participants (see also Eckert, Leonard, Richards, Aylward, Thomson, & Berninger, 2003, for similar findings concerning the inferior frontal gyrus, pars triangularis). The interaction reported by Pennington et al. (1999) was not affected by exclusion of iindividuals with a diagnosis of attention deficit hyperactivity disorder (ADHD) and persisted in the face of various statistical controls for age and IQ. That the insula was implicated in the group difference is of particular interest. Hynd, Semrud-Clikeman, Lorys, Novey, and Eliopulos (1990) reported that the insula was smaller in dyslexics than controls and Paulesu et al. (1996) found reduced PET (position emission tomography) activation in this region in adult (so-called compensated) dyslexics. The role of the insula is unclear, although Dronkers (1996) argued that it plays an important role in articulation.

THE PLANUM TEMPORALE

For many years, the different varieties of hemisphere-based (and mostly conceptually inadequate) theories of dyslexia concerned cerebral functional rather than neuro-anatomic organization. Then, in 1968, Geschwind and Levitsky measured the length of an area of the surface of the temporal lobe exposed by a knife-cut at the level of the Sylvian fissure. A particular region of this surface, the planum temporale, was said by Geschwind and Levitsky (1968) to be longer on the left side than the right side in 65 per cent of 100 brains. This finding seemed to support earlier observations on relatively small numbers of brains that the planum temporale "is typically larger on the left than the right" (Pfeifer, 1936, p. 539) and that the Sylvian fissure tends to be longer on the left side (Cunningham, 1892; Eberstaller, 1890; von Economo & Horn, 1930).

Since the publication of Geschwind and Levitsky's (1968) seminal paper, left–right asymmetry of the planum temporale (and related areas) has been noted by many other investigators using both post-mortem material (e.g. Aboitiz, Scheibel, & Zaidel, 1992; Kopp, Michel, Carrier, Biron, & Duvillard, 1977; Musiek & Reeves, 1990; Steinmetz, Rademacher, Jäncke, Huang, Thron, & Zilles, 1990b; Teszner, Tzvaras, Gruner, & Hécaen, 1972; Wada, Clarke, & Hamm, 1975; Witelson & Kigar, 1992) and *in vivo* neuroimaging techniques (e.g. Foundas et al., 1994; Good, Johnsrude, Ashburner, Henson, Friston, & Frackowiak, 2001; Habib, Robichon, Lévrier, Khalil, & Salamon, 1995; Karbe et al., 1995; Kulynych, Vladar, Jones, & Weinberger, 1994; Rossi et al., 1994; Steinmetz, Volkmann, Jäncke, & Freund, 1991). Occasionally, both methods have been used with the same brains (Steinmetz, et al., 1989). However, the morphology of this region is highly variable (Musiek & Reeves, 1990; Penhune, Zatorre, MacDonald, & Evans, 1996) and the proportion of cases showing a larger planum temporale on the left has varied both with the kind of measurement undertaken and the technique used. In fact, definition and hence measurement of the planum temporale is not uniform across studies (Beaton, 1997; Galaburda et al., 1987; Shapleske, Rossell, Woodruff, & David, 1999; Steinmetz et al., 1990b), yet the precise area delineated as the planum is crucial in determining the results that are obtained (Zetzsche et al., 2001).

A question of particular importance concerns how the anterior and posterior borders of the planum are defined. The anterior border is normally taken as being formed by the sulcus immediately posterior to the transverse gyrus of Heschl, which appears to be larger on the left

than the right side (Good et al., 2001; Leonard et al., 2001; Musiek & Reeves, 1990; Penhune et al., 1996). Sometimes, however, there is a second transverse gyrus, although the relative frequency of this gyrus is not easy to determine as it depends upon the distance from the mid-sagittal plane at which the observation is made (Leonard et al., 1998). Should a second transverse gyrus be included as part of the planum or be excluded? If a second transverse gyrus is more common on the right side (Campain & Minkler, 1976; Pfeifer, 1936; Von Economo & Horn, 1930; but see Musiek & Reeves, 1990), then exclusion of a second gyrus will more often lead to under-estimation of the size of the planum in the right hemisphere. Conversely, inclusion of a second gyrus of Heschl will more frequently lead to over-estimation of the size of right planum temporale and thus to reduced left–right asymmetry. In their seminal study, Geschwind and Levitsky (1968) included cortex posterior to the first transverse (Heschl's) gyrus on the left but posterior to a second transverse gyrus (if present) on the right.

With regard to the posterior border of the planum, this is usually (but not always) measured in relation to the termination of the Sylvian fissure. Some investigators include tissue lying beyond the point at which this fissure bifurcates (in many but not all brains) into the posterior ascending and descending rami (where both of these are in fact present; see Steinmetz et al., 1990b). Other investigators have regarded the point of bifurcation as the posterior border of the planum. Another issue concerns how to deal with the nonregular surface of the planum. Despite its name, the planum temporale is not in fact a plane surface, but is a convoluted region (Barta et al., 1995; Shapleske et al., 1999)—should tissue in the depths of the sulci be included or excluded from measurement?

A further problem relates to the possibility that the plana on left and right sides are inclined at different angles with respect to the coronal plane. The right side, particularly the terminal part of the Sylvian fissure, is thought to angulate upwards more sharply than the left (Cunningham, 1892; Rubens, Mahowald, & Hutton, 1976). This has implications for the magnitude of any asymmetry between the left and right planum that is revealed using horizontal magnetic resonance imaging (MRI) sections. A final question concerns whether to measure the length or the area of the planum or to quantify the amount of underlying grey matter and thereby assess the total volume of brain tissue in this region. Discussion of such issues is dealt with in a lucid paper by Barta and colleagues (1995). Excellent summaries of findings and reviews of methodological aspects of planum measurement are provided by Shapleske et al. (1999) and by Zetzsche et al. (2001).

It turns out that the magnitude and even direction of asymmetry between left and right planum temporale depends upon how the planum is defined and on how it is measured. Loftus, Tramo, Thomas, Green, Nordgren, and Gazzaniga (1993) adopted a single definition of the planum but used two algorithms to measure its area. One algorithm took account of the folding of the cortical surface, while the other did not. A left–right asymmetry was found only using the algorithm that did not take into account the folding and curvature of the cortical surface. Differences in the extent of planum asymmetry as between-area and volume measurements in the same individuals are discussed by Barta et al. (1995).

More recently, Zetzsche et al. (2001) compared the results obtained for three different definitions of the planum temporale using a method that calculates grey matter volume. The total extent of the planum was divided into an anterior portion and a posterior portion. The definition of the anterior portion varied according to the position of the posterior border of this segment. In the first definition, this was defined (somewhat unusually) as the end of Heschl's gyrus; in the second, the border was taken as the point at which "the horizontal ramus of the PT [planum temporale] turns into the ascending ramus"; on the third definition, the posterior border was taken as "the bifurcation where the SF (Sylvian fissure) splits into an upward and downward oriented ramus". In the case of each definition, the total volume (anterior plus posterior portions of the planum temporale) was the same.

Using the first definition of the posterior border of the anterior planum temporale, there was a significant rightward asymmetry of the anterior portion and a significant leftward asymmetry of the posterior portion. The rightward asymmetry of the anterior portion is surprising (given the literature) and was attributed by Zetzsche et al. (2001) to the fact that the ascending part of the planum temporale often commences more anteriorly (in relation to Heschl's gyrus) on the right than the left side and hence contains more tissue. Using the second definition of the planum, there was a non-significant leftward asymmetry of both the anterior and posterior portions. Using the third definition, there was a significant leftward asymmetry only in the anterior region. Thus the direction and magnitude of asymmetry of the anterior portion of the planum temporale (which in the past was often all that was measured) depended upon the precise definition of the borders of the planum that were adopted. Such diversity, together with differences in the dimension measured (length, area or volume), may help to explain discrepancies within the literature.

Despite the many definitional and interpretive difficulties regarding the size (and role) of the planum temporale, this area of the brain has exerted a peculiar fascination over researchers. Since the planum temporale (part of Brodmann's area 22) is close to the primary auditory receiving area and contains part of the area known to be involved in certain language functions, it has often been proposed (e.g. Galaburda, LeMay, Kemper, & Geschwind, 1978a) that anatomical asymmetry of the planum temporale in some way underlies the functional asymmetry between the brain whereby most people speak and understand language with the left rather than the right cerebral hemisphere (language lateralization).

Moffat, Hampson, and Lee (1998) studied a group of 16 left-handers: They reported that all nine participants who showed a right ear advantage on a dichotic fused word test—purportedly indicating left hemisphere speech (see Zatorre, 1989)—had a larger left than right planum temporale. In contrast, of seven left-handers who showed a left ear advantage (right hemisphere speech?), three showed the same pattern but four showed a larger right than left planum temporale. If ear differences can be taken to accurately reflect hemispheric representation of speech processes (and it is a big "if"), then these data do not suggest that right hemisphere speech corresponds consistently to a larger right planum. On the other hand, if a dichotic right ear advantage is regarded as typical, then an atypical ear advantage might be asociated with a random distribution of planum asymmetry, while the typical ear advantage is associated with a consistent bias in direction of planum asymmetry towards the left hemisphere (as Annett's right shift theory, discussed in Chapter 8, might predict; see Annett, 1992b).

Foundas et al. (1994) found a larger right- than left-sided planum temporale (rightward asymmetry) in a patient who was shown by the Wada test to have right-sided speech, while in 11 patients with left hemisphere speech lateralization the neuro-anatomic asymmetry favoured the left side. However, the individual with right-sided speech was said to be a non-right-hander. Since handedness has been related by some authors to planum asymmetry (see below and review by Beaton, 1997), the question arises as to the significance of this observation: is the anatomic asymmetry related to language lateralization or to non-right-handedness?

The fact that approximately 90 per cent of us (more on some estimates) speak with the left side of the brain (Knecht et al., 2000a)—not 65 per cent, the proportion of brains with a longer left planum as reported by Geschwind and Levitsky (1968) and Musiek and Reeves (1990)—tends to have been ignored. Admittedly, other investigators have reported a more pronounced left-sided bias in anatomical asymmetry than did Geschwind and Levitsky (1968), but a discrepancy between frequency of planum asymmetry and estimated frequency of left-sided speech production in right-handers remains.

Furthermore, the fact that the planum temporale forms part of the classical area of Wernicke (but see Bogen & Bogen, 1976), suggesting that it is more likely to be involved in auditory receptive aspects of language rather than in output processes (but see Karbe, Herholz, Weber-Luxenburger, Ghaemi, & Heiss, 1998), has been largely overlooked. Finally, recent suggestions (but see Yeni-Komshian & Benson, 1976) of

leftward asymmetry in the planum temporale of the chimpanzee (Gannon, Holloway, Broadfield, & Braun, 1998; Hopkins, Marino, Rilling, & MacGregor, 1998; Pilcher, Hammock, & Hopkins, 2001) raise difficulties for the view that human planum asymmetry is specifically related to speech (Beaton, 1997, 2003).

In fact, the planum is not a single cytoarchitectonic area (Galaburda & Sanides, 1980; Galaburda, Sanides, & Geschwind, 1978b). It may be that only a part of it, area Tpt in the terminology of Galaburda and Sanides (1980), is related to language lateralization (see Galaburda et al., 1987). According to Galaburda and Sanides (1980), who examined three brains post-mortem, "Area Tpt ... corresponds in location and appearance to Economo's [sic] and Koskinas's TA1 ('25) [sic] and Brodmann's area 22 at its posterior end ('09). Area Tpt often extends beyond the caudal end of the temporal lobe to occupy variable amounts of suprasylvian [sic] cortex" (p. 609). That is, area 22 extends beyond the boundaries of the planum temporale as usually measured (see Witelson, Glezer, & Kigar, 1995).

The fact that TA1 tissue extends into the parietal lobe adds a possible complication to any functional interpretation of the role of the planum temporale in studies in which it is identified by gross neuro-anatomy. In a study to determine the cytoarchitectonic structure of the parietal lobe of eight human brains, Eidelberg and Galaburda (1984) found a significant positive correlation between direction of planum temporale asymmetry and asymmetry of a sub-region of the inferior parietal lobule (corresponding to Brodmann's area 39 in the angular gyrus), although they noted "marked individual variability in the architectonic profile of the human angular gyrus, with great differences between specimens in the assignment of total angular gyrus cortex in two specific sub-areas" (p. 849). As first reported by Dejerine (1891), lesions of the angular gyrus on the left may produce alexia and agraphia (Friedman, Ween, & Albert, 1993; Henderson, 1986).

In making the assumption that neuro-anatomic asymmetry of the planum and speech lateralization are related, no-one has attempted to explain why a greater amount of brain tissue on one side should lead to speech and language being "attracted" to this side rather than the other. Nor is it obvious why a leftward asymmetry of the planum temporale is balanced, at least in right-handers, by a rightward asymmetry in adjacent tissue of the parietal cortex, the so-called planum parietale (Jäncke, Schlaug, Huang, & Steinmetz, 1994; see also area PEG of Eidelberg & Galaburda, 1984), which (in most brains) forms the posterior wall of the posterior ascending ramus of the Sylvian fissure (anterior surface of the supra-marginal gyrus). As this region forms part of the inferior parietal lobule, it is possible that this area on the right side is involved in visuo-spatial or attentional functions (Beaton, 2003; Jäncke et al., 1994). On the left, there is some evidence from a PET study that it is activated during verbal working memory tasks (Paulesu, Frith, & Frackowiak, 1993) and in writing (Penniello et al., 1995), which does not exclude the possibility that other areas are also involved in one or other of these functions (see, for example, Petrides, Alivisatos, Evans, & Meyer, 1993).

Despite difficulties in relating asymmetry of the planum temporale to hemispheric lateralization of speech, it is conceivable that the planum (or some part of it) is an important region of the brain in language-processing tasks by virtue of connecting the frontal and superior temporal areas on the left side of the brain (Karbe et al., 1998). Certainly, Heschl's gyrus, which is connected to the planum temporale, has extensive connections with posterior as well as frontal and sub-cortical areas of the brain (Musiek & Reeves, 1990). However, using functional MRI, Binder, Frost, Hammeke, Rao and Cox (1996) found that there was equal activation in the left planum to words and tone sequences during passive listening and greater activation to tones than to words during active listening. These findings suggest that the region is involved in auditory procesing generally as opposed to linguistic processing specifically. Consistent with this possibility, Jäncke and Steinmetz (1993) failed to find any correlation between extent of planum asymmetry and degree of ear asymmetry in a verbal dichotic listening task despite finding an association between planum asymmetry and handedness in the same

participants. Binder et al. (1996) did not report activation patterns from the right hemisphere and thus their findings are neutral with respect to hypotheses about the significance of asymmetry of the planum. It is therefore of interest that Karbe et al. (1995) noted that the extent of leftward anatomical asymmetry of the planum as measured by MRI correlated inversely with left-sided PET activation of a part of Brodmann's area 22 (part of the planum) on the left.

While the functional significance of asymmetry of the planum temporale is not clear, it is worth noting that Rumsey, Donohue, Brady, Nace, Giedd, and Andreason (1997a) found in a group of adult males significant correlations between a measure of planum asymmetry and scores on a number of verbal tests, including estimated verbal IQ, paragraph reading, and reading and spelling of nonwords. Similar correlations were not observed in matched dyslexic men. Leonard, Lombardino, Mercado, Browd, Breier, and Agee (1996) reported a significant correlation between scores on a test of phonemic awareness and degree of leftward asymmetry of the planum (as measured by the horizontal segment of the Sylvian fissure, i.e. excluding the vertical segment) in normal children aged 5–9 years, although the relationship was not present among older children (who were all skilled readers). Extent of leftward asymmetry of the planum was accounted for largely by variation in the size of the right planum (see also Galaburda et al., 1987). A shorter left than right planum (as measured by extreme sagittal slices) was found by Hynd et al. (1990) in all but one of a group of 10 dyslexics (3 of whom were left-handed). The reverse pattern of asymmetry was seen in 7 of 10 normal controls and in 7 of 10 attention deficit/hyperactivity disordered controls. The length of the right planum did not differ significantly between groups but the left planum was significantly shorter in dyslexics than in either of the two control groups. Regardless of group membership, those individuals with atypical asymmetry had a significantly lower mean verbal comprehension score (Semrud-Clikeman, Hynd, Novey, & Eliopulos, 1991) than those with typical (left-sided) asymmetry. All these findings are consistent with the idea that direction and magnitude of planum asymmetry have some implication for cognitive function.

Eckert, Lombardino, and Leonard (2001) measured planum asymmetry, total brain volume and the volume of the anterior (or motor) bank of the central sulcus in a representative sample of normal school children. For the sample considered as a whole, there was no correlation between planum asymmetry (measured by excluding the tissue in the depths of the posterior ascending and descending rami) and a measure of phonological awareness (derived from factor analysis of scores on a number of tests). Removal of 12 children said to be non-right-handed, however, led to a significant correlation between the phonological measure and planum asymmetry for the remainder of the sample ($n = 27$). Multiple regression revealed that phonological skill was uniquely predicted by planum asymmetry after controlling for socio-economic status and the effects of a positive family history of reading difficulty. It was said that the association was mediated largely by the size of the right planum temporale, which correlated negatively and significantly with the phonological score, while there was no correlation between the latter and the size of the left planum.

While these results for verbal ability are interesting, several notes of caution are warranted. First, the purely arbitrary split into right-handed and non-right-handed groups (on the basis of a handedness assessment, which I have criticized before) resulted in an approximately 2 : 1 ratio of right- to left-handers. Though all such splits are arbitrary, this is a somewhat lower ratio than one might expect (see Beaton, 2003). Second, the correlation between left and right planum size was not presented and no test of the difference between any correlations was carried out. Third, although brain volume was measured, it was not included in any of the analyses undertaken. Fourth, although several neuro-anatomic measures were taken (and presumably examined for their association with cognitive measures), no corrections for multiple testing were employed.

Asymmetry of the planum temporale has been reported to be present in the brains of fetuses (Chi, Dooling, & Gilles, 1977) and newborns (Witelson & Pallie, 1973) as well as adults. On the basis of their post-mortem material, Wada, Clarke, and Hamm (1975) declared that asymmetry was more pronounced in adult than in infant brains. This finding has been attributed by Preis, Jäncke, Schmitz-Hillebrecht, and Steinmetz (1999) to the fact that Wada et al. excluded a second transverse gyrus of Heschl (supposedly more common on the right), which, argue Preis et al. (1999), should properly be included in the definition and measurement of the planum temporale. According to these authors, there is little or no evidence from neuro-imaging data that asymmetry of the planum temporale (or planum parietale) varies with post-natal age from 3 to 14 years (or with brain volume). If a second transverse gyrus develops on the right some time after the first transverse gyrus, they argue, exclusion of this gyrus would tend to lead to an under-estimation of the extent of leftward planum asymmetry in younger compared with older specimens. This must be an error. Failure to take account of a second Heschl's gyrus on the right would lead to an under-estimation of the size of the right planum temporale and hence to an over-estimation, rather than an under-estimation, of the extent of leftward asymmetry.

Preis et al. (1999) found greater leftward planum asymmetry in girls than boys aged 3–14 years, but no such difference in their other studies. Shapleske et al. (1999) conclude with regard to normals that "PT asymmetry does appear to be influenced by gender but the sample sizes studied to date lack adequate statistical power to detect differences" (p. 41), a conclusion not at variance with Beaton's (1997) summary of the relevant literature. More recently, greater asymmetry was reported for males in a very large-scale study by Good et al. (2001), although a definition of the planum is not given. For further discussion of possible differences between the sexes in structural and functional brain organization in normal adults and in dyslexia, see Beaton (1997), Shapleske et al. (1999) and Lambe (1999).

Planum asymmetry and handedness

One reason for the considerable research interest that has been devoted to the planum temporale is that there have been reports linking planum asymmetry to handedness (Foundas, Leonard, Gilmore, & Heilman, 1995; Foundas, Leonard, & Hanna-Pladdy, 2002; Habib et al., 1995; Jäncke et al., 1994; Karbe et al., 1995; Steinmetz et al., 1991; see also Barta et al., 1995; Tzourio, Nkanga-Ngila, & Mazoyer, 1998; for a review, see Beaton, 1997; Good et al., 2001), which, in turn, relates in some way to language lateralization (Annett, 1975, 2002; Knecht et al., 2000b; McManus, 1985; McManus & Bryden, 1992; Rasmussen & Milner, 1977), although not all studies have found a relationship (e.g. Good et al., 2001; Musolino & Dellatolas, 1991). Whether it is degree or direction of handedness (or both) that relates to planum asymmetry is not yet clear (Beaton, 1997). More studies are clearly needed to tease out the relations between handedness, speech lateralization and asymmetry of the planum temporale.

Zetzsche et al. (2001) measured hand preference and hand skill in their participants, all of whom were right-handed. Zetzsche et al. (2001) correlated handedness scores with neuroanatomic asymmetry and reported a significant positive correlation between hand preference as measured by the Edinburgh Handedness Inventory (Oldfield, 1971) and volume of posterior planum designated according to one of three definitions of the planum temporale. The more right-handed participants were, the greater the volume of the posterior planum. The latter was defined as tissue posterior to the bifurcation of the Sylvian fissure into an upward and downward ramus (termed the planum parietale by Jäncke et al., 1994). The statistical significance of the correlation was lost when a conservative Bonferroni correction for multiple tests was applied. Nonetheless, given that the sample was restricted to right-handers, the finding is of heuristic interest.

At one time, the idea that language lateralization may relate to hand posture in writing (Levy & Reid, 1976) was much debated (for a summary, see Beaton, 1985), although in recent years this idea has been largely (but not entirely) neglected as a result of negative findings from lateralized visual reaction time (McKeever, 1979; McKeever & Van Hoff, 1979; Moscovitch & Smith, 1979), sodium amytal (Volpe, Sidtis, & Gazzaniga,

1981) and dichotic listening (Peters & McGrory, 1987) studies. The idea was that an upright posture indicated that the hand used for writing was controlled from the ipsilateral cerebral hemisphere, while an inverted or twisted posture was controlled contralaterally. In this context, the term "control" was used to refer to the hemisphere specialized for written language. Foundas et al. (1995b) noted that in three left-handers who used an inverted posture there was leftward planum asymmetry, while among five left-handers using an upright writing posture planum asymmetry favoured the right side. These findings do not conflict with the general belief that, as a group, left-handers are more likely to have reversed (rightward) asymmetry or not to exhibit anatomic asymmetry to the same extent as right-handers. That is, the plana of left-handers are said, on average, to be more symmetrical in size than the plana of right-handers. The same has been said to be true of dyslexics.

The planum temporale and dyslexia

In a much-quoted series of papers, Galaburda and his colleagues reported that the planum temporale was symmetrical in seven adult brains of purportedly dyslexic individuals (including one diagnosed by Orton) studied post-mortem (Galaburda & Kemper, 1979; Galaburda et al., 1985; Humphreys et al., 1990). However, as well as showing apparently symmetrical plana, the studies of Galaburda and colleagues revealed other cortical abnormalities, including ectopias and microgyria, especially in the inferior or third frontal gyrus (Broca's area)—although this is rarely commented upon—and peri-Sylvian areas of the left hemisphere. Ectopias are abnormalities of cell migration between different cortical layers and were also reported by Drake (1968) to be present post-mortem in the brain of the learning-disabled boy Billy referred to previously. "Polymicrogyria is defined by the presence in the cerebral cortex of an area containing mutiple, narrow, short, curved gyri occupying a variable extent of the cortical surface. When the affected area is small and limited in the number of abnormal gyri, the condition may be referrred to plainly as microgyria" (Rosen et al., 1989, p. 237, footnote 1).

It is not clear what should be concluded from the histological findings, since these abnormalities are also found at autopsy, though to a lesser extent, in some proportion of brains (more frequently in the right hemisphere) from neurologically normal individuals (Kaufmann & Galaburda, 1989). It was suggested by Galaburda et al. (1985) that focal dysgenesis in dyslexic brains might lead either directly to cognitive deficit or indirectly to restructuring of connections between associated cortical areas. This theory was thought to be supported by the case of a single rat, which was fortuitously found to have a type of microgyria in association with an abnormal pattern of callosal terminations (Rosen et al., 1989)!

The findings of Galaburda and his colleagues concerning symmetry of the planum in the brains of dyslexic adults excited much comment as they seemed to vindicate Orton's view that reading disability is associated with anomalies of hemispheric dominance. I have previously expressed concern about the method of assessment of symmetry in some cases and the specificity of diagnosis in others (Beaton, 1997). It is therefore important to have independent confirmation of the findings reported by Galaburda and his collaborators. While I know of no other postmortem study of planum (a)symmetry in dyslexia, several *in vivo* studies related to this issue have now been reported.

The earliest relevant studies invoved certain measurements of the width of the posterior part of the brain on computed tomography (CT) scans. These indicated that among dyslexics, rightward asymmetry (Hier, LeMay, Rosenberger, & Perlo, 1978) or symmetry (Haslam, Dalby, Johns, & Rademaker, 1981) was relatively frequent. Subsequently, similar results were obtained in investigations of the volume (Rumsey, Dorwart, Vermess, Denckla, Kruesi, & Rapoport, 1986) or area (Duara et al., 1991; Hynd et al., 1990; Kushch et al., 1993) of the planum temporale or related regions using other neuroimaging techniques. Not all investigators, however, have reported such effects. One study found no difference between nine young adult dyslexics and two control groups of readers in the length of the planum (Leonard et al., 1993), while another

failed to find a difference between 17 dyslexic and 14 control children in the area of the planum (Schultz et al., 1994). Similarly, no significant difference in surface area of the planum (regardless of whether the posterior ascending ramus was included) was found between 28 dyslexic college students and 15 controls by Leonard et al. (2001).

I have reviewed elsewhere (Beaton, 1997) the literature relating planum asymmetry to dyslexia (see also Hynd & Semrud-Clikeman, 1989; Morgan & Hynd, 1998). While the results of individual studies vary somewhat, it is uncritically accepted by many authors that dyslexia is in some way associated with a pattern of planum asymmetry that is subtly different from that of nondyslexic individuals. Planum asymmetry is believed to be more often reversed in direction and/or reduced in size among dyslexics in comparison with non-dyslexics. One study in particular has been frequently cited as demonstrating that the planum temporale tends to be symmetrical in dyslexia. Larsen, Höien, Lundberg, and Ödegaard (1990) compared 19 dyslexic young adults with 17 control readers. The planum temporale was reconstructed from coronal image slices and found to be symmetrical in 13 of the 19 dyslexic readers but in only five of the control readers. The reason for the frequency of citation of this paper probably has more to do with the classification of the dyslexic participants than with the methodological adequacy of the study.

Larsen et al. (1990) distinguished between "phonological dysfunction" and "orthographic dysfunction". One dyslexic person was said to show "pure orthographic dysfunction" and had asymmetrical plana; four individuals showing "phonological dysfunction", and seven of nine cases showing both "phonological and orthographic dysfunction", had symmetrical plana. These results have been cited as showing that phonological dyslexia is associated with symmetrical plana. However, the definition of orthographic dysfunction (difficulty in reading tachistoscopically exposed words) cannot be taken as indicating a pure orthographic deficit, while the definition of phonological dysfunction was limited to comparatively poor performance on a single test, that of nonword reading. Using the same definition of "phonological deficit", Leonard et al. (2001) reported leftward asymmetry of the planum (including the posterior ascending ramus) in both dyslexic adults and their controls (see also Eckert et al., 2003).

In my earlier review of planum asymmetry and dyslexia, I expressed the view that future studies should provide data on the distribution of planum asymmetry, not just present mean scores that obscure different degrees and directions of asymmetry. I also commented that investigators have often not matched dyslexic and control groups well for handedness, gender and IQ. However, a recent MRI study of brain asymmetry took into account the much-debated distinction between dyslexic and "garden variety" readers. Dalby, Elbro, and Stødkilde-Jørgensen (1998) defined retarded readers as those whose nonverbal IQ (Raven's progressive matrices) was below the 10th per centile and dyslexics were drawn from "two special schools for dyslexics" (plus one participant originally regarded as a normally reading control who was found to have "severe problems with phonological recoding in reading"). Although Dalby et al. (1998) did not attempt to measure the planum temporale, one of their measures, the depth of the Sylvian fissure as seen in coronal MRI slices of the brain, relates to the planum in so far as it measures the width of the planum on each slice. This measure did not distinguish between the three groups of participants for either the left or the right hemisphere. However, a neuro-anatomic difference was found between 17 dyslexics and 12 normally reading control participants in one aspect of the size of the temporal lobes. When the measure was left–right asymmetry in the combined cortical and subcortical tissue in the temporal lobes, the dyslexics differed from the normally reading controls. The latter had a mean value indicating a greater extent of tissue on the left than the right, whereas the former had on average more tissue on the right than the left. Comparing the number of individuals with leftward versus rightward or zero asymmetry revealed a significant difference between the dyslexic and normal readers. Symmetry or rightward asymmetry was more common among the dyslexics than the controls.

Furthermore, the 17 dyslexics were said to differ significantly from six poor readers who showed a similar distribution of left–right asymmetry to the normal controls. The difference between dyslexic and normal readers was present when differences in IQ between these groups were statistically controlled (by comparing not raw reading scores but residuals after regressing reading on nonverbal IQ).

In the above study by Dalby et al. (1998), left–right asymmetry in combined cortical and subcortical tissue of the temporal lobe correlated significantly with a measure of phonemic analysis or segmentation, namely indicating which of a set of four alternative words contained a sound in the same position as a target word. The greater the asymmetry in favour of the left side, the higher the phonemic analysis score. This is reminiscent of the finding reported by Leonard et al. (1996) that size of the planum temporale (in its horizontal extent) correlated with phonemic awareness scores in 5- to 12-year-old children.

Using a three-dimensional MRI technique that, unlike other studies of dyslexics, took account of the surface structure of the brain, Green et al. (1999) measured the area of a region they refer to as the "caudal infrasylvian" suface (cIS) in eight right-handed adult male dyslexics and a similar number of controls matched for age, handedness and education. This region contains the planum temporale as usually defined but includes tissue in the depths of the posterior ascending ramus (PAR), the terminal ascending (vertical) segment of the Sylvian fissure, which is often excluded from measurement. When two gyri of Heschl were present on one or other side (which was the case for two of the controls and four of the dyslexics), both gyri were excluded from the measurement. Green et al. found that the total surface area of the brain did not differ between the groups. There was no hemispheric difference in area of the cIS within either group and there was no significant group-by-hemisphere interaction. Expressing cIS either as a proportion of total hemispheric surface area or in terms of an asymmetry coefficient did not alter this pattern.

Lack of asymmetry between the hemispheres in dyslexics (and in controls) is consistent with another study that included tissue from the PAR (that is, the surface of the supramarginal gyrus) in the measurements and used an algorithm that takes account of surface curvature (Rumsey et al., 1997a). Among control participants, the tissue in the depth of the PAR is often larger on the right than the left side of the brain (Gauger, Lombardino & Leonard, 1997; Jäncke et al., 1994; Leonard et al., 2001), which may balance a leftward asymmetry of the anterior portion of the planum temporale. The results of the studies of Rumsey et al. (1997a) and Green et al. (1999) strongly suggest that if the planum is measured so as to include the PAR, and if the surface curvature of the brain is taken into account, then there is no significant asymmetry between the left and right temporal planum in either dyslexics or controls.

However, in the study of Green et al. (1999), the total area of the cIS was significantly greater in the dyslexic group (although the significance value was not adjusted for multiple testing, which might well have abolished the significant effect). Moreover, if the sign (direction) of the asymmetry coefficient was ignored, the dyslexic participants as a group had markedly, and significantly, lower absolute asymmetry scores than the controls. Green et al. (1999) suggested that a larger cIS area in dyslexics than controls might result from more exuberant growth of neuropil, from the addition of cortical columns or from less involution during cortical embryogenesis.

Some of the above studies are at odds with those that suggest a consistent leftward asymmetry in both controls and dyslexics (Leonard et al., 1993, 2001; Schultz et al., 1994) or in controls only (Larsen et al., 1990). Recently, Heiervang et al. (2000) reported finding equivalent degrees of leftward planum asymmetry in 20 dyslexic boys (aged 10–12 years) and 20 controls, but a somewhat smaller planum area on the left side of the dyslexics than in the controls. The right-sided planum did not differ between groups. Only two individuals in each group were classified as being left-handed and both groups showed a right ear advantage in a dichotic listening test. There were no correlations between dichotic listening scores and planum asymmetry (but see Hugdahl,

Heiervang, Ersland, Lundervold, Steinmetz, & Smievoll, 2003). The dyslexic group showed a significantly larger region of tissue on the right side in the area termed the planum parietale (Jäncke et al., 1994). A smaller left planum in the majority of dyslexic participants (but not all) is also apparent in reports by Kushch et al. (1993) and by Hynd et al. (1990). It can be inferred also from the report of Rumsey et al. (1997a).

How can symmetrical or reversed planum asymmetry account for dyslexia? Clearly, it cannot, on its own, "explain" the occurrence of (any kind of) dyslexia, since a good proportion of normal individuals have this pattern of brain organization without being dyslexic. Indeed, the incidence of atypical (a)symmetry is higher than the probable incidence of dyslexia. However, one way of making sense of reversed asymmetry or symmetry is in terms of Annett's right-shift theory discussed in Chapter 8. In some proportion of the population, namely those of rs−− genotype, planum asymmetry may be distributed entirely by chance, whereas in those who possess the hypothesized right-shift gene one would expect, in most cases, leftward asymmetry of the planum.

Asymmetry of the planum temporale has been investigated not only with regard to dyslexia but also in individuals having a diagnosis of specific language impairment (SLI). In general, the thrust of this work has also been taken as showing more frequent rightward asymmetric or symmetric brains in SLI children than in controls (Gauger et al., 1997; Plante, Swisher, Vance, & Rapcsak, 1991), which might be expected on the view that there is a genetic link between at least some form of SLI and reading disability (Bishop, 2001). On the other hand, as outlined above, evidence that dyslexic brains are characterized by symmetry rather than asymmetry is, to say the least, equivocal. It is probable, given the issues surrounding measurement and definition of the planum, that the same applies to SLI individuals (but see Eckert & Leonard, 2003).

How anatomic asymmetry between the left and right sides of the brain arises in the normal course of events is unclear (various ideas are discussed in Chapter 8). Nor is it known how, if at all, this process is perturbed in cases of dyslexia, although Stein (1991) was of the opinion that "The fundamental abnormality of dyslexics is . . . probably related to the genetics of hemispheric specialization" (p. 187). What is undeniable is that the left and right sides of the brain do not develop independently of one another. Galaburda, Rosen, and Sherman (1990) maintained that "Callosal connections are most certainly at the core of interhemispheric relationships" (p. 530).

The left and right sides of the brain are connected by the corpus callosum and other inter-hemispheric commissures. There may well be an intimate connection between asymmetry in the size of the planum at the two sides and the size of the callosum and, in particular, between those parts of it thought to connect the superior temporal lobes (see Aboitiz, Scheibel, Fisher, & Zaidel, 1992). Indeed, Moffat et al. (1998) reported that there was a positive correlation between the size of the planum temporale on the left and a number of mid-callosal areas. Planum asymmetry correlated significantly with callosal area such that a larger leftward asymmetry was associated with a larger callosal area.

INTER-HEMISPHERIC TRANSFER AND THE CORPUS CALLOSUM

The adult human corpus callosum is a band of approximately 174–177 million fibres (Tomasch, 1954) connecting the two sides of the brain. It is the largest band of fibres joining left and right cerebral cortices and consists of fibres of differing thickness. Thin fibres (> 1 μm after shrinkage) are most dense in the anterior callosum (genu) and mid-splenium and large-diameter fibres (> 5 μm after shrinkage) are proportionally more numerous in the posterior mid-body, where they connect primary and secondary sensory (and possibly motor) areas of the hemispheres (Aboitiz et al., 1992). According to a post-mortem study on the "brains of three men in their fifties" carried out by Tomasch (1954), approximately 40 per cent of callosal axons are unmyelinated, the highest proportion of these being in the splenium. The callosum grows rapidly during ontogenesis. The

total number of callosal axons present during the 10th week of fetal life (as estimated from crown–rump length) of one specimen was estimated to be 13,000; this increased in a 5-month-old child to 144 million fibres (Luttenberg, 1965). By the 8th fetal month (at the latest), myelinization has begun in the genu and anterior portion of the trunk. By the 5th post-partum month, myelinization can be seen to be more extensive in dorsal than ventral aspects of the callosum and is relatively retarded in the rostrum and splenium compared with more anterior regions (Luttenberg, 1966). There is some evidence from a small-scale twin study that the size and shape of the adult callosum is determined by both genetic and environmental factors (Oppenheim et al., 1989), as appears to be the case for the gyral pattern of the cortex (Bartley et al., 1997) and, so it has been claimed, for the surface area of the planum temporale (see Steinmetz et al., 1995).

The corpus callosum continues to grow long after birth. Indeed, one MRI study that measured the size of the callosum twice in the same individuals over a period of approximately 2 years suggests that growth of this structure is not complete until the mid-twenties are reached (Pujol, Vendrell, Junqué, Martí-Vilalta, & Capdevila, 1993). Different segments of the callosum may mature at different rates. In a study of 114 children and adolescents aged 4–18 years Giedd et al. (1996) noted that the anterior segments (rostrum and genu) did not differ significantly between preschool children and 18-year-olds or adults aged 20–40 years, whereas the posterior and middle segments (splenium, isthmus and body of callosum) increased in size as a function of age (uncorrected for total callosal area or total cerebral volume). In a subsequent longitudinal study, children and adolescents were, when possible, scanned at different ages. This study confirmed that callosal growth between the ages of about 5 and 18 years occurs primarily in posterior regions (Giedd et al., 1999). Conversely, with increasing age beyond 30 years or so, there appears to be a disproportionate decrease in the size of the anterior four-fifths of the callosum relative to the posterior fifth (Parashos, Wilkinson, & Coffey, 1995).

No effect of gender (after covarying for total cerebral volume) was observed in the studies by Giedd et al. (1996, 1999), although some work has related size of this structure to both gender and handedness (for reviews, see Beaton, 1997; Bishop & Wahlsten, 1997; Driesen & Raz, 1995). The literature is conflicting, not least because of methodological inadequacies and relatively low numbers of participants in some studies. Moffat et al. (1998) reported that nine left-handed males who showed a dichotic right ear advantage had a significantly larger mean area of one posterior callosal sub-region than 34 right-handers or seven left-handers showing a left ear advantage. However, Peters, Oeltze, Seminowicz, Steinmetz, Koeneke, and Jäncke (2002) found neither sex nor handedness effects in a neuro-imaging study of 184 healthy brains. Similar findings were reported by Good et al. (2001) in a study of 465 adults. Giedd et al. (1999) point out that "sex differences are subtle and depend on whether adjustments are made for the approximately 11% difference in total cerebral volume" (p. 581).

The role of the corpus callosum as elucidated by the classic split-brain studies is predominantly to convey information from one cerebral hemisphere to the other (Gazzaniga, 2000). Some authors (e.g. De Lacoste-Utamsing & Holloway, 1982; Witelson, 1985; Witelson & Nowakowski, 1991) have suggested that a larger callosal area implies more fibres and hence a greater capacity for inter-hemispheric transfer. Lamantia and Rakic (1990) observed no relation between callosal size and number of axons in monkey brains, but a relationship in human post-mortem material between callosal area and the number of fibres coursing through a given portion of the callosum was reported (although only for small fibres, those < 3 millimicrons in diameter) by Aboitiz et al. (1992). However, it does not necessarily follow that efficiency of inter-hemispheric transfer increases as a direct function of fibre number. At the present time, I know of no research that has addressed this point directly, although Hellige, Taylor, Lesmes, and Peterson (1998) found a significant positive correlation in 30 adult men between the mid-sagittal area of the corpus callosum (apparently uncorrected for total

brain volume) and number of left (but not right) visual hemifield errors in nonsense syllable (CVC) identification. They suggested that a larger callosum may be associated with increased functional separation of the hemispheres. Similarly, Clarke, Lufkin, and Zaidel (1993) proposed that regional callosal size is positively related to functional inter-hemispheric inhibition. Others, however, have made the contrary suggestion, namely that a small callosum is associated with greater functional separation (see Lassonde, Bryden, & Demers, 1990). In line with such ideas, O'Kusky et al. (1988), Hines, McAdams, Chiu, Bentler, and Lipcamon (1992) and Yazgan, Wexler Kinsbourne, Peterson, and Leckman (1995), all reported negative correlations between overall callosal area and asymmetry in performance at the left and right ears on a dichotic listening task. In a group of left-handers, Moffat et al. (1998) found that left-ear scores on a fused dichotic word test were negatively and significantly correlated with the area of the isthmus of the callosum (higher scores were associated with a smaller area), although this would not have survived correction for multiple testing.

Dyslexia and inter-hemispheric transfer

Based on their neuro-anatomical work investigating asymmetry in rats and humans, Galaburda et al. (1987, 1990) suggested that asymmetrical brains are characterized by less callosal connectivity than symmetrical brains (see also Aboitiz et al., 1992; Rosen, Sherman, & Galaburda, 1991). As they believed that dyslexic brains are more symmetrical than non-dyslexic brains, their hypothesis implies that dyslexic brains have a greater density of inter-hemispheric connections (greater callosal connectivity) and, consequently, an increased capacity for transfer of information between the two sides. This hypothesis is at odds with suggestions by other researchers who have argued on the basis of purely behavioural motor and tactile tasks, and somewhat less securely on the basis of visual (mainly tachistoscopic half-field) and dichotic auditory tasks held to involve an inter-hemispheric transfer component (see Beaton, 1985), that there is some deficit of inter-hemispheric transfer or integration of sensory information in dyslexia (Davidson, Leslie, & Saron, 1990; Gross-Glenn & Rothenberg, 1984; Hermann, Sonnabend, & Zeevi, 1986; Vellutino, Steger, Harding, & Phillips, 1975).

The corpus callosum and bimanual coordination tasks

Certain bimanual motor tasks are said to be performed more poorly by dyslexics than by controls. Several authors have hypothesized that the deficits are related to an impairment of inter-hemispheric transfer and thereby to the corpus callosum. There is direct evidence from work with patients who have undergone surgical division of the corpus callosum that the integrity of (at least the anterior section) of this structure is essential for coordinated performance on certain bimanual tasks (Preilowski, 1972, 1975; Tuller & Kelso, 1989; Zaidel & Sperry, 1977). There is also evidence that the anterior callosum is enlarged in experienced musicians (Schlaug, Jäncke, Huang, Staiger, & Steinmetz, 1995), in whom differences between the hands on a peg-moving task are reduced in comparison with non-musicians (Beaton & Coleman, unpplublished; Jäncke, Schlaug, & Steinmetz, 1997). Among people born without a corpus callosum, various deficits of motor function have been noted (e.g. Ferris & Dorsen, 1975; Jakobson, Servos, Goodale, & Lassonde, 1994; Jeeves & Silver, 1988; Meerwaldt, 1983; Silver & Jeeves, 1994). Thus involvement of the callosum in some bimanual functions may be considered reasonably well established (for a brief review, see Beaton, Hugdahl, & Ray, 2000), although it should be kept in mind that other areas of the brain, particularly frontal and medial–frontal cortex and the cerebellum, are important for certain bimanual actions (Jäncke, Peters, Himmelbach, Nösselt, Shah, & Steinmetz, 2000; Picard & Strick, 1996; Serrien & Wiesendanger, 2000; Stephan et al., 1999). Moreover, even commissurotomized patients (in whom the corpus callosum has been surgically sectioned) can carry out with ease familiar bimanual coordination tasks, such as tying shoelaces, in the immediate post-operative period and can make spatially uncoupled movements, such as simultaneously drawing a circle and a square (Franz, Waldie, &

Smith, 2000). However, Eliassen, Baynes, and Gazzaniga (2000) showed that the operation significantly impaired the temporal coupling of movements in a bimanual reaction time task in so far as there was a large increase in the variability with which so-called "simultaneous" movements were initiated by the left and right hands. Subsequently, Kennerley and his collaborators reported that lack of temporal coupling of the two hands occurred only when three callosotomy patients carried out a continuous bimanual tapping task and not when they made discrete bimanual movements (Kennerley, Diedrichsen, Hazeltine, Semjen, & Ivry, 2002). The nature of the task thus appears to be crucial in showing whether there is any deficit after commissurotomy.

BIMANUAL COORDINATION DEFICITS IN DYSLEXIA: THE CALLOSAL DEFICIT HYPOTHESIS

Badian and Wolff (1977) compared the performance of 28 reading-disabled boys aged 8–13 years with normative data on tests of unimanual and bimanual-alternating tapping. The two groups performed similarly with each hand alone whether tapping in time to a metronome or not. In the condition in which they had to tap with each hand alternately in time to a metronome, however, dyslexics were more variable (i.e. were less able to keep time) than controls with the left hand but not with the right. They performed significantly more poorly in the alternating condition than in the single hand conditions (control data are not presented). Although nine of the 28 dyslexic boys were judged to be left-handed, there were no significant effects (or interactions) attributable to handedness. It was suggested on the basis of split-brain findings (Kreuter, Kinsbourne, & Trevarthen, 1972) that the results indicated some impairment of inter-hemispheric cooperation.

In a later study, the findings of Badian and Wolff (1977) were replicated with slightly older reading-disabled and control participants of the same age (mean age approximately 13 years). In this study (Klicpera, Wolff, & Drake, 1981), it was observed in a bimanual asymmetrical tapping condition (in which each hand tapped at a different rate) that "retarded readers but not normal controls intermittently moved both hands simultaneously for three or four taps in a sequence, as if they could not suppress unintended mirror movements from the leading to the non-leading hand" (p. 621). Taken together with other results showing differences between disabled and normal readers only in bimanual conditions, it was argued that the findings "indicate that temporal co-ordination of asymmetrical motor commands, rather than the concurrent use of the two hands or control of peripheral movement speed, was the primary source of motor deficits in retarded readers" (p. 622). The results were taken as raising the possibility that "impaired mechanisms of interhemispheric communication account for both reading retardation and motor deficits" (p. 622)

In a study of 20 reading-disabled boys (mean age 12.2 years, average or above-average intelligence, two left-handed), Wolff et al. (1984) reported results similar to those of Badian and Wolff (1977), in that bimanual alternating taps entrained to 184 beats per minute (but not 92 beats per minute) were carried out with greater variability and less accuracy in this group compared with age-matched controls. This time, unimanual taps in time to a metronome were also performed less efficiently by the poor readers. In neither unimanual nor bimanual tapping conditions was timing by the left hand more variable than timing by the right. The poor readers also were slower than the controls in repeating single-item and three-item strings of syllables. Wolff et al. (1984) suggested that "speed-timing thresholds may be one nodal point of impaired function which is manifested behaviorally in temporal order perception, memory for sequences and coordinated action" (p. 599).

In a further study of bimanual motor functions in adolescent (age 13–18 years) and adult dyslexics, Wolff, Michel, Ovrut, and Drake (1990), reported that compared with normal readers and learning-disabled students without neurological impairments, motor deficits (as defined by tapping variability) among dyslexics were seen only in tasks of asynchronous and alternating tapping (more pronounced in the asynchronous condition) and not when synchronous tapping was required. These deficits were observed in approximately 50 per cent of the participants and only at fast rates of tapping. It was suggested that:

> Either an excess of bilateral excitations or the failure to suppress unintended mirror movements should in principle interfere with bimanual performance in tasks that require the rapid and continuous integration of timed responses between the two sides of the body. Whether similar deficiencies of interhemispheric communication also contribute to the reading impairment and language impairment of dyslexic subjects can not be deduced from the study of bimanual coordination alone.
> (Wolff et al., 1990, p. 357)

Wolff et al. (1990) point to the fact that surgical division of the corpus callosum has little effect on the reading fluency of adults, from which one might conclude that impaired efficiency of interhemispheric communication is not a significant factor in developmental dyslexia. They go on to suggest, therefore, that:

> variations in the dynamics of interhemispheric interaction, rather than neuroanatomically specified structural deficits, may be the factor that accounts for the temporal resolution deficits of dyslexic subjects during interlimb coordination, as well as for deficits in other time-dependent functions distributed across both hemispheres that are directly involved in learning to read.
> (Wolff et al., 1990, p. 357)

In a subsequent study with nine adult dyslexics and nine controls, Rousselle and Wolff (1991) confirmed that dyslexics did not differ from controls in unimanual tapping performance in time to a metronome. When synchronous and alternating asymmetrical bimanual tapping was called for, dyslexics performed in a similar manner to controls—that is, with similar variability in timing (specifically, in variability of phasing "computed as the mean deviation of measured relative phase from the theoretically specified relative phase" (p. 910). There was, however, one difference. Whereas the controls showed a significant tendency to "lead" (i.e. tap first) with the preferred right hand, the dyslexics showed no such effect. During a condition in which participants had to tap in a bimanual asymmetrical manner, one hand tapping at twice the rate of the other (1 : 2 or 2 : 1), both groups tended to revert to a symmetrical tapping mode (1 : 1). Following such a shift, the right hand of the controls showed less phasing variability (i.e. greater stability of inter-tap interval) than the left hand, but the dyslexics showed no such between-hand effect. Rousselle and Wolff (1991) argued that "Either a stronger intrinsic coupling of the two hands during rhythmic performance, or a more symmetrical distribution of motor control for bimanual skills in dyslexic subjects [,] could have accounted for these group differences" (pp. 918–919).

According to Wolff (1993), the motor tasks that most clearly discriminated dyslexic individuals and controls in his research all involved the integration of asymmetric or asynchronously timed movements between the right and left hands to achieve a desired goal. He argued that "Performance of such bimanual tasks depends upon the suppression or inhibition of unintentional bilateral coactivation of homotopic muscles on both sides of the body, or 'mirror movements', and therefore presumably on efficient transmission of motor commands between the hemispheres" (p. 92).

It is interesting that Wolff (1993) did not regard the findings obtained by him and his collaborators as pointing to a cerebellar deficit, as others might have done (see Chapter 6). Wolff writes:

> The temporal variables that clearly discriminated dyslexic subjects from normal readers in our studies were *timing precision*, *response frequency*, and their interactions.

Because . . . the cerebellar hemispheres have sometimes been identified as a domain-general neurological locus for the control of timing precision, we might then conclude . . . that the impaired temporal resolution of dyslexic subjects identified a dysfunction of the cerebellar hemispheres. Yet, even 8–9 year old dyslexic children performed as well as normal controls on tasks of *unimanual* finger tapping, so that our findings do not justify the conclusion of a basic deficit in timing precision in DD [developmental dyslexia].

(Wolff, 1993, pp. 91–92, emphasis in original)

Somewhat similar deficits in bimanual coordination among dyslexic adults have also been seen as being consistent with an impairment of callosal function (Moore, Brown, Markee, Theberge, & Zvi, 1995). Note, incidentally, that any hemispheric transfer deficit need not imply an impairment of the fibres of the corpus callosum. There could be some deficiency of function (or reduction in number) of the cells of origin in one or other hemisphere or of the cells on which callosal fibres synapse (Denckla, 1985).

Gladstone et al. (1989) noted that "No study to date has shown the differences in intermanual coordination between normal and impaired readers to be independent of rapid motor sequencing ability" (p. 237). These authors, therefore, carried out a study based on the task devised by Preilowski (1972) for studying inter-hemispheric integration in commissurotomized patients. The task involved using two knobs, controlled by left and right hands, to operate a single cursor. In some circumstances, each hand needed to turn the knobs in the same direction, either clockwise or anticlockwise, to succeed. In other circumstances, the two hands had to turn the knobs in opposite (mirror) directions, one turning clockwise and the other turning counter-clockwise. Right-handed dyslexic boys (n = 18, mean age 12.08 years) were slower and less accurate in the latter condition than age-matched controls, left hand errors being especially frequent when the participants were prevented from seeing their hands. Under these circumstances, dyslexics (but not controls) tended to revert to turning both knobs in the same direction. Unlike the controls, the dyslexic boys were significantly slower in the mirror-movements condition than when the knobs had to be turned in the same direction. Gladstone et al. explained their findings with reference to a model in which inter-hemispheric collaboration is compromised in dyslexia but there is also a degree of anomalous organization of ipsilateral manual control. The ipsilateral fibres were said to convey commands for movements that are spatially identical, rather than mirror-image as in controls.

In an attempt to discover whether there is a slowing down of inter-hemispheric transfer of neural impulses in dyslexia, Davidson et al. (1990) employed a crossed–uncrossed reaction time paradigm. This involves presenting visual information to one side of a central fixation point and requiring a response from the hand on the same side (uncrossed or ipsilateral response) or the opposite side (crossed or contralateral response). On the assumption that in humans (Gazzaniga, Bogen, & Sperry, 1967) as well as monkeys (Brinkman & Kuypers, 1972, 1973) a distal manual response (involving the fingers) is controlled unilaterally from the opposite cerebral hemisphere, uncrossed manual responses can be initiated from the hemisphere in receipt of the lateralized visual information. A crossed manual response, however, would require at least one more callosal synaptic relay, since the receiving and initiating cortical regions are in opposite hemispheres. The fact that uncrossed responses have been shown to be at least a few milliseconds faster than crossed responses has been regarded as providing support for this model of inter-hemispheric transfer. A variation on the paradigm is based on the assumption that in right-handers a stimulus appearing in the left visual hemifield elicits a vocal response from the left hemisphere and this will take a measurably longer time than if the stimulus were to appear in the right hemifield (Filbey & Gazzaniga, 1969).

Because the crossed versus uncrossed manual reaction time paradigm confounds measures of inter-hemispheric transfer with stimulus–response spatial compatibilty effects, several authors have required their participants to cross their hands such that the right hand responds to the left of the midline and the left hand to the right of the midline. Even without this manipulation, it is argued (Berlucchi, Aglito, Marzi, & Tassinari, 1995) that the paradigm measures at least some aspect of inter-hemispheric transmission time (ITT). Estimates of ITT vary typically from about 2 to 10 msec but may extend to 30 msec depending upon the precise experimental circumstances (for a review, see Bashore, 1981). Those for manual reaction time tend to be more reliable than those for vocal reaction time (St. John, Shields, Krahn, & Timney, 1987; but see Brysbaert, 1994) and are typically less than 10 msec. These values are approximately consistent with estimates (e.g. Rugg, 1982: Rugg, Lines, & Milner, 1984; Saron & Davidson, 1989) based on latency differences between evoked potential components recorded simultaneously over the left and right sides of the head to stimuli presented to one or other visual half-field.

Davidson et al. (1990) used both the standard and the modified paradigms in an attempt to measure transfer time in reading-disabled and chronological-age controls. No difference between the groups was found in the speed of transfer. The experiment was also carried out with tactile stimuli applied to the left or right leg (on the assumption that the stimulation was lateralized predominantly to the contralateral hemisphere). The participants were required to respond to the stimulation by lifting their index finger off a contact switch. As in the visual condition, the participants maintained central fixation and kept their chins on a chinrest. Again, there was no group difference in inter-hemispheric transmission time.

In the visual condition, participants in both groups showed faster mean reaction times with the left hand to stimuli presented on the left of fixation and with the right hand to stimuli on the right of fixation whether the hands were crossed or not. This supports a neuro-anatomic model of response time effects. In the tactile condition, an equivalent pattern was obtained when the hands were uncrossed but with crossed hands the right hand was faster to stimulation of the left leg and the left hand to stimulation of the right leg. Spatial compatibility thus appears to have been a more decisive factor in the tactile than in the visual condition. In any event, the lack of any group difference in either the visual or tactile condition, combined with measures of inter-hemispheric transfer time consistent with previous research with normal readers, provides no evidence for the thesis that transfer time is increased in dyslexia. In contrast, increased inter-hemispheric transfer times were reported for dyslexic college students in a study in which transfer times were derived from visual evoked potentials recorded while participants carried out a letter-matching task (Markee, Brown, Moore, & Theberge, 1996).

Finger localization and dyslexia

A body of research using different paradigms suggests that inter-hemispheric transfer is, if not slower, then less efficient in reading-disabled individuals than in controls. One task that has been widely used is cross-hand finger localization. In this task, the experimenter touches one or more fingers of one of the participant's hands and the participant responds by indicating in some way, by using the thumb for example, where he or she has been touched. In the within-hand condition, participants use the same hand to respond as was stimulated by the experimenter. In the cross-hand condition, the opposite hand from that stimulated is used for responding. The assumption is that touching one hand stimulates primarily or exclusively the somatosensory cortex of the contralateral hemisphere. Comparison of points touched on left and right hands is usually taken to require an intact corpus callosum, since so-called split-brain or commissurotomized patients cannot do this even though within-hand localization is unimpaired (Volpe, Sidtis, Holtzman, Wilson, & Gazzaniga, 1982) and patients with lesions of restricted segments of the central section of the callosum fail or perform poorly on this task (e.g. Geffen, Nilsson, Quinn, & Teng, 1985) as on other tasks involving tactile transfer between the hands (e.g. Benton, Sahar, & Moscovitch, 1984; Dimond, Scammell, Brouwers, & Weeks, 1977). Thus an impairment specifically in the cross-hand

localization condition as undertaken by neurologically intact individuals has been regarded by some as indicating a loss of information during inter-hemispheric transfer.

Quinn and Geffen (1986) showed that cross-hand localization was less accurate than within-hand hand localization and that the magnitude of the cross-hand deficit decreased with age in normally reading children aged 5–11 years. Since myelination of the corpus callosum is not thought to be complete until early adulthood (Yakovlev & Lecours, 1967), these data have been viewed as consistent with the idea that inter-hemispheric callosal transfer improves with age. Nonetheless, even normal adults show a cross-hand deficit compared with unimanual performance if the task is made difficult enough (Beaton & Yearley, unpublished).

It is well established that the ability to accurately localize stimulation of the fingers (finger agnosia) is compromised in children with impaired brain function (Benton, 1955). Finger recognition deficits have been found also in some studies of reading disability (e.g. Sparrow & Satz, 1970) and performance on finger localization tasks has been shown in some studies to predict later reading ability among normal school children (e.g. Fletcher, Taylor, Morris, & Satz, 1982; Lindgren, 1978). In terms of the callosal deficit hypothesis, impairment specifically involving the cross-hand condition relative to the within-hand condition was found for dyslexic adolescents by Gross-Glenn and Rothenberg (1984) and was reported for a sub-group of (supposedly phonologically deficient) young Italian dyslexic children by Fabbro, Pesenti, Facoetti, Bonanomi, Libera, and Lorusso (2001).

Moore, Brown, Markee, Theberge, and Zvi (1996) examined cross-hand transfer of finger localization in 21 college dyslexic students and controls (who also participated in the visual evoked potential study of Markee et al., 1996). Both groups made significantly fewer correct responses in the cross-hand than within-hand condition and fewer correct responses when four fingers were stimulated than when three were stimulated. There was no significant group-by-response hand interaction. When all participants were re-grouped according to their scores on a test of rhyming fluency, however, the interaction was significant because of a smaller number of correct scores in the cross-hand condition among those low in rhyming fluency. This suggests that inter-manual transfer of finger localization information is more efficient among those with higher rhyming skills.

In my own laboratory, Amanda Puddifer and I used the finger localization task with a group of reading-disabled children (mean age 10 years 4 months; mean reading age 7 years 2 months) and controls matched for chronological and reading age ($n = 8$ for each group). Participants indicated where their fingers had been touched by repeating the sequence using the thumb of the same or the opposite hand. Tests of nonword reading and phoneme deletion established that the disabled readers and the controls matched for reading age were each lower in phonological awareness scores than the controls matched for chronological age but did not differ from each other. All three groups showed reduced accuracy in the cross-hand compared with the within-hand conditions, but the extent of inter-manual transfer was considerably less for the controls matched for reading age and the disabled readers than for the controls matched for chronological age. Across all participants combined, there were significant negative correlations between per cent transfer and performance on both nonword reading and phoneme deletion tasks. Reading age and finger localization performance on the same hand were significantly correlated but not if chronological age was controlled. However, the correlation between reading age and performance in the cross-hand conditions remained significant even after taking account of chronological age. On the face of it, these findings support the view that the extent of tactile information transfer across the corpus callosum is related to phonological ability.

The findings outlined above support the view that inter-hemispheric transfer of information relevant to finger localization performance is compromised in dyslexic children and adults. However, explanations other than defective inter-hemispheric transfer have been proposed to account for at least some of the reduction in performance in the cross-hand condition by dyslexic compared with control readers. Specifically, dyslexics may (like younger normal readers) have a reduced capacity to construct visuo-spatial representations that can be used to carry out the task. McKinney (1964) performed an experiment in which children aged 4–8 years were instructed to close their eyes and were touched lightly on a finger of the right hand. After 3 sec, they were asked to "point to" the finger that had been touched (presumably with the opposite, left, hand though this is not specified in the report). There were three conditions: (A) right hand placed palm upwards and remaining in that position; (B) right hand palm upwards while finger touched but turned over (palm downwards) before response given, (C) right hand touched while palm upwards, hand turned over (palm downwards) and then returned to original position (palm upwards). McKinney reported that there were more errors in condition B (mirror-image condition) than in condition A. Results in the control condition (C) showed that that this could not be attributed to the motor movement involved in turning over the hand. McKinney (1964) suggested that "a visual image of the hand was elicited when the finger was stimulated tactually" (p. 99). Since only two of a small group ($n = 9$) of blind children showed the same performance decrement in condition B, McKinney concluded: "Clearly, a young child's hand schema is a predominantly visual image" (pp. 99–100).

It could be argued that in using a single hand for both stimulation and response, simple discrimination of where on the finger one has been stimulated is sufficient for accurate performance. However, if a response is to be made by the opposite hand, then, as well as touch discrimination, an awareness of the relative position of the fingers is also required. The experiment carried out by McKinney (1964) was repeated with 5-year-old children by Quinn and Geffen (1986), who distinguished between responses made by the opposite hand and those made by the same hand as that stimulated (using the thumb of that hand to indicate which finger had been touched). In the event, the children's performance using the opposite hand to that stimulated (cross-hand condition) was better (though not significantly so) in the mirror-image condition than in the other (spatially aligned) condition. In the same-hand condition, performance was significantly impaired when the hand was turned over before responding, in comparison with not turning over the hand. The results were taken as indicating that, even in the same-hand condition, awareness of finger topography (that is, of where the fingers are in space) is necessary for accurate perform-ance (as otherwise the experimental manipula-tions would not have been expected to have any effect). Quinn and Geffen (1986) concluded: "the increase in errors on the same hand with fin-ger positions reversed suggests that the 5-yr-old children may have a limited ability to perceive fin-ger topography unimanually; the further increase in errors with the opposite hand response sug-gests that there is also a loss of topographic information during interhemispheric transfer" (pp. 802–803). However, Pipe (1991) has ques-tioned whether inter-hemispheric transfer need be invoked to explain poorer cross-hand than within-hand localization performance.

In Pipe's (1991) study, children were presented in one condition with a model hand on which to make their responses with the same hand as that which had been stimulated. The fingers of the model hand were in the mirror-image positions to those of the stimulated hand but this condition does not require inter-hemispheric transfer of tactile information. In another condition, chil-dren responded with the hand opposite to the one that had been stimulated by successively opposing the thumb with the fingers that had been stimu-lated on the other hand. In this condition, too, the fingers are, of course, in mirror-image positions. Pipe found that whether children used a model to respond with their stimulated hand or used their opposite hand to indicate their response did not affect accuracy of performance. This was equally poor in both conditions and significantly worse than in the within-hand condition in which chil-dren indicated with thumb and finger the sequence of finger stimulation on that same hand. Pipe concluded that her results "did not support the notion that developmental changes in crossed finger localization result from inefficient transfer

of tactile information between the hemispheres ... Rather, it seems likely that task demands account for the poorer performance of all three age groups on the crossed and model tasks com-pared to the uncrossed task" (p. 342).

In a second study in my laboratory, conducted by Rebecca Edwards and myself, dyslexic adult students and control students were administered the same-hand and cross-hand finger localization tasks. Participants responded in both the con-ventional mode and using photographs of the left and right hand on which to respond. That is, we extended Pipe's set-up to include a condition in which a photograph (hereafter a model) was used to test same-hand and cross-hand conditions of stimulation. In the conditions in which a model was used, the model's hand was in the same orien-tation (palm upwards) as in the stimulating situ-ation. Participants indicated on the model which fingers had been touched and in what sequence. In the within-hand condition, the fingers of the model were aligned with those of the partici-pant's hand. In the cross-hand condition, the fin-gers of the model were in mirror-image positions (as they are in reality). These model conditions were compared with the conventional situation in which the participant used the thumb to indicate the sequence of stimulation on either the same or opposite hand.

What we found overall was that dyslexic stu-dents made significantly more errors than con-trols and that in the cross-hand (but not within-hand) condition, both groups made more errors using the conventional response mode than using the models. While this finding is consistent with the idea that some information is lost during inter-hemispheric transfer in both dyslexics and controls, we obtained no evidence from this group of adult students to suggest that this was any greater for dyslexics than controls. On the other hand, dyslexics generally benefited more from the models than did the controls. We also found that for both groups scores on a phonological test (spoonerisms) correlated significantly with accur-acy on cross-hand finger localization scores.

Jorm et al. (1986) suggested that finger local-ization might be "classed under phonological processing to the extent that it requires the child to learn numerical labels for the fingers" (p. 52). It is quite possible that participants engage in covert finger-counting, labelling or other strategies that may (or may not) make the task overall more difficult for dyslexics. Post-experimental enquiry elicited the information that our dyslexic adult students tended to eschew visual strategies in favour of verbal ones. This may help to explain the correlation we found between extent of intermanual transfer and scores on the spoonerism task and, by extension, other reports of a correlation between transfer and phonological tasks.

Until recently, it was difficult to see how a callosal transfer deficit could bring about the specific problems of reading and writing characteristic of dyslexia. However, a possible link between callosal transfer and cognitive processes relevant to dyslexia is suggested by the finding that at least some individuals in whom the corpus callosum is congenitally absent have shown impairments on a word fluency task requiring production of words beginning with a given letter, a phonological cue, or in retrieving words from rhyme cues (Dennis, 1981; Jeeves & Temple, 1987), as well as in certain other aspects of phonological processing (Temple & Ilsley, 1993; Temple, Jeeves, & Villaroya, 1989; 1990) and sentence comprehension (Sanders, 1989). Agenesis of the corpus callosum is not a single genetic syndrome (Dobyns, 1996). Whether these impairments are found in all acallosal individuals due merely to the absence of the corpus callosum or whether they can be attributed to associated cerebral pathology cannot be decided on the basis of the data presently available.

MORPHOLOGY OF THE CORPUS CALLOSUM IN DYSLEXIA

In addition to hypothesized deficits in callosal function, a number of neuro-imaging studies have suggested that there may be a structural difference between the callosa of dyslexic and non-dyslexic individuals. However, like the studies of planum temporale asymmetry, the results of morphological studies of the corpus callosum are conflicting.

Duara et al. (1991) reported that the sagittally scanned cross-sectional area of the splenium (variously designated in the literature as the posterior fifth or quarter of the callosum) was significantly larger in 21 dyslexic adults than in 29 controls after correction for total brain size. Larsen, Höien, Lundberg, and Ödegaard (1992) found no difference between dyslexic and control adolescents either in total callosal area (uncorrected for brain size) or in the splenium as a proportion of the total callosal area. Hynd et al. (1995) noted a smaller genu in 16 dyslexic than in 16 control participants but the two groups were not well matched for age, IQ or handedness, all of which have been putatively related to callosal size (see Beaton, 1997).

Rumsey et al. (1996) examined the anterior, middle and posterior thirds of the callosum in dyslexic and control adults. There were no group differences in absolute size of any segment. However, using total callosal area as a covariate, the area of the posterior third of the callosum (isthmus and splenium) as visualized on a low-resolution scanner was larger in the 21 dyslexic men than in 19 matched controls. This effect was not significant if the covariate was mid-brain sagittal area; neither the absolute mid-sagittal brain area nor the total mid-sagittal area of the corpus callosum differed significantly between the groups. All participants were said to be right-handed on the basis of a 12-item battery of physical and neurological tests, although one of the dyslexics wrote with his left hand.

Neuro-anatomical studies of the corpus callosum in dyslexia were reviewed by Beaton (1997). One study found a larger splenium in dyslexics (Duara et al., 1991), one found a smaller genu in dyslexics (Hynd et al., 1995) and one found no difference between dyslexics and controls (Larsen et al., 1992). Given concerns over a number of methodological factors, I concluded that "it is clearly too early to draw firm conclusions regarding callosal morphology in dyslexia" (p. 304).

Since my earlier review, an enlarged callosum (except for the genu and splenium) has been reported by Robichon and Habib (1998) for 16 dyslexic men in comparison with 12 controls. The strength of the magnet was greater than that used by Hynd et al. (1990) and Rumsey et al. (1996) and the same as that used in the remaining studies. The tracings were digitized and magnified to a standard anterior–posterior length to control for individual differences in brain size. The size of each callosal region was measured in relation to the total mid-sagittal callosal area. Total callosal area and isthmus tended to be relatively larger in right-handed dyslexics and non-right-handed controls than in non-right-handed dyslexics and right-handed controls, the group-by-hand interaction being significant. However, there was no statistical partialling out of variance due to IQ, which might relate to callosal size (Strauss, Wada, & Hunter, 1994).

In the study by Robichon and Habib (1998), correlations between scores on a test of sound categorization were significant for two callosal sub-regions. The number of errors made on a test of nonword reading correlated significantly with mid-sagittal area of an anterior sub-region of the callosum (posterior to genu); the results were similar for a sound categorization test and for errors in reading comprehension. Errors in sound categorization also correlated with area P1 (central trunk callosum) and with two indices of callosal shape, "circularity" and "slenderness". Finally, there was a significant correlation between nonword reading and slenderness. However, correlation data for the control group were not presented and no adjustment in the probability level accepted ($p < 0.05$) was made for carrying out multiple statistical tests.

In another more recent study, the largest to date of its kind, the area of the corpus callosum was measured in a sub-set of individuals from the Colorado Twin Study. To avoid the problem of related data, reading-disabled individuals were compared with normally reading controls (who were not twinned with the disabled readers) such that 75 reading-disabled individuals (all from separate pairs of twins) were compared with 22 unrelated control participants. Neither total callosal area nor any sub-division as measured using a high-resolution scanner differed between the two groups (Pennington et al., 1999). These results were not affected by exclusion of individuals who also carried a diagnosis of ADHD.

An even more recent study found no difference between 20 right-handed dyslexic boys and 20 controls in total area of the callosum or in any of its segments (von Plessen et al., 2002), although it was reported that the shape of the posterior mid-body was significantly different in the two groups.

To summarize the above findings, at least seven studies have measured *in vivo* the size of the corpus callosum in dyslexic participants. Three studies reported larger callosal segments in dyslexics than controls (Duara et al., 1991; Robichon & Habib, 1998; Rumsey et al., 1996), one reported a smaller genu in dyslexics (Hynd et al., 1990) and three reported no difference between dyslexics and controls (Larsen et al., 1992; Pennington et al., 1999; von Plessen et al., 2002; see also Cowell, Jernigan, Denenberg, & Tallal, 1995, who found no difference between controls and children diagnosed as having specific language impairment). While it is conceivable that individuals diagnosed as dyslexic by different criteria differ in their callosal morphology, it is unlikely that this is the explanation for the discrepancy in findings reported in the neuro-imaging literature.

I know of no post-mortem studies of the callosum in dyslexia. In one recent study of the brains of 10 elderly deceased persons, direct anatomical measures of the mid-sagittal callosal surface did not differ from those estimated from magnetic resonance imaging provided the image slices were thin (Peters, Jäncke, & Zilles, 2000). It is probable, therefore, that post-mortem studies based on small numbers would do little if anything to resolve the inconsistency seen in imaging studies of dyslexic brains.

The meaning of any difference that may exist between dyslexics and controls in the size of the corpus callosum is unclear. Variation in callosal size may be determined by one or more of a variety of histological factors, including absolute number of fibres, extent of myelinization, fibre thickness or packing density. These, in turn, may reflect experiential (see Schlaug et al., 1995) and/ or constitutional factors affecting the cells of origin of callosal axons. If found to be reliable, differences between dyslexic and non-dyslexic participants in the size of the corpus callosum may therefore relate to one or more of a number of factors that differ as between controls and dyslexics. However, given that individual variation in callosal size is striking (Giedd et al., 1996, 1999; Parashos et al., 1995), large samples of participants are required to adequately assess morphological characteristics of the callosum in relation to other variables. The literature on callosal morphology in dyslexia has tended to use small numbers of participants. Only the study by Pennington et al. (1999) may be considered to have used a sufficiently large number of participants, and this study showed no difference between poor readers and controls.

BEYOND THE CORTEX

The focus so far in this chapter has been on gross neuro-anatomic investigations of dyslexia; differences been dyslexics and controls in the size or asymmetry of a variety of structures have been proposed. The regions involved have included the frontal gyrus, the planum temporale and the corpus callosum. Anomalies of cerebellar structure and function have also been said to relate to dyslexia (see Chapter 10). In short, it is possible that there are very widespread morphological variations in the brains of dyslexic compared with non-dyslexic adults (see Brown, Eliez, Menon, Rumsey, White, & Reiss, 2001). However, there is no certainty about any of the proposed differences between dyslexic and non-dyslexic brains— a sobering thought given the amount of research conducted to date.

As well as differences between skilled and dyslexic readers in gross neuro-anatomic features, malformations of microscopic structure have been said to be present in the brains of dyslexic adults (Galaburda & Kemper, 1979; Galaburda et al., 1985; Humphreys et al., 1990). In recent years, a novel technique known as diffusion tensor magnetic resonance imaging has been developed that allows investigators to distinguish between grey matter and underlying white matter. It was used recently with six adult poor readers and the results point to some abnormality of white matter

structure in the temporo-parietal region bilaterally. This emerged without there being any indication of gross anatomical differences between such readers and controls. There was a significant relationship (on one-tailed tests) in the left hemisphere of both poor readers and control readers between structural characteristics of the white matter and scores on a test of nonword reading (Klingberg et al., 2000). These authors suggested that "Variability in the microstructure of the white matter tracts connecting temporo-parietal cortex and other cortices would affect communication between these areas and could thereby impair the coordination of visual and phonological codes that is necessary for skilled reading" (p. 497).

Cortical regions of the brain do not operate in isolation from sub-cortical regions. In the male (but not female) rat, cortical injury produced early in life by means of a probe cooled to a very low temperature (−70°C) produced a significant change in the distribution of cell size in the dorsal nuclei of the medial geniculate body (Herman et al., 1997). There was an associated behavioural impairment on an auditory sequence discrimination task in the male rats. It is therefore possible that the cortical anomalies reported in dyslexia can be related to the presence of sub-cortical malformations.

It is commonplace to talk of aphasia as resulting from a cortical lesion. D'Esposito and Alexander (1995) pointed out, however, "That a *purely* cortical lesion—even a macroscopic one—can produce standard Broca's or Wernicke's aphasia has never been demonstrated" (p. 41, emphasis in original). Most cortical lesions encroach to some extent on underlying sub-cortical structures. In this context, it is of interest to note that in one family with inherited speech and language impairment (along with other oral–praxic impairment), affected family members show anomalies of structure and function at a variety of sub-cortical sites, particularly the caudate nucleus (Watkins et al., 2002b).

The thalamus has been reported to show a left–right anatomical difference in normal brains (Eidelberg & Galaburda, 1982) and at least some parts of this structure are undoubtedly related to language functions (Brown, 1975; for reviews, see Crosson, 1984, 1985, 1999). Lesions to left lateral thalamic nuclei produce dysnomia, a phenomenon that may bear some relation to the naming difficulties frequently seen in dyslexics (see Chapter 5). Recently, left pulvinar damage has been associated with a highly specific naming impairment for medical terms (Crosson, Moberg, Boone, Gonzalez-Rothi, & Raymer (1997). More generally, aphasia can occur following damage to a variety of sub-cortical sites involving the striatal-capsular region, peri-ventricular white matter and the thalamus (Crosson, 1999; D'Esposito & Alexander, 1995).

In a group of 14 Parkinson patients, Hugdahl, Wester, and Asbjørnsen (1990b) reported that left- but not right-sided thalamotomy produced a dramatic reduction in recall from both ears in dichotic listening. In addition, left-sided stimulation prior to removal produced an improvement in right ear recall and right-sided stimulation produced an improved (but not significant) left ear recall. Wester and Hugdahl (1997) subsequently reported results from a larger group of patients showing that high-intensity ventrolateral thalamic stimulation on the left impaired (rather than improved) recall of a list of dichotically presented words. These findings suggest that the thalamus on the left may be involved in an attentional or alerting mechanism. If so, it would not be surprising to find that there are perturbations of some aspects of thalamic structure and function in dyslexia.

Consistent with this idea, Livingstone et al. (1991) found proportionally fewer large cells in a particular region of the lateral geniculate nucleus of five "dyslexic" brains, those previously reported to show post-mortem cortical malformations (and symmetry of the planum temporale), than in five control brains. The distribution of cells of different size was subsequently also reported to be abnormal in the medial geniculate nucleus of the same brains.

The medial geniculate nucleus (MGN) is the auditory equivalent of the lateral geniculate nucleus (LGN) in the visual system (see Chapter 12). The MGN receives fibres from the olivary body, part of the auditory pathway, and projects to the superior temporal gyrus, the primary auditory receiving area. Galaburda and Livingstone (1993) reported that whereas control brains showed relatively more large cells in the left than the right MGN, the five "dyslexic" brains showed an asymmetry in the opposite direction. Unfortunately, the statistical significance of these findings is unclear from the details provided in their paper. A later report (Galaburda, Menard, & Rosen, 1994) stated that "Using difference scores between the hemispheres (right minus left) as a dependent measure, we found an interaction between hemisphere and diagnosis. Specifically, there was significant right–left asymmetry in the dyslexic but not the nondyslexic group, with dyslexics having smaller left than right MGN neurons" (p. 8011). However, finding that two groups of difference scores are statistically different according to a non-parametric test does not establish that there is a significant asymmetry in one group but not in the other. Nor is this established by the series of chi-square analyses undertaken, although admittedly the data are suggestive.

Although cell size distribution in the lateral and medial geniculate nuclei might differ as between dyslexics and normal readers, the gross anatomy of the thalamus may not be unusual in dyslexia. Pennington et al. (1999) investigated brain morphometry using MRI in a subset of twins from the Colorado Twin Study. A randomly chosen number of 75 unrelated reading-disabled participants were compared with 22 unrelated controls who were normal readers. After taking account of differences between the sexes (together with age and IQ), there was no difference between the two groups in the volume of any of a number of sub-cortical structures, including the thalamus. However, some PET and functional MRI studies have revealed differences between dyslexics and controls in activation levels of the thalamus (Brunswick McCroy, Price, Frith, & Frith, 1999; Roush, 1995), which supports the view that the thalamus may function abnormally in dyslexia.

It is with investigations of brain function as opposed to structure that the next chapter is concerned.

10

Functional Brain Imaging and Reading

As well as neuro-anatomic and behavioural studies aimed at elucidating the biological bases of dyslexia, in recent years there has been increasing interest in functional brain studies of reading and reading disability (see Pugh et al., 2000a). Neuroimaging studies of dyslexia extend previous electroencephalographic (EEG) and evoked potential (EP) investigations (largely of cerebral laterality differences between good and poor readers) and link with imaging studies of auditory and visual verbal processing in normal readers. Readers interested in early EEG studies may wish to consult the paper by Duffy and McAnulty (1985) and for more recent work papers by Ackerman, McPherson, Oglesby, and Dykman (1998), Rippon and Brunswick (2000) and Leisman (2002).

POSITRON EMISSION TOPOGRAPHY

Positron emission tomography (PET) is a technique whereby brain activity is monitored "online". Brain activity is associated with an increase in metabolic activity of neurons leading to dilation of blood vessels. Blood flow increases to those parts of the brain where the activity occurs. Cerebral blood flow, oxygen and glucose metabolism are relatively high in those regions of the brain active at any given moment, the total flow of blood being distributed throughout the brain in response to the demands placed upon it in different regions. However, the local increase in blood flow exceeds the oxygen requirement of the local tissue. Local or regional changes (increases or decreases) in blood flow can be tracked by introducing a radioactive tracer with a short half-life, such as air mixed with xenon-133 gas or water labelled with positron-emitting oxygen ($^{15}O_2$), into the bloodstream (Frackowiak & Friston, 1994). It takes about 30 sec for the tracer to enter the brain and it is during the following 30 sec or so when radiation rises to a maximum that a picture of regional cerebral blood flow is obtained (Frith & Friston, 1997). This short interval of time obviously limits the duration of the cognitive operations that it is possible to monitor.

Radioactive atoms decay by emission of positively charged particles (positrons), which, after travelling a finite distance, come to rest and interact with negatively charged particles (electrons). In doing so, the two particles are annihilated, their mass being converted into two photons travelling in opposite directions. Annihilation photons are detected by devices using radiation detectors that record an event only when two photons arrive simultaneously. The PET scanner has a ring of scintillation detectors that detect the emitted radioactivity in a given plane through the brain. The use of several rings of detectors allows measurement of radioactivity in different planes and the positron annihilation source points are reconstructed tomographically to produce an image. During radioactive decay, the tracer emits positrons at a rate dependent upon its relative concentration. Since the relationship between local blood flow and radioactivity is known (and nearly linear), the amount of emitted radioactivity at each of a number of locations provides an indication of regional cerebral blood flow.

Differences between any two experimental conditions in blood flow or metabolism at particular locations in the brain are displayed in colour on a computerized image, differences in colour corresponding to differences in activity. However, according to Friston, Frith, Liddle, Dolan, Lammertsma, and Frackowiak (1990), "One obstacle to the interpretation of regional data is the confounding effect of global changes ... an individual with intrinsically high global activity might show a larger, lower, or the same local increase during activation as a subject with low global activity" (pp. 458–459). The independence of an effect due to experimental condition from the confounding linear effect of global activity satisfies the requirements of an analysis of covariance. Friston et al. (1990) therefore recommend removal of differences in global blood flow between individuals by means of analysis of covariance prior to displaying differences in activation patterns between conditions. They point out that changes associated with a particular activation can be partitioned into global and local effects according to two models. One model assumes that an increase in local activity depends upon the level of global activity; the other assumes that local effects are independent of global effects. Friston et al. tested these models on data from 24 scans performed on four individuals

and concluded that their data favoured the second model.

The images from an individual brain are transformed to a standard size and shape by reference to a standard brain atlas or stereotactic coordinate system and are often averaged over a number of individuals. This ignores the considerable inter-individual differences that exist in the size and configuration of the brain's convolutions (Rademacher, et al., 1993; Steinmetz & Seitz, 1991). The images obtained using standard techniques do not show local topographic detail. Yet given that there are characteristic relationships between major cytoarchitectonic areas—which show individual variation—and topographic landmarks (gyri and sulci) on individual brains, it might be more reliable to use these, rather than standard brain atlases, in functional mapping studies (Rademacher et al., 1993). On the other hand, some allowance for individual differences in gyral anatomy can be made by mathematical techniques, such as smoothing the data by a Gaussian filter (Jenkins & Frackowiak, 1993). For short, non-technical accounts of PET, the interested reader is referred to Petersen and Fiez (1993), Frackowiack and Friston (1994) and Frith and Friston (1997).

FUNCTIONAL MAGNETIC RESONANCE IMAGING

An alternative technique for measuring brain activity is functional magnetic resonance imaging (fMRI). Essentially, fMRI responses reflect haemodynamic changes in magnetic susceptibility. The assumption is that changes in blood flow are closely correlated with changes in fMRI activity. The exact nature of the relationship between fMRI responses and the underlying neural activity is unclear at present but simultaneous fMRI and intra-cortical electrophysiological recordings in monkey by Logothetis, Pauls, Augath, Trinath, and Oeltermann (2001) suggest that fMRI "activation may actually reflect more the neural activity related to the input and the local procesing in any given area, rather than the spiking activity commonly thought of as the output of the area" (p. 151). Activation of a particular brain area may represent either excitation or inhibition—it is not possible to tell which. A major difference between PET and fMRI, apart from the use of radiation in the former, is that the images during fMRI are collected in sequential slices. This means that activity at the beginning and end of the sequence is recorded at slightly different times.

During the past decade, PET and fMRI techniques have been widely applied to the study of reading disability. These normally take the form of comparing patterns of regional blood flow between dyslexic and non-dyslexic groups. Although it might appear that the use of standard neuro-imaging techniques will lead to the same results in different laboratories, there are at least two major sources of difference that may give rise to discrepancy between the results reported from different investigators (or from the same investigators at different times). One concerns the baseline or control levels of activation in different brain regions against which experimental manipulations are tested. Changes in blood flow are shown as an increase or decrease in relation to this control. What counts as a statistically significant change in activation of a particular area can vary with the views of different investigators. Thus activation of a particular area in one study but not another may reflect not differential activation of brain regions in the two studies, but rather different criteria for determining what is a statistically significant change in regional brain activity.

It is also important to remember that "A functional area of the brain is not a task area: there is no 'tennis forehand area' to be discovered. Likewise, no single area of the brain is devoted to a very complex function; neither 'attention' nor 'language', for example, is localized in a particular Brodmann area or lobe. Any task or 'function' utilizes a complex and distributed set of brain areas" (Petersen & Fiez, 1993, p. 513). One advantage that functional imaging studies have over classic studies of brain-damaged patients is that the former enable an investigator to consider the possible contribution to a given function or task of many brain areas simultaneously, whereas

lesion studies (singly if not collectively) are necessarily more restricted in what they can tell us about neuro-anatomic localization of function. However, often one receives the impression that imaging studies show "too much" simultaneous activation—one cannot see the wood for the trees. This impression is even more compelling if one attempts to combine results from several studies ostensibly investigating the same issue.

A second major concern is that it is not always (if ever) possible to know the nature or content of an individual participant's cognitive processes at any given moment, even though the experimental instructions attempt to control this. While the neural representation underlying the same cognitive process may differ as between dyslexics and controls, perhaps due to early anomalies of function and/or neuro-anatomy in the former, differences between any two groups of participants in patterns of regional cerebral blood flow may relate to any of a number of differences between the two groups. These may involve the cognitive strategies employed in carrying out the experimental tasks, the level of difficulty experienced, the degree of anxiety felt in response to the experimental procedure, or to differences in IQ or other variables (Flowers, Wood, & Naylor, 1991). It is possible to control statistically for individual differences in variables such as IQ or handedness, but it is far more difficult to bring strategy differences under experimenter control.

The same kind of consideration applies with equal force to the subtractive approach to analysing functional activation patterns, the approach used in the majority of neuro-imaging studies. The logic of the argument is that brain activation specific to a particular cognitive component can be isolated by comparing two conditions that supposedly differ only in so far as one task requires a single additional cognitive component relative to the other task (see Pugh et al., 1997).

For example, reading a word aloud might be thought to involve activating visual, semantic and phonological representations of that word. Silent reading might be held to require only visual and semantic representations. Subtracting activation under a silent reading condition from activation produced by reading aloud might therefore be expected to isolate the pattern of brain activation associated with accessing a phonological representation. But what if phonological representations are automatically accessed even if not required by the silent reading task? And what if information processing takes place not sequentially but in parallel, or cascade? In short, isolating brain activation associated with different components of cognitive processing requires a level of componential specification that goes beyond present-day cognitive theory and a degree of methodological sophistication and control that taxes experimental ingenuity to the utmost (for discussion of this and other methodological issues, see Démonet, Wise, & Frackowiak, 1993; Sergent, Zuck, Lévesque, & MacDonald, 1992). As Sergent et al. expressed the problems:

> Given the less than adequate understanding of the actual decomposition of cognitive tasks ... the identification of anatomical–functional correlations of higher order cognitive operations is exposed to several difficulties ... Even if computational models postulate a fractionation of cognitive functions into subcomponent processes ... designing a task that specifically taps a restricted set of subprocesses does not guarantee that other operations are not conjointly performed during its performance. This is particularly true of verbal stimuli in which human adults have acquired such considerable expertise that their processing unfolds in an automatic and obligatory manner at different levels simultaneously ... More processes are performed than strictly required by the specific demands of a verbal task, which implies more activation of cerebral structures than would theoretically ... be sufficient to carry out the task.
>
> (Sergent et al., 1992, pp. 69, 78)

Fiez and Petersen (1998) reviewed neuro-imaging studies of word reading. Taking only nine studies, these authors calculated that there was a total of 147 foci of activation, of which "104 were determined to represent a commonly found activation" (p. 915). Another way of looking at this is to say that approximately one-third of foci were *not* commonly found areas of activation. Even though the commonly found foci fell into clusters, it is difficult for someone familiar with the literature to avoid the feeling that the number of regions activated during single-word reading would be even greater if more studies were included. It is possible to attempt to relate common areas of activation to particular cognitive processes, as Fiez and Petersen (1998) did in suggesting that the left frontal operculum relates to the process of orthographic-to-phonological conversion. However, this barely extends the kind of broad structure–function correlation suggested by lesion studies and leaves unexplained the relatively large proportion of activation foci that were not commonly found.

Despite the popular notion of neuro-imaging techniques laying bare the machinery of the brain, only a theoretically motivated cognitive analysis can provide some insight as to the different components involved in a given task or function and hence of the kind of computational operations that a particular brain region undertakes. In a highly thoughtful review of how the results of fMRI and PET studies are interpreted, Bub (2000) pointed out that "functional imaging is confronted with a host of methodological difficulties that must be navigated successfully before the technique can be used to provide a testing ground for neuropsychological and neurophysiological theories of higher cognitive function" (p. 482).

Bub (2000) argued that one should not be seduced by "the hidden tendency to assume that the pattern of activation seen in the final image is a literal description of neurons firing to a particular task demand" (p. 468). It is important to appreciate that if the same region of the brain is activated to the same extent in both a "control" condition and an "experimental" condition, this will not show up as a regional difference when the two conditions are compared. That is, lack of PET activation does not mean lack of brain activity. Thus the patterns of activation reported in published papers do not necessarily identify in their entirety those neural areas involved in a given task. Moreover, "a pattern of significantly activated brain areas does not provide information about the interregional relationships" (Karbe et al., 1998, pp. 114–115). Distinguishing those regions that are differentially activated in two or more experimental conditions may shed little or no light on the total functional organization or brain circuitry involved in particular cognitive operations.

With the above reservations in mind, I turn now to the relevant literature. In doing so, it should be remembered that establishing the direction of causation of any differences in patterns of brain activation between dyslexic and non-dyslexic readers is problematic. Castro-Caldas, Petersson, Reis, Stone-Elander, and Ingvar (1998) have reported that adults who had never learned to read exhibit a different pattern of PET activation than control participants carrying out the same tasks. As the functionally illiterate participants were presumably entirely normal from a neurological point of view, these findings dictate caution in interpreting activation differences between dyslexic and control readers. They may reflect cognitive or strategy differences rather than differences in the functional organization of the brain consequent upon some anomaly of neurological development.

PET STUDIES AND DYSLEXIA

The past decade has seen a considerable number of PET studies examining differences between dyslexic and non-dyslexic adult readers. Rumsey et al. (1992) reported that in comparison with 14 controls, 14 dyslexic men showed reduced activation at the left temporo-parietal region in response to a simple task in which they had to press a button if two words rhymed. However, the dyslexics showed increased activation at the right temporal region. Hagman, Wood, Buchsbaum, Tallal, Flowers, and Katz (1992) also found increased activation in 10 dyslexic adults in response to a task in which they had to identify an auditorily presented target CV nonsense syllable when it was presented within a stream of dis-

tractors. This time, the increase was not confined to the right hemisphere but occurred at medial temporal lobe sites bilaterally. There were no group differences at more lateral sites.

The dyslexic participants in the study by Hagman et al. (1992) also took part in a study conducted by Flowers et al. (1991), in which they listened to a list of common nouns and were requested to make a bimanual finger response whenever they heard a word that was written with four letters. Among 69 controls, this task activated Wernicke's area and activation was correlated with task accuracy. This finding was replicated in a second group of 83 participants who varied in reading ability but who were drawn from a "reading centre". In an area immediately posterior to Wernicke's region, 23 readers described as either non-reading-disabled or good readers were seen to show reduced flow in comparison with 33 reading-disabled participants. Whereas group differences at Wernicke's area were entirely accounted for by differences in overall reading ability, those at the more posterior temporo-parietal site remained even after this factor was taken into account. Flowers et al. concluded that there is a "shift" towards a more posterior focus of activation in poor compared with good readers in response to the experimental task. However, of the 83 participants in total, seven were said to be left-handed and six ambidextrous. Although handedness was examined in relation to right hemisphere flow in this entire group, there is nothing in the report concerning the handedness composition of the poor readers. Nor was handedness apparently controlled statistically (as were age, gender and IQ) in assessing the difference between poor and "good" readers in level of activation at the temporo-parietal site. It is therefore possible that a difference in handedness contributed to the group difference in activation.

One study of 17 right-handed dyslexic adult men (including three who participated in the study by Rumsey et al., 1992) showed (as a group) processing abnormalities in the mid-posterior temporal lobes bilaterally (Rumsey, Nace, Donohue, Wise, Maisog, & Andreason, 1997c). The tasks in the PET study included reading aloud pseudowords (said to involve phonological processing) and irregular/inconsistent words (e.g. *save* versus *have*, reflecting orthographic processes). Dyslexics showed more widespread activation and de-activation than controls, attributed by the authors to greater subjective difficulty for the dyslexics, and reduced activation in posterior temporal/inferior parietal regions relative to controls, especially in the "phonological" condition and especially on the left side.

Differences in regional cerebral blood flow between the phonological and orthographic processing tasks might be taken as indicating the two different pathways identified in so-called dual-route theory as lexical and sub-lexical routes to pronunciation. The underlying basis of dual-route theory, it will be remebered (see Chapter 2), is that familiar, irregular words are processed by a different (orthographic) mechanism than are novel letter strings pronounceable according to a set of "correspondence" rules relating sub-word segments of the letter string (such as letter, grapheme, syllable, rime or other unit) to discrete phonological units. Although modern connectionist accounts of single-word reading (discussed briefly in Chapter 2) do not make this assumption, basing all reading on a single mechanism, there is some evidence (Baluch & Besner, 1991; Monsell, Patterson, Graham, Hughes, & Milroy, 1992; see also Weekes, Capetillo-Cunliffe, Rayman, Iacoboni, & Zaidel, 1999) that individuals differ in their relative reliance on lexical and sub-lexical strategies (or, in connectionist terms, on the relative strength of the weights between orthographic and phonological units for different kinds of word).

Participants in the PET study of Rumsey et al. (1997c) were also given a test of syntactical processing. They were asked to indicate by a button press whether the meaning of each of a pair of sentences expressed in different syntactic forms was identical or not (Rumsey et al., 1994). Dyslexics (*n* = 15) showed activation patterns in left frontal and temporal regions similar to those shown by controls. In a parietal region (in the vicinity of the angular and supramarginal gyri), dyslexics showed a rightward asymmetry of activation, whereas controls showed greater left

hemisphere activation. When the participants were requested to lie still with their eyes closed (presumably thinking of nothing in particular), the dyslexics showed reduced blood flow to this region on the left in comparison with the controls. Although lack of correction for the multiple statistical testing procedures demand caution in interpreting these findings, the indication of abnormal parietal activation in dyslexics is of special interest, since the left angular gyrus has long been thought, on the basis of neuropsychological studies, to be involved in reading (Dejerine, 1891; Henderson, 1986).

According to Horwitz, Rumsey, and Donohue (1998), among the 14 control normal readers in the PET study of Rumsey et al. (1997c) activation of the left (but not the right) angular gyrus region was significantly associated with activation of extra-striate and temporal cortical regions in response to reading aloud single irregular and nonsense words. This was referred to as "functional connectivity". Among the 17 dyslexics, there was no significant association between angular gyrus activation and activation of the other areas. It should be noted, though, that the significance of the differences between groups in the relevant correlations was not formally tested. In a subsequent publication it was reported that, among controls, regional blood flow volume in the left angular gyrus was significantly correlated with reading skill but inversely correlated in dyslexics (Rumsey, Horwitz, Donohue, Nace, Maisog, & Andreason, 1999). This was seen as confirming the important role of the angular gyrus in normal readers and its probable impairment in developmental (as opposed to acquired) dyslexia.

Among controls but not dyslexics in the study of Rumsey et al. (1997c), there were interesting correlations between degree of left–right activation of anterior temporal/inferior frontal regions during syntactic processing and scores on several tests, including reading and spelling. A greater degree of leftward asymmetry of activation was associated with better performance. The same applied to the correlation between asymmetry of activation and performance on the syntactic processing task. These findings are consistent with the idea that dyslexic persons show less functional asymmetry than controls.

In a much quoted study, Paulesu et al. (1996) observed that in comparison with controls, a small group of adult (compensated) dyslexic men with residual phonological processing difficulties showed reduced or absent PET activation of Wernicke's area, the cerebellum and the left insular region in response to a letter-rhyming task. On a task involving memory for single letters, control participants showed fairly widespread activation of regions in the left hemisphere, including Broca's and Wernicke's areas and the insula, while the dyslexics showed reduced activation in Broca's area and no activation of the insula. Paulesu et al. suggested that the insula acts as a bridge between anterior and posterior language processing areas and that there is reduced connectivity in dyslexia. In contrast, Rumsey et al. (1997c) found increased activation in the insula region bilaterally in dyslexics compared with controls. The difference in results might relate to better performance on word and nonword reading tasks by the dyslexics in the study of Paulesu et al. than in the study of Rumsey et al. or to some unidentified difference in the composition of the dyslexic groups in the two studies. Alternatively, the findings might relate to methodological differences. For example, Rumsey et al. (1997c) used simple visual fixation as a control task, whereas Paulesu et al. (1996) had their participants judge whether a Korean letter (an unfamiliar visual pattern to the participants) was similar to a target letter presented on the screen.

Brunswick et al. (1999) reported that while reading words and pseudo-words aloud, six adult (compensated) dyslexic students showed significantly reduced PET activation (relative to a rest condition) in the left posterior inferior temporal region (and left frontal operculum and bilaterally in the cerebellum) in comparison with control participants. Compared with six other adult dyslexic students and controls, they also showed this pattern when reading silently (relative to a feature detection condition using the same stimuli). Since the left posterior inferior temporal region (Brodmann's area 37) has been implicated in phonological processing tasks (Price, Moore, & Frack-

owiak, 1996; but see also Petersen, Fox, Snyder, & Raichle, 1990), the authors suggested that this area (together with the left frontal operculum) is important in the specification or retrieval of phonological information and both areas "may have a special role in the lexical retrieval process during reading" (p. 1913). Brunswick et al. (1999) saw their findings as being "consistent with dyslexia involving a core deficit in accessing phonological word forms" (p. 1913). Brunswick et al. also found that, while reading aloud, dyslexics showed reduced activation relative to control readers in the left and mid-line cerebellum, left thalamus and medial extra-striate cortex. This was not seen during silent or implicit reading.

fMRI STUDIES AND DYSLEXIA

Using fMRI, Shaywitz et al. (1998) failed to confirm the PET finding of reduced activation of the insula in adult dyslexics reported by Paulesu et al. (1996). Participants carried out visually presented single-letter rhyming, nonword rhyming, semantic categorization, letter case and line orientation same–different matching tasks, the latter being a baseline subtraction condition against which activation in the other conditions was measured. In comparison with 32 non-impaired controls, 29 dyslexic readers were said not to show an equivalent increase in activation in posterior brain regions (Wernicke's area, angular gyrus, striate and extra-striate cortex) in going from letter-case matching (e.g. bbBb versus bbBb) to single-letter rhyming (e.g. T versus V) to nonword rhyming (e.g. *jete* versus *keat*) tasks. These three tasks were considered to reflect increasing degrees of phonological processing. A comparatively reduced level of activation in posterior brain regions is consistent with Rumsey and co-workers' findings but, in contrast to Rumsey et al. (1997c), Shaywitz et al. (1998) also observed increased activation in dyslexics compared with controls in frontal regions (including Broca's area). Shaywitz et al. argued that "these brain activation patterns provide evidence of an imperfectly functioning system for segmenting words into their phonologic constituents . . . The pattern of relative underactivation in posterior brain regions contrasted with relative overactivation in anterior regions may provide a neural signature for the phonologic difficulties characterizing dyslexia" (p. 2640). Certainly the dyslexic participants in this investigation were significantly poorer at nonword reading than the controls and made more errors on the nonword rhyming task. What the data do not show, however, is how well the dyslexics performed on tests of real word reading and thus how specific the nonword deficits were. It is also not clear why dyslexics should have shown lower activation of Brodmann's area 17, the primary visual receiving area, than the controls if their difficulty was purely phonological.

In addition to the above findings, Shaywitz et al. (1998) found significant hemispheric differences in the angular gyrus and Brodmann's area 37 ("the posterior aspect of the inferior and middle temporal gyri and anterior aspect of the lateral occipital gyrus"). Across all tasks, normal readers showed greater left- than right-sided activation, whereas the dyslexics showed the opposite pattern. Greater activation on the right side is an unexpected though not isolated finding (see Simos, Breier, Fletcher, Bergman, & Papanicolaou, 2000), but the results for dyslexics support the PET findings of Brunswick et al. (1999) in showing lower left-sided activation during reading in comparison with controls.

Pugh et al. (2000b) reported further analysis of fMRI data obtained from the same 29 adult dyslexic readers and 32 normal control readers as in Shaywitz et al. (1998). Regression analyses showed that, for normal readers, there were significant correlations between activation in the angular gyrus of the left hemisphere and activation at temporal and occipital lobe sites during performance of the four remaining tasks. Dyslexics showed the same pattern of "functional connectivity" between the angular gyrus and other sites for the single-letter reading and letter-case tasks but not for the remaining tasks. For the right hemisphere, the dyslexic readers showed significant correlations for all four tasks; the control group showed the same pattern for all but the

letter-case task, which yielded a non-significant correlation. The authors argued that:

> The most plausible explanation for these left hemisphere findings is the hypothesis . . . positing a basic weakness in phonological representations. This linguistic deficit limits DYS[lexic] readers' ability to build efficient structures within the angular gyrus that link orthographic codes computed in the extra-striate areas of the occipital lobe to phonological codes represented in the superior temporal gyrus.
> (Pugh et al., 2000b, pp. 54–55)

For a number of reasons, functional activation studies of dyslexics almost invariably involve adults rather than children and men rather than women. As differences between the sexes have been reported in the patterns of brain activation shown in response to visually presented language tasks (Shaywitz et al., 1995), restricting investigations largely to males is an unfortunate limitation (see Lambe, 1999). A lack of functional activation studies with children is cause for even greater regret as it is during childhood, before compensatory strategies have been acquired, that one would most expect to find critical differences between dyslexics and controls. In a rare fMRI study carried out with children, German-speaking dyslexics showed under-activation in left inferior temporal regions, as has been found with adults, but frontal regions (Broca's area in particular) were also under-activated in comparison with control readers (Georgiewa et al., 1999). More recently, the results of a large-scale fMRI study of a wide range of English-speaking readers, including impaired and non-impaired readers, have been reported. This study involved children and adolescents of both sexes aged 7–18 years. During nonword reading, the non-impaired readers showed greater activation than impaired readers at a number of fronto-temporal (including Broca's area) and more posterior (including posterior middle temporal gyrus and anterior middle occipital gyrus) sites in both the left and right hemisphere. There was, however, no difference between the groups in activation of the insula (Shaywitz et al., 2002). It was argued that these findings demonstrate that "the dysfunction in left hemisphere posterior reading circuits is already present in dyslexic children and cannot be ascribed simply to a lifetime of poor reading" (p. 107) as might be inferred from the results of studies with adult dyslexics.

Shaywitz et al. (2002) also reported that non-word reading performance correlated significantly with activation of posterior regions of the brain, particularly of the left hemisphere, and that this could not be attributed to age. They took this to suggest that "the left occipitotemporal region may be a critical component of a neural system for skilled reading" (p. 107).

FURTHER NEURO-ELECTRIC TECHNIQUES

Positron emission tomography and functional magnetic resonance imaging are only two of a number of neuro-imaging techniques and are the ones that have been most used with neurologically intact volunteers (for application of neuro-imaging techniques in clinical contexts, see Moseley, 1995). While they are useful in delineating different brain areas that are simultaneously activated during cognitive activity, they both lack good temporal resolution. It is estimated that there is a lag of 5–8 sec between a change in neural activity and the associated change in blood flow (Frith & Friston, 1997). Electroencephalography (EEG) is low in spatial resolution but much more sensitive to when events occur in time, electrophysiological responses occurring within milliseconds rather than seconds of a stimulus event. The nature of the relationships between such EEG characteristics as event-related potentials (ERPs) and particular cognitive events are as uncertain as they are for PET and fMRI, but the temporal resolution of the former makes the study of ERPs useful in certain situations (for application to developmental language disorders, see Leppänen & Lyytinen, 1997; Molfese, 2000; Molfese, Molfese & Espy, 1999). Transcranial magnetic stimulation (TMS) is a technique which interferes transiently with activity in focal brain

regions over a period of milliseconds (Hallett, 2000). It can be applied repetitively and has obvious potential for testing neuroanatomical and temporally based information processing theories of dyslexia but as yet has been little used in this regard.

Magnetoencephalography (MEG), otherwise known as magnetic source imaging (MSI), detects not the electric activity of brain cells but the minute magnetic fields associated with brain activity. Magnetoencephalography has relatively good spatial resolution and excellent temporal resolution. Using this technique, Salmelin, Service, Kiesilä, Uutela, and Salonen (1996) compared the time course of cortical activation in six adult (Finnish) dyslexics and eight controls as they passively viewed single words and nonwords (that is, no response was required). Whereas the controls showed a sharp activation in the left inferior temporo-occipital region at about 180 msec post-onset, dyslexics either failed to show any activation or showed a considerably later response. It was argued that this demonstrated an impairment of the area concerned with word-form perception or recognition. Within 200–400 msec, the left temporal lobe, including Wernicke's area, was said to be strongly activated in controls but not dyslexics.This was considered to be consistent with impaired phonological processing in this region of the brain of dyslexics as reported in the PET study by Rumsey et al. (1992). A left inferior frontal region was also activated within 400 msec in four of the six dyslexics but none of the eight controls. This is reminiscent of the finding of Brunswick et al. (1999), who reported over-activation (while reading words and nonwords) in the left pre-motor area in dyslexics compared with controls.

Using MEG and a passive oddball paradigm, the functional organization of the auditory cortex of the left hemisphere in 11 dyslexic and nine control children (aged 8–14 years) was studied by Heim et al. (2000). Although the topographical distribution of the first major peak of activity (M80) was identical in both groups, a later peak (M120) occurred more anteriorly in dyslexics than controls. This was the case with both pure tone and consonant-vowel stimuli leading Heim et al. (2000) to conclude that the two groups of children differed with regard to the functional organization of their auditory cortex on the left.

Simos et al. (2000) tested 10 dyslexic children (aged 10–17 years) and eight controls using MEG on visual and auditory word discrimination tasks (the exact details of which are not clear from the report). The main findings were that during the visual task, nine of the 10 dyslexics showed reduced activation in left temporo-parietal regions in comparison with the controls. Among the dyslexics, this was accompanied by increased activation in the right temporo-parietal region. As a group, the controls showed significantly greater left hemisphere activation, whereas the dyslexics showed significantly greater activation on the right side. On the auditory task both groups showed the same profile of activation. These findings support those of Shaywitz et al. (1998) using PET.

Taking advantage of MEG's good temporal resolution, Simos et al. (2000) examined the time course of brain activation during the two tasks. Generally speaking, in both participant groups activation was first apparent in basal temporal areas of the left hemisphere. In the control group this was followed by temporo-parietal activation in the same hemisphere, but in the dyslexic group basal temporal activation was followed by activation in the temporo-parietal region of the *right* hemisphere. The authors discussed their findings in terms of an aberrant pattern of functional connectivity between the areas normally involved in reading, but clearly strategy differences between the two groups of readers might be implicated. It might also be worth noting that the mean IQ score of the control group was one standard deviation (not less than 0.5 SD as stated in the text) higher than the mean score of the dyslexic group (with reference to the distribution of the latter group) but this was not taken into account in any of the statistical analyses that were undertaken. Nonetheless, the results reported by Simos et al. represent a potentially valuable contribution given that they apply to younger dyslexics (and show greater inter-individual consistency) than is normally the case in imaging studies.

In a subsequent report, Simos and his collaborators demonstrated that the aberrant activation profiles of eight dyslexic children were reversed after an intensive remediation programme lasting 80 h (Simos et al., 2002). This implies that what one is seeing in functional neuro-imaging studies of dyslexia are not the consequences of an irreversible "hard-wired" deficit, but the reflection of concurrent cognitive processes (see also Temple et al., 2003).

From this brief review of neuro-imaging studies, it would appear that during reading-related tasks there is often an under-activation, suggesting some processing abnormality, of posterior temporo-parietal areas in the left hemisphere of dyslexics. In addition, some studies, but not all, have found increased activation in left frontal areas in dyslexics compared with controls (Brunswick et al., 1999; Pugh et al., 2000a; Shaywitz et al., 1998). In some studies, increased activation has also been reported for posterior areas of the right hemisphere of dyslexics (e.g. Hagman et al., 1992; Rumsey et al., 1992, 1997a; Simos et al., 2000), possibly indicating a compensatory mechanism, at least in adult dyslexics. Differences between studies may relate in some respects to differences between individual dyslexics that are obscured in the group comparisons reported to date.

Because there is still considerable uncertainty as to the precise localization of specific components of reading in normal readers (see Cohen et al., 2000; Howard et al., 1992; Indefrey et al., 1997; Poldrack, Wagner, Prull, Desmond, Glover, & Gabrieli, 1999; Pugh et al., 1996; Rumsey, Horowitz, Donohue, Nace, Maisog, & Andreason, 1997b), the findings do not at present permit one to arrive with confidence at any more detailed conclusions with regard to dyslexia. Nonetheless, the findings in the round support the long-held view based on purely behavioural studies that there is some left-hemisphere deficit in dyslexia. Certain findings, such as that implicating dysfunction of the insula, if confirmed, may in due course lead to useful hypotheses regarding functional abnormalities of cortical circuitry and even of neuro-anatomy. With regard to the latter, in a recent structural MRI study, Eliez, Rumsey,

Giedd, Schmitt, Patwardhan, and Reiss (2000) reported that the volume of the temporal lobe was significantly reduced in 16 dyslexic men (who had previously taken part in the study of Rumsey et al., 1997c) in comparison with 14 control participants. This volume reduction was said to be attributable to a reduction in grey matter but not white matter and to be more pronounced on the left side than on the right. No group differences were seen in the superior temporal gyrus alone (or in frontal, parietal or occipital lobes, or in the cerebellum). While this finding supports the view of bilateral temporal lobe dysfunction that emerges from functional neuro-imagery research, it is perhaps noteworthy that the authors do not relate their anatomic measures to pseudoword reading scores—implying, perhaps, that there was no significant correlation—or any other cognitive measure. Leonard et al. (2001) also used MRI to assess hemispheric volume from sagittal images in dyslexic men and reported that a relatively low cerebral volume (grey and white matter combined) was correlated with scores on tests of listening comprehension and the verbal analogies sub-tests of the Woodcock-Johnson battery.

Neuro-imaging research has pointed to subtle abnormalities of functional organization of the cortex, particularly of the left hemisphere, in dyslexics. Other brain areas, however, also have been implicated in some studies. (A useful summary and guide to brain areas activated in studies involving various aspects of visual word recognition is provided by Grigorenko, 2001.) In particular, there is increasing interest in the possible role of the cerebellum in dyslexia.

THE CEREBELLUM AND DYSLEXIA

There are connections between the cortex and the cerebellum via the thalamus and the pons. Recent neuro-psychological and neuro-imaging evidence has been interpreted as showing that the cerebellum participates not only in motor functions and certain kinds of learning (e.g. Holmes, 1917, 1939; Ito, 1993), but also in a variety of cognitive and language functions (Allen, Buxton, Wong, &

Courchesne, 1997; De Schutter & Maex, 1996; Fabbro, Moretti, & Bava, 2000; Leiner, Leiner, & Dow, 1989, 1993; Levisohn, Cronin-Galomb, Schmahmann, 2000; Mariën, Engelborghs, Fabbro, & De Deyn, 2001; Riva & Giorgi, 2000; Schmahmann & Sherman, 1998), including reading (Brunswick et al., 1999; Fulbright et al., 1999; Moretti, Bava, Torre, Antonello, & Cazzato, 2002). Damage to certain parts of the cerebellum is associated not only with defects of articulation and other motor aspects of speech, but with other, arguably more cognitive, aspects of speech and language. In addition to language functions being affected by damage to the cerebellum, PET and other studies have shown activation of parts of this structure, especially on the right, during word retrieval and other verbal tasks. It is perhaps not surprising, therefore, that the cerebellum has been investigated in the context of dyslexia using neuro-imaging and other techniques

The role of the cerebellum in cognition is, however, a contentious issue (Glickstein, 1993; Ivry, 1997; Thach, 1996). For example, it has been suggested that experiments purporting to demonstrate a role for the cerebellum in cognition confound the experimental and control tasks in terms of the number of response alternatives (Ivry, 1997). An alternative to the view that the cerebellum plays a cognitive role in language and other tasks is that "cerebellar activation reflects the preparation of all of the possible responses" (Ivry, 1997, p. 569). Ivry asks: "Is this cognition?" (p. 569). It may be that the cerebellum has a modulatory role such that certain linguistic deficits arise as a result of reduced activation of areas of the left cerebral hemisphere—that is, through a mechanism of crossed cerebello-cerebral diaschisis (Mariën et al., 2001).

In a recent PET study, Nicolson, Fawcett, Berry, Jenkins, Dean, and Brooks (1999) measured brain activation levels while six adult dyslexics and six controls performed motor tasks. The tasks involved carrying out a sequence of finger movements with the right hand with the eyes closed. In one condition, the sequence was highly over-learned; in another condition, participants learned a new sequence. Compared with a resting condition, controls showed greater activation than dyslexics in the right cerebellum (which projects to the left cerebral hemisphere) during performance of both the over-learned task and during acquisition of the novel sequence. In contrast, the dyslexics showed greater activation than the controls in frontal and pre-frontal areas while learning the novel sequence. When activation during performance of the pre-learned sequence was compared with that during the novel sequence, controls showed significantly greater activation than dyslexics in the middle frontal gyrus on the left, while the dyslexics showed significantly greater activation than controls in frontal and pre-frontal cortex.

Rae et al. (1998) reported evidence of a biochemical asymmetry in the cerebellum of dyslexic men but not in controls. Although Rae et al. (1998) interpreted their magnetic resonance spectroscopy findings in terms of "an altered pattern of cell density in the cerebellum of a dyslexic individual" (p. 1852), they did not measure cell size directly. However, Finch, Nicolson, and Fawcett (2002) have recently reported the results of a neuro-anatomic study suggesting that there are fewer small cells and more large cells both in the inferior olive (part of the auditory pathway) and in the cerebellum of "dyslexic" brains compared with control brains. They did not find any significant cerebellar asymmetry.

The brains examined by Finch et al. (2002) were the four male brains reported on by Galaburda et al. (1985) and included in the reports of Livingstone et al. (1991) and Galaburda et al. (1994). Although it is of interest to note the results of Finch et al. alongside those of the other investigations, there are some doubts as to whether these specimens can be considered representative of dyslexic brains in general (Beaton, 1997). In addition, certain other aspects of the study by Finch et al. are less than ideal. The number of brains examined was low, dyslexics and controls were not well-matched and the diagnostic criteria for dyslexia are not provided. Some relevant information is given in Galaburda et al. (1985) but the details are sketchy.

In another recent report on cerebellar morphology in dyslexia, Rae et al. (2002) used MRI with 11 adult male dyslexics and nine controls. Among

the controls there was a significant left–right asymmetry in grey matter (the proportion of right grey matter to total cerebellar volume being greater than the proportion of left grey matter to total volume) but among the dyslexics there was no such asymmetry. The authors saw their finding of no cerebellar asymmetry in dyslexics as being consistent with previous reports of symmetrical temporal plana in dyslexia (but see Beaton, 2002). Leonard et al. (2001) reported that the posterior lobe of the cerebellum was larger on the right than on the left in a group of college-age dyslexics compared with controls, although the group difference in asymmetry did not survive statistical correction for multiple comparisons. The anterior lobe of the cerebellum on the right was smaller in the dyslexics than the controls, a finding recently replicated with dyslexic children (Eckert et al., 2003).

Among dyslexics, there was said in the abstract to the paper by Rae et al. (2002, p. 1285) to be a correlation between "the degree of cerebellar symmetry" and "the severity of dyslexics' phonological decoding deficit. Those with more symmetric cerebella made more *errors* on a nonsense word reading measure of phonological decoding ability" (emphasis added). However, the relevant error data are not presented in the body of the paper, although it is stated (Rae et al., p. 1287) that "nonsense word reading *time* correlated significantly with the grey matter symmetry ratio (left grey/total volume) in dyslexics but not in controls" (emphasis added). Despite the reference in the abstract to more errors being made by those with symmetric cerebella, there is nothing in the text of the paper about error scores in nonsense word reading. For this to be the case and for it to be also true that "nonsense word reading time correlated significantly with the grey matter symmetry ratio (left grey/total volume) in dyslexics", there would need to have been a speed versus accuracy trade-off. As this is highly unlikely—dyslexics tend to be both slow and inaccurate at reading nonsense words—the most probable conclusion to be drawn is either that Rae et al. (2002) have misinterpreted their own results or that there is an error in the way in which their data have been reported in their paper.

A summary of the cerebellar hypothesis of dyslexia (see Chapter 6) was presented by Nicolson, Fawcett, and Dean (2001). The reader is referred to commentaries on this paper and to Beaton (2002) and Bishop (2002) for further discussion of the hypothesis.

Dyslexia is commonly thought of as a developmental disorder of language, but this was not always so. The following two chapters are devoted to a consideration of visual aspects of dyslexia.

11

Visual Aspects of Dyslexia

VISUO-PERCEPTUAL FACTORS IN READING AND DYSLEXIA

Learning to read undoubtedly involves some measure of perceptual learning. A child has to learn to discriminate between visually similar shapes and to perceive initially unfamiliar patterns that have to be associated with the sounds making up words (see Samuels & Anderson, 1973). It is perhaps not surprising, therefore, that at one time it was common (see Vellutino, 1979) to think of dyslexia as involving a difficulty in inter-sensory (cross-modal) integration (Beaumont, Thomson, & Rugg, 1981; Birch & Belmont, 1964; Gooddy & Reinhold, 1961) or some form of visuo-perceptual impairment (see Ingram, 1963; Lovell et al., 1964; Silver & Hagin, 1964; Vellutino, 1979; Vernon, 1957), although the precise nature of the putative perceptual deficit was rarely made explicit (Stanovich, 1988a). Indeed, the suggestion of a visuo-perceptual impairment was often made purely on the basis of relatively poor performance on visuo-constructive tasks or performance sub-tests of intelligence scales. Hermann (1959) held that "difficulties in reading and writing can be viewed as the result of an impairment of Gestalt function ... which is impeded ... because there is primarily a disturb-ance of directional function" (p. 144). The latter he treated "primarily as a matter of optic–spatial orientation", while admitting the involvement of "chronological aspects, especially in relation to sequence" (p. 145). Drew (1956) regarded the dyslexia shown by three members of the same family as "due to a basic defect in Gestalt recognition which interferes with visual–verbal comprehension" (p. 457).

Birch and Belmont (1965) reported that performance on an auditory–visual (cross-modal) matching task varied with level of reading "readiness". In criticizing this study, Bryden (1972) showed that poor readers were impaired relative to age- and IQ-matched controls on same–different tasks that did not involve matching across sensory modalities (as well as those that did). He therefore concluded that "The failing of poor readers, extending as it does to tasks involving both auditory and visual presentation, and both sequential and spatial patterns, must be an even more general one" (p. 831), which he thought might involve verbal coding. None the less, there remained a widespread belief that faulty visual perception was largely responsible for difficulty in learning to read.

In an influential classification, Boder (1971, 1973) distinguished what she called "dyseidetic" from "dysphonetic" dyslexics (and those of a mixed category). Dyseidetics formed only 9 per cent of Boder's sample, but her scheme of classification led many to persist in thinking of dyslexia in terms primarily of problems in the domain of visuo-spatial processing.

Interest in this aspect of dyslexia has gradually declined following publication of Vellutino's (1979) monograph, in which he concluded that visuo-perceptual deficits do not generally play a significant role in reading disability (see also Vellutino & Scanlon, 1991). Instead, Vellutino emphasized speech-related problems, thereby encouraging the huge investment of research time and energy that has continued for over two decades. Nonetheless, some workers have continued to emphasize visual and visuo-perceptual problems experienced by some dyslexics. These have usually been found along with verbal deficits rather than occurring as isolated impairments among disabled readers (e.g. Watson & Willows, 1995). The following sections summarize research related to visual and ocular aspects of reading and dyslexia.

The act of reading places demands on the eye as well as the brain. The eyes do not pick up information passively but are moved in saccades to register information at particular locations in space during fixation. The role of eye movements in reading (see Reichle, Polatsek, Fisher, & Rayner, 1998) has a voluminous literature in its own right. It is perhaps not surprising, then, that considerable effort has been expended on investigating ocular factors in reading disability. However, the results of investigations into eye movements and other ocular factors in dyslexia have been attended by considerable controversy. Interest in this area has tended to fluctuate, centring on different aspects of visual function at different times, perhaps because of the inconsistency in findings. A selective but relatively uncritical summary of studies of oculomotor and other visual factors that have been related to reading performance is provided by Kulp and Schmidt (1996).

As might be expected, concern with ocular sidedness and mixed- or crossed-laterality dominated the literature at one time. Summarizing his own research, Dearborn wrote:

The preponderance of the clinical cases of (1) left-eyedness and (2) lack of ocular and manual dominance, and (3) of mixed conditions of ocular and manual dominance, e.g., left-eyedness associated with right-handedness or ambidexterity warrant an account. . . of the etiology of deplexia [*sic*] and "congenital alexia" . . . The primary reason why the above described conditions are associated and . . . may in some cases be the cause of special difficulties in learning to read and write is that they produce uncertainty about the correct ordering or sequence of letters in word forms, and result in the storing up in the mind of faulty and mutilated images of words . . . The dextral sequence of eye movements is kinesthetically the essence of reading. Left-eyed children may tend to move in the opposite direction, to begin at the wrong end of words or to reverse the order or even to perceive letters in the wrong way as in seeing b as d, or boy as dog.

(Dearborn, 1931, p. 704)

Subsequent research into the role of eye movements in reading, which has continued to the present day, probably originated with this paper.

EYE MOVEMENTS AND DYSLEXIA

Some poor readers appear to show abnormal eye movements while reading connected text (Adler-Grinberg & Stark, 1978; Rayner, 1978; Zangwill & Blakemore, 1972) but movement patterns have not generally been found to be abnormal during other kinds of task (Adler-Grinberg & Stark, 1978; Brown et al., 1983; Stanley, Smith, & Howell, 1983). Contrary findings were obtained by Pavlidis (1981) using a visual tracking task. He reported that the eye movements of dyslexics were abnormal (for a critique, see Stanley et al., 1983 and reply by Pavlidis, 1983; rejoinder by Smith et al., 1983). A careful replication of this work by Olson, Kliegl, and Davidson (1983) failed to find evidence of an overall impairment of eye movement patterns among dyslexics, although these authors did observe individual differences in "ocular efficiency" within both dyslexic and non-dyslexic readers.

On the other hand, Martos and Vila (1990) reported that "dyslexics" (defined as having a reading age 2 years behind chronological age and IQ higher than 95) but not "retarded readers" (same reading–chronological age discrepancy but IQ between 75 and 90) differed from normal readers on a visual tracking task. Eden et al. (1994) also found that dyslexics differed from normally reading controls (but not other poor readers) in a number of aspects of eye movement control on non-reading tasks. Specifically, differences were found in vergence (convergence and divergence) amplitude, saccadic and pursuit movement tasks as well as in fixation stability. Levinson (1990) emphasized that measures of vertical nystagmus (as an indication of cerebellar–vestibular dysfunction) may have diagnostic significance in dyslexia and other learning disabilities (see also Levinson, 1988).

Eye movement studies rarely distinguish between dyslexic sub-types. It is therefore at least possible that different sub-types have different eye movement patterns. Zoccolotti et al. (1999) compared eye movement patterns between four surface dyslexic Italian boys and normally reading controls of approximately the same age. These authors wrote that "While the controls read a text with a few large saccades coupled with short fixations, dyslexics scanned the same text with numerous saccades of very small amplitude and spent more time in fixations. Such fractionation of the reading material into shorter segments seems consistent with the use of a sub-lexical reading procedure" (p. 206).

Whether abnormal eye movements are a cause or a consequence (or simply a correlate) of the reading problem is difficult to say. The fact that pursuit motor movements were abnormal in the studies by Adler-Grinberg and Stark (1978) and Eden et al. (1994), even though such movements are not involved in reading, perhaps suggests that abnormal control mechanisms are not simply a consequence of reading failure. The general consensus in the literature, however, appears to

favour the view that abnormal eye movements are a consequence rather than a cause of a reading disability (Morris & Rayner, 1991; Stanovich, 1986). The findings of a very recent study of the eye movements of two brain-damaged patients with the acquired reading disorder known as letter-by-letter reading is consistent with this view. The patients' eye movements were shown not to be different from those of control participants during non-reading tasks but different during reading (Behrmann, Shomstein, Black, & Barton, 2001). However, the pattern of eye movements during reading was similar to that exhibited by normal readers under difficult reading conditions, which suggests that eye movements reflect the level of difficulty in processing textual material.

In an early review, Tinker (1958) argued that "eye movement patterns merely reflect ease or difficulty of reading, efficient or poor reading performance, and degree of comprehension, rather than cause good or poor reading" (p. 224), a conclusion thought "justified" by Rayner (1978) and echoed by Stanovich (1986). The latter wrote: "When skilled readers are forced to read material too difficult for them, their eye movement patterns deteriorate and approximate those of the less skilled reader. The eye movement patterns of the latter look more fluent when they are allowed to read easier material. In short, the level of reading determines the nature of the eye movement patterns, not the reverse" (Stanovich, 1986, p. 365).

The question arises, then, as to the appropriate control group for dyslexic readers. Age-matched control readers will be better readers and any ocular difference between the groups may be a function of reading experience. As a result, the eye patterns of dyslexics may appear immature, that is to say similar to those of younger readers, even if steps are taken to ensure (e.g. Adler-Grinberg & Stark, 1978) that both normal and poor readers are presented with material appropriate to their reading level. Clearly, reading-age control groups are required in this area of reading research as in others, although they have been used comparatively infrequently.

Hyönä and Olson (1995) compared dyslexic children with reading-age controls. The eye movements of both groups were related to length and frequency of the texts they were asked to read but the effects were similar for dyslexics and non-dyslexics, leading Hyönä and Olson to conclude that eye movement patterns reflect difficulty in word recognition. Nonetheless, differences in eye movements between dyslexic children and normal readers (but not between dyslexics and "retarded" readers), irrespective of the supposed difficulty level of two (Spanish) texts, have been reported by Martos and Vila (1990), but no evidence that the relevant texts actually differed in difficulty was presented. Nor was any analysis of an interaction between text difficulty and reading ability undertaken; perusal of the data suggests there was none. The most parsimonious conclusion appears, therefore, to be that eye movement patterns are a function of the subjective difficulty of the material being read and that any given text is likely to be more difficult for poor readers than for nomal readers of a given age.

It is by no means clear precisely how erratic eye movements relate to poor reading. The results of a study by Eden et al. (1994) showed that although poor vergence control by dyslexics always accompanied poor phonological ability (as assessed by a Pig Latin task), poor fixation control was observed both in the presence and in the absence of phonological difficulties. Poor fixation control may relate in some way to complaints by some dyslexics that print appears blurred to them. It is difficult to know what to make of such complaints, as many normal readers, including the author, find that on occasion text swims before their eyes, especially if the material being read is less than fully absorbing.

Attention and eye movements

Lennerstrand, Ygge, and Jacobsson (1993) briefly report a study with Swedish poor readers showing that during pursuit movements the amplitude of the movement of left and right eyes is more asymmetrical among poor readers than controls. They suggest that:

It is possible that the variations noted between dyslexics and normal readers in the control of saccades during reading are related to differences between groups in the timing and sequence of saccadic movements. Normally saccadic movements are produced in two stages of attention: an engaged state during fixation and a disengaged stage during casual looking around.

(Lennerstrand et al., 1993, p. 238)

Lennerstrand et al. suggest that dyslexia may involve "insufficient control over the attentional system, which in turn leads to insufficient control over saccadic eye movements in reading", the larger asymmetries in poor readers than controls being due to "the saccadic system working more in the disengaged state" (p. 238).

It is reasonable to assume that directing the so-called "attentional spotlight" during the period of learning to read is a task that is not automatic but has to be accomplished by the nervous system through learning. Fischer and Weber (1990) used the distinction between engaged and disengaged visual attention when investigating eye movements of dyslexics. In the engaged state saccades are inhibited, as for example during fixation on an object of interest. When attention is disengaged, the "saccade generating system is disinhibited" (p. 805). It was argued that a normal pattern of eye movements requires a switching between engaged and disengaged attention. Fischer and Weber (1990) monitored eye movements while their participants fixated a small white square and made saccades to small red squares presented randomly to either side of fixation. They found that more than half of the dyslexic children exhibited unstable fixation of the white square and as a group the dyslexics made faster saccades than normal control children. The authors concluded that "The major problem of the dyslexic children appears to be the timing of saccades [but] . . . the real deficit is not in the eye-movement system as such but in the attentional system . . . The overall picture seems to be that dyslexics can easily switch to the disengaged state" (pp. 816–817). The implication seems to be that dyslexics are less able to engage attention than to disengage. Unfortunately, a reading-age control group was not employed in this study, so it is impossible to say whether the pattern of performance shown by the dyslexic particpants is a cause, consequence or correlate of their reading experience. In subsequent work by Fischer and his collaborators some, but not all, (discrepancy-defined) dyslexic children have been found to show impaired voluntary eye movement control (anti-saccades), but not in making "normal" saccadic eye movements, in comparison with age-matched normally-reading peers (Biscaldi, Fischer, & Hartnegg, 2000; Fischer, Hartnegg, & Mokler, 2000). The deficit improves with daily practice in carrying out the experimental tasks which were used but "it remains open to which [sic] extent the training effects transfer to reading and/or spelling skills" (Fischer & Hartnegg, 2000, p. 541). Given the absence of reading age controls and the fact that many dyslexics performed as well as controls on the experimental tasks (which did not involve reading), the conservative interpretation must be that there is little or no evidence at present that impaired voluntary eye movement control is a causal factor in dyslexia.

ORTHOPTIC AND BINOCULAR FACTORS IN READING

Dunlop (1972) described a test of what she referred to as the "reference" eye in binocular viewing. The test was said to evaluate whether the left or the right eye's view predominated in a person's percept of the binocular visual field. Dunlop and her colleagues reported a higher incidence of crossed hand-reference eye laterality among dyslexic than control readers (Dunlop, 1976; Dunlop, Dunlop, & Fenelon, 1973), but these results were not replicated by Bishop, Jancey, and Steel (1979). Based on the concept of a reference eye, Dunlop and Dunlop (1974) presented a theory intended to explain confusion between mirror-image letters, which they saw as a central problem in dyslexia. In many respects, their theory is reminiscent of Orton's views, but as I have pointed out elsewhere (Beaton, 1985), the theoretical underpinnings of their theory are weak. In addition, others (Goulandris, McIntyre,

Snowling, Bethel, & Lee, 1998; Newman, Wadsworth, Archer, & Hockly, 1985) have failed to support the finding of a relationship between performance on the Dunlop reference eye test and reading and spelling ability. Some of the inconsistency in findings may relate to the fact that there appears to be a high degree of subjectivity regarding administration and interpretation of this and similar tests. Although results are apparently more reliable when the test is conducted by experienced users, this obviously introduces an element of variability into the proceedings.

A variation of the Dunlop test was devised by Stein and Fowler (1982), who reported that 54 per cent of their 354 backward readers had failed to establish "ocular motor dominance" in comparison with only one of 80 normal readers. Backwardness in reading was only tested formally in 80 poor readers and was defined as a reading age 18 months behind chronological age with IQ being 90 or above. Ocular dominance was defined using synoptophore tubes, which allowed the participants to view two slides, one with each eye, such that initially the two images were fused. The tubes were gradually separated and the eyes diverged to maintain a single percept until fusion broke down. At this point, part of the image presented to one eye appeared to move, while the whole of the other image remained stable. This eye was then referred to as the dominant eye.

Newman et al. (1985) used the same ocular dominance test as Stein and Fowler (1982) to examine 298 children from a variety of schools. Although the proportion of reading children found to have "unstable ocular dominance" was very similar to that reported by Stein and Fowler, this proportion did not vary as a function of reading or spelling ability (corrected for mental age).

Rather than compare normal and poor readers of the same age, it might be more appropriate to compare children at the same level of reading ability, since conceivably performance on the Dunlop test or synoptophore is related to reading experience. On the other hand, a reading-age matched design does not control for other factors associated with general maturation. Bigelow and McKenzie (1985) compared two groups of 14 children each who differed in chronological age

(10.0 years versus 8.2 years) but had virtually the same mean reading age (8.4 and 8.3 years). The older aged children thus had a discrepancy of about 20 months between chronological and reading age. This group of children were said to show a significantly higher frequency of unstable ocular dominance (64 per cent) than the younger group (21 per cent). Since the groups were similar in reading ability, this result suggests that reading experience alone does not relate to performance on the synoptophore test. Participant selection details are not provided other than that the children were "selected from six primary schools" (p. 331), so it is not possible to compare poor readers in the studies by Bigelow and McKenzie (1985) and Newman et al. (1985).

Stein and Fowler (1985) reported that among dyslexics who showed an unfixed or unstable reference eye, monocular occlusion (of the left eye) frequently led both to the development of a fixed reference eye and to an improvement in reading. This improvement was said to be greater than that shown by individuals who already had a fixed reference eye at the start of the experiment or who failed to develop one during the period of occlusion. It was also greater than that shown by a "placebo" group who wore spectacles with plain glass rather than an occluding lens.

In addition to an unstable reference eye, Stein and his colleagues have suggested that binocular vergence control is unstable in some dyslexic readers (two-thirds of the 39 dyslexic children aged 8–11 years whose eye movements were actually recorded by Stein, Riddell, & Fowler, 1988) and that this may interfere with accurate spatial localization of letters (see Stein, 1991; Stein & Fowler, 1982, 1985, 1993; Stein et al., 1988), an ability that is likely to be important in reading. One might question whether it is accurate spatial localization *per se* or relative letter localization that is important for reading. In any event, Wilsher (1985) criticized several aspects of Stein and Fowler's (1985) study to which a reply was given by Stein, Riddell, and Fowler (1985).

A more extensive critique of Stein and Fowler's (1985) paper was published by Bishop (1989b), who criticized the notion that unstable vergence control is relevant to dyslexia. She pointed out that there is evidence that the Dunlop test (or the Stein and Fowler modification) is related both to IQ scores and age. Lower age or IQ is associated in each case with a greater frequency of unstable or unfixed reference eye and with lower scores on reading tests. Bishop (1989b) re-analysed the data of Stein and Fowler (1985), noting that participants who began with an unfixed reference eye at the start of the study but then acquired a stable eye had higher initial reading scores than those who already had a stable reference eye. The more severe the initial problem, the less progress was made. Bishop's re-analysis led her to conclude that "there is no evidence that monocular occlusion with unfixed reference results in improved reading scores . . . There is a significant relationship between development of stable reference and improvement in reading, but this is explicable in terms of differences in initial reading ability" (p. 214).

Bishop's conclusions were contested by Stein and Fowler (1993), who re-analysed their data and argued that Bishop's conclusions were based on an inappropriate statistical model. Nonetheless, they agreed that "the size of the reading gain of children who converted from unstable to stable binocular control was dependent on their initial reading age" (p. 41). However, Stein and Fowler felt that "the fact that they made any reading gains at all was certainly the result of their improved binocular control. For if their binocular control did not improve, then their reading did not either, whatever their initial reading age" (p. 41).

Demonstrating a relationship between poor binocular control and poor reading does not constitute evidence of a causal relationship. The fact that a substantial proportion of normal readers have an unfixed reference eye suggests that this cannot be regarded as a necessary or even sufficient cause of poor reading. Stein and Fowler (1993), however, argued that when "normal" children have been shown to have unstable binocular control, they have also been found on average to be reading at a level "4–6 months below their peers with stable responses; they were therefore in reality 'low normal' readers. This is of course what our theory predicts" (p. 34).

Although consistent with a causal interpretation this does not, of course, prove a causal relationship between the two variables. Stein and Fowler (1993) considered the causal nature of the relationship between binocular control and poor reading to be established by their occlusion study (Stein & Fowler, 1985) and by the fact that dyslexics matched for IQ and reading age to younger normal children have poorer binocular control. However, while this is more consistent with the view that unstable binocular control causes poor reading than with the reverse interpretation, it leaves open the possibility that in dyslexics both poor binocular control and poor reading are caused by a third unknown factor.

There is no obvious explanation for the discrepancies in the findings obtained by different investigators. It is possibly relevant to note that the children studied by Stein and Fowler (1982) had been referred to a hospital ophthalmology department and such children may be more likely to have been suspected of having visual problems than the children studied by Newman et al. (1985), who selected their children "from various schools selected to participate in a larger study of reading. None of the children had been referred to any clinic for reading difficulties" (p. 228).

One possible confounding factor in orthoptic studies is that performance on the reference eye test may relate to attentional ability, which may have varied between the different groups tested. It is also possible that performance on the Dunlop test varies with instructions and different test administrators (see Stein & Fowler, 1993, for further details relevant to the study by Newman et al., 1985).

It is important to appreciate that Stein and his colleagues have not argued that all dyslexics have vergence control problems or that this is the only cause of poor reading. What they do claim is that in some proportion of poor readers (of both high and low IQ), "visual problems" are found either alone or in combination with linguistic or verbal problems such as poor phonological awareness (Eden et al., 1995a). Poor readers who show exclusively (or predominantly) visual problems are referred to by Stein and co-workers as visual dyslexics, although a precise definition of visual

dyslexia is not offered. Nor is it clear how so-called visual dyslexia relates to performance on the (modified) Dunlop test (Bishop, 1989b).

The most usual research strategy in this area has been to compare dyslexic and control readers in terms of the relative frequency of individuals with and without a dominant or reference eye within the two groups. An alternative strategy is to compare groups matched for age, IQ and reading or spelling ability but differing in whether or not they "pass" or "fail" the Dunlop test. This is the approach adopted by Cornelissen, Bradley, Fowler, and Stein (1991, 1992). Groups of children thus distinguished were found to differ in the errors that they made in reading. Specifically, Cornelissen et al. (1991) tested children suspected of reading difficulty on three lists of words matched for linguistic complexity. Stimuli were presented in decreasing size of print. As print size decreased, so errors increased. Those children who did not have a stable reference eye showed a significant increase in the proportion of errors that were nonwords (referred to as neologisms) rather than real words.

Cornelisen et al. (1991) suggested that the group without a stable reference eye made more neologisms than did children with a stable reference eye because of diplopia (double vision) and binocular retinal rivalry. They maintained that "It is clear that binocular instability of this sort could lead to children experiencing visual confusion and perceiving incorrect letter sequences, which they could translate as nonwords" (p. 760). In a subsequent paper, it was reported that reading with one eye rather than two reduced the proportion of nonword reading errors as a proportion of the total number of errors that were made (Cornelissen et al., 1992).

A problem in motor control of the two eyes and/or in binocular sensory fusion in children who "fail" the Dunlop test might relate to the larger number of nonword error scores recorded in the binocular viewing condition. Cornelissen, Munro, Fowler, and Stein (1993) recorded binocular eye movements while children and adults read single words (of a fixed size) "appropriate for their reading ability". Although children generally made more vergence errors than adults, the data suggested that "poor vergence control during reading is not the immediate cause of the nonword error effect found among children who fail the Dunlop test" (p. 786).

Subsequently, Cornelissen, Bradley, Fowler, and Stein (1994) argued that visual confusion might be expected to make it difficult to learn the visual pattern of words and such children might therefore tend to rely on a more phonologically based strategy. They tested this idea by looking at mis-spellings of words by children referred to an orthoptic clinic because of reading difficulties. Despite being well-matched for age, verbal IQ, reading and spelling age and rhyming ability, those who "failed" the Dunlop test made significantly more phonologically plausible spelling errors than those who "passed" (Cornelissen et al., 1994). They did not make more errors overall. Cornelissen et al. (1994) propose that "intermittent visual confusion of text may be sufficient to destabilize the 'visual memory map' sufficiently to make it unreliable" (p. 723).

Regardless of whether "visual confusion" is at the root of differences between the two groups, the fact that the proportion of phonologically plausible errors made depended upon whether or not binocular control was stable supports the idea that performance on the Dunlop and related tests is in some way related to aspects of literacy. On the other hand, a recent study (Goulandris et al., 1998) using a battery of orthoptic tests with 20 dyslexic and 20 reading-age matched controls failed to find orthoptic tests (including the Dunlop test) that discriminated between the two groups. One possibility is that the dyslexics in the study of Goulandris et al. had primarily phonological, rather than visual, problems; another is that the number of dyslexics studied was not large (Stein, Richardson, & Fowler, 1998). Yet even if both these were true, the conflicting results reported in the literature mean that the putative relevance of orthoptic factors in dyslexia remains unclear, as do the reasons for the discrepant findings reported. Not everyone is convinced that investigations of ocular factors in cases of reading disability are worthwhile. A particular barrier to the general acceptance that ocular factors play any role at all in dyslexia is that many children with conspicuous visual problems still learn to read and to spell perfectly adequately (see Olson, Connors, & Rack, 1991). Nevertheless, in view of the many anecdotal reports and the findings reviewed here, it is wise to remain open to the possibility that certain orthoptic factors are related to poor reading in some cases (for brief reviews, see Stein, 1991, 1992, 1993; Stein & Fowler, 1993).

THE USE OF COLOURED LENSES AND OVERLAYS IN READING

Reports that many children with reading difficulties complain of text blurring or swimming in front of their eyes frequently appear in the popular press, together with claims of how this can be ameliorated. In the scientific community, however, considerable uncertainty surrounds the issue of so-called scotopic sensitivity syndrome (for a brief account, see Irlen, 1994; for a critical appraisal, see Solan, 1990; Solan & Richman, 1990) and the use of tinted lenses or filters in the remediation of reading difficulties.

Some studies have reported that lenses or filters improve the comprehension (O'Connor, Sofo, Kendall, & Olsen, 1990; Williams, Lecluyse, & Rock-Faucheux, 1992) or reading rate or accuracy of some children (Jeanes et al., 1997; Kyd, Sutherland, & McGettrick, 1992; O'Connor et al., 1990; Tyrrell, Holland, Dennis, & Wilkins, 1995), whether or not they are dyslexic, while others have found no improvement in any of these measures (Blaskey, Scheiman, Parisi, Ciner, Gallaway, & Selznick, 1990; Menacker, Breton, Breton, Radcliffe, & Gole, 1993; Saint-John & White, 1988). From research by Wilkins and his colleagues, it has emerged that children who find colour helpful usually have migraine in the family, leading Wilkins (1996) to suggest that "the effects of coloured lenses [may] have more to do with symptoms of eye-strain and headache than with reading [*per se*]" (p. 6, emphasis in original).

In one study of the effects of coloured overlays on rate of reading, Jeanes et al. (1997) used a nonsense passage of randomly arranged common words so as to eliminate cues from semantic and linguistic context. The participants were children who had been been given an overlay one year previously. The primary school sample was divided into those children ($n = 11$) who were still using it when the study was performed and those who by then had abandoned its use ($n = 19$). It was found for the first group that reading rate was significantly faster using their preferred coloured overlay than reading without it, but for those who were not using it reading rate was equivalent in the two conditions. The latter result is, of course, somewhat uninformative, as it could be taken to imply either that the maximum benefit had been gained before the start of the study, and was maintained even without the overlay being used, or that the overlay had not been used sufficiently long for any possible benefit to have occurred. In fact, the reading rate of those who had abandoned the overlay was slower than that of those who had maintained it, so the first explanation is unlikely. Conversely, the fact that the group that had carried on using the overlays for a year appeared to be faster than the other group might be taken to indicate that it had had some beneficial effect, but as no initial data were presented this cannot be asserted with confidence. In any event, it does not follow from an improvement in rate of reading a meaningless passage that any useful increase in reading proficiency had been achieved over the period of use of the overlay (although, of course, it might have been). It must be acknowledged, of course, that the concern might not have been to "improve" reading so much as to reduce any visual "discomfort" the children experienced. It is also worth noting that "Although the individuals who used coloured overlays . . . clearly had a visual difficulty with reading, few were dyslexic according to customary definition" (p. 547). It may be that coloured lenses "work" for children diagnosed as reading-disabled according to one particular set of criteria but not for children diagnosed according to different criteria (Pammer & Lovegrove, 2001).

Different colours are preferred by different children and this idiosyncratic preference, though stable and reliable according to Jeanes et al. (1997), is difficult to explain. It also appears that the same colour may not be chosen for an overlay as for a lens, a fact accounted for by Jeanes et al. as follows:

> The overlay provides one coloured surface in a visual field containing many differently coloured surfaces, and the eyes are adapted to white light. When coloured glasses are worn the entire visual field is coloured, the eyes adapt to the colour, and, partly as a result of that adaptation, the colour is discounted by mechanisms similar to those that underlie colour constancy. If the effects of the tint are central (cortical) rather than peripheral (ocular), as proposed by Wilkins (1995), one might very well expect differences in the colour chosen for overlays and for lenses.
>
> (Jeanes et al., 1997, p. 533)

An important distinction that has not always been observed in the literature is between efficacy in improving reading level or reading speed and simply reducing apparent strain or visual discomfort (which is not to say that the latter aim is not in itself desirable). Even with regard to rate of reading alone, discrepant results may arise from differences in test conditions and stimulus material used. Wilkins (1996) pointed out that "Colour has its greatest benefit with text that is small and closely spaced. With more conventional text, the effects on reading speed take time to appear and do so only when the reader is beginning to tire" (p. 6).

A further difficulty in evaluating the putative benefits of coloured filters and overlays is that subjective reports of "improvement" or "increased comfort" may represent purely a placebo effect (Cotton & Evans, 1990; Fitzgerald, 1989; Solan & Richman, 1990) and do not necessarily relate to any objective improvement in reading accuracy or ability. Menacker et al. (1993), for example, could find no evidence for improvement in a group of 24 dyslexic readers aged 8–12 years tested with different coloured lenses despite the children being able to select those lenses that "subjectively made reading easier". As a rule, one does not know the extent to which inclusion of children in a study leads not only to motivational changes but to increased (or, for that matter, decreased) parental interest in their children's reading, which might account for any apparent changes in reading performance.

O'Connor et al. (1990) claimed to control for placebo effects in a study of reading-impaired children designated as "scotopic" or "non-scotopic". Among a group of "scotopic" children—designated on the basis that they "displayed definite scotopic signs *and* displayed marked improvement in reading performance with a particular colored transparency overlay" (p. 599, emphasis in original)—those assigned to a treatment condition incorporating their preferred coloured filtered showed an improvement in reading rate and accuracy compared with children assigned either to an inappropriate colour or to a transparent filter. The "scotopic" children assigned to their preferred colour also improved in comparison with "non-scotopic" children assigned either coloured or transparent filters. However, as only the first group were assigned to a condition that would lead them to expect an improvement, a placebo effect cannot in fact be ruled out, an ever-present problem in this field (see also Robinson & Conway, 1990). Children given a clear transparency actually showed a regression effect, which clearly raises questions about the source of the effectiveness of the colour filters in the "scotopic" group. Parker (1990), reviewing the papers by Robinson and Conway (1990), O'Connor et al. (1990) and Blaskey et al. (1990), suggested that "the diagnostic procedure itself may act as a potent treatment in itself" (p. 619).

The fact that the theoretical basis of coloured lenses or overlays as methods of remediation is "largely a matter of conjecture" (Tyrrell et al., 1995) naturally creates uncertainty over the abundant anecdotal evidence that such methods are effective. One idea put forward is that particular colours could affect the relative transmission of information within the magnocellular and parvocellular divisions of the visual system (see below), a view hinted at by Irlen herself (Irlen, 1994). Broadband "blue" light has been said to enhance reading performance, whereas broadband "red" light decreases performance. Blue light was hypothesized to facilitate the normal time course of activity in the so-called transient (magno) system, whereas red light was thought to attenuate such activity. Coloured filters would thus be expected to modulate the relative timing of information transmission in the transient and sustained (parvo) systems (Williams et al., 1992). On the other hand, Pammer and Lovegrove (2001) could find little or no evidence that activity in the transient visual system (see below) of adults or children (including disabled readers) is differentially influenced by different coloured stimuli. This led them to doubt "the wisdom of pursuing research into the remedial implications of broadband color for reading disabled children … when the basis of such [positive] reports remains a mystery" (p. 499). However, Skottun (2001) has criticized the use of the Ternus test used by Pammer and Lovegrove (2001), arguing from an analysis of the properties of the test that "to use the Ternus test to assess magnocellular function, both generally and specifically in dyslexic readers, is problematic" (p. 1456).

Where it is claimed that overlays or lenses are effective, a question arises as to whether this is due to a particular colour or to a change in luminance or contrast brought about by the coloured filter (Lopez, Yolton, Kohl, Smith, & Saxerud, 1994). It is unlikely that the simple reduction in contrast produced by an overlay is responsible for any benefit, since grey overlays—which reduce the contrast by an amount equivalent to that of coloured overlays—are not effective (Jeanes et al., 1997). The source of any improvement is difficult to identify. Wilkins (1993) admitted that "The physiological basis for efficacy of the tints is uncertain but may relate to a selective impairment of achromatic or color-opponent channels" (p. 435). He has speculated that the visual distortions provoked by some kinds of stimuli reflect some "minimal hyperexcitability" of cortical neurones. The effect of the coloured overlays is to change the pattern of excitation in hyperexcitable regions of cortex preventing the spread of such excitation (see Tyrrell et al., 1995; Wilkins, 1995).

RETINAL FACTORS IN DYSLEXIA

Although most workers concentrate on presumed brain mechanisms underlying dyslexic phenomena, it has been suggested that retinal factors may be involved in at least some cases.

The two classes of photoreceptors, rods used in twilight vision and cones used for colour vision, are not equally distributed across the retina. Rods are proportionally more frequent in the periphery, whereas red and green sensitive cones are concentrated at and close to the centre or fovea of the retina (though blue sensitive cones, which are absent from the fovea, are found more peripherally; Polyak, 1957). The classic study is that of Østerberg (1935), who examined a single human eye and estimated that there are between 110,000,000 and 125,000,000 rods and between 6,300,000 and 6,800,000 cones in the human retina. He showed that "At a short distance from the middle of the fovea … the rods begin to make their appearance, and their number increases regularly and markedly to a distance of about 4–5 mm from the centre. Here the rod count reaches a well-defined maximum and then it falls off gradually towards the ora serrata" (p. 75). On the other hand, cones are more dense in the centre and rapidly decline, becoming "less abrupt when the rods begin to appear. Then for a long distance, from a point 2–3 mm from the centre to 3–4 mm from the ora serrata, the curve falls quite gradually though very little, so that here it is almost horizontal" (p. 75). A more recent study of four human retinas found that cones are more dense in the nasal than the temporal hemi-retina (Curcio, Sloan, Packer, Hendrickson, & Kalina, 1987), confirming Østerberg's own observations. Visual acuity for fine detail is greatest in central vision, whereas detection thresholds for brief flashes of light are lower (indicating greater sensitivity) in the periphery of vision.

In an experiment on letter recognition, Geiger and Lettvin (1987) noted a more gradual decline in performance in moving from central vision to the periphery among compensated adult dyslexics than among controls. In fact, the dyslexics showed better letter recognition than the controls at certain retinal eccentricities, although poorer recognition than controls at eccentricities closer to (but not at) the fovea (central vision). This pattern was explained in terms of the differential use of peripheral versus central vision by dyslexic and normal readers, since the results of a training regime with one severely dyslexic individual showed a shift to a more normal pattern of recognition performance. Shaywitz and Waxman (1987) suggest that attentional strategies might have distinguished the two groups. However, the findings were interpreted by Grosser and Spafford (1989) as suggesting that dyslexics have an anomaly in the spatial distribution of their photoreceptors, cones being found more peripherally in dyslexics than in non-dyslexics. They tested this hypothesis by plotting colour-sensitive zones across the field of vision, finding that 14 college-age dyslexics were more successful than 14 controls at detecting colours in the periphery. However, it is not clear from their report that differential eye movement patterns cannot explain their findings. On the other hand, Zoccolotti et al. (1999) compared letter recognition at different retinal eccentricities between four (surface) dyslexic Italian boys and normally reading controls. Despite finding significant differences in eye movement patterns, there was no difference between dyslexics and controls in the function relating accuracy of response to eccentricity.

Other methodological problems with the study by Grosser and Spafford (1989) include the fact that the colour targets were hand-held and moved by someone who was not "blind" to the hypothesis under study. Furthermore, the fact that the results for their control participants show considerable variation in colour detection across retinal eccentricities that do not vary in cone density, suggests (Cohn, 1989) that their experimental task has little to do with the relative distribution of cones (and hence rods) in moving from central to peripheral vision.

In a subsequent study, Grosser and Spafford (1990) reported that the detection thresholds for faint spots of light presented against a low level of background illumination were significantly lower (on a one-tail test) for proficient than for impaired readers in the periphery. They argued that this was consistent with an increase in the number of cones, and correspondingly reduced number of rods, in the peripheral retina of poor readers. However, Grosser and Spafford did not present data for the central region of vision, so the specificity of any peripheral anomaly cannot be assessed. Moreover, given the level of background illumination (which was not dark), it is likely that cones as well as rods contributed to the detection of an incremental change in light level during the detection task (Stuart & Lovegrove, 1992a). Other criticisms of the hypothesis that dyslexics have an anomalous distribution of photoreceptors (see also Spafford & Grosser, 1991) have been made by Cohn (1989) and by Stuart and Lovegrove (1992a). The latter believe that improved chromatic detection thresholds and reduced incremental detection thresholds in dyslexics can both be explained by reference to the properties of an impaired neural system (the transient or magnocellular sub-division of the visual system; see below) rather than the photoreceptor system. In a reply, Grosser and Spafford (1992) suggest that:

> the bridge between our approach and that of others favoring the "transient" system might well be that the rods are the receptors initiating the rapid onset of responding in the magnocellular, transient pathway ... [our hypothesis is that] the parvocellular system is almost entirely fed by cones whereas both kinds of receptors drive magnocellular cells (with the rapid onset of early transient system responding being based on the highly light sensitive rods).
>
> (Grosser & Spafford, 1992, pp. 118, 119)

This view, too, was criticized by Stuart and Lovegrove (1992b), who argued that the empirical work reported by Grosser and Spafford could not be "convincingly tied to rod function" and, more importantly, that "transient responses are a property of neurons, not photoreceptors" (p. 649).

The Grosser–Spafford hypothesis is not the only one to focus on retinal factors. Carroll, Mullaney, and Eustace (1994) tested 41 reading-disabled individuals and found that a sub-group of 12 showed poorer (i.e. slower) dark adaptation than controls in the periphery, but not at the centre, of vision. Peripheral dark adaptation is (initially at least) a function of the rods of the retina, which require high concentrations of docosahexaenoic acid (DHA) and other fatty acids for normal functioning. Docosahexaenoic acid, a polyunsaturated fatty acid found in fish oil, evening primrose oil and other oils, has been suggested as "the factor associated with improved visual/neural performance of supplemented infants compared with those fed standard formula" (Makrides, Neumann, Simmer, Pater, & Gibson, 1995, p. 1467).

In a brief report, Stordy (1995) stated that 10 adult dyslexics showed "poorer" dark adaptation than controls but following a one-month regime of DHA supplement, four out of five dyslexics (and one of four controls) showed an "improvement". She stated that "DHA supplements given to dyslexics can also be associated with improvements in reading ability" (p. 385), but in an unpublished study in my laboratory Mary Duke and I found no evidence that a monthly regime of fish oil had any effect on either central or peripheral letter detection in a small group of dyslexic adults. It should be acknowledged, however, that we made no determination of our participants' dark adaptation curves. In a second report, Stordy (2000) provides the dark adaptation data on which the earlier communication is based and claims that, as a group, 15 developmentally dyspraxic children also showed an improvement in motor skills after 4 months of "supplementation with a patented mixture of tuna oil, evening primrose oil, thyme oil, and vitamin E" (p. 324S). However, no placebo control group was included in this study, which seriously undermines confidence in the result.

It may well be that any role that highly unsaturated fatty acids play in dyslexia is not confined to the retina but operates at different sites or systems throughout the central nervous system. A brain imaging study using phosphorus-31 magnetic resonance spectroscopy to assess brain biochemistry reported results consistent with the idea that phospholipid metabolism is abnormal in dyslexic adults (Richardson, Cox, Sargentoni, & Puri, 1997).

Taylor, Higgins, Calvin, Easton, McDaid, and Richardson (2000) reported that clinical signs of fatty acid deficiency were on average higher in 74 dyslexic than in 31 control adult males (but not females). Severity of presumed fatty acid deficiency was significantly correlated with scores on an adult dyslexia checklist, which covered a wide range of behaviour associated with dyslexia. Similar results were reported by Richardson et al. (2000) for 97 dyslexic children aged 8–12 years. Among the latter, approximately one-third of the sample were considered to have relatively high levels of fatty acid deficiency. Among male dyslexic children, the correlation between fatty acid deficiency scores and reading and spelling ability were significant. Unfortunately, no control data from non-dyslexic children were reported in this study and the measure of presumed fatty acid deficiency was not objective but based on a checklist of symptoms (such as excessive thirst, frequent urination, dry skin or hair) completed by parents. In both studies, the possibility exists (and was acknowledged by the authors) that the effects reported are related not to dyslexia *per se* but to the possible confounding presence of attention deficit hyperactivity disorder with which dyslexia is frequently associated and which has been linked to fatty acid deficiency (Stevens et al., 1995).

The above studies do not fall into the mainstream of research in dyslexia. At present, the results are correlational rather than causal, although Taylor and Richardson (2000) and Stein (2000) have presented ideas as to how fatty acid metabolism might relate to the magnocellular system (see Chapter 12) and hence to dyslexia and other neurodevelopmental disorders.

This chapter has considered the putative contribution of different aspects of visual and ocular function to the manifestation of reading problems. Although advocates of oculo-visual theories of reading impairment are not numerous within the scientific community, exaggerated claims in support of remedial interventions based on their views have occasionally appeared in the popular press. Perhaps because of this, "mainstream" dyslexia researchers have tended to give such views a sceptical and sometimes hostile reception. One problem is that certain interventions appear to lack a convincing theoretical rationale. In recent years, however, there has been a growing interest in the respective roles of the magnocellular and parvocellular divisions of the visual system and their interaction in dyslexia. Aspects of magnocellular function, in particular, have received a great deal of attention and arguably can be related top a wide range of visual and oculomotor abnormalities seen in poor readers. The following chapter considers the magnocullar deficit hypothesis of dyslexia.

12

The Magnocellular Deficit Hypothesis

Notwithstanding the mass of evidence pointing to a core phonological deficit in dyslexia (Stanovich, 1988b), many findings suggestive of early or low-level visual processing anomalies have been reported in recent years. For example, it has been reported that young disabled readers, as well as adult dyslexics (Winters, Patterson, & Shontz,1989), differ from age-matched controls in showing increased durations of visible persistence (Badcock & Lovegrove, 1981; Lovegrove et al., 1980b; Stanley & Hall, 1973; but see Hogben et al., 1995) and lower critical flicker-fusion thresholds (Lovegrove et al., 1986; Talcott, Hansen, Willis-Owen, McKinnell, Richardson, & Stein, 1998).

There are also (inconsistent) findings of differences between reading-disabled and control children in the pattern of their contrast sensitivity functions for gratings of different spatial frequencies (Lovegrove, Bowling, Badcock, & Blackwood, 1980a; Lovegrove, Martin, Bowling, Blackwood, Badcock, & Paxton, 1982; Spafford, Grosser, Donatelle, Squillace, & Dana, 1995; but see Gross-Glenn et al., 1995). These differences themselves have been found in some studies to vary as a function of luminance (Martin & Love-

grove, 1984) or spatial frequency (e.g. Lovegrove et al., 1982), which suggests a possible link with a particular component of the visual processing system (but see Skottun, 2000).

THE MAGNOCELLULAR SUB-DIVISION OF THE VISUAL SYSTEM

There is a fairly close correspondence between the properties of a psychophysically identified transient component of the human visual system (Kulikowski & Tolhurst, 1973) on the one hand and, on the other, the characteristics of a particular sub-division of the visual system identified in animals by neurophysiologists and known as the magnocellular sub-division. Similarly, there are close similarities between a psychophysically identified sustained system and a second neurophysiological sub-division, the parvocellular sub-division (see Hogben, 1996; Lovegrove, 1996). Many of the visual deficits reported in dyslexia have been taken as indicating some impairment in the transient channel or magnocellular sub-division of the visual system. [Although the terms sustained and parvocellular (parvo for short) or transient and magnocellular (magno) are not strictly synonymous, they have been used interchangeably in the dyslexia literature].

Basic neuroanatomy of the visual system

The behaviour of the visual system of humans is sufficiently similar to that of rhesus monkeys for the latter to be taken as a useful (though not perfect) model of the human visual system. What follows is based upon the monkey visual system (ignoring certain species differences) and is thought to apply to humans unless specified otherwise.

When light strikes the eye, a chemical reaction occurs whereby the pigments in the light-sensitive photoreceptors, rods and cones, at the back of the retina are bleached. This sets up activity in layers of cells, which, in turn, project to a layer of cells known as retinal ganglion cells, the axons of which form the optic nerve (see Figure 3). Retinal ganglion cells are of two main kinds (P cells and M cells) classified on the basis of their neurophysiological reponse properties. In the rhesus macaque monkey (*Maccaca fascicularis*), magno (or M) retinal ganglion cells are dominated by rod input, especially at low luminance (Lee, Smith, Pokorny, & Kremers, 1997). This suggests that they are not much concerned with colour, a conclusion supported by other evidence. It has been reported that in the macque monkey, the ratio of the number of parvo to magno cells at 80° eccentricity is 4 : 1 but closer to 40 : 1 in the fovea (Connolly & Van Essen, 1984). This implies that magno cells are relatively more numerous in the periphery compared with the central retina. The same may be true of humans (Dacey, 1993), although the evidence is far from compelling (see Drasdo, Thompson, & Deeley, 1991). In fact, even in the monkey the view that the proportion of magno cells increases with eccentricity has been questioned (Livingstone & Hubel, 1988a).

From each eye of the monkey, relatively large retinal ganglion cells (M cells) project ipsilaterally or contralaterally to large cells in the next relay station on the way to the cortex, the lateral geniculate nucleus (LGN) of the thalamus. A small proportion of M cells also projects to the superior colliculus, as does a third class of rarely encountered ganglion cell (Shapley & Perry, 1986). The contralateral eye projects to layer 1 of the the ventral aspect of LGN, the ipsilateral eye to layer 2 of the LGN. The retinal ganglion nerves synapse (chemically connect) with large geniculate cells that project to the visual or striate cortex (V1) at the back of the brain, whence a network of other fibres feeds forward (and back) to terminate in different extra-striate visual centres or regions. These pathways constitute the magnocellular division of the visual system. Other, smaller retinal ganglion cells (P cells), which comprise approximately 80 per cent of retinal ganglion cells (Perry, Oehler, & Cowey, 1984), project to small cells in the dorsal LGN (contralaterally to layers 4 and 6, ipsilaterally to layers 3 and 5), which, in turn, project to the cortex and form the parvocellular division (Hubel & Wiesel, 1977; Leventhal, Rodieck, & Dreher, 1981; Livingstone & Hubel, 1988b; Zeki, 1993). As well as the magno and parvo routes to V1 via the LGN, there is evidence of a third route (the K or koniocellular route) in many primate and mammalian species, but its functions are as yet unclear (Casagrande, 1994, 1999). It may have a role to play in chromatic modulation of luminance-detecting mechanisms (Troscianko et al., 1996), as well as in the processing of fast-moving stimuli (Morand et al., 2000).

Fibres from the magnocellular (magno or M pathway) and parvocellular (parvo or P pathway) sub-divisions are physically segregated (rather like the small copper wires that are contained within differently coloured sheaths in the electric supply system) not only at the lateral geniculate nucleus, but perhaps to some degree also at the primary visual cortex (V1) of the brain. Projections from the different layers of the LGN arrive at different layers in the primary visual cortex (V1). Neurones in layer IVCα of the primary visual cortex receive projections from the magnocellular layers of the lateral geniculate nucleus and project to layer IVB of V1, whereas neurones in layer IVCβ receive projections from parvocellular layers. Until recently, layer IVCβ cells were thought not to project to IVB but only to the more superficial layers (2 and 3) of the primary visual cortex (V1).

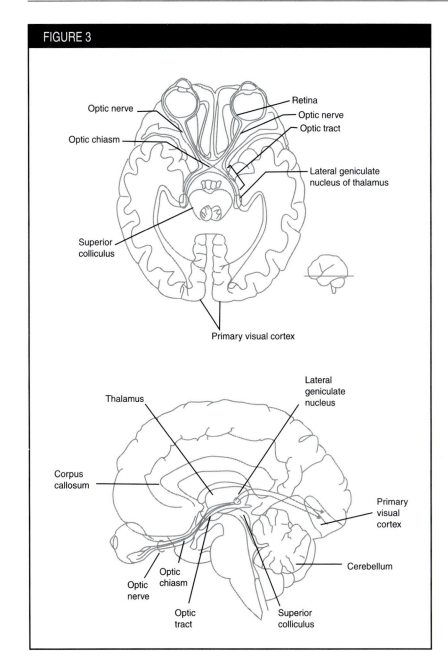

Figure 3 Pathway from retina to lateral geniculate nucleus and visual cortex

However, it now seems possible that both magno and parvo input converge on layer IVB cells (Sawatari & Callaway, 1996; see also note 12 of Yabuta, Sawatari, & Callaway, 2001), although the relevant findings are based on only five morphologically identified neurones. In any case, the magno and parvo neurones in V1 providing input to extra-striate areas V2 and V3 are spatially intermingled (Yabuta, et al., 2001). There is also evidence that magno and parvo input to V1 is merged in the output from V1 to V2 (Sincich & Horton, 2002). Thus the idea that magno and parvo streams remain physically segregated should not be pushed too far. As Shapley (1990) put it, magno and parvo pathways "may start out parallel but they converge".

The primary visual cortex (V1) provides input to other areas of the brain (Callaway, 1998; Shapley, 1990). Cells from layer IVB of V1 project to the so-called thick stripe region of area V2, to V3 and to the middle-temporal region (Felleman & Van Essen, 1987), which, in turn, projects to V4 and the posterior parietal area (Desimone & Ungerleider, 1986).

As well as cells of the magno stream having larger cell bodies than those of the parvo stream, the magno and parvo systems have distinctive neurophysiological properties that underlie differences in function. M cell receptive fields are larger than those of P cells, reflecting spatial summation over a larger pool of photoreceptors (rods and cones). Consequently, M cells are more sensitive than P cells to low spatial frequencies (coarser visual details), to overall changes in space-averaged luminance and to low contrast. They are relatively insensitive to colour differences. Because of their smaller receptive fields, P cells respond optimally to high spatial frequencies (fine detail). They are also sensitive to colour. The axons of M cells are heavily myelinated and their conduction velocities are high; M cells tend to respond primarily to the onset and offset of a stimulus, whereas P cells give a more sustained response (Livingstone & Hubel, 1988b; Merigan & Maunsell, 1993).

Lesions to M pathway cells of the macaque monkey LGN reduce the animal's contrast sensitivity to stimuli of low spatial or high temporal frequency (Merigan, Byrne, & Maunsell, 1991a) and impair sensitivity to motion (Merigan & Maunsell, 1990; Schiller, Logothetis, & Charles, 1990). Lesions affecting the parvocellular system of the monkey LGN impair perception of colour, texture and pattern (Merigan, Katz, & Maunsell, 1991b; Schiller et al., 1990). Thus while the magno system appears to be concerned primarily with detection of movement of objects in the world, the parvo system is more concerned with analysis of form and colour. Having said this, it should be noted that in a major review of the field, Merrigan and Maunsell (1993; see also Merrigan et al., 1991a) were reluctant to accept that the M pathway is concerned with motion perception *per se*; rather, they concluded that "the M pathway is not specialized for motion perception, but is specialized for the transmission of middle and high velocity stimuli that are important to some functions of the parietal visual stream" (p. 394).

In the monkey, there is a small area known as MT or V5 in the posterior bank of the superior temporal sulcus, which, together with the adjacent medial superior temporal area (MST), is considered to be specialized for the perception of visual motion (Zeki, 1973). Chemical lesions made in this region grossly impair the animal's ability to detect direction of motion, at least in the short term (Newsome & Paré, 1988). Area MT receives input from M cells via layer IVB of area V1 (Merigan & Maunsell, 1993) but also receives some indirect parvo input via the thick stripes of V2 and, probably, from V3 (Movshon & Newsome, 1996).

The magnocellular division of the visual system is usually thought of as terminating in the motion-sensitive area of the temporal lobe. In fact, from here fibres connect with the posterior parietal cortex via the medial superior temporal (MST) and ventral intraparietal (VIP) areas (Maunsell & Van Essen, 1983; see also Livingstone & Hubel, 1988b; Merigan & Maunsell, 1993). Areas V2 and V3 may also play a role in motion perception, since a good proportion of cells in V3 at least are sensitive to direction of movement (Felleman & Van Essen, 1987). Areas MT and V4 are reciprocally connected (Maunsell & Van Essen 1983; Ungerleider & Desimone, 1986), as indeed are MT and other extra-striate areas (Ungerleider & Desimone, 1986). There are also descending projections from MT to several sub-cortical sites, including the basal ganglia, thalamus, superior colliculus and pons (Maunsell & Van Essen, 1983; Merigan & Maunsell, 1993). The latter projects to lobe VII of the cerebellum. Most of these areas (including the cerebellum) have been implicated in the generation and control of eye movements (Maunsell & Van Essen, 1983).

Neuropsychological evidence from brain-damaged patients (Riddoch, 1917; Zeki, 1991; Zihl, von Cramon, & Mai, 1983; Zihl, von

Cramon, Mai, & Schmid, 1991) and investigations with neurologically intact volunteers using
PET (Zeki, Watson, Lueck, Friston, Kennard, &
Frackowiack, 1991) and fMRI imaging (Tootell et
al., 1995), as well as these two techniques combined (Watson et al., 1993), have revealed that in
the human brain, too, there is an area that can be
regarded as a centre for detection of movement.
This area (referred to as MT/V5) lies at the junc-
tion of the ascending limb of the inferior temporal sulcus with the lateral occipital sulcus
(Watson et al., 1993) "and not in the middle temporal region of the human cerebral cortex"
(Beckers & Zeki, 1995, p. 50). In addition to the
geniculo-striate route, there is evidence in humans
of a sub-cortical route to V5 that bypasses V1
(Beckers & Zeki, 1995; Ffytche, Guy & Zeki,
1995, 1996; Holliday, Anderson, & Harding,
1997) and presumably originates in the superior
colliculus. As with the monkey (Ungerleider &
Desimone, 1986), it is probably as well to think of
area MT/V5 as being only one component of a
system capable of handling movement information. Other areas "downstream" of MT almost
certainly contribute to the processing of different
aspects of motion information. Indeed, not only
cortical areas appear to be implicated in movement perception. Nawrot and Rizzo (1998) have
reported that midline lesions of the cerebellum
impaired discrimination of direction of movement when patients were tested 2 years after their
cerebellar stroke while Ivry & Diener (1991)
found that damage to the cerebellum impaired
perception of velocity. One should remember,
however, that there are reciprocal connections
between the cerebellum and a number of cortical
areas leading to a dynamic interplay between
these different regions of the brain (Junck, Gilman, Rothley, Betley, Koeppe & Hichwa, 1988).

Dorsal and ventral streams

The route from primary visual cortex (V1) projecting to the so-called thick stripe region of V2,
V3 and the middle-temporal and parietal regions
is known as the dorsal stream or route. The route
from the so-called "blobs" and "inter-blobs"
region of V1 projecting to V4 and inferior temporal cortex via the inter-stripe and thin stripe

regions of V2, respectively (Felleman & Van
Essen, 1987), is referred to as the ventral stream.
Traditionally, the ventral stream has been
regarded as critical for object identification,
whereas the dorsal stream has been seen as
important for processing the spatial location of
objects (Desimone & Ungerleider, 1989; Mishkin,
& Ungerleider 1982). These two systems have
been dubbed the "what?" and "where?" systems.
More recently, the dorsal stream has been re-
conceptualized as being important for the visual
control of actions (Goodale & Milner, 1992).
Such characterizations of the dorsal and ventral
streams (for review see Creem & Proffitt, 2001)
have been criticized by Previc (1990), who suggested that these two routes relate to near and
far vision, respectively, via specialization of
lower and upper visual fields (upper and lower
retina).

The relationship between the dorsal route and
the M pathway on the one hand and between the
ventral route and P pathway on the other was
discussed by Merigan and Maunsell (1993). Their
view was that despite extensive connections
between the two sub-divisions, there is some reason to believe that the major contribution to the
dorsal route is from the magnocellular division
(Maunsell, Nealy, & DePriest, 1990; Merigan and
Maunsell, 1993). Merigan and Maunsell concluded from their review of the evidence that:

> The M pathway seems to dominate the par-
> ietal [dorsal] pathway, although some P
> pathway contributions are found. On the
> other hand, both the M and P pathways
> contribute appreciably to the temporal
> [ventral] pathway. The segregation of the P
> and M pathways in extra-striate cortex
> appears to consist mainly of a partial exclu-
> sion of P contributions from the parietal
> pathway.
> (Merigan & Maunsell, 1993, p. 390)

However, the report of Sawatari and Callaway
(1996) that both magno and parvo input converge
on layer IVB cells in V1 and the recent finding
that magno and parvo input to V1 is merged in

the output from V1 to V2 (Sincich & Horton, 2002) suggest some modification of this view.

DYSLEXIA AND THE MAGNO SYSTEM

The idea that at least some dyslexics have an impairment of the magno pathway arises in part from reports that they show deficits in performing the kinds of task that research suggests is undertaken by this pathway (for reviews see, Hogben, 1997; Lovegrove, 1991, 1996; Lovegrove & Williams, 1993; Lovegrove et al., 1986; Stein, 1991, 1993, 2001; Stein & Walsh, 1997).

In comparison with controls, poor readers have been reported in some studies (Borsting et al., 1996; Evans, Drasdo, & Richards, 1994; Felmingham & Jakobson, 1995; Lehmkuhle, Garzia, Turner, Hash, & Baro, 1993; Livingstone et al., 1991; Lovegrove et al., 1982; Martin & Lovegrove, 1984, 1987) but not others (Gross-Glenn et al., 1995; Hayduk, Bruck, & Cavanagh, 1996; Johannes, Kussmaul, Münte, & Mangun, 1996; Smith, Early, & Grogan 1986; Vanni, Uusitalo, Kiesila, Hari, 1997; Walther-Müller, 1995) to show increased reaction time, decreased evoked potentials or reduced sensitivity to stimuli of low spatial or high temporal frequency, especially at low levels of luminance, which emphasize the magnocellular contribution to vision (Lee et al., 1997). In one study, the difference in sensitivity to temporal frequency between dyslexics and controls increased as the frequency of flicker of a sinusoidal grating increased (Felmingham & Jakobson, 1995). This is highly suggestive of a magnocellular pathway deficit.

A study by Evans et al. (1994) is notable for a number of features. First, dyslexics were defined in terms of the difference between actual reading performance and that expected on the basis of age and IQ. There were relatively large numbers of dyslexic and control participants and a careful investigation of both ocular and visual processing factors was made. Finally, a visual search task was included. The results showed that in comparison with age- and IQ-matched controls, dyslexics had a similar frequency of refractive errors but reduced visual acuity (as measured by ophthalmic charts) and reduced contrast sensitivity for stationary low and medium spatial frequency sine-wave gratings. Of more interest, perhaps, dyslexics also showed reduced sensitivity to a homogeneous green field flickering at 10 Hz and were slower to find a target digit from among an array of digits.

If there is a deficit in the transient or magnocellular system, it is in processing moving stimuli that one would expect to find it. Such an impairment was demonstrated in dyslexic children by Cornelissen, Richardson, Mason, Fowler, and Stein (1995) and in six adult dyslexic males by Eden, VanMeter, Rumsey, Maisog, Woods, and Zeffiro (1996). The latter reported that the dyslexics were significantly poorer than eight control participants in discriminating between the velocities of moving stimuli. That is, participants saw two sets of moving dots, each set being presented for 1 sec one after the other, and they had to indicate whether the second set of dots was moving more rapidly or more slowly than the first set. In a study by Felmingham and Jakobson (1995), dyslexics were less efficient at detecting the presence of a single letter defined purely in terms of the relative movement of dots forming part of a random-dot display. This cannot be attributed to a straightforward letter-recognition deficit, as dyslexics were able to identify the same letters presented in a stationary format.

Talcott et al. (1998) compared the responses of 18 adult dyslexic readers with 18 matched controls on two tests believed to reflect M pathway function: thresholds for detecting coherent direction of motion in random dot kinematograms (RDK) and critical flicker fusion (CFF), the highest frequency at which a temporally modulated stimulus (i.e. flickering light) can be detected at 100 per cent luminance contrast. It was reported that the coherent motion detection thresholds of dyslexics were significantly higher than those of controls, indicating that dyslexics required more randomly spaced dots to be moving in a coherent direction before they were able to detect the direction of movement (see also Everatt, Bradshaw, & Hibbard, 1999). The critical or threshold frequencies of the dyslexic participants were significantly lower than those of the controls—that is, the dyslexics were less good at detecting flicker (see also Lovegrove et al., 1986).

As well as being impaired on velocity discrimination tasks, functional MRI in the study by Eden et al. (1996) showed that in dyslexic participants, unlike controls, area V5 in the left and right hemispheres was not activated in response to moving stimuli. This was the case for all six dyslexic participants, each of whom showed bilateral activity in V5. Similar, although less clear-cut, findings have been reported by Demb, Boynton, and Heeger (1998b; see also Demb, Boynton, & Heeger, 1997). The failure of moving stimuli to elicit activation in area V5 of dyslexics cannot be attributed to an overall problem with their visual system, since they showed normal responses to stationary stimulus patterns in other visual areas (V1 and V2).

Using magnetoencephalography (MEG), Vanni et al. (1997) found that similar responses were evoked in area V5 of Finnish adult dyslexic and control participants by a low-brightness stimulus that shifted position slightly back and forth every 45 msec. It is possible that the different methodologies (MEG versus fMRI) account for the discrepancy in findings reported by Eden et al. (1996) and Vanni et al. (1997). Alternatively, it may be that the faster movement of the stimulus in the study by Vanni et al. led to equal degrees of activation in dyslexics and controls. Clearly, stimulus parameters such as speed, luminance contrast, spatial frequency and illumination level will have to be investigated carefully in future studies.

Early work tended to examine contrast sensitivity for stationary stimuli of low spatial frequency and/or for stimuli flickering at relatively high temporal frequency. Both have been regarded as reflecting functions of the transient (magno) system. However, rarely have these two "tests" been presented together to the same individual: In the study by Evans et al. (1994), the results did not correlate highly. In another investigation, however, performance of five dyslexic college students and five controls on a test of velocity discrimination (putatively a transient

system or magno function) correlated with contrast sensitivity within both groups combined (Demb, Boynton, Best, & Heeger, 1998a). The dyslexics were significantly worse on the motion discrimination task but the difference between groups in contrast sensitivity for a low frequency grating (0.4 cycle/degree) was not significant.

Despite many positive findings, there have been failures to support the magno deficit hypothesis. For example, the study by Gross-Glenn et al. (1995) produced results difficult to reconcile with this hypothesis. Contrast sensitivity for horizontal sine-wave gratings was measured in 21 carefully diagnosed adult dyslexics and 21 control readers matched for gender, age, education and handedness. Measures were taken at two spatial frequencies, 0.6 cycles/degree and 12 cycles/degree, designed to stimulate transient and sustained systems, respectively. Sensitivity at these two frequencies was measured both when stimulus onsets and offsets were abrupt (termed "unramped") and when they were gradual ("ramped") and for various stimulus durations. With gradual stimulus onsets and offsets, there were no differences between dyslexics and controls at either spatial frequency (nor at an intermediate frequency of 4.0 cycles/degree). With abrupt onsets and offsets, dyslexics had lower contrast sensitivity relative to the controls only for 12 cycles/degree and at short stimulus durations (under 100 msec), but not at the longer durations (between 100 and 1000 msec). A magno system deficit would predict a difference between dyslexics and controls at the low spatial frequency (0.6 cycles/degree) rather than at 12 cycles/degree.

Among control observers, differences in sensitivity to high and low spatial frequencies have been seen as reflecting differences between the sustained and transient systems in temporal summation. Given the results of their study, it was suggested by Gross-Glenn et al. (1995) that "more sluggish temporal summation may account for the reduced sensitivity of the dyslexic observers" (p. 158). However, the fact that there was no difference between dyslexics and controls in sensitivity for low spatial frequency gratings, and that the increase in sensitivity for unramped stimuli (transient onsets and offsets) over ramped stimuli was similar for dyslexics and controls, does not suggest that dyslexics are specifically impaired in detecting stimulus transients. Gross-Glenn et al. conclude: "There is no evidence, therefore, in our data that dyslexic readers have reduced sensitivity to stimulus transients. This appears to conflict with the notion of a transient system deficit in dyslexia" (p. 159). It should be noted, however, that this does not undermine the finding that stimulus duration, *per se*, was important at high (but not low) spatial frequency, a finding that Gross-Glenn et al. see as being indicative of a sustained system deficit on the following grounds. While:

> ... brief stimuli have larger amplitudes at higher temporal frequencies [and thus might be thought to be processed within the transient system], the largest amplitudes for profiles of both brief stimuli and longer lasting stimuli are still found at very low temporal frequencies. Therefore one shall have to be careful not to equate detection of brief stimuli with high temporal frequencies or to assume that detection of such stimuli is mediated by the transient system ... Because the sustained system has its highest sensitivity to low temporal frequencies, deficits associated with brief high-spatial frequency stimuli, like the ones we observed, are consistent with a deficit in the sustained system.
>
> (Gross-Glenn et al., 1995, p. 161,
> legend to figure 6)

Gross-Glenn et al. (1995) also used a forward-masking condition in their experiment to evaluate the proposal that the sustained system is inhibited by the transient system. There is, in fact, some doubt about this idea (see below). In any event, Gross-Glenn et al. found no difference between their participant groups in susceptibility to forward masking at any spatial frequency, which they saw as further evidence against the transient or magno deficit hypothesis.

In an excellent critique of the literature on contrast sensitivity in dyslexia, Skottun (2000) makes the point that some studies not only fail to support the magno deficit hypothesis, but actually provide evidence that is difficult to reconcile with this hypothesis. His main criticism of the investigations that he reviews is that they have often failed to bear in mind that contrast sensitivity is a measure of contrast detection and that what holds for measurement of contrast threshold cannot be applied without qualification to situations involving supra-threshold stimuli. Skottun notes that psychophysical studies indicate that "The spatial frequency at which detection switches from the transient system to the sustained system" is about 1.5 cycles/degree or lower. He continues:

> It is quite clear that when using supra-threshold stimuli of sufficiently high power it is possible to elicit sustained system responses to stimuli having frequencies well below 1.5 c/deg and transient system responses to stimuli well above 1.5 c/deg. Failure to distinguish between threshold and suprathreshold data may therefore lead to incorrect conclusions regarding the origin of any given observed deficit.
>
> (Skottun, 2000, p. 113)

A second reason given by Skottun for scepticism regarding a magnocellular deficit is that some experiments have revealed that:

> Lesions restricted to magnocellular layers have relatively little effect on the overall contrast sensitivity ... Reductions in contrast sensitivity following such lesions are mainly apparent when contrast sensitivity is determined using stimuli having *both* low spatial (e.g. 1 c/deg) and high temporal frequencies (e.g. 10 Hz) ... reduced contrast sensitivity to either low spatial frequency or high temporal frequency stimuli is by itself an imperfect indicator of a magnocellular deficit ... The fact that magnocellular deficits manifest themselves only at certain spatial frequencies makes it important to map the spatial-frequency dependence of any sensitivity loss.
>
> (Skottun, 2000, pp. 113–114, emphasis in original).

In Skottun's (2000) opinion, it is important for the magno deficit hypothesis "to demonstrate that the magnitude of the sensitivity loss increases with temporal frequency and decreases with spatial frequency" (p. 117).

Skottun (2000) reviewed nearly two dozen studies. He concluded that only four of 22 studies are in agreement with the the magno deficit hypothesis, 11 provide evidence against the hypothesis (those that have found deficits only at high spatial frequencies) and seven studies have provided inconclusive results. Skottun therefore argued that "the evidence from contrast sensitivity studies for a magnocellular deficit is highly conflicting" (p. 118) and that "It seems that the evidence from the temporal contrast sensitivity studies is also quite conflicting. Like the spatial data, the temporal studies do not provide unequivocal support for the presence of a magnocellular deficit in dyslexia" (p. 120).

Despite Skottun's insightful critique of the contrast sensitivity literature in relation to dyslexia, certain findings showing a relationship between magno function and some aspects of reading suggest that it would be premature to dismiss the hypothesis as undeserving of further attention. In particular, investigations measuring aspects of movement perception might be thought to provide more unequivocal support for a magno deficit hypothesis, although Kronbichler et al. (2002) recently failed to find evidence of a movement discrimination deficit in Austrian dyslexic boys. Even with regard to such experiments, however, Skottun notes that recent neurophysiological experiments (Sawatari & Callaway, 1996) have revealed that parvocellular input to the motion-sensitive area of the cortex (MT/V5) is greater than was originally believed (see above):

> Thus a deficit in motion perception uncovered using a stimulus which has the potential to activate both the magnocellular and parvocellular systems (meaning the vast majority of suprathreshold luminance stimuli, including random dots . . .) can not be unambiguously attributed to the magnocellular subcortical pathway as the deficit

could be parvocellular or could be of cortical origin.

(Skottun, 2000, p. 124)

Such a cortical origin might include area MT/V5, of course, or regions that provide input to it. In this connection, Eden et al. (1996) found a deficit in area MT of dyslexic adults but no deficit in the primary visual area (V1). Skottun (2000) argues that had "the deficit in the motion area been the result of a subcortical magnocellular deficit, this deficit would presumably have been passed to MT through V1. In which case [sic] one would have expected to see deficits also in V1" (p. 124). However, the presence of a deficit in area MT, together with the absence of a deficit in V1, is entirely consistent with recent evidence that there is input to area MT, which bypasses V1 (Beckers & Zeki, 1995; Ffytche et al., 1995; Holliday et al., 1997).

The thrust of Skottun's review is that there is little compelling evidence for a deficit in dyslexia that can be related exclusively to the magnocellular system. This does not invalidate the findings said to support the hypothesis even if it casts considerable doubt on their interpretation within the framework of the transient/sustained or magnocellular/parvocellular divisions of the visual system. The findings themselves remain to be explained.

The relation of transient/sustained or magno/parvo systems to reading

Hayduk et al. (1996) pointed out that the transient/magno system deficit hypothesis "is supported by a limited number of paradigms which are not representative of normal reading conditions" (p. 1009). This begs the question of exactly what the relation is between the findings obtained with such paradigms and the processes involved in reading. That there is such a relation is suggested by the finding of a correlation between performance on tests of putative magno function and various reading tasks.

Cornelissen, Hansen, Hutton, Evangelinou, and Stein (1998b) presented a motion detection task to a group of 58 unselected children aged 9–11 years. Performance on this task correlated with the proportion of orthographically inconsistent reading errors, termed "letter" errors (such as reading *victim* as *vikim*, suspect as *subpact*, swift as *sweef*, where the response includes a sound not contained in the target word), that were made on a task of regular word reading even when IQ, reading age and phonological awareness were taken into account. This result held even with the exclusion of 17 children whose reading age was at least 2 years behind their chronological age. It was argued that letter errors reflect a problem in correctly encoding the position of letters within words and that this information is carried by the magno system, since, in a different experiment, 24 students identified as "poor" coherent motion detectors made more such letter errors than 24 "good" coherent motion detectors (Cornelissen, Hansen, Gilchrist, Cormack, Essex, & Frankish, 1998a). Impaired magnocellular function, it was suggested (Cornelissen, et al., 1998b), might lead to a degraded encoding of letter position during reading such that "positional uncertainty of this kind could cause letters or parts of letters to be lost or duplicated, or even incorrectly bound together, leading to a scrambled or nonsense version of what is actually printed on the page. When children try to read aloud what they see under these circumstances ... their utterances should contain sounds not represented in the printed word" (p. 473).

In another study of motion detection thresholds carried out with adult dyslexics and controls, the participants were given tests of nonword reading (Talcott et al., 1998). Within each of the participant groups, poorer performance on the putative tests of M pathway function was associated with more nonword naming errors. Indeed, the authors reported that "nearly 48% of the variance in nonword naming could be predicted from the subjects' overall M-pathway sensitivity on our two temporal perception tasks" (p. 198). Motion (speed) discrimination thresholds (but not those for contrast detection) have been reported to correlate with the reading rate for words on the Nelson-Denny test of reading (Demb et al., 1998a). This same group (Demb et al., 1997) found a significant positive correlation between reading rate and level of brain response recorded by fMRI in the middle temporal region

and between reading comprehension and brain activity in a number of extra-striate sites (V2, V3, V3A, V4). There were no correlations with single-word reading or spelling measures.

Motion perception, dyslexia and brain activation

Demb et al. (1998b) used fMRI to monitor levels of brain activation while two diagonal sinusoidal gratings were presented at low luminance and at five different contrast levels. The gratings were in different parts of the visual field and moved simultaneously towards or away from the fixation point at different speeds. The participants' task was to identify the faster-moving grating. Brain activation was monitored and compared with a test condition in which flickering (contrast-reversing) sinusoidal stimuli were presented at the same contrast levels but higher mean luminance. The participants were five dyslexic students (mean age 22 years) and five normally reading controls. Consistent with the magno deficit hypothesis, relative brain activation for the middle temporal region and primary visual cortex was significantly higher in the control group than in the dyslexic group for the moving stimuli but not for the control stimuli. Group differences in overall visual function or in attention or motivation can therefore not explain the results for the moving stimuli condition. Furthermore, for both brain regions, but especially the temporal region, there was a significant negative correlation across all participants between extent of brain activation and sensitivity to movement (speed discrimination threshold). The higher the brain activation, the lower the threshold—that is, the better the performance.

The finding of a group difference in brain activation as early in the visual system as the striate or visual cortex (V1)—that is, "downstream" of the middle temporal area—is consistent with the idea that the deficit may arise at a pre-cortical (geniculate or retinal) level. In this context, it is of interest that Livingstone et al. (1991) found smaller cells in the magnocellular layer of the LGN in a limited set of five brains of dyslexic adults compared with five control brains (see Chapter 9). They also found a reduced visual

evoked potential under conditions of low luminance and high temporal frequency in five
(different) dyslexics, consistent with an M pathway deficit, although the finding of a reduced
response specific to dyslexia was not replicated in
a group of dyslexic adults and children (median
age 13.5 years) by Victor, Conte, Burton, and
Nass (1993).

Visual evoked response latencies to the onset
of a moving checkerboard pattern, but not to pat-
tern-reversal of another checkerboard, were
found by Kubová, Kuba, Peregrin, and Nováková
(1995) to be slower in a group of 20 purportedly
dyslexic children (neither age nor diagnostic criteria are given) compared with age-matched controls. This was viewed as being consistent with a
magnocellular deficit in dyslexia. Lehmkuhle et
al. (1993) found that dyslexics had longer latencies and smaller amplitude in certain components of the electrophysiological response at the
scalp evoked by a low-frequency sine-wave
target presented against a flickering background.
No differences between dyslexics and controls
were observed with targets of high spatial frequency or with a uniform stationary background. These findings were also interpreted as
evidence in favour of the magnocellular deficit
hypothesis. However, no difference between six
adult dyslexics and six controls in the visual
evoked potential to rapidly reversing checkerboard patterns was found by Johannes et al.,
(1996).

Although not discussed within the framework
of the M pathway hypothesis, earlier reports of
differences between dyslexic boys and controls in
evoked potentials recorded from the scalp (especially over the left hemisphere) in reponse to
stimulation from a flashing strobe light (Duffy,
Denckla, Bartels, & Sandini, 1980), or of reduced
P150 and P350 components of the visual evoked
response to word-by-word presentation of sentences   among-language   impaired/reading-
disabled children (Neville, Coffey, Holcomb, &
Tallal, 1993), might bear some relation to an
impaired magno pathway.

The results of a number of studies, then, provide some evidence to link movement-related
(putatively magnocellular) functions to reading in

some way (Everatt et al., 1999; Slaghuis & Ryan,
1999), but exactly what leads to poor motion processing in dyslexia is not known—there are a
number of conceivable mechanisms (Walther-
Müller, 1995). One possible explanation of dyslexics' poorer coherence thresholds as determined
from random dot kinematograms (RDK) is that
they have a problem in detecting stimuli of short
duration; another is that the problem lies in integrating spatial and/or temporal responses of cells
in the M pathway and/or the cortical regions to
which they project. Talcott, Hansen, Assoku, and
Stein (2000a) varied the spatial and temporal
properties of the stimuli present in RDK stimuli
seen by 10 adult dyslexic viewers and 10 control
participants. In one experiment the duration of
the dots was varied and in another the density
of the dots was varied. Increasing the duration of
the stimuli between successive screen presentations (refreshes) did not improve dyslexics' performance, over and above that seen for controls,
as might have been expected on the basis that they
have a problem with short-duration stimuli. The
second manipulation did affect dyslexics' performance, increasing dot density led to improved
performance (i.e. lower coherence thresholds) as
it did in controls. Talcott et al. (2000a) suggested
that "dyslexics' performance may improve
because the increased motion signal can accumulate in cells tuned for that particular direction of
motion" (p. 941).

Motion perception deficits are not found in all
dyslexics (Everatt et al., 1999) nor with all movement-related tasks. Furthermore, any impairment
observed may relate not to reduced sensitivity in
detecting motion per se but to an impairment in
the perceptual integration of movement information (Raymond & Sorensen, 1998). In a study of
seven adult dyslexic participants, Hill and Raymond (2002) presented random dot kinematograms in which the dots moved coherently either
in one direction (unidirectional motion) or in two
perpendicular directions (bidirectional motion).
In the unidirectional condition, the dyslexics performed as well as controls but in the bidirectional
condition six out of the seven were significantly
impaired. Since no deficit was found in the standard unidirectional condition, it was argued that

"these findings provide little support for theories that posit a low-level disruption of motion processing mechanisms (i.e. a pre-striate magno, or motion input deficit). Rather, they are best explained by hypothesising a higher-order deficit in integration and segmentation of motion information possibly involving extra-striate cortical areas of the brain" (p. 1201). Hill and Raymond suggest that the dyslexic participants "may have had greater difficulty than controls in attending to and therefore reporting the direction of the two motion components" (p. 1201).

The consequences of a magno system deficit

If it is granted that there is an impairment of movement detection in dyslexia and that this implicates the magno system (bearing in mind Skottun's reservations), how might a magnocellular deficit lead to difficulties in learning to read and to spell? Breitmeyer and Ganz (1976) and Breitmeyer (1993) suggested that in the brief interval between successive fixations of a visual scene, when vision is impaired due to saccadic suppression (for reviews, see Matin, 1974; Volkman, 1986), the magnocellular or transient system suppresses or masks activity in the parvocellular or sustained system. The effect would be to ensure that the images received during each fixation would not interfere with each other. However, recent research has provided evidence for the opposite effect, that during saccades the magnocellular system is selectively suppressed (Burr, Morrone, & Ross, 1994; see also reviews by Ross, Burr, & Morrone, 1996; Volkman, Riggs, White, & Moore, 1978), which rather undermines Breitmeyer's theory.

If the magno pathway is selectively suppressed during sacaddic eye movements, this will have the effect of reducing the perception of motion (Ross, et al., 1996). This might help to explain why we are not aware of a blurred image during saccades but see clearly only what we fixate upon. As Ross et al. (1996) put it, "Suppressing the M-system prevents what would otherwise be an alarming rush of motion every time we made a saccade" (p. 6). Suppression of the magno pathway during saccades may thus be the means whereby stimuli from successive fixations are maintained in such a form as to allow the information to be processed and represented in some abstract code, thereby allowing a continuous rather than a disjointed record of what we perceive. Any anomalous operation of the suppression mechanism in relation to the magno system would thus be expected to have consequences for reading.

A different view on how an impaired magno system might affect reading was expressed by Talcott et al. (1998). "It is not suggested that dyslexics' lowered contrast sensitivity at low luminances and low spatial but high temporal frequencies interferes directly with their reading, but rather indirectly, perhaps via effects on visible persistence, visual stability, or eye movements" (p. 191). They are not the only authors to implicate eye movements. Borsting et al. (1996) pointed to the observation that in cases of acquired "dysphonesia" (in Boder's terminology) there is involvement of the insula of the temporal lobe. These authors also referred to PET findings (Anderson, Jenkins, Brooks, Hawken, Frackowiak, & Kennard, 1994) implicating the insula in saccadic eye movements. They therefore suggested that "dysphonesia may result in an abnormal saccade mechanism that could adversely effect [sic] reading" (p. 1052). Of course, they can hardly be suggesting that "dysphonesia" *causes* abnormal eye movements; rather, the two must be caused by some third variable, which, by implication, is a "faulty" insula. The fact that at least one PET study has found an inactive left insula in dyslexic adults compared with controls (Paulesu et al., 1996) is therefore of interest in this context.

Stein and his colleagues have argued that deficits in the M pathway might cause problems with binocular fixation (Stein, 1992; Stein & Walsh, 1997). In a recent paper, Stein has reiterated this argument as follows:

One problem that constantly bedevils the hypothesis that dyslexics have impaired magnocellular function is that people find it very difficult to understand how a system devoted to detecting visual motion could possibly be relevant to reading. After all, we don't usually have to track moving targets when reading; the page is usually kept stationary. In fact, the retinal images of print are not stationary, and many dyslexic children complain that letters seem to move around when they are trying to read, i.e. their visual world is highly unstable. This is because during reading visual images are actually very far from being stationary on the retina, and dyslexics fail to compensate for this … We believe that their unstable visual perceptions are the result of the insensitivity of their visual magnocellular systems.

(Stein, 2000, p. 111).

If dyslexics have longer fixations, shorter saccades and more regressions than controls (Rayner, 1978), this might be to compensate for a reduced ability to distinguish the offset of one fixation from the onset of the next—that is, for a deficit in temporal order judgements (TOJ; see Chapter 6), as suggested by May et al. (1988). These workers noted that deficient transient processing "may represent the initial flaw which results in a TOJ problem" (p. 922). On the basis of reports of abnormally long latencies of evoked visual potentials in dyslexics, Lehmkuhle et al. (1993) argued that deficiency of the magnocellular pathway in dyslexia "involves a slowing of response in this pathway" (p. 995), which Lehmkuhle (1993) suggested might perturb the "normal timing of the visual system" (p. 91).

It is possible that visual deficits of one kind or other are not found in all dyslexics but only in some and perhaps only within a particular subtype. Borsting et al. (1996) and Ridder et al. (1997) found contrast sensitivity for low spatial and high temporal frequency (suggestive of a magnocellular deficit) to be reduced in some (predominantly) adult dyslexics compared with controls, but not in those said to comprise a subgroup of dyslexics who, on Boder's (1973) scheme, were "dyseidetic" dyslexics. Similarly, Spinelli, Angelelli, De Luca, Di Pace, Judica, and Zoccolotti (1997) found no evidence for a transient system deficit in a group of Italian children said to be surface dyslexics (on the basis that they were generally slow readers but not selectively

impaired in reading nonwords and were significantly impaired in comprehending and discriminating homophonic sentences). These children did, however, show a significant reduction in sensitivity to stationary stimuli of high spatial frequency, which would not be expected on the magnocellular deficit hypothesis.

A further possibility is that visual deficits are found only in dyslexic individuals who have attentional deficits or only when the diagnosis of dyslexia is based on reading accuracy, as is usual with English-speaking participants, rather than on reading fluency or speed (Kronbichler et al., 2002).

The magnocellular deficit hypothesis and phonological impairments

The fact that visual anomalies have been observed in dyslexics with a primarily phonological rather than orthographic impairment (see also Eden et al., 1996; Lovegrove et al., 1982) might be taken as implying that the visual deficit observed is a correlate rather than a direct cause of the poor reading. Eden et al. (1996) suggested that the coexistence of a visual impairment and a phonological deficit in dyslexia "may be due to the presence of an underlying deficit in systems that have in common the processing of temporal properties of stimuli" (p. 69). This suggestion is clearly related to the idea that there may be analogues to the transient/sustained visual channels or magno/parvo pathways in other sensory sub-systems, as proposed by a number of other authors (Farmer & Klein, 1995; Livingstone et al., 1991; Tallal et al., 1993). May et al. (1988) went so far as to suggest that "Subtle but ubiquitous problems in transient subsystems in all the senses and the motor system could lead to the myriad of sensory, motor, perceptual and cognitive deficiencies which have been observed in the reading disabled" (p. 923).

The claim that relatively low-level visual deficits of the transient or magnocellular system are found in association with reading difficulties has often been seen as standing in opposition to the evidence that phonological deficits are the core causal problem in dyslexia. But there is no fundamental incompatibility between these two views of the origins of dyslexics' difficulties. It has been argued that visual and language difficulties may co-occur in dyslexia (Slaghuis, Lovegrove, & Davidson, 1993; Slaghuis et al., 1996; see also Cestnick & Coltheart, 1999). Conceivably, both are the result of a third underlying factor involving sensory processing. Cornelissen et al. (1998b) suggested that many of the component skills of reading are distributed independently and continuously in the population and that impaired magnocellular function as well as problems of phonological awareness may affect how children learn to read.

According to Stein and Walsh (1997), "Slight impairments of mLGN (magnocellular laminae of the lateral geniculate nucleus) performance or organization might . . . multiply up to greater deficits in PPC (posterior parietal cortex) function. The PPC is known to be important for normal eye movement control, visuo-spatial attention and peripheral vision—all important components of reading" (p. 149). Hari, Renvall, & Tanskanen (2000) have proposed that a magnocellular deficit in providing input to the right parietal lobe "would impair processing of stimulus sequences as a result of sluggish attention shifting" (p. 1378). These authors reported that, in comparison with controls, dyslexic adults show a form of "minineglect" evidenced by slower stimulus processing in the left visual hemifield. They argued that hypofunction of the right parietal lobe "can be related to sluggishness of attentional capture and shifting, as well as to modified spatial distribution of attention" (p. 1378). Omtzigt, Hendriks, and Kolk (2002) compared identification of isolated letters presented to normal adult readers in central and parafoveal vision under conditions said to favour either the parvo system (colour contrast between letters and background) or the magno system (low luminance contrast). Identification rates in central vision did not differ between these two conditions but for flanking letters was better in the low luminance contrast condition than in the colour contrast condition. It was argued that this supports the view that the magno system is involved in the selection of letters to be attended to and that "a magnocellular deficit may contribute to reading disability by

hindering identification of letters presented among other letters" (p. 1889).

A somewhat similar interpretation as to the relevance of an impaired magno system in dyslexia was suggested by Vidyasagar and Pammer (1999), who reported that in a visual search task (for a unique conjunction of features) dyslexics (defined in terms of a reading lag of 2 or more years behind age-matched controls) were significantly impaired compared with controls when the stimulus set to be searched was large (> 70 items) but not when it was relatively small (< 36 items). They argued that this was attributable to a magnocellular deficit because "the M-mediated dorsal stream performs a vital function in focussing spatial attention" (p. 1286) but the inference is weak at best. As discussed earlier, the idea that the dorsal stream is dominated by input from the magno system has been challenged by recent findings. Moreover, Hayduk et al. (1996) found no evidence that dyslexic children differed from controls specifically on visual search tasks (for a single feature) that depended upon the transient system. Rather, dyslexics made more errors and tended overall to be slower on a few tasks that tapped both transient and sustained systems. However, these authors cautioned that the comorbidity of dyslexia and attentional problems "poses a potentially serious confound to research into the existence of visual deficits in dyslexia" (p. 1011).

The hypothesis of a magnocellular deficit in dyslexia has generated considerable scepticism and controversy (see Hayduk et al., 1996; Hulme, 1988; Lovegrove, 1991; Skottun, 1997, 2000; Walther-Müller, 1995). There are, of course, two aspects to this claim. One is that the deficit can be attributed to the functions of a particular subdivision of the visual system; the other is that the visual deficits, by whatever pathway they are mediated, play a causal role in dyslexia. While intervention studies have confirmed the role of phonological skills in learning to read, comparable evidence as to the causal role of visual deficits is lacking. Whether low-level visual processing differences between disabled readers are consequent upon the reading deficit—that is, due to lack of reading experience—as opposed to the two variables being causally related in the reverse direction or simply correlated by virtue of a third common factor, might be examined using a reading-age matched group of control participants. Though common, indeed standard practice, in language-based studies of dyslexia, reading-age control groups have hardly ever been adopted in investigations of visually based deficits. One reason for this may be that children are expected to show improvement with age on visual tasks so a reading-age design may give dyslexic readers an advantage (Eden, Stein, Wood, & Wood, 1995b). Of course, the obvious way of assessing whether there is any such advantage in a particular study is also to include a chronological-age matched control group, as in language-based studies.

Given that language and visual anomalies have been reported to co-occur in some dyslexics, at least, perhaps further speculation is in order. It is well known that in listening to someone speak, we take account of how their lips move. McGurk and MacDonald (1976) showed this experimentally by presenting a face with the mouth saying one thing at the same time as participants heard something different spoken over loudspeakers. Participants reported hearing a sound that was a compromise between the auditory and visual stimuli.

Could it be that early in childhood development a subtle magno deficit in processing lip movements leads to errors in perceiving or categorizing the phonemes of speech? This might entail a weakness or incompleteness in the phonological representations of words, a state of affairs postulated by some authors to characterize dyslexia (Shankweiler et al., 1992; Snowling & Hulme, 1994; Swan & Goswami, 1997a, 1997b). Certainly patient L.M. who has damage to area V5 (and midline cerebellum) has a severe motion processing deficit and is impaired at speech reading (Campbell, Zihl, Massaro, Munhall, & Cohen, 1997), while both child and adult "compensated" dyslexics show a deficit in matching speech sounds to the correct picture of the corresponding articulatory movements (Griffiths & Frith, 2002). Although not discussed in these terms, the results of an experiment by de Gelder

and Vroomen (1998) are consistent with the idea that a subtle magnocellular deficit may impair the ability to derive phonological information from vision. These authors found that 14 poor readers were impaired in speech reading in comparison with both age-matched and reading-level matched controls.

A magno deficit and asymmetry of the planum temporale

Finally, the relation of a putative magnocellular deficit to neuro-anatomic factors merits brief discussion. Given that planum temporale symmetry or reversed asymmetry and a magnocellular deficit have both been hypothesized to underlie dyslexic difficulties in some way, it is of interest to ask whether these two "anomalies" tend to co-occur in the same individual.

Mention was made above of a study by Livingstone et al. (1991), who reported abnormalities of the magnocellular but not parvocellular layers of the lateral geniculate nucleus. The brains examined by Livingstone et al. (1991) were said to be "symmetrical" as far as the planum temporale was concerned (Galaburda et al., 1985; Humphreys et al., 1990). Symmetry has been said to characterize dyslexia, particularly of the phonological variety (Larsen, et al., 1990), although this cannot be considered well established (see Chapter 9).

The question of the co-occurrence of magno deficits and planum (a)symmetry was taken up by Best and Demb (1999), who investigated planum asymmetry in five dyslexics from a study by Demb et al. (1998b) who all showed reduced brain activity in area MT in response to stimuli designed to elicit strong activation. All five dyslexics showed leftward planum asymmetry when this was measured according to the criteria developed by Steinmetz and his colleagues, which includes tissue in the depth of the sulci (including Heschl's sulcus) as well as the posterior ascending ramus (PAR). When the measurement technique was similar to that employed by Rumsey and her colleagues (which excludes the PAR and does not take account of small sulci on the surface of the planum), one dyslexic individual was classified as having symmetrical plana and one as having rightward asymmetry, the remaining three showing leftward asymmetry. Using a method similar to that employed in post- mortem studies, such as the classic study of Geschwind and Levitsky (1968), which excludes all sulcal tissue, there were again three individuals with leftward asymmetry. Thus in this sample of dyslexic participants, it appears that there is no obvious association between anomalous planum asymmetry, however defined, and putative magnocellular deficits in dyslexia. Similarly, six dyslexics studied by Eden et al. (1996), who all showed deficits in motion sensitivity, were drawn from a group among whom the majority were known to have normal leftward planum asymmetry (Rumsey et al., 1997a). It thus seems unlikely that there is any relation between magno deficits and planum symmetry, although according to Stein (1994) "one can speculate that magnocellular input and lateralisation characteristics are causally connected; in other words that the favoured access of magnocellular input to the left hemisphere is what causes it to become the language hemisphere and the planum temporale to be larger on that side" (p. 247).

While there are to my knowledge no data directly related to Stein's suggestion, a study investigating cell size asymmetry in the visual cortex is of some interest in the present context. On the assumption that layer IVCα of primary visual cortex receives input from magnocellular layers of the LGN, while layer IVCβ receives parvocellular input, it was anticipated by Jenner et al. (1999) that cells in layer IVCα of dyslexic brains would differ from those of control brains while cells in layer IVCβ would not. Using the same five brains from dyslexics as used in the study by Livingstone et al. (1991), Jenner et al. (1999) reported that over all cortical layers combined there was no hemispheric asymmetry in mean cross-sectional neuronal area of the primary visual cortex (V1 or Brodmann's area 17) in dyslexic brains, unlike the leftward asymmetry seen in control brains. The hemisphere-by-group interaction was statistically significant. Subsequent analyses suggested that this pattern occurred for both layers IVCα and IVCβ. On the other hand, within-hemisphere comparisons in each (small) group revealed no

significant difference between dyslexic and control brains for either hemisphere. Using a laterality coefficient to control for individual differences in brain size, asymmetry in cell size (as opposed to mean cross-sectional area) was compared between dyslexics and non-dyslexics. Again, non-dyslexics were significantly more biased towards the left than were dyslexics over all cortical layers combined and in layer IVCα alone but not apparently in layer IVCβ. Furthermore, there was no significant difference in cell size for either hemisphere between dyslexic and non-dyslexic brains. The differences between dyslexic and non-dyslexic brains were interpreted in terms of the size (rather than the packing density) of neurones, non-dyslexics being said to have larger neurones in the left than the right hemisphere and dyslexics having similar sized neurones in the two hemispheres.

While the histological findings from the dyslexic brains are interesting, a note of caution is warranted. The five brains used formed part of the series of brains that were used in previous studies of the planum temporale (Galaburda et al., 1985; Humphreys et al., 1990), lateral (Livingstone et al., 1991) and medial (Galaburda & Livingstone, 1993) geniculate nuclei and cerebellum (Finch et al., 2002). I have drawn attention elsewhere (Beaton, 1997) to uncertainties regarding the diagnosis of dyslexia and other questions with regard to these brains (see Chapter 9). Be that as it may, Jenner et al. (1999) were careful to acknowledge that the differences which they report between dyslexic and control individuals might reflect different reading experience rather than be a cause of poor reading.

From this review of the magnocellular deficit hypothesis, it might be thought that researchers are interested only in relatively low-level or early visual processing by dyslexics (see, for example, Kruk & Willows, 2001). While this is true of the bulk of current research into visual functions in dyslexia, a recent report (Lewis & Frick, 1999) that dyslexics are impaired (but see Williams & Bologna, 1985) in grouping non-letter stimuli according to the Gestalt principles of continuation and similarity is likely to promote further interest in higher-level perceptual processes as they apply to reading. These include visual search (see Casco & Prunetti, 1996) and grouping or graphemic parsing strategies (Bock, Monk, & Hulme, 1993; Joubert & Lecours, 2000; Rey, Ziegler, & Jacobs, 2000). The ease with which fluent reading is accomplished by skilled adult readers should not blind us to the complexities of the cognitive operations involved. These include visual as well as phonological processes. The latter have dominated research in recent years; perhaps the next decade will see an increase in studies devoted to greater understanding of the former.

13

Concluding Comments

So far in this book, I have reviewed a large number of findings obtained using a wide range of methodologies. In this final chapter, I identify some of the themes and issues that arise from this research.

By and large, the scientific literature refers either to poor readers or to dyslexics without distinguishing between these categories of poor reader unless that is the principal aim of the investigation. Consequently, a central and unresolved issue concerns how developmental dyslexia should be conceptualized.

WHO IS DYSLEXIC?

Although it is usually assumed that a low level of cognitive ability is not the cause of reading problems, it is common to exclude from research samples of poor readers those individuals whose IQ is much below average. The vast bulk of research, therefore, applies to children (and adults) who in most cases will meet a discrepancy definition of dyslexia. Such a definition requires evidence of a marked disparity between measured intellectual ability on the one hand and an individual's level of reading and/or spelling on the other. Criticisms of discrepancy definitions of dyslexia were dis-

cussed in Chapter 1. Perhaps in part because of these criticisms, it is becoming more common in practice, if not in research, to ignore IQ, or a discrepancy between IQ and reading level, in deciding whether someone is in need of special educational provision. The assumption, usually tacit but sometimes explicit, is that if there are no differences in reading-related cognitive processes between discrepancy-defined dyslexics and those poor readers who do not show any discrepancy between their actual reading and that predicted (for example, on the basis of a regression equation), then there is no reason to regard these two classes of poor reader as importantly different from each other. Consequently, there is in some quarters an increasing unwillingness to use the term dyslexia, which, it is feared, might lead to resources being made available to some children but not to others.

While the aim of ensuring equal and fair treatment of all children with literacy problems, regardless of their intellectual ability, is clearly laudable, it does not necessarily follow that a profound discrepancy between intellectual ability and reading and spelling attainment is of no significance whatsoever. In today's knowledge-based society, it is of increasing rather than diminishing importance that individuals constantly acquire new information, much of which will come from the written word. It does not seem to me improbable that the greater one's intellectual ability, the greater will be the likely need to acquire such information in the course of work that one find's fulfilling. It follows that the greater the discrepancy between a person's intellect and their ability to acquire new information by reading, or to communicate their own ideas in writing, the greater will be the handicap imposed by difficulties in the sphere of written language.

This is not to argue that our tools for assessing intellectual ability are perfect (they are not, but that is a separate issue); rather, it is to recognize that the practical consequences of poor reading and spelling are likely to differ as a function of what has traditionally been termed intelligence. If this is true, then it is not being inequitable to argue that a discrepancy between IQ and reading is relevant to how the child (or adult) with literacy difficulties might best be supported. This does not necessarily mean, of course, that a discrepancy should be part of the *definition* of dyslexia. However, one possible advantage of carrying out an IQ assessment is that it may show a profile on the different sub-scales that is of diagnostic and/or prognostic significance. For example, low scores on the Arithmetic, Coding, Information Processing and Digit Span sub-scales of the Wechsler Intelligence Scale-Children (WISC), in comparison with high scores on the remaining sub-scales (producing the so-called Acid profile) might, along with other information, be highly suggestive of a phonological processing and/or memory deficit. Rather than overall IQ, it is the precise pattern of strengths and weaknesses, together with information about reading and writing skills, that is relevant to a diagnosis and, possibly, to remediation.

Two further points can be made with regard to abandoning discrepancy definitions of dyslexia. First, although research to date has not revealed conspicuous cognitive differences between discrepancy-defined and garden-variety poor readers (other than that implicit in the categorization of these two groups), this does not mean that theoretically interesting differences between the groups will not be found if the discrepancy used is that between, say, listening comprehension and

literacy level, rather than between overall IQ and attainment in reading and writing. Even if overall IQ scores and listening comprehension generally correlate well, leading one to expect little effect of substituting listening comprehension for IQ, the size of the correlation is likely to be attenuated for dyslexics. A discrepancy between listening comprehension and reading level, therefore, might have some discriminative or predictive power, possibly in combination with IQ if not alone. In this context, incidentally, it is instructive to reproduce an observation made by a 10-year-old boy quoted by Orton (1925): "Mother says there is something about me because you could read anything to me and I'd git it right away, but if I read it myself I couldn't git it" (p. 593). Parents regard a speech versus reading comprehension discrepancy as relevant to a diagnosis of dyslexia, even if "clever folks" do not.

The second point to be made is that despite the lack of relevant cognitive differences between discrepancy-defined dyslexics and other poor readers reported in most studies, this has not been a universal finding (see Chapter 1). Moreover, some biological research suggests that neuroanatomic profiles are related to whether or not there is an IQ-reading discrepancy (see below). Furthermore, at least one study has found differences in auditory sensory processing between groups of normal school children categorized in terms of their non-verbal ability and literacy level (Talcott et al., 2002). These findings suggest that it may be premature to dismiss overall intellectual ability as being in no way related to other variables that might discriminate between different groups of poor reader.

The significance of IQ is not the only issue relevant to the question of how dyslexia should be conceptualized. For many years, the field was dominated by exclusionary definitions according to which someone was regarded as dyslexic if their reading was inexplicably poor in relation to their general intellectual ability. The keyword here is "inexplicably". Provided there was no known organic, neurological, psychiatric, emotional, educational, motivational or other potential cause of the low level of literacy, then a "diagnosis" of dyslexia was deemed appropriate. It remains true that in most, if not all, samples of poor readers collected for research purposes, individuals with a background suggestive of medical or socio-educational problems are specifically excluded. Although this can be justified in the interest of reducing heterogeneity in the sample under investigation, the utility of this procedure for practical, as opposed to research, purposes is less clear.

An argument can be made that exclusionary criteria are unnecessarily restrictive. Two examples from my own experience help to illustrate this. One case concerns a highly intelligent student, the daughter of qualified professional parents who have always provided a stimulating and supportive family background. I shall refer to the student as Ellie, although this is not her real name. At nursery and early primary school, Ellie was always well towards the top of her class and had no problems in learning to read and to write or to do simple arithmetic. At the age of 5½ years, Ellie caught chicken pox and suffered two epileptic convulsions in association with a high fever. It is assumed that she suffered from an encephalitic episode caused by the varicella-zoster virus. Recovery was medically normal but from this time on Ellie experienced great difficulty in reading, writing and arithmetic. Although showing slow but gradual improvement, she experienced persistent difficulty over her entire school career. Despite this, her motivation and academic achievements were such that she was accepted on to a degree course, which she is currently pursuing. There is a large discrepancy between her IQ and her attainment in reading and spelling. On standard IQ tests, Ellie has consistently scored in the superior range. Her spelling ability was recently re-assessed (when she was 18 years of age) and said to be approximately equivalent to that of the average 11-year-old. Her mathematical skills remain weak. Ellie's phonological skills have never been particularly poor and she has no conspicuous impairment in verbal short-term memory. Her literacy skills may be characterized as showing the pattern of surface dyslexia and dysgraphia. Within this context, there is nothing to distinguish her reading and writing performance from that of other poor readers who

might be (or have been) termed developmental surface dyslexics. Given that there is no history of poor reading within the family, that Ellie's twin brother never experienced any problems of this kind, that Ellie was clearly performing well above the level of her peers before her illness, it seems reasonable to describe Ellie as a case of acquired developmental surface dyslexia/dysgraphia. Applying traditional exclusionary criteria, however, would deny Ellie a diagnosis of developmental dyslexia on the basis of the presumed encephalitic episode.

The second case which I believe illustrates difficulty with rigid application of traditional exclusionary criteria concerns a young lady whom I shall call Helen. After a difficult upbringing, during which she appears to have lacked intellectual stimulation, Helen and her sisters were adopted by a professional couple who have since provided a loving, secure and stimulating home environment. At the time of her adoption at 9 years of age, Helen was said to have a restricted vocabulary, as did her sisters. For example, they did not know the names of common colours. However, when I visited their home some years later when Helen was 16 years old, their vocabulary was not noticeably impoverished. In conversation Helen and her younger sister were talkative and friendly, although both showed some slight abnormalities of articulation. This was more noticeable on formal testing of nonword repetition. Both girls were poor on tasks of phoneme deletion and exchange as well as in digit span. Reading and spelling were severely impaired. The picture was that of phonological dyslexia/dysgraphia. I did not formally assess Helen's IQ but my guess, and that of her adoptive parents, was that her score would be about average for her age. Reading and spelling were well below what might have been expected for someone of this IQ. In terms of classical exclusionary criteria, Helen would be denied a diagnosis of developmental dyslexia on the basis of her early family circumstances. Yet the pattern of performance exhibited by Helen was not conspicuously different from that of other developmentally dyslexic children. It is likely (but cannot be proved) that Helen's reduced literacy skills can be attributed, at least in part, to her early upbringing (and perhaps in part to recurrent bouts of "glue ear" from which she apparently suffered).

The cases of both Ellie and Helen illustrate persistent difficulties in learning to read and to spell that are not obviously different in kind from those of other children for whom no conspicuous cause of their dyslexia has been identified. But lack of a conspicuous cause does not imply absence of a cause. It does not seem defensible to me to apply the label developmental dyslexia only to those cases for which no obvious cause can be found, but to exclude those cases where we can hazard a strong guess as to the likely causal agent(s).

A point related to the issue of who should be called dyslexic concerns the range of cognitive impairments to which the term dyslexia should be applied. Some people have argued that dyslexia is "nothing but" poor reading and spelling (see Chapter 1). An alternative position argues that dyslexia is not simply poor reading or spelling alone but rather is a syndrome or pattern of difficulties. One alternative to defining dyslexia by exclusion, then, is to employ inclusionary criteria. Other criteria that could be invoked might include difficulties in speech perception and/or production, motor problems, poor coordination, slowness in naming objects or in distinguishing left from right, and so on (see Chapters 5 and 6). This would correspond to a clinical "definition" or "feel" of dyslexia. One might take the view that to be classed as dyslexic, a poor reader should be reading not only at a level below that to be expected on the basis of some agreed set of criteria (age, educational provision, IQ or whatever), but should *in addition* have either a phonological deficit and/or be deficient in one or more of a specified set of other skills. This seems to be the position that in practice is implicitly or explicitly adopted when children (or adults) are assessed by many (but by no means all) professionals in the field. But what is one then to make of a person who has the requisite profile *except* that he or she reads at a satisfactory level? Is such a person "dyslexic"? And is such an approach really any better than one that simply regards all poor readers (by whatever criterion) as dyslexic? What is the justification for distinguishing between poor readers on the one hand and "clinically" defined dyslexics (who have additional deficits) on the other?

It is an empirical point whether dyslexics defined in terms of "additional" criteria differ in any theoretically meaningful way from "non-dyslexic" poor readers. Yet, to my knowledge, no-one has compared "clinically" defined dyslexics with impaired readers defined purely in terms of a low level of literacy skill. To be sure, poor readers who do, and those who do not, exhibit some discrepancy between reading skill and their level of cognitive performance more generally have been compared between themselves (see Chapter 1), but neither has been compared with "clinically" defined dyslexics. It might turn out, for example, that the latter show more severe or less tractable reading difficulties than other groups.

The question of how different categories of poor readers should be defined is not purely semantic. The literature on both cognitive and biological aspects of dyslexia is replete with effects that are found for some members of the participant group or population sampled but not for others. It is important to know whether such diversity can be linked to an individuals's particular characteristics. One such characteristic, likely to be more intensively investigated in the future, is a participant's attentional performance. My guess is that it will prove highly relevant to differences between sub-groups of poor readers (see, for example, Rudel, 1985; Talcott et al., 2002).

WHAT CAUSES DYSLEXIA?

Questions of definition and nomenclature are bound up with issues of causation. What is required, in my view, is not a definition of dyslexia based on the absence of any identifiable cause(s), but a theory of causation, at either the cognitive or biological level. If one knew for certain that X and Y were (jointly or independently) a cause (or causes) of relatively poor literacy skill in any individual case, then classification according to cause would provide a theoretically justified (though not necessarily useful) means of differentiating between different groups of poor readers. From this perspective, it is useful to distinguish between distal and proximal causes (Jackson & Coltheart, 2001). A proximal cause is the link in a causal chain immediately before the event (such as poor reading of nonwords) that one wishes to explain. This will be at a cognitive level, but not all cognitive causes are proximal—they might be distal. Poor nonword reading might be due to inadequate knowledge of letters, the proximal cause, but this might in turn be due to poor phonemic awareness, a distal cause. This may in turn be attributed to a biological, say genetic, factor. In saying this, it needs to be clear that many, if not most, of the cognitive and biological factors identified as being related to poor reading by the research discussed in this book can not yet be attributed an unequivocal causal role, proximal or distal. Rather, they have the staus of correlates of impaired reading performance (see Bishop, 2002).

The view from cognition

From a cognitive perspective, most people would probably argue that impaired phonemic awareness is a core, perhaps *the* core, deficit in dyslexia. While this phonological deficit hypothesis (discussed in Chapter 4) enjoys considerable currency, it is far from clear how the fundamental deficit should be characterized. As a consequence of the findings obtained by Morais and colleagues showing that non-literate adults are impaired at deleting or adding phonemes (phones) to spoken words (and especially nonwords), it is usually conceded that there is a reciprocal relationship between reading and phonemic awareness rather than that phoneme awareness itself derives from reading. However, some children appear not to realize that a spoken word's onset and rime may be uncoupled, or that the final or initial phoneme can be deleted from a word, until they have at least some ability to read or have received some minimal level of reading instruction. In general, performance on phoneme deletion and phoneme synthesis tasks seems to develop in parallel with reading, suggesting that these skills fail to develop without appropriate instruction and experience of print. If so, then the argument that poor phonological awareness

causes poor reading is more complex than is usually supposed. As Morais et al. (1979) noted: "it is not right to say that awareness of the phonetic structure of speech is a precondition for starting to learn to read and write. The precondition for the acquisition of these skills is not phonetic awareness as such but the cognitive capacity for 'becoming aware' during the first stages of the learning process" (p. 330).

Certainly, phoneme segmentation deficits alone cannot account for all manifestations of phonological difficulty in dyslexic children (Landerl & Wimmer, 2000) or adults. Dutch dyslexic children experience problems on phoneme deletion tasks but these rarely persist into adulthood (de Gelder & Vroomen, 1991) as they often do for dyslexic readers of the more opaque English orthography (Bruck, 1992; Gottardo et al., 1997). Despite their lack of explicit segmentation problems, Dutch adult dyslexics remain poor at nonword reading. Similarly, research with Austrian dyslexic children suggests that although by the end of the third grade at school they have mastered the relatively consistent correspondence that exists between letters and sounds in German, they too are still very slow at reading nonwords. As with acquired phonological dyslexia (Beauveis & Dérouesné 1985; Dérouesné & Beauvois, 1979), such findings imply that "selective impairment of nonword reading can occur for reasons other than phonological impairment" (Coltheart, 1996, p. 755) and suggest that one should distinguish between explicit phonological awareness and other phonological abilities (Fowler, 1991; Hulme & Snowling, 1992; Wagner et al., 1994; Windfuhr & Snowling, 2001).

One view is that tasks such as verbal short-term memory (see Chapter 4) and confrontation or serial naming tasks (Chapter 5) make direct or unconscious use of the phonological representations underlying performance, whereas phoneme or syllable segmentation tasks require conscious awareness of the phonological forms of words. For example, a child may be able to indicate that he or she knows the initial sound of a word or nonword yet perform poorly on an initial-phoneme deletion task (Bruck & Treiman, 1990). It might also be relevant that most phonological awareness tasks are more cognitively complex than the task of identifying individual phonemes.

Fowler noted that:

> There is growing evidence that the phonological problems of poor readers often extend beyond the level of awareness ... Memory, perception, articulation, and lexical access have been implicated in reading disability; all ultimately depend on phonological representations, yet none obviously requires phoneme awareness ... a failure to gain access to phonemic segments is associated not with general metacognitive inadequacies, but with a host of other subtle phonological deficits, involving the formation, retrieval, and maintenance of phonological representations. Although the difficulties have been attributed variously to "weak", "fragile", or "underspecified" representations, arrived at via "inefficient" phonological processing, there has been little attempt to further define these terms or to reconcile these individual differences within the current theory of phonological development.
>
> (Fowler, 1991, pp. 101–102).

More recently, however, Ramus (2001) attempted to analyse the level of phonological representation that is likely to be impaired in dyslexics. He argues that a sub-lexical (rather than lexical) deficit is the most likely locus of impairment in that it can explain the deficits that have been reported in a wide range of speech-related tasks, including, as the research reviewed in Chapters 4, 5 and 6 of this monograph demonstrates, short-term or working memory, meta-phonological awareness, speech perception and phonological learning, as well as reading. A deficit purely at the lexical level would have difficulty explaining impairment in the orthographic–phonological conversion route and hence in explaining why most dyslexics find nonword reading difficult. On the other hand, argues Ramus, a deficit at a sub-lexical level (itself not a single level) would lead to difficulty in orthographic–phonological conversion, in building up a phonological lexicon and in a range of

other tasks. Note, incidentally, that phonology may be impaired on the input side, the output side or both. Griffiths and Snowling (2001) argue that it is in retrieval processes operating on phonological representations that dyslexics are impaired.

Ramus (2001) notes: "Perhaps the greatest paradox of the phonological deficit hypothesis is that it should predict that dyslexics have trouble speaking and understanding speech, since these involve both lexical and sub-lexical representations" (p. 205). He acknowledges that:

> Dyslexics do indeed have subtle difficulties in speech perception and production, but they are mild enough not to be noticeable in real-life situations. Certainly, it may happen that the phonological deficit is severe enough to provoke noticeable language difficulties. But then it is likely that the child will be characterized as having a specific-language impairment, rather than just dyslexia.
>
> (Ramus, 2001, p. 205)

I disagree with Ramus. I submit that the oral deficits of some dyslexics *are* noticeable in real life. How specific, then, is the "specific learning difficulty", developmental dyslexia? Should it be regarded as separate from other developmental disorders of language?

Impairments of (many) dyslexics in object naming, in verbal memory and in fluency of speech output on their own do not justify a diagnosis of specific language impairment, but in cases where these are allied to sufficiently severe syntactic and/or semantic problems they may do so. The nature of any fundamental phonological deficit in dyslexia is therefore bound up with questions of differential diagnosis. It is likely that at least two independent factors contribute to overall efficiency of reading: phonological ability and general verbal skill. Consideration of phonological factors to the exclusion of semantic and syntactic factors (see Chapter 5) might be to take an artificially restricted view of dyslexic difficulties. Dyslexia and specific language impairment have several features in common. Any decision as to whether they are "lumped" together or "split" may be entirely arbitrary (which is not to assert that dyslexia is simply a less *severe* form of specific language impairment).

Whether, and if so how, dyslexia differs from other developmental disorders of language will, I believe, be a question that receives considerable attention over the next few years. So, too, will be the issue of specifying the nature of the phonological deficit, since both its exact nature and its functional locus within a fully articulated cognitive model of reading have yet to be clearly established. Not that all dyslexic deficits relate to phonology. The research reviewed in this monograph suggests that there is a "surface" type of dyslexia (see Chapter 4) that does not involve a phonological deficit (at least at the level of segmental phonological analysis). Compared with the vast amount of research relevant to impaired phonological processing, there has been relatively little work concerned with how orthographic (whole-word) representations are established in learning to read. Conversely, little is known about how this process is compromised in cases of surface dyslexia. Further detailed research of this sub-type affords many opportunities for future investigation.

How should research proceed?

At present, the dual-route model discussed in Chapter 2 provides a useful framework for exploring reading difficulties, though some have argued that it does not provide an appropriate developmental context. Nor, argue others, do box-and-arrow models of this kind present sufficiently well-specified accounts as to how the different components operate. It is, I submit, counterproductive to oppose box-and-arrow models with connectionist-type models—the two approaches are not antithetical but complementary. Before applying a fine-grained approach—as taken by theorists of a connectionist-type persuasion—to any particular cognitive task, one must know what there is to be explained or modelled in the first place. In my view, models of the dual-route variety are a useful first step in conceptualizing the different skills that underlie normal reading and that are impaired in cases of dyslexia.

Efficient reading and spelling depend upon a range of component skills. It is therefore to be expected that a number of different deficits can bring about impairment of literacy skills. Cognitive models that specify the different components of reading, their mode of operation and the relationships between them, have been employed with conspicuous success in investigations of reading impairments resulting from brain damage. Such cognitive neuropsychological models have been applied in only a few (admittedly unusual) cases of developmental dyslexia (see Temple, 1997a, 1997b). I would like to see this kind of approach, as opposed to the correlational group studies approach, adopted far more widely in research into the nature and functional loci of developmental dyslexic deficits. As testimony to the potential value of a model-driven approach, one need only think of how frequently, and to what effect, nonwords have been employed as stimuli in experimental investigations of dyslexia. Arguably, this would never have occurred without the guiding principle of a "route" or pathway specialized for processing novel letter strings yet "beginning readers encounter novel words on almost every page they read" (Gough et al., 1992, p. 35).

I am far from being the first to advocate taking the same approach to developmental as to acquired forms of dyslexia. Ellis (1979) expressed himself as being "of the firm opinion that real advances in the understanding of developmental reading difficulties will occur only if the same approach is adopted" (p. 418). This view was rejected by Jorm (1979b), who considered "a case study approach unwise unless the subject population is such a small one that only single cases can be obtained" (p. 432). More than 20 years on, the group study approach has prevailed. There are, however, a number of arguments favouring a single-case study approach. As the pros and cons of intensive single-case versus group studies have been argued in a more general arena, there is no need for these to be reiterated here. Suffice it to say that the practice of averaging scores over what is universally admitted to be a heterogeneous collection of dyslexic individuals may obscure important differences between them and the means, perhaps, will be representative of very few of them.

I believe that a cognitive neuropsychological approach would prove helpful to practitioners as well as researchers, since it has the great merit of drawing attention to the individual nature of dyslexics' difficulties. More than 40 years ago, Vernon (1962) recommended the study of individual cases of reading difficulty to ascertain "exactly what it is that each backward reader is unable to do or has failed to learn . . . that is to say, we must study these children as individuals, and the peculiar nature of their disability" (p. 143). Fractionating developmental dyslexia according to impairments in particular components of a model of reading arguably offers a way around the definitional impasse imposed by certain traditional practices and ways of thinking. While this runs the risk of leading to a proliferation of "subtypes" of dyslexia, since impairment to different components of the cognitive architecture underlying reading may theoretically produce different "symptoms", it focuses attention on measurable features of impaired and intact function rather than on exclusionary aspects of reading disability. In short, a cognitive neuropsychology of developmental dyslexia would be more productive in the long run than the practice of simply attaching the label "dyslexia". As Temple (1997b) put it: "cognitive neuropsychology applied to the developmental disorders can play an important role in constraining the viable theories of normal developmental and cognitive psychology" (p. 327)

In reviewing the contributions of authors to a special issue of the journal *Cognition*, Bertelson (1986) wrote: "The problem of possible biological roots of reading disorders is one that none of the contributors to the present issue addresses . . . The question is rather one of research strategy. We need a good description of reading performance at its own behavioral level before the relation of that description to aspects belonging to other levels of description can be fruitfully examined" (p. 5). It is my firm belief that a developmental cognitive neuropsychology of reading will provide the best description and that the time is now ripe for a convergence of biological and cognitive approaches to understanding dyslexia.

As an example of convergence between cognitive and biological approaches to reading, consider a neuro-imaging study by Simos et al. (2002). Using magnetic source imaging, these investigators linked sub-lexical (assembled) phonological processing to activation of the posterior area of the left superior temporal gyrus (Wernicke's area) but not to activation of the middle temporal gyrus. Conversely, exception word reading was said to be associated with activation of the posterior area of the middle temporal gyrus on the left side but not with activation of the superior temporal gryrus. Although the double-dissociation was not quite as clear-cut as this implies, the findings exemplify the kind of approach to linking cognitive models with specific brain areas that modern technology makes possible (once inconsistencies in findings from different studies are resolved!). From the above model, one would predict that dyslexics with difficulty in reading nonwords will show a different pattern of activation from controls in the superior temporal gyrus, whereas surface dyslexics will show an unusual pattern of middle temporal activation.

The view from biology

The past 15 years or so have seen a continuing increase in research effort aimed at identifying the biological underpinnings of dyslexia. The second part of this monograph reviewed a large number of studies relating to different anatomical structures and systems, which, at one time or another, have been said to distinguish poor readers from controls. Heterogeneity in the symptomatology of reading difficulties is mirrored in the number of anatomical structures and brain areas that have been identified as being in some way involved in dyslexia. These include the retina (Chapter 11), cerebellum (Chapters 6 and 10), corpus callosum (Chapter 9) and posterior cortex of the left hemisphere (Chapter 10), as well as the magnocellular division of the visual system (Chapter 12) and perhaps of other sensory modalities as well.

Since most individuals with optical defects successfully learn to read, retinal factors can probably be discounted as contributing significantly to most cases of dyslexia. The cerebellar deficit hypothesis cannot be so easily dismissed.

The arguments supporting the idea that some dyslexic symptoms are related to a deficiency in cerebellar function are not overwhelming, but they are sufficiently strong that one should keep an open mind (Beaton, 2002). However, to my knowledge, no-one has reported acquired alexia to occur as a consequence solely of damage to the cerebellum (but see Moretti et al., 2002 and Chapter 10); in contrast, focal cortical lesions may produce frank dyslexic and/or dysgraphic symptoms. Nor have cerebellar lesions been reported to interfere with segmental language skills, impairment of which, according to some authors, constitutes the core deficit of dyslexia. This suggests that the cerebellum is not directly involved in central aspects of dyslexia, although conceivably it is more critical for the early development of reading skills than for their subsequent maintenance.

Perhaps the cerebellum can be related more readily to peripheral or secondary dyslexic deficits rather than to core deficits. It is well-known that dyslexia and dyspraxia (developmental in-co-ordination syndrome) often co-occur and it is in relation to deficits of fine and gross movements that links between dyslexia and cerebellar functions might be most apparent. Certainly, motor deficits are problematic for any theory implicating purely phonological problems in the aetiology of dyslexia. However, as with other structures putatively related to dyslexia, one must be cautious in viewing an "impaired" cerebellum as anything other than a correlate, as opposed to a cause, of dyslexic symptoms (Bishop, 2002).

Whatever the linguistic status of the cerebellum, there is little doubt that it has an important role to play in certain aspects of temporal processing, especially in relation to the control of movement. It has been hypothesized recently that the cerebellum is specifically involved in generating time-specific signals predicting the outcome of movement of the eyes and limbs (Miall & Reckess, 2002), where discontinuous rather than continuous smooth movements are involved (Spencer, Zelaznik, Diedrichsen, & Ivry, 2003). Efficient timing is crucial to accurate motor coordination and control (for recent papers, see the special issue of *Brain and Cognition*, Volume 48, Number 1, 2002). However, the similarity

between the temporal deficits found following cerebellar lesions and those observed in dyslexia is not always clear. To say that some dyslexics have problems in certain aspects of temporal processing (see Chapter 6) and that damage to the cerebellum also produces temporal problems may not in fact be to say very much if the problems are of two very different kinds. Much of the work on temporal processing in dyslexia discussed in Chapter 6 has involved the perception or discrimination of short temporal intervals or rapidly occurring events. This might be viewed as investigating input variables in dyslexia. Studies of timing functions of the cerebellum, on the other hand, have tended to concern themselves with motor control (but see Ackermann, Gräber, Hertrich, & Daum, 1997, 1999), that is, ostensibly with output factors.

It has been difficult to replicate some of the so-called "cerebellar" effects that have been reported for dyslexic participants, such as difficulty in carrying out concurrent balancing and counting tasks. On the other hand, deficits in various bimanual motor tasks have consistently been reported to occur in dyslexia. It is not clear that these relate in any straightforward way to those occurring in the context of cerebellar damage, although I am inclined to think that there is a connection (see Beaton, 2002). A different structure, the corpus callosum, has therefore provided an alternative focus for investigators interested in bimanual motor deficits in dyslexia (see Chapter 9). The link between the callosum and movement of the hands again seems to depend upon timing control processes. Kennerley et al. (2002) used a bimanual tapping task with three commissurotomy patients. The patients' hands were temporally coupled when the task was intermittent but became uncoupled when the movements were continuous. This points to a role for the callosum in at least some aspects of timing control of the two hands. Are impaired motor skills in some dyslexics due to an impaired callosal transfer system that also manifests itself in poor reading?

It is often said that Dejerine (1892) was the first to draw attention to the role of the corpus callosum in reading. In fact, he attributed little to this structure, tending rather to emphasize the importance of the disconnection, between the angular gyrus on the left and visual input from both the left hemisphere and the intact right hemisphere, produced by damage to the left occipital lobe of his patient, Monsieur C. Given the functions of the corpus callosum as revealed by the classic and more recent commissurotomy studies (Gazzaniga, 2000), it strikes me as unlikely that this structure is crucially involved in the core elements of dyslexic symptomatology. In saying this, I am mindful of the work of Temple and her colleagues on phonological deficits in acallosal individuals (see Chapter 9). However, there is no single mechanism underlying agenesis of the corpus callosum and the condition is often accompanied by a wide range of other abnormalities (Lassonde & Sauerwein, 2003). In my view, there is little reason to suppose that the language-related deficits that have been reported are caused solely by absence of the corpus callosum.

Some authors have claimed that the experience of reading and writing influences callosal morphology (Castro-Caldas et al., 1999; Habib, Robichon, Chanoine, Démonet, Frith, & Frith, 2000). It is unlikely, however, that the eventual size or shape of the corpus callosum is affected only by environmental factors. Genetic factors together with pre-natal concentrations of gonadal hormone (see Moffat et al., 1997) probably influence its growth, possibly along with that of other brain systems that are related to reading.

For a good number of years, researchers investigating the biological underpinnings of dyslexia (and cerebral laterality) were motivated by the hormonal theory developed by Geschwind and his collaborators (see Chapter 8), although interest in the theory has declined noticeably in recent years. Perhaps it is inevitable when any theory constructed on a grand scale falls into relative obscurity that many of the associated ideas instantly lose their popularity. Yet it does not seem to me too far-fetched to retain in some form the notion that events occurring during critical periods of gestation are causally linked to a range of neurodevelopmental disorders. As Behan and Geschwind (1985b) point out, "the intratuterine environment plays a major role in many cases in determining the course of development of the nervous system and other bodily systems" (p. 17). Evidence consistent with some factor relevant to early uterine experience was presented in the introduction to the second part of this book.

I do not know of any research that has attempted to link direct measurement of uterine hormonal concentrations with dyslexia in later life (I was once refused funding for such an investigation). To be sure, the work of Grimshaw and her collaborators mentioned in Chapter 8 is a start but these investigators were unable to carry out a large-scale study and were not explicitly concerned with dyslexia.

It may be that all component skills relevant to reading and spelling, and the biological factors that underpin them, are continuously and independently distributed throughout the population in a Gaussian or normal fashion. Neurodevelopmental disorders such as dyslexia probably develop from a random combination of a number of biological risk factors, including gestational factors. Each in isolation may be of relatively slight influence, but together they substantially increase susceptibility to the disorder being manifest, particularly in the presence of environmental risks. Perhaps undue difficulty in learning to read is experienced when an individual is at the tail end of "too many" distributions.

The original version of the hormonal hypothesis attempted to account for a raised incidence of left-handedness among learning-disabled children, including dyslexics. Despite increasing scepticism in some quarters, I am convinced that there is some link between those factors that determine handedness and those that provide some of the neural underpinnings of speech and hence reading. Interest in handedness in relation to reading and dyslexia has a long history (see Chapter 8). Research from my laboratory and elsewhere points to a strong link between hand skill asymmetry and reading ability in unselected school children. Whatever influences handedness also seems to affect reading (see Annett, 2002).

Most researchers appear to agree (but see Bishop, 2001) that there is a genetic influence on handedness (see Beaton, 2003, for an overview of theories of handedness). From the findings reviewed in Chapter 7, it is clear that there is also a genetic factor at work in many, perhaps most, cases of developmental dyslexia. At present, we do not know the mode of operation of the relevant gene(s) or how genetic and environmental factors interact in individual cases to produce problems in the development of literacy. As Olson (2002) puts it: "When we do find genes that account for some percentage of the group reading deficit, there is much further work to be done to understand how those genes influence brain development and activity in ways that make reading and other related skills difficult to learn" (Olson, 2002, p. 156).

Genes may adversely affect hormonal secretion, gyral development, hemispheric asymmetry, callosal morphology, cortical and cerebellar function and any of a host of other biological systems, but there is no need for unallayed pessimism. Estimates of the strength of a genetic influence on reading (for example, a heritability coefficient) apply to groups of people, not to individuals. Moreover, different samples or populations of participants give rise to different estimates. Olson (2002) notes that the celebrated Colorado study excludes a particularly difficult school region and that "If that environmental range had been broader (e.g. by including the Denver schools), it is likely that our estimates of genetic influence would have been lower, and the influence from shared family and school environment would have been higher" (p. 149). This points up the fact that heritability estimates apply only to a particular sample of people at a particular time in a particular environment. They say nothing about the ways in which genes and environment interact in the development of processes such as reading. Gayán and Olson (2001) point out that "It is important to recognize the possibility that at least part of the genetic influence on reading deficits may be through differences in environmental selection, and this may have implications for remediation" (p. 504). People who have a genetically based difficulty in learning to read may choose to read less than normally reading children from the same environment. Indeed, Gayán and Olson (2001) give the hypothetical example of two dizygotic twins, one of whom has a genetically based reading difficulty while the other does not. This might lead them to choose very different levels of exposure to print and reading practice even within the same home or school. As Gayán and Olson (2001) point out, "Evidence for genetic influences on deficits in reading and related skills should not discourage our best efforts toward environmental intervention and remediation" (p. 504).

The hormonal hypothesis of cerebral lateralization was intended to account not only for an excess of left-handedness in dyslexia, but also for the supposed absence of left–right asymmetry of the planum temporale. This area of the brain has received a good deal of attention in relation to dyslexia, as was discussed in Chapter 9. Although much of the work reviewed can be criticized on methodological grounds, and planum asymmetry may well have been over-emphasized in the past (Beaton, 1997; Habib & Robichon, 2003), it remains possible that asymmetry of the planum temporale, or other anatomic asymmetry, is related in some way or other to verbal ability (Eckert & Leonard, 2003) and to asymmetry at a behavioural level.

It is also possible that different neuro-anatomical or neuro-physiological profiles (see Chapters 9 and 10) will eventually distinguish not only dyslexics from normal readers but different dyslexic sub-types from each other or those with dyslexia defined in one way from those with the condition defined according to different criteria. Phonological awareness scores have been related to the size and asymmetry of the planum temporale in young children (Leonard et al., 1996). Perhaps dyslexics with primarily phonological difficulties differ in subtle aspects of cerebral (or cerebellar) morphology from those whose difficulties are less severe in this regard. It is equally possible that dyslexics with "additional" difficulties (perhaps in the semantic or syntactic domains or involving motor control or attention) can be differentiated neuro-anatomically or neuro-physiologically from those whose problems are restricted purely to reading and spelling. Eckert and Leonard (2003) suggest that anomalous asymmetry of the planum temporale (that is, rightward asymmetry or symmetry) is characteristic of language-impaired individuals who do not show a discrepancy between reading level and verbal ability or IQ, whereas anomalous planum (a)symmetry does not predict dyslexia in individuals who do show such a discrepancy. Summarizing their own research and that of others, Eckert and Leonard (2003) state: "We feel the congruity of the anatomical evidence from three different samples suggests that specific (discrepant) reading disability and reading disability associated with oral language impairment have different anatomical phenotypes" (p. 670).

Chicken or egg?

Examination of Einstein's brain led Witelson, Kigar, and Harvey (1999) to suggest that "variation in specific cognitive functions may be associated with the structure of brain regions mediating those functions" (p. 2152). Seen in this light, the idea that discrepancy-defined dyslexics might have a different physiological or neuro-anatomical signature from other poor readers may not be so very far-fetched. It seems plausible to assume that as a result of gene–environment interactions there are, in principle, identifiable neuro-anatomical and neuro-physiological patterns that differentiate between the "dyslexic" brain (or certain varieties of the "dyslexic" brain) and the "normal" brain. Such patterns would not, of themselves, constitute biological causes of dyslexia but, like planum asymmetry or individual gyral anomalies (see Chapter 7), would be markers for the condition. It is likely that many areas of the brain are implicated in the genesis of dyslexia—different parts of the brain do not work, or develop, in isolation from each other. It will be necessary in future, therefore, to focus not on a single brain area, but to consider the patterns associated with a number of regions combined (see Leonard et al., 2001).

The functional neuro-imaging studies reviewed in Chapter 10 point to different patterns of activation of certain regions of the left (and sometimes right) cerebral hemisphere in dyslexics and controls, but the significance of such findings is not clear. As with all such investigations, the data are correlational in nature. Evidence of the direction of causality is lacking. The question of which came first, the dyslexia or the various neurophysiological (and anatomical) "anomalies" (if confirmed), has still to be answered. Does some congenital defect in brain function or anatomy influence the way in which dyslexics' brains are wired or is it that dyslexics perform many experimental tasks in characteristically different ways from controls? Alternatively, has there been a functional reorganization of the brain as a result of dyslexics' experience? Castro-Caldas and colleagues have argued on the basis of PET studies with literate and non-literate participants that learning to read and to write in childhood permanently influences organization of the adult brain in regard to processing the sounds of speech (Castro-Caldas et al., 1998). Similarly, Paulesu et al. (2000) reported different patterns of activation in English and Italian readers while reading words and nonwords. Some caution is necessary in interpreting this finding as the Italians were faster overall, but it is consistent with the possibility that how the brain organizes itself is at least, in part, a function of the orthographic depth of the script to which it is most frequently exposed (see Chapter 4).

Frith (1997) discussed the possible connections between biological, cognitive and behavioural levels of description as they relate to dyslexia. One of a number of possible schemes outlined by Frith (1997) relates a genetically determined abnormality of the peri-Sylvian region to a core cognitive deficit in phonological processing and the latter to behavioural manifestations, namely poor performance in reading, naming, phonological awareness and verbal memory. Frith suggests that some other impairments (for example, in visual motion detection) might be regarded as associated problems "resulting from some abnormality before differentiation into different brain components occurred" (p. 13), rather than as primary functional deficits. In short, problems of visual motion sensitivity might be seen as a biological marker for dyslexia. Hogben (1997), too, suggests that visual deficits might be "an accidental concomitant of, or marker for, reading disability" (p. 68). If so, they might pave the way for the early detection of dyslexia before the age at which reading difficulties normally become apparent (Frith & Frith, 1996).

As outlined in Chapter 12, a major theoretical view of dyslexia is that it stems from a deficit in the magnocellular division of the visual system (and perhaps of analogues in other sensory modalities—see Grant, Zangaladze, Thiagarajah, & Sathian, 1999). The magnocellular division of the visual system is thought to be largely concerned with visual motion processing. However, performance on tasks designed to tap this aspect of magnocellular function appears to relate to performance in certain tasks in the auditory domain (which does not prove that either kind of task is actually carried out by the magno pathway or its auditory equivalent). In view of the putative deficits of dyslexics in visual motion sensitivity, it would be of great interest to determine whether they are impaired on tasks involving auditory movement detection.

There is some reason to believe that the functions of the visual magno system are more closely related to the operations of those (sub-lexical, phonological) processes that underlie performance on pseudo-word reading (Borsting et al., 1966; Ridder et al., 1997; Talcott et al., 1998) than to the reading of real words by means of an orthographic (lexical) mechanism (Cestnick & Coltheart, 1999; Spinelli et al., 1997;—but see Skottun, 2001). On the other hand, after removal of the effects of IQ and overall reading ability, Talcott et al. (2000b) found a relationship between auditory frequency modulation sensitivity and a composite measure of phonological processing in a small ($n = 32$) opportunity sample of normal 10-year-old school children. They also reported a strong relationship between visual motion processing and orthographic (lexical) processing skills. Although the specificity of these findings was not replicated in a much larger study of 350 normal children aged 7–11 years, relationships between level of literacy (average performance across reading and spelling measures from the revised British Abilities Scale) and both visual motion processing (coherence thresholds) and auditory frequency discrimination performance were confirmed (Talcott et al., 2002). Findings such as these suggest that the effect of an inef-

ficient magno system on reading (if indeed the magno system is specifically involved) is not purely visual. An extension of the magnocellular deficit to include certain kinds of problem within the auditory domain would seem, at least on the surface, to provide a plausible account of some of the speech perception and other auditory impairments of dyslexics that have been reported. Once again, though, the causal rather than correlational nature of any magnocellular impairment remains to be established.

It is interesting that some of the research on visual aspects of dyslexia has used tasks which, in other contexts, have been seen as applying to a different domain of functioning. Studies of critical-flicker fusion, for example, have been regarded either as investigations of visual function or as contributing to research on the temporal aspects of perception. How the relevant *data* are used and integrated into a given conceptual scheme will be determined by the theoretical approach adopted. There is no reason, for example, why certain aspects of dyslexia (or of normal reading) might not be seen as visual *and* temporal (as many authors have recognized), but there is often a discernible polarization of attitude. Dyslexia becomes a problem *either* of vision *or* of temporal order.

Given the (controversial) evidence for a visual magnocellular impairment in dyslexia, for a temporal processing deficit (Farmer & Klein, 1995; Habib, 2000) and for impairment in gross and fine motor control, it might be that a combined magno-cerebellar, or more likely magno-cortical-cerebellar, deficit can account for a good proportion of the range of impairments seen in dyslexia. The cerebellum receives massive (sometimes said to be predominantly magno) input from the posterior parietal cortex and it is involved in controlling certain types of eye movement as well as in motor control more generally (Stein & Glickstein, 1992).

One might envisage visual aspects of dyslexia as being related to inefficiency of the magnocellular system, problems of oculo-motor function (see Chapter 11), motor performance and balance as linked to abnormalities within the cerebellum, and phonological deficits as related to cortical regions of the left hemisphere (see Stein, 2000). Indeed, the notion of a circuit that is widely distributed across the brain has considerable intuitive appeal. Damage to particular parts might lead to relatively discrete difficulties, while damage to a number of parts at once would entail a wide variety of difficulties. This would fit well with the notion of a dyslexic "syndrome" that applies to some individuals and a more circumscribed language-related problem confined to reading and spelling in others. Think of an inverted cone boring into an onion. The depth to which the cone penetrates the onion represents the severity of some biological factor or aggregate of factors—genetic, hormonal, structural or infectious—while the different layers of the onion represent a range of skills, some of which, but not all, are directly linked to reading. The more the cone penetrates the onion, the greater the range of skills affected.

I began this monograph by suggesting that speech and written language represent the pinnacles of evolutionary achievement. But if speech is the characteristic of *Homo sapiens* that sets us so far apart from other animals, and if reading is to a very large extent parasitic upon speech mechanisms, why is it that so many people have such difficulty in learning to read? I confess I do not know the answer. Perhaps speech and language processes are inimical to the efficient execution of other skills upon which humankind has depended in the past. There may be an uneasy trade-off between language and non-verbal skills such that at the level of the individual the one develops at the expense of the other, but in the population as a whole both are maintained in balance by evolutionary pressure (see Annett, 2002). Whatever the reason for so many people having problems in learning to read, we should be compassionate towards their difficulties. Critchley (1970) pointed out that under appropriate circumstances all of us show some features of dyslexic behaviour: "To extract the meaningful content of a printed or written text is a problem which varies according to the innate obscurity of the subject matter. This statement holds true independently of cerebral pathlogy. Thus, confronted with a text sufficiently recondite or elusive, every normal subject is a potential alexic" (p. 4). The ability to read fluently and with comprehension is a unique achievement of the human brain and not one to be taken lightly or for granted. It has made us what we are.

References

Aboitiz, F., Scheibel, A. B., Fisher, R. S., & Zaidel, E. (1992). Individual differences in brain asymmetries and fiber composition in the human corpus callosum. *Brain Research*, *598*, 154–161.

Ackerman, P. T., Dykman, R. A., & Gardner, M. Y. (1990). Counting rate, naming rate, phonological sensitivity, and memory span: major factors in dyslexia. *Journal of Learning Disabilities*, *23*, 325–327 and 319.

Ackerman, P. T., Dykman, R. A., Oglesby, M., & Newton, J. E. O. (1995). EEG power spectra of dysphonetic and non-dysphonetic poor readers. *Brain and Language*, *49*, 140–152.

Ackerman, P. T., McPherson, B. D., Oglesby, M., & Dykman, R. A. (1998). EEG power spectra of adolescent poor readers. *Journal of Learning Disabilities*, *31*, 83–90.

Ackermann, H., Gräber, S., Hertrich, I., & Daum, I. (1997). Categorical speech perception in cerebellar disorders. *Brain and Language*, *60*, 323–331.

Ackermann, H., Gräber, S., Hertrich, I., & Daum, I. (1999). Cerebellar contributions to the perception of temporal cues within the speech and nonspeech domain. *Brain and Language*, *67*, 228–241.

Adams, M. J. (1990). *Beginning to read: thinking and learning about print*. Cambridge, MA: MIT Press.

Adlard, A., & Hazan, V. (1998). Speech perception in children with specific reading difficulties (dyslexia). *Quarterly Journal of Experimental Psychology*, *51*, 153–177.

Adler-Grinberg, D., & Stark, L. (1978). Eye movements, scanpaths, and dyslexia. *American Journal of Optometry and Physiological Optics*, *55*, 557–570.

Aguiar, L., & Brady, S. (1991). Vocabulary acquisition and reading ability. *Reading and Writing: An Interdisciplinary Journal*, *3*, 413–425.

Ahissar, M., Protopapas, A., Reid, M., & Merzenich, M. M. (2000). Auditory processing parallels reading abilities in adults. *Proceedings of the National Academy of Sciences, USA*, *97*, 6832–6837.

Albanese, E., Merlo, A., Albanese, A., & Gomez, E. (1989). Anterior speech region. *Archives of Neurology*, *46*, 307–310.

Allen, G., Buxton, R. B., Wong, E. C., & Courchesne, E. (1997). Attentional activation of the cerebellum independent of motor involvement. *Science*, *275*, 1940–1943.

Anderson, T. J., Jenkins, I. H., Brooks, D. J., Hawken, M. B., Frackowiak, R. J., & Kennard, C. (1994). Cortical control of saccades and fixation in man: A PET study. *Brain*, *117*, 1073–1084.

Andrews, S. (1989). Frequency and neighbourhood effects on lexical accesss: activation or search? *Journal of Experimental Psychology: Learning, Memory and Cognition*, *15*, 802–814.

Annett, M. (1970). Handedness, cerebral dominance and the growth of intelligence. In D. J. Bakker & P. Satz (Eds.), *Specific reading disability: advances in theory and method* (pp. 61–79). Rotterdam: Rotterdam University Press.

Annett, M. (1975). Hand preference and the laterality of cerebral speech. *Cortex*, *11*, 305–328.

Annett, M. (1976). A co-ordination of hand skill and

preference replicated. *British Journal of Psychology*, *67*, 587–592.

Annett M. (1978). Genetic and nongenetic influences on handedness. *Behavior Genetics*, *8*, 227–249.

Annett, M. (1985). *Left, right, hand, brain: the right shift theory*. Hove, UK: Lawrence Erlbaum Associates Ltd.

Annett, M. (1991). Speech lateralisation and phonological skill. *Cortex*, *27*, 583–593.

Annett, M. (1992a). Phonological processing and right minus left hand skill. *Quarterly Journal of Experimental Psychology*, *44A*, 33–46.

Annett, M. (1992b). Parallels between asymmetries of planum temporale and of hand skill. *Neuropsychologia*, *30*, 951–962

Annett, M. (1993). Handedness and educational success: the hypothesis of a genetic balanced polymorphism with hetrozygote advantage for laterality and ability. *British Journal of Developmental Psychology*, *11*, 359–370.

Annett, M. (1995a). The right shift theory of a genetic balanced polymorphism for cerebral dominance and cognitive processing. *Cahiers de Psychologie Cognitive/Current Psychology of Cognition*, *14*, 1–53.

Annett, M. (1995b). The fertility of the right shift theory of a genetic balanced polymorphism for cerebral dominance and cognitive processing. *Cahiers de Psychologie Cognitive/Current Psychology of Cognition*, *14*, 427–480.

Annett, M. (1996). Laterality and types of dyslexia. *Neuroscience and Behavioural Reviews*, *20*, 631–636.

Annett, M. (1999a). Eye dominance in families predicted by the right shift theory. *Laterality*, *4*, 167–172.

Annett, M. (1999b). Handedness and lexical skills in undergraduates. *Cortex*, *35*, 357–372.

Annett, M. (2000). Predicting combinations of left and right asymmetries. *Cortex*, *36*, 485–505.

Annett, M. (2002). *Handedness and brain asymmetry: the right shift theory*. Hove, UK: Psychology Press.

Annett, M., Eglinton, E., & Smythe, P. (1996). Types of dyslexia and the shift to dextrality. *Journal of Child Psychology and Psychiatry*, *37*, 167–180.

Annett, M., & Kilshaw, D. (1983). Right and left hand skill, II. Estimating the parameters of the distribution of L–R differences in males and females. *British Journal of Psychology*, *74*, 269–281.

Annett, M., & Kilshaw, D. (1984). Lateral preference and skill in dyslexics: implications of the right shift theory. *Journal of Child Psychology and Psychiatry*, *25*, 327–377.

Annett, M., & Manning, M. (1990). Reading and a bal-

anced polymorphism for laterality and ability. *Journal of Child Psychology and Psychiatry*, *31*, 511–529.

Annett, M., & Manning, M. (1994). Corrigendum—reading and a balanced polymorphism for laterality and ability. *Journal of Child Psychology and Psychiatry*, *35*, 573–575.

Annett, M., & Turner, A. (1974). Laterality and the growth of intellectual abilities. *British Journal of Educational Psychology*, *44*, 37–46.

Ans, B., Carbonnel, S., & Valdois, S. (1998). A connectionist multiple-trace memory model for polysyllabic reading. *Psychological Review*, *105*, 678–723.

Aro, M., Aro, T., Ahonen, T., Räsänen, T., Hietala, A., & Lyytinen, H. (1999). The development of phonological abilities and their relation to reading acquisition: case studies of six Finnish children. *Journal of Learning Disabilities*, *32*, 457–463.

Avons, S. E., Wragg, C. A., Cupples, L., & Lovegrove, W. J. (1998). Measures of phonological short-term memory and their relationship to vocabulary development. *Applied Psycholinguistics*, *19*, 583–601.

Backman, J. E., Mamen, M., & Ferguson, H. B. (1984). Reading level design: conceptual and methodological issues in reading research. *Psychological Bulletin*, *96*, 560–568.

Badcock, D., & Lovegrove, W. (1981). The effects of contrast, stimulus duration, and spatial frequency on visible persistence in normal and specifically disabled readers. *Journal of Experimental Psychology: Human Perception and Performance*, *7*, 495–505.

Baddeley, A. D. (1986). *The psychology of memory*. London: Harper International.

Baddeley, A. D. (1990). *Human memory: theory and practice*. Hove, UK: Lawrence Erlbaum Associates Ltd.

Baddeley, A. D., Ellis, N. C., Miles, T. R., & Lewis, V. J. (1982). Developmental and acquired dyslexia: a comparison. *Cognition*, *11*, 185–199.

Baddeley, A., & Gathercole, S. (1992). Learning to read: the role of the phonological loop. In J. Alegria, D. Holender, J. J. de Morais, & M. Radeau (Eds.), *Analytic approaches to human cognition* (pp. 153–167). Amsterdam: Elsevier.

Baddeley, A., Gathercole, S., & Papagno, C. (1998). The phonological loop as a language learning device. *Psychological Review*, *105*, 158–173.

Baddeley, A. D., & Hitch, G. (1974). Working memory. In G. A. Bower (Ed.), *The psychology of learning and motivation* (Vol. 8, pp. 47–90). New York: Academic Press.

Baddeley, A. D., Logie, R. H., & Ellis, N. C. (1988).

Characteristics of developmental dyslexia. *Cognition, 29*, 197–228.

Baddeley, A. D., Thomson, N., & Buchanan, M. (1975). Word length and the structure of short-term memory. *Journal of Verbal Learning and Verbal Behavior, 14*, 575–589.

Badian, N. A., & Wolff, P. H. (1977). Manual asymmetries of motor sequencing in boys with reading disability. *Cortex, 13*, 343–349.

Bakan, P. (1971). Handedness and birth order. *Nature, 229*, 195.

Bakan, P. (1977). Left handedness and birth order revisited. *Neuropsychologia, 15*, 837–839.

Bakan, P., Dibb, G., & Reed, P. (1973). Handedness and birth stress. *Neuropsychologia, 15*, 837–840.

Bakker, D. J. (1967). Temporal order, meaningfulness, and reading ability. *Perceptual and Motor Skills, 24*, 1027–1030.

Bakker, D. J. (1970). Temporal order perception and reading retardation In D. J. Bakker & P. Satz (Eds.), *Specific reading disability: advances in theory and method* (pp. 81–96). Rotterdam: Rotterdam University Press.

Bakker, D. J. (1992). Neuropsychological classification and treatment of dyslexia. *Journal of Learning Disabilities, 25*, 102–109.

Bakker, D. J., Smink, T., & Reitsma, P. (1973). Ear dominance and reading ability. *Cortex, 9*, 301–312.

Bakwin, H. (1973). Reading disability in twins. *Developmental Medicine and Child Neurology, 15*, 184–187.

Baldeweg, T., Richardson, A., Watkins, S., Foale, C., & Gruzelier, J. (1999). Impaired auditory frequency discrimination in dyslexia detected with mismatch evoked potentials. *Annals of Neurology, 45*, 495–503.

Baluch, B., & Besner, D. (1991). Strategic use of lexical and nonlexical routines in visual word recognition: evidence from oral reading in Persian. *Journal of Experimental Psychology: Learning, Memory and Cognition, 17*, 644–652

Baron, J. (1979). Orthographic and word-specific mechanisms in children's reading of words. *Child Development, 50*, 60–72.

Baron, J., & Strawson, C. (1976). Use of orthographic and word-specific knowledge in reading words aloud. *Journal of Experimental Psychology: Human Perception and Performance, 2*, 386–393.

Barron, R. W. (1986). Word recognition in early reading: a review of the direct and indirect access hypotheses. *Cognition, 24*, 93–119.

Barry, C. (1992). Interactions between lexical and assembled spelling (in English, Italian and Welsh). In C. Sterling & C. Robson (Eds.), *Psychology, spelling and education* (pp. 71–86). Clevedon, UK: Multilingual Matters.

Barry, C., & Seymour, P. H. K. (1988). Lexical priming and sound-to-spelling contingency effects in nonword spelling. *Memory and Cognition, 40*, 5–40.

Barta, P. E., Petty, R. G., McGilchrist, I., Lewis, R. W., Jerram, M., Casanova, M. F., Powers, R. E., Brill, L. B., II, & Pearson, G. D. (1995). Asymmetry of the planum temporale: methodological considerations and clinical associations. *Psychiatry Research Neuro-imaging, 61*, 137–150.

Bartlett, C. W., Flax, J., Yabut, O., Hirsch, L., Li, W., Tallal, P., & Brzustwcz, L. (2000). A genome-scan for linkage of specific language impairment: report on chromosomes 1, 6 and 15. *American Journal of Human Genetics, 67* (suppl. 1), 309.

Bartley, A. J., Jones, D. W., & Weinberger, D. R. (1997). Genetic variability of human brain size and cortical gyral patterns. *Brain, 120*, 257–269.

Bashore, T. R. (1981). Vocal and manual reaction time estimates of interhemispheric transmission time. *Psychological Bulletin, 89*, 352–368.

Basso, A., & Corno, M. (1994). Semantic errors in transcoding tasks in shallow orthographies: a retrospective study on 502 Italian vascular patients. *Journal of Neurolinguistics, 8*, 149–156.

Bateson, P. (2002). The corpse of a wearisome debate. *Science, 297*, 2212–2213.

Beaton, A. A. (1985). *Left side, right side: a review of laterality research.* London: Batsford/New Haven, CT: Yale University Press.

Beaton, A. A. (1995). Hands, brains and lateral thinking: an overview of the right shift theory. *Cahiers de Psychologie Cognitive/Current Psychology of Cognition, 14*, 481–495.

Beaton, A. A. (1997). The relation of planum temporale asymmetry and morphology of the corpus callosum to handedness, gender, and dyslexia: a review of the evidence. *Brain and Language, 60*, 255–322.

Beaton, A. A. (2002). Dyslexia and the cerebellar deficit hypothesis. *Cortex, 38*, 479–490.

Beaton, A. A. (2003). The nature and determinants of handedness. In: K. Hugdahl & R. J. Davidson (Eds.), *The asymmetrical brain* (pp. 105–158). Cambridge, MA: MIT Press.

Beaton, A. A., Buck, R., & Williams, C. (2001, March). Reading — Welsh and English: is there life left in the orthographic depth hypothesis. Paper presented at the *Centenary Conference of the British Psychological Society*, Glasgow, UK.

Beaton, A. A., Hugdahl, K., & Ray, P. (2000). Lateral asymmetries and interhemispheric transfer in aging: a review and some new data. In M. K. Mandal, M. B. Bulman-Fleming, & G. Tiwari (Eds.), *Side bias: a neuropsychological perspective* (pp. 101–152). Dordrecht: Kluwer Academic.

Beaton, A. A., McDougall, S. M. & Singleton, C. (Eds.) (1997a). Dyslexia in literate adults. *Journal of Research in Reading: special issue, 20*.

Beaton, A. A., McDougall, S. M., & Singleton, C. (1997b). Humpty Dumpty grows up? Diagnosing dyslexia in adults. *Journal of Research in Reading, 20*, 1–12.

Beaton, A. A., Puddifer, A., & Edwards, R. (2004). Interhemispheric transfer of tactile information in dyslexia. (submitted)

Beaton, A. A., Ved, R., & Guest, J. (1994). Semantic errors of naming, reading, writing and drawing following left hemisphere infarction. *Cognitive Neuropsychology, 14*, 459–478.

Beaumont, J. G., Thomson, M., & Rugg, M. (1981). An intrahemispheric integration deficit in dyslexia. *Current Psychological Research, 1*, 185–198.

Beauvois, M.-F., & Dérouesné, J. (1985). The "phonemic stage" in nonlexical reading. In K. E. Patterson, J. C. Marshall, J. C. & M. Coltheart (Eds.), *Surface dyslexia: neuropsychological and cognitive studies of phonological reading* (pp. 15–34). Hove, UK: Lawrence Erlbaum Associates.

Beckers, G., & Zeki, S. (1995). The consequence of inactivating areas V1 and V5 on visual motion perception. *Brain, 118*, 49–60.

Behan, P. O., & Geschwind, N. (1985a). Hemispheric laterality and immunity. In R. Guillemin, M. Cohen, & T. Melnechuk (Eds.), *Neural modulation of immunity* (pp. 73–80). New York: Raven Press.

Behan, P., & Geschwind, N. (1985b). Dyslexia, congenital anomalies, and immune disorders: the role of the fetal environment. *Annals of the New York Academy of Sciences, 457*, 13–18.

Behrmann, M., Shomstein, S. S., Black, S. E., Barton, J. J. S. (2001). The eye movements of pure alexic patients during reading and nonreading tasks. *Neuropsychologia, 39*, 983–1002.

Belmont, L., & Birch, H. G. (1965). Lateral dominance, lateral awareness, and reading disability. *Child Development, 36*, 57–71.

Ben-Dror, I., Pollatsek, A., & Scarpati, S. (1991). Word identification in isolation and in context by college dyslexic students. *Brain and Language, 40*, 471–490.

Bentin, S., Sahar, A., & Moscovitch, M. (1984). Intermanual information transfer in patients with lesions in the trunk of the corpus callosum. *Neuropsychologia, 22*, 601–611.

Benton, A. L. (1955). Development of finger-localization capacity in school children. *Child Development, 26*, 225–230.

Berker, E. A., Berker, A. H., & Smith, A. (1986). Translation of Broca's 1865 report: localization of speech in the third left frontal convolution. *Archives of Neurology, 43*, 1065–1072.

Berlin, R. (1887). *Eine besondere Art der Wortblindheit: Dyslexia*. Wiesbaden: J. F. Bergmann.

Berlucchi, G., Aglito, S., Marzi, C. A., Tassinari, G. (1995). Corpus callosum and simple visuomotor integration. *Neuropsychologia, 33*, 923–936.

Bertelson, P. (1986) The onset of literacy: liminal remarks. *Cognition, 24*, 1–30.

Bertelson, P., de Gelder, B., Tfouni, L. V., & Morais, J. (1989). Metaphonological abilities of adult illiterates: new evidence of heterogeneity. *European Journal of Cognitive Psychology, 1*, 239–250.

Besner, D., & Smith, M. C. (1992). Basic processes in reading: is the orthographic depth hypothesis sinking? In R. Frost & L. Katz (Eds.), *Orthography, phonology, morphology, and meaning* (pp. 45–66). Amsterdam: North-Holland/Elsevier.

Besner, D., Twilley, L., McCann, R. S., & Seergobin, K. (1990). On the association between connectionism and data: are a few words necessary? *Psychological Review, 97*, 432–446.

Best, M., & Demb, J. B. (1999). Normal planum temporale asymmetry in dyslexics with a magnocellular pathway deficit. *NeuroReport, 10*, 607–612.

Betancur, C., Vélez, A., Cabanieu, G., Le Moal, M., & Neveu, P. J. (1990). Association between left-handedness and allergy: a reappraisal. *Neuropsychologia, 28*, 223–227.

Bigelow, E. R., & McKenzie, B. E. (1985). Unstable ocular dominance and reading ability. *Perception, 14*, 329–335.

Binder, J. R., Frost, J. A., Hammeke, T. A., Rao, S. M., & Cox, R. W. (1996). Function of the left planum temporale in auditory and linguistic processing. *Brain, 119*, 1239–1247.

Birch, H. G., & Belmont, L. (1964). Auditory–visual integration in normal and retarded readers. *American Journal of Orthopsychiatry, 34*, 852–861.

Birch, H. G., & Belmont, L. (1965). Auditory–visual integration, intelligence and reading ability in school children. *Perceptual and Motor Skills, 20*, 293–305.

Bird, J., Bishop, D. V. M., & Freeman, N. H. (1995). Phonological awareness and literacy development in children with expressive phonological impairments. *Journal of Speech and Hearing Research, 38,* 446–462.

Biscaldi, M., Fischer, B., & Hartnegg, K. (2000). Voluntary saccadic control in dyslexia. *Perception, 29,* 509–521.

Bisgaard, M. L., Eiberg, H., Møller, N., Niebuhr, E., & Mohr, J. (1987). Dyslexia and chromosome 15 heteromorphism: negative lod score in a Danish material. *Clinical Genetics, 32,* 118–119.

Bishop, D. V. M. (1980). Handedness, clumsiness and cognitive ability. *Developmental Medicine and Child Neurology, 22,* 569–579

Bishop, D. V. M. (1983). How sinister is sinistrality? *Journal of the Royal College of Physicians of London, 17,* 161–172.

Bishop, D. V. M. (1984). Using non-preferred hand skill to investigate pathological left-handedness in an unselected population. *Developmental Medicine and Child Neurology, 26,* 214–226.

Bishop, D. V. M. (1986). Is there a link between handedness and hypersensitivity? *Cortex, 22,* 289–296.

Bishop, D. V. M. (1989a). Does hand proficiency determine hand preference? *British Journal of Psychology, 80,* 191–199.

Bishop, D. V. M. (1989b). Unfixed reference, monocular occlusion, and developmental dyslexia—a critique. *British Journal of Ophthalmology, 73,* 209–215.

Bishop, D. V. M. (1990a). Handedness, clumsiness and developmental language disorders. *Neuropsychologia, 28,* 681–690.

Bishop, D. V. M. (1990b). *Handedness and developmental disorder.* Oxford: Blackwell Scientific.

Bishop, D. V. M. (1991). Developmental reading disabilities: the role of phonological processing has been overemphasised. *Mind and Language, 6,* 97–101.

Bishop, D. V. M. (1997). *Uncommon understanding: development and disorders of language comprehension in children.* Hove, UK: Psychology Press.

Bishop, D. V. M. (2001). Individual differences in handedness and specific speech and language impairment: evidence against a genetic link. *Behavior Genetics, 31,* 339.

Bishop, D. V. M. (2002). Cerebellar abnormalities in developmental dyslexia: cause, correlate or consequences? *Cortex, 38,* 491–498.

Bishop, D. V. M., & Adams, C. (1990). A prospective study of the relationship between specific language impairment, phonological disorders and reading retardation. *Journal of Child Psychology and Psychiatry, 31,* 1027–1050.

Bishop, D. V. M., Bishop, S. J., Bright, P., James, C., Delaney, T., & Tallal, P. (1999a). Different origin of auditory and phonological processing problems in children with language impairment: evidence from a twin study. *Journal of Speech, Language and Hearing Research, 42,* 155–168.

Bishop, D. V. M., Carlyon, R. P., Deeks, J. M., & Bishop, S. J. (1999b). Auditory temporal processing impairment: neither necessary nor sufficient for causing language impairment in children. *Journal of Speech, Language and Hearing Research, 42,* 1295–1310.

Bishop, D. V. M., & Edmundson, A. (1986). Is otitis media a major cause of specific developmental language disorders? *British Journal of Disorders of Communication, 21,* 321–338.

Bishop, D. V. M., & Edmundson, A. (1987). Specific language impairment as a maturational lag: evidence fom longitudinal data on language and motor development. *Developmental Medicine and Child Neurology, 29,* 442–459.

Bishop, D. V. M., Jancey, C., & Steel, A. (1979). Orthoptic status and reading disability. *Cortex, 15,* 659–666.

Bishop, D. V. M., & Leonard, L. B. (Eds.) (2000). *Speech and language impairments in children: causes, characteristics, intervention and outcome.* Hove, UK: Psychology Press.

Bishop, D. V. M., North, T., & Donlan, C. (1995). Genetic basis of specific language impairment: evidence from a twin study. *Developmental Medicine and Child Neurology, 37,* 56–71.

Bishop, D. V. M., & Robson, J. (1989). Unimpaired short-term memory and rhyme judgement in congenitally speechless individuals: implications for the notion of articulatory coding. *Quarterly Journal of Experimental Psychology, 41,* 123–140.

Bishop, K. M., & Wahlsten, D. (1997). Sex differences in the human corpus callosum: myth or reality? *Science and Behavioural Reviews, 21,* 581–601.

Blachman, B. A. (1991). Phonological awareness: implications for prereading and early reading instruction. In S. A. Brady & D. P. Shankweiler (Eds.), *Phonological processes in literacy: A tribute to Isabelle Y. Liberman* (pp. 29–36). Hillsdale, NJ: Lawrence Erlbaum Associates Inc.

Blaskey, P., Scheiman, M., Parisi, M., Ciner, E. B., Gallaway, M., & Selznick, R. (1990). The effectiveness of Irlen filters for improving reading performance: a pilot study. *Journal of Learning Disabilities*, *23*, 604–612.

Blom, E. C. (1928). Mirror-writing. *Psychological Bulletin*, *25*, 582–594.

Bock, J. M., Monk, A. F., & Hulme, C. (1993). Perceptual grouping in visual word recognition. *Memory and Cognition*, *21*, 81–88.

Boder, E. (1971). Developmental dyslexia: prevailing diagnostic concepts and a new diagnostic approach. In H. R. Myklebust (Ed.), *Progress in learning disabilities* (Vol. 2, pp. 293–321). New York: Grune & Stratton.

Boder, E. (1973). Developmental dyslexia: a diagnostic approach based on three atypical reading–spelling patterns. *Developmental Medicine and Child Neurology*, *15*, 663–687.

Bogen, J. E., & Bogen, G. M. (1976). Wernicke's region — where is it? *Annals of the New York Academy of Sciences*, *280*, 834–843.

Borsting, E., Ridder, W. H., Dudeck, K., Kelley, C., Matsui, L., & Motoyama, J. (1996). The presence of a magnocellular defect depends on the type of dyslexia. *Vision Research*, *36*, 1047–1053.

Borstrøm, I., & Elbro, C. (1997). Prevention of dyslexia in kindergarten: effects of phoneme awareness training with children of dyslexic parents. In C. Hulme & M. Snowling (Eds.), *Dyslexia: biology, cognition and intervention* (pp. 235–253). London: Whurr Publishers.

Bourassa, D. C., McManus, I. C., & Bryden, M. P. (1996). Handedness and eye dominance: a meta-analysis of their relationship. *Laterality*, *1*, 5–34.

Bowers, P. G., & Wolf, M. (1993). Theoretical links among naming speed, precise timing mechanisms and orthographic skill in dyslexia. *Reading and Writing: An Interdisciplinary Journal*, *5*, 69–85.

Bowey, J. A. (1986). Syntactic awareness in relation to reading skill and ongoing reading comprehension monitoring. *Journal of Experimental Child Psychology*, *41*, 282–299.

Bowey, J. A. (1990a). Orthographic onsets and rimes as functional units of reading. *Memory and Cognition*, *18*, 419–427.

Bowey, J. A. (1990b). On rhyme, language, and children's reading. *Applied Psycholinguistics*, *11*, 439–448.

Bowey, J. A. (1994). Phonological sensitivity in novice readers and nonreaders. *Journal of Experimental Child Psychology*, *58*, 134–159.

Bowey, J. A. (1996a). On the association between phonological memory and receptive vocabulary in five-year-olds. *Journal of Experimental Child Psychology*, *63*, 44–78.

Bowey, J. A. (1996b). Phonological sensitivity as a proximal contributor to phonological recoding skills in children's reading. *Australian Journal of Psychology*, *48*, 113–118.

Bowey, J. A. (1997). What *does* nonword repetition measure? A reply to Gathercole and Baddeley. *Journal of Experimental Child Psychology*, *67*, 295–301.

Bowey, J. A. (1999). The limitations of orthographic rime analogies in beginners' word reading: a reply to Goswami. *Journal of Experimental Child Psychology*, *72*, 220–231.

Bowey, J. A., Cain, M. T., & Ryan, S. M. (1992). A reading-level design study of phonological skills underlying fourth-grade children's word reading difficulties. *Child Development*, *63*, 999–1011.

Bowey, J. A., & Francis, J. (1991). Phonological analysis as a function of age and exposure to reading instruction. *Applied Psycholinguistics*, *12*, 91–121.

Bowey, J. A., & Hansen, J. (1994). The development of orthographic rimes as units of word recognition. *Journal of Experimental Child Psychology*, *58*, 465–488.

Bowey, J. A., & Patel, R. K. (1988). Meta-linguistic ability and early reading achievement. *Applied Psycholinguistics*, *9*, 367–383.

Bowey, J., & Underwood, N. (1996). Further evidence that orthographic rime usage in nonword reading increases with word-level reading proficiency. *Journal of Experimental Child Psychology*, *63*, 526–562.

Bowey, J. A., Vaughan, L., & Hansen, J. (1998). Beginning readers' use of orthographic analogies in word reading. *Journal of Experimental Child Psychology*, *68*, 108–133.

Bradley, L., & Bryant, P. E. (1978). Difficulties in auditory organization as a possible cause of reading backwardness. *Nature*, *271*, 746–747.

Bradley, L., & Bryant, P. E. (1983). Categorizing sounds and learning to read — a causal connection. *Nature*, *301*, 419–421.

Bradlow, A. R., Kraus, N., Nicol, T. G., McGee, T. J., Cunningham, J., Zecker, S. G., & Carrell, T. D. (1999). Effects of lengthened format transition duration on discrimination and neural representation of synthetic CV syllables by normal and learning-disabled children. *Journal of the Acoustical Society of America*, *106*, 2086–2096.

Bradshaw, J. L., Nettleton, N. C., Wilson, L., & Burden, V. (1985). Mirror-reading in right and left handers: are sinistrals really superior? *Brain and Language*, *26*, 322–331.

Brady, S. (1986). Short-term memory, phonological

processing, and reading ability. *Annals of Dyslexia*, *36*, 138–153.

Brady, S. A. (1991). The role of working memory in reading disability. In S. A. Brady & D. P. Shankweiler (Eds.), *Phonological processes in literacy: a tribute to Isabelle Y. Liberman* (pp. 129–151). Hillsdale, NJ: Lawrence Erlbaum Associates Inc.

Brady, S. A., & Shankweiler, D. P. (Eds.) (1991). *Phonological processes in literacy: a tribute to Isabelle Y. Liberman*. Hillsdale, NJ: Lawrence Erlbaum Associates Inc.

Brady, S., Shankweiler, D., & Mann, V. (1983). Speech perception and memory coding in relation to reading ability. *Journal of Experimental Child Psychology*, *35*, 345–367.

Brandt, J., & Rosen, J. J. (1980). Auditory phonemic perception in dyslexia: categorical identification and discrimination of stop consonants. *Brain and Language*, *9*, 324–337.

Breier, J. I., Gray, L. C., Fletcher, J. M., Foorman, B., & Klaas, P. (2002). Perception of speech and non-speech stimuli by children with and without reading disability and attention deficit disorder. *Journal of Experimental Child Psychology*, *82*, 226–250.

Breitmeyer, B. G. (1993). Sustained (P) and transient (M) channels in vision: a review and implications for reading. In D. M. Willows, R. S. Kruk & E. Corcos (Eds.), *Visual processes in reading and reading disabilities* (pp. 95–110). Hillside, NJ: Lawrence Erlbaum Associates Inc.

Breitmeyer, B. G., & Ganz, L. (1976). Implications of sustained and transient channels for theories of visual pattern masking, saccadic suppression, and information processing. *Psychological Review*, *83*, 1–36.

Bridgeman, B. (1987). Is the dual-route theory possible in phonetically regular languages? *Brain and Behavioral Sciences*, *10*, 331–332.

Briggs, G. G., Nebes, R. D., & Kinsbourne, M. (1976). Intellectual differences in relation to personal and family handedness. *Quarterly Journal of Experimental Psychology*, *28*, 591–601.

Brinkman, J., & Kuypers, H. G. J. M. (1972). Split-brain monkeys: cerebral control of ipsilateral and contralateral arm, hand, and finger movements. *Science*, *176*, 536–539.

Brinkman, J., & Kuypers, H. G. J. M. (1973). Cerebral control of contralateral and ipsilateral arm, hand and finger movements in the split-brain rhesus monkey. *Brain*, *96*, 653–674.

British Dyslexia Association (1995). *The dyslexia handbook*: Reading, UK: British Dyslexia Association.

Broadbent, W. H. (1872). On the cerebral mechanism of speech and thought. *Transactions of the Royal Medical and Chirurgical Society*, *15*, 145–194.

Broadbent, W. H. (1896). Note on Dr. Hinshelwood's communication on word-blindness and visual memory. *Lancet*, 4 January, p. 18.

Broca, P. (1861). Remarques sur le siège de la faculté du langage articulé suivies d'une observation d'aphémie (perte de la parole). *Bulletins de la Société Anatomique de Paris*, *6*, 330–357.

Broca, P. (1863). Localisations des fonctions cérébrales — siège du langage articulé. *Bulletins de la Société d'Anthropologie de Paris*, *4*, 200–204.

Broca, P. (1865). Sur le siège de la faculté du langage articulé. *Bulletins de la Société d'Anthropologie de Paris*, *6*, 337–393.

Broom, Y. M., & Doctor, E. A. (1995). Developmental phonological dyslexia: a case study of the efficacy of a remediation programme. *Cognitive Neuropsychology*, *12*, 725–766.

Brown, B., Haegerstrom-Portnoy, G., Adams, A. J., Yingling, C. D., Galin, D., Herron, J., & Marcus, M. (1983). Predictive eye movements do not discriminate between dyslexic and control children. *Neuropsychologia*, *21*, 121–128.

Brown, G. D. A. (1987). Resolving inconsistency: a computational model of word naming. *Journal of Memory and Language*, *26*, 1–23.

Brown, G. D. A. (1997). Connectionism, phonology, reading, and regularity in developmental dyslexia. *Brain and Language*, *59*, 207–235.

Brown, G. D. A., & Deavers, R. (1999). Units of analysis in nonword reading: evidence from children and adults. *Journal of Experimental Child Psychology*, *73*, 208–242.

Brown, G. D. A., & Hulme, C. (1995). Modelling item length effects in memory span: no rehearsal needed? *Journal of Memory and Language*, *34*, 594–621.

Brown, G. D. A., Preece, T., & Hulme, C. (2000). Oscillator-based memory for serial order. *Psychological Review*, *107*, 127–181.

Brown, G. D. A., & Watson, F. (1994). Spelling-to-sound effects in single word reading. *British Journal of Psychology*, *85*, 181–202.

Brown, J. (1975). On the neural organization of language: thalamic and cortical relationships. *Brain and Language*, *2*, 18–30.

Brown, P., & Besner, D. (1987). The assembly of phonology in oral reading: a new model. In M. Coltheart (Ed.). *Attention and performance XII. The psychology of reading* (pp. 471–489). Hove, UK: Lawrence Erlbaum Associates.

Brown, W. E., Eliez, S., Menon, V., Rumsey, J. M., White, C. D., & Reiss, A. L. (2001). Preliminary evidence of widespread morphological variations of the brain in dyslexia. *Neurology, 56*, 781–783.

Bruce, D. J. (1964). The analysis of word sounds by young children. *British Journal of Educational Psychology, 34*, 158–170.

Bruck, M. (1990). Word recognition skills of adults with childhood diagnosis of dyslexia. *Developmental Psychology, 26*, 439–454.

Bruck, M. (1992). Persistence of dyslexics' phonological awareness deficits. *Developmental Psychology, 28*, 874–886.

Bruck, M., & Genesee, F. (1995). Phonological awareness in young second language learners. *Journal of Child Language, 22*, 307–324.

Bruck, M., & Treiman, R. (1990). Phonological awareness and spelling in normal children and dyslexics: the case of initial consonant clusters. *Journal of Experimental Child Psychology, 50*, 156–178.

Bruck, M., & Treiman, R. (1992). Learning to pronounce words: the limitations of analogies. *Reading Research Quarterly, 27*, 374–389.

Brunswick, N., McCroy, E., Price, C. J., Frith, C. D., & Frith, U. (1999). Explicit and implicit processing of words and pseudowords by adult developmental dyslexics. *Brain, 122*, 1901–1917.

Bryant, P. E. (1985). The question of prevention. In M. Snowling (Ed.), *Children's written language difficulties: assessment and management* (pp. 43–55). Windsor: NFER-Nelson.

Bryant, P. E. (1998). Sensitivity to onset and rhyme does predict young children's reading: a comment on Muter, Hulme, Snowling, and Taylor (1997). *Journal of Experimental Child Psychology, 71*, 29–37.

Bryant, P. E., & Bradley, L. (1980). Why do children sometimes write words which they can not read? In U. Frith (Ed.), *Cognitive processes in spelling* (pp. 355–370). London: Academic Press.

Bryant, P., & Bradley, L. (1985). *Children's reading problems: psychology and education*. Oxford: Blackwell.

Bryant, P., & Goswami, U. (1986). Strengths and weaknesses of the reading level design: a comment on Backman, Mamen and Ferguson. *Psychological Bulletin, 100*, 101–103.

Bryant, P., & Impey, L. (1986) The similarities between normal readers and developmental and acquired dyslexics. *Cognition, 24*, 121–137.

Bryant, P., MacLean, M., & Bradley, L. (1990a).

Rhyme, language and children's reading. *Applied Psycholinguistics, 11*, 237–252.

Bryant, P., MacLean, M., & Bradley, L. (1990b). Comments on "Rhyme, language, and children's reading". *Applied Psycholinguistics, 11*, 449–450.

Bryant, P. E., MacLean, M., Bradley, L. L., & Crossland, J. (1989). Nursery rhymes, phonological skills and reading. *Journal of Child Language, 16*, 407–428.

Bryant, P. E., MacLean, M., Bradley, L. L., & Crossland, J. (1990c). Rhyme and alliteration, phoneme detection, and learning to read. *Developmental Psychology, 26*, 429–438.

Bryden, M. P. (1972). Auditory–visual and sequential–spatial matching in relation to reading ability. *Child Development, 43*, 824–832.

Bryden, M. P. (1988). Does laterality make any difference? Thoughts on the relation between cerebral asymmetry and reading. In D. L. Molfese & S. Segalowitz (Eds.), *Brain Lateralization and Development in Children* (pp. 509–525). New York: Guilford Press.

Bryden, M. P., McManus, I. C., & Bulman-Fleming, M. B. (1994a). Evaluating the empirical support for the Geschwind-Behan-Galaburda model of cerebral lateralization. *Brain and Cognition, 26*, 103–167.

Bryden, M. P., McManus, I. C., & Bulman-Fleming, M. B. (1994b). GBG, BMB, R & L, X & Y . . . reply to commentaries. *Brain and Cognition, 26*, 312–326.

Brysbaert, M. (1994). Behavioural estimates of inter-hemispheric transmission time and the signal detection method: a reappraisal. *Perception and Psychophysics, 56*, 479–490.

Bub, D. N. (2000). Methodological issues confronting PET and fMRI studies of cognitive function. *Cognitive Neuropsychology, 17*, 467–484.

Burgess, N., & Hitch, G. J. (1999). Memory for serial order: a network model of the phonological loop and its timing. *Psychological Review, 106*, 551–581.

Burden, V. (1989). A comparison of priming effects on the nonword spelling performance of good and poor spellers. *Cognitive Neuropsychology, 6*, 43–65.

Burr, D. C., Morrone, M. C., & Ross, J. (1994). Selective suppression of the magnocellular visual pathway during saccadic eye movements. *Nature, 371*, 511–513.

Burt, C. (1958). *The Backward Child*. London: University of London Press.

Bus, A. G., & van Ijzendoorn, M. H. (1999). Phonological awareness and early reading: a meta analysis of experimental training studies. *Journal of Educational Psychology, 91*, 403–414.

Byrne, B., & Fielding-Barnsley, R. (1989). Phonemic awareness and letter knowledge in the child's acquisition of the alphabetic principle. *Journal of Educational Psychology*, *81*, 313–321.

Byrne, B., & Fielding-Barnsley, R. (1990). Acquiring the alphabetic principle: a case for teaching recognition of phoneme identity. *Journal of Educational Psychology*, *82*, 805–812.

Byrne, B. & Fielding-Barnsley, R. (1995). Evaluation of a program to teach phonemic awareness to young children: a 2- and 3-year follow-up and a new preschool trial. *Journal of Educational Psychology*, *87*, 488–503.

Byrne, B., Fielding-Barnsley, R., & Ashley, L. (2000). Effects of pre-school phoneme identity training after six years: outcome level distinguished from rate of response. *Journal of Educational Psychology*, *92*, 659–667.

Callaway, E. M. (1998). Local circuits in primary visual cortex of the macaque monkey. *Annual Review of Neuroscience*, *21*, 47–74.

Campain, R., & Minkler, J. (1976). A note on the gross configurations of the human auditory cortex. *Brain and Language*, *3*, 318–323.

Campbell, R. (1983). Writing nonwords to dictation. *Brain and Language*, *19*, 153–178.

Campbell, R. (1985). When children write nonwords to dictation. *Journal of Experimental Child Psychology*, *40*, 133–151.

Campbell, R., & Butterworth, B. (1985). Phonological dyslexia and dysgraphia in a highly literate subject: a developmental case with associated deficits of phonemic processing and awareness. *Quarterly Journal of Experimental Psychology*, *37A*, 435–475.

Campbell, R., & Sais, E. (1995). Accelerated metalinguistic (phonological) awareness in bilingual children. *British Journal of Developmental Psychology*, *13*, 61–68.

Campbell, R., Zihl, J., Massaro, D., Munhall, K., & Cohen, M. M. (1997). Speechreading in the akinetopsic patient, L.M. *Brain*, *120*, 1793–1803.

Capener, N. (1952) Leonardo's left hand. *Lancet*, 19 April, pp. 813–814.

Caramazza, A. (1986). On drawing inferences about the structure of normal cognitive systems from the analysis of patterns of impaired performance: the case for single-patient studies. *Brain and Cognition*, *5*, 41–66.

Caramazza, A., & McCloskey, M. (1988). The case for single-patient studies. *Cognitive Neuropsychology*, *5*, 517–528.

Caravolas, M., & Bruck, R. (1993). The effect of oral and written language input on children's phonological awareness: a cross-linguistic study. *Brain and Language*, *55*, 1–30.

Cardon, L. R., Smith, S. D., Fulker, D. W., Kimberling, W. J., Pennington, B. F., & DeFries, J. C. (1994). Quantitative trait locus for reading disability on chromosome 6. *Science*, *266*, 276–279.

Cardon, L. R., Smith, S. D., Fulker, D. W., Kimberling, W. J., Pennington, B. F., & DeFries, J. C. (1995). Quantitative trait locus for reading disability: correction. *Science*, *268*, 1553.

Carmon, A., & Nachshon, I. (1971). Effect of unilateral brain damage on perception of temporal order. *Cortex*, *7*, 410–418.

Carpenter, A. F., Georgopoulos, A. P., & Pellizzer, G. (1999). Motor cortical encoding of serial order in a context-recall task. *Science*, *283*, 1752–1757.

Carroll, T. A., Mullaney, P., & Eustace, P. (1994). Dark adaptation in disabled readers screened for scotopic sensitivity syndrome. *Perceptual and Motor Skills*, *78*, 131–141.

Casagrande, V. A. (1994). A third parallel visual pathway to primate area V1. *Neuroscience*, *17*, 305–310.

Casagrande, V. A. (1999). The mystery of the visual system K pathway. *Journal of Physiology*, *517*, 630.

Casco, C., & Prunetti, E. (1996). Visual search of good and poor readers: effects with targets having single and combined features. *Perceptual and Motor Skills*, *82*, 1155–1167.

Castles, A., & Coltheart, M. (1993). Varieties of developmental dyslexia. *Cognition*, *47*, 149–180.

Castles, A., & Coltheart, M. (1994). Cognitive neuropsychology and rehabilitation. In J. Riddoch & G. W. Humphreys (Eds.), *Cognitive neuropsychology and cognitive rehabilitation* (pp. 13–37). Hillsdale, NJ: Lawrence Erlbaum Associates Inc.

Castles, A., & Coltheart, M. (1996). Cognitive correlates of developmental surface dyslexia: a single case study. *Cognitive Neuropsychology*, *13*, 25–50.

Castles, A., Datta, H., Gayán, J., & Olson, R. K. (1999). Varieties of developmental reading disorder: genetic and environmental influences. *Journal of Experimental Child Psychology*, *72*, 73–94.

Castles, A., & Holmes, V. M. (1996). Subtypes of developmental dyslexia and lexical acquisition. *Australian Journal of Psychology*, *48*, 130–135.

Castro-Caldas, A., Miranda, P., Carmo, I., Reis, A., Leote, F., Ribeiro, C., & Ducla-Soares, E. (1999). The influence of learning to read and write on the morphology of the corpus callosum. *European Journal of Neurology*, *6*, 23–28.

Castro-Caldas, A., Petersson, K. M., Reis, A., Stone-

Elander, S., & Ingvar, M. (1998). The illiterate brain: learning to read and write during childhood influences the functional organization of the adult brain. *Brain, 121*, 1053–1063.

Cataldo, S., & Ellis, N. C. (1988). Interactions in the development of spelling, reading and phonological skills. *Journal of Research in Reading, 11*, 86–109.

Catts, H. W. (1986). Speech production/phonological deficits in reading-disordered children. *Journal of Learning Disabilities, 19*, 504–508.

Catts, H. W. (1989a). Defining dyslexia as a developmental language disorder. *Annals of Dyslexia, 39*, 50–63.

Catts, H. W. (1989b). Speech production deficits in developmental dyslexia. *Journal of Speech and Hearing Disorders, 54*, 422–428.

Catts, H. W. (1993). The relationship between speech-language impairments and reading disabilities. *Journal of Speech and Hearing Research, 36*, 948–958.

Cestnick, L., & Coltheart, M. (1999). The relationship between language-processing and visual-processing deficits in developmental dyslexia. *Cognition, 71*, 231–255.

Chaney, C. (1992). Language development, metalinguistic skills, and print awareness in 3-year-old children. *Applied Psycholinguistics, 13*, 485–514.

Chavance, M., Dellatolas, G., Bousser, M. G., Amor, B., Grardel, B., Kahan, A., Kahn, M. F., Le Floch, J. P., & Tchobroutsky, G. (1990). Handedness, immune disorders and information bias. *Neuropsychologia, 28*, 429–441.

Chi, J. G., Dooling, E. C., & Gilles, F. H. (1977). Left–right asymmetries of the temporal speech areas of the human fetus. *Archives of Neurology, 34*, 346–348.

Cholfin, J. A., Curtiss, S. R., Shields, D. W., Kornblum, H. I., & Geschwind, G. H. (2000). A dominantly inherited speech and language disorder not linked to the *SPCH1* locus on chromosome 7q31. *Annals of Neurology, 48*, 418.

Cipolotti, L., & Warrington, E. K. (1995). Semantic memory and reading abilities: a case report. *Journal of the International Neuropsychological Society, 1*, 104–110.

Clark, M. M. (1970). *Reading difficulties in schools.* Harmondsworth: Penguin.

Clark, M. M., & Plante, E. (1998). Morphology of the inferior frontal gyrus in developmentally language-disordered adults. *Brain and Language, 61*, 288–303.

Clarke, J. M., Lufkin, R. B., & Zaidel, E. (1993). Corpus callosum morphometry and dichotic listening peformance: individual differences in functional hemispheric inhibition? *Neuropsychologia, 31*, 1503–1513.

Cohen, L., Dehaene, S., Naccache, L., Lehéricy, S., Dehaene-Lambertz, G., Henaff, M. A., & Michel, F. (2000). The visual word form area: spatial and temporal characterization of an initial stage of reading in normal subjects and posterior split-brain patients. *Brain, 123*, 291–307.

Cohn T. E. (1989). Are rods and cones of dyslexics anomalous? *Perceptual and Motor Skills, 69*, 91–94.

Coltheart, M. (1978). Lexical access in simple reading tasks. In G. Underwood (Ed.). *Strategies of information processing* (pp. 151–216). London: Academic Press.

Coltheart, M. (1980). Deep dyslexia: a review of the syndrome. In M. Coltheart, K. E. Patterson, & J. C. Marshall (Eds.). *Deep dyslexia* (pp. 23–47). London: Routledge & Kegan Paul.

Coltheart, M. (1982). The psycholinguistic analysis of acquired dyslexias: some illustrations. *Philosophical Transactions of the Royal Society of London, B, 298*, 151–164.

Coltheart, M. (1985). Cognitive neuropsychology and the study of reading. In M. I. Posner & O. S. M. Marin (Eds.), *Attention and Performance XI* (pp. 3–37). Hillsdale, NJ: Lawrence Erlbaum Associates Inc.

Coltheart, M. (1987). Varieties of developmental dyslexia: a comment on Bryant and Impey. *Cognition, 27*, 97–101.

Coltheart, M. (1996). Phonological dyslexia: past and future issues. *Cognitive Neuropsychology, 13*, 749–762.

Coltheart, M., Curtis, B., Atkins, P., & Haller, M. (1993). Models of reading aloud: dual-route and parallel-distributed-processing approaches. *Psychological Review, 100*, 589–608.

Coltheart, M., Masterson, J., Byng, S., Prior, M., & Riddoch, J. (1983). Surface dyslexia. *Quarterly Journal of Experimental Psychology, 35A*, 469–495.

Coltheart, M., & Rastle, K. (1994). Serial processing in reading aloud: evidence for dual route models of reading. *Journal of Experimental Psychology: Human Perception and Performance, 20*, 1197–1211.

Coltheart, M., Rastle, K., Perry, C., Langdon, R., & Ziegler, J. (2001). DRC: a dual route cascaded model of visual word recognition and reading aloud. *Psychological Review, 108*, 204–256.

Coltheart, V., & Leahy, J. (1992). Children's reading of nonwords: effects of regularity and consistency.

Journal of Experimental Psychology: Learning, Memory and Cognition, 18, 718–729.

Coltheart, V., & Leahy, J. (1996). Procedures used by beginning and skilled readers to read unfamiliar letter strings. *Australian Journal of Psychology, 48*, 124–129.

Compton, D. L., DeFries, J. C., & Olson, R. K. (2001). Are RAN- and phonological awareness-deficits additive in children with reading disabilities? *Dyslexia, 7*, 125–149.

Connolly, M., & Van Essen, D. (1984). The representation of the visual field in parvicellular and magnocellular layers of the lateral geniculate nucleus in the macaque monkey. *Journal of Comparative Neurology, 226*, 544–564.

Content, A., Kolinsky, R., Morais, J., & Bertelson, P. (1986). Phonetic segmentation in prereaders: effect of corrective information. *Journal of Experimental Child Psychology, 42*, 49–72.

Corballis, M. C., & Beale, I. L. (1993). In D. M. Willows, R. S. Kruk, & E. Corcos (Eds.), *Visual processes in reading and reading disabilities* (pp. 57–73). Hove, UK: Lawrence Erlbaum Associates Ltd.

Coren S., & Halpern, D. F. (1991). Left-handedness: a marker for decreased survival fitness. *Psychological Bulletin, 109*, 90–106.

Coren, S., & Searleman, A. (1990). Birth stress and left-handedness: the rare trait marker model. In S. Coren (Ed.), *Left-handedness: behavioral implications and anomalies* (pp. 3–32). Amsterdam: North-Holland/Elsevier.

Coren, S., Searleman, A., & Porac, C. (1986). Rate of physical maturation and handedness. *Developmental Neuropsychology, 2*, 17–23.

Corkin, S. (1974). Serial-ordering deficits in inferior readers. *Neuropsychologia, 12*, 347–354.

Cornelissen, P., Bradley, L., Fowler, S., & Stein, J. (1991). What children see affects how they read. *Developmental Medicine and Child Neurology, 33*, 755–762.

Cornelissen, P., Bradley, L., Fowler, S., & Stein, J. (1992). Covering one eye affects how some children read. *Developmental Medicine and Child Neurology, 34*, 296–304.

Cornelissen, P., Bradley, L., Fowler, S., & Stein, J. (1994). What children see affects how they spell. *Developmental Medicine and Child Neurology, 36*, 716–727.

Cornelissen, P. L., Hansen, P. C., Bradley, L., & Stein, J. F. (1996). Analysis of conceptual confusions between nine sets of consonant–vowel sounds in normal and dyslexic adults. *Cognition, 59*, 275–306.

Cornelissen, P. L., Hansen, P. C., Gilchrist, I., Cormack, F., Essex, J., & Frankish, C. (1998a). Coherent motion detection and letter position encoding. *Vision Research, 38*, 2181–2191.

Cornelissen, P. L., Hansen, P. C., Hutton, J. L., Evangelinou, V., & Stein, J. F. (1998b). Magnocellular visual function and children's single word reading. *Vision Research, 38*, 471–482.

Cornelissen, P., Munro, N., Fowler, S., & Stein, J. (1993). The stability of binocular fixation during reading in adults and children. *Developmental Medicine and Child Neurology, 35*, 777–787.

Cornelissen, P., Richardson, A., Mason, A., Fowler, S., & Stein, J. (1995). Contrast sensitivity and coherent motion detection measured at photopic luminance levels in dyslexics and controls. *Vision Research, 35*, 1483–1494.

Coslett, H. B. (1991). Read but not write "idea": evidence for a third reading mechanism. *Brain and Language, 40*, 425–443.

Cossu, G., Rossini, F., & Marshall, J. C. (1993). When reading is acquired but phonemic awareness is not: a study of literacy in Down's syndrome. *Cognition, 46*, 129–138.

Cossu, G., Shankweiler, D., Liberman, I. Y., Katz, L., & Tola, G. (1988). Awareness of phonological segments and reading ability in Italian children. *Applied Psycholinguistics, 9*, 1–16.

Cotton, M. M., & Evans, K. M. (1990). A review of the use of Irlen (tinted) lenses. *Australian and New Zealand Journal of Ophthalmology, 18*, 307–312.

Cowan, N., Keller, T. A., Hulme, C., Roodenrys, S., McDougall, S., & Rack, J. (1994). Verbal memory span in children: speech timing clues to the mechanisms underlying age and word length effects. *Journal of Memory and Language, 33*, 234–250.

Cowell, P. E., Jernigan, T. L., Denenberg, V. H., & Tallal, P. (1995). Language and learning impairment and prenatal risk: an MRI study of the corpus callosum and cerebral volume. *Journal of Medical Speech-Language Pathology, 3*, 1–13.

Crawford, S. G., Kaplan, B. J., & Kinsbourne, M. (1994). Are families of children with reading difficulties at risk for immune disorders and nonright-handedness? *Cortex, 30*, 281–292.

Creem, S. H., & Proffitt, D. R. (2001). Defining the cortical visual systems: "What", "Where", and "How". *Acta Psychologica, 107*, 43–68.

Critchley, M. (1928). *Mirror-writing*. London: Kegan Paul, Trench, Trubner & Co.

Critchley, M. (1970). *The Dyslexic Child*. London: Heinemann Medical.

Crosson, B. (1984). Role of the dominant thalamus in language: a review. *Psychological Bulletin, 96*, 491–517.

Crosson, B. (1985). Subcortical language functions in language: a working model. *Brain and Language, 25*, 257–292.

Crosson, B. (1999). Subcortical mechanisms in language: lexical–semantic mechanisms and the thalamus. *Brain and Cognition, 40*, 414–438.

Crosson, B., Moberg, P. J., Boone, J. R., Gonzalez-Rothi, L. J., & Raymer, A. (1997). Category-specific naming deficit for medical terms after dominant thalamic/capsular hemorrhage. *Brain and Language, 60*, 407–442.

Crow, T. J., Crow, L. R., Done, D. J., & Leask, S. (1998). Relative hand skill predicts academic ability: global deficits at the point of hemispheric indecision. *Neuropsychologia, 36*, 1275–1282.

Cuetos, F., Valle-Arroyo, F., & Suarez, M.-P. (1996). A case of phonological dyslexia in Spanish. *Cognitive Neuropsychology, 13*, 1–24.

Cunningham, D. J. (1892). *Contribution to the surface anatomy of the cerebral hemispheres*. Cunningham Memoires No. VII. Dublin: Royal Irish Society.

Curcio, A. C., Sloan, K. R., Packer, O., Hendrickson, A. E., & Kalina, R. E. (1987). Distribution of cones in human and monkey retina: individual variability and radial asymmetry. *Science, 236*, 579–582.

Dacey, D. (1993). The mosaic of midget ganglion cells in the human retina. *Journal of Neuroscience, 13*, 5334–5335.

Dalby, M. A., Elbro, C., & Stødkilde-Jøgensen, H. (1998). Temporal lobe asymmetry and dyslexia: an *in vivo* study using MRI. *Brain and Language, 62*, 51–69.

Dale, P. S., Simonoff, E., Bishop, D. V. M., Eley, T. C., Oliver, B., Price, T. S., Purcell, S., Stevenson, J., & Plomin, R. (1998). Genetic influence on language delay in two-year old-children. *Nature Neuroscience, 1*, 324–328.

Davidson, R. J., Leslie, S. C., & Saron, C. (1990). Reaction time measures of interhemispheric transfer time in reading disabled and normal children. *Neuropsychologia, 28*, 471–485.

Davis, C. J., Gayán, J., Knopik, V. S., Smith, S. D., Cardon, L. R., Pennington, B. F., Olson, R. K., & De Fries, J. C. (2001). Etiology of reading difficulties and rapid naming: the Colorado twin study of reading disability. *Behavior Genetics, 31*, 625–635.

Dearborn, W. F. (1929). The aetiology of so-called congenital word-blindness. *Psychological Bulletin, 26*, 178–179.

Dearborn, W. F. (1931). Ocular and lateral dominance in dyslexia. *Psychological Bulletin, 28*, 704–705.

Deavers, R. P., & Brown, G. D. A. (1997a). Rules versus analogies in children's spelling: evidence for task dependence. *Reading and Writing: An Interdisciplinary Journal, 9*, 339–361.

Deavers, R. P., & Brown, G. D. A. (1997b). Analogy-based strategies for nonword reading in dyslexia: effects of task. *Dyslexia, 3*, 135–156.

De Bastiani, P., Barry, C., & Carreras, M. (1988). Mechanisms for reading nonwords: evidence from a case of phonological dyslexia in an Italian reader. In G. Denes, C. Semenza, & P. Bisiacchi, (Eds.), *Perspectives on cognitive neuropsychology* (pp. 253–267). Hove, UK: Larewnce Erlbaum Associates Ltd.

Decker, S. N., & Bender, B. G. (1988). Converging evidence for multiple genetic forms of reading disability. *Brain and Language, 33*, 197–215.

DeFries, J. C. (1992). Genetics and dyslexia: An overview: In M. Snowling, & M. Thomson, (Eds.), *Dyslexia: integrating theory and practice* (pp. 3–20). London: Whurr Publishers.

DeFries, J. C., & Alarcón, M. (1996). Genetics of specific reading disability. *Mental Retardation and Developmental Disabilities Research Reviews, 2*, 39–47.

DeFries, J. C., Alarcón, M., & Olson, R. K. (1997). Genetic aetiologies of reading and spelling deficits: developmental differences. In C. Hulme, & M. Snowling, (Eds.), *Dyslexia: biology, cognition and intervention* (pp. 20–37). London: Whurr Publishers.

DeFries, J. C., & Fulker, D. W. (1985). Multiple regression analysis of twin data. *Behaviour Genetics, 15*, 467–473.

DeFries, J. C., Fulker, D. W., & LaBuda, M. C. (1987). Evidence for a genetic aetiology in reading disability of twins. *Nature, 329*, 537–539

DeFries, J. C., Singer, S. M., Foch, T. T., & Lewitter, F. I. (1978). Familial nature of reading disability. *British Journal of Psychiatry, 132*, 361–367.

de Gelder, B., & Vroomen, J. (1991). Phonological deficits: beneath the surface of reading-acquisition problems. *Psychological Research, 53*, 88–97.

de Gelder, B., & Vroomen, J. (1998). Impaired speech perception in poor readers: evidence from hearing and speech reading. *Brain and Language, 64*, 269–281.

Dejerine, M. J. (1891). Sur un cas de cécité verbale avec

agraphie, suivi d'autopsie. *Mémoires de la Société de Biologie, 3,* 197–201.

Dejerine, M. J. (1892). Contribution a l'étude anatomo-pathologique et clinique des différentes variétés de cécité verbale. I. Cécité verbale avec agraphie ou troubles très marqués de l'écriture. II. Cécité verbale pure avec intégrité de l'écriture spontanée et sous dictée. *Mémoires de la Société de Biologie, 4,* 61–90.

de Jong, P. F., & Van der Leij, A. (1999). Specific contributions of phonological abilities to early reading acquisition: results from a Dutch latent variable longitudinal study. *Journal of Educational Psychology, 91,* 450–476.

de Jong, P. F., Seveke, M.-J., & Van Veen, M. (2000). Phonological sensitivity and the acquisition of new words in children. *Journal of Experimental Child Psychology, 76,* 275–301.

De Lacoste-Utamsing, M. C., & Holloway, R. L. (1982). Sexual dimorphism in the human corpus callosum. *Science, 216,* 1431–1432.

Dellatolas, G., Annesi, I., Jallon, P., Chavance, M., & Lellouch, J. (1990). An epidemiological reconsideration of the Geschwind-Galaburda theory of cerebral lateralization. *Archives of Neurology, 47,* 778–782.

Dellatolas, G., Curt, F., Dargent-Paré, C., & De Agostini, M. (1998). Eye dominance in children: a longitudinal study. *Behaviour Genetics, 28,* 187–195.

Demb, J. B., Boynton, G. M., Best, M., & Heeger, D. J. (1998a). Psychophysical evidence for a magnocellular pathway deficit in dyslexia. *Vision Research, 38,* 1555–1559.

Demb, J. B., Boynton, G. M., & Heeger, D. J. (1997). Brain activity in visual cortex predicts individual differences in reading performances. *Proceedings of the National Academy of Sciences, USA, 94,* 13363–13366.

Demb, J. B., Boynton, G. M., & Heeger, D. J. (1998b). Functional magnetic resonance imaging of early visual pathways in dyslexia. *Journal of Neuroscience, 18,* 6939–6951.

Démonet, J.-F., Wise, R., & Frackowiak, R. S. J. (1993). Language functions explored in normal subjects by positron emission tomography: a critical review. *Human Brain Mapping, 1,* 39–47.

Denckla, M. B. (1985). Motor coordination in dyslexic children: theoretical and clinical implications. In F. H. Duffy, & N. Geschwind, (Eds), *Dyslexia: a neuroscientific approach to clinical evaluation* (pp. 184–195). Boston, MA: Little, Brown, & Co.

Denckla, M. B., & Rudel, R. G. (1976a). Rapid "automatized" naming (R.A.N.): dyslexia differentiated from other learning disabilities. *Neuropsychologi, 14,* 471–479.

Denckla, M. B., & Rudel, R. G. (1976b). Naming of object-drawings by dyslexic and other learning disabled children. *Brain and Language, 3,* 1–15.

Denckla, M. B., Rudel, R. G., & Broman, M. (1981). Tests that discriminate between dyslexic and other learning-disabled boys. *Brain and Language, 13,* 118–129.

Denenberg, V. H. (1999). A critique of Mody, Studdert-Kennedy, and Brady's "Speech perception deficits in poor readers: Auditory processing or phonological coding?" *Journal of Learning Disabilities, 32,* 379–383.

Dennis, M. (1981). Language in a congenitally acallosal brain. *Brain and Language, 12,* 33–53.

De Partz, M.-P. (1986). Re-education of a deep dyslexic patient: rationale of the method and results. *Cognitive Neuropsychology, 3,* 149–177.

Dérouesné, J., & Beauvois, M.-F. (1979). Phonological processing in reading: data from alexia. *Journal of Neurology, Neurosurgery and Psychiatry, 42,* 1125–1132.

De Schutter, E., & Maex, R. (1996). The cerebellum: cortical processing and theory. *Current Opinion in Neurobiology, 6,* 759–764.

Desimone, R., & Ungerleider, L. G. (1986). Multiple visual areas in the caudal superior temporal sulcus of the macaque. *Journal of Comparative Neurology, 248,* 164–189.

Desimone, R., & Ungerleider, L. G. (1989). Neural mechanisms of visual perception in monkeys. In F. Boller & J. Grafman (Eds.), *Handbook of neuropsychology,* (Vol. 2, pp. 267–299). Amsterdam: Elsevier.

D'Esposito, M., & Alexander, M. P. (1995). Subcortical aphasia: distinct profiles following putaminal hemorrhage. *Neurology, 45,* 38–41.

Dimond, S. J., Scammell, R. E., Brouwers, E. Y. M., & Weeks, R. (1977). Functions of the centre section (trunk) of the corpus callosum in man. *Brain, 100,* 543–562.

Dobbins, D. A. (1988). Yule's "hump" revisited. *British Journal of Educational Psychology, 58,* 338–344.

Dobyns, W. B. (1996). Absence makes the search grow longer. *American Journal of Human Genetics, 58,* 7–16.

Dollaghan, C., Biber, M., & Campbell, T. (1993). Constituent syllable effects in a nonsense-word repetition task. *Journal of Speech and Hearing Research, 36,* 1051–1054.

Downey, J. E. (1933). Laterality of function. *Psychological Bulletin*, *30*, 109–142.

Drake, W. E. (1968). Clinical and pathological findings in a child with developmental learning disability. *Journal of Learning Disability*, *1*, 486–502.

Drasdo, N., Thompson, C. M., & Deeley, R. J. (1991). Psychophysical evidence of two gradients of neural sampling in peripheral vision. In A. Valberg, and B. B. Lee (Eds.), *From pigments to perception* (pp. 189–192). New York: Plenum Press.

Drew, A. L. (1956). A neurological appraisal of familial congenital word-blindness. *Brain*, *79*, 440–460.

Driesen, N. R., & Raz, N. (1995). The influence of sex, age, and handedness on corpus callosum morphology: a meta analysis. *Psychobiology*, *23*, 240–247.

Dronkers, N. F. (1996). A new brain region for coordinating speech articulation. *Nature*, *384*, 159–161.

Duara, B., Kushch, A., Gross-Glenn, K., Barker, W. W., Jallad, B., Pascal, S., Lowenstein, D. A., Sheldon, J., Rabin, M., Levin, B., & Lubs, H. (1991). Neuroanatomic differences between dyslexic and normal readers on magnetic resonance imaging scans. *Archives of Neurology*, *48*, 410–416.

Duffy, F. H., Denckla, M. B., Bartels, P. H., & Sandini, G. (1980). Dyslexia: regional differences in brain electrical activity by topographic mapping. *Annals of Neurology*, *7*, 412–420.

Duffy, F. H., & McAnulty, G. B. (1985). Brain electrical activity mapping (BEAM): the search for a physiological signature of dyslexia. In F. H. Duffy, & N. D. Geschwind (Eds.), *Dyslexia: a neuroscientific approach to clinical evaluation* (pp. 105–123). Boston, MA: Little, Brown, & Co.

Duncan, L. G., Seymour, P. H. K., & Hill, S. (1997). How important are rhyme and analogy in beginning reading? *Cognition*, *63*, 171–208.

Dunlop, D. B. (1972). The binocular basis of dyslexic confusion. *Australian Orthoptic Journal 12*, 16–20.

Dunlop, D. B. (1976). The changing role of orthoptics in dyslexia. *British Orthoptic Journal*, *33*, 22–28.

Dunlop, D. B., & Dunlop, P. (1974). New concepts of visual laterality in relation to dyslexia. *Australian Journal of Ophthalmology*, *2*, 101–112.

Dunlop, D. B., Dunlop, P., & Fenelon, B. (1973). Vision laterality analysis in children with reading disability: the results of new techniques of examination. *Cortex*, *9*, 227–236.

Dykman, R. A., & Ackerman, P. T. (1992). Diagnosing dyslexia: IQ regression plus cut-points. *Journal of Learning Disabilities*, *25*, 574–576.

Eberstaller, O. (1890). *Das Stirnhirn*. Vienna Urban & Schwarzenberg.

Eckert, M. A. & Leonard, C. M (1999). *Heritability of Heschl's gyrus duplication: a neural risk factor for dyslexia*. Paper presented at the annual conference of the Cognitive Neuroscience Society, Washington D.C.

Eckert, M. A., & Leonard, C. M. (2003). Developmental disorders: dyslexia. In K. Hugdahl & R. J. Davidson, (Eds.), *The asymmetrical brain* (pp. 651–679). Cambridge, MA: MIT Press.

Eckert, M. A., Leonard, C. M., Richards, T. L., Aylward, E. H., Thomson, J., & Berninger, V. W. (2003). Anatomical correlates of dyslexia: frontal and cerebellar findings. *Brain*, *126*, 482–494.

Eckert, M. A., Lombardino, L. J., & Leonard, C. M. (2001). Planar asymmetry tips the phonological playground and environment raises the bar. *Child Development*, *72*, 988–1002.

Eden, G. F., Stein, J. F., Wood, H. M., & Wood, F. B. (1994). Differences in eye movements and reading problems in dyslexic and normal children. *Vision Research*, *34*, 1345–1358.

Eden, G. F., Stein, J. F., Wood, H. M., & Wood, F. B. (1995a). Temporal and spatial processing in reading disabled and normal children. *Cortex*, *31*, 451–468.

Eden, G. F., Stein, J. F., Wood, M. H., & Wood, F. B. (1995b). Verbal and visual problems in reading disability. *Journal of Learning Disabilities*, *28*, 272–290.

Eden , G. F., VanMeter, J. W., Rumsey, J. M., Maisog, J. M., Woods, R. P., & Zeffiro, T. A. (1996). Abnormal processing of visual motion in dyslexia revealed by functional brain imaging. *Nature*, *382*, 66–69.

Edwards, S., & Beaton, A. A. (1996). Howzat?! Why is there an over-representation of left-handed bowlers in professinal cricket in the UK? *Laterality*, *1*, 45–50.

Efron, R. (1963a). The effect of handedness on the perception of simultaneity and temporal order. *Brain*, *86*, 261–284.

Efron, R. (1963b). The effect of stimulus intensity on the perception of simultaneity in right- and left-handed subjects. *Brain*, *86*, 285–294.

Eglinton, E., & Annett, M. (1994). Handedness and dyslexia: a meta-analysis. *Perceptual and Motor Skills*, *79*, 1611–1616.

Ehri, L. C. (1980). The development of orthographic images. In U. Frith, (Ed.), *Cognitive processes in spelling* (pp. 311–338). London: Academic Press.

Ehri, L. C. (1987). Learning to read and spell words. *Journal of Reading Behavior*, *19*, 5–31.

Ehri, L. C. (1989). The development of spelling knowledge and its role in reading acquisition and reading disability. *Journal of Learning Disabilities, 22,* 356–365.

Ehri, L. C. (1992a). Reconceptualizing the development of sight word reading and its realationship to recoding. In P. H. Gough, L. C. Ehri, & R. Treiman, (Eds.), *Reading acquisition* (pp. 107–143). Hillsdale, NJ:. Lawrence Erlbaum Associates IWC.

Ehri, L. C. (1992b). The development of reading and spelling in children: an overview. In M. Snowling & M. Thomson (Eds.), *Dyslexia: integrating theory and practice* (pp. 63–79). London: Publishers.

Ehri, L. C. (1995). Phases of development in learning to read words by sight. *Journal of Research in Reading, 18,* 116–125.

Ehri, L. C. (1997). Learning to read and to spell are one and the same, almost. In C. A. Perfetti, L. Rieben, & M. Fayol (Eds.), *Learning to Spell: Research, Theory and Practice across Languages* (pp. 237–269). Mahwah, NJ: Lawrence Erlbaum Associates Inc.

Ehri, L. C., & Robbins, C. (1992). Beginners need some decoding skill to read words by analogy. *Reading Research Quarterly, 27,* 12–26.

Ehri, L. C., & Saltmarsh, J. (1995). Beginning readers outperform older disabled readers in learning to read by sight. *Reading and Writing: An Interdisciplinary Journal, 7,* 295–326.

Ehri, L. C., & Wilce, L. S. (1985). Movement into reading: is the first stage of printed word learning visual or phonetic? *Reading Research Quarterly, 20,* 163–179.

Eidelberg, D., & Galaburda, A. M. (1982). Symmetry and asytmmetry in the human posterior thalamus. 1. Cytoarchitectonic analysis in normal persons. *Archives of Neurology, 39,* 325–332.

Eidelberg, D., & Galaburda, A. M. (1984). Inferior parietal lobule: divergent architectonic asymmetries in the human brain. *Archives of Neurology, 41,* 843–852.

Eimas, P. D., Siqueland, E. R., Jusczyk, P. W., & Vigorito, J. (1971). Speech perception in infants. *Science, 171,* 303–306.

Elbro, C. (1996). Early linguistic abilities and reading development: a review and a hypothesis. *Reading and Writing: An Interdisciplinary Journal, 8,* 453–485.

Elbro, C., Nielsen, I., & Petersen, D. K. (1994). Dyslexia in adults: evidence for deficits in nonword reading and in the phonological representation of lexical items. *Annals of Dyslexia, 44,* 205–226.

Eliassen, J. C., Baynes, K., & Gazzaniga, M. S. (2000). Anterior and posterior callosal contributions to simultaneous bimanual movements of the hands and fingers. *Brain, 123,* 2501–2511.

Eliez, S., Rumsey, J. M., Giedd, J. N., Schmitt, J. E., Patwardhan, A. J., & Reiss, A. L. (2000). Morphological alteration of temporal lobe gray matter in dyslexia: an MRI study. *Journal of Child Psychology and Psychiatry, 41,* 637–644.

Elliott, C. D., Murray, D. J., & Pearson, L. S (1979). *The British Ability Scales* (1st edn). Windsor: NFER-Nelson.

Ellis, A. W. (1979). Developmental and acquired dyslexia: some observations on Jorm (1979). *Cognition, 7,* 413–420.

Ellis, A. W. (1984). *Reading, writing and dyslexia: a cognitive analysis.* (1st edn). Hove, UK: Lawrence Erlbaum Associates Ltd.

Ellis, A. W. (1985). The cognitive neuropsychology of developmental (and acquired) dyslexia: a critical survey. *Cognitive Neuropsychology, 2,* 169–205.

Ellis, A. W. (1987). Intimations of modularity, or, the modelarity of mind: doing cognitive neuropsychology without syndromes. In M. Coltheart, G., Sartori, & R. Job, (Eds.), *The cognitive neuropsychology of language* (pp. 397–408). London: Lawrence Erlbaum Associates Ltd.

Ellis, A. W. (1993). *Reading, writing and dyslexia: a cognitive analysis* (2nd edn). Hove, UK: Lawrence Erlbaum Associates Ltd.

Ellis, A. W., McDougall, S. J. P., & Monk, A. F. (1996a). Are dyslexics different? I. A comparison between dyslexics, reading age controls, poor readers and precocious readers. *Dyslexia, 2,* 31–58.

Ellis, A. W., McDougall, S. J., & Monk, A. (1996b). Are dyslexics different? II. Individual differences among dyslexics, reading age controls, poor readers and precocious readers. *Dyslexia, 2,* 59–68.

Ellis, A. W., McDougall, S. J., & Monk, A. (1997). Are dyslexics different? III. Of course they are! *Dyslexia, 3,* 2–8.

Ellis, N. C. (1990). Reading, phonological skills and short-term memory: interactive tributaries of development. *Journal of Research in Reading, 13,* 107–122.

Ellis, N. C., & Beaton, A. A. (1993). Factors affecting the learning of foreign language vocabulary: imagery keyword mediators and phonological short-term memory. *Quarterly Journal of Experimental Psychology, 46A,* 533–558.

Ellis, N. C., & Large, B. (1987). The development of

reading: as you seek so shall you find. *British Journal of Psychology, 78*, 1–28.

Ellis, N. C., & Miles, T. R. (1978). Visual information processing as a determinant of reading speed. *Journal of Reading Research, 1*, 108–120.

Ellis, N. C., & Sinclair, S. (1996). Working memory in the acquisition of vocabulary and syntax: putting language in good order. *Quarterly Journal of Experimental Psychology, 49A*, 234–250.

Evans, B. J. W., Drasdo, N., & Richards, I. L. (1994). An investigation of some sensory and refractive visual factors in dyslexia. *Vision Research, 34*, 1913–1926.

Everatt, J., Bradshaw, M. F., & Hibbard, P. B. (1999). Visual processing and dyslexia. *Perception, 28*, 243–254.

Fabbro, F., Moretti, R., & Bava, A. (2000). Language impairments in patients with cerebellar lesions. *Journal of Neurolinguistics, 13*, 173–188.

Fabbro, F., Pesenti, S., Facoetti, A., Bonanomi, M., Libera, L., & Lorusso, M. L. (2001). Callosal transfer in different types of developmental dyslexia. *Cortex, 37*, 65–74.

Fagerheim, T., Raeymaekers, P., Tønnessen, F. E., Pedersen, M., Tranebjaerg, L., & Lubs, H. A. (1999). A new gene (DYX3) for dyslexia is located on chromosome 2. *Journal of Medical Genetics, 36*, 664–669.

Falzi, G., Perrone, P., & Vignolo, L. A. (1982). Right–left asymmetry in anterior speech regions. *Archives of Neurology, 39*, 239–240.

Farmer, M. E., & Klein, R. M. (1995). The evidence for a temporal processing deficit linked to dyslexia: a review. *Psychonomic Bulletin and Review, 2*, 460–493.

Fawcett, A. J., & Nicolson, R. I. (1992). Automatisation deficits in balance for dyslexic children. *Perceptual and Motor Skills, 75*, 507–529.

Fawcett, A. J., & Nicolson, R. I. (1995). Persistent deficits in motor skill of children with dyslexia. *Journal of Motor Behaviour, 27*, 235–240.

Fawcett, A. J., & Nicolson, R. I. (1999). Performance of dyslexic children on cerebellar and cognitive tests. *Journal of Motor Behaviour, 31*, 68–78.

Feldman, L. B., & Turvey, M. T. (1983). Word recognition in Serbo-Croatian is phonologically analytic. *Journal of Experimental Psychology: Human Perception and Performance, 9*, 288–298.

Felleman, D. J., & Van Essen, D. C. (1987). Receptive field properties of neurons in area V3 of macaque monkey extra-striate cortex. *Journal of Neurophysiology, 57*, 889–920.

Felmingham, K. L., & Jakobson, L. S. (1995). Visual and visuomotor performance in dyslexic children. *Experimental Brain Research, 106*, 467–474.

Felsenfeld, S., & Plomin, R. (1997). Epidemiological and offspring analysis of developmental speech disorders using data from the Colorado Adoption Project. *Journal of Speech, Language and Hearing Research, 40*, 778–791.

Felton, R. H., Naylor, C. E., & Wood, F. B. (1990). Neuropsychological profile of adult dyslexics. *Brain and Language, 39*, 485–497.

Ferris G. M., & Dorsen, M. (1975). Agenesis of the corpus callosum. 1. Neuropsychological studies. *Cortex, 11*, 95–122.

Ffytche, D. H., Guy, C. N., & Zeki, S. (1995). The parallel visual motion inputs into areas V1 and V5 of human cerebral cortex. *Brain, 118*, 1375–1394.

Field, L. L., & Kaplan, B. J. (1998). Absence of linkage of phonological coding dyslexia to chromosome 6p23-p21.3 in a large family data set. *American Journal of Human Genetics, 63*, 1448–1456.

Fiez, J. A., & Petersen, S. E. (1998). Neuro-imaging studies of word reading. *Proceedings of the National Academy of Sciences, USA, 95*, 914–921.

Filbey, R. A., & Gazzaniga, M. S. (1969). Splitting the normal brain with reaction time. *Psychonomic Science, 17*, 335–336.

Fildes, L. G. (1921). A psychological inquiry into the nature of the condition known as word-blindness. *Brain, 44*, 286–307.

Fildes, L. G., & Myers, C. S. (1921). Left-handedness and the reversal of letters. *British Journal of Psychology, 12*, 273–278.

Finch, A. J., Nicolson, R. I., & Fawcett, A. J. (2002). Evidence for a neuroanatomical difference within the olivo-cerebellar pathway of adults with dyslexia. *Cortex, 38*, 529–539.

Finucci, J. M., Guthrie, J. T., Childs, A. L., Abbey, H., & Childs, B. (1976). The genetics of specific reading disability. *Annals of Human Genetics, 40*, 1–23.

Fischer, B., & Hartnegg, K. (2000). Effects of visual training on saccade control in dyslexia. *Perception, 29*, 531–542.

Fischer, B., & Weber, H. (1990). Saccadic reaction times of dyslexic and age-matched normal subjects. *Perception, 19*, 805–818.

Fischer, B., Hartnegg, K., & Mokler, A. (2000). Dynamic visual perception of dyslexic children. *Perception, 29*, 523–530.

Fischer, F. W., Liberman, I. Y., & Shankweiler, D. (1978). Reading reversals and developmental dyslexia: a further study. *Cortex, 14*, 496–510.

Fisher, J. H. (1905). Case of congenital word-blindness

(inability to learn to read). *Ophthalmic Review, 24*, 315–318.

Fisher, S. E., Marlow, A. J., Lamb, J., Maestrini, E., Williams, D. F., Richardson, A. J., Weeks, D. E., Stein, J. F., & Monaco, A. P. (1999). A quantitative-trait locus on chromosome 6p influences different aspects of developmental dyslexia. *American Journal of Human Genetics, 64*, 146–156.

Fisher, S. E., Vargha-Khadem, F., Watkins, K. E., Monaco, A. P., & Pembret, M. (1998). Localisation of a gene implicated in a severe speech and language disorder. *Nature Genetics, 18*, 168–170.

Fisher, S. E., Francks, C., Marlow, A. J., MacPhie, I. L., Newbury, D. F., Cardon, L. R., Ishakawa-Brush, Y., Richardson, A. J., Talcott, J. B., Gayán, J., Olson, R. K., Pennington, B. F., Smith, S. D., DeFries, J. C., Stein, J. F., & Monaco, A. P. (2002). Independent genome-wide scans identify a chromosome 18 quantitative-trait locus influencing dyslexia. *Nature Genetics, 30*, 86–91.

Fitch, R. H., Berrebi, A. S., Cowell, P. E., Schrott, L. M., Denenberg, V. H. (1990). Corpus callosum: effects of neocortical hormones on sexual dimorphism in the rat. *Brain Research, 515*, 111–116.

Fitch, R. H., Miller, S., & Tallal, P. (1997). Neurobiology of speech perception. *Annual Review of Neuroscience, 20*, 331–353.

Fitzgerald, A. (1989). Tinted lenses and dyslexia: a review of the literature. *Australian Orthoptic Journal, 25*, 1–6.

Flannery, K. A., & Liederman, J. (1995). Is there really a syndrome involving the co-occurrence of neurodevelopmental disorder, talent, non-right handedness and immune disorder among children? *Cortex, 31*, 503–515.

Fletcher, J. M., Espy, K. A., Francis, D. J., Davidson, K. C., Rourke, B. P., & Shaywitz, S. (1989). Comparison of cut-off and regression-based definitions of reading disabilities. *Journal of Learning Disabilities, 22*, 334–338 and 355.

Fletcher, J. M., Taylor, H. G., Morris, R., & Satz, P. (1982). Finger recognition skills and reading achievement: a developmental neuropsychological analysis. *Developmental Psychology, 18*, 124–132.

Fletcher, J. M., Shaywitz, S. E., Shankweiler, D. P., Katz, L., Liberman, I. Y., Stuebing, K. K., Francis, D. J., Fowler, A. E., & Shaywitz, B. A. (1994a). Cognitive profiles of reading disability: comparisons of discrepancy and low achievement definitions. *Journal of Educational Psychology, 86*, 6–23.

Fletcher, J. M., Stuebing, K. K., Shaywitz, B. A., Shaywitz, S. E., Rourke, B. P., & Francis D. J. (1994b). Validity of the concept of dyslexia: alternative approaches to definition and classification. In K. P. van den Bos, L. S. Siegel, D. J. Bakker, & D. L. Share (Eds.), *Current directions in dyslexia research* (pp. 31–43). Lisse: Swets & Zeitlinger.

Fletcher-Flinn, C. M., & Thompson, G. B. (2000). Learning to read with underdeveloped phonemic awareness but lexicalised phonological recoding: a case study of a 3-year-old. *Cognition, 74*, 177–208.

Flowers, D. L., Wood, F. B., & Naylor, C. E. (1991). Regional cerebral blood flow correlates of language processes in reading disability. *Archives of Neurology, 48*, 637–643.

Flynn, J. M., Deering, W., Goldstein, M., & Rahbar, M. H. (1992). Electrophysiological correlates of dyslexic subtypes. *Journal of Learning Disabilities, 25*, 133–141.

Foundas, A. L., Eure, K. F., Luevano, L. F., & Weinberger, D. R. (1998a). MRI asymmetries of Broca's area: the pars triangularis and pars opercularis. *Brain and Language, 64*, 282–296.

Foundas, A. L., Leonard, C. M., Gilmore, R., Fennell, E., & Heilman, K. M. (1994). Planum temporale asymmetry and language dominance. *Neuropsychologia, 32*, 1225–1231.

Foundas, A. L., Leonard, C. M., Gilmore, R. L., Fennell, E. B., & Heilman, K. M. (1996). Pars triangularis asymmetry and language dominance. *Proceedings of the National Academy of Sciences, USA, 93*, 719–722.

Foundas, A. L., Leonard, C. M., Gilmore, R., & Heilman, K. M. (1995). Morphologic cerebral asymmetries and handedness: the pars triangularis and planum temporale. *Archives of Neurology, 52*, 501–507.

Foundas, A. L., Leonard, C. M., & Hanna-Pladdy, B. (2002). Variability in the anatomy of the planum temporale and posterior ascending ramus: do right- and left-handers differ? *Brain and Language, 83*, 403–424.

Fowler, A. E. (1991). How early phonological development might set the stage for phoneme awareness. In S. A. Brady & D. P. Shankweiler (Eds.), *Phonological processes in literacy: a tribute to Isabelle Y. Liberman* (pp. 97–117). Hillsdale, NJ: Lawrence Erlbaum Associates Inc.

Fox, B., & Routh, D. K. (1976). Phonemic analysis and synthesis as word attack skills. *Journal of Educational Psychology, 68*, 70–74.

Fox, B., & Routh, D. K. (1983). Reading disability, phonemic analysis, and dysphonetic spelling: a follow-up. *Journal of Clinical Child Psychology, 12*, 28–32

Fox, B., & Routh, D. K. (1984). Phonemic analysis and synthesis as word attack skills: revisited. *Journal of Educational Psychology, 76*, 1059–1064.

Frackowiak, R. S. J., & Friston, K. J. (1994). Functional neuroanatomy of the human brain: positron emission tomography — a new neuroanatomical technique. *Journal of Anatomy, 184*, 211–225.

Frank, J., & Levinson, H. (1973). Dysmetric dyslexia and dyspraxia. *Journal of the American Academy of Child Psychiatry, 12*, 690–701.

Fransella, F., & Gerver, D. (1965). Multiple regression equations for predicting reading age from chronological age and WISC verbal I.Q. *British Journal of Educational Psychology, 35*, 86–89.

Franz, A. E., Waldie, K. E., & Smith, M. J. (2000). The efect of callosotomy on novel versus familiar bimanual actions: a neural dissociation between controlled and automatic processes? *Psychological Science, 11*, 82–85.

Fredman, G., & Stevenson, J. (1988). Reading processes in specific reading retarded and reading backward 13-year-olds. *British Journal of Developmental Psychology, 6*, 97–108.

Freud, S. (1953). *On aphasia: a critical study* (translated by E. Stengel). London: Imago Publishing. (Original work published 1891)

Friedman, R. F., Ween, J. E., & Albert, M. L. (1993). Alexia. In K. M. Heilman & E. Valenstein (Eds.), *Clinical neuropsychology* (pp. 37–62). New York: Oxford University Press.

Friston, K. J., Frith, C. D., Liddle, P. F., Dolan, R. J., Lammertsma, A. A., & Frackowiak, R. S. J. (1990). The relationship between global and local changes in PET scans. *Journal of Cerebral Blood Flow and Metabolism, 10*, 458–466.

Frith, C., & Friston, K. J. (1997). Studying brain function with neuro-imaging. In M. Rugg (Ed.), *Cognitive neuroscience* (pp. 169–195). Hove, UK: Psychology Press.

Frith, C., & Frith, U. (1996). A biological marker for dyslexia. *Nature, 382*, 19–20.

Frith, U. (1980). Unexpected spelling problems. In U. Frith (Ed.), *Cognitive processes in spelling* (pp. 495–515). London: Academic Press.

Frith, U. (1985). Beneath the surface of developmental dyslexia. In K. E. Patterson, J. C. Marshall, & M. Coltheart (Eds.), *Surface dyslexia* (pp. 301–322). London: Lawrence Erlbaum Associates Ltd.

Frith, U. (1986). A developmental framework for developmental dyslexia. *Annals of Dyslexia, 36*, 69–81.

Frith, U. (1997). Brain, mind and behaviour in dyslexia. In C. Hulme & M. Snowling (Eds), *Dyslexia: biology, cognition and intervention* (pp. 1–19). London: Whurr Publishers.

Frith, U., Landerl, K., & Frith, C. (1995). Dyslexia and verbal fluency: more evidence for a phonological deficit. *Dyslexia, 1*, 2–11.

Frith, U., Wimmer, H., & Landerl, K. (1998). Differences in phonological recoding in German- and English-speaking children. *Scientific Studies of Reading, 2*, 31–54.

Frost, R. (1998). Toward a strong phonological theory of visual word recognition: true issues and false trails. *Psychological Bulletin, 123*, 71–99.

Frost, R., Katz, L., & Bentin, S. (1987). Strategies for visual word recognition and orthographical depth: a multilingual comparison. *Journal of Experimental Psychology: Human Perception and Performance, 13*, 104–115.

Froster, U., Schulte-Körne, G., Hebebrand, J., & Remschmidt, H. (1993). Cosegregation of balanced translocation (1;2) with retarded speech development and dyslexia. *Lancet, 342*, 178–179.

Fry, M. A., Johnson, C. S., & Muehl, S. (1970). Oral language production in relation to reading achievement among select second graders. In D. J. Bakker & P. Satz (Eds.), *Specific reading disability: advances in theory and method* (pp. 123–146). Rotterdam: Rotterdam University Press.

Fulbright, R. K., Jenner, A. R., Mencl, W. E., Pugh, K. R., Shaywitz, B. A., Shaywitz, S. E., Frost, S. J., Skudlarski, P., Constable, R. T., Lacadie, C. M., Marchione, K. E., & Gore, J. C. (1999). The cerebellum's role in reading. *American Journal of Neuroradiology, 20*, 1925–1930.

Funnell, E. (1983). Phonological processes in reading: new evidence from acquired dyslexia. *British Journal of Psychology, 74*, 159–180.

Funnell, E., & Davison, M. (1989). Lexical capture: a developmental disorder of reading and spelling. *Quarterly Journal of Experimental Psychology, 41A*, 471–487.

Galaburda, A. M., Corsiglia, J., Rosen, G. D., & Sherman, G. F. (1987). Planum temporale asymmetry: reappraisal since Geschwind and Levitsky. *Neuropsychologia, 25*, 853–868.

Galaburda, A. M., & Kemper, T. L. (1979). Cytoarchitectonic abnormalities in developmental dyslexia: a case study. *Annals of Neurology, 6*, 94–100.

Galaburda, A. M., LeMay, M., Kemper, T. L., &

Geschwind, N. (1978a). Right–left asymmetries in the brain: structural differences between the hemispheres may underlie cerebral dominance. *Science, 199*, 852–856.

Galaburda, A., & Livingstone, M. (1993). Evidence for a magnocellular defect in developmental dyslexia. *Annals of the New York Academy of Sciences, 682*, 70–82.

Galaburda, A. M., Menard, M. T., & Rosen, G. T. (1994). Evidence for aberrant auditory anatomy in developmental dyslexia. *Proceedings of the National Academy of Sciences, USA, 91*, 8010–8013.

Galaburda, A. M., Rosen, G. D., & Sherman, G. F. (1990). Individual variability in cortical organization: its relationship to brain laterality and implications to function. *Neuropsychologia, 28*, 529–546.

Galaburda, A., & Sanides, F. (1980). Cytoarchitectonic organization of the human auditory cortex. *Journal of Comparative Neurology, 190*, 597–610.

Galaburda, A. M., Sanides, F., & Geschwind, N. (1978b). Human brain: cytoarchitectonic left–right asymmetries in the temporal speech region. *Archives of Neurology, 35*, 812–817.

Galaburda, A. M., Sherman, G. F., Rosen, G. D., Aboitiz, F., & Geschwind, N. (1985). Developmental dyslexia: four consecutive patients with cortical anomalies. *Annals of Neurology, 18*, 222–233.

Gallagher, A., Frith, U., & Snowling, M. (2000). Precursors of literacy delay among children at genetic risk of dyslexia. *Journal of Child Psychology and Psychiatry, 41*, 203–213.

Galuske, R. A. W., Schlote, W., Bratzke, H., & Singer, W. (2000). Interhemispheric asymmetries of the modular structure in human temporal cortex. *Science, 289*, 1946–1949.

Gannon, P. J., Holloway, R. L., Broadfield, D. C., Braun, A. R. (1998). Asymmetry of chimpanzee planum temporale: humanlike pattern of Wernicke's brain language area homolog. *Science, 279*, 220–222.

Gardner, R. A., & Broman, M. (1979). The Purdue pegboard: normative data on 1334 school children. *Journal of Clinical Child Psychology*, Fall, pp. 156–162.

Gates, A. I., & Bond, G. Y. (1936). Relation of handedness, eye-sighting and acuity dominance to reading. *Journal of Educational Psychology, 27*, 450–456.

Gathercole, S. E. (1995). Is nonword repetition a test of phonological memory or long-term knowledge? It all depends on the nonwords. *Memory and Cognition, 23*, 83–94.

Gathercole, S. E., & Adams, A. M. (1994). Children's phonological working memory: contributions of long-term knowledge and rehearsal. *Journal of Memory and Language, 33*, 627–688.

Gathercole, S. E., Adams, A. M., & Hitch, G. J. (1994a). Do young children rehearse? An individual differences analysis. *Memory and Cognition, 22*, 201–207.

Gathercole, S. E., & Baddeley, A. D. (1987). The process underlying segmental analysis. *European Bulletin of Cognitive Psychology, 7*, 462–464.

Gathercole, S. E., & Baddeley, A. D. (1989). Evaluation of the role of phonological STM in the development of vocabulary in children: a longitudinal study. *Journal of Memory and Language, 28*, 200–213.

Gathercole, S. E., & Baddeley, A. D. (1990a). The role of phonological memory in vocabulary acquisition: a study of young children learning new names. *British Journal of Psychology, 81*, 439–454.

Gathercole, S. E., & Baddeley, A. D. (1990b). Phonological memory deficits in language disordered children: is there a causal connection? *Journal of Memory and Language, 29*, 336–360.

Gathercole, S. E., & Baddeley, A. D. (1997). Sense and sensitivity in phonological memory and vocabulary development: a reply to Bowey (1996). *Journal of Experimental Child Psychology, 67*, 290–294.

Gathercole, S. E., Hitch, G. J., Service, E., & Martin, A. J. (1997). Phonological short-term memory and new word learning in children. *Developmental Psychology, 33*, 966–979.

Gathercole, S. E., & Martin, A. J. (1996). Interactive processes in phonological memory. In S. E. Gathercole (Ed.), *Models of short-term memory* (pp. 73–100). Hove, UK: Psychology Press.

Gathercole, S. E., Willis, C. S., & Baddeley, A. D. (1991a). Differentiating phonological memory and awareness of rhyme: reading and vocabulary development. *British Journal of Psychology, 82*, 387–406.

Gathercole, S. E., Willis, C. S., Baddeley, A. D., & Emslie, H. (1994b). The children's test of nonword repetition: a test of phonological working memory. *Memory, 2*, 103–127.

Gathercole, S. E., Willis, C. S., Emslie, H., & Baddeley, A. D. (1991b). The influence of number of syllables and wordlikeness on children's repetition of nonwords. *Applied Psycholinguistics, 12*, 349–367.

Gauger, L. M., Lombardino, L. J., & Leonard, C. M. (1997). Brain morphology in children with specific language impairment. *Journal of Speech, Language and Hearing Research, 40*, 1272–1284.

Gayán, J., & Olson, R. K. (2001). Genetic and environmental influences on orthographic and phonological skills in children with reading disabilities. *Developmental Neuropsychology, 20,* 483–507.

Gayán, J., Smith, S. D., Cherny, S. S., Cardon, L. R., Fulker, D. W., Brower, A. M., Olson, R. K., Pennington, B. R., & DeFries, J. C. (1999). Quantitative-trait locus for specific language and reading deficits on chromosome 6p. *American Journal of Human Genetics, 64,* 157–164.

Gazzaniga, M. S. (2000). Does the corpus callosum enable the human condition? *Brain, 123,* 1293–1326.

Gazzaniga, M. S., Bogen, J. E., & Sperry, R. W. (1967). Dyspraxia following division of the cerebral commissures. *Archives of Neurology, 16,* 606–612.

Geffen, G., Nilsson, J., Quinn, K., & Teng, E. L. (1985). The effect of lesions of the corpus callosum on finger localization. *Neuropsychologia, 23,* 497–514.

Geiger, G., & Lettvin, J. Y. (1987). Peripheral vision in persons with dyslexia. *New England Journal of Medicine, 316,* 1238–1243.

Georgiewa, P., Rzanny, R., Hopf, J. M., Knab, R., Glauche, V., Kaiser, W., & Blanz, B. (1999). FMRI during word processing in dyslexics and normal reading children. *NeuroReport, 10,* 3459–3465.

Geschwind, N., & Behan, P. O. (1982). Left-handedness: association with immune disease, migraine, and developmental learning disorder. *Proceedings of the National Academy of Sciences, USA, 79,* 5097–5100.

Geschwind, N., & Behan, P. O. (1984). Laterality, hormones and immunity. In N. Geschwind & A. Galaburda (Eds.), *Cerebral dominance: the biological foundations* (pp. 211–224). Cambridge, MA: Harvard University Press.

Geschwind, N., & Galaburda, A. (1985a). Cerebral lateralization. Biological mechanisms, associations, and pathology: I. A hypothesis and a program for research. *Archives of Neurology, 42,* 428–459.

Geschwind, N., & Galaburda, A. (1985b). Cerebral lateralization. Biological mechanisms, associations, and pathology: II. A hypothesis and a program for research. *Archives of Neurology, 42,* 521–552.

Geschwind, N., & Galaburda, A. (1985c). Cerebral lateralization. Biological mechanisms, associations, and pathology: III. A hypothesis and a program for research. *Archives of Neurology, 42,* 634–654.

Geschwind, N., & Galaburda, A. M. (1987). *Cerebral lateralization: biological mechanisms, associations and Pathology.* Cambridge, MA: MIT Press.

Geschwind, N., & Levitsky, W. (1968). Human brain: left–right asymmetries of the temporal speech region. *Science, 161,* 186–187.

Geurts, C. H., & Mulder, T. W. (1994). Attention demands in balance recovery following lower limb amputation. *Journal of Motor Behaviour, 26,* 162–170.

Giedd, J. N., Blumenthal, J., Jeffries, N. O., Rajapakse, J., Vaituzis, A. C., Liu, H., Berry, Y. C., Tobin, M., Nelson, J., & Castellanos, F. X. (1999). Development of the human corpus callosum during childhood and adolescence: a longitudinal MRI study. *Progress in Neuropharmacological and Biological Psychiatry, 23,* 571–588.

Giedd, J. N., Rumsey, J. M., Castellanos, F. X., Rajapakse, J. C., Kaysen, D., Vaituzis, A. C., Vauss, Y. C., Hamburger, S. D., & Rapoport, J. L. (1996). A quantitative MRI study of the corpus callosum in children and adolescents. *Developmental Brain Research, 91,* 274–280.

Gilbert, A. N., & Wysocki, C. J. (1992). Hand preference and age in the United States. *Neuropsychologia, 30,* 601–608.

Gilger, J. W., & Pennington, B. F. (1995). Why associations among traits do not necessarily indicate their common etiology: a comment on the Geschwind-Behan-Galaburda model. *Brain and Cognition, 27,* 89–93.

Gilger, J. W., Pennington, B. F., Green, P., Smith, S. M., & Smith, S. D. (1992). Reading disability, immune disorders and non-right-handedness: twin and family studies of their relations. *Neuropsychologia, 30,* 209–227.

Gilger, J. W., Pennington, B. F., Harbeck, R. J., DeFries, J. C., Kotzin, B., Green, P., & Smith, S. (1998). A twin and family study of the association between immune system dysfunction and dyslexia using blood serum immunoassay and survey data. *Brain and Cognition, 36,* 310–333.

Gladstone, M., Best, C. T., & Davidson, R. J. (1989). Anomalous bimanual coordination among dyslexic boys. *Developmental Psychology, 25,* 236–246.

Glass, P., Bulas, D. I., Wagner, A. E., Rajasingham, S. R., Civitello, L. A., & Coffman, C. E. (1998). Pattern of neuropsychological deficit at age five years following neonatal unilateral brain injury. *Brain and Language, 63,* 346–356.

Glickstein, M. (1993). Motor skills but not cognitive tasks. *Trends in Neuroscienc, 16,* 450–451.

Glushko, R. J. (1979). The organization and activation of orthographic knowledge in reading aloud. *Journal of Experimental Psychology: Human Perception and Performance, 5,* 674–691.

Godfrey, J. J., Syrdal-Lasky, A. K., Millay, K. K., & Knox, C. M. (1981). Performance of dyslexic children on speech perception tests. *Journal of Experimental Child Psychology, 32*, 401–424.

Goldman, P. S., Lodge, A., Hammer, L. R., Semmes, J., & Mishkin, M. (1968). Critical flicker frequency after unilateral temporal lobectomy in man. *Neuropsychologia, 6*, 355–363.

Gombert, J. E., Bryant, P., & Warrick, N. (1997). Children's use of analogy in learning to read and spell. In C. A. Perfetti, L., Reiben, & M. Fayol (Eds.), *Learning to spell: research, theory, and practice across languages* (pp. 221–235). Mahwah, NJ: Lawrence Erlbaum Associates Inc.

González, J. E. J., & Valle, I. H. (2000). Word identification and reading disorders in the Spanish language. *Journal of Learning Disabilities, 33*, 44–60.

Good, C. D., Johnsrude, I., Ashburner, J., Henson, R. N. A., Friston, K. J., & Frackowiak, R. S. J. (2001). Cerebral asymmetry and the effects of sex and handedness on brain structure: a voxel-based morphometric analysis of 465 normal adult human brains. *NeuroImage, 14*, 685–700.

Goodale, M., & Milner, A. D. (1992). Separate visual pathways for perception and action. *Trends in Neuroscience, 15*, 20–25.

Gooddy, W., & Reinhold, M. (1961). Congenital dyslexia and asymmetry of cerebral function. *Brain, 84*, 231–242.

Gopnik, M. (1990). Feature-blind grammar and dysphasia. *Nature, 344*, 715.

Gopnik M., & Crago, M. B. (1991). Familial aggregation of a developmental language disorder. *Cognition, 39*, 1–50.

Gordon, H. (1921). Left-handedness and mirror-writing, especially among defective children. *Brain, 43*, 313–368

Goswami, U. (1986). Children's use of analogy in learning to read: a developmental study. *Journal of Experimental Child Psychology, 42*, 73–83.

Goswami, U. (1988a). Orthographic analogies and reading development. *Quarterly Journal of Experimental Psychology, 40A*, 239–268.

Goswami, U. (1988b). Children's use of analogy in learning to spell. *British Journal of Developmental Psychology, 6*, 21–33.

Goswami, U. (1990a). A special link between rhyming skill and the use of orthographic analogies by beginning readers. *Journal of Child Psychology and Psychiatry, 31*, 301–311.

Goswami, U. (1990b). Phonological priming and orthographic analogies in reading. *Journal of Experimental Child Psychology, 49*, 323–340.

Goswami, U. (1991). Learning about spelling sequences: the role of onsets and rimes in analogies in reading. *Child Development, 62*, 1110–1123.

Goswami, U. (1993). Toward an interactive analogy model of reading development: decoding vowel graphemes in beginning reading. *Journal of Experimental Child Psychology, 56*, 443–475.

Goswami, U. (1997). Learning to read in different orthographies: phonological awareness, orthographic representations and dyslexia. In C. Hulme & M. Snowling (Eds.), *Dyslexia: biology, cognition and intervention.* (pp. 131–152). London: Whurr Publishers.

Goswami, U. (1999a). Orthographic analogies and phonological priming: a comment on Bowey, Vaughan, and Hansen (1998). *Journal of Experimental Child Psychology, 72*, 210–219.

Goswami, U. (1999b). Causal connections in beginning reading: the importance of rhyme. *Journal of Research in Reading, 22*, 217–240.

Goswami, U., & Bryant, P. (1990). *Phonological skills and learning to read.* Hove, UK: Lawrence Erlbaum Associates Ltd.

Goswami, U., & Bryant, P. (1992). Rhyme, analogy, and children's reading. In P. B. Gough, L. C. Ehri, & R. Treiman (Eds.), *Reading acquisition.* (pp. 49–63). Hove, UK: Lawrence Erlbaum Associates Ltd.

Goswami, U., & East, M. (2000). Rhyme and analogy in beginning reading: conceptual and methodological issues. *Applied Psycholinguistics, 21*, 63–93.

Goswami, U., Gombert, J. E., & de Barrera, L. F. (1998). Children's orthographic representations and linguistic transparency: nonsense word reading in English, French, and Spanish. *Applied Psycholinguistics, 19*, 19–52.

Goswami, U., & Mead, F. (1992). Onset and rime awareness and analogies in reading. *Reading Research Quarterly, 27*, 152–162.

Goswami, U., Porpodas, C., & Wheelwright, S. (1997). Children's orthographic representations in English and Greek. *European Journal of Psychology of Education, 12*, 273–292.

Goswami, U., Thomson, J., Richards, U., Stainthorp, R., Hughes, D., Rosen, S., & Scott, S. K. (2002). Amplitude envelope onsets and developmental dyslexia: a new hypothesis. *Proceedings of the National Academy of Sciences, USA, 99*, 10911–10916.

Goswami, U., Ziegler, J. C., Dalton, L., & Schneider, W. (2001). Pseudohomophone effects and phonological recoding procedures in reading development in English and German. *Journal of Memory and Language, 45*, 648–664.

Gottardo, A., Siegel, L. S., & Stanovich, K. E. (1997). The assessment of adults with reading disabilities: what can we learn from experimental tasks? *Journal of Research in Reading, 20,* 42–54.

Gottardo, A., Stanovich, K. E., & Siegel, L. S. (1996). The relationships between phonological sensitivity, syntactic processing, and verbal working memory in the reading performance of third-grade children. *Journal of Experimental Child Psychology, 63,* 563–582.

Gough, P. B., & Hillinger, M. L. (1980). Learning to read: an unnatural act. *Bulletin of the Orton Society, 30,* 179–196.

Gough, P. B., Juel, C., & Griffith, P. L. (1992). Reading, spelling, and the orthographic cipher. In P. B. Gough, L. C. Ehri, & R. Treiman (Eds.), *Reading acquisition,* (pp. 35–48). Hove, UK: Lawrence Erlbaum Associates Ltd.

Gough, P. B., & Tunmer, W. E. (1986). Decoding reading and reading disability. *Remedial and Special Education, 7,* 6–10.

Gough, P. B., & Walsh, M. A. (1991). Chinese, Phoenicians, and the orthographic cipher of English. In S. A. Brady & D. P. Shankweiler (Eds.), *Phonological processes in literacy: a tribute to Isabelle Y. Liberman* (pp. 199–209). Hillsdale, NJ: Lawrence Erlbaum Associates Inc.

Goulandris, N., McIntyre, A., Snowling, M., Bethel, J.-M. & Lee, J. P. (1998). A comparison of dyslexic and normal readers using orthoptic assessment procedures. *Dyslexia, 4,* 30–48.

Goulandris, N. K., & Snowling, M. J. (1991). Visual memory deficits: a plausible case of developmental dyslexia? Evidence from a single case. *Cognitive Neuropsychology, 8,* 127–154.

Grainger, J. (1992). Orthographic neighbourhoods and visual word recognition. In R. Frost & L. Katz (Eds.), *Orthography, phonology, morphology, and meaning* (pp. 131–146). Amsterdam: Elsevier.

Grant, A. C., Zangaladze, A., Thiagarajah, M. C., & Sathian, K. (1999). Tactile perception in developmental dyslexia: a psychophysical study using gratings. *Neuropsychologia, 37,* 1201–1211.

Greaney, K. T., Tunmer, W. E., & Chapman, J. W. (1997). Effects of rime-based orthographic analogy training on the word recognition skills of children with reading disability. *Journal of Educational Psychology, 89,* 645–651.

Green, R. L., Hutsler, J. J., Loftus, W. C., Tramo, M. J., Thomas, C. E., Silberfarb, A. W., Nordgren, R. E., Nordgren, R. A., & Gazzaniga, M. S. (1999). The caudal infrasylvian surface in dyslexia: novel magnetic resonance imaging-based findings. *Neurology, 53,* 974–981.

Griffiths, P. (1991). Word-finding ability and design fluency in developmental dyslexia. *British Journal of Clinical Psychology, 30,* 47–60.

Griffiths, S., & Frith, U. (2002). Evidence for an articulatory awareness deficit in adult dyslexics. *Dyslexia, 8,* 14–21.

Griffiths, Y., & Snowling, M. (2001). Auditory word identification and phonological skills in dyslexic and average readers. *Applied Psycholinguistics, 22,* 419–439.

Griffiths, Y., & Snowling, M. (2002). Predictors of exception word and nonword reading in dyslexic children: the severity hypothesis. *Journal of Educational Psychology, 94,* 34–43.

Grigorenko, E. L. (2001). Developmental dyslexia: an update on genes, brains, and environments. *Journal of Child Psychology and Psychiatry, 42,* 91–125.

Grigorenko, E. L., Wood, F. B., Golovyan, L., Meyer, M., Romano, C., & Pauls, D. (2003). Continuing the search for dyslexia genes on 6p. *American Journal of Medical Genetics Part B (Neuropsychiatric Genetics) 118B,* 89–98.

Grigorenko, E. L., Wood, F. B., Meyer, M. S., Pauls, J. E. D. Hart, L. A., & Pauls, D. L. (2001). Linkage studies suggest a possible locus for developmental dyslexia on chromosome 1p. *American Journal of Medical Genetics (Neuropsychiatric Genetics), 105,* 120–129.

Grigorenko, E. L., Wood, F. B., Meyer, M. S., Hart, L. A., Speed, W. C., Shuster, A., & Pauls, D. L. (1997). Susceptibility loci for distinct components of developmental dyslexia on chromosomes 6 and 15. *American Journal of Human Genetics, 60,* 27–39.

Grigorenko, E. L., Wood, F. B., Meyer, M. S., & Pauls, D. (2000). Chromosome 6p influences on different dyslexia-related cognitive processes: further confirmation. *American Journal of Human Genetics, 66,* 715–723.

Grimshaw, G. M., Bryden, M. P., &. Finegan, J.-A. K. (1995). Relations between prenatal testosterone and cerebral lateralization in children. *Neuropsychology, 9,* 68–79.

Grodzinsky, Y., Pinango, M.-M., Zurif, E., & Drai, D. (1999). The critical role of group studies in neuropsychology: comprehension regularities in Broca's aphasia. *Brain and Language, 67,* 134–147.

Grosser, G. S., & Spafford, C. S. (1989). Perceptual evidence for an anomalous distribution of rods and cones in the retinas of dyslexics: a new hypothesis. *Perceptual and Motor Skills, 68,* 683–698.

Grosser, G. S., & Spafford, C. S. (1990). Light sensitivity in peripheral retinal fields of dyslexic and proficient readers. *Perceptual and Motor Skills, 71*, 467–477.

Grosser, G. S., & Spafford, C. S. (1992). Reply to Stuart and Lovegrove's question, "Visual processsing deficits in dyslexia: receptors or neural mechanisms?". *Perceptual and Motor Skills, 75*, 115–120.

Gross-Glenn, K., & Rothenberg, S. (1984). Evidence for deficit in interhemispheric transfer of information in dyslexic boys. *International Journal of Neuroscience, 24*, 23–35.

Gross-Glenn, K., Skottun, B. C., Glenn, W., Kusch, A., Lingua, R., Dunbar, M., Jallad, B., Lubs, H. A., Levin, B., Rabin, M., Parke, L. A., & Duara, R. (1995). Contrast sensitivity in dyslexia. *Visual Neuroscience, 12*, 153–163.

Guthrie, J. T. (1973a). Reading comprehension and syntactic responses in good and poor readers. *Journal of Educational Psychology, 65*, 294–299.

Guthrie, J. T. (1973b). Models of reading and reading disability. *Journal of Educational Psychology, 65*, 9–18.

Habib, M. (2000). The neurological basis of developmental dyslexia: an overview and working hypothesis. *Brain, 123*, 2373–2399.

Habib, M., Espesser, R., Rey, V., Giraud, K., Bruas, P., & Gres, C. (1999). Training dyslexics with acoustically modified speech: evidence of improved phonological performance. *Brain and Cognition, 40*, 143–146.

Habib, M., & Robichon, F. (2003). Structural correlates of brain asymmetry: studies in left-handed and dyslexic individuals. In K. Hugdahl & R. J. Davidson (Eds.), *The asymmetrical brain* (pp. 681–716). Cambridge, MA: MIT Press.

Habib, M., Robichon, F., Chanoine, V., Démonet, J.-F., Frith, C., & Frith, U. (2000). The influence of language learning on brain morphology: the "callosal effect" in dyslexics differs according to native language. *Brain and Language, 74*, 520–524.

Habib, M., Robichon, F., Lévrier, O., Khalil, R., & Salamon, G. (1995). Diverging asymmetries of temporo-parietal cortical areas: a reappraisal of Geschwind/Galaburda theory. *Brain and Language, 48*, 238–258.

Habib, M., Touze, F., & Galaburda, A. (1990). Intrauterine factors in sinistrality: a review. In S. Coren (Ed.), *Left-handedness: behavioral implications and anomalies* (pp. 99–130). Amsterdam: North-Holland/Elsevier.

Hagman, J. O., Wood, F., Buchsbaum, M. S., Tallal, P., Flowers, L., & Katz, W. (1992). Cerebral brain metabolism in adult dyslexic subjects assessed with positron emission tomography during performance of an auditory task. *Archives of Neurology, 49*, 734–739.

Hallet, M. (2000). Transcranial magnetic stimulation and the human brain. *Nature, 406*, 147–150.

Hallgren, B. (1950). Specific dyslexia ("congenital word-blindness"): a clinical and genetic study. *Acta Psychiatrica et Neurologica* (suppl. 65), 1–287.

Hanley, J. R. (1997). Reading and spelling impairments in undergraduate students with developmental dyslexia. *Journal of Research in Reading, 20*, 22–30.

Hanley, J. R., & Gard, F. (1995). A dissociation between developmental surface and phonological dyslexia in two undergraduate students. *Neuropsychologia, 33*, 909–914.

Hanley, J. R., Hastie, K., & Kay, J. (1992). Developmental surface dyslexia and dysgraphia: an orthographic processing impairment. *Quarterly Journal of Experimental Psychology, 44A*, 285–319.

Hanley, R., Reynolds, C., & Thornton, A. (1997). Orthographic analogies and developmental dyslexia. *British Journal of Psychology, 88*, 423–440.

Hansen, J., & Bowey J. A. (1994). Phonological analysis skills, verbal working memory, and reading ability in second grade children. *Child Development, 65*, 938–950.

Hansen, O., Nerup, J., & Holbek, B. (1986). A common genetic origin of specific dyslexia and insulin-dependent diabetes mellitus? *Hereditas, 105*, 165–167.

Hansen, O., Nerup, J., & Holbek, B. (1987). Further indication of a possible common genetic origin of specific dyslexia and insulin-dependent diabetes mellitus? *Hereditas, 107*, 257–258.

Hardyck, C. (1977). Laterality and intellectual ability: a just not noticeable difference. *British Journal of Educational Psychology, 47*, 305–311.

Hardyck, C., & Petrinovich, L. F. (1977). Left-handedness. *Psychological Bulletin, 84*, 385–404.

Hari, R., & Kiesilä, P. (1996). Deficit of temporal auditory processing in dyslexic adults. *Neuroscience Letters, 205*, 138–140.

Hari, R., Renvall, H. & Tanskanen, T. (2001). Left minineglect in dyslexic adults. *Brain, 124*, 1373–1380.

Hari, R., Sääskilahti, A., Helenius, P., & Uutela, K. (1999). Non-impaired auditory phase locking in dyslexic adults. *NeuroReport, 10*, 2347–2348.

Harm, M. W., & Seidenberg, M. S. (1999). Phonology, reading acquisition, and dyslexia: insights from connectionist models. *Psychological Review, 106,* 491–528.

Harm, M. W., & Seidenberg, M. S. (2001). Are there orthographic impairments in phonological dyslexia? *Cognitive Neuropsychology, 18,* 71–92.

Harris, A. J. (1957). Lateral dominance, directional confusion, and reading disability. *Journal of Psychology, 44,* 283–294.

Harris, A. J. (1974). *Harris tests of lateral dominance.* New York: Psychological Corporation.

Harris, L. J. (1991). Cerebral control for speech in right-handers and left-handers: an analysis of the views of Paul Broca, his contemporaries and his successors. *Brain and Language, 40,* 1–50.

Haslam, R. H. A., Dalby, J. T., Johns, R. D., & Rademaker, A. W. (1981). Cerebral asymmetry in developmental dyslexia. *Archives of Neurology, 38,* 679–682.

Haslum, M. N. (1989). Predictors of dyslexia? *Irish Journal of Psychology, 10,* 622–630.

Hatcher, P. J., & Hulme, C. (1999). Phonemes, rhymes, and intelligence as predictors of children's responsiveness to remedial reading instruction: evidence from a longitudinal intervention study. *Journal of Experimental Child Psychology, 72,* 130–153.

Hatcher, P. J., Hulme, C., & Ellis, A. W. (1994). Ameliorating early reading failure by integrating the teaching of reading and phonological skills: the phonological linkage hypothesis. *Child Development, 65,* 41–57.

Hayduk, S., Bruck, M., & Cavanagh, P. (1996). Low-level visual processing skills of adults and children with dyslexia. *Cognitive Neuropsychology, 13,* 975–1015.

Hayes, T. L., & Lewis, D. A. (1995). Anatomical specialization of the anterior motor speech area: hemispheric differences in magnopyramidal neurons. *Brain and Language, 49,* 289–308.

Head, H. (1926). *Aphasia and kindred disorders of speech.* Cambridge: Cambridge University Press.

Heath, S. M., Hogben, J. H., & Clark, C. D. (1999). Auditory temporal processing in disabled readers with and without oral language delay. *Journal of Child Psychology and Psychiatry, 40,* 637–647.

Heiervang, E., Hugdahl, K., Steinmetz, H., Smievoll, I., Stevenson, J., Lund, A., Ersland, L., & Lundervold, A. (2000). Planum temporale, planum parietale and dichotic listening in dyslexia. *Neuropsychologia, 38,* 1704–1713.

Heilman, K. M., Voeller, K., & Alexander, A. W. (1996). Developmental dyslexia: a motor-articulatory feedback hypothesis. *Annals of Neurology, 39,* 407–412.

Heim, S., Eulitz, C., Kaufmann, J., Füchter, I., Pantev, C., Lamprecht-Dinnesen, A., Matulat, P., Scheer, P., Borstel, M., & Elbert, T. (2000). Atypical organisation of the auditory cortex in dyslexia as revealed by MEG. *Neuropsychologia, 38,* 1749–1759.

Helenius, P., Uutela, K., & Hari, R. (1999). Auditory stream segregation in dyslexic adults. *Brain, 122,* 907–913.

Hellige, J. B., Taylor, K. B., Lesmes, L., & Peterson, S. (1998). Relationships between brain morphology and behavioural measures of hemispheric asymmetry and interhemispheric interaction. *Brain and Cognition, 36,* 158–192.

Henderson, V. W. (1986). Anatomy of posterior pathways in reading: a reassessment. *Brain and Language, 29,* 119–133.

Herman, A. E., Galaburda, A. M., Fitch, R. H., Carter, A. R., & Rosen, G. D. (1997). Cerebral microgyria, thalamic cell size and auditory temporal processing in male and female rats. *Cerebral Cortex, 7,* 453–464.

Hermann, H. T., Sonnabend, N. L., & Zeevi, Y. Y. (1986). Interhemispheric coordination is compromised in subjects with developmental dyslexia. *Cortex, 22,* 337–358.

Hermann, K. (1959). *Reading disability: a medical study of word-blindness and related handicaps.* Copenhagen: Munksgaard.

Hiemenz, J. R., & Hynd, G. W. (2000). Sulcal/gyral pattern morphology of the perisylvian language region in developmental dyslexia. *Brain and Language, 74,* 113–133.

Hier, D. B., LeMay, M., Rosenberger, P. B., & Perlo, V. P. (1978). Developmental dyslexia: evidence for a sub-group with a reversal of cerebral asymmetry. *Archives of Neurology, 35,* 90–92.

Hildreth, G. (1934). Reversals in reading and writing. *Journal of Educational Psychology, 25,* 1–20.

Hill, E. L. (1998). A dyspraxic deficit in specific language impairment and developmental coordination disorder: evidence from hand and arm movements. *Developmental Medicine and Child Neurology, 40,* 388–395.

Hill, N. I., Bailey, P. J., Griffiths, Y. M., & Snowling, M. J. (1999). Frequency acuity and binaural masking release in dyslexic listeners. *Journal of the Acoustical Society of America, 106,* 53–59.

Hill, G. T., & Raymond, J. E. (2002). Deficits of motion transparency perception in adult developmental dyslexics with normal unidirectional motion sensitivity. *Vision Research*, 1195–1203.

Hines, M., McAdams, L. A., Chiu, L., Bentler, P. M., & Lipcamon, J. (1992). Cognition and the corpus callosum: verbal fluency, visuo-spatial ability, and language lateralization related to midsagittal surface areas of callosal subregions. *Behavioral Neuroscience, 106*, 3–14.

Hinshelwood, J. (1895). Word-blindness and visual memory. *Lancet*, 21 December, pp. 1564–1570.

Hinshelwood, J. (1896). A case of dyslexia: a peculiar form of word-blindness. *Lancet*, 21 November, pp. 1451–1454.

Hinshelwood, J. (1898). A case of "word" without "letter" blindness. *Lancet*, 12 February, pp. 422–425.

Hinshelwood, J. (1899). "Letter" without "word" blindness. *Lancet*, 14 January, pp. 83–86.

Hinshelwood, J. (1900). Congenital word-blindness. *Lancet*, 26 May, pp. 1506–1508.

Hinshelwood, J. (1907). Four cases of congenital word-blindness occurring in the same family. *British Medical Journal*, 2 November, pp. 1229–1232.

Hinshelwood, J. (1917). *Congenital word-blindness*. London: H. K. Lewis.

Hinton, G. E., Plaut, D. C., & Shallice, T. (1993). Simulating brain damage. *Scientific American, 269*, 76–82.

Hinton, G. E., & Shallice, T. (1991). Lesioning an attractor network: investigations of acquired dyslexia. *Psychological Review, 98*, 74–95.

Hiscock, M., & Kinsbourne, M. (1982). Laterality and dyslexia: a critical view. *Annals of Dyslexia, 32*, 177–228.

Hitch, G. J., & Halliday, M. S. (1983). Working memory in children. *Philosophical Transactions of the Royal Society of London, B, 302*, 325–340.

Ho, C. S.-H., & Bryant, P. E. (1997). Phonological skills are important in learning to read Chinese. *Developmental Psychology, 33*, 946–951.

Ho, C. S.-H., Chan, D. W.-O., Tsang, S.-M., & Lee, S.-H. (2002). The cognitive profile and multiple deficit hypothesis in Chinese developmental dyslexia. *Developmental Psychology, 38*, 543–553.

Hogben, J. H. (1996). A plea for purity. *Australian Journal of Psychology, 48*, 172–177.

Hogben, J. H. (1997). How does a visual transient deficit affect reading? In C. Hulme & M. Snowling (Eds.), *Dyslexia: biology, cognition and intervention* (pp. 59–71). London: Whurr Publishers.

Hogben, J. H., Rodino, I. S., Clark, C. D., & Pratt, C. (1995). A comparison of temporal integration in

children with a specific reading disability and normal readers. *Vision Research, 35*, 2067–2074.

Hohn, W. E., & Ehri, L. C. (1983). Do alphabet letters help prereaders acquire phonemic segmentation skill? *Journal of Educational Psychology, 75*, 752–762.

Hohnen, B., & Stevenson, J. (1999). The structure of genetic influences on general cognitive, language, phonological, and reading abilities. *Developmental Psychology, 35*, 590–603.

Høien, T., Lundberg, I., Stanovich, K. E., & Bjaalid, I.-K. (1995). Components of phonological awareness. *Reading and Writing: An Interdisciplinary Journal, 7*, 171–188.

Holliday, I. E., Anderson, S. J., & Harding, G. F. A. (1997). Magnetoencephalographic evidence for non-geniculostriate visual input to human cortical area V5. *Neuropsychologia, 35A*, 1139–1146.

Holligan, C., & Johnston, R. (1988). The use of phonological information by good and poor readers in memory and reading tasks. *Memory and Cognition, 16*, 522–532.

Holmes, G. (1917). Functional localization in the cerebellum. *Brain, 40*, 531–535.

Holmes, G. (1939). The cerebellum of man. *Brain, 62*, 1–30.

Holmes, V. M., & Standish, J. M. (1996). Skilled reading with impaired phonology: a case study. *Cognitive Neuropsychology, 13*, 1207–1222.

Hopkins, W. D., Marino, L., Rilling, J. K., & MacGregor, L. A. (1998). Planum temporale asymmetries in great apes revealed by magnetic resonance imaging (MRI). *NeuroReport, 12*, 2913–2918.

Horwitz, B., Rumsey, J. M., & Donohue, B. C. (1998). Functional connectivity of the angular gyrus in normal reading. *Proceedings of the National Academy of Sciences, of the USA, 95*, 8939–8944.

Howard, D., & Best, W. (1996). Developmental phonological dyslexia: real word reading can be completely normal. *Cognitive Neuropsychology, 13*, 887–934.

Howard, D., & Best, W. (1997). Impaired nonword reading with normal word reading: a case study. *Journal of Research in Reading, 29*, 55–65.

Howard, D., Patterson, K., Wise, R., Brown, W. D., Friston, K., Weiller, C., & Frackowiak, R. (1992). The cortical localization of the lexicons. *Brain, 115*, 1769–1782.

Huang, H. S., & Hanley, R. J. (1995). Phonological awareness and visual skill in learning to read Chinese and English. *Cognition, 54*, 73–98.

Hubel, D., & Wiesel, T. (1977). Functional architecture

of macaque monkey visual cortex. *Proceedings of the Royal Society of London, B, 198*, 1–59.

Hugdahl, K., & Andersson, B. (1987). Dichotic listening and reading acquisition in children: a one-year follow-up. *Journal of Clinical and Experimental Neuropsychology, 9*, 631–649.

Hugdahl, K., Heiervang, E., Ersland, L., Lundervold, A., Steinmetz, H., & Smievoll, A. I. (2003). Significant relation between MR measures of planum temporale area and dichotic processing of syllables in dyslexic children. *Neuropsychologia, 41*, 666–675.

Hugdahl, K., Heiervang, E., Nordby, H., Smievoll, A. I., Steinmetz, H., Stevenson, J., & Lund, A. (1998). Central auditory processing, MRI morphometry and brain laterality: applications to dyslexia. *Scandinavian Audiology, 27* (Supplement 49), 26–34.

Hugdhal, K., Synnevåg, B., & Satz, P. (1990a). Immune and auto-immune diseases in dyslexic children. *Neuropsychologia, 28*, 673–679.

Hugdhal, K., Synnevåg, B., & Satz, P. (1991). Immune and auto-immune diseases in dyslexic children: erratum. *Neuropsychologia, 29*, 211.

Hugdahl, K., Wester, K., & Asbjørnsen, A. (1990b). The role of the felt and right thalamus in language asymmetry: dichotic listening in Parkinson patients undergoing stereotactic thalamotomy. *Brain and Language, 39*, 1–13.

Hulme, C. (1988). The implausibility of low-level visual deficits as a cause of children's reading difficulties. *Cognitive Neuropsychology, 5*, 369–374.

Hulme, C., Maughan, S., & Brown, G. D. A. (1991). Memory for familiar and unfamiliar words: evidence for a long-term memory contribution to short-term memory span. *Journal of Memory and Language, 30*, 685–701.

Hulme, C., Muter, V., & Snowling, M. (1998). Segmentation does predict early progress in learning to read better than rhyme: a reply to Bryant. *Journal of Experimental Child Psychology, 71*, 39–44.

Hulme, C., & Roodenrys, S. (1995). Practitioner review: verbal working memory development and its disorders. *Journal of Child Psychology and Psychiatry, 36*, 373–398.

Hulme, C., Roodenrys, S., Schweikert, R., Brown, R., Martin, S., & Stuart, G. (1997). Word frequency effects on short-term memory tasks: evidence for a redintegration process in immediate serial recall. *Journal of Experimental Psychology: Learning, Memory and Cognition, 23*, 1217–1232.

Hulme, C., & Snowling, M. (1992). Deficits in output

phonology: an explanation of reading failure? *Cognitive Neuropsychology, 9*, 47–72.

Hulme, C., Thomson, N., Muir, C., & Lawrence, A. (1984). Speech rate and the development of short-term memory span. *Journal of Experimental Child Psychology, 38*, 241–253.

Humphreys, G. W., & Evett, L. J. (1985). Are there independent lexical and non-lexical routes in word processing? An evaluation of the dual-route theory of reading. *Behavioral and Brain Sciences, 8*, 689–705.

Humphreys, P., Kaufmann, W. E., & Galaburda, A. M. (1990). Developmental dyslexia in women: neuropathological findings in three patients. *Annals of Neurology, 28*, 727–738.

Hurford, D. P. (1991). The possible use of IBM-compatible computers and digital-to-analog conversion to asess children for reading disabilities and to increase their phonemic awareness. *Behavior Research Methods, Instruments and Computers, 23*, 319–323.

Hurford, D. P., & Sanders, R. E. (1990). Assessment and remediation of a phonemic discrimination deficit in reading disabled second and fourth graders. *Journal of Experimental Child Psychology, 50*, 396–441.

Hynd, G. (1992). Neurological aspects of the balance model. *Journal of Learning Disabilities, 25*, 110–112 and 123.

Hynd, G. W., Hall, J., Novey, E. S., Eliopulos, D., Black, K., Gonzalez, J. J., Edmonds, J. E., Riccio, C., & Cohen, M. (1995). Dyslexia and corpus callosum morphology. *Archives of Neurology, 52*, 32–37.

Hynd, G. W., & Hiemenz, J. R. (1997). Dyslexia and gyral morphology variation. In: C. Hulme & M. Snowling (Eds.), *Dyslexia: biology, cognition and intervention* (pp. 38–58). London: Whurr Publishers.

Hynd, G. W., & Semrud-Clikeman, M. (1989). Dyslexia and brain morphology. *Psychological Bulletin, 106*, 447–482.

Hynd, G. W., Semrud-Clikeman, M., Lorys, A. R., Novey, E. S., & Eliopulos, D. (1990). Brain morphology in developmental dyslexia and attention deficit/hyperactivity disorder. *Archives of Neurology, 47*, 919–926.

Hyönä, J., & Olson, R. K. (1995). Eye fixation patterns among dyslexic and normal readers: effects of word length and word frequency. *Journal of Experimental Psychology: Learning, Memory and Cognition, 21*, 1430–1440.

Indefrey, P., Kleinschmidt, A., Merboldt, K.-D., Krüger, G., Brown, C., Hagoort, P., & Frahm, J. (1997). Equivalent responses to lexical and nonlexical visual stimuli in occipital cortex: a functional magnetic resonance imaging study. *NeuroImage, 5*, 78–81.

Ingram, T. T. S. (1963). Delayed development of speech with special reference to dyslexia. *Proceedings of the Royal Society of Medicine, 56*, 199–203.

Ingram, T. T. S., & Mason, A. W. (1965). Child care in general practice. *British Medical Journal, 20*, 463–465.

Inman, W. S. (1924). An enquiry into the origin of squint, left-handedness and stammer. *Lancet, 2* August, pp. 211–215.

Ireland, W. (1881). On mirror-writing and its relation to left-handedness and cerebral disease. *Brain, 4*, 361–367.

Irlen, H. L. (1994). Scotopic sensitivity/Irlen syndrome hypothesis and explanation of the syndrome. *Journal of Behavioural Optometry, 5*, 65–66.

Isaacs, E., Christie, D., Vargha-Khadem, F., & Mishkin, M. (1996). Effects of hemispheric side of injury, age at injury, and presence of seizure disorder on functional ear and hand asymmetries in hemiplegic children. *Neuropsychologia, 34*, 127–137.

Ito, M. (1993). Movement and thought: identical control mechanisms by the cerebellum. *Trends in Neuroscience, 16*, 448–450.

Ivry, M. (1997). Cerebellar timing systems. *International Review of Neurobiology, 41*, 555–573.

Ivry, R. B., & Diener, H. C. (1991). Impaired velocity perception in patients with lesions of the cerebellum. *Journal of Cognitive Neuroscience, 3*, 355–366.

Ivry, R. B., & Keele, S. W. (1989). Timing functions of the cerebellum. *Journal of Cognitive Neuroscience, 1*, 136–152.

Jackson, N. E., & Butterfield, E. C. (1989). Reading-level-match designs: myths and realities. *Journal of Reading Behavior, 21*, 387–412.

Jackson, N. E., & Coltheart, M. (2001). *Routes to reading success and failure: toward an integrated cognitive psychology of atypical reading*: Hove, UK: Psychology Press.

Jacobs, B., Schall, M., & Scheibel, A. B. (1993). A quantitative dendritic analysis of Wernicke's area in humans. II. Gender, hemispheric, and environmental factors. *The Journal of Comparative Neurology, 327*, 97–111.

Jakobson, L. S., Servos, P., Goodale, M. A., & Lassonde, M. (1994). Control of proximal and distal components of prehension in callosal agenesis. *Brain, 117*, 1107–1113.

Jamison, C. S. (1988). Palmar dermatoglyphics of dyslexia. *American Journal of Physical Anthropology, 76*, 505–513.

Jäncke, L., Peters, M., Himmelbach, M., Nösselt, T., Shah, J., & Steinmetz, H. (2000). fMRI study of bimanual coordination. *Neuropsychologia, 38*, 164–174.

Jäncke, L., Schlaug, G., Huang, Y., & Steinmetz, H. (1994). Asymmetry of the planum parietale. *NeuroReport, 5*, 1161–1163.

Jäncke, L., Schlaug, G., & Steinmetz, H. (1997). Hand skill asymmetry in professional musicians. *Brain and Cognition, 34*, 424–432.

Jäncke, L., & Steinmetz, H. (1993). Auditory lateralization and planum temporale asymmetry. *Cognitive Neuroscience and Neuropsychology, 5*, 169–172.

Jeanes, R., Busby, A., Martin, J., Lewis, E., Stevenson, N., Pointon, D., & Wilkins, A. (1997). Prolonged use of coloured overlays for classroom reading. *British Journal of Psychology, 88*, 531–548.

Jeeves, M. A., & Silver, P. H. (1988). The formation of finger grip during prehension in an acallosal patient. *Neuropsychologia, 26*, 153–159.

Jeeves, M. A., & Temple, C. M. (1987). A further study of language function in callosal agenesis. *Brain and Language, 32*, 325–335.

Jenkins, I. H., & Frackowiak, R. S. J. (1993). Functional studies of the human cerebellum with positron emission tomography. *Revue Neurologique (Paris), 149*, 647–653.

Jenner, A. R., Rosen, G. D., & Galaburda, A. M. (1999). Neuronal asymmetries in primary visual cortex of dyslexic and nondyslexic brains. *Annals of Neurology, 46*, 189–196.

Job, R., Peresotti, F., & Cusinato, A. (1998). Lexical effects in naming pseudowords in shallow orthographies: further empirical data. *Journal of Experimental Psychology: Human Perception and Performance, 24*, 622–630.

Johannes, S., Kussmaul, C. L., Münte, T. F., & Mangun, G. R. (1996). Developmental dyslexia: passive visual stimulation provides no evidence for a magnocellular processing defect. *Neuropsychologia, 34*, 1123–1127.

Johnson, D. J., & Myklebust, H. R. (1967). *Learning disabilities: educational principles and practices*. New York: Grune & Stratton.

Johnson, N. F. (1992). On the role of cohorts or neighbours in visual word recognition. In R. Frost & L. Katz (Eds.), *Orthography, phonology, morphology, and meaning* (pp. 147–164). Amsterdam: North-Holland/ Elsevier.

Johnston, R. S. (1982). Phonological coding in dyslexic readers. *British Journal of Psychology*, *73*, 455–460.

Johnston, R. S., & Anderson, M. (1998). Memory span, naming speed, and memory strategies in poor and normal readers. *Memory*, *6*, 143–163.

Johnston, R. S., Anderson, M., & Holligan, C. (1996). Knowledge of the alphabet and awareness of phonemes. *Reading and Writing: An Interdisciplinary Journal*, *8*, 217–234.

Johnston, R. S., Rugg, M. D., & Scott, T. (1987a). The influence of phonology on good and poor readers when reading for meaning. *Journal of Memory and Language*, *26*, 57–68.

Johnston, R. S., Rugg, M. D., & Scott, T. (1987b). Phonological similarity effects, memory span and developmental reading disorders: the nature of the relationship. *British Journal of Psychology*, *78*, 205–211.

Jones, G. (1983). On double-dissociation of function. *Neuropsychologia*, *21*, 397–400.

Jorm, A. F. (1979a). The cognitive and neurological basis of developmental dyslexia: a theoretical framework and review. *Cognition*, *7*, 19–33.

Jorm, A. F. (1979b). The nature of the reading deficit in developmental dyslexia: a reply to Ellis. *Cognition*, *7*, 421–433.

Jorm, A. F. (1983). Specific reading retardation and working memory: a review. *British Journal of Psychology*, *74*, 311–342.

Jorm, A. F., & Share, D. L. (1983). Phonological recoding and reading acquisition. *Applied Psycholinguistics*, *4*, 103–147.

Jorm, A. F., Share, D. L., MacLean, R., & Matthews, R. G. (1984). Phonological recoding skills and learning to read: a longitudinal study. *Applied Psycholinguistics*, *5*, 201–207.

Jorm, A. F., Share, D. L., MacLean, R., & Matthews, R. (1986). Cognitive factors at school entry predictive of specific reading retardation and general reading backwards: a research note. *Journal of Child Psychology and Psychiatry*, *27*, 45–54.

Joubert, S. A., & Lecours, A. R. (2000). The role of sublexical graphemic processing in reading. *Brain and Language*, *72*, 1–13.

Juel, C., Griffith, P. L., & Gough, P. B. (1986). Acquisition of literacy: a longitudinal study of children in first and second grade. *Journal of Educational Psychology*, *78*, 243–255.

Junck, L., Gilman, S., Rothley, J. R., Betley, A. T.,

Koeppe, R. A., & Hichwa, R. D. (1988). A relationship between metabolism in frontal lobes and cerebellum in normal subjects studied with PET. *Journal of Cerebral Blood Flow and Metabolism*, *8*, 774–782.

Jusczyk, P. W. (1994). Infant speech perception and the development of the mental lexicon. In J. Goodman & H. C. Nusbaum (Eds.), *The development of speech perception: the transition from speech sounds to spoken words* (pp. 227–270). Cambridge, MA: MIT Pess.

Kail, R. (1992). Processing speed, speech rate, and memory. *Developmental Psychology*, *28*, 899–904.

Kail, R., & Hall, L. K. (1994). Processing speed, naming speed, and reading. *Developmental Psychology*, *30*, 949–954.

Kamhi, A. G. (1992). Response to historical perspective: a developmental language perspective. *Journal of Learning Disabilities*, *25*, 48–52.

Kamhi, A. G., Catts, H. W., & Mauer, D. (1990). Explaining speech production deficits in poor readers. *Journal of Learning Disabilities*, *23*, 632–636.

Kaplan, D. E., Gayán, J., Ahn, J., Won, T.-W., Pauls, D., Olson, R. K., DeFries, J. C., Wood, F., Pennington, B. F., Page, G. P., Smith, S. D., & Gruen, J. R. (2002). Evidence for linkage and association with reading disability, on 6p21.3–22. *American Journal of Human Genetics*, *70*, 1287–1298.

Karbe, H., Herholz, K., Weber-Luxenburger, G., Ghaemi, M., & Heiss, W. D. (1998). Cerebral networks and functional brain asymmetry: evidence from regional metabolic changes during word repetition. *Brain and Language*, *65*, 108–121.

Karbe, H., Würker, M., Herholz, K., Ghaemi, M., Pietrzyk, U., Kessler, J., & Heiss, W. (1995). Planum temporale and Brodmann's area 22. *Archives of Neurology*, *52*, 869–874.

Katz, R. (1986). Phonological deficiencies in children with reading disability: evidence from an object naming task. *Cognition*, *22*, 225–257.

Katz, R., & Feldman, L. B. (1983). Relation between pronunciation and recognition of printed words in deep and shallow orthographies. *Journal of Experimental Psychology: Learning, Memory and Cognition*, *9*, 157–166.

Katz, R., & Frost, R. (1992). Reading in different orthographies: the orthographic depth hypothesis. In R. Frost & L. Katz (Eds.), *Orthography, phonology, morphology, and meaning* (pp. 67–84). Amsterdam: North-Holland/Elsevier.

Kaufmann, W. E., & Galaburda, A. M. (1989). Cerebrocortical microdysgenesis in neurologically normal subjects: a histopathologic study. *Neurology, 39,* 238–244.

Kawi, A. A., & Pasamanick, B. (1958). Association of factors of pregnancy with reading disorders in childhood. *Journal of the American Medical Association, 16,* 1420–1423.

Kay, J., & Marcel, A. (1981). One process, not two, in reading aloud: lexical analogies do the work of non-lexical rules. *Quarterly Journal of Experimental Psychology, 33A,* 397–413.

Kennerley, S. W., Diedrichsen, J., Hazeltine, E., Semjen, A., & Ivry, R. (2002). Callosotomy patients exhibit temporal uncoupling during continuous bimanual movements. *Nature Neuroscience, 5,* 376–381.

Kerr, J. (1897). School hygiene in its mental, moral and physical aspects. *Journal of the Royal Statistical Society, LX,* 613–680.

Kimura, D. (1993). *Neuromotor mechanisms in human communication.* Oxford: Oxford University Press.

Kimura, D., & Watson, N. (1989). The relation between oral movement control and speech. *Brain and Language, 37,* 565–590.

Kinsbourne, M., Rufo, D. T., Gamzu, E., Palmer, R. L., & Berliner, A. K., (1991). Neuropsychological deficits in adults with dyslexia. *Developmental medicine and child neurology, 33,* 763–775.

Kinsbourne, M., & Warrington, E. K. (1963). Developmental factors in reading and writing backwardness. *British Journal of Psychology, 54,* 145–156.

Kirk, S. A. (1934). A study of the relation of ocular and manual preference to mirror-reading. *Journal of Genetic Psychology, XLIV,* 192–205.

Kirtley, C., Bryant, P., MacLean, M., & Bradley, L. (1989). Rhyme, rime and the onset of reading. *Journal of Experimental Child Psychology, 48,* 224–245.

Klein, D., Behrmann, M., & Doctor, E. (1994). The evolution of deep dyslexia: evidence for the spontaneous recovery of the semantic reading route. *Cognitive Neuropsychology, 11,* 579–611.

Klein, S. K., & Rapin, I. (1993). Intermittent conductive hearing loss and language development. In D. V. M. Bishop & K. Mogford (Eds.), *Language development in exceptional circumstances* (pp. 96–97). Hove: Lawrence Erlbaum Associates Ltd.

Klicpera, C., Wolff, P. H., & Drake, C. (1981). Bimanual co-ordination in adolescent boys with reading retardation. *Developmental Medicine and Child Neurology, 23,* 617–625.

Klingberg, T., Hedehus, M., Temple, E., Salz, T., Gabrieli, J. D. E., Moseley, M. E., & Poldrack, R. A. (2000). Microstructure of temporo-parietal white matter as a basis for reading ability: evidence from diffusion tensor magnetic resonance imaging. *Neuron, 25,* 493–500.

Knecht, S., Deppe, M., Dräger, B., Bobe, L., Lohmann, H., Flöel, A., Ringelstein, E. -B., & Henningsen, H. (2000a). Language lateralization in healthy humans. *Brain, 123,* 74–81.

Knecht, S., Dräger, B., Deppe, M., Bobe, L., Lohmann, H., Flöel, A., Ringelstein, E. -B., & Henningsen, H. (2000b). Handedness and language dominance in healthy humans. *Brain, 123,* 2512–1518.

Knopik, V. S., Alarcón, M., & DeFries, J. C. (1997). Comorbidity of mathematics and reading deficits: evidence for a genetic etiology. *Behaviour Genetics, 27,* 447–453.

Knott, K., Patterson, K., & Hodges, J. (2000). The role of speech production in auditory–verbal short-term memory: evidence from progressive fluent aphasia. *Neuropsychologia, 38,* 125–142.

Kopp, N., Michel, F., Carrier, H., Biron, A., & Duvillard, P. (1977). Etude de certaines asymétries hémisphériques du cerveaux. *Journal of the Neurological Sciences, 34,* 349–363.

Korhonen, T. T. (1995). The persistence of rapid naming problems in children with reading disabilities: a nine-year follow-up. *Journal of Learning Disabilities, 28,* 232–239.

Kraus, N., McGee, T. J., Carrell, T. D., Zecker, S. G., Nicol, T. G., & Koch, D. B. (1996). Auditory neurophysiologic responses and discrimination deficits in children with learning problems. *Science, 273,* 971–973.

Kreuter, C., Kinsbourne, M., & Trevarthen, C. (1972). Are deconnected cerebral hemispheres independent channels? A preliminary study of the effect of unilateral loading on bilateral finger tapping. *Neuropsychologia, 10,* 453–461.

Kronbichler, M., Hutzler, F., & Wimmer, H. (2002). Dyslexia: verbal impairments in the absence of magnocellular impairments. *Cognitive Neuroscience and Neuropsychology, 13,* 617–620.

Kruk, R. S., & Willows, D. M. (2001). Backward pattern masking of familiar and unfamiliar materials in disabled and normal readers. *Cognitive Neuropsychology, 18,* 19–37.

Kubová, Z., Kuba, M., Peregrin, J., & Nováková, V. (1995). Visual evoked potential evidence for magnocellular system deficit in dyslexia. *Physiological Research, 44,* 87–89.

Kujala, T., Myllyviita, K., Tervaniemi, M., Alho, K., Kallio, J., & Näätänen, R. (2000). Basic auditory dysfunction in dyslexia as demonstrated by brain activity measurements. *Psychophysiology*, *37*, 262–266.

Kulikowski, J. J., & Tolhurst, D. J. (1973). Psychophysical evidence for sustained and transient detectors in human vision. *Journal of Physiology*, *232*, 149–162.

Kulp, M. T., & Schmidt, P. P. (1996). Effect of oculomotor and other visual skills on reading performance: a literature review. *Optometry and Vision Science*, *73*, 283–292.

Kulynych, J. J., Vladar, K., Jones, D. W., & Weiberger, D. R. (1994). Gender differences in the normal lateralization of the supratemporal cortex: MRI surface-rendering morphometry of Heschl's gyrus and the planum temporale. *Cerebral Cortex*, *4*, 107–118.

Kushch, A., Gross-Glenn, K., Jallad, B., Lubs, H., Rabin, M., Feldman, E., & Duara, R. (1993). Temporal lobe surface area measurements of MRI in normal and dyslexic readers. *Neuropsychologia*, *31*, 811–821.

Kussmaul, A. (1877). Die Störungen der Sprache. In H. von Ziemssen (Ed.), *Cyclopedia of the Practice of Medicine*, Vol. IX (translated by J. A. McCreery). New York: William Wood.

Kyd, L. J. C., Sutherland, G. F. M., & McGettrick, P. M. (1992). A preliminary appraisal of the Irlen screening process for scotopic sensitivity syndrome and the effect of Irlen coloured overlays on reading. *British Orthoptic Journal*, *49*, 25–30.

Laasonen, M., Tomma-Halme, J., Lahti-Nuuttila, P., Service, E., & Virsu, V. (2000). Rate of information segregation in developmentally dyslexic children. *Brain and Language*, *75*, 66–81.

Lai, C. S. L., Fisher, S. E., Hurst, J. A., Vargha-Khadem, F., & Monaco, A. P. (2001). A forkhead-domain gene is mutated in a severe speech and language disorder. *Nature*, *413*, 519–523.

Lahita, R. G. (1988). Systemic lupus erythematosus: learning disability in the male offspring of female patients and relationship to laterality. *Psychoneuroendocrinology*, *13*, 385–396.

Laing, E., & Hulme, C. (1999). Phonological and semantic processes influence beginning readers' ability to learn and read words. *Journal of Experimental Child Psychology*, *73*, 183–207.

Lamantia, A. -S., & Rakic, P. (1990). Cytological and quantitative characteristics of four cerebral commissures in the rhesus monkey. *Journal of Comparative Neurology*, *291*, 520–537.

Lambe, E. K. (1999). Dyslexia, gender, and brain imaging. *Neuropsychologia*, *37*, 521–536.

Lambon-Ralph, M., Ellis, A., & Franklin, S. (1995).

Semantic loss without surface dyslexia. *Neurocase*, *1*, 363–369.

Landerl, K. (1997). Word recognition in English and German dyslexics: a direct comparison. In C. K. Leong & R. M. Joshi (Eds.), *Cross language studies of learning to read and spell* (pp. 121–137). Dordrecht: Kluwer.

Landerl, K. (2001). Word recognition deficits in German: more evidence from a representative sample. *Dyslexia*, *7*, 183–196.

Landerl, K., Frith, U., & Wimmer, H. (1996). Intrusion of orthographic knowledge on phoneme awareness: strong in normal readers, weak in dyslexic readers. *Applied Psycholinguistics*, *17*, 1–14.

Landerl, K., & Wimmer, H. (2000). Deficits in phoneme segmentation are not the core problem of dyslexia: evidence from German and English children. *Applied Psycholinguistics*, *21*, 243–262.

Landerl, K., Wimmer, H., & Frith, U. (1997). The impact of orthographic consistency on dyslexia: a German–English comparison. *Cognition*, *63*, 315–334.

Larsen, J. P., Höien, T., Lundberg, I., & Ödegaard, H. (1990). MRI evaluation of the size and symmetry of the planum temporale in adolescents with developmental dyslexia. *Brain and Language*, *39*, 289–301.

Larsen, J. P., Höien, T., Lundberg, I., & Ödegaard, H. (1992). Magnetic resonance imaging of the corpus callosum in developmental dyslexia. *Cognitive Neuropsychology*, *9*, 123–134.

Lashley, K. S. (1951). The problem of serial order in behavior. In L. A. Jeffress (Ed.), *Cerebral mechanisms in behavior* (pp. 112–136). New York: Wiley.

Lassonde, M., Bryden, M. P., & Demers, P. (1990). The corpus callosum and cerebral speech lateralization. *Brain and Language*, *38*, 195–206.

Lassonde, M., & Sauerwein, H. (2003). Agenesis of the corpus callosum. In K. Hugdahl & R. J. Davidson (Eds.), *The asymmetrical brain* (pp. 619–649). Cambridge, MA: MIT Press.

Laxon, V., Masterson, J., & Coltheart, M. (1991). Some bodies are easier to read: the effect of consistency and regularity on children's reading. *Quarterly Journal of Experimental Psychology*, *43A*, 793–824.

Laxon, V., Masterson, J., & Moran, R. (1994). Are children's representation of words distributed? Effects of orthographic neighbourhood size, consistency and regularity of naming. *Language and Cognitive Processes*, *9*, 1–27.

Layton, L., Deeny, K., Upton, G., & Tall, G. (1998). A pre-school training programme for children with poor phonological awareness: effects on reading and spelling. *Journal of Research in Reading, 21*, 36–52.

Leather, C. V., & Henry, L. A. (1994). Working memory span and phonological awareness tasks as predictors of early reading ability. *Journal of Experimental Child Psychology, 58*, 88–111.

Lee, B. B., Smith, V. C., Pokorny, J., & Kremers, J. (1997). Rod inputs to macaque ganglion cells. *Vision Research, 37*, 2813–2828.

Leek, M. R., & Brandt, J. F. (1983). Lateralization of rapid auditory sequences. *Neuropsychologia, 21*, 67–77.

Lefly, D. L., & Pennington, B. F. (1991). Spelling errors and reading fluency in compensated adult dyslexics. *Annals of Dyslexia, 41*, 143–162.

Lehmkuhle, S. (1993). Neurological basis of visual processes in reading. In D. M. Willows, R. S. Kruk, & E. Corcos (Eds.), *Visual processes in reading and reading disabilities* (pp. 77–94). Hove, UK: Lawrence Erlbaum Associates Ltd.

Lehmkuhle, S., Garzia, R. P., Turner, L., Hash, T., & Baro, J. A. (1993). A defective visual pathway in children with reading disability. *New England Journal of Medicine, 328*, 989–996.

Leiner, H. C., Leiner, A. L., & Dow, R. S. (1989). Reappraising the cerebellum: what does the hindbrain contribute to the forebrain? *Behavioural Neuroscience, 103*, 998–1008.

Leiner, H. C., Leiner, A. L., & Dow, R. S. (1993). Cognitive and language functions of the human cerebellum. *Trends in Neuroscience, 16*, 444–447.

Leisman, G. (2002). Coherence of hemisphere function in developmental dyslexia. *Brain and Cognition, 48*, 425–451.

Lenel, J. C., & Cantor, J. H. (1981). Rhyme recognition and phonemic perception in young children. *Journal of Psycholinguistic Research, 10*, 57–67.

Lennerstrand, G., Ygge, J., & Jacobsson, C. (1993). Control of binocular eye movements in normals and dyslexics. *Annals of the New York Academy of Sciences, 682*, 231–239.

Leonard, C. M., Eckert, M. A., Lombardino, L. J., Oakland, T., Kranzler, J., Mohr, C. M., King, W. M., & Freeman, A. (2001). Anatomical risk factors for phonological dyslexia. *Cerebral Cortex, 11*, 148–157.

Leonard, C. M., Lombardino, L. J., Mercado, L. R., Browd, S. R., Breier, J. I., & Agee, O. F. (1996). Cerebral asymmetry and cognitive development in children: a magnetic resonance imaging study. *Psychological Science, 7*, 89–95.

Leonard, C. M., Puranik, C., Kuldau, J. M., & Lom-

bardino, L. J. (1998). Normal variation in the frequency and location of human auditory cortex landmarks. Heschl's gyrus: where is it? *Cerebral Cortex, 8*, 397–406.

Leonard, C. M., Voeller, K. K. S., Lombardino, L. J., Morris, M. K., Hynd, G. W., Alexander, A. W., Andersen, H. G., Garofalakis, M., Honeyman, J. C., Mao, J., Agee, F., & Staab, E. V. (1993). Anomalous cerebral structure in dyslexia revealed with magnetic resonance imaging. *Archives of Neurology, 50*, 461–469.

Leong, C. K. (1999). Phonological and morphological processing in adult students with learning/reading disabilities. *Journal of Learning Disabilities, 32*, 224–238.

Leppänen, P. H. T., & Lyytinen, H. (1997). Auditory event-related potentials in the study of developmental language-related disorders. *Audiology and Neuro-otology, 2*, 308–340.

Leslie, L., & Calhoon, A. (1995). Factors affecting children's reading of rimes: reading ability, word frequency, and rime-neighbourhood size. *Journal of Educational Psychology, 87*, 576–586.

Leslie, S. C., Davidson, R. J., & Batey, O. B. (1985). Purdue pegboard performance of disabled and normal readers: unimanual versus bimanual differences. *Brain and Language, 24*, 359–369.

Leventhal, A. G., Rodieck, R. W., & Dreher, B. (1981). Retinal ganglion cell classes in the Old World monkey: morphology and central projections, *Science, 213*, 1139–1142.

Levinson, H. N. (1980). *Dyslexia: a solution to the riddle*. Berlin: Springer-Verlag.

Levinson, H. N. (1988). The cerebellar vestibular basis of learning disabilities in children, adolescents and adults: hypothesis and study. *Perceptual and Motor Skills, 67*, 983–1006.

Levinson, H. N. (1990). Diagnostic value of cerebellar–vestibular tests detecting learning disabilities, dyslexia, and attention deficit disorder. *Perceptual and Motor Skills, 71*, 67–82.

Levisohn, L., Cronin-Galomb, A., & Schmahmann, J. D. (2000). Neuropsychological consequences of cerebellar tumour resection in children: cerebellar cognitive affective syndrome in a paediatric population *Brain, 123*, 1041–1050.

Leviton, A., & Kilty, T. (1979). Seasonal variation in the birth of left-handed schoolgirls. *Archives of Neurology, 36*, 115–116.

Levy, J. (1969). Possible basis for the evolution of lateral specialization of the human brain. *Nature, 224*, 614–615.

Levy, J., & Reid, M. (1976). Variations in writing posture and cerebral organization. *Science, 194*, 337–339.

Lewis, B. A. (1992). Pedigree analysis of children with phonology disorders. *Journal of Learning Disabilities, 25*, 586–597.

Lewis, B. A., & Thompson, L. A. (1992). A study of developmental speech and language disorders in twins. *Journal of Speech, Language, and Hearing Research, 35*, 1086–1094.

Lewis, J. P., & Frick, R. W. (1999). Row blindness in Gestalt grouping and developmental dyslexia. *Neuropsychologia, 37*, 385–393.

Lewis, R. S., & Harris, L. J. (1990). Handedness, sex, and spatial ability. In S. Coren (Ed.), *Left-handedness: behavioural implications and anomalies* (pp. 319–341). Amsterdam: North-Holland/Elsevier.

Lewitter, F. I., DeFries, J. C., & Elston, R. C. (1980). Genetic models of reading disability. *Behavior Genetics, 10*, 9–30.

Liberman, A. M. (1993). In speech perception, time is not what it seems. In: P. Tallal, A. M. Gallaburda, R. R. Llinás, & C. von Euler (Eds.) *Temporal information processing in the nervous system: special reference to dyslexia and dysphasia* (pp. 264–271). New York Academy of Sciences: New York.

Liberman, A. M., Cooper, F. S., Shankweiler, D. P., & Studdert-Kennedy, M. S. (1967). Perception of the speech code. *Psychological Review, 74*, 431–461.

Liberman, A., & Mattingly, I. G. (1985). The motor theory of speech revised. *Cognition, 21*, 1–36.

Liberman, I. Y., Shankweiler, D., Fischer, F. W., & Carter, B. (1974). Explicit syllable and phoneme segmentation in the young child. *Journal of Experimental Child Psychology, 18*, 201–212.

Liberman, I. Y., Shankweiler, D., Orlando, C., Harris, K., & Bell-Berti, F. (1971). Letter confusions and reversals of sequence in the beginning reader: implications for Orton's theory of developmental dyslexia. *Cortex, 7*, 127–142.

Licht, R. (1994). Electrocortical correlates of reading disability subtypes. In K. P. van den Bos, L. S. Siegel, D. J. Bakker, & D. Share (Eds), *Current directions in dyslexia research* (pp. 117–133). Lisse: Swets & Zeitlinger.

Lichtheim, L. (1885). On aphasia. *Brain, 7*, 433–484.

Liederman, J., & Flannery, K. A. (1994). Fall conception increases the risk of neurodevelopmental disorder in offspring. *Journal of Clinical and Experimental Neuropsychology, 16*, 754–768.

Liégeois-Chauvel, C., de Graaf, J. B., Laguitton, V., & Chauvel, P. (1999). Specialization of left auditory cortex for speech perception in man depends on temporal coding. *Cerebral Cortex, 9*, 484–496.

Lindgren, S. D. (1978). Finger localization and the prediction of reading disability. *Cortex, 14*, 87–101.

Lindgren, S. D., De Renzi, E., & Richman, L. C. (1985). Cross-national comparisons of developmental dyslexia in Italy and the United States. *Child Development, 56*, 1404–1417.

Livingston, R., Adam B. S., & Bracha, H. S. (1993). Season of birth and neurodevelopmental disorders: summer birth is associated with dyslexia. *Journal of the American Academy of Child and Adolescent Psychiatry, 32*, 612–616.

Livingstone, M. S., & Hubel, D. H. (1988a). Do the relative mapping densities of the magno-and parvocellular systems vary with eccentricity? *Journal of Neuroscience, 8*, 4334–4339.

Livingstone, M., & Hubel, D. (1988b). Segregation of form, colour, movement, and depth: anatomy, physiology, and perception. *Science, 240*, 740–749.

Livingstone, M. S., Rosen, G. D., Drislane F. W., & Galaburda, A. M. (1991). Physiological and anatomical evidence for a magnocellular defect in developmental dyslexia. *Proceedings of the National Academy of Sciences, USA, 88*, 7943–7947.

Llinás, R. (1993). Is dyslexia a dyschronia? In P. Tallal, A. Galaburda, R. R. Llinas, & C. von Euler (Eds.), Temporal information processing in the nervous system: special reference to dyslexia and dysphasia. *Annals of the New York Academy of Sciences, 682*, 48–56.

Locke, J. L., Hodgson, J., Macaruso, P., Roberts, J., Lambrecht-Smith, S., & Guttentag, C. (1997). The development of developmental dyslexia. In C. Hulme & M. Snowling (Eds.), *Dyslexia: biology, cognition and intervention* (pp. 97–107). London: Whurr Publishers.

Loftus, W. C., Tramo, M. J., Thomas, C. E., Green, R. L., Nordgren, R. A., & Gazzaniga, M. S. (1993). Three-dimensional quantitative analysis of hemispheric asymmetry in the human superior temporal region. *Cerebral Cortex, 3*, 348–355.

Logethetis, N. K., Pauls, J., Augath, M. A., Trinath, T., & Oeltermann, A. (2001). Neurophysiological investigation of the basis of the fMRI signal. *Nature, 412*, 150–157.

Lopez, R., Yolton, R. L., Kohl, P., Smith, D. L., & Saxerud, M. H. (1994). Comparison of Irlen scotopic sensitivity Syndrome test results to academic and visual performance data. *Journal of the American Optometric Association, 65,* 705–714.

Lovegrove, B. (1996). Dyslexia and a transient/magnocellular pathway deficit: the current situations and future directions. *Australian Journal of Psychology, 48,* 167–171.

Lovegrove, W. J. (1991). Is the question of the role of visual deficits as a cause of reading disabilities a closed one? Comments on Hulme. *Cognitive Neuropsychology, 8,* 435–441.

Lovegrove, W. J., Bowling, A., Badcock, D., & Blackwood, M. (1980a). Specific reading disabilities: differences in contrast sensitivity as a function of spatial frequency. *Science, 210,* 439–440.

Lovegrove, W. J., Heddle, M., & Slaghuis, W. (1980b). Reading disability: spatial frequency specific deficits in visual information store. *Neuropsychologia, 18,* 111–115.

Lovegrove, W., Martin, F., Bowling, A., Blackwood, M., Badcock, D., & Paxton, S. (1982). Contrast sensitivity functions and specific reading disability. *Neuropsychologia, 20,* 309–315.

Lovegrove, W. J., Martin, F., & Slaghuis, W. L. (1986). A theoretical and experimental case for a visual deficit in specific reading disability. *Cognitive Neuropsychology, 3,* 225–227.

Lovegrove, W. J., & Williams, M. C. (1993). In D. R. Willows, R. S. Kruk, & E. Corcos (Eds.), *Visual processes in reading and reading disabilities* (pp. 311–327). Hillside, NJ: Lawrence Erlbaum Associates Inc.

Lovell, K., Shapton, D., & Warren, N. S. (1964). A study of some cognitive and other disabilities in backward readers of average intelligence as assessed by a non-verbal test. *British Journal of Educational Psychology, 34,* 58–64.

Lovett, M. W., Borden, S. L., DeLuca, T., Lacerenza, L., Benson, N. J., & Brackstone, D. (1994). Treating the core deficits of developmental dyslexia: evidence of transfer of learning after phonologically- and strategy-based reading training programs. *Developmental Psychology, 30,* 805–822.

Lovett, M. W., Lacerenza, L., Borden, S. L., Frijters, J. C., Steinbach, K. A., & De Palma, M. (2000). Components of effective remediation for developmental reading disabilities: combining phonological and strategy based instruction to improve outcomes. *Journal of Educational Psychology, 92,* 263–283.

Lovett, M. W., Ransby, M. J., Hardwick, N., Johns, M. S., & Donaldson, S. A. (1989). Can dyslexia be treated? Treatment-specific and generalized treatment effects in dyslexic children's response to remediation. *Brain and Language, 37,* 90–121.

Lubs, H. A., Rabin, M., Feldman, E., Jallad, B. J., Kusch, A., Gross-Glenn, K., Duara, R., & Elston, R. C. (1993). Familial dyslexia: genetic and medical findings in eleven three generation families. *Annals of Dyslexia, 43,* 44–60.

Lundberg, I. (1989). Lack of phonological awareness — a critical factor in dyslexia. In C. von Euler, I. Lundberg, & R. Lennardstrand (Eds.), *Brain and reading* (pp. 221–231). London: Macmillan.

Lundberg, I., Frost, J., & Petersen, O. P. (1988). Effects of an extensive program for stimulating phonological awareness in pre-school children. *Reading Research Quarterly, 23,* 263–284.

Lundberg, I., & Høien, T. (1989). Phonemic deficits: a core symptom of developmental dyslexia? *Irish Journal of Psychology, 10,* 579–592.

Lundberg, I., Olofsson, A., & Wall, S. (1980). Reading and spelling skills in the first school years predicted from phonemic awareness skills in kindergarten. *Scandinavian Journal of Psychology, 21,* 159–173.

Luttenberg, J. (1965). Contribution to the fetal ontogenesis of the corpus callosum in man. II. *Folio Morphologica, 13,* 136–144.

Luttenberg, J. (1966). Contribution to the fetal ontogenesis of the corpus callosum in man. III. Myelinization in the corpus callosum. *Folio Morphologica, 14,* 192–199.

Lyytinen, H. (1997). In search of the precursors of dyslexia: a prospective study of children at risk for reading problems. In C. Hulme, & M. Snowling (Eds.), *Dyslexia: biology, cognition and intervention* (pp. 97–107). London: Whurr Publishers.

MacDonald, G. W., & Cornwall, A. (1995). The relationship between phonological awareness and reading and spelling achievement eleven years later. *Journal of Learning Disabilities, 28,* 523–527.

MacKain, K., Studdert-Kennedy, M., Spieker, S., & Stern, D. (1983). Specific reading disability: identification of an inherited form through linkage analysis. *Science, 219,* 1345–1349.

MacLean, M., Bryant, P. E., & Bradley, L. (1987). Ryhmes, nursery rhymes and reading in early childhood. *Merill-Palmer Quarterly, 33,* 255–282.

Macmillan, M. B. (2002). Rhyme and reading: a critical review of the research methodology. *Journal of Research in Reading, 25,* 4–42.

MacPherson, W. B., Ackerman, P. T., Oglesby, D. M., & Dykman, R. A. (1996). Event-related brain potentials elicited by rhyming and non-rhyming pictures differentiate sub-groups of reading disabled adolescents. *Integrative Physiological and Behavioral Science, 31,* 3–17.

Makita, K. (1968). The rarity of reading disability in Japanese children. *American Journal of Orthopsychiatry, 38,* 599–614.

Makrides, M., Neumann, M., Simmer, K., Pater, J., & Gibson, R. (1995). Are long-chain polyunsaturated fatty acids essential nutrients in infancy? *The Lancet, 345,* 1463–1468.

Mamen, M., Ferguson, H. B., & Backman, J. E. (1986). No difference represents a significant finding: the logic of the reading level design. A response to Bryant and Goswami. *Psychological Bulletin, 100,* 104–106.

Manis, F. R., Custodio, R., & Szeszulski, P. A. (1993). Development of phonological and orthographic skill: a 2-year longitudinal study of dyslexic children. *Journal of Experimental Child Psychology, 56,* 64–86.

Manis, F. R., McBride-Chang, C., Seidenberg, M. S., Keating, P., Doi, L. M., Munson, B., & Peterson, A. (1997). Are speech perception deficits associated with developmental dyslexia? *Journal of Experimental Child Psychology, 66,* 211–235.

Manis, F. R., Seidenberg, M. S., Doi, L. M., McBride-Chang, C., & Petersen, A. (1996). On the bases of two subtypes of developmental dyslexia. *Cognition, 58,* 157–195.

Manis, F. R., Szeszulski, P. A., Howell, M. J., & Horn, C. C. (1986). A comparison of analogy- and rule-based decoding strategies in normal and disabled readers. *Journal of Reading Behavior, 18,* 203–218.

Mann, V. A. (1986). Phonological awareness: the role of reading experience. *Cognition, 24,* 65–92.

Mann, V. A. (1991). Are we taking too narrow a view of the conditions for development of phonological awareness? In S. A. Brady & D. P. Shankweiler (Eds.), *Phonological processes in literacy: a tribute to Isabelle Y. Liberman* (pp. 55–64). Hillsdale, NJ: Lawrence Erlbaum Associates Inc.

Mann, V. A., & Liberman, I. Y. (1984). Phonological awareness and verbal short-term memory. *Journal of Learning Disabilities, 17,* 592–599.

Mann, V., Liberman, I. Y., & Shankweiler, D. (1980). Children's memory for sentences and word strings in relation to reading ability. *Memory and Cognition, 8,* 329–335.

Mariën, P., Engelborghs, S., Fabbro, F., & De Deyn, P. P. (2001). The lateralized linguistic cerebellum: a review and a new hypothesis. *Brain and Language, 79,* 580–600.

Mark, L. S., Shankweiler, D. P., Liberman, I. Y., & Fowler, C. A. (1977). Phonetic recoding and reading difficulty in beginning readers. *Memory and Cognition, 5,* 623–629.

Markee, T., Brown, W. S., Moore, L. H., & Theberge, D. C. (1996). Callosal function in dyslexia: evoked potential interhemispheric transfer time and bilateral field advantage. *Developmental Neuropsychology, 12,* 409–428.

Marsh, G., Desberg, P., & Cooper, J. (1977). Developmental changes in reading strategies? *Journal of Reading Behaviour, 9,* 391–394.

Marsh, G., Friedman, M. P., Welch, V., & Desberg, P. (1981). A cognitive-developmental theory of reading acquisition. In G. E. Mackinnon & T. G. Waller (Eds.), *Reading research: advances in theory and practice* (Vol. 3, pp. 199–221). New York: Academic Press.

Marshall, J. C. (1983). Review of Levinson, H. N. (1980). Dyslexia: a solution to the riddle. Berlin: Springer-Verlag. *Journal of Researchin Reading, 6,* 72–73.

Marshall, J. C. (1985) On some relationships between acquired and developmental dyslexias. In F. H. Duffy & N. Geschwind (Eds.), *Dyslexia: a neuroscientific approach to clinical evaluation* (pp. 55–66). Bostow, MA: Little, Brown, & Co.

Marshall, J. C., & Newcombe, F. (1973) Patterns of paralexia: a psycholinguistic approach. *Journal of Psycholinguistic Research, 2,* 175–199.

Martin, F., & Lovegrove, W. (1984). The effects of field size and luminance on contrast sensitivity differences between specifically reading disabled and normal children. *Neuropsychologia, 22,* 73–77.

Martin, F., & Lovegrove, W. (1987). Flicker contrast sensitivity in normal and specifically disabled readers. *Perception, 16,* 215–221.

Martino, G., & Winner, E. (1995). Talents and disorders: relationships among handedness, sex and college major. *Brain and Cognition, 29,* 66–84.

Martos, F. J., & Vila, J. (1990). Differences in eye movements control among dyslexic, retarded and normal readers in the Spanish population. *Reading and Writing: An Interdisciplinary Journal, 2,* 175–188.

Masterson, J., Hazan, V., & Wijayatilake, L. (1995). Phonemic processing problems in developmental phonological dyslexia. *Cognitive Neuropsychology, 12,* 233–259.

Masterson, J., Laxon, V., & Stuart, V. (1992). Beginning reading with phonology. *British Journal of Psychology, 83,* 1–12.

Matin, E. (1974). Saccadic suppression: a review and an analysis. *Psychological Bulletin, 81*, 899–917.

Mattis, S., French, J. H., & Rapin, I. (1975). Dyslexia in children and young adults: three independent neuropsychological syndromes. *Developmental Medicine and Child Neurology, 17*, 150–163.

Maughan, B. (1995). Annotation: long term outcomes of developmental reading problems. *Journal of Child Psychology and Psychiatry, 36*, 357–371.

Maunsell, J. H., Nealey, T. A., & DePriest, D. D. (1990). Magnocellular and parvocellular contributions to responses in the middle temporal visual area (MT) of the macaque monkey. *Journal of Neuroscience, 10*, 3323–3334.

Maunsell, J. H. R., & Van Essen, D. C. (1983). The connections of the middle temporal visual area (MT) and their relationship to a cortical hierarchy in the macaque monkey. *Journal of Neuroscience, 3*, 2563–2586.

May, J. G., Williams, M. C., & Dunlap, W. P. (1988). Temporal order judgements in good and poor readers. *Neuropsychologia, 20*, 917–924.

Mayringer, H., & Wimmer, H. (2002). No deficits at the point of hemispheric indecision. *Neuropsychologia, 40*, 701–704.

McAnally, K. I., Hansen, P. C., Cornelissen, P. L., & Stein, J. F. (1997). Effect of time and frequency manipulation on syllable perception in developmental dyslexics. *Journal of Speech, Language and Hearing Research, 40*, 912–924.

McAnally, K. I., & Stein, J. F. (1996). Auditory temporal coding in dyslexia. *Proceedings of the Royal Society of London, 263*, 961–965.

McBride-Chang, C. (1995). What is phonological awareness? *Journal of Educational Psychology, 87*, 179–192.

McBride-Chang, C. (1996). Models of speech perception and phonological processing in reading. *Child Development, 67*, 1836–1856.

McBride-Chang, C., Wagner, R. K., & Chang, L. (1997). Growth modelling of phonological awareness. *Journal of Educational Psychology, 89*, 621–630.

McClelland, J., & Rummelhart, D. E. (1981). An interactive activation model of context effects in letter perception. 1. An account of basic findings. *Psychological Review, 88*, 375–407.

McDougall, S. J. P., & Ellis, A. W. (1994). On the problems of comparing dyslexics with other groups of readers (and the quest for the cognitive basis of dyslexia). *Early Child Development and Care, 101*, 33–49.

McDougall. S. J. P., & Donohoe, R. (2002). Reading ability and memory span: long-term memory contributions to span for good and poor readers. *Reading and Writing: An Interdisciplinary Journal, 15*, 359–387.

McDougall, S., Hulme, C., Ellis, A., & Monk, A. (1994). Learning to read: the role of short-term memory and phonological skills. *Journal of Experimental Child Psychology, 58*, 112–133.

McFie, J. (1952). Cerebral dominance in cases of reading disability. *Journal of Neurology, Neurosurgery and Psychiatry, 15*, 194–199.

McGurk, H., & MacDonald, J. W. (1976). Hearing lips and seeing voices. *Nature, 264*, 746–748.

McKeever, W. F. (1979). Handwriting posture in left-handers: sex, familial sinistrality and language laterality correlates. *Neuropsychologia, 17*, 429–444.

McKeever, W. F., & Van Hoff, A. L. (1979). Evidence of a possible isolation of left hemisphere visual and motor areas in sinistrals employing an inverted handwriting posture. *Neuropsychologia, 17*, 445–455.

McKinney, J. P. (1964). Hand schema in children. *Psychonomic Science, 1*, 99–100.

McManus, I. C. (1983). Pathologic left-handedness: does it exist? *Journal of Communication Disorders, 16*, 315–344.

McManus, I. C. (1985). Handedness, language dominance and aphasia: a genetic model. *Psychological Medicine* (monograph suppl. 8), 1–40.

McManus, I. C. (1991). The genetics of dyslexia. In J. F. Stein (Ed.), *Vision and visual dysfunction, vol. 13* (pp. 94–112). London: Macmillan.

McManus, I. C. (2002). *Right hand, left hand*. London: Weidenfeld & Nicolson.

McManus, I. C., & Bryden, M. P. (1991). The Geschwind-Galaburda theory of cerebral lateralization: developing a formal, causal model. *Psychological Bulletin, 110*, 237–253

McManus, I. C., & Bryden, M. P. (1992). The genetics of handedness, cerebral dominance and lateralization. In I. Rapin & S. Segalowitz (Eds.), *Handbook of neuropsychology: 10. Developmental neuropsychology* (pp. 115–144). Amsterdam: Elsevier.

McManus, I. C., & Mascie-Taylor, C. G. N. (1983). Biosocial correlates of cognitive abilities. *Journal of Biosocial Science, 15*, 289–306.

McManus, I. C., Porac, C., Bryden, M. P., & Boucher, R. (1999). Eye-dominance, writing hand, and throwing hand. *Laterality, 4*, 173–192.

McManus, I. C., Shergill, S., & Bryden, M. P. (1993). Annett's theory that individuals heterozygous for the right shift gene are intellectually advantaged: theoretical and empirical problems. *British Journal of Psychology, 84*, 517–537.

McPhillips, M., Hepper, P. G., & Mulhern, G. (2000). Effects of replicating primary-reflex movements on specific reading difficulties in children: a randomised, double-blind, controlled trial. *Lancet, 335*, 537–541.

Meerwaldt, J. D. (1983). Disturbances of spatial perception in a patient with agenesis of the corpus callosum. *Neuropsychologia, 21*, 161–165.

Melekian, B. A. (1990). Family characteristics of children with dyslexia. *Journal of Learning Disabilities, 23*, 386–391.

Menacker, S. J., Breton, M. E., Breton, M. L., Radcliffe, J., & Gole, A. (1993). Do tinted lenses improve the reading performance of dyslexic children? *Archives of Ophthalmology, 111*, 213–218.

Menell, P., McAnally, K. I., & Stein, J. F. (1999). Psychophysical sensitivity and physiological response to amplitude modulation in adult dyslexic listeners. *Journal of Speech, Language and Hearing Research, 42*, 797–803.

Menyuk, P. (1978). Linguistic problems in children with developmental dysphasia. In M. A. Wyke (Ed.), *Developmental dysphasia* (pp. 135–158). London: Academic Press.

Merigan, W. H., Byrne, C. E., & Maunsell, J. H. (1991a). Does primate motion perception depend on the magnocellular pathway? *Journal of Neuroscience, 11*, 3422–3429.

Merigan, W. H., Katz, L. M., & Maunsell, J. H. (1991b). The effects of parvocellular lateral geniculate lesions on the acuity and contrast sensitivity of macaque monkeys. *Journal of Neuroscience, 11*, 994–1001.

Merigan, W. H., & Maunsell, J. H. R. (1990). Macaque vision after magnocellular lateral geniculate lesions. *Visual Neuroscience, 5*, 347–352.

Merigan, W. H., & Maunsell, J. H. R. (1993). How parallel are the primate visual pathways? *Annual Review of Neuroscience, 16*, 369–402.

Merzenich, M. M., Jenkins, W. M., Johnston, P., Schreiner, C., Miller, S. L., & Tallal, P. (1996). Temporal processing deficits of language-learning impaired children ameliorated by training. *Science, 271*, 77–81.

Metsala, J. (1997). Spoken word recognition in reading disabled children. *Journal of Educational Psychology, 89*, 159–169.

Metsala, J., Stanovich, K., & Brown, G. D. A. (1998). Regularity effects and the phonological deficit

model of reading disabilities: meta-analytic review. *Journal of Educational Psychology, 90*, 279–293.

Meyer, M. S., Wood, F. B., Hart, L. A., & Felton, R. H. (1998). Selective predictive value of rapid automatized naming in poor readers. *Journal of Learning Disabilities, 31*, 106–117.

Miall, R. C., & Reckess, G. Z. (2002). The cerebellum and the timing of coordinated eye and hand tracking. *Brain and Cognition, 48*, 212–226.

Michas, I. C., & Henry, L. A. (1994). The link between phonological memory and vocabulary acquisition. *British Journal of Developmental Psychology, 12*, 147–163.

Miles, E. (1995). Can there be a single definition of dyslexia? *Dyslexia, 1*, 37–45.

Miles, T. R. (1957). Contributions to intelligence testing and the theory of intelligence. 1. On defining intelligence. *British Journal of Educational Psychology, 27*, 153–165.

Miles, T. R. (1982). *The Bangor dyslexia test.* Cambridge: Learning Development Aids.

Miles, T. R. (1986). On the persistence of dyslexic difficulties into adulthood. In G. T. Pavlidis & D. F. Fisher (Eds.), *Dyslexia: its neuropsychology and treatment* (pp. 149–163). Chichester: Wiley.

Miles, T. R. (1992). On determining the prevalence of dyslexia. In M. J. Snowling & M. E. Thomson (Eds.), *Dyslexia: integrating theory and practice* (pp. 144–153). London: Whurr Publishers.

Miles, T. R. (1993a). *Dyslexia: the pattern of difficulties,* (2nd edn.) London: Whurr Publishers.

Miles, T. R. (1993b). *Understanding dyslexia.* Bath: Amethyst Books.

Miles, T. (1994). A proposed taxonomy and some consequences. In A. Fawcett & R. Nicolson (Eds.), *Dyslexia in children: multidisciplinary perspectives* (pp. 195–214). London: Harvester Wheatsheaf.

Miles, T. R., & Gibbons, S. L. (2002). Colour naming in dyslexic and non-dyslexic adults. *Dyslexia Review, 13*, 4–6.

Miles, T. R., & Haslum, M. N. (1986). Dyslexia: anomaly or normal variation? *Annals of Dyslexia, 36*, 103–117.

Miles, T. R., Haslum, M. N., & Wheeler, T. J. (1998). Gender ratio in dyslexia. *Annals of Dyslexia, 48*, 27–55.

Miles, T. R., Haslum, M. N., & Wheeler, T. J. (2001). The mathematical abilities of ten year olds. *Annals of Dyslexia, 51*, 299–321.

Miles, T. R., & Miles, E. (1990). *Dyslexia: a hundred years on.* Buckingham: Open University Press.

Mills, L., & Rollman, G. B. (1979). Left hemisphere

selectivity for processing duration in normal subjects. *Brain and Language*, *7*, 320–335.

Mills, L., & Rollman, G. B. (1980). Hemispheric asymmetry for auditory perception of temporal order. *Neuropsychologia*, *18*, 41–47.

Mishkin, M., & Ungerleider, L.G. (1982). Contribution of striate inputs to the visuospatial functions of parieto-preoccipital cortex in monkeys. *Behavioral Brain Research*, *6*, 57–77.

Mitterer, J. O. (1982). There are at least two kinds of poor readers: whole-word poor readers and recoding poor-readers. *Canadian Journal of Psychology*, *36*, 445–461.

Mody, M., Studdert-Kennedy, M., & Brady, S. (1997). Speech perception deficits in poor readers: auditory processing or phonological coding? *Journal of Experimental Child Psychology*, *64*, 199–231.

Moffat, S. D., & Hampson, E. (1996). Salivary testosterone levels in left- and right-handed adults. *Neuropsychologia*, *34*, 225–233.

Moffat, S. D., Hampson, E., & Lee, D. H. (1998). Morphology of the planum temporale and corpus callosum in left handers with evidence of left and right hemisphere speech representation. *Brain*, *121*, 2369–2379.

Moffat, S. D., Hampson, E., Wickett, J. C., Vernon, P. A., & Lee, D. H. (1997). Testosterone is correlated with regional morphology of the human corpus callosum. *Brain Research*, *767*, 297–304.

Molfese, D. L. (2000). Predicting dyslexia at 8 years of age using neonatal brain responses. *Brain and Language*, *72*, 238–245.

Molfese, D. L., Molfese, V. J., & Espy, K. A. (1999). The predictive use of event-related potentials in language development and the treatment of language disorders. *Developmental Neuropsychology*, *16*, 373–377.

Money, J. (1962). Dyslexia: a post-conference overview. In Money, J. (Ed.). *Reading disability: progress and research needs in dyslexia* (pp. 9–34). Johns Hopkins Press: Baltimore.

Monroe, M. (1928). Methods for diagnosis and treatment of cases of reading disability. *Genetic Psychology Monographs*, *4*, 333–456.

Monroe, M. (1932). *Children who cannot read*. Chicago, IL: University of Chicago Press.

Monsell, S., Patterson, K. E, Graham, A., Hughes, C. H., & Milroy, R. (1992). Lexical and sub-lexical translation of spelling to sound: strategic anticipation of lexical status. *Journal of Experimental Psychology: Learning, Memory and Cognition*, *18*, 452–467.

Moore, L. H., Brown, W. S., Markee, T. E., Theberge, D. C., & Zvi, J. C. (1995). Bimanual coordination in dyslexic adults. *Neuropsychologia*, *33*, 781–793.

Moore, L. H., Brown, W. S., Markee, T. E., Theberge, D. C., & Zvi, J. C. (1996). Callosal transfer of finger localization information in phonologically dyslexic adults. *Cortex*, *32*, 311–322.

Morais, J., Alegria, J., & Content, A. (1987). The relationships between segmental analysis and alphabetic literacy: an interactive view. *Cahiers de Psychologie Cognitive/Current Psychology of Cognition*, *7*, 415–438.

Morais, J., Bertelson, P., Cary, L., & Alegria, J. (1986). Literacy training and speech segmentation. *Cognition*, *24*, 45–64.

Morais, J., Cary, L., Alegria, J., & Bertelson, P. (1979). Does awareness of speech as a sequence of phones arise spontaneously? *Cognition*, *7*, 323–331.

Morand, S., Thut, G., Grave de Peralta, R., Clarke, S., Khateb, A., Landis, T., & Michel, C. M. (2000). Electrophysiological evidence for fast visual processing through human koniocellular pathway when stimuli move. *Cerebral Cortex*, *10*, 817–825.

Moretti, R., Bava, A., Torre, P., Antonello, R. M., & Cazzato, G. (2002). Reading errors in patients with cerebellar vermis lesions. *Journal of Neurology*, *249*, 461–468.

Morgan, A. E., & Hynd, G. W. (1998). Dyslexia, neurolinguistic ability, and anatomical variation of the planum temporale. *Neuropsychology Review*, *8*, 79–93.

Morgan, W. P. (1896). A case of congenital word-blindness. *British Medical Journal*, 7 November, p. 1378.

Morris, D. W., Robinson, L., Turic, D., Duke, M., Webb, V., Milham, C., Hopkin, E., Pound, K., Fernando, S., Easton, M., Hamshere, M., Williams, N., McGuffin, P., Stevenson, J., Krawczak, M., Owen, M. J., O'Donovan, M. C., & Williams, J. (2000). Family-based association mapping provides evidence for a gene for reading disability on chromosome 15q. *Human Molecular Genetics*, *9*, 843–848.

Morris, R. D., Stuebing, K. K., Fletcher, J. M., Shaywitz, S. E., Lyon, G. R., Shankweiler, D. P., Katz, L., Francis, D. J., & Shaywitz, B. A. (1998). Subtypes of reading disability: variability around a phonological core. *Journal of Educational Psychology*, *90*, 347–373.

Morris, R. K., & Rayner, K. (1991). Eye movements in skilled reading: implications for developmental dyslexia. In Stein, J. (Ed.). *Vision and visual dyslexia* (*vision and visual dysfunction, Vol. 13*) (pp. 233–242). London: Macmillan Press Ltd.

Moscovitch, M., & Smith, L. C. (1979). Differences in neural organisation between individuals with inverted and non-inverted handwriting postures. *Science*, *205*, 710–712.

Moseley, I. (1995). Imaging the adult brain. *Journal of Neurology Neurosurgery and Psychiatry*, *58*, 7–21.

Movshon, J. A., & Newsome, W. T. (1996). Visual response properties of striate cortical neurons projecting to area MT in macaque monkeys. *Journal of Neuroscience*, *16*, 7733–7741.

Munhall, K. G. (1994). Review of Hammond, G. (Ed.), *Cerebral control of speech and limb movements*. Amsterdam: North-Holland/Elsevier Science. *Brain and Language*, *46*, 174–177.

Munro, L. (1932). An unusual combination of left-handedness and stammer. *Lancet*, 9 January, pp. 84–85.

Murray, B. A. (1998). Gaining alphabetic insight: is phoneme manipulation skill or identity knowledge causal? *Journal of Educational Psychology*, *90*, 461–475.

Musiek, F. E., & Reeves, A. G. (1990). Asymmetries of the auditory areas of the cerebrum. *Journal of the American Academy of Audiology*, *1*, 240–245.

Musolino, A., & Dellatolas, G. (1991). Asymétries du cortex cérébral chez l'homme évaluées *in vivo* par angiographie stéréotaxique-stéréoscopique. *Revue Neurologique*, *147*, 35–45.

Muter, V., Hulme, C., Snowling, M., & Taylor, S. (1997). Segmentation, not rhyming, predicts early progress in learning to read. *Journal of Experimental Child Psychology*, *65*, 370–396.

Muter, V., & Snowling, M. (1998). Concurrent and longitudinal predictors of reading: the role of metalinguistic and short-term memory skills. *Reading Research Quarterly*, *33*, 320–337.

Muter, V., Snowling, M., & Taylor, S. (1994). Orthographic analogies and phonological awareness: their role and significance in early reading development. *Journal of Child Psychology and Psychiatry*, *35*, 293–310.

Naidoo, S. (1972). *Specific dyslexia: the research report of the ICAA Word Blind Centre for Dyslexic Children*. London: Pitman.

Nagarajan, S., Mahncke, H., Salz, T., Tallal, P., Roberts, T., & Merzenich, M. (1999). Cortical auditory signal processing in poor readers. *Proceedings of the National Academy of Sciences, USA*, *96*, 6483–6488.

Natale, N. (1977). Perception of nonlinguistic auditory rhythms by the speech hemisphere. *Brain and Language*, *4*, 32–44.

Nation, K. (1999). Reading skills in hyperlexia: a developmental perspective. *Psychological Bulletin*, *125*, 338–355

Nation, K., Allen, R., & Hulme, C. (2001). The limitations of orthographic analogy in early reading development: performance on the clue-word task depends on phonological priming and elementary decoding skill, not the use of orthographic analogy. *Journal of Experimental Child Psychology*, *80*, 75–94.

Nation, K., & Hulme, C. (1996). The automatic activation of sound-letter knowledge: an alternative interpretation of analogy and priming effects in early spelling development. *Journal of Experimental Child Psychology*, *63*, 416–435.

Nation, K., & Hulme, C. (1997). Phonemic segmentation, not onset-rime segmentation, predicts early reading and spelling skills. *Reading Research Quarterly*, *32*, 154–167.

Nation, K., & Snowling, M. (1997). Assessing reading difficulties: the validity and utility of current measures of reading skill. *British Journal of Educational Psychology*, *67*, 359–370.

Nation, K., & Snowling, M. J. (1998). Individual differences in contextual facilitation: evidence from dyslexia and poor reading comprehension. *Child Development*, *69*, 996–1011.

Nation, K., & Snowling, M. J. (2000). Factors influencing syntactic awareness skills in normal readers and poor comprehenders. *Applied Psycholinguistics*, *21*, 229–241.

Nawrot, M., & Rizzo, M. (1998). Chronic motion perception deficits from midline cerebellar lesions in human. *Vision Research*, *38*, 2219–2224.

Neville, H. J., Coffey, S. A., Holcomb, P. J., & Tallal, P. (1993). The neurobiology of sensory and language processing in language-impaired children. *Journal of Cognitive Neuroscience*, *5*, 235–253.

Newcombe, F. G., Ratcliff, G. G., Carrivick, P. J., Hiorns, R. W., Harrison, G. A., & Gibson, J. B. (1975). Hand preference and I.Q. in a group of Oxfordshire villages. *Annals of Human Biology*, *2*, 235–242.

Newman, S. P., Wadsworth, J. F., Archer, R., & Hockly, R. (1985). Ocular dominance, reading, and spelling ability in school children. *British Journal of Ophthalmology*, *69*, 228–232.

Newsome, W. T., & Paré, E. B. (1988). A selective impairment of motion perception following lesions of the middle temporal visual area (MT). *Journal of Neuroscience, 8*, 2201–2211.

Newton, P. K., & Barry, C. (1997). Comprehension effects in word production but not word comprehension in deep dyslexia. *Cognitive Neuropsychology, 14*, 481–509.

Nicholls, M. E. R. (1996). Temporal processing asymmetries between the cerebral hemispheres: evidence and implications. *Laterality, 1*, 97–137.

Nicolson, R. I. (1996). Developmental dyslexia: past, present and future. *Dyslexia, 2*, 190–207.

Nicolson, R. I., & Fawcett, A. J. (1990). Automaticity: a new framework for dyslexia research? *Cognition, 35*, 159–182.

Nicolson, R. I., & Fawcett, A. J. (1994a). Comparison of Deficits in cognitive and motor skills among children with dyslexia. *Annals of Dyslexia, 44*, 147–163.

Nicolson, R. I., & Fawcett, A. J. (1994b). Reaction times and dyslexia. *Quarterly Journal of Experimental Psychology, 47A*, 29–48.

Nicolson, R. I., & Fawcett, A. J. (1995a). Dyslexia is more than a phonological disability. *Dyslexia, 1*, 19–36.

Nicolson, R. I., & Fawcett, A. J. (1995b). Comparison of deficit severity across skills: Towards a taxonomy for dyslexia. In A. Fawcett & R. Nicolson (Eds.), *Dyslexia in children: multidisciplinary perspectives* (pp. 215–239). London: Harvester Wheatsheaf.

Nicolson, R. I., Fawcett, A. J., Berry, E. L., Jenkins, I. H., Dean, P., & Brooks, D. J. (1999). Association of abnormal cerebellar activation with motor learning difficulties in dyslexic adults. *Lancet, 353*, 1662–1667.

Nicolson, R. I., Fawcett, A. J., & Dean, P. (1995). Time estimation deficits in developmental dyslexia: evidence of cerebellar involvement. *Proceedings of the Royal Society of London, 259*, 43–47.

Nicolson, R. I., Fawcett, A. J., & Dean, P. (2001). Developmental dyslexia: the cerebellar deficit hypothesis. *Trends in Neuroscience, 24*, 508–511.

Nittrouer, S. (1999). Do temporal processing deficits cause phonological processing problems? *Journal of Speech, Language and Hearing Research, 42*, 925–942.

Nopola-Hemmi, J., Myllyluoma, B., Haltia, T., Taipale, M., Ollikainen, V., Ahonen, T., Voutilainen, A., Kere, J. & Widén, E. (2001). A dominant gene for developmental dyslexia on chromosome 3. *Journal of Medical Genetics, 38*, 658–664.

Nopola-Hemmi, J., Taipale, M., Haltia, T., Lehesjoki, A.- E., Voutilainen, A., & Kere, J. (2000). Two trans-locations of chromosome 15q associated with dyslexia. *Journal of Medical Genetics, 37*, 771–775.

Norrie, E. (1954). Ordblindhedens (dyslexiens) arvegang. *Laesepaedagogen, 261*, (as cited by Hermann, 1959).

Norris, D. (1994). A quantitative multiple-levels model of reading aloud. *Journal of Experimental Psychology: Human Perception and Performance, 20*, 1212–1232.

Nöthen, M. M., Schulte-Körne, G., Grimm, T., Cichon, S., Vogt, I. R., Müller-Myhsok, B., Propping, P., & Remschmidt, H. (1999). Genetic linkage analysis with dyslexia; evidence for linkage of spelling disability to chromosome 15. *European Child Adolescent Psychiatry, 8*, Supplement 3, 56–59.

Oakhill, J. (1982). Constructive processes in skilled and less skilled comprehenders' memory for sentences. *British Journal of Psychology, 73*, 13–20.

O'Boyle, N., & Benbow, C. P. (1990). Handedness and its relationship to talent. In S. Coren (Ed.), *Left-handedness: behavioral implications and anomalies* (pp. 343–372). Amsterdam: North-Holland/Elsevier Science.

Obrzut, J. E., Boliek, C. A., & Bryden, M. P. (1997). Dichotic listening, handedness, and reading ability: a meta-analysis. *Developmental Neuropsychology, 13*, 97–110.

O'Callaghan, M. J., Burn, Y. R., Mohay, H. A., Rogers, Y., Tudehope, D. I. (1993). Handedness in extremely low birth weight infants. *Cortex, 29*, 629–637

O'Connor, P. D., Sofo, F., Kendall, L., & Olsen, G. (1990). Reading disabilities and the effects of colored filters. *Journal of Learning Disabilities*, 23, 597–603.

Ognjenovic, V., Lukatela, G., Feldman, L. B., & Turvey, M. T. (1983). Misreadings by beginning readers of Serbo-Croation. *Quarterly Journal of Experimental Psychology, 35A*, 97–111.

Ojemann, G. A., & Mateer, C. (1979). Human language cortex: localisation of memory, syntax and sequential motor–phoneme identification systems. *Science, 205*, 1401–1403.

Ojemann, R. H. (1931). Studies in handedness II. Testing bimanual handedness. *Journal of Educational Psychology, 21*, 695–702.

O'Kusky, J., Strauss, E., Kosaka, B., Wada, J., Li, D., Druhan, M., & Petrie, J. (1988). The corpus callosum is larger with right cerebral hemisphere speech dominance. *Annals of Neurology, 24*, 379–383.

Oldfield, R. C. (1971). The assessment and analysis of

handedness: the Edinburgh Inventory. *Neuropsychologia, 9*, 87–113.

Olofsson, A., & Niedersøe, J. (1999). Early language development and kindergarten phonological awareness as predictors of reading problems: from 3 to 11 years of age. *Journal of Learning Disabilities, 32*, 464–472.

Olson, D. R. (1996). Towards a psychology of literacy: on the relations between speech and writing. *Cognition, 60*, 83–104.

Olson, R. K. (2002). Dyslexia: nature and nurture. *Dyslexia, 8*, 143–159.

Olson, R., Connors, F., & Rack, J. (1991). Eye movements in dyslexic and normal readers. In J. Stein (Ed.), *Vision and visual dyslexia* (*Vision and Visual Dysfunction, Vol. 13*) (pp. 235–250). London: Macmillan.

Olson, R. K., Kliegl, R., & Davidson, B. J. (1983). Dyslexic and normal readers' eye movements. *Journal of Experimental Psychology: Human Perception and Performance, 9*, 816–825.

Olson, R., Wise, B., Conners, F., Rack, J., & Fulker, D. (1989). Specific deficits in component reading and language skills: genetic and environmental influences. *Journal of Learning Disabilities, 22*, 339–348.

Omtzigt, D., Hendriks, A. W., & Kolk, H. H. (2002). Evidence for magnocellular involvement in the identification of flanked letters. *Neuropsychologia, 40*, 1881–1890.

Öney, B., & Durgunoğlu, A. Y. (1997). Beginning to read in Turkish, a phonologically transparent orthography. *Applied Psycholinguistics, 18*, 1–15.

Oppenheim, J. S., Skerry, J. E., Tramo, M. J., & Gazzaniga, M. S. (1989). Magnetic resonance imaging morphology of the corpus callosum in monozygotic twins. *Annals of Neurology, 26*, 100–104.

Orton, S. T. (1925). "Word-blindness" in school children. *Archives of Neurology and Psychiatry, 14*, 581–615.

Orton, S. T. (1928). A physiological theory of reading disability and stuttering in children. *New England Journal of Medicine, 199*, 1046–1052.

Orton, S. T. (1937). *Reading, writing and speech problems in children.* London: Chapman & Hall.

Osborne, R. T., Gregor, A. J., & Miele, F. (1968). Heritability of factor V: verbal comprehension. *Perceptual and Motor Skills, 26*, 191–202.

Østerberg, G. (1935). Topography of the layer of rods and cones in the human retina. *Acta Ophthalmologica, 6* (supplement), 1–102.

Palmer, R. E., & Corballis, M. C. (1996). Predicting reading ability from handedness measures. *British Journal of Psychology, 87*, 609–620.

Palmer, S. (2000). Phonological recoding deficit in working memory of dyslexic teenagers. *Journal of Research in Reading, 23*, 28–40.

Pammer, K., & Lovegrove, W. (2001). The influence of color on transient system activity: implications for dyslexia research. *Perception and Psychophysics, 63*, 490–500.

Parashos, I. A., Wilkinson, W. E., & Coffey, C. E. (1995). Magnetic resonance imaging of the corpus callosum: predictors of size in normal adults. *Journal of Neuropsychiatry and Clinical Neurosciences, 7*, 35–41.

Parker, R. M. (1990). Power, control, and validity in research. *Journal of Learning Disabilities, 23*, 613–620.

Parson, B. S. (1924). *Lefthandedness: a new interpretation.* New York: Macmillan.

Patterson, K. (1986). Lexical but nonsemantic spelling? *Cognitive Neuropsychology, 3*, 341–367.

Patterson, K., & Behrmann, M. (1997). Frequency and consistency effects in a pure surface dyslexic patient. *Journal of Experimental Psychology: Human Perception and Performance, 23*, 1217–1231.

Patterson, K., Marshall, K. J. C., & Coltheart, M. (Eds.), (1985). *Surface dyslexia: neuropsychological and cognitive studies of phonological reading.* Hillsdale, NJ: Lawrence Erlbaum Associates Inc.

Patterson, K., & Morton, J. (1985). From orthography to phonology: an attempt at an old interpretation. In K. Patterson, K. J. C. Marshall, & Coltheart (Eds.), *Surface dyslexia: neuropsychological and cognitive studies of phonological reading* (pp. 335–359). Hillsdale, NJ: Lawrence Erlbaum Associates Inc.

Paulesu, E., Démonet, J.- F., Fazio, F., McCrory, E., Chanoine, V., Brunswick, N., Cappa, S. F., Cossu, G., Habib, M., Frith, C. D., & Frith, U. (2001). Dyslexia: cultural diversity and biological unity. *Science, 291*, 2165–2167.

Paulesu, E., Frith, C. D., & Frackowiak, R. S. J. (1993). The neural correlates of the verbal component of working memory. *Nature, 362*, 342–343.

Paulesu, E., Frith, U., Snowling, M., Gallagher, A., Morton, J., Frackowiak, R. S. J., & Frith, C. D. (1996). Is developmental dyslexia a disconnection syndrome? Evidence from PET scanning. *Brain, 119*, 143–157.

Paulesu, E., McCrory, E., Fazio, F., Menoncello, L., Brunswick, N., Cappa, S. F., Cotelli, M., Cossu, G., Corte, F., Lorusso, M., Pesenti, S., Gallagher, A.,

Price, C., Frith, C. D., & Frith, U. (2000). A cultural effect on brain function. *Nature Neuroscience, 3,* 91–97.

Pavlidis, G. Th. (1981). Do eye movements hold the key to dyslexia? *Neuropsychologia, 19,* 57–64.

Pavlidis, G. Th. (1983). Erratic sequential eye-movements in dyslexics: comments and reply to Stanley et al. *British Journal of Psychology, 74,* 189–193.

Peereman, R., & Content, A. (1995). Neighbourhood size effect in naming: lexical activation or sub-lexical correspondences? *Journal of Experimental Psychology: Learning, Memory, and Cognition, 21,* 409–421.

Penhune, V. B., Zatorre, R. J., MacDonald, J. D., & Evans, A. C. (1996). Interhemispheric anatomical differences in human primary auditory cortex: probabilistic mapping and volume measurement from magnetic resonance scans. *Cerebral Cortex, 6,* 661–672.

Penniello, M.-J., Lambert, J., Eustache, F., Petit-Taboué, M. C., Barr, L., Viader, F., Lechevalier, B., & Baron, J.-C. (1995). A PET study of the functional neuroanatomy of writing impairment in Alzheimer's disease: the role of the left supra-marginal and left angular gyri. *Brain, 118,* 697–706.

Pennington, B. F. (1990). Annotation: the genetics of dyslexia. *Journal of Child Psychology and Psychiatry, 31,* 193–201.

Pennington, B. F. (1997). Using genetics to dissect cognition. *American Journal of Human Genetics, 60,* 13–16.

Pennington, B. F. (1999). Toward an integrated understanding of dyslexia: genetic, neurological, and cognitive mechanisms. *Development and Psychopathology, 11,* 629–654.

Pennington, B. F., Filipek, P. A., Lefly, D., Churchwell, J., Kennedy, D. N., Simon, J. H., Filley, C. M., Galaburda, A., Alarcon, M., & DeFries, J. C. (1999). Brain morphometry in reading-disabled twins. *Neurology, 53,* 723–729.

Pennington, B. F., Gilger, J. W., Olson, R. K., & DeFries, J. C. (1992). The external validity of age- versus IQ-discrepancy definitions of reading disability: lessons from a twin study. *Journal of Learning Disabilities, 25,* 562–573.

Pennington, B. F., Gilger, J. W., Pauls, D., Smith, S. A., Smith, S. D., & DeFries, J. C. (1991a). Evidence for major gene transmission of developmental dyslexia. *Journal of the American Medical Association, 266,* 1527–1534.

Pennington, B. F., Smith, S. D., Kimberling, W. J.,

Green, P. A., & Haith, M. M. (1987). Left-handedness and immune disorders in familial dyslexics. *Archives of Neurology, 44,* 634–639.

Pennington, B. F., Van Orden, G., Kirson, D., & Haith, M. (1991b). What is the causal relation between verbal STM problems and dyslexia? In S. A. Brady & D. P. Shankweiler (Eds.), *Phonological processes in literacy: a tribute to Isabelle Y. Liberman* (pp. 173–186). Hillsdale, NJ: Lawrence Erlbaum Associates Inc.

Pennington, B. F., Van Orden, G. C., Smith, S. D., Green, P. A., & Haith, M. M. (1990). Phonological processing skills and deficits in adult dyslexics. *Child Development, 61,* 1753–1758.

Perfetti, C. (1985). *Reading ability.* Oxford: Oxford University Press.

Perfetti, C. A. (1992). The representation problem in reading acquisition. In P. B. Gough, L. C. Ehri, & R. Treiman (Eds.), *Reading acquisition* (pp. 145–174). Hillsdale, NJ: Lawrence Erlbaum Associates Inc.

Perfetti, C. A., Beck, I., Bell, L. C., & Hughes, C. (1987). Phonemic knowledge and learning to read are reciprocal: a longitudinal study of first grade children. *Merrill-Palmer Quarterly, 33,* 283–319.

Perin, D. (1983). Phonemic segmentation and spelling. *British Journal of Psychology, 74,* 129–144.

Perry, V. H., Oehler R., & Cowey, A. (1984). Retinal ganglion cells that project to the dorsal lateral geniculate nucleus in the macaque monkey. *Neuroscience, 12,* 1101–1123.

Peters, M. (1983). RT to tactile stimuli presented ipsi- and contralaterally to the responding hand. *Quarterly Journal of Experimental Psychology, 35A,* 397–410

Peters, M. (1990). Subclassification of non-pathological left-handers poses problems for theories of handedness. *Neuropsychologia, 28,* 279–289.

Peters, M., Jäncke, L., & Zilles, K. (2000). Comparison of overall brain volume and midsagittal corpus callosum surface area as obtained from NMR scans and direct anatomical measures: a within-subject study on autopsy brains. *Neuropsychologia, 38,* 1375–1381.

Peters, M., & McGrory, J. (1987). Dichotic listening performance and writing posture in right- and left-handers. *Brain and Language, 32,* 253–264.

Peters, M., Oeltze, S., Seminowicz, D., Steinmetz, H., Koeneke, S., & Jäncke, L. (2002). Division of the corpus callosum into subregions. *Brain and Cognition, 50,* 62–72.

Petersen, S. E., & Fiez, J. A. (1993). The processing of single words studied with positron emission tomography. *Annual Review of Neuroscience, 16,* 509–530.

Petersen, S. E., Fox, P. T., Snyder, A. Z., & Raichle, M. E. (1990). Activation of extra-striate and frontal cortical areas by visual words and word-like stimuli. *Science, 249,* 1041–1044.

Peterson, M. E., & Haines, L. P. (1992). Orthographic analogy training with kindergarten children: effects on analogy use, phonemic segmentation, and letter-sound knowledge. *Journal of Reading Behaviour, 24,* 109–127.

Petrides, M., Alivisatos, B., Evans, A. C., & Meyer, E. (1993). Dissociation of human mid-dorsolateral from posterior dorsolateral frontal cortex in memory processing. *Proceedings of the National Academy of Sciences, USA, 90,* 873–877.

Petryshen, T. L., Kaplan, B. J., Fu Lui M., & Field, L. L. (2000). Absence of significant linkage between phonological coding dyslexia and chromosome 6p23–21.3, as determined by the use of quantitative-trait methods: confirmation of qualitative analysis. *American Journal of Human Genetics, 66,* 708–714.

Petryshen, T. L., Kaplan, B. J., Fu Lui, M., Schmill de French, N., Tobias, R., Hughes, M. L., & Field, L. L. (2001). Evidence for a susceptibility locus on chromosome 6q influencing phonological coding dyslexia. *American Journal of Medical Genetics* (*Neuropsychiatric Genetics*), *105,* 507–517.

Pfeiffer, R. A. (1936). Pathologie der Hörstrahlung und der corticalen Hörsphäre. In O. Bumke & O. Förster (Eds.), *Handbuch der Neurologie* (Vol. 6, pp. 533–626). Berlin: Springer-Verlag.

Picard, N., & Strick, P. L. (1996). Motor areas of the medial wall: a review of their location and functional activation. *Cerebral Cortex, 6,* 342–353.

Pilcher, D. L., Hammock, E. A. D., & Hopkins, W. D. (2001). Cerebral volumetric asymmetries in non-human primates: a magnetic resonance study. *Laterality, 6,* 165–179.

Pipe, M. E. (1988). Atypical laterality and retardation. *Psychological Bulletin, 104,* 343–347.

Pipe, M.-E. (1991). Developmental changes in finger localization. *Neuropsychologia, 29,* 339–342.

Plante, E., Swisher, L., Vance, R., & Rapcsak, S. (1991). Anatomical correlates of normal and impaired language in a set of dizygotic twins. *Brain and Language, 41,* 52–66.

Plaut, D. (1995). Double dissociation without modularity: evidence from connectionist neuropsychology. *Journal of Clinical and Experimental Neuropsychology, 17,* 291–321.

Plaut, D. C., McClelland, J. L., Seidenberg, M. S., & Patterson, K. (1996). Understanding normal and impaired word reading: computational principles in quasi-regular domains. *Psychological Review, 103,* 56–115.

Poldrack, R. A., Wagner, A. D., Prull, M. W., Desmond, J. E., Glover, G. H., & Gabrieli, J. D. E. (1999). Functional specialization for semantic and phonological processing in the left inferior prefrontal cortex. *NeuroImage, 10,* 15–35.

Polyak, S. (1957). *The vertebrate visual system.* Chicago, IL: University of Chicago Press.

Porac, C. (1997). Eye preference patterns among left-handed adults. *Laterality, 2,* 305–316.

Porpodas, C. D. (1999). Patterns of phonological and memory processing in beginning readers and spellers of Greek. *Journal of Learning Disabilities, 32,* 406–416.

Poskiparta, E., Niemi, P., & Vauras, M. (1999). Who benefits from training in linguistic awareness in the first grade, and what components show training effects? *Journal of Learning Disabilities, 32,* 437–446.

Pratt, A. C., & Brady, S. (1988). Relation of phonological awareness to reading disability in children and adults. *Journal of Educational Psychology, 80,* 319–323.

Preilowski, B. (1972). Possible contribution of the anterior forebrain commissures to bilateral motor co-ordination. *Neuropsychologia, 10,* 267–277.

Preilowski, B. (1975). Bilateral motor interaction: perceptual–motor performance of partial and complete split-brain patients. In K J. Zulch, D. Creutzfeld, & G. C. Galbraith (Eds.), *Cerebral localization* (pp. 115–132). New York: Springer-Verlag.

Preis, S., Jäncke, L., Schmitz-Hillebrecht, J., & Steinmetz, H. (1999). Child age and planum temporale asymmetry. *Brain and Cognition, 40,* 441–452.

Preis, S., Schittler, P., & Lenard, H.-G. (1997). Motor performance and handedness in children with developmental language disorder. *Neuropediatrics, 28,* 324–327.

Previc, F. H. (1990). Functional specialization in the lower and upper visual fields in humans: its ecological origins and neurophysiological implications. *Behavioral and Brain Sciences, 13,* 519–575.

Previc, F. H. (1993). Abnormal motoric laterality in strabismus and a hypothesis concerning its neurological origins. *International Journal of Neuroscience, 68,* 19–31.

Price, C. J., Moore, C. J., & Frackowiak, R. S. (1996). The effect of varying stimulus rate and duration on brain activity during reading. *Neuroimage, 3,* 40–52.

Pugh, K. R., Mencl, W. E., Jenner, A. R., Katz, L., Frost, S. J., Lee, J. R., Shaywitz, S. E., & Shaywitz, B. A. (2000a). Functional neuro-imaging studies of reading and reading disability (developmental dyslexia). *Mental Retardation and Developmental Disabilities Research Review, 6,* 207–213.

Pugh, K. R., Mencl, W. E., Shaywitz, B. A., Shaywitz, S. E., Fulbright, R. K., Constable, R. T., Skudlarski, P., Marchione, K. E., Jenner, A. R., Fletcher, J. M., Liberman, A. M., Shankweiler, D. P., Katz, L., Lacadie, C., & Gore, J. C. (2000b). The angular gyrus in developmental dyslexia: task-specific differences in functional connectivity within posterior cortex. *Psychological Science, 11,* 51–56.

Pugh, K. R., Shaywitz, B. A., Shaywitz, S. E., Constable, R. T., Skudlarski, P., Fulbright, R. K., Bronen, R. A., Shankweiler, D. P., Katz, L., Fletcher, J. M., & Gore, J. C. (1996). Cerebral organization of component processes in reading. *Brain, 119,* 1221–1238.

Pugh, K. R., Shaywitz, B. A., Shaywitz, S. E., Shankweiler, D. P., Katz, L., Fletcher, J. M., Skudlarski, P., Fulbright, R. K., Constable, R. T., Bronen, R. A., Lacadie, C., & Gore, J. C. (1997). Predicting reading performance from neuro-imaging profiles: the cerebral basis of phonological effects in printed word identification. *Journal of Experimental Psychology: Human Perception and Performance, 23,* 299–318.

Pujol, J., Vendrell, P., Junqué, C., Martí-Vilalta, J. L., & Capdevila, A. (1993). When does human brain development end? Evidence of corpus callosum growth up to adulthood. *Annals of Neurology, 34,* 71–75.

Quinn, K., & Geffen, G. (1986). The development of tactile transfer of information. *Neuropsychologia, 24,* 793–804.

Rabin, M., Wen, X. L., Hepburn, M., Lubs, H. A., Feldman, E., & Duara, R. (1993). Suggestive linkage of developmental dyslexia to chromosome 1p34–p36. *Lancet, 342,* 178.

Rack, J. P. (1985). Orthographic and phonetic coding in developmental dyslexia. *British Journal of Psychology, 76,* 325–340.

Rack, J. P. (1997). Issues in the assessment of developmental dyslexia in adults: theoretical and applied perspectives. *Journal of Research in Reading, 20,* 66–76.

Rack, J. P., Hulme, C., & Snowling, M. J. (1993). Learning to read: a theoretical synthesis. *Advances in Child Development and Behaviour, 24,* 99–127.

Rack, J. P., Hulme, C., Snowling, M. J., & Wightman, J. (1994). The role of phonology in young children learning to read words: the direct mapping hypothesis. *Journal of Experimental Child Psychology, 57,* 42–71.

Rack, J. P., & Olson, R. K. (1993). Phonological deficits, IQ and individual differences in reading disability: genetic and environmental influences. *Developmental Review, 13,* 269–278.

Rack, J. P., Snowling, M. J., & Olson, R. K. (1992). The nonword reading deficit in developmental dyslexia: a review. *Reading Research Quarterly, 27,* 29–53.

Rademacher, J., Caviness, V. S., Steinmetz, H., & Galaburda, A. M. (1993). Topographical variation of the human primary cortices: implications for neuroimaging, brain mapping, and neurobiology. *Cerebral Cortex, 3,* 313–329.

Rae, C., Harasty, J., Dzendrowsky, T. E., Talcott, J. B., Simpson, J. M., Blamire, A. M., Dixon, R. M., Lee, M. A., Thompson, C. H., Styles, P., Richardson, A. J., & Stein, J. F. (2002). Cerebellar morphology in developmental dyslexia. *Neuropsychologia, 46,* 1285–1292.

Rae, C., Lee, M. A., Dixon, R. M., Blamire, A. M., Thompson, C. H., Styles, P., Talcott, J., Richardson, A. J., & Stein, J. F. (1998). Metabolic abnormalities in developmental dyslexia detected by ^{1}H magnetic resonance spectroscopy. *Lancet, 351,* 1849–1852.

Raine, A., Hulme, C., Chadderton, H., & Bailey, P. (1991). Verbal short-term memory span in speech-disordered children: implications for articulatory coding in short-term memory. *Child Development, 62,* 415–423.

Ramus, F. (2001). Outstanding questions about phonological processing in dyslexia. *Dyslexia, 7,* 197–216.

Rasmussen, T., & Milner, B. (1977). The role of early left-brain injury in determining lateralization of cerebral speech functions. *Annals of the New York Academy of Sciences, 299,* 355–369.

Rastle, K., & Coltheart, M. (1998). Whammies and double whammies: the effect of length on nonword reading. *Psychonomic Bulletin and Review, 5,* 277–282.

Rastle, K., & Coltheart, M. (1999a). Serial and strategic effects in reading aloud. *Journal of Experimental Psychology: Human Perception and Performance, 25,* 482–503.

Rastle, K., & Coltheart, M. (1999b). Lexical and nonlexical phonological priming in reading aloud. *Journal of Experimental Psychology: Human Perception and Performance, 25,* 461–481.

Rastle, K., & Coltheart, M. (2000a). Lexical and non-lexical print-to-sound translation of disyllabic words and nonwords. *Journal of Memory and Language, 42*, 342–364.

Rastle, K., & Coltheart, M. (2000b). Serial processing in reading aloud: reply to Zorzi. *Journal of Experimental Psychology: Human Perception and Performance, 26*, 1232–1235.

Rastle, K., Harrington, J., Coltheart, M., & Palethorpe, S. (2000). Reading aloud begins when the computation of phonology is complete. *Journal of Experimental Psychology: Human Perception and Performance, 26*, 1178–1191.

Raymond, J. E., & Sorensen, R. (1998). Visual motion perception in children with dyslexia: normal detection but abnormal integration. *Visual Cognition, 5*, 389–404.

Rayner, K. (1978). Eye movements in reading and information processing. *Psychological Bulletin, 85*, 618–660.

Read, C., Zhang, Y.-F., Nie, H.-Y., & Ding, B.-Q. (1986). The ability to manipulate speech sounds depends on knowing alphabetic writing. *Cognition, 24*, 31–44.

Reason, R., Frederickson, N., Heffernan, M., Martin, C., & Woods, K. (1999). *Report by a working party of the Division of Educational and Child Psychology of the British Psychological Society*. Leicester: British Psychological Society.

Reed, M. (1989). Speech perception and discrimination of brief auditory cues in reading disabled children. *Journal of Experimental Child Psychology, 48*, 270–292.

Reichle, E. D., Polatsek, A., Fisher, D. L., & Rayner, K. (1998). Toward a model of eye movement control in reading. *Psychological Review, 105*, 125–157.

Reitsma, P. (1983). Printed word learning in beginning readers. *Journal of Experimental Child Psychology, 36*, 321–339.

Resch, F., Haffner, J., Parzer, P., Pfueller, U., Strehlow, U., & Zerahn-Hartung, C. (1997). Testing the hypothesis of the relationships between laterality and ability according to Annett's right-shift theory: findings in an epidemiological sample of young adults. *British Journal of Psychology, 88*, 621–635.

Rey, A., Ziegler, J. C., & Jacobs, A. M. (2000). Graphemes are perceptual reading units. *Cognition, 75*, B1–B12.

Reynolds, C. A., Hewitt, J. K., Erickson, M. T., Silberg, J. L., Rutter, M., Simonoff, E., Meyer, J., & Eaves, L. J. (1996). The genetics of children's oral reading performance. *Journal of Child Psychology and Psychiatry, 37*, 425–434.

Richardson, A. J., Calvin, C. M., Clisby, C., Schoenheimer, D. R., Montgomery, P., Hall, J. A., Hebb, G., Westwood, E., Talcott, J. B., & Stein, J. (2000). Fatty acid deficiency signs predict the severity of reading and related difficulties in dyslexic children. *Prostaglandins, Leukotrienes and Essential Fatty Acids, 63*, 69–74.

Richardson, A. J., Cox, I. J., Sargentoni, J. & Puri, B. K. (1997). Abnormal cerebral phospholipid metabolism in dyslexia indicated by phosphorus-31 magnetic resonance spectroscopy. *NMR in Biomedicine, 10*, 309–314.

Richardson, S. O. (1992). Historical perspectives on dyslexia. *Journal of Learning Disabilities, 25*, 40–47.

Richman, L. C., & Kitchell, M. M. (1981). Hyperlexia as a variant of developmental language disorder. *Brain and Language, 12*, 203–212.

Ridder, W. H., Borsting, E., Cooper, M., McNeel, B., & Huang, E. (1997). Not all dyslexics are created equal. *Optometry and Vision Science, 74*, 99–104.

Riddoch, G. (1917). Dissociation of visual perceptions due to occipital injuries, with especial reference to appreciation of movement. *Brain, 40*, 15–57.

Rippon, G., & Brunswick, N. (2000). Trait and state EEG indices of information processing in developmental dyslexia. *International Journal of Psychophysiology, 36*, 251–265.

Riva, D., & Giorgi, C. (2000). The cerebellum contributes to higher functions during development: evidence from a series of children surgically treated for posterior fossa tumours. *Brain, 123*, 1051–1061.

Roberts, L., & McDougall, S. (2003). What do children do in the rime-analogy task? An examination of the skills and strategies used by early readers. *Journal of Experimental Child Psychology, 84*, 310–337.

Robichon, F., & Habib, M. (1998). Abnormal callosal morphology in male adult dyslexics: relationships to handedness and phonological abilities. *Brain and Language, 62*, 127–146.

Robinson, G. L. W., & Conway, R. N. F. (1990). The effects of Irlen colored lenses on students' specific reading skills and their perception of ability: a 12-month validity study. *Journal of Learning Disabilities, 23*, 589–596.

Robinson, G. M., & Solomon, D. J. (1974). Rhythm is processed by the speech hemisphere. *Journal of Experimental Psychology, 102*, 508–511.

Rodgers, B. (1983). The identification and prevalence of specific reading retardation. *British Journal of Educational Psychology, 53*, 369–373.

Rogerson, P. A. (1994). On the relationship between

handedness and season of birth for men. *Perceptual and Motor Skills, 79,* 499–506.

Rohl, M., & Pratt, C. (1995). Phonological awareness, verbal working memory and the acquisition of literacy. *Reading and Writing: An Interdisciplinary Journal, 7,* 327–360.

Roodenrys, S., Hulme, C., Alban, J., Ellis, A. W., & Brown, G. D. A. (1994). Effects of word frequency and age of acquisition on short-term memory span. *Memory and Cognition, 22,* 695–701.

Roodenrys, S., Hulme, C., & Brown, G. (1993). The development of short-term memory span: separable effects of speech rate and long-term memory. *Journal of Experimental Child Psychology, 56,* 431–442.

Rose, S. A., Feldman, J. F., Jankowski, J. J., & Futterweit, L. R. (1999). Visual and auditory temporal processing, cross-modal transfer, and reading. *Journal of Learning Disabilities, 32,* 256–266.

Rosen, G. D., Galaburda, A. M., & Sherman, G. F. (1989). Cerebrocortical microdysgenesis with anomalous callosal connections: a case study in the rat. *International Journal of Neuroscience, 47,* 237–247.

Rosen, G. D., Sherman, G. F., & Galaburda, A. M. (1991). Ontogenesis of neocortical asymmetry: a [³H]thymidine study. *Neuroscience, 2,* 779–790.

Ross, G., Lipper E. G., & Auld, P. A. M. (1987). Hand preference of four-year-old children: its relationship to premature birth and neurodevelopmental outcome. *Developmental Medicine and Child Neurology, 29,* 615–622.

Ross, J., Burr, D., & Morrone, C. (1996). Suppression of the magnocellular pathways during saccades. *Behavioural Brain Research, 80,* 1–8.

Rossi, A., Serio, A., Petruzzi, C., Schiazza, G., Mattei, P., Mancini, F., & Casacchia, M. (1994). Three-dimensional in vivo planum temporale reconstruction. *Brain and Language, 47,* 68–95.

Roush, W. (1995). Arguing over why Johnny can't read. *Science, 267,* 1896–1898.

Rousselle, C., & Wolff, P. H. (1991). The dynamics of bimanual coordination in developmental dyslexia. *Neuropsychologia, 29,* 907–924.

Rozin, P., Poritsky, S., & Sotsky, R. (1971). American children with reading problems can easily learn to read English represented by Chinese characters. *Science, 171,* 1264–1267.

Rubens, A. B., Mahowald, M. W., & Hutton, J. T. (1976). Asymmetry of the lateral (Sylvian) fissures in man. *Neurology, 26,* 620–624.

Rudel, R. G. (1985). The definition of dyslexia: lan-

guage and motor deficits. In F. H. Duffy & N. Geschwind (Eds.), *Dyslexia: a neuroscientific approach to clinical evaluation* (pp. 33–53). Boston, MA: Little, Brown, & Co.

Rugg, M. D. (1982). Electrophysiological studies. In J. G. Beaumont (Ed.), *Divided visual field studies of cerebral organisation* (pp. 129–146). London: Academic Press.

Rugg, M., Lines, C. R., & Milner, A. D. (1984). Visual evoked potentials to lateralized visual stimuli and the measurement of interhemispheric transmission time. *Neuropsychologia, 22,* 215–225.

Ruiz, A., Ansaldo, A. I., & Lecours, A. R. (1994). Two cases of deep dyslexia in unilingual hispanophone aphasics. *Brain and Language, 46,* 245–256.

Rumsey, J. M., Andreason, P., Zametkin, A. J., Aquino, T., King, A. C., Hamburger, S. D., Pikus, A., Rapoport, J. L., & Cohen, R. M. (1992). Failure to activate the left temporoparietal cortex in dyslexia. *Archives of Neurology, 49,* 527–534.

Rumsey, J. M., Andreason, P., Zametkin, A. J., King, A. C., Hamburger, S. D., Aquino, T., Hanahan, A. P., Pikus, A., & Cohen R. M. (1994a). Right fronto-temporal activation by tonal memory in dyslexia: an O¹⁵ PET study. *Biological Psychiatry, 35,* 171–180.

Rumsey, J. M., Casanova, M., Mannheim, G. B., Patronas, N., DeVaughn, N., Hamburger, S. D., & Aquino, T. (1996). Corpus callosum morphology, as measured with MRI, in dyslexic men. *Biological Psychiatry, 39,* 769–775.

Rumsey, J. M., Donohue, B. C., Brady, D. R., Nace, K., Giedd, J. N., & Andreason, P. A. (1997a). Magnetic resonance imaging study of planum temporale asymmetry in men with developmental dyslexia. *Archives of Neurology, 54,* 1481–1489.

Rumsey, J. M., Dorwart, R., Vermess, M., Denckla, M. B., Kruesi, M. J. P., & Rapoport, J. L. (1986). Magnetic resonance imaging of brain anatomy in severe developmental dyslexia. *Archives of Neurology, 43,* 1045–1046.

Rumsey, J. M., Horwitz, B., Donohue, B. C., Nace, K., Maisog, J. M., & Andreason, P. (1997b). Phonological and orthographic components of word recognition: a PET–rCBF study. *Brain, 120,* 739–759.

Rumsey, J. M., Horwitz, B., Donohue, B. C., Nace, K. L., Maisog, J. M., & Andreason, P. (1999). A functional lesion in developmental dyslexia: left angular gyral blood flow predicts severity. *Brain and Language, 70,* 187–204.

Rumsey, J. M., Nace, K., Donohue, B., Wise, D., Maisog, J. M., & Andreason, P. (1997c). A positron emission tomographic study of impaired word recognition and phonological processing in dyslexic men. *Archives of Neurology, 54,* 562–573.

Rumsey, J. M., Zametkin, A. J., Andreason, P. A., Hanahan, A. P., Hamburger, S. D., Aquino, T., King, A. C., Pikus, A., & Cohen, R. M. (1994b). Normal activation of fronto-temporal language cortex in dyslexia as measured with oxygen-15 positron emission tomography. *Archives of Neurology, 51,* 27–38.

Rutter, M., Tizard, J., & Whitmore, K. (1970). *Education, Health & Behaviour.* London: Longman.

Rutter, M., & Yule, W. (1975). The concept of specific reading retardation. *Journal of Child Psychology and Psychiatry, 16,* 181–197.

Saigal, S., Rosenbaum, P., Szatmari, P., & Hoult, L. (1992). Non-right handedness among ELBW and term children at eight years in relation to cognitive function and school performance. *Developmental Medicine and Child Neurology, 34,* 425–433.

Saint-John, L. M., & White, M. A. (1988). The effect of coloured transparencies on the reading performance of reading-disabled children. *Australian Journal of Psychology, 40,* 403–411.

Salcedo, J. R., Spiegler, B. J., Gibson, E., & Magilavy, D. B. (1985). The auto-immune disease systemic lupus erythematosus is not associated with left-handedness. *Cortex, 21,* 645–647.

Salmelin, R., Service, E., Kiesilä, P., Uutela, K., & Salonen, O. (1996). Impaired visual word processing in dyslexia revealed with magnetoencephalography. *Annals of Neurology, 40,* 157–162.

Sampson, O. C. (1975). Fifty years of dyslexia: a review of the literature, 1925–75. I. Theory. *Research in Education, 14,* 15–32.

Samuels, S. J., & Anderson, R. H. (1973). Visual recognition memory, paired-associate learning, and reading achievement. *Journal of Educational Psychology, 65,* 160–167.

Samuelsson, S. (2000). Converging evidence for the role of occipital regions in orthographic processing: a case of developmental surface dyslexia. *Neuropsychologia, 38,* 351–362.

Sanders, R. J. (1989). Sentence comprehension following agenesis of the corpus callosum. *Brain and Language, 37,* 59–72.

Saron, C. D., & Davidson, R. J. (1989). Visual evoked potential measures of interhemispheric transfer time-humans *Behavioural Neuroscience, 103,* 1115–1138.

Satz, P., (1972). Pathological left-handedness: an explanatory model. *Cortex, 8,* 121–135.

Satz, P., & Fletcher, J. M. (1987). Left-handedness and dyslexia: an old myth revisited. *Journal of Pediatric Psychology, 12,* 291–298.

Satz, P., & Soper, H. V. (1986). Left-handedness, dyslexia, and auto-immune disorder: a critique. *Journal of Clinical and Experimental Neuropsychology, 8,* 453–458.

Savage, R., & Stuart, M. (1998). Sub-lexical inferences in beginning reading: medial vowel digraphs as functional units of transfer. *Journal of Experimental Child Psychology, 69,* 85–108.

Sawatari, A., & Callaway, E. M. (1996). Convergence of magno- and parvocellular pathways in layer 4B of macaque primary visual cortex. *Nature, 380,* 442–446.

Scarborough, H. S. (1984). Continuity between childhood dyslexia and adult reading. *British Journal of Psychology, 75,* 329–348.

Scarborough, H. S. (1989). Prediction of reading disability from familial and individual differences. *Journal of Educational Psychology, 81,* 101–108.

Scarborough, H. S. (1990). Very early language deficits in dyslexic children. *Child Development, 61,* 1728–1743.

Schachter, S. C., Galaburda, A. M., & Ransil, B. J. (1993). Associations of dyslexia with epilepsy, handedness, and gender. In P. Tallal, A. M. Galaburda, R. R. Llinás, & C. von Euler (Eds.), Temporal information processing in the nervous system. *Annals of the New York Academy of Sciences, 682,* 402–403.

Schilder, P. (1944). Congenital alexia and its relation to optic perception. *Journal of Genetic Psychology, 65,* 67–88.

Schiller, P. H., Logothetis, N. K., & Charles, E. R. (1990). Role of the colour-opponent and broad-band channels in vision. *Visual Neuroscience, 5,* 321–346.

Schlaug, G., Jäncke, L., Huang, Y., Staiger, J. F., & Steinmetz, H. (1995). Increased corpus callosum size in musicians. *Neuropsychologia, 33,* 1047–1055.

Schmahmann, J. D., & Sherman, J. D. (1998). The cerebellar cognitive affective syndrome. *Brain, 121,* 561–579.

Schneider, W., Roth, E., & Ennemoser, M. (2000). Training phonological skills and letter knowledge in children at risk for dyslexia: a comparison of three kindergarten intervention programs. *Journal of Educational Psychology, 92,* 284–295.

Schneider, W., & Shiffrin, R. M. (1977). Controlled and automatic information processing: I. Detection, search, and attention. *Psychological Review*, *54*, 1–88.

Schonell, F. J. (1935). Diagnostic tests for specific disabilities in school subjects. In *Yearbook of Education*. London: Evans.

Schulte-Körne, G., Deimel, W., Bartling, J., & Remschmidt, H. (1998a). Auditory processing and dyslexia: evidence for a specific speech processing deficit. *NeuroReport*, *9*, 337–340.

Schulte-Körne, G., Deimel, W., Müller, K., Gutenbrunner, C., & Remschmidt, H. (1996). Familial aggregation of spelling disability. *Journal of Child Psychology and Psychiatry*, *37*, 817–822.

Schulte-Körne, G., Grimm, T., Nöthen, M. M., Müller-Myhsok, B., Cichon, S., Vogt, I. R., Propping, P., & Remschmidt, H. (1998b). Evidence for linkage of spelling disability to chromosome 15. *American Journal of Human Genetics*, *63*, 279–282.

Schultz, R. T., Cho, N. K., Staib, L. H., Kier, L. E., Fletcher, J. M., Shaywitz, S. E., Shankweiler, D. P., Karz, L., Gore, J. C., Duncan, J. S., & Shaywitz, B. A. (1994). Brain morphology in normal and dyslexic children: the influence of age and sex. *Annals of Neurology*, *35*, 732–739.

Schwartz, M. F., Marin, O. S. M., & Saffran, E. M. (1979). Dissociations of language function in dementia: a case study. *Brain and Language*, *7*, 277–306.

Schwartz, M. F., Saffran, E. M., & Marin, O. S. M. (1980). Fractionating the reading process in dementia. In M. Coltheart, K. E. Patterson, & J. C. Marshall (Eds.), *Deep dyslexia* (pp. 259–269). London: Routledge & Kegan Paul.

Searleman, A., Coren, S., & Porac, C. (1989). Relationship between birth order, birth stress, and lateral preferences: a critical review. *Psychological Bulletin*, *105*, 397–408.

Searleman, A., & Fugagli, K. (1987). Suspected autoimmune disorders and left-handedness: evidence from individuals with diabetes, Crohn's disease and ulcerative colitis. *Neuropsychologia*, *25*, 367–374.

Sears, C. R., Hino, Y., & Lupker, S. J. (1995). Neighbourhood size and neighbourhood frequency effects in word recognition. *Journal of Experimental Psychology: Human Perception and Performance*, *21*, 876–900.

Sebastián-Gallés, N. (1991). Reading by analogy in a shallow orthography. *Journal of Experimental Psychology: Human Perception and Performance*, *17*, 471–477.

Seidenberg, M. S. (1992). Dyslexia in a computational model of word recognition in reading. In P. B. Gough, R. C. Ehri, & R. Treiman (Eds.), *Reading acquistion* (pp. 243–273). Hillsdale, NJ: Lawrence Erlbaum Associates Inc.

Seidenberg, M. S. (1993). A connectionist modelling approach to word recognition and dyslexia. *Psychological Science*, *4*, 299–304.

Seidenberg, M. S., & McClelland, J. L. (1989). A distributed, developmental model of word recognition and naming. *Psychological Review*, *96*, 523–568.

Seidenberg, M. S., & McClelland, J. L. (1990). More words but still no lexicon: reply to Besner et al. (1990). *Psychological Review*, *97*, 447–452.

Seidenberg, M. S., Plaut, D. C., Petersen, A. S., McClelland, J. L., & McRae, K. (1994). Nonword pronunciation and models of word recognition. *Journal of Experimental Psychology: Human Perception and Performance*, *20*, 1177–1196.

Seidenberg, M. S., & Tanenhaus, M. K. (1979). Orthographic effects on rhyme monitoring. *Journal of Experimental Psychology: Human Learning and Memory*, *5*, 546–554.

Seldon, H. L. (1981a). Structure of human auditory cortex. I. Cytoarchitectonics and dendritic distributions. *Brain Research*, *229*, 277–294.

Seldon, H. L. (1981b). Structure of human auditory cortex. II. Axon distributions and morphological correlates of speech perception. *Brain Research*, *229*, 295–310.

Semrud-Clikeman, M., Guy, K., Griffin, J. D., & Hynd, G. W. (2000). Rapid naming deficits in children and adolescents with reading disabilities and attention deficit hyperactivity disorder. *Brain and Language*, *74*, 70–83.

Semrud-Clikeman, M., Hynd, G. W., Novey, E. S., & Eliopulos, D. (1991). Dyslexia and brain morphology: relationships between neuroanatomical variation and neurolinguistic tasks. *Learning and Individual Differences*, *3*, 225–242.

Sénéchal, M., LeFevre, J.-A., Hudson, E., & Lawson, E. P. (1996). Knowledge of storybooks as a predictor of young children's vocabulary. *Journal of Educational Psychology*, *88*, 520–536.

Sergent, J., Zuck, E., Lévesque, M., & MacDonald, B. (1992). Positron emission tomography study of letter and object processing: empirical findings and methodological considerations. *Cerebral Cortex*, *2*, 68–80.

Serrien, D. J., & Wiesendanger, M. (2000). Temporal control of a bimanual task in patients with cerebellar dysfunction. *Neuropsychologia*, *38*, 558–565.

Service, E. (1992). Phonology, working memory, and

foreign-language learning. *Quarterly Journal of Experimental Psychology, 45A,* 21–50.

Service, E. (1998). The effect of word length on immediate serial recall depends on phonological complexity, not articulatory duration. *Quarterly Journal of Experimental Psychology, 51A,* 283–304.

Service, E., & Kohonen, V. (1995). Is the relation between phonological memory and foreign language learning accounted for by vocabulary acquisition? *Applied Psycholinguistics, 16,* 155–172.

Seymour, P. H. K. (1986) *Cognitive analysis of dyslexia.* London: Routledge & Kegan Paul.

Seymour, P. H. K. (1987a). Developmental dyslexia: a cognitive experimental analysis. In M. Coltheart, J. Sartori, & R. Job (Eds.), *The cognitive neuropsychology of language.* (pp. 351–395). Hove: Lawrence Earlbaum Associates Ltd.

Seymour, P. H. K. (1987b). How might phonemic segmentation help reading development? *Cahiers de Psychologie Cognitive/European Bulletin of Cognitive Psychology, 7,* 504–508.

Seymour, P. H. K. (1990). Developmental dyslexia. In M. W. Eysenck (Ed.), *Cognitive psychology: an international review* (pp. 135–196). Chichester, uk: Wiley.

Seymour, P. H. K. (1997). Foundations of orthographic development. In C. A. Perfetti, L. Rieben, & M. Fayol (Eds.), *Learning to spell: research, theory, and practice across languages* (pp. 319–337). Mahwah, NJ: Lawrence Erlbaum Associates Inc.

Seymour, P. H. K., Aro, M., & Erskine, J. (2003). Foundation literacy in European orthographies. *British Journal of Psychology, 94,* 143–174.

Seymour, P. H. K., & Bunce, F. (1994). Application of cognitive models to remediation in cases of developmental dyslexia. In M. J. Riddoch & G. W. Humphreys (Eds.), *Cognitive neuropsychology and cognitive rehabilitation* (pp. 349–377). Hove, UK: Lawrence Erlbaum Associates Ltd.

Seymour, P. H. K., & Duncan, L. G. (1997). Small versus large unit theories of reading acquisition. *Dyslexia, 3,* 125–134.

Seymour, P. H. K., Duncan, L. G., & Bolik F. M. (1999). Rhymes and phonemes in the common unit task: replications and implications for beginning reading. *Journal of Research in Reading, 22,* 113–130.

Seymour, P. H. K., & Elder, L. (1986). Beginning reading without phonology. *Cognitive Neuropsychology, 3,* 1–36.

Seymour, P. H. K., & Evans, H. M. (1993). The visual (orthographic) processor and developmental dys-

lexia. In D. Willows, R. Kruk, & E. Corcos (Eds.), *Visual processes in reading and reading disabilities* (pp. 347–376). Hillsdale, NJ: Lawrence Erlbaum Associates Inc.

Seymour, P. H. K., & Evans, H. M. (1994a). Levels of phonological awareness and learning to read. *Reading and Writing: An Interdisciplinary Journal, 6,* 221–250.

Seymour, P. H. K., & Evans, H. M. (1994b). Sources of constraint and individual variations in normal and impaired spelling. In G. D. A. Brown & N. C. Ellis (Eds.), *Handbook of spelling: theory, process and intervention* (pp. 129–153). Chichester, uk: Wiley.

Seymour, P. H. K., & MacGregor, C. J. (1984). Developmental dyslexia: a cognitive experimental analysis of phonological, morphemic and visual impairments. *Cognitive Neuropsychlogy, 1,* 43–82.

Shallice, T., & McCarthy, R. (1985). Phonological reading: from patterns of impairment to possible procedures. In K. Patterson, J. C. Marshall, & J. Morton, (Eds.), *Surface dyslexia: neuropsychological and cognitive studies of phonological reading* (pp. 361–398). Hillsdale, NJ: Lawrence Erlbaum Associates Inc.

Shallice, T., Warrington, E. K., & McCarthy, R. (1983). Reading without semantics. *Quarterly Journal of Experimental Psychology, 35A,* 111–138.

Shankweiler, D., Crain, S., Brady, S., & Macaruso, P. (1992). Identifying the causes of reading disability. In P. H. Gough, L. C. Ehri, and R. Treiman (Eds.), *Reading acquisition* (pp. 275–306). Hillsdale, NJ: Lawrence Erlbaum Associates Inc.

Shankweiler, D., Liberman, I. Y., Mark, L. S., Fowler, C. A., & Fischer, F. W. (1979). The speech code and learning to read. *Journal of Experimental Psychology: Human Learning and Memory, 5,* 531–545.

Shapiro, J., Nix, G. W., & Foster, S. F. (1990). Auditory perceptual processing in reading disabled children. *Journal of Research in Reading, 13,* 122–132.

Shapleske, J., Rossell, S. L., Woodruff, P. W. R., & David, A. S. (1999). The planum temporale: a systematic, quantitative review of its structural, functional and clinical significance. *Brain Research Reviews, 29,* 26–49.

Shapley, R. (1990). Visual sensitivity and parallel retinocortical channels. *Annual Review of Psychology, 41,* 635–658.

Shapley, R., & Perry, V. H. (1986) Cat and monkey retinal ganglion cells and their visual functional roles. *Trends in Neuroscience, 9,* 229–235.

Share, D. L. (1995). Phonological recoding and self-teaching: *sine qua non* of reading acquisition. *Cognition, 55*, 151–218.

Share, D. L. (1999). Phonological recoding and orthographic learning: a direct test of the self-teaching hypothesis. *Journal of Experimental Child Psychology, 72*, 95–129.

Share, D. L., McGee, R., McKenzie, D., Williams, S., & Silva, P. A. (1987). Further evidence relating to the distinction between specific reading retardation and general reading backwardness. *British Journal of Developmental Psychology, 5*, 35–44.

Shaywitz, B. A., Fletcher, J. M., Holahan, J. M., & Shaywitz, S. E. (1992b). Discrepancy compared to low achievement definitions of reading disability: results from the Connecticut longitudinal study. *Journal of Learning Disabilities, 25*, 639–648.

Shaywitz, B. A., Shaywitz, S. E., Pugh, K. R., Constable, R. T., Skudlarski, P., Fulbright, R. K., Bronen, R. A., Fletcher, J. M., Shankweiler, D. P., Katz, L., & Gore, J. C. (1995). Sex differences in the functional organization of the brain for language. *Nature, 373*, 607–609.

Shaywitz, B. A., Shaywitz, S. E., Pugh, K. R., Mencl, E., Fulbright, R. K., Skudlarski, P., Constable, R. T., Marchione, K. E., Fletcher, J. M., Lyon, G. R., & Gore, J. C. (2002). Disruption of posterior brain systems for reading in children with developmental dyslexia. *Biological Psychiatry, 52*, 101–110.

Shaywitz, B. A., & Waxman, S. G. (1987). Dyslexia. *New England Journal of Medicine, 316*, 1268–1270.

Shaywitz, S. E., Escobar, M. D., Shaywitz, B. A., Fletcher, J. M., & Makuch, R. (1992a). Evidence that dyslexia may represent the lower tail of a normal distribution of reading ability. *New England Journal of Medicine, 326*, 145–150.

Shaywitz, S. E., Shaywitz, B. A., Fletcher, J. M., & Escobar, M. D. (1990). Prevalence of reading disability in boys and girls. *Journal of the American Medical Association, 264*, 998–1002.

Shaywitz, S. E., Shaywitz, B. A., Pugh, K. R., Fulbright, R. K., Constable, R. T., Mencl, W. E., Shankweiler, D. P., Liberman, A. M., Skudlarski, P., Fletcher, J. M., Katz, L., Marchione, K. E., Lacadie, C., Gatenby, C., & Gore, J. C. (1998). Functional disruption in the organisation of the brain for reading in dyslexia. *Proceedings of the National Academy of Sciences*, USA, *95*, 2636–2641.

Sherwin, I., & Efron, R. (1980). Temporal ordering deficits following anterior temporal lobectomy. *Brain and Language, 11*, 195–203.

Siegel, L. S. (1988). Evidence that IQ scores are irrelevant to the definition and analysis of reading disability. *Canadian Journal of Psychology, 42*, 201–215.

Siegel, L. S. (1989a). IQ is irrelevant to the definition of learning disabilities. *Journal of Learning Disabilities, 22*, 469–478.

Siegel, L. S. (1989b). Why we do not need intelligence test scores in the definition and analysis of learning disabilities. *Journal of Learning Disabilities, 22*, 514–518.

Siegel, L. S. (1992). An evaluation of the discrepancy definition of dyslexia. *Journal of Learning Disabilities, 25*, 618–629.

Siegel, L. S. (1999). Issues in the definition and diagnosis of learning disabilities: a perspective on Guckenberger v. Boston University. *Journal of Learning Disabilities, 32*, 304–319.

Siegel, L. S., & Himel, N. (1998). Socio-economic status, age and the classification of dyslexics and poor readers: the dangers of using IQ scores in the definition of reading disability. *Dyslexia, 4*, 90–104.

Siegel, L. S., & Ryan, E. B. (1988). Development of grammatical sensitivity, phonological, and short-term memory skills in normally achieving and learning disabled children. *Developmental Psychology, 24*, 28–37.

Siegel, L. S., & Ryan, E. B. (1989). Subtypes of developmental dyslexia: the influence of definitional variables. *Reading and Writing, 1*, 257–287.

Siegel, L. S., Share, D., & Geva, E. (1995). Evidence for superior orthographic skills in dyslexics. *Psychological Science, 6*, 250–255.

Silver, A. A., & Hagin, R. A. (1964). Specific reading disability: follow-up studies. *American Journal of Orthopsychiatry, 34*, 95–102.

Silver, P. H., & Jeeves, M. A. (1994). Motor coordination in callosal agenesis. In M. Lassonde & M. A. Jeeves (Eds.). *Callosal agenesis: a natural split brain? Advances in behavioural biology, 42*, 207–219.

Simos, P. G., Breier, J. I., Fletcher, J. M., Bergman, E., & Papanicolaou, A. C. (2000). Cerebral mechanisms involved in word reading in dyslexic children: a magnetic source imaging approach. *Cerebral Cortex, 10*, 809–816.

Simos, G. P., Breier, J. I., Fletcher, J. M., Foorman, B. R., Castillo, E. M., & Papanicolaou, A. C. (2002). Brain mechanisms for reading words and pseudo words: an integrated approach. *Journal of Cognitive Neuroscience, 12*, 297–305.

Simos, P. G., Fletcher, J. M., Bergman, E., Breier, J. I., Foorman, B. R., Castillo, E. M., Davis, R. N., Fitzgerald, M., & Papanicolaou, A. C. (2002).

Dyslexia-specific brain activation profile becomes normal following succesful remedial training. *Neurology*, *58*, 1203–1213.

Sincich, L. C., & Horton, J. C. (2002). Divided by cytochrome oxidase: a map of the projections from V1 to V2 in macaques. *Science*, *295*, 1734–1737.

Skottun, B. C. (1997). Some remarks on the magnocellular deficit theory of dyslexia. *Vision Research*, *37*, 965–966.

Skottun, B. C. (2000). The magnocellular deficit theory of dyslexia: the evidence from contrast sensitivity. *Vision Research*, *40*, 111–127.

Skottun, B. C. (2001) On the use of the Ternus test to assess magnocellular function. *Perception*, *30*, 1449–1457.

Sladen, B. K. (1970). Inheritance of dyslexia. *Bulletin of the Orton Society*, *20*, 30–40.

Slaghuis, W. L., Lovegrove, W. J., & Davidson, J. A. (1993). Visual and language processing deficits are concurrent in dyslexia. *Cortex*, *29*, 601–615.

Slaghuis, W. L., & Ryan, J. F. (1999). Spatio-temporal contrast sensitivity, coherent motion, and visible persistence in developmental dyslexia. *Vision Research*, *39*, 651–668.

Slaghuis, W. L., Twell, A. J., & Kingston, K. R. (1996). Visual and language processing disorders are concurrent in dyslexia and continue into adulthood. *Cortex*, *32*, 413–438.

Smith, A. T., Early, F. T., & Grogan, S. C. (1986). Flicker masking and developmental dyslexia. *Perception*, *15*, 473–482.

Smith, S. D., Kimberling, W. J., Pennington, B. F., & Lubs, H. A. (1983). Specific reading disability: identification of an inherited form through linkage analysis. *Science*, *219*, 1345–1347.

Smith, S. D., Pennington, B. F., Kimberling, W. J., & Ing, P. S. (1990). Familial dyslexia: use of genetic linkage data to define subtypes. *Journal of the American Academy of Child and Adolescent Psychiatry*, *29*, 204–213.

Smythe, P. (2000). Aspects of phonological processing in sub-groups of left- and right-handedness. Unpublished PhD thesis, University of Leicester.

Snowling, M. J. (1980). The development of grapheme–phoneme correspondences in normal and dyslexic readers. *Journal of Experimental Child Psychology*, *29*, 294–305.

Snowling, M. J. (1981). Phonemic defects in developmental dyslexia. *Psychological Research*, *43*, 219–234.

Snowling, M. J. (1987). *Dyslexia: a cognitive developmental perspective*, 1st edn. Oxford: Blackwell.

Snowling, M. J. (1995). Phonological processing and developmental dyslexia. *Journal of Research in Reading*, *18*, 132–138.

Snowling, M. J. (2000a). *Dyslexia: a cognitive developmental perspective*, 2nd edn. Oxford: Blackwell.

Snowling, M. J. (2000b). Language and literacy skills: who is at risk and why? In D. V. M. Bishop & L. B. Leonard (Eds.), *Speech and language impairments in children: causes, characteristics, intervention and outcome* (pp. 245–259). Hove, UK: Psychology Press.

Snowling, M. J. (2001). From language to reading and dyslexia. *Dyslexia*, *7*, 37–46.

Snowling, M., Bishop, D. V. M., & Stothard, S. E. (2000). Is pre-school language impairment a risk factor for dyslexia in adolescence? *Journal of Child Psychology and Psychiatry*, *41*, 587–600.

Snowling, M. J., Bryant, P. E., & Hulme, C. (1996a). Theoretical and methodological pitfalls in making comparisons between developmental and acquired dyslexia: some comments on A. Castles & M. Coltheart (1993). *Reading and Writing: An Interdisciplinary Journal*, *8*, 443–451.

Snowling, M., Chiat, S., & Hulme, C. (1991). Words, nonwords, and phonological processes: some comments on Gathercole, Willis, Emslie, and Baddeley. *Applied Psycholinguistics*, *12*, 369–373.

Snowling, M., Gallagher, A., & Frith, U. (2003). Family risk of dyslexia is continuous: Individual differences in the precursors of reading skill. *Child Development*, *74*, 358–373.

Snowling, M., Goulandris, N., Bowlby, M., & Howell, P. (1986a). Segmentation and speech perception in relation to reading skill: a developmental analysis. *Journal of Experimental Child Psychology*, *41*, 489–507.

Snowling, M., Goulandris, N., & Defty, N. (1996b). A longitudinal study of reading development in dyslexic children. *Journal of Educational Psychology*, *88*, 653–669.

Snowling, M., & Hulme, C. (1989). A longitudinal study of developmental phonological dyslexia. *Cognitive Neuropsychology*, *6*, 379–401.

Snowling, M., & Hulme, C. (1994). The development of phonological skills. *Philosophical Transactions of the Royal Society of London*, *346*, 21–27.

Snowling, M. J., Hulme, C., Smith, A., & Thomas, J. (1994). The effects of phonetic similarity and list length on children's sound categorization performance. *Journal of Experimental Child Psychology*, *58*, 160–180.

Snowling, M. J., & Nation, K. A. (1997). Language, phonology, and learning to read. In C. Hulme & M.

Snowling (Eds.), *Dyslexia: biology, cognition and intervention* (pp. 153–166). London: Whurr Publishers.

Snowling, M., Nation, K., Moxham, P., Gallagher, A., & Frith, U. (1997). Phonological processing skills of dyslexic students in higher education: a preliminary report. *Journal of Research in Reading, 20*, 31–41.

Snowling, M., Stackhouse J., & Rack, J. (1986b). Phonological dyslexia and dysgraphia—developmental analysis. *Cognitive Neuropsychology, 3*, 309–339.

Snowling, M., Van Wagtendonk, B., & Stafford, C. (1988). Object-naming deficits in developmental dyslexia. *Journal of Research in Reading, 11*, 67–85.

Solan, H. A. (1990). An appraisal of the Irlen technique of correcting reading disorders using tinted overlays and tinted lenses. *Journal of Learning Disabilities, 23*, 621–623 and 626.

Solan, H. A., & Richman, J. (1990). Irlen lenses: a critical appraisal. *Journal of the American Optometric Association, 61*, 789–796.

Spafford, C., & Grosser, G. S. (1991). Retinal differences in light sensitivity between dyslexic and proficient reading children: new prospects for optometric input in diagnosing dyslexia. *Journal of the American Optometric Association, 62*, 610–615.

Spafford, C. S., Grosser, G. S., Donatelle, J. R., Squillace, S. R., & Dana, J. P. (1995). Contrast sensitivity differences between proficient and disabled readers using colored lenses. *Journal of Learning Disabilities, 28*, 240–252.

Sparrow, S. S., & Satz, P. (1970). Dyslexia, laterality and neuropsychological development. In D. J. Bakker & P. Satz (Eds.), *Specific reading disability: advances in theory and method* (pp. 41–60). Rotterdam: Rotterdam University Press.

Spencer, L., & Hanley, R. (2003). Effects of orthographic transparency on reading and phoneme awareness in children learning to read in Wales. *British Journal of Psychology, 94*, 1–28.

Spencer, M. C., Zelaznik, H. N., Diedrichsen, J., & Ivry, R. B. (2003). Disrupted timing of discontinuous but not continuous movements by cerebellar lesions. *Science, 300*, 1436–1439.

Spiegler, B. J., & Yeni-Komshian, G. H. (1983). Incidence of left-handed writing in a college population with reference to family patterns of hand preference. *Neuropsychologia, 21*, 651–659.

Spinelli, D., Angelelli, P., De Luca, M., Di Pace, E., Judica, A., & Zoccolotti, P. (1997). Developmental surface dyslexia is not associated with deficits in the transient visual system. *NeuroReport, 8*, 1807–1812.

St. John, R., Shields, C., Krahn, P., & Timney, B. (1987). The reliability of estimates of interhemispheric transmission times derived from unimanual and verbal response latencies. *Human Neurobiology, 6*, 195–202.

Stackhouse, J. (2000). Barriers to literacy development in children with speech and language difficulties. In D. V. M. Bishop & L. B. Leonard (Eds.), *Speech and language impairments in children: causes, characteristics, intervention and outcome* (pp. 73–97). Hove, UK: Psychology Press.

Stackhouse, J., & Wells, B. (1997). How do speech and language problems affect literacy development? In C. Hulme & M. Snowling (Eds.), *Dyslexia: biology, cognition and intervention* (pp. 212–234). London: Whurr Publishers.

Stage, S. A., & Wagner, R. K. (1992). Development of young children's phonological and orthographic knowledge as revealed by their spellings. *Developmental Psychology, 28*, 287–296.

Stahl, S. A., & Murray, B. A. (1994). Defining phonological awareness and its relationship to early reading. *Journal of Educational Psychology, 86*, 221–234.

Stainthorp, R., & Hughes, D. (1998). Phonological sensitivity and reading: evidence from precocious readers. *Journal of Research in Reading, 21*, 53–68.

Stanley, G., & Hall, R. (1973). Short term visual information processing in dyslexics. *Child Development, 44*, 841–844.

Stanley, G., Smith, G. A., & Howell, E. A. (1983). Eye-movements and sequential tracking in dyslexic and control children. *British Journal of Psychology, 74*, 181–187.

Stanovich, K. E. (1986). Matthew effects in reading: some consequences of individual differences in the acquisition of literacy. *Reading Research Quarterly, 21*, 360–406.

Stanovich, K. E. (1988a). The right and wrong places to look for the cognitive locus of reading disability. *Annals of Dyslexia, 38*, 154–177.

Stanovich, K. E. (1988b). Explaining the differences between the dyslexic and the garden-variety poor reader: the phonological-core variable-difference model. *Journal of Learning Disabilities, 21*, 590–604.

Stanovich, K. E. (1989). Various varying views on variation. *Journal of Learning Disabilities, 22*, 366–369.

Stanovich, K. E. (1991). Discrepancy definitions of reading disability: has intelligence led us astray? *Reading Research Quarterly, 26*, 7–29.

Stanovich, K. E. (1992). Speculation on the causes and consequences of individual differences in early reading acquisition. In P. B. Gough, L. C. Ehri, & R.

Treiman (Eds.), *Reading acquistion* (pp. 307–342). Hillsdale, NJ: Lawrence Erlbaum Associates Inc.

Stanovich, K. E. (1994a). Annotation: does dyslexia exist? *Journal of Child Psychology and Psychiatry*, *35*, 579–595.

Stanovich, K. E. (1994b). Are discrepancy-based definitions of dyslexia empirically defensible? In K. P. van den Bos, L. S. Siegel, D. J. Bakker, & D. L. Share (Eds.), *Current directions in dyslexia research* (pp. 15–30). Lisse: Swets & Zeitlinger.

Stanovich, K. E., Cunningham, A. E., & Freeman, D. J. (1984). Intelligence, cognitive skills and early reading progress. *Reading Research Quarterly*, *19*, 278–303.

Stanovich, K. E., Nathan, R. G., & Zolman, J. E. (1988). The developmental lag hypothesis in reading: longitudinal and matched reading level comparisons. *Child Development*, *59*, 71–86.

Stanovich, K. E., & Siegel, L. S. (1994). Phenotypic performance profile of children with reading disabilities: a regression-based test of the phonological-core variable-difference model. *Journal of Educational Psychology*, *86*, 24–53.

Stanovich, K. E., Siegel, L. S., & Gottardo, A. (1997a). Progress in the search for dyslexia subtypes. In C. Hulme & M. Snowling (Eds.), *Dyslexia: biology, cognition and intervention* (pp. 108–130). London: Whurr Publishers.

Stanovich, K. E., Siegel, L.S., & Gottardo, A. (1997b). Converging evidence for phonological and surface subtypes of reading disability. *Journal of Educational Psychology*, *89*, 114–127.

Steenhuis, R. E., Bryden, M. P., & Schroeder, D. H. (1993). Gender, laterality, learning difficulties and health problems. *Neuropsychologia*, *31*, 1243–1254.

Steffens, M. L., Eilers, E. R., Gross-Glenn, K., & Jallad, B. (1992). Speech perception in adult subjects with familial dyslexia. *Journal of Speech and Hearing Research*, *35*, 192–200.

Stein, J. F. (1991). Visuospatial sense, hemispheric asymmetry and dyslexia. In J. F. Stein (Ed.), *Vision and visual dyslexia* (*Vision and Visual Dysfunction, Vol. 13*), (pp. 181–188). London: MacMillan.

Stein, J. F. (1992). Vision and language. In M. Snowling & M. Thomson (Eds.), *Dyslexia: integrating theory and practice* (pp. 31–43). London: Whurr Publishers.

Stein, J. F. (1993). Visuospatial perception in disabled readers. In D. M. Willows, R. S. Kruk, & E. Corcos (Eds.), *Visual processes in reading and reading disabilities* (pp. 331–346). Hillsdale, NJ: Lawrence Erlbaum Associates Inc.

Stein, J. (1994). Developmental dyslexia, neural timing and hemispheric lateralisation. *International Journal of Psychophysiology*, *18*, 241–249.

Stein, J. (2000). The neurobiology of reading difficulties. *Prostaglandins, Leukotrienes and Essential Fatty Acids*, *63*, 109–116.

Stein, J. (2001). The magnocellular theory of developmental dyslexia. *Dyslexia*, *7*, 12–36.

Stein, J. F., & Fowler, S. (1982). Diagnosis of dyslexia by means of a new indicator of eye dominance. *British Journal of Ophthalmology*, *66*, 332–336.

Stein, J., & Fowler, S. (1985). Effect of monocular occlusion on visuomotor perception and reading in dyslexic children. *Lancet*, 13 July pp. 69–73.

Stein, J. F., & Fowler, M. (1993). Unstable binocular control in dyslexic children. *Journal of Research in Reading*, *16*, 30–45.

Stein, J. F., & Glickstein, M. (1992). Role of cerebellum in visual guidance of movement. *Physiological Reviews*, *72*, 967–1017.

Stein, J., Richardson, A., & Fowler, S. (1998). Comparison of dyslexic and normal readers using orthoptic assessment procedures (letter). *Dyslexia*, *4*, 109–110.

Stein, J. F., Riddell, P. M., & Fowler, S. (1985). Replying to: dyslexia and monocular occlusion. *Lancet*, 19 October, pp. 883–884.

Stein, J. F., Riddell, P. M., & Fowler, S. (1988). Disordered vergence control in dyslexic children. *British Journal of Ophthalmology*, *72*, 162–166.

Stein, J., & Walsh, V. (1997). To see but not to read: the magnocellular theory of dyslexia. *Trends in Neuroscience*, *20*, 147–152.

Steinmetz, H. (1996). Structure, function and cerebral asymmetry: *in vivo* morphometry of the planum temporale. *Neuroscience and Behavioural Reviews*, *20*, 587–591.

Steinmetz, H., Ebeling, U., Huang, Y., & Kahn, T. (1990a). Sulcus topography of the parietal opercular region: an anatomic and MR study. *Brain and Language*, *38*, 515–533.

Steinmetz, H., Herzog, A., Schlaug, G., Huang, Y., & Jäncke, L. (1995). Brain (a)symmetry in monozygotic twins. *Cerebral Cortex*, *5*, 296–300.

Steinmetz, H., Rademacher, J., Huang, Y., Hefter, H., Zilles, K., Thron, A., & Freund, H.-J. (1989). Cerebral asymmetry: MR planimetry of the human planum temporale. *Journal of Computer Assisted Tomography*, *13*, 996–1005.

Steinmetz, H., Rademacher, J., Jäncke, L., Huang, Y., Thron, A., & Zilles, K. (1990b). Total surface of temporoparietal intrasylvian cortex: diverging left–

right asymmetries. *Brain and Language*, *39*, 357–372.

Steinmetz, H., & Seitz, R. J. (1991). Functional anatomy of language processing: neuro-imaging and the problem of individual variability. *Neuropsychologia*, *29*, 1149–1161.

Steinmetz, H., Volkmann, J., Jäncke, L., & Freund, H.-J. (1991). Anatomical left–right asymmetry of language-related temporal cortex is different in left- and right-handers. *Annals of Neurology*, *29*, 315–319.

Stephan, K. M., Binkofski, F., Halsband, U., Dohle, C., Wunderlich, G., Schnitzler, A., Tass, P., Posse, S., Herzog, H., Sturm, V., Zilles, K., Seitz, R. J., & Freund, H.-J. (1999). The role of ventral medial wall motor areas in bimanual co-ordination: a combined lesion and activation study. *Brain*, *122*, 351–368.

Stephenson, S. (1907). Six cases of congenital word-blindness affecting three generations of one family. *Ophthalmoscope*, *5*, 482–484.

Stevens, L. J., Zentall, S. S., Deck, J. L., Abate, M. L., Watkins, B. A., Lip, S. R., & Burgess, J. R. (1995). Essential fatty acid metabolism in boys with attention-deficit hyperactivity disorder. *American Journal of Clinical Nutrition*, *62*, 761–768.

Stevenson, H. W., Stigler, J. W., Lucker, G. W., Lee, S., Hsu, C., & Kitamura, S. (1982). Reading disabilities: the case of Chinese, Japanese and English. *Child Development*, *53*, 1164–1181.

Stevenson, J. (1988). Which aspects of reading ability show a "hump" in their distribution? *Applied Cognitive Psychology*, *2*, 77–85.

Stevenson, J., Graham, P., Fredman, G., & McLoughlin, V. (1987). A twin study of genetic influences on reading and spelling ability and disability. *Journal of Child Psychology and Psychiatry*, *28*, 229–247.

Stirling, E. G., & Miles, T. R. (1988). Naming ability and oral fluency in dyslexic adolescents. *Annals of Dyslexia*, *38*, 50–72.

Stone, B., & Brady, S. (1995). Evidence for phonological processing defects in less-skilled readers. *Annals of Dyslexia*, *45*, 51–78.

Stordy, B. J. (1995). Benefit of docosahexaenoic acid supplements to dark adaptation in dyslexics. *Lancet*, *346*, 385.

Stordy, J. (2000). Dark adaptation, motor skills, docosahexaenoic acid, and dyslexia. *American Journal of Clinical Nutrition*, *71*, 323S–326S.

Stothard, S. E., & Hulme, C. (1992). Reading comprehension difficulties in children: the role of language comprehension and working memory skills. *Reading and Writing: An Interdisciplinary Journal*, *4*, 245–256.

Stothard, S. E., & Hulme, C. (1995). A comparison of phonological skills in children with reading comprehension difficulties and children with decoding difficulties. *Journal of Child Psychology and Psychiatry*, *36*, 399–408.

Stothard, S. E., Snowling, M. J., & Hulme, C. (1996). Deficits in phonology but not dyslexic? *Cognitive Neuropsychology*, *13*, 641–672.

Strain, E., Patterson, K. E., & Seidenberg, M. S. (1995). Semantic effects in single word naming. *Journal of Experimental Psychology: Learning, Memory and Cognition*, *21*, 1140–1154.

Strauss, E., Wada, J., & Hunter, M. (1994). Callosal morphology and performance on intelligence tests. *Journal of Clinical and Experimental Neuropsychology*, *16*, 79–83.

Stromswold, K. (1998). Genetics of spoken language disorders. *Human Biology*, *70*, 297–324.

Stromswold, K. (2001). The heritability of language: a review and meta-analysis of twin, adoption, and linkage studies. *Language*, *77*, 647–723.

Stuart G. W., & Lovegrove, W. J. (1992a). Visual processing deficits in dyslexia: receptors or neural mechanisms. *Perceptual and Motor Skills*, *74*, 187–192.

Stuart G. W., & Lovegrove, W. J. (1992b). Still no evidence for a photoreceptor-level abnormality in dyslexia. *Perceptual and Motor Skills*, *75*, 648–650.

Stuart, M. (1990). Processing strategies in a phoneme deletion task. *Quarterly Journal of Experimental Psychology*, *42A*, 305–327.

Stuart, M., & Coltheart, M. (1988). Does reading develop in a sequence of stages? *Cognition*, *30*, 139–181.

Stuart, M., & Masterson, J. (1992). Patterns of reading and spelling in 10-year-old children related to pre-reading phonological abilities. *Journal of Experimental Child Psychology*, *54*, 168–187.

Stuart, M., Masterson, J., & Dixon, M. (2000). Spongelike acquisition of sight vocabulary in beginning readers? *Journal of Research in Reading*, *23*, 12–27.

Stuart, M., Masterson, J., Dixon, M., & Quinlan, P. (1999). Inferring sub-lexical correspondences from sight vocabulary: evidence from 6- and 7-year-olds. *Quarterly Journal of Experimental Psychology*, *52A*, 353–366.

Studdert-Kennedy, M., & Mody, M. (1995). Auditory temporal perception deficits in the reading-impaired: a critical review of the evidence. *Psychonomic Bulletin and Review, 2,* 508–514.

Swan, D., & Goswami, U. (1997a). Phonological awareness deficits in developmental dyslexia and the phonological representations hypothesis. *Journal of Experimental Child Psychology, 66,* 18–41.

Swan, D., & Goswami, U. (1997b). Picture naming deficits in developmental dyslexia: the phonological representations hypothesis. *Brain and Language, 56,* 334–353.

Swanson, H. L. (1999). Reading comprehension and working memory in learning-disabled readers: is the phonological loop more important than the executive system? *Journal of Experimental Child Psychology, 72,* 1–31.

Swanson, H. L., Ashbaker, M. H., & Lee, C. (1996). Learning-disabled readers' working memory as a function of processing demands. *Journal of Experimental Child Psychology, 61,* 242–275.

Swisher, L., & Hirsh, I. J. (1972). Brain damage and the ordering of two temporally successive stimuli. *Neuropsychologia, 10,* 137–152.

Symmes, J. S., & Rapoport, D. (1972). Unexpected reading failure. *American Journal of Orthopsychiatry, 42,* 82–91.

Taipale, M., Kaminen, N., Nopola-Hemmi, J., Haltia, T., Myllyluoma, B., Lyytinen, H., Muller, K., Kaaranen, M., Lindsberg, P. J., Hannnula-Jouppi, K., & Kere, J. (2003). A candidate gene for developmental dyslexia encodes a nuclear tetratricopeptide repeat domain protein dynamically regulated in brain. *Proceedings of the National Academy of Sciences of the USA, 100,* 11553–11558.

Talcott, J. B., Hansen, P. C., Assoku, E. L., & Stein, J. F. (2000a). Visual motion sensitivity in dyslexia: evidence for temporal and energy integration deficits. *Neuropsychologia, 38,* 935–943.

Talcott, J. B., Hansen, C., Willis-Owen, C., McKinnell, I. W., Richardson, A. J., & Stein, J. F. (1998). Visual magnocellular impairment in adult developmental dyslexics. *Neuro-ophthalmology, 20,* 187–201.

Talcott, J. B., Witton, C., Hebb, G. S., Stoodley, C. J., Westwood, E. A., France, S. J., Hansen, P. C., & Stein, J. F. (2002). On the relationship between dynamic visual and auditory processing and literacy skills: results from large primary-school study. *Dyslexia, 8,* 204–225.

Talcott, J. B., Witton, C., McLean, M. F., Hansen, P. C., Rees, A., Green, G. G. R., & Stein, J. F. (1999). Can sensitivity to auditory frequency modulation predict children's phonological and reading skills? *NeuroReport, 10,* 2045–2050.

Talcott, J. B., Witton, C., McLean, M. F., Hansen, P. C., Rees, A., Green, G. G. R., & Stein, J. F. (2000b). Dynamic sensory sensitivity and children's word decoding skills. *Proceedings of the National Academy of Sciences, USA, 97,* 2952–2957.

Tallal, P. (1980). Auditory temporal perception, phonics and reading disabilities in children. *Brain and Language, 9,* 182–198.

Tallal, P. (1984). Temporal or phonetic processing deficit in dyslexia? That is the question. *Applied Psycholinguistics, 5,* 167–169.

Tallal, P. (1999). Children with language impairment can be accurately identified using temporal processing measures: a response to Zhang and Tomblin. *Brain and Language, 69,* 222–229.

Tallal, P., Allard, L., Miller, S., & Curtiss, S. (1997). Academic outcomes of language impaired children. In C. Hulme & M. Snowling (Eds.), *Dyslexia: biology, cognition and intervention* (pp. 167–181). London: Whurr Publishers.

Tallal, P., Miller, S. L., Bedi, G., Byma, G., Wang, X., Nagarajan, S. S., Schreiner, C., Jenkins, W. M., & Merzenich, M. M. (1996). Language comprehension in language-learning impaired children improved with acoustically modified speech. *Science, 271,* 81–84.

Tallal, P., Miller, S., & Fitch, R. H. (1993). Neurobiological basis of speech: a case for the preeminence of temporal processing. In P. Tallal, A. M. Galaburda, R. R. Llinás, & C. von Euler (Eds.), *Temporal information processing in the nervous system. Annals of the New York Academy of Sciences, 682,* 27–47.

Tallal, P., Miller, S., & Fitch, R. H. (1995). Neurobiological basis of speech: a case for pre-eminence of temporal processing. *Irish Journal of Psychology, 16,* 194–219.

Tallal, P., & Newcombe, F. (1978). Impairment of auditory perception and language comprehension in dysphasia. *Brain and Language, 5,* 13–24.

Tallal, P., & Piercy, M. (1973). Developmental aphasia: impaired rate of non-verbal processing as a function of sensory modality. *Neuropsychologia, 11,* 389–398.

Tallal, P., & Piercy, M. (1974). Developmental aphasia: rate of auditory processing and selective impairment of consonant perception. *Neuropsychologia, 12,* 83–93.

Tallal, P., & Piercy, M. (1975). Developmental aphasia: the perception of brief vowels and extended stop consonants. *Neuropsychologia, 13,* 69–74.

Tallal, P., & Piercy, M. (1978). In M. A. Wyke (Ed.),

Developmental dysphasia (pp. 63–84). London: Academic Press.

Tallal, P., & Stark, R. E. (1982). Perceptual/motor profiles of reading impaired children with or without concomitant oral language deficits. *Annals of Dyslexia, 32*, 163–176.

Tallal, P., Stark, R. E., & Mellits, E. D. (1985a). Identification of language-impaired children on the basis of rapid perception and production skills. *Brain and Language, 25*, 314–322.

Tallal, P., Stark, R. E., & Mellits, E. D. (1985b). The relationship between auditory temporal analysis and receptive language development: evidence from studies of developmental language disorder. *Neuropsychologia, 23*, 527–534.

Tan, U., & Tan, M. (1999). Incidences of asymmetries for the palmar grasp reflex in neonates and hand preference in adults. *NeuroReport, 10*, 3253–3256.

Tan, U., & Tan, M. (2001). Testosterone and grasp–reflex differences in human neonates. *Laterality, 6*, 181–192.

Tankle, R. S., & Heilman, K. M. (1982). Mirror-reading in right- and left-handers. *Brain and Language, 17*, 124–132.

Tankle, R. S., & Heilman, K. M. (1983). Mirror-writing in right-handers and in left-handers. *Brain and Language, 19*, 115–123.

Taylor, H. G., Satz, P., & Friel, J. (1979). Developmental dyslexia in relation to other childhood reading disorders: significance and clinical utility. *Reading Research Quarterly, 15*, 84–101.

Taylor, K. E. T., & Richardson, A. J. (2000). Visual function, fatty acids and dyslexia. *Prostaglandins, Leukotrienes and Essential Fatty Acids, 63*, 89–93.

Taylor, K. E. T., Higgins, C. J., Calvin, C. M., Easton, T., McDaid, A. M., & Richardson, A. J. (2000). Dyslexia in adults is associated with clinical signs of fatty acid deficiency. *Prostaglandins, Leukotrienes and Essential Fatty Acids, 63*, 75–78.

Temple, C. M. (1985a). Reading with partial phonology: developmental phonological dyslexia. *Journal of Psycholinguistic Research, 14*, 523–541.

Temple, C. M. (1985b). Surface dyslexia: variation within a syndrome. In K. E. Patterson, J. C. Marshall, & M. Coltheart (Eds.), *Surface dyslexia: neuropsychological and cognitive studies of phonological reading* (pp. 269–288). Hove, UK: Lawrence Erlbaum Asociates Ltd.

Temple, C. M. (1987). The nature of normality, the deviance of dyslexia and the recognition of rhyme: a reply to Bryant and Impey (1986). *Cognition, 27*, 103–108.

Temple, C. M. (1988). Developmental dyslexia and dysgraphia persistence in middle age. *Journal of Communication Disorders, 21*, 189–207.

Temple, C. M. (1990). Foop is still floop: a six year follow-up of phonological dyslexia and dysgraphia. *Reading and Writing: An Interdisciplinary Journal, 2*, 209–221.

Temple, C. M. (1997a). Cognitive neuropsychology and its application to children. *Journal of Child Psychology and Psychiatry, 38*, 27–52.

Temple, C. M. (1997b). *Developmental cognitive neuropsychology*. Hove, UK: Psychology Press.

Temple, C., & Ilsley, J. (1993). Phonemic discrimination in callosal agenesis. *Cortex, 29*, 341–348.

Temple, C., Jeeves, M., & Villaroya, O. (1989). Ten pen men: rhyming skills in two children with callosal agenesis. *Brain and Language, 37*, 548–564.

Temple, C., Jeeves, M., & Villaroya, O. (1990). Reading in callosal agenesis. *Brain and Language, 39*, 235–253.

Temple, C. M., & Marshall, J. C. (1983). A case study of developmental phonological dyslexia. *British Journal of Psychology, 74*, 517–533.

Temple, E., Deutsch, G. K., Poldrack, R. A., Miller, S. L., Tallal, P., Merzenich, M., & Gabrieli, J. D. E. (2003). Neural deficits in children with dyslexia ameliorated by behavioral remediation: evidence from functional MRI. *Proceedings of the National Academy of Sciences, USA, 100*, 2860–2865.

Teszner, D., Tzavaras, A., Gruner, J., & Hécaen, H. (1972). L'asymétrie droite-gauche du planum temporale: à propos de l'étude anatomique de 100 cerveaux. *Revue Neurologique*, 444–449.

Teuber, H.-L. (1955). Physiological psychology. *Annual Review of Psychology, 6*, 267–296.

Thach, W. T. (1996). On the specific role of the cerebellum in motor learning and cognition: clues from PET activation and lesion studies in man. *Behavioral and Brain Sciences, 19*, 411–431.

Thomas, C. J. (1905). Congenital "word-blindness" and its treatment. *Ophthalmoscope, 5*, 380–385.

Thompson, G. B., Cottrell, D. S., & Fletcher-Flinn, C. M. (1996). Sub-lexical orthographic–phonological relations early in the acquisition of reading: the knowledge sources account. *Journal of Experimental Child Psychology, 62*, 190–222.

Thomson, M. (1975). Laterality and reading attainment: research Notes. *British Journal of Educational Psychology, 45*, 317–321.

Thomson, M. E. (1982). The assessment of children with specific reading difficulties (dyslexia) using the

British Ability Scales. *British Journal of Psychology*, *73*, 461–478.

Thorstad, G. (1991). The effect of orthography on the acquisition of literacy skills. *British Journal of Psychology*, *82*, 527–537.

Tinker, M. A. (1958). Recent studies of eye movements in reading. *Psychological Bulletin*, *55*, 215–231.

Tomasch, J. (1954). Size, distribution, and number of fibres in the human corpus callosum. *Anatomical Record*, *119*, 119–135.

Tomblin, J. B., & Buckwalter, P. R. (1998). Heritability of poor language achievement among twins. *Journal of Speech, Language and Hearing Research*, *41*, 188–199.

Tønnessen, F. E. (1997a). How can we best define "dyslexia"? *Dyslexia*, *3*, 78–92.

Tønnessen, F. E. (1997b). Testosterone and dyslexia. *Pediatric Rehabilitation*, *1*, 51–58.

Tønnessen, F. E., Løkken, A., Høien, T., & Lundberg, I. (1993). Dyslexia, left-handedness, and immune disorders. *Archives of Neurology*, *50*, 411–416.

Tootell, R. B. H., Reppas, J. B., Kwong, K. K., Malach, R., Born, R. T., Brady, T. J., Rosen, B. R., & Belliveau, J. W. (1995). Functional analysis of human MT and relayed visual cortical areas using magnetic resonance imaging. *Journal of Neuroscience*, *15*, 3215–3230.

Torgesen, J. K. (1989), Why IQ *is* relevant to the definition of learning disabilities. *Journal of Learning Disabilities*, *22*, 484–486.

Torgesen, J. K., & Davis, C. (1996). Individual difference variables predict the response to training in phonological awareness. *Journal of Experimental Child Psychology*, *63*, 1–21.

Torgesen, J. K., Morgan, S. T., & Davis, C. (1992). Effects of two types of phonological awareness training on word learning in kindergarten children. *Journal of Educational Psychology*, *84*, 364–370.

Torgesen, J., Rashotte, C., Greenstein, J, Houck, G., & Portes, P. (1987). Academic difficulties of learning disabled children who perform poorly on memory span tasks. In H. L. Swanson, K. D. Gadow, & A. Poling (Eds.), *Advances in Learning and Behavioral Disabilities. 2: Memory and Learning Disabilities* (pp. 305–333). Greenwich, CT: JAI Press.

Torgesen, J. K., & Wagner, R. K. (1992). Language abilities, reading acquisition, and developmental dyslexia: limitations and alternative views. *Journal of Learning Disabilities*, *25*, 577–581.

Torgesen, K. J., Wagner, R. K., Balthazar, M., Davis, C., Morgan, S., Simmonds, K., Stage, S., & Zirps,

F. (1989). Developmental and individual differences in performance on phonological synthesis tasks. *Journal of Experimental Child Psychology*, *47*, 491–505.

Toth, G., & Siegel, L. S. (1994). A critical evaluation of the IQ–achievement discrepancy based definition of dyslexia. In K. P. van den Bos, L. S. Siegel, D. J. Bakker, & D. L. Share (Eds.), *Current directions in dyslexia research* (pp. 45–70). Lisse: Swets & Zeitlinger.

Travis, L. E., & Johnson, W. (1934). Stuttering and the concept of handedness. *Psychological Review*, *41*, 534–562.

Treiman, R. (1983). The structure of spoken syllables: evidence from novel word games. *Cognition*, *15*, 49–74.

Treiman, R. (1985). Onsets and rimes as units of spoken syllables: evidence from children. *Journal of Experimental Child Psychology*, *39*, 161–181.

Treiman, R. (1986). The division between onsets and rimes in English syllables. *Journal of Memory and Language*, *25*, 476–491.

Treiman, R. (1992). The role of intrasyllabic units in learning to read and spell. In P. B. Gough, L. C. Ehri, & R. Treiman (Eds.), *Reading acquistion* (pp. 65–106). Hillsdale, NJ: Lawrence Erlbaum Associates Inc.

Treiman, R. (1994). Use of consonant names in beginning spelling. *Developmental Psychology*, *30*, 567–580.

Treiman, R., & Cassar, M. (1996). Effects of morphology on children's spelling of final consonant clusters. *Journal of Experimental Child Psychology*, *63*, 141–170.

Treiman, R., Goswami, U., & Bruck, M. (1990). Not all nonwords are alike: implications for reading development and theory. *Memory and Cognition*, *18*, 559–567.

Treiman, R., & Hirsh-Pasek, K. (1985). Are there qualitative differences in reading behaviour between dyslexics and normal readers? *Memory and Cognition*, *13*, 357–364.

Treiman, R., Mullennix, J., Bijeljac-Babic, R., & Richmond-Welty, E. D. (1995). The special role of rimes in the description, use, and acquisition of English orthography. *Journal of Experimental Psychology: General*, *124*, 107–136.

Treiman, R., & Rodriguez, K. (1999). Young children use letter names in learning to read words. *Psychological Science*, *10*, 334–338.

Treiman, R., & Tincoff, R. (1997). The fragility of the alphabetic principle: children's knowledge of letter names can cause them to spell syllabically rather than alphabetically. *Journal of Experimental Child Psychology, 64,* 425–451.

Treiman, R., Tincoff, R., & Richmond-Welty, E. D. (1996). Letter names help children to connect print and speech. *Developmental Psychology, 32,* 505–514.

Treiman, R., Tincoff, R., Rodriguez, K., Mouzaki, A., & Francis, D. J. (1998). The foundations of literacy: learning the sounds of letters. *Child Development, 69,* 1524–1540.

Treiman, R., & Zukowski, A. (1988). Units in reading and spelling. *Journal of Memory and Language, 27,* 466–477.

Treiman, R., & Zukowski, A. (1991). Levels of phonological awareness. In S. Brady & D. Shankweiler (Eds.), *Phonological processes in literacy: a tribute to Isabelle Y. Liberman* (pp. 67–83). Hillsdale, NJ: Lawrence Erlbaum Associates Inc.

Treiman, R., & Zukowski, A. (1996). Children's sensitivity to syllables, onsets, rimes, and phonemes. *Journal of Experimental Child Psychology, 62,* 193–215 (erratum: *62,* 432).

Troia, G. A. (1999). Phonological awareness intervention research: a critical review of the experimental methodology. *Reading Research Quarterly, 34,* 28–52.

Troscianko, T., Davidoff, J., Humphreys, G., Landis, T., Fahle, M., Greenlee, M., Brugger, P., & Phillips, W. (1996). Human colour discrimination based on a non-parvocellular pathway. *Current Biology, 6,* 200–210.

Tucha, O., Aschenbrenner, S., & Lange, K. W. (2000). Mirror-writing and handedness. *Brain and Language, 73,* 432–441.

Tuller, B., & Kelso, J. A. S. (1989). Environmentally-specified patterns of movement coordination in normal and split-brain subjects. *Experimental Brain Research, 75,* 306–316.

Tunmer, W. E., Herriman, M. L., & Neasdale, A. R. (1988). Meta-linguistic abilities and beginning reading. *Reading Research Quarterly, 23,* 134–158.

Tunmer, W. E., & Hoover, W. A. (1992). Cognitive and linguistic factors in learning to read. In P. B. Gough, L. C. Ehri, & R. Treiman (Eds.), *Reading acquistion* (pp. 175–214). Hillsdale, N.J: Lawrence Erlbaum Associates Inc.

Tunmer, W. E., Neasdale, A. R., & Wright, A. D. (1987). Syntactic awareness and reading acquisition. *British Journal of Developmental Psychology, 5,* 25–34.

Turner, M. (1997). *Psychological assessment of dyslexia.* London: Whurr Publishers.

Turvey, M. T., Feldman, L. B., & Lukatela, G. (1984). The Serbo-Croatian orthography constrains the reader to a phonologically analytic strategy. In: L. Henderson (Ed.), *Orthography and reading: perspectives for cognitive psychology, neuropsychology, and linguistics* (pp. 81–89). Hove, UK: Lawrence Erlbaum Associates Ltd.

Tyrrell, R., Holland, K., Dennis, D., & Wilkins, A. (1995). Coloured overlays, visual discomfort, visual search and classroom reading. *Journal of Research in Reading, 18,* 10–23.

Tzeng, O. J. L., & Wang, W. S.-Y. (1984). Search for a common neurocognitive mechanism for language and movements. *American Journal of Physiology, 246,* 904–911.

Tzourio, N., Nkanga-Ngila, B., & Mazoyer, B. (1998). Left planum temporale surface correlates with functional dominance during story listening. *NeuroReport, 9,* 829–833.

Ungerleider, L. G., & Desimone, R. (1986). Cortical connections of visual area MT in the macaque. *Journal of Comparative Neurology, 248,* 190–222.

Uylings, B. M., Malofeeva, L. I., Bogolepova, I. N., Amunts, K., & Zilles, K. (1998). Broca's language area from a neuroanatomical and developmental perspective. In C. M. Brown & P. Hagoort (Eds.). *The neurocognition of language* (pp. 319–336). Oxford: Oxford University Press.

Vaid, J., & Stiles-Davis, J. (1989). Mirror-writing: an advantage for the left-handed? *Brain and Language, 37,* 616–627.

Van der Leij, A., & Van Daal, V. (1999). Automization aspects of dyslexia: speed limitations in word identification, sensitivity to increasing task demands, and orthographic compensation. *Journal of Learning Disabilities, 32,* 417–428.

Van der Wissel, A., & Zegers, F. E. (1985). Reading retardation revisited. *British Journal of Developmental Psychology, 3,* 3–9.

Van Ijzendoorn, M. H., & Bus, A. G. (1994). Meta-analytic confirmation of the nonword reading deficit in developmental dyslexia. *Reading Research Quarterly, 29,* 267–275.

Vanni, S., Uusitalo, M. A., Kiesila, P., & Hari, R. (1997). Visual motion activates V5 in dyslexics. *NeuroReport, 8,* 1939–1942.

Van Orden, G. C., Pennington, B. F., & Stone, G. O. (1990). Word identification in reading and the promise of subsymbolic psycholinguistics. *Psychological Review, 97,* 488–522.

Van Strien, J. W., & Bouma, A. (1995). Sex and familial

sinistrality differences in cognitive abilities. *Brain and Cognition*, *27*, 137–146.

Velay, J.-L., Daffaure, V., Giraud, K., & Habib, M. (2002). Interhemispheric sensorimotor integration in pointing movements: a study on dyslexic adults. *Neuropsychologia*, *40*, 827–834.

Vellutino, F. R. (1979). *Dyslexia: theory and research*. Cambridge, MA: MIT Press.

Vellutino, F. R., & Scanlon, D. M. (1991). The pre-eminence of phonologically based skills in learning to read. In S. A. Brady & D. P. Shankweiler (Eds.), *Phonological processes in literacy: a tribute to Isabelle Y. Liberman* (pp. 237–252). Hillsdale, NJ: Lawrence Erlbaum Associates Inc.

Vellutino, F. R., Scanlon, D. M., & Lyon, G. R. (2000). Differentiating between difficult-to-remediate and readily remediated poor readers: more evidence against the IQ–achievement discrepancy definition of reading disability. *Journal of Learning Disabilities*, *33*, 223–238.

Vellutino, F. R., Scanlon, D. M., Sipay, E. R., Small, S. G., Pratt, A., Chen, R., & Denckla, M. B. (1996). Cognitive profiles of difficult-to-remediate and readily remediated poor readers: early intervention as a vehicle for distinguishing between cognitive and experiential deficits as basic causes of specific reading disability. *Journal of Educational Psychology*, *88*, 601–638.

Vellutino, F. R. Steger, J. A., Harding, C. J., & Phillips, F. (1975). Verbal versus non-verbal paired-associates learning in poor and normal readers. *Neuropsychologia*, *13*, 75–82.

Vernon, M. D. (1957). *Backwardness in reading*. Cambridge: Cambridge University Press.

Vernon, M. D. (1960). The investigation of reading problems today. *British Journal of Educational Psychology*, *30*, 146–154.

Vernon, M. D. (1962). Specific dyslexia. *British Journal of Educational Psychology*, *32*, 143–150.

Victor, J. D., Conte, M. M., Burton, L., & Nass, R. D. (1993). Visual evoked potentials in dyslexics and normals: failure to find a difference in transient or steady-state responses. *Visual Neuroscience*, *10*, 939–946.

Vidyasagar, T. R., & Pammer, K. (1999). Impaired visual search in dyslexia relates to the role of the magnocellular pathway in attention. *NeuroReport*, *10*, 1283–1287.

Volkman, F. C. (1986). Human visual suppression. *Vision Research*, *26*, 1401–1416.

Volkman, F. C., Riggs, L. A., White, K. D., & Moore, R. K. (1978). Perception of suprathreshold stimuli during saccadic eye movements. *Vision Research*, *18*, 1193–1199.

Volpe, B., Sidtis, J. J., & Gazzaniga, M. S. (1981). Can left-handed writing posture predict cerebral language laterality? *Archives of Neurology*, *38*, 637–638.

Volpe, B., Sidtis, J., Holtzman, J., Wilson, D., & Gazzaniga, M. (1982). Cortical mechanisms involved in praxis: observations following partial and complete section of the corpus callosum in man. *Neurology*, *32*, 645–650.

von Economo, C., & Horn, L. (1930). Über Windungsreliefs, Maße und Rindenarchitektonik der Supratemporalfläche: ihre individuellen und ihre Seitenunterschiede. *Zeitschrift für die gesamte Neurologie und Psychiatrie*, *130*, 678–757.

von Plessen, K., Lundervold, A., Duta, N., Heiervang, E., Klauschen, F., Smievoll, A. I., Ersland, L., & Hugdahl, K. (2002). Less developed corpus callosum in dyslexic subjects — a structural MRI study. *Neuropsychologia*, *40*, 1035–1044.

Waber, D. P., Weiler, M. D., Wolff, P. H., Bellinger, D., Marcus, D. J., Ariel, R. Forbes, P., & Wypij, D. (2001). Processing of rapid auditory stimuli in school-age children referred for evaluation of learning disorders. *Child Development*, *72*, 37–49.

Wada, J., Clarke, R., & Hamm, A. (1975). Cerebral hemispheric asymmetry in humans: cortical speech zones in 100 adults and 100 infant brains. *Archives of Neurology*, *32*, 239–246.

Wadsworth, S. J., DeFries, J. C., Stevenson, J., Gilger, J. W., & Pennington, B. F. (1992). Gender ratios among reading-disabled children and their siblings as a function of parental impairment. *Journal of Child Psychology and Psychiatry*, *33*, 1229–1239.

Wadsworth, S. J., Gillis, J. J., DeFries, J. C., & Fulker, D. W. (1989). Differential genetic aetiology of reading disability as a function of age. *Irish Journal of Psychology*, *10*, 509–520.

Wadsworth, S. J., Knopic, V. S., & DeFries, J. C. (2000a). Reading disability in boys and girls: no evidence for a differential genetic etiology. *Reading and Writing: An Interdisciplinary Journal*, *13*, 133–145.

Wadsworth, S. J., Olson, R. K., Pennington, B. F., & DeFries, J. C. (2000b). Differential genetic etiology of reading disability as a function of IQ. *Journal of Learning Disabilities*, *33*, 192–199.

Wagner, R. K., & Torgesen, J. K. (1987). The nature of phonological processing and its causal role in the acquisition of reading skills. *Psychological Bulletin*, *101*, 192–212.

Wagner, R. K., Torgesen, J. K., Laughon, J. K., Simmons, P., & Rashotte, C. A. (1993). Development of young readers' phonological processing abilities. *Journal of Educational Psychology, 85*, 83–103.

Wagner, R. K., Torgesen, J. K., & Rashotte, C. A. (1994). Development of reading-related phonological processing abilities: new evidence of bidirectional causality from a latent variable longitudinal study. *Developmental Psychology, 30*, 73–87.

Walther-Müller, P. U. (1995). Is there a deficit of early vision in dyslexia? *Perception, 24*, 919–936.

Walton, P. D. (1995). Rhyming ability, phoneme identity, letter-sound knowledge, and the use of orthographic analogy by prereaders. *Journal of Educational Psychology, 87*, 587–597.

Waters, G. S., & Seidenberg, M. S. (1986). Spelling–sound effects in reading: time-course and decisiion criteria. *Memory and Congnition, 13*, 557–572.

Watkins, K. E., Dronkers, N. F., & Vargha-Kadem, F. (2002a). Behavioural analysis of an inherited speech and language disorder: comparison with acquired aphasia. *Brain, 125*, 452–464.

Watkins, K. E., Vargha-Khadem, F., Ashburner, J., Passingham, R. E., Connelly, A., Friston, K. J., Frackowiak, R. S. J., Mishkin, M., & Gadian, D. G. (2002b). MRI analysis of an inherited speech and language disorder: structural brain abnormalities. *Brain, 125*, 465–478.

Watson, B. U., & Miller, T. K. (1993). Auditory perception, phonological processing, and reading ability/disability. *Journal of Speech and Hearing Research, 36*, 850–863.

Watson, C., & Willows, D. M. (1995). Information-processing patterns in specific reading disability. *Journal of Learning Disabilities, 28*, 216–231.

Watson, J. D. G., Myers, R., Frackowiak, R. S. J., Hajnal, J. V., Woods, R. P., Mazziotta, J. C., Shipp, S., & Zeki, S. (1993). Area V5 of the human brain: evidence from a combined study using positron emission tomography and magnetic resonance imaging. *Cerebral Cortex, 3*, 79–94.

Weekes, B. S., & Robinson, G. A. (1997). Semantic anomia without surface dyslexia. *Aphasiology, 11*, 813–825.

Weekes, N. Y., Capetillo-Cunliffe, L., Rayman, J., Iacoboni, M., & Zaidel, E. (1999). Individual differences in the hemispheric specialization of dual route variables. *Brain and Language, 67*, 110–133.

Werker, J. F., & Tees, R. C. (1984). Cross-language speech perception. *Infant Behavior and Development, 7*, 49–63.

Werker, J. F., & Tees, R. C. (1987). Speech perception in severely disabled and average reading children. *Canadian Journal of Psychology, 41*, 48–61.

Wernicke, C. (1974). *Der aphasische Symtomencomplex: Eine Psychologisches studie auf Anatomischer Basis.* Breslau: Cohn & Weigert.

Wester, K., & Hugdahl, K. (1997). Thalamotomy and thalamic stimulation: effects on cognition. *Stereotactic and Functional Neurosurgery, 69*, 80–85.

Whitaker, H. A., & Selnes, O. A. (1976). Anatomic variations in the cortex: individual differences and the problem of the localization of language functions. *Annals of the New York Academy of Sciences, 280*, 844–856.

Whitehurst, G. J., & Fischel, J. E. (2000). Reading and language impairments in conditions of poverty. In: D. V. M. Bishop & L. B. Leonard (Eds.), *Speech and language impairments in children: causes, characteristics, intervention and outcome* (pp. 53–71). Hove, UK: Hove: Psychology Press.

Whitehurst, G. J., & Lonigan, C. J. (1998). Child development and emergent literacy. *Child Development, 69*, 848–872.

Whittington, J. E., & Richards, P. N. (1987). The stability of children's laterality prevalences and their relationship to measures of performance. *British Journal of Educational Psychology, 57*, 45–55.

Wilding, J. (1989). Developmental dyslexics do not fit in boxes: evidence from the case studies. *European Journal of Cognitive Psychology, 1*, 105–127.

Wilding, J. (1990). Developmental dyslexics do not fit in boxes: evidence from six new case studies. *European Journal of Cognitive Psychology, 2*, 97–131.

Wilkins, A. (1993). Reading and visual discomfort. In D. M. Willows, R. R. Kruk, & E. Corcos (Eds.), *Visual processes in reading and reading disabilities* (pp. 435–456). Hillsdale, NJ: Lawrence Erlbaum Associates Inc.

Wilkins, A. J. (1995). *Visual Stress.* Oxford: Oxford University Press.

Wilkins, A. (1996). Helping reading with colour. *Dyslexia Review, 7*, 4–7.

Williams, M. C., & Bologna, N. B. (1985). Perceptual grouping in good and poor readers. *Perception and Psychophysics, 38*, 367–384.

Williams, M. C., Lecluyse, K., & Rock-Faucheux, A. (1992). Effective interventions for reading disability. *Journal of the American Optometric Association, 3*, 411–417.

Willows, D. M., & Ryan, E. B. (1986). The development of grammatical sensitivity and its relationship to early reading achievement. *Reading Research Quarterly, 21*, 253–266.

Wilsher, C.R. (1985). Dyslexia and monocular occlusion. (Letter). *The Lancet*, 19 October.

Wimmer, H. (1990). A premature refutation of the logographic stage assumption: a critical comment on Stuart & Coltheart (1988). *British Journal of Developmental Psychology*, 8, 201–203.

Wimmer, H. (1993). Characteristics of developmental dyslexia in a regular writing system. *Applied Psycholinguistics*, *14*, 1–33.

Wimmer, H. (1996a). The nonword reading deficit in developmental dyslexia: evidence from children learning to read German. *Journal of Experimental Child Psychology*, *61*, 80–90.

Wimmer, H. (1996b). The early manifestation of developmental dyslexia: evidence from German children. *Reading and Writing: An Interdisciplinary Journal*, *8*, 171–188.

Wimmer, H., & Goswami, U. (1994). The influence of orthographic consistency on reading development: word recognition in English and German children. *Cognition*, *51*, 91–103.

Wimmer, H., & Hummer, P. (1990). How German speaking first graders read and spell: doubts on the importance of the logographic stage. *Applied Psycholinguistics*, *11*, 349–368.

Wimmer, H., & Landerl, K. (1997). How learning to spell German differs from learning to spell English. In C. A. Perfetti, L. Rieben, & M. Fayol (Eds.), *Learning to spell: research, theory, and practice across languages* (pp. 81–96). Mahwah, NJ: Lawrence Erlbaum Associates Inc.

Wimmer, H., Landerl, K., Linortner, R., & Hummer, P. (1991). The relationship of phonemic awareness to reading acquisition: more consequence than precondition but still important. *Cognition*, *40*, 219–249.

Wimmer, H., Landerl, K., & Schneider, W. (1994). The role of rhyme awareness in learning to read regular orthography. *British Journal of Developmental Psychology*, *12*, 469–484.

Wimmer, H., Mayringer, H., & Landerl, K. (2000). The double-deficit hypothesis and difficulties in learning to read a regular orthography. *Journal of Educational Psychology*, *92*, 668–680.

Wimmer, H., Mayringer, H., & Raberger, T. (1999). Reading and dual-task balancing: evidence against the automatization deficit explanation of developmental dyslexia. *Journal of Learning Disabilities*, *32*, 473–478.

Windfuhr, K. L., & Snowling, M. J. (2001). The relationship between paired associate learning and phonological skills in normally developing readers. *Journal of Experimental Child Psychology*, *80*, 160–173.

Winters, R. L., Patterson, R., & Shontz, W. (1989). Visual persistence and adult dyslexia. *Journal of Learning Disabilities*, *22*, 640–645

Wise, B. W., Olson, R. K., & Treiman, R. (1990). Subsyllabic units in computerized reading instruction: onset-rime vs postvowel segmentation. *Journal of Experimental Child Psychology*, *49*, 1–19.

Wise, R. J. S., Greene, J., Büchel, C., & Scott, S. K. (1999). Brain regions involved in articulation. *Lancet*, *353*, 1057–1061.

Witelson, S. F. (1977). Developmental dyslexia: two right hemispheres and none left. *Science*, *195*, 309–311.

Witelson, S. F. (1985). The brain connection: the corpus callosum is larger in left-handers. *Science*, *229*, 665–668.

Witelson, S. F. (1991). Neural sexual mosaicism: sexual differentiation of the human temporo-parietal region for functional asymmetry. *Psychoneuroendocrinology*, *16*,131–153.

Witelson, S. F., Glezer, I. I., & Kigar, D. L. (1995). Women have greater density of neurons in posterior temporal cortex. *Journal of Neuroscience*, *15*, 3418–3428.

Witelson, S. F., & Kigar, D. L. (1992). Sylvian fissure morphology and asymmetry in men and women: bilateral difference in relation to handedness. *Journal of Comparative Neurology*, *323*, 326–340.

Witelson, S. F., Kigar, D. L., & Harvey, T. (1999). The exceptional brain of Albert Einstein. *Lancet*, *353*, 2149–2153.

Witelson, S. F., & Nowakowski, R. S. (1991). Left out axons make men right: a hypothesis for the origin of handedness and functional asymmetry. *Neuropsychologia*, *29*, 327–333.

Witelson, S. F., & Pallie, W. (1973). Left hemisphere specialization for language in the newborn. *Brain*, *96*, 641–646.

Witton, C., Talcott, J. B., Hansen, P. C., Richardson, A. J., Griffiths, T. D., Rees, A., Stein, J. F., & Green, G. G. R. (1998). Sensitivity to dynamic auditory and visual stimuli predicts nonword reading ability in both dyslexic and normal readers. *Current Biology*, *8*, 791–797.

Witty, P. A., & Kopel, D. (1936). Sinistral and mixed manual–ocular behaviour in reading disability. *Journal of Educational Psychology*, *27*, 119–134.

Wolf, M. (1986). Rapid alternating stimulus naming in the developmental dyslexias. *Brain and Language*, *27*, 360–379.

Wolf, M. (1991). Naming speed and reading: the contribution of the cognitive neurosciences. *Reading Research Quarterly, 26*, 123–141.

Wolf, M., Bally, H., & Morris, R. (1986). Automaticity, retrieval processes, and reading: a longitudinal study in average and impaired readers. *Child Development, 57*, 988–1000.

Wolf, M., & Bowers, P. G. (1999). The double-deficit hypothesis for the developmental dyslexias. *Journal of Educational Psychology, 91*, 415–438.

Wolf, M., & Goodlass, H. (1986). Dyslexia, dysnomia, and lexical retrieval: a longitudinal investigation. *Brain and Language, 28*, 154–168.

Wolf, M., & Obregón, M. (1992). Early naming deficits, developmental dyslexia, and a specific deficit hypothesis. *Brain and Language, 42*, 219–247.

Wolff, P. H. (1993). Impaired temporal resolution in developmental dyslexia. *Annals of the New York Academy of Sciences, 682*, 87–103.

Wolff, P. H., Cohen, C., & Drake, C. (1984). Impaired motor timing control in specific reading retardation. *Neuropsychologia, 22*, 587–600.

Wolff, P. H., & Melngailis, I. (1994). Family patterns of developmental dyslexia: clinical findings. *American Journal of Medical Genetics, 54*, 122–131.

Wolff, P. H., Michel, G. F., Ovrut, M., & Drake, C. (1990). Rate and timing precision of motor coordination in developmental dyslexia. *Developmental Psychology, 26*, 349–359.

World Federation of Neurology (1968). Report of research group on developmental dyslexia and world illiteracy. *Bulletin of the Orton Society, 18*, 21–22.

Wright, B. A., Lombardino, L. J., King, W. M., Puranik, C. S., Leonard, C. M., & Merzenich, M. M. (1997). Deficits in auditory temporal and spectral resolution in language-impaired children. *Nature, 387*, 176–178.

Wyke, M. A. (Ed.) (1978) *Developmental dysphasia.* London: Academic Press.

Yabuta, N. H., Sawatari, A., & Callaway, E. M. (2001). Two functional channels from primary visual cortex to dorsal visual cortical areas. *Science, 292*, 297–300.

Yakovlev, P. I., & Lecours, A. R. (1967). The myelogenetic cycles of regional maturation of the brain. In A. Monkowski (Ed.), *Regional development of the brain in early life* (pp. 3–70). Oxford: Blackwell.

Yap, R. L., & Van der Leij, A. (1994). Testing the automization deficit hypothesis of dyslexia via a dual task paradigm. *Journal of Learning Disabilities, 27*, 660–665.

Yavas, M. S., & Gogate, L. J. (1999). Phoneme aware-

ness in children: a function of sonority. *Journal of Psycholinguistic Research, 28*, 245–260.

Yazgan, M. Y., Wexler, B. E., Kinsbourne, M., Peterson, B., & Leckman, J. F. (1995). Functional significance of individual variations in callosal area. *Neuropsychologia, 33*, 769–779.

Yeni-Komshian, G. H., & Benson, D. A. (1976). Anatomical study of cerebral asymmetry in the temporal lobe of humans, chimpanzees, and rhesus monkeys. *Science, 192*, 387–389.

Yopp, H. K. (1988). The validity and reliability of phonemic awareness tests. *Reading Research Quarterly, 23*, 159–177.

Young, A. W., & Ellis, A. W. (1981). Asymmetry of cerebral hemispheric function in normal and poor readers. *Psychological Bulletin, 89*, 183–190.

Yuill, N., & Oakhill, J. (1991). *Children's problems in text comprehension: an experimental investigation.* Cambridge. Cambridge University Press.

Yule, W., Rutter, M., Berger, M., & Thompson, J. (1974). Over- and under-achievement in reading: distribution in the general population. *British Journal of Educational Psychology, 44*, 1–12.

Zabell, C., & Everatt, J. (2002) Surface and phonological subtypes of adult developmental dyslexia. *Dyslexia, 8*, 160–177.

Zaidel, D., & Sperry, R. W. (1977). Some long-term motor effects of cerebral commissurotomy in man. *Neuropsychologia, 15*, 193–204.

Zangwill, O. L. (1962). Dyslexia in relation to cerebral dominance. In J. Money (Ed.), *Reading disability: progress and research needs in dyslexia* (pp. 103–113). Baltimore, MD: Johns Hopkins University Press.

Zangwill, O. L. (1978). The concept of developmental dysphasia. In M. A. Wyke (Ed.), *Developmental dysphasia* (pp. 1–11). London: Academic Press.

Zangwill, O. L., & Blakemore, C. (1972). Dyslexia: reversal eye-movements during reading. *Neuropsychologia, 10*, 371–373.

Zatorre, R. J. (1989). Perceptual asymmetry on the dichotic fused words test and cerebral speech lateralization determined by the carotid sodium amytal test. *Neuropsychologia, 27*, 1207–1219

Zeffiro, T., & Eden, G. (2001). The cerebellum and dyslexia: perpetrator or innocent bystander? *Trends in Neurosciences, 24*, 512–513.

Zeki, S. M., (1973). Functional organization of a visual area in the posterior bank of the superior temporal sulcus of the rhesus monkey. *Journal of Physiology, 236*, 549–573.

Zeki, S. (1991). Cerebral akinetopsia (visual motion blindness): a review. *Brain, 114*, 811–824.

Zeki, S. (1993). A Vision of the Brain. Oxford: Blackwell Scientific Publications.

Zeki, S., Watson, J. D. G., Lueck, C. J., Friston, K. J., Kennard, C., & Frackowiak, R. S. J. (1991). A direct demonstration of functional specialization in human visual cortex. *Journal of Neuroscience, 11,* 641–649.

Zerbin-Rüdin, E. (1967). Kongenitale wortblindheit oder speczifische dyslexie (Congenital word-blindness). *Bulletin of the Orton Society, 17,* 47–56.

Zetzsche, T., Meisenzahl, E. M., Preuss, U. W., Holder, J. J., Kathmann, N., Leinsinger, G., Hahn, K., Hegerl, U., & Möler, H.-J. (2001). *In-vivo* analysis of the human planum temporale (PT): does the definition of PT borders influence the results with regard to cerebral asymmetry and correlation with handedness? *Psychiatry Research: Neuro-imaging, 107,* 99–115.

Zhang, X., & Tomblin, J. B. (1998). Can children with language impairment be accurately identified using temporal processing measures? A simulation study. *Brain and Language, 65,* 395–403.

Ziegler, J. C., Perry, C., & Coltheart, M. (2000). The DRC model of visual word recognition and reading aloud: an extension to German. *European Journal of Cognitive Psychology, 12,* 413–430.

Ziegler, J. C., Perry, C., Jacobs, A. M., & Braun, M. (2001). Identical words are read differently in different languages. *Psychological Science, 12,* 379–384.

Zihl, J., von Cramon, D., & Mai, N. (1983). Selective disturbance of movement after bilateral brain damage. *Brain, 106,* 313–340.

Zihl, J., von Cramon, D., Mai, N., & Schmid, Ch. (1991). Disturbance of movement vision after bilateral posterior brain damage: further evidence and folow up observations. *Brain, 114,* 2235–2252.

Zinna, D. R., Liberman, I. Y., & Shankweiler, D. (1986). Children's sensitivity to factors influencing vowel reading. *Reading Research Quarterly, 21,* 465–480.

Zoccolotti, P., De Luca, M., Di Pace, E., Judica, A., Orlandi, M., & Spinelli, D. (1999). Markers of developmental surface dyslexia in a language (Italian) with high grapheme–phoneme correspondence. *Applied Psycholinguistics, 20,* 191–216.

Zoccolotti, P., Matano, A., Deloche, G., Cantagallo, A., Passadori, A., Leclerq, M., Braga, L., Cremelle, N., Pittau, P., Renom, M., Rousseaux, M., Truche, A., Fimm, B., & Zimmerman, P. (2000). Patterns of attentional impairment following closed head injury: a collaborative European study. *Cortex, 36,* 93–107.

Zorzi, M., Houghton, G., & Butterworth, B. (1998). Two routes or one in reading aloud? A connectionist dual-process model. *Journal of Experimental Psychology, 24,* 1131–1161.

Zurif, E. B., & Carson, G. (1970). Dyslexia in relation to cerebral dominance and temporal analysis. *Neuropsychologia, 8,* 351–361.

Zurif, E. B., Gardner, H., & Brownell, H. (1989). The case against the case against group studies. *Brain and Cognition, 10,* 237–255.

Zurif, E., Swinney, D., & Fodor, J. A. (1991). An evaluation of the assumption underlying the single-patient only position in neuropsychological research. *Brain and Cognition, 16,* 198–210.

Author Index

Subject Index